The Original **CATFANCY**

CAT BIBLE

Sandy Robins

with Arnold Plotnick MS, DVM, ACVIM, Lorraine Shelton, and Sarah Hartwell

I-5
EST. 2013
·PRESS·

Project Team
Editor: Tom Mazorlig
Copy Editor: Joann Woy
Indexer: Elizabeth Walker
Design: Mary Ann Kahn

i-5 PUBLISHING, LLC™
Chief Executive Officer: Mark Harris
Chief Financial Officer: Nicole Fabian
Vice President, Chief Content Officer: June Kikuchi
General Manager, i5 Press: Christopher Reggio
Editorial Director, i5 Press: Andrew DePrisco
Art Director, i5 Press: Mary Ann Kahn
Digital General Manager: Melissa Kauffman
Production Director: Laurie Panaggio
Production Manager: Jessica Jaensch
Marketing Director: Lisa MacDonald

Library of Congress Cataloging-in-Publication Data
Robins, Sandy.
 The original cat fancy cat bible : the definitive source for all things cat / by Sandy Robins, with Dr. Arnold Plotnick, Sarah Hartwell, and Lorraine M. Shelton.
    pages cm
 Includes bibliographical references and index.
 ISBN 978-1-933958-79-8 (alk. paper)
 1. Cats. I. Title.
 SF442.R57 2014
 636.8--dc23
        2013044507

This book has been published with the intent to provide accurate and authoritative information in regard to the subject matter within. While every precaution has been taken in the preparation of this book, the author and publisher expressly disclaim any responsibility for any errors, omissions, or adverse effects arising from the use or application of the information contained herein. The techniques and suggestions are used at the reader's discretion and are not to be considered a substitute for veterinary care. If you suspect a medical problem, consult your veterinarian.

i-5 Publishing, LLC™
3 Burroughs, Irvine, CA 92618
www.facebook.com/i5press
www.i5publishing.com

Printed and bound in China
14 15 16 17   1 3 5 7 9 8 6 4 2

Table of Contents

Dedication

For my parents, Eddy Robins (1917–2007) and Rennette
Robins (1937–2007), who taught me to love and respect all
animals and who made sure that while I was growing up our
home was always filled with a furry menagerie that included
cats with quirky traits and endearing personalities

What makes a book a *cat bible*? It takes a quintessential resource to reveal who cats are, document the history of the human-feline bond, celebrate the roles cats have played in our civilization from mouser to muse, provide a background on all the breeds, and teach you how to keep your purring soul mates healthy and happy. This book *is* that ultimate resource, and *Cat Fancy* is proud to present it to you. Like a cherished family bible, you will want to read it, study it, and keep it handy in your home.

Award-winning writer Sandy Robin's fun and lively voice engages you throughout this beautiful volume, while acclaimed veterinarian Arnold Plotnick enlightens you on the latest feline health issues, and preeminent experts Sarah Hartwell and Lorraine Shelton explore the world of cat breeds.

The great American writer, Mark Twain, had much to say about cats and fancied himself a feline expert. Of course, he had much more to say about humans, which was much less flattering than what he had to say about cats. In fact, in 1894 he penned: "Of all God's creatures there is only one that cannot be made the slave of the lash. That one is the cat. If man could be crossed with the cat it would improve man, but it would deteriorate the cat."

Notable people throughout history knew what those of you who picked up this volume already know: Cats command respect. From their amazing athletic abilities and superhuman senses to their loving head butts bestowed on their favorite people, felines have earned the admiration of Abraham Lincoln, Florence Nightingale, Isaac Newton, Leonardo da Vinci, Ernest Hemingway, and John Lennon, to name a few.

As you peruse these pages, perhaps with kitty on your lap, you will gain a fresh understanding and appreciation for your feline friend that will serve to enhance your relationship. Enjoy the read and every moment you spend with your beloved companion, who shares your heart and home!

— By Susan Logan-McCracken

Acknowledgments

Up front, a very special thanks to my colleague and Facebook friend Arnold Plotnick, DVM, for authoring the health section of this book in such an informative yet easy-to-read style and to Sarah Hartwell and Lorraine Shelton for their expertise in the breeds section.

This book is truly a *magnum opus,* and behind the scenes were literally dozens of world experts who collectively gave graciously of their very valuable time to impart their knowledge. The list is too long to thank everyone individually—you all know who you are—but I have to mention the following people (in no particular order): longstanding friend and go-to person Prof. Nick Dodman, head of the small animal behavior clinic at the Cummings School of Veterinary Medicine at Tufts University; cat behaviorist Marilyn Krieger (whom I had on speed dial); veterinarians Drew Weigner (my mentor and friend), Brent Mayabb, Manager of

Education and Development at Royal Canin USA, who fielded numerous top-priority emails with lightning-speed efficiency, and my new BFF Dennis Jewel, a nutritional scientist at Hills Pet Nutrition, who told me I need to step away from my desk and get out more, and his colleague Edisa Chasin, who arranged for me to include certain of the company's excellent nutritional charts in this publication; the newest of my pet foodie friends Pete Brace and Betsy Berger from Merrick PetCare who taught me the true meaning of their slogan about pet food, namely "food worthy of a fork". A big thank you to my own cats' purrsonal veterinarian Dr. Jeff Glass of Irvine, California, who remains on the cutting edge of veterinary medicine and thus keeps me informed; to Prof. Leslie A. Lyons, former Professor of Genetics at the School of Veterinary Medicine at UC Davis who is now attached to the University of Missouri for overseeing my chapter on genetics—her research in the field of cat genetics has put a new perspective on the history of feline domestication; to my legal interns, Sara Junks and Robin Fae Katz from Texas Tech University School of Law, who walked me through the maze of cat laws; to Joan Miller for her wonderful perspective of all things cat; and to *Cat Fancy* editor Susan Logan for her perennial support and friendship—she is a gem!

A book titled *The Original Cat Bible* has to have a truly outstanding editor to put everything in place. I was privileged to work with the *crème de la crème* of editors, namely Jarelle Stein who elevated her editing craft into an art form! She was meticulous. Nothing escaped her and she certainly knows how to re-arrange a wobbly sentence! Apart from being good at her job, following up on my research and giving me valuable input, she is also a Cat Person. Say no more! And a big thank you to Tom Mazorlig, who did the final edit on this book. Tom "discovered" me at a conference and was instrumental in my very first book deal.

I am lucky to have an amazing agent, Erin Niumata of the Folio Literary Agency who has played a pivotal role in guiding my career, and a big thank you I-5 Publishing's acquisitions editor Andrew DePrisco, who gave me *carte blanche* with this manuscript (that's an author's dream!).

Another special thank you to my husband, Mike Sandler, and son Evan, who share my love of cats and took over numerous household duties (including litter box scoop patrol) so that I could put my time and energy into researching and writing this book. It goes without saying that my daughter Cherri and her husband Nick are cat people and I know my grandbaby Cali will be taught to love and respect all animals too.

Purrs and head butts to the feline researchers who tried and tested games, foods, and accessories and endorsed them as suitable to be included in this book: my beautiful, green-eyed Fudge, my "wild child" Ziggy, Cherri's cats Isabella, and Mr. Poopy Pants, Esq.; my best friend Gail's three irrepressible felines, This, That, and The Other. And finally, my feline muses, Nibbi (1976 – 1990), the beautiful Muffin (? – 2005), and Cali (1990–2009). They continue to inspire me every day.

Introduction

I t's official. Cats are the world's most popular companion animals. More than 95.6 million felines live in American homes, and more than 600 million cats live among people around the world. Anyone lucky enough to share his or her home with a feline will concur that cats inherently understand their roles as beloved companions. While they certainly don't need statistics to back up this claim to popularity, data substantiating it does exist, coming from a slew of diverse resources, such as internationally recognized historians, archaeologists, zoologists, geneticists, and animal behaviorists who have tracked the history of the domestic cat back some 10,000 years.

Throughout history, cat lovers have described their feline companion as many things—loving, empathetic, intuitive, curious, funny, mysterious, fussy, dictatorial, autonomous, duplicitous, and prophetic. William Shakespeare in his play *The Merchant of Venice* even referred to cats as "necessary." And no cat lover will argue with that.

Cats come in all sizes, shapes, and colors and display a wide array of endearing character traits. Different breeds often display different characteristics. That's why it's important to study the breeds and learn as much as you can about them when you are looking for a companion cat that will suit your personality and your lifestyle. Of course, you may not get the chance to choose—stray cats have been known wander up to the people of their choice and "adopt" them with no more fanfare than a look that says "What's for supper?"

Although felines have a reputation for being aloof—and can put on award-winning performances as lofty monarchs—they actually thrive on human interaction and make fabulous affectionate companions. However, every relationship based on love and companionship comes with enormous responsibility built on understanding and tolerance. Cats need both mental and physical stimulation provided by toys and games and by interaction with other felines and, of course, with the humans who love and care for them.

Fortunately, more and more owners are coming to understand that domestic cats are worthy of the best we can afford to give them. The entrepreneurial world has caught on to this desire to provide for our cats and take them with us when we travel. Now cats are both showered with comforts at home and have the welcome mat rolled out for them throughout much of the travel and leisure industry. And their world is getting even better with a strong population of animal-welfare advocates speaking out against cruelty and a national effort to humanely curb the stray cat population. We're getting closer to a truly pet-friendly, no-kill nation and ensuring that each and every cat has a loving home.

From choosing a breed to making a feline-friendly home to contributing to a feline-friendly world, *The Original Cat Bible* contains it all. Everything you've ever wanted to learn about cats is right here in these pages. It covers the "Old Testament" in terms of historical facts detailing how cats came to live among us, the role they have played in different cultures (including American popular culture), the personality and character traits of the different breeds and laws pertaining to felines. While the "Mew Testament" (in *catemporary* cat speak) covers current attitudes about the importance of diet and good grooming, highlights the many ways in which to enrich your cat's life, outlines how to understand their behaviors and body language, catalogs the wonderful state-of-the-art veterinary medicine that mimics human treatments as well as home lifestyle accessories that improve feline health and well-being. On top of all of that, we'll discuss the latest trends from traveling with cats to the feline social-networking mania, careers with cats, and even how to get your cat a job.

Chapter 1

The History and Development of the Modern Cat

The only mystery about the cat is why it ever decided to become a domestic animal

— Sir Compton Mackenzie

nlike other domestic animals, such as the dog and the horse, the cat is self-domesticated. Its history shows that cats chose to live in close proximity to people and not the other way around. People domesticated other animals to help humankind in some way—by providing food and clothing, such as milk and wool, or by assisting people in their work, through, for example, herding and hunting, as dogs were trained to do. By contrast, people have wisely made no concerted efforts to mold cats to any kind of task, and cats have certainly done as little as possible to mold themselves. Perhaps that is why, if domesticated cats are forced into a situation in which they have to fend for themselves, their natural survival and hunting instincts kick in. British zoologist Juliet Clutton-Brock, a leading authority in the history of feline domesticity, describes the domestic cat as an "exploiter of humans." Today, cat lovers readily acknowledge this facet of a cat's personality, claiming that while dogs have *masters*, cats have *staff*.

Ancestors of the Cat

The origins of the domestic cat date back about 60 million years to a forest-dwelling, short-legged, long-bodied mammal with a small head (and hence a small brain) called a *miacid*, one of the first mammalian carnivores. All carnivorous mammals (which definitely include cats) are said have descended from the miacid, which came into being after the dinosaurs became extinct and allowed

▶ *Dinictis felina* is an early catlike mammal found in North America more than 20 million years ago.

new forms of mammals to evolve and flourish. The first of the miacid's descendents to resemble a modern-day cat was called a *Dinictis*, a lynx-size animal with catlike incisor teeth. However, it was a weasel-like creature called the *Proailurus*, which came along some 30 million years ago, that could lay claim to the title of first true cat. This was the first known member of the family Felidae, which includes all the cats—big and small, living and extinct.

By 20 million years ago, the *Proailurus* had evolved into the *Pseudaelurus*. According to paleontologists, the slender proportions and short legs of these animals suggested that they were agile climbers. Some time between 6 and 10 million years ago, *Pseudaelurus* had spread out and evolved into four branches, or subfamilies, of cats. The Machairodontinae branch produced saber-toothed cats, such as the *Smilodon*, which eventually became extinct. The subfamily Pantherinae produced all modern-day big cats (such as leopards, lions, and tigers). The subfamily Felinae came into being as well; all of today's small cats, including the domestic cat, belong to this family. Standing aloof from the other cats, in a subfamily of its own, the Acinonychinae is the modern-day cheetah. (Some cats don't play well with others.) Felinae or Acinoychinae may be the most recently evolved of the subfamilies, but the exact timing of all this evolution is still uncertain.

▼Big cats, including lions, are in a different subfamily than domestic cats.

Climbing Trees in South America

There were no ancestors of cats in South America until the Isthmus of Panama formed to connect it to North America, and the animals crossed over. Today, South America is home to the ultimate tree-climbing wildcat known as the margay, which lives in the rain forests. The margay is able to walk down a tree trunk with the same grace as she ascended because she has flexible ankles in her hind legs, which allow her back feet to rotate up to 180 degrees.

The Big Cats

Large cats who roar (they have a specialized hyoid bone at the base of their tongues that gives them this ability) were once labeled by the genus *Panthera* (lions, tigers, leopards, snow leopards, clouded leopards, and jaguars are all part of this genus). Recently, the big cats have been split into a three different genera: *Uncia* (the snow leopard), *Neofelis* (two species of clouded leopards), and *Panthera* (all the rest). Whereas big cats are currently concentrated in specific geographic locations, their ancestors roamed across many parts of the world. Today's lions, for instance, are native to Africa, with a very small population in India, but their ancestors once inhabited Europe, southeastern and north central Asia, and North and Central America. Leopards, found only in certain regions of Africa and Asia these days, had ancestors who lived throughout Europe, Africa, and Asia and on the island of Java. Fossils of cheetahs have also been found in France.

The Small Cats

All small wild cats who purr and growl but don't roar fall were considered to be in the genus *Felis*. Recent research has split up the small cats into several genera. Scientists today think that there could have been anywhere between twenty-six and thirty-seven small wildcats in this group. Remains of the African wildcat (*Felis silvestris lybica*), which is considered the progenitor of the domestic cat, have been found as far north as Scotland, as far south as South Africa, and as far east as Mongolia.

This small subspecies has a tan, striped (tabby) coat and is roughly the size of a modern domestic cat. Although scientists long believed that this cat stood at the top of the domestic cat's family tree, they were not able to establish this fact until the twenty-first century.

In 2000, research scientist Carlos A. Driscoll, then working at the US National Cancer Institute's Laboratory of Genomic Diversity, gathered DNA samples from 979 wildcats and domestic cats from Europe, the Middle East, southern Africa, Azerbaijan, Kazakhstan, and Mongolia. Because wildcats are very territorial and not nomadic, Driscoll wanted to find out if the genetic composition of these groups would vary according

▼ Scientists think that our pet cats were domesticated from the various subspecies of wildcat, *Felis silvestris*. A southern African wildcat is pictured.

Leslie Lyons's research on cat genetics shows that the domestic cat evolved from wildcats somewhere in the Middle East.

and his colleagues thus concluded that the origins of domestic cats were from a single locale—the Middle East. Researchers believe that only one species of wildcat was domesticated because other species hunted larger game or their habitats did not coincide with the regions where people were farming.

This hypothesis was confirmed by the work of geneticist Leslie Lyons and her team working at the Center for Companion Animal Health, School of Veterinary Medicine at the University of California, Davis. (Dr. Lyons now works at the University of Missouri.) Lyons and her team had collected samples of cheek cells from more than 1,000 cats for their study. Lyons had done much of her research in Egypt but also collected information from Turkey and Lebanon. With the aid of the

to their geographic location but remain stable within each group. He hypothesized that if the DNA of domestic cats more closely resembled that of one of the wildcat populations, then he would have evidence for where (if not when) feline domestication began.

Driscoll's results, published in 2007, revealed five distinct lineages. Four of them corresponded directly with four of the known subspecies of wildcats and the specific places in which they lived: *F. s. silvestris* (European wildcat, Europe), *F. s. bieti* (Chinese mountain wildcat, China), *F. s. ornata* (Asiatic wildcat, Central Asia), and *F. s. cafra* (South African wildcat, southern Africa). The fifth group included not only the fifth known subspecies of wildcat, *F. s. lybica* (African wildcat), found in the Middle East, but also bore a genetic resemblance to hundreds of domestic cats who were sampled (both purebred and mixed-breed) from the United States, the United Kingdom, and Japan. Genetically, *F. s. lybica* wildcats sampled from Israel, the United Arab Emirates, and Saudi Arabia were virtually indistinguishable from the domestic cats. Driscoll

▼Ancient Egyptians famously revered cats. They even mummified them so they would come with their owners to the afterlife..

American military, the team did manage to get samples of cats from throughout Iraq, as well. She and her team concluded, as Driscoll had, that the domestic cat evolved from the African wildcat in the Middle East. Although the political situation in Pakistan made it difficult for Lyons to do research in the Indus Valley, she has studied cats throughout India and Southeast Asia and believes that although the cat breeds of Southeast Asia are very distinct, they probably did come from the west (that is, from the Middle East). She conjectures that they were isolated during periods in history when rulers such as Genghis Khan closed off routes of discovery and that they remained isolated until explorers such as Marco Polo started opening up trade routes to the New World. In isolation, distinctions evolved.

Timeline of Feline Domestication

As British author Terry Pratchett once said: "In ancient times cats were worshipped as gods; they have not forgotten this." If we're seeking someone to blame for fostering this lofty feline attitude, we need look no further than the ancient Egyptians, who not only adored their cats but also deified them. Over the years, archaeologists and historians have unearthed treasures depicting the lifestyle of those who lived along the banks of the Nile thousands of years ago, including paintings showing cats in very domestic situations: sitting on chairs, eating out of bowls, and even wearing collars. These researchers of the past have also found paintings and statues of the common cat's depiction as the incarnation of the goddess Bast.

Because of this, researchers long theorized that the Egyptians were responsible for the first domesticated cats. However, archaeological finds since the turn of the twenty-first century, coupled with the latest genetic research (see above), have led to a revision of the domestication timeline and place, showing that feline domestication in fact predates this Egyptian adulation by some 4,000 years. This research has zeroed in on the Middle Eastern Fertile Crescent (the agricultural region often dubbed the Cradle of Civilization), as well as on the equally fertile Indus Valley between India

and Pakistan and the lush banks of the Yellow River in China. Consequently, history books are currently being rewritten to state that feline domestication is synonymous with the history of agriculture.

Because these three areas all had excellent water sources, history documents that nomadic tribes started to put down roots there, building permanent homes to raise their livestock and to cultivate the land. Consequently, the precursors of today's domestic cats, with their penchant for hunting small animals such as rats and mice, realized that they could find an endless supply of food in these settlements. It was the perfect symbiotic relationship. So the settlers encouraged the cats to stay and keep the stores of grains and food intact from rodent scavengers. Some cats adapted to this living arrangement and became tame.

In 2004, French archaeologists Professor Jean Guilaine, of the Centre d'Anthropologie in Toulouse, France, and Dr. Jean-Denis Vigne, of the National Museum of Natural History in Paris, unearthed what is now thought to be the earliest evidence of humans keeping cats as pets. On the Mediterranean island of Cyprus, archaeologists discovered a grave, believed to be approximately 9,500 years old, containing human remains, a collection of various items such as crude tools and seashells, and the skeleton of a cat of about eight months old. The body of the cat faced west in similar conformation to the human remains.

Mummified Cats

So many mummified cats were excavated from Bubastis and other Egyptian excavation sites during the 1900s that they were shipped by the boatload to England and Europe, where they were ground up and used as fertilizer. Some that were later discovered intact are now on display in the Natural History Museum in London.

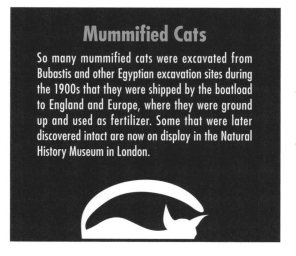

The cat specimen closely resembled the African wildcat. Vigne and his team concluded that because cats were not indigenous to the islands in the Mediterranean, early felines must have been taken there by boat. This, coupled with the burial discovery, suggested that a human–animal bond existed between people and cats.

Other pertinent discoveries include an ivory cat statuette found in the Fertile Crescent that also suggests that cats were commonplace in the homes of the settlers there. Furthermore, teams working near Baghdad and in Israel found remains of a house mouse, Mus musculus domesticus, that was thought to have been an ideal source of food for felines that lived around people because this species of mouse was unable to thrive in nature and gravitated to human homes and grain silos.

Since these archaeological finds, scientists and geneticists—including Leslie Lyons and Carlos Driscoll—have conducted independent research and concluded that feline domestication began in the Cradle of Civilization and spread out to places such as Egypt over thousands of years. These scientists managed to more accurately plot the timeline of feline domestication, which now indicates that images, paintings, and mummified remains of cats found in Egypt could be about 6,000 years younger than the remains of the cat found on Cyprus. Although ancient Egyptians are no longer considered the originators of feline domestication, they did play a crucial role in the domestication process, giving cats the status that they still have in our lives today.

From the Old World to the New

There's no question that cats had their historical heyday during the era of the New Kingdom, some 3,000 years ago, when the Egyptians literally put cats on pedestals and worshipped them. Egyptians believed that the common cat was the incarnation of Bast, the goddess of fertility, love, pleasure, and dance and protector from all evil. By day, she appeared with the head of a cat and the body of a woman and rode through the sky with her father, the sun god Ra. At night, she was known as Bastet and could transform completely into a cat. With her amazing night vision, she protected Ra against his greatest enemy, the serpent Apep.

▼ Archaeologists found a 9,500-year-old grave containing a man and a cat in Cyprus. Cats still roam the island today.

A temple built in Bast's honor in the city of Bubastis was adorned with cat statues and became home to many cats. When they died, they were mummified and buried in the temple. Such was Bast's influence that Egyptian law forbade killing or hurting a cat; the punishment for such a crime was death. The Egyptians were so devoted to their cats that, for centuries, it was even against the law to export them. They were, however, smuggled out by Phoenician traders, first to Greece and then later to destinations throughout the Roman Empire.

According to German-born Frederick Zeuner (1905–1963), a distinguished archaeologist at the University of London's Institute of Archaeology and author of *A History of Domesticated Animals* (1963), the coming of Christianity to Egypt loosened the restrictions on the exportation of sacred animals and allowed the barter and exchange of cats with the Romans. After the fall of the Roman Empire, which extended across Britain and western Europe, came the Early Middle Ages (fifth to tenth century AD). During this period, numerous Anglo-Saxon kingdoms were established in Britain. A large number of cat remains have been excavated from these Saxon sites, leading researchers to believe that the domestic cat was introduced to this area by the Roman conquerors and lived on with the Saxons (see chapter 3).

During this period, the value of the cat was stated in the famous Laws of Hywel Dda, the Welsh king who lived in the early 900s. His laws were translated into modern English in the nineteenth century and revealed "the price of a cat is four pence. Her qualities are to see, to hear, to kill mice, to have her claws whole, and to nurse and not devour her kittens. If she is deficient in any one of these qualities, one third of her price must be returned."

Throughout the Middle Ages, cats were included on voyages of discovery and trade expeditions to do the same job as they did in the Fertile Crescent: keep vermin and snakes at bay. This penchant for pest control helped the domesticated feline conquer the world. Despite the atrocities of the Papal Inquisition during this time, which led to the killing of cats as so-called servants of Satan and evil witches (see

▲ Bastet was an Egyptian goddess who is depicted as a cat or as a cat-headed woman.

chapter 3 for a further discussion on cats and religion), many people considered it good luck to have cats aboard ship, and cats consequently traveled far and wide. Christopher Columbus reportedly had cats on his ships when he set sail to find a shorter route to India in 1492 and ran into what would be called the New World (later, the Americas). The colonists who established Jamestown, Virginia (1607), and the pilgrims who arrived on the Mayflower (1620) were also said to have brought cats with them for luck and pest control.

From the Barn to the Hearth

Little written documentation exists regarding domesticated cats during the eighteenth and nineteenth centuries. What we do know supports the idea that people originally kept cats for practical reasons, as mousers. However, some of these cats no

The Cat That Walked by Himself

Author Rudyard Kipling's story called "The Cat That Walked by Himself," which appears in his famous book *Just So Stories*, tells of the first man and woman to collect animals to help them. The dog joins the family to help the man hunt. The horse is employed to carry the man. The cow is brought into the family to provide milk. The cat watches all this secretly and finally makes a deal with the woman, whereby he will keep the baby amused and catch mice when necessary; in return, he will be allowed to live in the cave, drink the milk, and lie next to the fire. The deal is entirely in the cat's favor because no working hours are specified. In his contract, the cat agrees to be kind to babies and hunt mice when it suits him. Kipling writes: "but when the moon gets up and night comes, he is the cat that walks by himself, and all places are alike to him. Then he goes out to the wet, wild woods or up the wet wild trees or on the wet wild roofs, waving his wild tail and walking by his wild lone, just the same as before."

doubt found places for themselves in warm kitchens and were allowed to remain inside. (Anyone who has ever enjoyed the company of a cat knows how capable a cat is of winning hearts.)

Author Katherine C. Grier, in her book *Pets in America* (2006), states that cats were becoming acceptable pets during the late 1800s, particularly for women and young girls. During this era, families were increasingly photographed with their pet cats. Felines were also appearing in children's stories, such as Lewis Carroll's *Alice in Wonderland*, which indicates that cats were sharing living space with families and playing a more prominent role in domestic life. Nevertheless, cats were far less celebrated pets than dogs (and even birds and fish) and continued to be regarded more as the family mouser until the 1950s.

People began to spend more on their pets in general after the Second World War, when they could concentrate on domestic life and even earn

▼ Cats have sailed all over the world. Sailors welcome them onboard for their prowess as ratters.

some disposable incomes. Small mom-and-pop feed stores started rethinking their roles in the marketplace and began catering more specifically to pet needs, with items such as food bowls, beds, and collars. Some even sold boxes and bags of sand so that cats wouldn't have to go outside in inclement weather.

In 1947, Minnesotan Edward Lowe, who sold clay absorbents to garage owners to soak up gasoline spills, was asked by his neighbor Kay Draper if she could try some of his absorbent clay to replace the ashes she was using in her cat's box. He obliged, and Draper was so excited with the results that Lowe decided to market this new cat box filler. He trademarked the words *kitty kitter* and, with his product, changed the course of history for domestic cats. Today, for many cats in America, domestication means having an exclusively indoor lifestyle made possible by Edward Lowe's invention and others like it.

The World's First Spokescat

Morris, the orange tabby who is the spokescat for 9Lives cat food, has been one of the most recognizable feline faces in the United States since 1969. The first Morris was rescued from a Chicago animal shelter by trainer Bob Martwick in 1968. He was twenty minutes away from being euthanized! He eventually became an honorary director of StarKist Foods, with the power to veto any cat-food flavor he didn't like. He was invited by President Richard Nixon to cosign (with a paw print) the National Animal Protection Bill. In 2006, the spokescat spearheaded a national campaign to find homes for 1 million cats. This was achieved by June 2008. The current Morris spokescat is the fifth orange tabby to hold this position. He lives in California with Hollywood cat trainer Rose Ordile.

By the 1980s, the pet business had become an industry of international proportions. In the United States, it is now an economic force that rakes in billions of dollars annually and outsells toys, jewelry, and candy combined. By this time, most people stopped serving table scraps to their cats and started looking for proper cat food to meet the nutritional demands of their charges and products to improve their cats' health and well-being. In 2004, a market research analyst named Pam Danziger, an internationally recognized expert in understanding the mind of the consumer, published a report called *Why People Buy Things for Their Pets*. She made the point that Americans no longer simply have pets—they have animal companions, or, more specifically, furry family members.

Current statistics from the *National Pet Owners Survey*, published by the American Pet Products Association (APPA), highlight that more than 80 percent of American cat owners call themselves "pet parents." In this role, they want only the best for their kith and kin in terms of a lifestyle that mimics their own. (This same survey shows that many of the 86.4 million cats living in the United States live in multicat households [two to three cats], demonstrating how welcome cats are in the American home.)

It is clear that, in tracing the history of the domesticated cat, the feline has evolved from a working companion animal (one that worked for her own benefit) to a beloved companion.

Although many cats live in a state of domestic bliss, modern domestic life has produced a dark side, too, with hundreds of human-dependent cats being abandoned and left to fend for themselves. This has also created a social problem: feral cat colonies. Thus, while researchers continue with their insatiable thirst for additional knowledge to learn more about the ancestors of the felines that inhabit our homes and have a place in our hearts today, other scientists are trying to resolve the issue of unwanted or stray cats. They (and many other cat lovers) hope to create a world where every domestic cat has a loving home.

The History of Cats in Our World

Chapter 2

Cat Welfare and Rescue

*The worst sin towards our fellow creatures is
not to hate them, but to be indifferent to them.
That's the essence of inhumanity.*

— George Bernard Shaw

The history of animal welfare has its roots in Great Britain. Led by renowned British abolitionist William Wilberforce, a group of reformers founded the world's first animal welfare charity organization, the Society for the Prevention of Cruelty to Animals, in London in 1824. Initially, the society sought to protect farm animals. The organization's inspectors, the first of their kind, were sent out to markets and slaughterhouses to discover whether animals were receiving humane treatment (even in the methods used for killing). They also oversaw treatment of animals used to pull carriages for transport. In its first year, the organization took sixty-three offenders to court. Queen Victoria bestowed royal status on the society in 1840, making it the Royal Society for the Prevention of Cruelty to Animals. Today, this organization operates around the world.

In 1866, on the other side of the Atlantic, American diplomat Henry Bergh established the American

▶ Henry Bergh established the American Society for
the Prevention of Cruelty to Animals in 1866.

Society for the Prevention of Cruelty to Animals "to provide effective means for the prevention of cruelty to animals throughout the United States, based on the belief that animals are entitled to kind and respectful treatment at the hands of humans, and must be protected under the law." At the time of Bergh's death twenty years later, thirty-eight states had animal anticruelty laws in place.

Primary motivating factors for the society's foundation were changes in how animals were being treated in cities and towns and people's growing awareness of that treatment. This awareness led to the establishment of the first municipal shelters for animals and later to nonprofit rescues and private shelters. As pedigreed cats became more popular, breed rescue organizations formed to rescue specific breeds.

From the beginning, one huge problem for animal welfare workers was the ever-growing populations of feral cats. In the early 1900s, the feral cat population began to grow explosively because it was increasingly difficult to catch feral cats, let alone attempt to socialize them and try to find them homes. Consequently, animal control officers would go on massive hunts, rounding up cats, poisoning them or shooting them, extermination methods that sadly still exist in many places to this day.

The History of Shelters and Rescues

Prior to the latter half of the nineteenth century, numerous animals, including livestock such as pigs and chickens, as well as dogs and cats, had been allowed to roam the streets of the United States. Often, it was merely an economical way of feeding livestock: Butchers, for example, let their pigs wander and scavenge as a means of fattening themselves up before the kill. The same held true for chickens. Neither animal was dangerous, although their droppings were messy and didn't enhance neighborhoods. Early American towns, though, often had dirt streets, and the main mode of transportation, after all, was horses.

Dogs, however, whether owned or "tramp" (feral), were another matter. They fought with one another and ran in packs, especially the feral ones.

People worried that they could be attacked by these dogs and were concerned about the diseases the animals were purported to carry. Towns employed dogcatchers to round the animals up and cruelly bludgeon them to death or drown them.

Cats, on the other hand, while ubiquitous in the same towns and cities, were regarded as "free spirits" and allowed to roam, living as ferals in the shadows of urban life. Because cats weren't likely to attack people and shied away from human contact, their uncontrolled populations grew. In fact, many small businesses and even government offices relied

The Animal Welfare Act

The Animal Welfare Act became law in 1966 and is monitored and enforced by the US Department of Agriculture. It is the only federal law in the United States that regulates the treatment of animals in research, during exhibition, during transport, and by dealers (pet stores).

It was originally designed to ensure the humane treatment of animals used in scientific studies, such as in the use of drug testing by pharmaceutical companies. Over the years, it has evolved to include the terms and conditions under which a dog or cat should be housed and protected when found stray. Under Chapter 54 of the Animal Welfare Act, Section 2158, a cat, when found stray, must be cared for and protected by the entity for no fewer than five days so as to allow for the original owner to recover the lost pet or allow for the pet to be adopted by a new owner. Beyond this five-day period, the cat may be sold to a licensed dealer and, in turn, purchased by a scientific research center for study in animal behavior, testing in experimental drugs, or even purchased for use in government services. The Act requires dealers to provide to the recipient written certification regarding each animal's background.

The Act has been amended six times (in 1970, 1976, 1985, 1990, 2002, and 2007) and is enforced by the USDA's Animal and Plant Health Inspection Service (APHIS).

The Act can be read in full at www.nal.usda.gov.

▲ The Bide-A-Wee Home was one of the early animal rescue shelters. It opened just after the turn of the twentieth century in New York.

on cats to keep rats and mice at bay to prevent them from damaging store merchandise and mail.

As the nineteenth century drew to a close, however, public officials began to focus on making cities healthier places to live, and one of the first ways of doing this was by cleaning up the streets and removing scavenging animals, including cats. Some cities established pounds, places where they could temporarily place the stray animals they had rounded up (impounding them), perhaps giving owners a few days to claim them, then disposing of the unclaimed ones efficiently "in bulk."

However, as people took pets into their homes and gave them "jobs"—dogs to protect their owners and cats to ward off vermin—animal lovers started to recognize the inhumane methods being used to dispose of unwanted canines and felines. In line with this enlightened trend of thought, the Women's Branch of the Pennsylvania American Society for the Prevention of Cruelty to Animals (ASPCA), founded in 1869, passed a motion to establish a refuge to house homeless animals where they could be kept until they found a home or, when that failed, disposed of more humanely. The group lobbied the mayor of Philadelphia and won control over the city's municipal pound. They also cared for the captured pets, giving them food and water as well as shelter. First, they introduced "painless killing of these animals with chloroform," and then they constructed a special chamber where they could destroy multiple animals simultaneously using carbon monoxide gas. The first "shelter" in America had been created.

Apart from branches of the ASPCA, other animal rescue and welfare organizations, such as the Animal Rescue League of Boston (1899) and the Bide-A-Wee Home in New York (1902), began to emerge. These groups offered pet owners rudimentary "services" and began to promote the idea that people should relinquish their pets rather than simply turn them loose to fend for themselves. Furthermore, these early animal activists made a concerted effort to try to re-home as may pets as possible.

Slowly, as more cities began to realize that the responsibility of animal control fell under a municipal umbrella, they established animal control units, usually working in conjunction with their police divisions.

Sadly, since these early beginnings, many shelters or pounds that function under municipal control today are still bleak places where animals are caged and given a few days' grace in the hope of being claimed; if not, they are euthanized.

Nonprofit Rescues and Private Shelters

In the 1950s, as a sense of normalcy once again began to prevail after the end of the Second World War, both dogs and cats found themselves increasingly accepted by families as pets and not necessarily just required to work in the household by guarding property or killing vermin. Slowly and unobtrusively, they gained the status of companion animals and became an integral part of family life.

This prompted animal lovers to question the operational procedures of city pounds and address the plight of the unfortunate creatures that ended up in those places. These animal advocates began taking homeless pets in and initiating efforts to re-home them. Where possible, advocates would get together, find someone who had an unused garage or barn, and open a small shelter there. Functioning as nonprofit organizations, they relied solely on the generosity of the public and volunteers for the financial and hands-on support to assist the animals in their care.

Such groups began applying for tax-exempt status under the terms of Section 501(c), the provision of the United States Internal Revenue code that gives such groups the right to exemption from federal and, in many cases, state taxes. These small groups were the forerunners of the many private shelters and rescue organizations that continue to work tirelessly to rescue pets from municipal pounds where they are usually doomed to die, giving the animals a second chance by finding them forever homes.

▲ The establishment of animal shelters and rescues became more common in the United States starting in the 1950s.

Breed Rescue Organizations

Mix-breed cats are not the only ones who wind up in shelters. Although you might not think it, given what they often cost, many pedigreed cats suffer a similar fate. Responsible breeders have been known to take back the cats they produce to find them other homes. In fact, most sales contracts include a clause stating that the buyer will return the cat to the breeder if the buyer decides not to keep the cat. Still, pedigreed cats do sometimes end up in shelters.

Faced with this growing problem, lovers of a particular breed have formed specific breed rescue organizations. Today, breed rescue groups exist for every recognized cat breed from Abyssinians to Sphynx cats, from Persians to Munchkins—and even for designer breeds, such as the Bengal and the Savannah.

It's a sad reality that there's such a growing need for breed rescue groups to exist in the first place. But thank goodness that they do because people aware of the certain characteristics and traits of a particular breed are dedicated to ensuring that these cats are adopted into the right homes the second time around.

Breed rescue organizations have earned an excellent reputation. At the same time, they are educating the public that anyone wanting to adopt a particular breed of pedigreed cat as a household pet should consider adopting from such an organization.

Breed rescue organizations are easy to find by simply "googling" them to locate a group in a specific area. Often, cat shows also allow breed rescues to bring cats who are up for adoption to such events. Alternatively, cat breeders themselves are always an excellent source of information.

Adoption Screenings

When it came to helping cats, these organizations had their hands full because, in many instances, the feral cats whom they had managed to trap were too wild to settle down to domestic life as a pet. They also had to deal with the growing problem of people adopting cats and then, in the event of a move, abandoning them to fend for themselves. Animal rescuers slowly began educating the public about adopting cats, beginning with the idea that adoption is a long-term responsibility. They also wanted cat lovers to recognize that domestic cats were much safer when allowed to live a strictly indoor existence rather than being allowed outside, where they were not only exposed to diseases but also could be attacked by other animals, killed in traffic, and, if not spayed or neutered, proliferate by the thousands.

Slowly, forward-thinking cat rescue volunteers started screening potential cat owners, actually visiting their homes to ensure that anyone adopting a cat from a shelter was in fact offering not only love and affection but also a truly secure place to live.

Simultaneously came the recognition that the only way to curb the numbers of animals consigned to both municipal and private shelters was to embark on a massive sterilization program to ensure that cats, in particular, would be prevented from giving birth to an annual litter of kittens. Consequently, it became common practice to spay or neuter all cats in a shelter prior to their adoption. Many shelters to this day rely on the generosity of veterinarians who donate their time and services to get this mammoth task done.

The adoption fee paid to the shelter helps to cover these costs. Shelter managers also believe that someone who is prepared to put money on the table to adopt a pet will be more serious in the commitment and responsibility to that animal.

Feral Cats

Feral cats are defined as cats who are unowned and unsocialized. Cats who once had homes but were abandoned—for any number of reasons—quickly turn feral to survive, and they add to the throngs of the unwanted. Sadly, feral populations continue to grow, not only in the United States but also around the world.

Today, it's not uncommon to find cat lovers feeding a group of ferals cats who live in the neighborhood. In some instances, groups of volunteers have banded together to feed colonies of these cats who continue to live in the underbelly of cities and towns all around the globe.

Shelter Wish List

Here are some much needed gifts you can give to your local animal shelter:

- washable comforters, blankets, and rugs
- grooming tools
- toys
- beds
- cat and kitten food (unopened)
- treats
- water and food bowls
- soft-sided carriers
- crates (all sizes)

Shelters also typically need equipment and supplies to help them provide quality, caring support for the animals they house, such as:

- large plastic garbage cans and 30-gallon trash bags
- all-purpose cleaning materials and odor removers
- paper towels, tissues, and toilet paper
- kitty litter
- mops and buckets with wringers
- plastic water pitchers, plastic utensils
- large plastic storage containers
- rolling storage carts
- office supplies, such as folders, pens, small notebooks, stamps, and paper
- baby weighing scale
- pet store gift certificates

Animal shelters gratefully accept donations of gently used items, too, such as towels, linens, bedding, and pet beds. You can also donate unwanted computers and kitchen items, such as microwaves and refrigerators.

Feral cat managers always appreciate the offer to help construct wooden doghouse-type structures for shelters. Food, as well as financial donations to pay for veterinary care when needed, is also appreciated.

Overpopulation in the cat world is a huge and growing problem because unspayed and unneutered cats continue to proliferate at an alarming rate. Female cats come into season in spring and summer, and such pregnancies culminate in what has become known as "kitten season" a mere sixty-three days later. An average litter is three to five kittens. To make matters worse, cats can reach sexual maturity at six months of age. Experts have done the math and claim that if a single female cat were to mate every time she came into season, and all her kittens were to survive and breed, she could be responsible for up to 21,000 extra cats in just seven years. It became obvious to volunteers who worked with ferals on a regular basis that the only way to curb and possibly control these feral populations was to attempt to sterilize these free-roaming felines.

Trap, Neuter, and Return/Release Programs

In the 1960s, British model and famous *Vogue* cover girl Celia Hammond used her celebrity to speak out against the fur trade and about the plight of feral cats in Britain. Hammond, an enthusiastic cat lover, learned how to trap feral cats to have them neutered and then returned to their environment, where they could continue to live but not continue to breed. She was solely responsible for setting up numerous low-cost spay and neutering clinics in Britain, and she fought and won many battles with local authorities to establish this method as a viable alternative to euthanasia.

By the 1970s, Hammond had opened a sanctuary where cats who could not be returned to their environments could live in peace. She re-homed thousands of neutered, vaccinated ferals; she also kept records of the neutered colonies and was able to document how, over time, these colonies could die out through the attrition of old age if no one added to their numbers by adding more cats.

Her system had a name—TNR—standing for trap, neuter, and return (also called trap, neuter, and release). It was rapidly recognized as a viable option by cat activists around the world who followed in her footsteps in countries such as Denmark, France, Israel, South Africa, and, finally, the United States.

▲ Breed rescues are great places to look for a new feline companion if you desire a specific breed but still want to adopt a homeless cat.

The Celia Hammond Animal Trust continues to run low-cost neuter/spay clinics in Britain for cats and dogs whose owners are on welfare or have low incomes, and Hammond herself continues to work tirelessly for ferals.

TNR in the United States

AnnaBell Washburn of Martha's Vineyard, Massachusetts, has been credited with being the first to practice feral cat management in the United States. In 1980, she founded the Pet Adoption and Welfare Service (PAWS) to help those animals adopted by summer visitors to the island who subsequently abandoned the animals when they packed up to go back home at the end of the season. In 1986, Washburn initiated the first TNR partnership with veterinarians when she accompanied veterinary students from the Cummings School of Veterinary Medicine at Tufts

University to help sterilize cats on Virgin Gorda in the British Virgin Islands.

During the 1980s, several feral cat programs were established around the country, including the Stanford Cat Network, which practiced TNR on the Stanford University campus and continues to manage the cat colony there. The San Francisco Society for the Prevention of Cruelty to Animals launched a major drive to reduce the number of animals being euthanatized in the San Francisco Bay area by offering free sterilization services. And, in fact, many people around the country were practicing TNR on a private basis and unknown to one another.

One such person was Ellen Perry Berkeley, who in 1982 published a book titled *Maverick Cats: Encounters with Feral Cats*, based on the cats living free in her home state of Vermont. Her close contact with them prompted her to study the problem of feral cats and encourage the idea of neutering. The book was hallmarked as a blueprint and was especially enlightening in the early days of TNR.

The first formal network for managing feral cats in the United States was created in 1990, when a former South African named Louise Holton, who had been practicing TNR in Johannesburg, South Africa and brought her methods to the United States, teamed up with Becky Robinson, another

How to Become a Foster Cat Parent

Fostering a cat or a litter of kittens so that they can eventually be adopted into forever homes is a very rewarding job. You're helping to shape these animals' futures so that they can settle into a permanent home. Fostering plays a very important role in the animal adoption system. If it weren't for many wonderful no-kill shelters, with their foster programs and dedicated foster parents who open up their homes and their hearts to these deserving cats, thousands more would be euthanized each year.

Often, when people think of fostering, they think of small kittens who need to be bottle-fed and nurtured until they are old enough to be adopted. In fact, many adult cats need care and attention too. Foster homes are also needed for pets in trouble—like those separated from their families during Hurricane Katrina. Many of those displaced pets landed in welcoming homes hundreds of miles away from their hometown and stayed with their foster families for months.

Becoming a foster parent is not a task for the faint-hearted. It's emotionally and physically demanding. It means being able to give lots of love and attention and a safe and secure environment to the cat in your care so that it can become a well-socialized, happy, and healthy animal. Some pets require special time-consuming medical attention, whereas others have behavioral issues and need time to learn to trust humans.

The best fostering situation is one in which there is at least one adult at home at all times. You also need transport to take your charge to the shelter on a regular basis for veterinary checkups and, possibly, for postoperative care.

Although the adoption shelter typically provides all the basic necessities like food and medication, it's necessary to make special preparations in the home to give your foster pet the best care. Often, this means setting aside a room and keeping foster pets apart from the rest of the animals in your household. This separation allows the fostered pets to settle in and adapt to a warm and loving environment. It also ensures that your own pets are not exposed to any health risks.

Foster pets have been known to ruin carpeting and couches, so their care environment is a great place to recycle your old furniture.

Of course, no cat can ever have too many toys, and foster parents are encouraged to spoil their charges by stocking up on lots of interactive toys such as lasers and wand toys, crinkly balls, and catnip mice.

A great way to find out whether you would make a good foster parent is to first become a volunteer at a local animal shelter. Most organizations require a prospective volunteer to go through their standard orientation program and become well-acquainted with the shelter and the foster system in general.

When fostering, it's important to remain somewhat emotionally detached and, when the time comes, to let your charge go to his or her permanent home knowing you have saved a life—and that you are ready to go through the process again.

▲ Unchecked, feral cat populations grow amazingly fast.

strong voice for America's unwanted cats, to form Alley Cat Allies (ACA). Their mission was simple: to end the killing of cats and lead a movement for their humane care. Today, the organization, headquartered in Bethesda, Maryland, has the support of more than 190,000 caregivers and supporters, continues to spearhead a progressive movement for the protection of all cats, and educates the public about the lives of cats.

Alley Cat Allies has been instrumental in animal control and shelter industry reform and humane treatment, calling for pounds and shelters around the country to keep public records of animal intake and kill rates, for public and mandatory government oversight, and for increased pound and shelter accountability. The group continues to develop educational materials on the care and protection of stray and feral cats and works with grassroots organizations around the world that look to ACA for guidance on how to abolish cruel policies and improve the lives of cats everywhere.

In 2000, Holton broke away from ACA to form Alley Cat Rescue, which has also grown to be another powerful force in educating people in the welfare of all cats—domestic, stray, and feral, as well as wild cat species living around the world. Most recently, she has led teams of volunteers into Mexico to spread the word about TNR to that country, setting up makeshift clinics and offering free spay and neutering to everyone who showed up with a pet.

Feral Cats and the Environment

One of the biggest problems that continues to jeopardize feral cat colonies is the cry that they are destructive to other wildlife, particularly birds. Bird lovers are often quick to blame feral cats for bird decimation, overlooking human causes for the birds' demise, such as industrial and residential development and the overuse of pesticides in farming. Consequently, proponents of feral cat protection continually fight local city ordinances, which are often unfair to the feline point of view.

In fact, two federal laws that protect endangered and migratory bird species, the Migratory Bird Treaty Act (MBTA) and the Endangered Species Act (ESA), were both passed by Congress in response to the widespread *human* destruction of birds, other species,

and their habitats—not because of cats. For feral cat activists, it is an ongoing battle to present their side of the story and make their voices heard.

Project Bay Cat, in Foster City, California, is an officially managed feral cat colony program that owes its success to the ongoing cooperation among the City of Foster City, a rescue group known as the Homeless Cat Network, and the community.

It came into being as a humane solution to help nearly 200 cats living along San Francisco Bay. A public meeting was called and Cimeron Morrissey, the driving force behind Project Bay Cat, explained how a program of trap, neuter, and return could help to stabilize the feral cat population and that a managed colony that was being well fed was not likely to hunt.

In a groundbreaking move, the City of Foster City decided to officially join hands with the Homeless Cat Network and the community to create Project Bay Cat, with the goal of balancing the humane treatment of the cat population and the needs of the City and the users of the waterfront.

The City created and installed signs along the trail explaining to the public that this was a managed colony and that any interference or animal abandonment is punishable by law. The Homeless Cat Network built special feeding stations along the trail. Setting up the project from the municipality's standpoint cost taxpayers a mere $500—the cost of the signs!

Volunteers, who have included doctors, lawyers, and even a millionaire entrepreneur, take turns to feed the cats on a daily basis. While Homeless Cat Network provides the food and necessary supplies, many of the volunteers pay for kibble and canned food themselves. Feeding by members of the public is discouraged because it makes it more difficult for the official caregivers to keep tabs on the cats and trap them when they need veterinary attention.

The Network's relationship with two veterinary hospitals has helped greatly. The hospitals spayed/neutered and vaccinated all the cats from Project

◀ Alley Cat Allies is one of a number of organizations that use the trap-neuter-release (TNR) method to humanely control feral cat populations.

Bay Cat, and they continue to treat any diseases and ailments on an ongoing basis.

Every year since the program was developed, the number of cats in the colony has declined. On the program's tenth anniversary, Project Bay Cat reported a 65 percent decline in the cat population due to natural attrition and adoption efforts. The program's organizers anticipate a continuation of the trend and anticipate that, one day, the colony will cease to exist. Project Bay Cat is a blueprint for success. The organization is happy to offer advice to anyone who wishes to emulate the concept in other cities in America or elsewhere in the world.

For her tireless work and determination to succeed, Cimeron Morrissey was named Animal Planet's Cat Hero of the Year in 2007.

Cat Rescue Today

In the twenty-first century, cat shelters featuring adoption programs, TNR, and feral cat management programs have become viable alternatives to euthanasia. Today, many educational resources offering advice to cat lovers on how to start a rescue group or offering assistance to established feral cat groups can be found on pet welfare organization websites such as those run by the ACA, Alley Cat Rescue, the Humane Society of the United States, and the ASPCA. The past decade has seen feral cat caregivers establish working relationships with local municipal animal control agencies that, in time, we hope, will lead to other success stories such as Project Bay Cat.

In addition, instead of just looking after unwanted cats, rescue groups are making a concerted effort to establish foster programs so that, where possible, cats and kittens in the rescue system can be properly socialized, which will make it much easier to find them forever homes.

Another positive side of cat rescue has been the establishment of retirement homes for elderly cats whose owners have passed away but had the foresight to make provision in their estates for their cats' lifelong care. Specific retirement establishments, such as the Blue Bell Foundation for Cats in Laguna Beach, California, are wonderful, homey environments staffed by volunteers who attend to the medical needs of these aging felines and give them lots of love and affection. It's a

▼ Project Bay Cat is a successfully managed colony of feral cats in Foster City, California, that demonstrates what can be accomplished when municipalities, cat lovers, and environmentalists work together.

▲ Hoarding is more than just having too many cats. It's a complex mental health issue that involves denying the inability to care for so many cats (or other animals).

Abuse, Cruelty, Hoarding, and Abandonment

Recent academic studies have shown that animal abuse and cruelty is often just a starting point for the perpetrators of these shameful acts, with many of these individuals moving on to commit other acts of violence and domestic abuse. This has helped animal rights activists call for more stringent laws to be put in place and for harsher punishments for crimes against animals.

Animal cruelty laws vary from state to state. In 2006, Maine became the first state in the country to introduce a law specifically allowing courts to include companion animals in domestic violence protective orders. Since then, similar laws have been passed in California, Colorado, Connecticut, Illinois, Louisiana, Nevada, New York, Tennessee, Vermont, Washington, and Puerto Rico. Of course, courts in other states can extend this protection to pets without a specific law.

There are more than 550 animal cruelty laws; the related penalties are listed on the ASPCA website, and it's an excellent up-to-date resource. This database, maintained by the ASPCA Government Affairs and Public Policy department, is easy to use because it allows you to select a specific state to access the relevant laws and even offers a keyword search function to find a specific topic. This can be useful when reporting an incident of animal abuse, helping to make local law enforcement officials aware that a legal course of action is available if, as is often the case, they are not familiar with lesser-known laws.

When reporting an incident of animal abuse, it's important to provide law enforcement with a concise, written, factual statement; include dates and approximate times; and, whenever possible, back this up with witness statements. It's also a good idea to try to photograph the abusive situation and date your pictures.

Hoarding

It is not clearly understood why people become animal hoarders. Early research pointed toward a variant of obsessive-compulsive disorder, but new

testament to their work that many of the cats in retirement homes are living well into their late teens and even their twenties.

Furthermore, sanctuaries that also offer a safe haven to homeless pets for the rest of their lives have opened around the country. One of the most famous is the Best Friends Animal Sanctuary in Kanab, Utah, which even invites pet lovers to come and stay and spend a volunteer vacation working with the cats, dogs, and a variety of other animals lucky enough to live there.

Animal rescue and welfare has changed dramatically since its conception in the late nineteenth century. Today, both shelter and feral cats have strong, humane voices championing their cause. Apart from the countless of volunteers who are undoubtedly the driving forces behind these many organizations countrywide, help has come from the veterinary community and from animal behaviorists who are stepping forward to educate cat owners on proper care. Veterinarians and behaviorists want to ensure that cats can stay in their homes, that they will not be relinquished because their owners are ignorant about how to give them the care they need and deserve.

▲ Unfortunately, many cats are abandoned to fend for themselves by owners who can no longer care for them.

studies and theories are leading toward attachment disorders in conjunction with personality disorders, paranoia, delusional thinking, depression, and other mental illnesses. Some animal hoarders began collecting after a traumatic event or loss, whereas others see themselves as "rescuers" who save animals from a life on the street.

The Hoarding of Animals Research Consortium, an independent group of academic researchers based in Massachusetts, gives the following criteria to define an animal hoarder. A hoarder is someone who:

- has more than the typical number of companion animals
- is unable to provide even minimal standards of nutrition, sanitation, shelter, and veterinary care, with this neglect often resulting in starvation, illness, and death.
- denies the inability to provide this minimum care and the impact of that failure on the animals, the household, and human occupants of the dwelling.

Laws about hoarding cats are covered by every state's Cruelty to Animals statute, which typically requires a caretaker to provide sufficient food and water, veterinary care, and a sanitary environment. Only one state, Illinois, currently has a legal definition of animal hoarding in its cruelty statute. With guidance from ASPCA, the Illinois Companion Animal Hoarder Act of 2001 was created to both delineate penalties and mandate psychological counseling for convicted companion animal hoarders. It also expands the tools police officers, humane societies, and judges have to combat animal neglect and cruelty.

Other items addressed in the bill include:

- Increasing the penalties for neglect, cruel treatment, aggravated cruelty, and animal torture. Animal neglect is raised to a Class B misdemeanor; cruel treatment becomes a Class A misdemeanor, aggravated cruelty becomes a Class 4 felony (1–3 years jail time), and animal torture becomes a Class 3 felony (3–5 years jail time).
- Allowing individuals who own animals that have been the victims of aggravated cruelty or torture to file a civil action for damages. Damages may include the monetary value of the animal; veterinary expenses incurred; any other expenses, including the emotional distress suffered by the owner; and punitive damages of up to $25,000 plus attorneys fees and court costs.
- Allowing police officers to seize vehicles used in dog fighting.
- Allowing humane societies to ask courts for security to be posted to help ease the financial burden associated with caring for impounded animals.
- Establishing an Illinois Animal Abuse Investigation Fund to help fund investigation of cruelty and neglect complaints.
- Mandating psychological counseling for juveniles convicted of animal cruelty.

Similar legislation has been submitted, but has not as yet become law, in the states of Vermont and New Mexico.

North Shore Animal League America

North Shore Animal League America, headquartered in Port Washington, New York, is the world's largest no-kill animal rescue and adoption organization. Since its inception in 1944, it has stayed true to its mission of saving lives, and it reaches out daily across the country to rescue, nurture, and facilitate the adoption of more than 20,000 pets into happy and loving homes every year.

Although proper records were not kept in the early years, the shelter's directors estimate that more than 56,000 felines have been given a second chance at love and a family life as a result of the league's rescue missions.

▲ Potential pet adopters waiting to enter North Shore Animal League's Emergency Rescue and Adoption Unit in New York City.

The first shelter operated by the league was a converted backyard garage. The efforts of the handful of volunteers that ran it went unnoticed until 1969, when a couple of animal lovers named Elisabeth and Alexander Lewyt attended a shelter meeting and decided to start a membership drive that subsequently launched the organization into the public spotlight and created the powerful force that it is today.

It was while visiting a local pound that Elizabeth Lewyt saw all the puppies, kittens, dogs, and cats about to be destroyed. Horrified by this destruction of innocent life, she paid all the pound fees, put all the pets in her station wagon, took them back to the shelter, and set about finding them all homes.

Today, the league is home to the Alex Lewyt Veterinary Medical Center, which provides twenty-four-hour veterinary care and annually tends to more than 10,000 outpatients. The center also administers over 27,000 vaccinations and performs more than 14,000 free spay-neuter procedures every year.

The league has also founded several programs that have improved the lives of countless pets, such as the SPAY/USA program, which has established a network of sterilization clinics nationwide that offer affordable spay and neutering services to anyone in need of assistance.

The league also offers a permanent home to many special-needs animals. Sometimes, an animal has to stay with the organization for life due to a severe medical condition. The Sponsorship program invites members of the public to "adopt" a pet, and their monthly donation goes to offset the costly medical and rehabilitative costs necessary to keep these orphans happy and healthy. The league sends monthly updates to donors, letting them know how their special pet is doing.

This organization has become a model of hope that others have copied, with the communal goal of one day making America a no-kill nation for any companion animals. For more information, go to www.AnimalLeague.org.

Abandonment

When the economy started to tank in 2008, plunging America into deep recession, people abandoned many cats and dogs when they abandoned the homes they could not longer afford to keep. Although abandoning animals is illegal in most states under anticruelty laws, these laws are often not rigidly enforced. Consequently, to deal with this crisis, lawmakers in California passed a law in January 2009 that made it mandatory for landlords and banks that found themselves in possession of foreclosed home to be responsible for any animals that owners had abandoned on the properties concerned. The law states that:

> Any person or private entity with whom a live animal has been "involuntarily deposited" must take charge of it and immediately notify animal control officials to retrieve the animal. An "involuntary deposit" includes the abandonment of a live animal on a property that has been vacated upon, or immediately preceding, the termination of a lease or foreclosure of the property.

Laws such as this highlight how far animal welfare has come in America. But there's still much work to be done.

The History of Cats in Our World

Chapter 3

Cats in Religion, Folklore, and Popular Culture

*I believe cats to be spirits come to earth.
A cat, I am sure, could walk on a
cloud without coming through.*

— Jules Verne

Throughout history, cats have been considered images of both good and evil, harbingers of both good luck and bad. They have been seen as spiritual beings in the religions of some societies and as unclean outcasts in those of others. Which and where, who and what, have changed over the centuries, having nothing to do with the true nature of cats and everything to do with the fears and fervent wishes of the people of a given place and time.

Cats have also fired the imagination of storytellers from the moment they first sauntered into human settlements, and, as a consequence, they have found themselves prominent actors in folktales, poetry, and other types of literature throughout time, down to and including the modern mystery novel. Their sleek, colorful, furry appearance, their supreme air of superiority and confidence, along with their effortless ability to charm and endear themselves have been captured and magnified by painters, sculptors, cartoonists, and moviemakers. They have been celebrated in children songs and danced their way across the stage in Broadway musicals. Cats, as is their way, have managed to make their presence felt.

▶ In ancient Egypt, newlyweds were given statues of Bast in the belief the goddess would protect them and bless them with children.

◄ In Norse mythology, the chariot of the goddess Freya was pulled by two large cats.

Cats in Religion and Mythology

Are they the embodiment or servants of gods? Or the sinister servants of Satan and witches? Should we revere them or revile them? That depends on whose religion/mythology you choose to believe.

Cats Revered

The ancient Egyptians worshipped cats based on their conviction that the common cat was the incarnation of Bast, the goddess of fertility, love, pleasure, and dance and the protector against all evil. The goddess was known as Bast by day, when she appeared with a cat's head and the body of a woman, and as Bastet by night, when she could transform completely into a cat. Newlyweds received a statue of Bastet with her tail wrapped around her body to the right, a gift to bless them with children and to ward off evil in their home. This statue is still a popular tourist souvenir sold in Egyptian street markets.

Romans may have acquired some of their first cats from Egypt around the fifth century BC, but they did not acquire the Egyptians' reverence for the domestic cat. What they did appreciate, however, was the cat's prowess as a vermin killer, and so they welcomed the cat on that practical basis. The cat rose no higher than that among the Romans, certainly not as high as spiritual status. When they marched to conquer northern Europe, Romans took cats with them, and many of these domestic cats found places among the native peoples, some of whom practiced religions closely associated with animals. Cats were incorporated into those practices.

The Nordic people already had their own cats—the Norwegian Forest Cat—most of them to be found among the common people, a few to be found mingling with the pantheon of Norse gods. Two large gray (some say black) cats pulled the chariot of Freya, beautiful goddess of love and fertility. Because of this belief, the Nordic people viewed domestic cats as Freya's emissaries on earth and believed that those who sheltered and fed a cat brought themselves good fortune.

Far to the east, domestic cats, believed to have been introduced to Japan from China in the sixth century CE, were valued in religious circles. Every temple owned two cats to prevent mice from gnawing through precious manuscripts. Emperor Ichijo, who reigned from 986 to 1011 CE, was purported to have been a great cat lover and insisted that felines should be pampered and respected for the "work" they did.

In Siam (present-day Thailand), Siamese cats were respected guardians of Buddhist temples. When a member of the royal family died, it was tradition to select one of these cats to receive the dead person's soul. The cat was then removed from the royal household and sent to one of the temples to spend the rest of her days living a ceremonial life of great luxury, with monks and priests as her servants. Once becoming temple cats, these select felines were supposed to have special powers and could intercede for the royal souls they carried. Siamese cats were held in such high esteem in Siam that no one except the king and other members of the royal family were permitted to own them.

Cats Reviled

Dark days began for the cat in Europe around the time of the fall of the Roman Empire in the fifth century CE, when other religious belief systems gained precedence in Europe. One of the new practices was Gnosticism, a system built on Greek philosophy that included some of the teachings of Christianity. It taught dualism, a separation between the material and spiritual world based on the principles of good and evil. In Gnosticism, and for the first time in religious history, the devil was portrayed as a black cat. In some circles, this unfortunate association persists to this day.

During the Early Middle Ages, the Catholic Church sought to spread Christianity and wipe out so-called pagan practices by native people. In 1231, Pope Gregory IX instituted the Papal Inquisition in an attempt to apprehend "heretics." The Inquisition turned, literally, into a witch hunt—and a cat hunt. Sir Edward of Norwich, the second Duke of York (1373–1415) made clear his belief in an association of felines with witchcraft and Satanism, a belief shared by many, when he wrote: "Of common wild cats, I need not speak much for every hunter in England knoweth them, and their falseness and malice are well known. But one thing I dare well say that if any beast hath the devil's spirit in him, without doubt it is the cat, both the wild and the tame."

Cats were captured, tortured, and killed by the hundreds of thousands during this period. In the fifteenth century, common people who owned cats were tortured and killed as well. Witch hunts and cat hunts continued to spread throughout Britain and Europe and across the ocean to the New World, where they culminated in the infamous Salem witch trials in Puritan Massachusetts in 1692. It was during this era that black cats in particular had their darkest hour because of their association with witches.

Following the Salem witch hunts, societal changes that lessened the feline association with evil occurred. Great Britain's Witchcraft Act of 1736 repealed laws in that country that allowed the persecution of people accused of being witches; in fact, this Act reflected a 180-degree shift in attitude. Under the new Act, officials were authorized to prosecute any person "pretending to exercise or use any kind of Witchcraft, Sorcery, Inchantment, or Conjuration." Evidently, because all intelligent, educated people now knew that there were no such things as witches, sorcerers, or conjurers, anyone claiming to have such powers only did so to "delude and defraud" and to extract money from the gullible. This dramatic change in view was certainly good news for cats as well. Eventually, people felt more comfortable about owning cats. During the ensuing Age of Enlightenment in Britain and Europe, various religious sects became less fanatical in their views about others, including cats.

The fact that common people once again considered cats useful because they helped control the rats and mice that spread the many diseases rife at the time strengthened this viewpoint. Their image was further improved, reaching a point where they were even perceived as a symbol of cleanliness because they spent so many hours fastidiously cleaning themselves.

However, despite these changes, because devil worship continued to exist (and still does), the association of felines with evil continued to endure, albeit it on a lesser scale.

▼ In the Middle Ages, cats—especially black cats—became associated with witchcraft and satanic worship, and many cats were killed because of this.

Cats in Reincarnation

The concept of rebirth can be found in the philosophies of the ancient Greeks, as well as in the Buddhist and Hindu religions. Interestingly, Hindu beliefs name the lion, the domestic cat's cousin, a sacred animal, along with cows and elephants. Hindu priests believe that, after death, the *atman* (soul) of a person or animal passes into a new body and a new life. The quality of this new life depends on how the person or animal lived in their previous lives. And because of the belief that a person can be reborn as any animal, including a cat, many Hindus are vegetarians.

It is the belief of both the Catholic Church and various branches of the Christian faith that although animals are to be respected, the life spirit that comes with their birth ends with their death. They are not reborn into another body.

Among the numerous legends that cat lovers like to hold on to support a belief in an afterlife for cats is the story that Baby Jesus wouldn't stop crying until a cat climbed into the manger and started to purr, sending him off to sleep. In gratitude, the Virgin Mary marked the cat's face with the first letter of her name.

▲ Statue of a Beckoning Cat at the entrance to a Hindu temple in Bali, Indonesia.

There's also a fable that says that the Prophet Mohammed, founder of Islam and an acknowledged cat lover, placed the *M* on a forehead of his favorite tabby. Yet, in spite of this, Islam makes no special mention of cats. The Muslim belief is that whereas people are judged for their actions in life, on Judgment Day, there is no afterlife for any animal—cats only live their lives here on earth.

There are a variety of Jewish views about an afterlife for human beings, but nothing in the Talmud relates to an afterlife for cats or animals in general. Nevertheless, the Jewish faith holds that all of God's creatures, big and small, are beloved of the Creator and insists on kindness to animals. Jews who closely follow traditional teachings or commandments do not eat until their animals have been fed.

Feline Folklore

Cats, as they would be the first to tell you, are endlessly fascinating. So it is not surprising that they have been cast in folktales from one side of the world to the other. And, despite the religious beliefs that linked cats to evil and bad luck during the Middle Ages, it's interesting to note that, for some cultures, they were also considered symbols of good fortune.

Asia

Not surprisingly, because so many cat breeds originated in the Far East, many legends and folktales are told of the cat here.

China

Chinese folklore claims that cats once ruled the world and had the power of speech. The story goes that they delegated this power to humans so that they could spend more time snoozing in the sun and manicuring their toenails. That's why they no longer speak and eye humans suspiciously when they hurry past, busying themselves with ridiculous daily tasks.

Japan

A popular souvenir around the world is the *Maneki Neko* or Beckoning Cat from Japan. This little ornament is considered a symbol of good luck and prosperity. Japanese legend says that a cat stood at the door of the Gotoku-ji Temple in Tokyo and raised her paw in the traditional Japanese beckoning gesture to a feudal lord who was passing by. He followed the cat into the temple and escaped being killed by a bolt of lightning that hit the ground where he had been standing.

▲The Maneki Neko, or Beckoning Cat, is a symbol of luck and prosperity in Japan. The statues are popular tourist souvenirs.

Today, there is a huge and growing exhibit of Maneki Neko figurines at the temple because visitors come to pay their respects and then leave another statue, thus adding to the collection. Maneki Neko statues can be found all over Japan and indeed around the world. Piggy banks are often created in the cat's likeness to invite wealth.

Malaysia

In Malaysia, people believed that cats would help their soul journey from hell to paradise, and the punishment for killing a cat was to carry as many coconut tree trunks as the cat had hairs.

According to other Malaysian legends, English soldier and traveler Sir James Brooke was given the right to rule Sarawak by the grateful Sultan of Brunei in 1841 as a reward for quelling a local uprising. Unsure of the town's Malay name, he looked to his local guide for help. The guide thought he was pointing at a feral cat, and he found himself proclaiming the name of the town to be *Kuching*, the Malay word for "cat." Today, this city

in East Malaysia honors felines, with a cat museum featuring a massive statue of a cat outside as well as many other huge feline statues around the city.

Thailand (Siam)

In the Thai province of Songktha, which is the gateway to Malaysia and Singapore, another huge feline statue sits on Samila beach, marking two tiny islands known as Ko Nu (Rat Island) and Ko Maeo (Cat Island). The local story proclaims that a dog, a cat, and a rat were sailing with a merchant on a sampan and stole his magic crystal. They tried to swim ashore but drowned and lost their lives. The rat and the cat became islands and the dog died on the shore and became the hill called Hin Khao Tang Kuan.

Another popular Siamese legend tells of a princess who was frightened of losing her rings while she bathed in a stream. She noticed her favorite cat sitting close by and decided to put her rings on the cat's tail because a kink in the tail would prevent them from falling off. Proponents of this myth like to believe that Siamese cats have kinks in their tails for this reason. It's a "fault" that modern breeders have been working to remove from their Siamese bloodlines, but ornamental cats with their tails in the air are still popular ring holders to this day.

Siamese King Ramu V was said to have given the breed known as the Korat its name. *Korat* means "gray cat"; Ramu V believed these cats were the color of rain clouds, and he decreed that they be carried in rituals to bring rain to the fields. This belief was also adopted in Indonesia.

Europe
Despite the persecution of cats during the Middle Ages, many positive folktales of cats are to be found.

England
The story of Dick Whittington, an adventurer who left India by ship with only a cat for "baggage" and went on to gain fame and fortune in London with his cat by his side, has inspired many to this day to believe that cats bring good luck. Whittington served three terms as Lord Mayor of London in the late fourteenth and early fifteenth century. The Whittington Hospital in the Borough of Islington in London is named after him, and a small statue of his cat sitting on a commemorative plaque can be found on Highgate Hill, alongside the hospital.

France
Local legend in the southwestern French town of La Romieu tells the story of Angeline, a fourteenth-century lover and savior of cats and a village heroine. Orphaned as a baby, she was adopted by another family, and she in turn adopted several of the stray village cats. They followed her to the fields where she worked (and they lounged), to the table where they shared her food, and to bed, where they all curled up together. Then came three years of harsh winters and drenching springs and summers, which meant no crops could be sown and food reserves ran out, bringing famine to the village. Desperate for any source of food, the villagers turned to the cat population. A determined

▲The name of the Malaysian city of Kuching is the Malay word for "cat," and there are many statues of cats throughout the city.

Angeline, with her adopted parents' approval, secreted away two of her cats, a male and a female, keeping them in the attic by day, releasing them to hunt for food by night. Angeline, her family, and much of the village survived the famine, and better seasons brought crops once again. Unfortunately, a new threat endangered the harvest—rats. Without the once-ubiquitous cats, nothing stood between the rodents and the crops. Then Angeline appeared, followed by the two cats she had protected—and their eighteen progeny. They set about taking care of the village's problem most enthusiastically. Thus, La Romieu was saved, thanks to a young girl's love for her cats and the cats' excellent skill at doing what comes naturally.

The coda to the legend: Maurice Serreau, a sculptor from Orléans, overheard a woman telling

▲The cat statues in La Romieu, France, honor a local legend of a young girl and her cats who saved the town from a plague of rats.

Angeline's story to her grandchildren. Taken by the tale, he decided to create a whimsical reminder of it by populating the town's square with sculptures of cats lounging, sitting, walking, and stalking.

Italy

An Italian legend dating back to the twelfth century tells of a rich merchant who fled the city of Aquileia and the wrath of Attila the Hun. Stopping along the coast of the Adriatic Sea, he asked a poor man to become his business partner in the hundreds of tiny islands that fill the sea. The man had no money, but he did have two cats, which were to become the foundation of the new business enterprise. The cats went to work on the rat-infested islands, winning the merchant high praise, and the business thrived. The merchant considered the cats his lucky charms, but he agreed to sell them for a fortune. The legend claims that this is why the city of Venice was free of the plague-infested mice that had killed thousands in the surrounding cities and towns. Later, during the Middle Ages, however, the mice and rats returned.

Poland

According to a Polish legend, a mother cat was crying at the bank of a river as she helplessly watched her kittens drown after accidently falling into the water while chasing butterflies. The willow trees on the river's banks helped save the kittens by dipping their branches into the water and bringing the kittens safely back to their mother. Since then, every spring, these willow trees sprout tiny fur-like buds at their tips, earning them the nickname "pussy willow."

North America

Cats of all sorts travel the mountains, deserts, plains, and valleys—as well as the buildings—of North America in folklore and legend.

Tennessee, United States

From Tennessee folklore comes the story of the Wampus Cat, said to be half woman and half mountain cat. This legend, told around campfires, is the story of a woman who decided to follow her husband when the men of her tribe went on a hunting trip because she wanted to spy on him and his fellow hunters. According to the laws of the tribe, it was absolutely forbidden for women to hear the sacred stories and see the men's magic. So, when the Indian woman was discovered, the medicine man of the tribe punished her by binding her into the mountain cat skin she wore, transforming her into a half woman and half mountain cat creature, and leaving her doomed to roam the hills, howling desolately in her desire to return to her human body. She is supposed to still haunt the hills of rural eastern Tennessee.

Southwestern United States

The bobcat-size Cactus Cat is said to be covered in hair-like thorns with long spines on its tail. This thorny creature is said to have terrorized lumberjacks in southwestern American lumber camps at the turn of the twentieth century. According to legend, the creature used its spines to slash cacti at night, allowing the juice to run from the plants. The Cactus Cat would leave the juice to ferment on the ground, then return to lap it all up and become intoxicated. Then the cat would shriek throughout the night, scaring those within range of its bloodcurdling sounds.

Washington, DC

The Demon Cat is a ghost cat said to haunt the government buildings on Capitol Hill in Washington, DC. At some time in the early 1800s, cats were brought into the basement of the Capitol buildings to kill the rats that infested its underground tunnels and basements. Legend states that the Demon Cat is a black feline that never left. It's said to still live in the basement crypt of the Capital, which was originally intended as a burial chamber for President George Washington.

Those who work on the Hill claim that the cat is seen before presidential elections and is a bad omen, heralding a tragedy. It was purportedly sighted before the assassinations of Abraham Lincoln and John F. Kennedy. Although usually the size of a house cat, the Demon Cat is alleged to

▲ According to Polish legend, the pussywillow tree saved kittens from drowning, and since then, the trees grow fuzzy buds in the spring.

be able to grow to the size of a tiger and pounce on unsuspecting victims.

Cats in Popular Culture

Ah, our feline muses. They have inspired enduring literature and art, as well as farcical cartoonish violence (think Tom and Jerry). They play a very prominent role in our popular culture, from Garfield, the lasagna-loving cartoon cat; to the iconic Catwoman, Batman's conflicted comic book and movie adversary and love interest; to the numerous fashion accessories that ailurophiles around the world are proud to wear. We commemorate real cats and the Krazy Kats on our postage stamps, so we can send their images out into the world to share with all our friends (and bill collectors).

Symbols of Good Luck

Black cats are a sign of bad luck, right? Or is it white cats? Well, it seems to depend on where in the world you live. Here are a few more beliefs about which cats are lucky or unlucky and when and why, all of which tell you more about people than about cats.

- To this day, sailors around the world believe that cats on board a ship bring good luck. Should a cat should fall overboard, a bad storm will brew up and sink the ship.

- In the northern parts of Europe, people believe that if a cat enters a house of her own volition, she brings good luck.

- Abyssinian folklore decrees that an unmarried girl who keeps a cat is a wealthy catch.

- The Japanese consider both tortoiseshell and white cats to be lucky; tricolor cats are thought to be lucky in Canada.

- Contrary to the religious beliefs of the Middle Ages, the English now consider a black cat to be symbol of good fortune and white cats to be omens of gloom and doom. In Scotland, a black kitten on the porch is a symbol of future happiness and riches.

- American folklore still aligns black cats with bad luck and, because the myth perpetuates, animal shelters often have trouble finding homes for pure black cats and kittens. Some shelters even refuse to allow black cats to be adopted during October because of sadistic feline rituals associated with Halloween.

- Russians consider blue (gray) cats to be symbols of good fortune, and young couples are encouraged to move into their first homes with a cat to bring them good luck.

- Other symbols of feline good luck in many places in the world include a cat appearing at a wedding and a sneezing cat.

▲ Sailors consider it good luck to have a cat on board.

Literature

Across the centuries many authors have loved cats. From *Aesop's Fables*, written in the sixth century BCE to the *Grimm's Fairytales* penned in the nineteenth century, cat stories have endured and continue to delight children. In more recent times, many have been adapted for both the stage and screen to reach an ever-increasing audience.

The story *Puss in Boots,* penned by French author Charles Perrault in 1697, about a cat who uses trickery and deceit to gain power, wealth, and the hand of a princess in marriage for his penniless master, is another fairytale that also continues to enthrall.

Puss makes an appearance in the third act of Tchaikovsky's ballet *The Sleeping Beauty* and has also starred in numerous pantomime versions regularly brought to the stage around the world. In England, this pantomime has almost received the status of a Christmas-time tradition. Puss has even had to learn how to lace on ice skates for on-ice versions of this perennial favorite.

Walt Disney honored this famous fictional feline with an animated black-and-white movie in 1922. In 2004, a new generation was introduced to Puss in the popular computer-animated *Shrek* movies, with the character Puss-in-Boots loosely based on Perrault's original feline. The cat made his appearance in the second *Shrek* film and also starred in *Shrek 3* and *Shrek 4.* Following on the success of these films, Puss got a starring role in a spin-off film called *Puss in Boots: The Story of an Ogre Killer,* in 2011.

Nineteenth-century writers and poets began celebrating cats as mysterious yet delightful characters in their works. Baudelaire wrote "mysterious cat, seraphic cat and strange cat" in his two poems *The Cat* and *Cats*. French writer Verlaine praised feline virtues in his work *La Femme et la Chatte* (The Woman and the Cat).

Other popular stories include Rudyard Kipling's *Just So Stories* and Louis Carroll's *Alice in Wonderland*, which immortalized the Cheshire Cat and its cheesy grin. Once again, Disney transformed Alice into a classic animated movie, and Cheshire Cat merchandise, from mugs to bed throws, continues to be popular souvenirs to take home from Disney theme parks around the world. In 2010, avant-garde film director Tim Burton made another film version of this classic tale, casting Johnny Depp as the Mad Hatter and Stephen Fry as the Cheshire Cat, and using the latest 3-D cinematic technology to perpetuate the story for future generations.

Poetry works such as Edward Lear's the *Owl and the Pussycat* and T. S. Eliot's whimsical poetry collection *Old Possum Book of Practical Cats* have also been adapted into other art forms. The latter was adapted into the musical *Cats* by Tim Rice and Sir Andrew Lloyd Webber and has been performed around the world in twenty languages. (See Songs of the Cat, page 48.)

In 1907, British author Beatrix Potter delighted children with her book *The Tale of Tom Kitten*, a story about three mischievous kittens named Tom Kitten, Mittens, and Moppet who ruin their mother Tabitha Twitchit's tea party. After she's groomed and dressed the threesome to receive company, they go out to play and lose their clothes to some puddle ducks. When their mother finds out, she banishes them to a bedroom, telling her guests they have measles. But they continue to disturb the tea party with their boisterous play in their upstairs bedroom. The story was adapted into an animated children's film in 1993.

▶ A balloon of Felix the Cat from the 2011 New Year's parade in London.

Today, writers such as Shirley Rousseau Murphy, author of the popular Joe Grey Mysteries, and Carole Nelson Douglas, with her protagonist cat Midnight Louie, continue to delight a growing audience of loyal readers who enjoy mysteries solved from a feline standpoint. Another popular writer is Rita Mae Brown who, along with her feline co-author Sneaky Pie, has authored many popular mystery stories.

Art

From the early statues of Bast created by Egyptian cat lovers to modern-day drawings by such popular feline artists as Martin Leman, statues and artwork featuring cats continue to be popular collectibles.

▲ Stamp from the United Kingdom commemorating Edward Lear's illustrated poem *The Owl and the Pussycat*.

Cats have been admired in Japanese and Chinese art and pottery for more than 2,000 years. In many examples of both ancient and modern Asian art and pottery, feline images have covered a full range of subject matter from religious connotations, such as the Indian goddess of fertility riding a cat, to scenes of domesticity that show cats as beloved and well-cared-for companions.

When nineteenth-century Swiss artist and cat lover Gottfried Mind (1768–1814) painted his cat Minette and her kittens in a beautiful watercolor piece, artists realized that cats were great subject matter. Mind was nicknamed "the cat's Raphael" for the way he captured the personality of his felines.

Both French impressionist artists Edouard Manet (1832–1883) and Auguste Renoir (1841–1919) painted posed portraits of people with their pets and paved the way for today's celebrity pet photographers, such as Jim Dratfield and Christopher Ameruoso, to practice their craft and capture wonderful poses of today's fabulous felines.

Comic Strips and Cartoons

American cartoonist George Herriman, who created Krazy Kat in 1910, is recognized as the originator of the cartoon cat. The strip focused on the strange "love triangle" between Krazy Kat, Ignatz Mouse, and a protective police dog named Officer Bull Pupp. It was first published in the *New York Evening Journal*, owned by newspaper tycoon William Randolph Hearst. The comic strip was animated several times, in 1916, in 1920, and again in 1925.

Felix the Cat, the creation of New Jersey cartoonist Otto Messmer, became a pop culture icon in the 1920s and was probably the first cartoon character cat to spawn an array of merchandise from stuffed toys to ceramic mugs. Felix gained further fame as the first image to be broadcast over the television airwaves. RCA Research Labs engineers creating the phenomenon of TV used a rotating Felix doll as their test model in their very first transmission on NBC. Felix was the first balloon to appear in the Macy's Thanksgiving Parade, and Felix's popularity has only increased over the decades.

Puss Gets the Boot was the title of the very first cartoon starring Tom, a Russian Blue tomcat, and his house-mouse sidekick, Jerry. This cartoon twosome was the creation of famous MGM studio animators William Hanna and Joseph Barbera and launched what came to be known in the cartoon movie industry as comic violence. The never-ending rivalry between Tom and Jerry was the theme for more than 110 cartoons produced by the studio between 1940 and 1957. The original series won

▼ Wax figure of Michelle Pfeiffer as Catwoman, a villain from the Batman comics and movies.

▲ Puss in Boots is another famous feline. This is a 1950s greeting card from the USSR.

seven Academy Awards in the Best Short Subject Cartoon category.

Another cartoon cat favorite who launched his screen career in the 1940s was the tuxedo cat named Sylvester and his canary nemesis Tweety. Creator Friz Freleng debuted this duo in the cartoon called *Life with Feathers* and introduced the world to a lisping cat who uttered the words "Thufferin' Thuccotash" throughout his career.

Three decades later, Garfield, created by Jim Davis, burst into homes across America in the cartoon strip that holds the Guinness Book of World Records for being the most syndicated newspaper comic strip of all time (and no doubt simultaneously boosted lasagna sales around the world). Since then, this pasta-eating feline has become a worldwide industry that includes full-length movies, a TV series, clothes bearing his likeness, and a vast array of decorating accessories from lamps to duvet covers.

The most recent cartoon cat to gain international recognition is Mooch, a feline drawn by Patrick McDonnell as one of the lead characters in his cartoon strip *Mutts*. This endearing character is best friend to a dog named Earl. Both characters were based on McDonnell's own pets, his calico cat MeeMow and Earl, his Jack Russell Terrier. Their friendship in this popular strip focuses on the differences between cats and dogs as pets and draws parallels between friends.

Cartoon cats continue to draw a loyal audience, with their timeless antics, friendships, and archenemies. Furthermore, the creative talents of their creators, with their endearing drawings and tongue-in-cheek wisdom, have turned cartoon cats into a veritable art form.

Movies

Cats have starred in numerous Disney movies, from those already mentioned to such animated favorites as *The Aristocats* and *The Lady and the Tramp*. And, over the years, many real felines have also had successful careers on the big screen. Today, cats are even making movies themselves.

▼ One of the most famous fictional cats is the Cheshire Cat from *Alice's Adventures in Wonderland*, here commemorated on a British stamp.

▲American stamp commemorating Krazy Kat, one of the first cartoon cats.

Animated Cats

One of the most celebrated animated cats to stalk the big screen is the Pink Panther. The opening title sequence of the original 1963 *The Pink Panther* film featured a pink panther, a cartoon cat with pink fur and the manners of an English aristocrat created by David H. DePatie and Friz Freleng. The story involved a sophisticated jewel thief (played by David Niven), a bumbling Inspector Clouseau (Peter Sellers), and a large diamond called the Pink Panther.

The animated Pink Panther proved just as popular with movie-goers as the film itself, leading film company executives to not only make film sequels, but also to create a series of animated cartoon shorts with light-hearted plots featuring the stylish pink cat who only becomes flustered or angry when obtuse or offensive humans or troublesome gadgets, rodents, or insects threaten the tranquility of his existence. The cartoons were produced for both TV and the big screen. This inadvertent feline film star remains a popular plush toy favorite with children, has appeared in numerous video games, and continues to star in the opening credit sequences of the Pink Panther films, the most recent being *The Pink Panther 2*, starring Steve Martin as the blundering Inspector Clouseau.

Real Cats

A Siamese cat named Pyewacket, who starred in the 1958 movie *Bell, Book, and Candle* with Kim Novak, won a PATSY (Picture Animal Top Star of the Year) award for the role. Audrey Hepburn's feline confidante, Cat, in the movie *Breakfast at Tiffany's* was also the recipient of this coveted award.

Songs of the Cat

The feline impact on classical composers includes Tchaikovsky's *Sleeping Beauty*, Maurice Ravel's *Les Berceuses du Chat*, and Igor Stravinsky's *Le Faucon et la Petite Chatte*.

In popular music, one of the most famous songs of all time is the "Siamese Cat Song," recorded by Peggy Lee in 1955 for the soundtrack of the Disney film *The Lady and the Tramp*. Over the years, numerous artists have covered it. When the cartoon cat and canary duo Sylvester and Tweety became popular on the silver screen, so did the song "I Tawt I Taw a Puddy Tat," recorded by voice actor (Sylvester the Cat *and* Tweety Bird, to name just two of many), comedian, and singer Mel Blanc.

In 1963, a group called The Rooftop Singers recorded the song "Tom Cat," and three years later singer/songwriter Norma Tanega had a hit with her song "Walking My Cat Named Dog," which has since been covered by a number of other artists. In 1967, British singer Petula Clark had a hit with the song "The Cat in the Window," which compares a cat trying to get out of a window with the singer wanting to fly away. *The Aristocats*, another Disney cartoon movie, had cat lovers humming the tune "Everybody Wants to Be a Cat." (Over the years, there have also been many popular songs with the word *cat* in the title, such as "What's New Pussycat?" by Tom Jones, that have nothing to do with felines.)

Apart from these works, cats had little impact on the music scene until the 1980s, when a new musical form, the rock opera, was born. The leading proponents of this musical form, Tim Rice and Andrew Lloyd Webber, transformed T. S. Eliot's *Old Possum's Book of Practical Cats* into the very successful musical called *Cats*, which to date has been the second longest-running musical on Broadway, from October 1982 until September 2000, a total of 7,485 performances.

▲ Many countries have featured cats on their stamps; the ones shown are from South Korea, Laos, and Bulgaria (left to right).

A Persian cat named Snowball proved a memorable sidekick in the James Bond film *Diamonds Are Forever* (1971). In a spoof of this Bond classic, *Austin Powers* (1997), actor Mike Myers starred as Dr. Evil, whose sidekick was a Sphynx cat named Mr. Bigglesworth.

And who can forget the handsome Himalayan named Jinx in the movies *Meet the Parents* (2000) and *Meet the Fockers* (2004)? These days, Hollywood talent scouts offer special "acting classes" to train cats for movie roles, as well as for successful careers in print and television commercials.

Behind-the-Camera Cats

In 2010, Friskies brand cat food fitted twenty-five cats around the country with special video cameras attached to their collars to film their daily lives. The purpose: to give cat owners an idea of life around the clock from the feline perspective. The feline repurrters included the author's cat, Fudge.

The result was a movie called *Cat Diaries: The First Ever Movie Filmed by Cats*, produced by Los Angeles-based director-producer Erik Denno and editor-director Jason Farrell. In true Hollywood fashion, the film was unveiled during a red-carpet event at The Grove's Pacific Theater in Los Angeles. Feline lovers such as Denise Richards and Larry King came to meet the celebricats. It was the perfect Tinseltown event. The film continues to be a huge hit on YouTube; as this book goes to press, there have been more than 1,734,500 viewings.

Stamps

Many countries around the world have issued stamps featuring felines. In 1974, Japan issued a series of nature conservation stamps that featured the Iromote Wild Cat. In 1983, New Zealand issued a set depicting different cat breeds. The Siamese has been featured in Thailand on numerous occasions, as well as in Britain—along with ginger cats and even the Cheshire Cat from *Alice in Wonderland*.

Fairytale cats have also featured prominently on world stamps over the years. *Puss in Boots* appeared in Hungary in 1960, Poland in 1968, and Monaco

Cats in Religion, Folklore, and Popular Culture

Meow Memes

Meme: a defining cultural idea or event shared around the world via the Internet.

There's no question that cat videos are the most watched category on the Internet. There are also the millions of cat photographs shared on social media at lightning speed. The feline meme queen is undoubtedly Grumpy Cat, whose photographs first appeared in 2012. In a mere six months, this kitty, whose real name is Tardar Sauce, went from Internet meme to IRL (in real life) celebrity in 2013. She's trademarked her name, launched a huge array of merchandise, become a spokes kitty for Friskies cat food, and also starred along with other internet kitty favorites Colonel Meow; Hamilton, the Hipster Cat; Oskar, the Blind Cat; and Nala in the world's first cat music video, a catchy little number called "It's Hard to Be A Cat At Christmas." The song was launched at the iconic Capitol Records recording studios in Hollywood in time for Christmas 2013 to draw attention to the plight of cats in shelters. Despite her down-in-the-mouth expressions, this petite and very placid kitty has a wonderfully sweet nature. She has earned a lot of kibble for her family in endorsement deals and deserves to lap up a life of luxury.

▲The author with Tardar Sauce, a.k.a. Grumpy Cat.

in 1978. A scene from the *Arabian Nights* featuring cats was immortalized on a 1965 stamp in Hungary, and Great Britain featured *The Tale of Tom Kitten* as part of a series commemorating author Beatrix Potter in 1993.

In 1982, the United States Postal Service issued a Christmas stamp with a kitten and puppy playing together. In 1998, images of a cat and a dog were included in the *Bright Eyes* stamp set that featured five pets, and again in 2002 on a stamp series issued as part of a spay or neuter awareness campaign.

In April 2010, a set of ten first-class stamps featuring five dogs and five cats adopted from a shelter in New Milford, Connecticut, called *Animal Rescue: Adopt a Shelter Pet*, went on sale. They were designed to increase public awareness about shelter pets and encourage pet adoption. To bring greater attention to the cause, the United States Postal Service teamed up with TV celebrity Ellen DeGeneres and Halo, a holistic pet care company co-owned by DeGeneres, who pledged to provide a million meals to shelter pets. All the pets featured on these stamps were adopted into forever homes.

Social Media

One of the most significant changes in the world of communications has been the advent of what is collectively known as *social media*. Sites such as Facebook allow people to interact on a personal basis and have spawned both canine and feline Internet web-based communities for pet lovers to meet and mingle in cyberspace. Catster.com is hugely popular with cat lovers because the site allows cats to have their own web pages and join groups to socialize and blog. Cats have their own Facebook pages, too, and YouTube allows cat owners to share the wild adventures of their cats with each other.

Twitter, Facebook, and Blogs

With the advent of Twitter in 2006, a social networking site that poses the question "What are you doing?," thousands of cat lovers came on board, all "tweeting" from their cat's perspective. Without doubt, the top cat on Twitter is a gray-and-white domestic shorthaired cat named Sockamillion, aka Sockington, who lives in Waltham, Massachusetts, with his computer administrator-owner Jason Scott. Scott started tweeting on Sockington's behalf in late

2007 and very quickly had more than a million and a half followers.

Not only is Sockington hugely entertaining, with such acerbic comments as "yeah this is love at first crunch I THINK THE KIBBLE AND I ARE GOING STEADY" and "SO WHAT'S WITH ALL THE HUB-BUB AROUND HERE some of us are trying to sleep for a decade or whatever you call until further notice," but he is also following in the footsteps of Romeo, another Twitter favorite feline, and using his celebrity to raise hundreds of thousands of dollars for shelter and abandoned cats.

Sockington, a stray Scott found in a Boston subway station, has had offers to endorse products and speak about causes. He has turned them all down so far; as Scott maintains on behalf of his feline, "What does a cat have to do with the war in Darfur?"

Romeo and his owner, Caroline Golon of Columbus, Ohio, have, at the time this book was written, raised more than $60,000 for various animal causes via different social media sites. The cat has his own blog at www.romeothecat.com, some 16,000 followers on Twitter, and some 5,000 friends on Facebook.

Social networking and blogging from the feline perspective has become so popular that Golon co-hosted the first Blogpaws conference for pet bloggers in 2010, which has since become a popular annual event.

Social media is bringing cat lovers from around the world together to form a very close-knit community. Via data-accessible phones or the mere click of a computer mouse, they are able to exchange ideas about the latest cat toys, food fads, and health information. The impact that these sites have had on raising money for shelter pets is huge and continues to grow.

YouTube

Cat videos have some of the highest numbers of viewer hits on this popular Internet channel and have produced many feline stars. Among them is Gizmo, the cat who flushes the toilet and watches the water disappear only to flush again and again and again… There are dozens of talking cats, catnip-infused cats…and then there's Simon's Cat—the amusing cartoon feline every cat lover can relate to, drawn by British illustrator Simon Tofield, who has created his own YouTube channel to showcase his fabulous feline.

◄ The author's cat, Fudge, participated in the filming of *Cat Diaries: The First Ever Movie Filmed by Cats.*

Chapter 4

Breed Development and Characteristics

Researchers believe that the Egyptians may have been the first selective cat breeders because they liked the looks of some cats as opposed to others. As far as the modern cat fancy is concerned, the selective breeding of cats to produce new and distinctive breeds dates to the latter part of the nineteenth century and coincided with the fascination of keeping a variety of different animals, including cats, as pets.

The breeding of cats in modern times first flourished in England, thanks to the efforts of a handful of enthusiasts including Harrison Weir, an English artist who not only loved cats but also had long been disturbed by the inattention and cruelty he had observed toward the animals. In fact, the first cat show, which took place at the Crystal Palace in London in July 1871, was organized by Harrison Weir to show cats off to the public, promote their welfare, and urge people to make a greater commitment to their breeding and thereby enhance the beauty and well-being of the domestic cat in general. Harrison Weir and his brother John served as judges at this event. In 1889, Harrison Weir wrote *Our Cats and All About Them,* describing and illustrating the varieties of the time in what is considered to be the first book ever written about pedigree cats.

In 1895, inspired by Weir's show at the Crystal Palace, Englishman James Hyde organized the first major cat show in America (up until this point, cat shows were small events, often a part of county fairs). The National Capital Cat Show, held at Madison Square Garden in New York City, boasted 176 entries. It gave the viewing public the opportunity to see

▶ The Siamese first came to the attention of Britain and the rest of the Western world at the very first cat show, held in London in 1871.

different breeds and form opinions about their favorites, which, in turn, inspired breeders to focus on producing those cats who scored highly in these popularity charts.

At the time of these shows, there were only two main types of cats. Cats from Britain, Europe, and America all had stocky bodies, large heads, short ears, and thick coats (a characteristic developed to cope with the cold climates where they originated). Both short- and longhaired varieties existed within this type. The second cat type came from the hot climates of Asia and had long legs, a slender body, large ears, and a short coat. This type included the Siamese, which made its debut to the British public at Mr. Weir's cat show.

The world of cats breeds, however, was about to expand dramatically. During the course of the twentieth century and the opening decades of the twenty-first, many a new cat breed made its bow onto the international stage of the cat fancy, including the curly-coated Cornish Rex, the peculiarly eared Scottish Fold, the jungle-spotted Bengal, and the hairless Sphynx. Other intriguing new breeds still dance impatiently in the wings, preparing to preen center stage.

Breeding the Breeds

Unlike in the dog world, where different dog breeds were developed to perform specific functions, the different breeds of cats developed primarily from the aesthetic preferences of their owners. Many of the first show cats were selectively bred for a brachycephalic head type—a shortening of the muzzle and broadening of the head, with large, wide-set eyes. It is thought that this form of selective breeding was chosen because of the similarity of this skull shape to that of human infants.

Selecting for a rare trait or a new mutation is also a way to develop cat breeds. In earlier times, for example, the blue coat color, genetically recessive to black coloration, naturally appeared in a cat population less frequently, so cats of this color were often given special care and their kittens passed on to those of prominent social status as cherished gifts. In this manner, the blue longhaired cat (known today as the blue Persian) became the preferred feline of Victorian royalty. In a similar manner, the pointed coloration of the Siamese and Birman cats first appeared as a rare oddity; these cats were quickly adopted by royalty and the religious elite of the Far East and kept apart from the common population. This practice of identifying and preserving natural mutations has been a part of cat history from the beginning of feline domestication.

Then there's the fact that even with environmental changes, uncontrolled breeding of stray cats, and specialized breeding programs, our feline companions still possess many of the distinguishing traits of their wild ancestors. Look at a cat sunning herself in the comfort of her home—stretching, rolling over, sitting up, and inspecting her toes—and then observe a lion in the grassy plains of Africa or a tiger in the jungles of India doing the exact same thing. In many ways, domestic cats are simply miniature versions of their bigger cousins. And several breeders have set out to develop cats who look like, as well as act like (to a

certain extent anyway), their wild cousins. Think Bengal and Toyger.

Breed Development and Registration

Domestic cats are not native to North America, so all cats in the Americas initially came with the explorers, colonists, and immigrants who came to the New World. These include the British/European Shorthairs that became the Domestic Shorthair cats and the Norwegian Forest Cats and Russian Longhairs (Siberians) that provided the foundation for the Domestic Longhair cats. Once domestic cats set their paws on American soil, their high reproductive rate allowed their populations to grow rapidly. Beginning in the late 1800s, cat owners began to selectively breed these native cats and keep records of their pedigrees, developing the first American breeds: the American Shorthair and the Maine Coon. In time, other breeds were imported from overseas. The first breeds for which registration records were kept (initially by England's National Cat Club, founded in 1887, and by the United States' Beresford Cat Club, founded in 1897)

▼ Some breeds, like the Bengal, have been bred to resemble mini versions of the great cats.

were the Longhair, Siamese, Russian Blue, Manx, Abyssinian, and the Domestic Shorthair (especially popular were the British Blue and silver tabby varieties). Initially, all cats with long hair, including the Angora, Persian, Russian Longhair, and Maine Coon, were registered as a single breed, categorized by color.

Pedigreed vs. Purebred Cat

The term *purebred* is rarely used within the cat fancy. Strictly speaking, a purebred cat is one whose ancestors over several generations are all the same breed. What is usually meant, however, when someone says purebred is *pedigreed*, meaning the cat's ancestry is recorded (although it may include ancestors of different breeds). A pedigree is written documentation of a cat's family tree, which allows the owner to trace her ancestry back several generations. Each breed of cat has its own breed standard, developed over time by committees in the breed. Cats who conform to these criteria are called pedigreed and thus can be registered with one or more cat registries.

Differences in size and conformation between cat breeds, unlike those between dog breeds, can be quite subtle. The difference between the Singapura (the world's smallest recognized cat breed; teacup Persians are even smaller, but are not recognized by registries) and the Maine Coon (the largest) is, at most, a fourfold difference. By contrast, dogs range from tiny 2-pound Chihuahuas to 300-plus-pound English Mastiffs. A written standard, in which different physical characteristics are assigned specific point values, defines the finer points of conformation, coat quality, and color for each cat breed.

The primary advantage to obtaining a well-bred pedigreed cat is predictability of temperament. Whether you are looking for a calm, quiet cat or a highly active, vocal cat, there is a cat breed that is sure to be perfect for you and your family.

▶ The Maine Coon is one of the sixteen breeds that the Cat Fanciers' Association has designated as natural or foundational.

Registration

Registering a cat is important to keep track of her lineage and is a requirement if the cat is going to be a contender in the show world. Unlike the breeding programs of other domestics such as dogs, horses, cattle, and sheep—some of which have been going on for thousands of years—most cat breeds were developed within the last 150 years, and many of the breeding programs have taken place in Europe and America. The Persian, Russian Blue, Siamese, Angora, and Manx were among the first cat breeds to be recognized by cat associations around the world.

Today, among the various cat registries throughout the world, documentation exists for nearly eighty international cat breeds. In the United States, the Cat Fanciers' Association (CFA), the largest cat fancy association in the country, only recognizes forty-two breeds. (They recognize forty pedigreed breeds for showing in the Champion Class and two breeds as Miscellaneous.) Of this number, the organization has designated sixteen cat breeds as "natural" or "foundation" breeds (described as a breed that bears no resemblance to another). These are the Abyssinian, American Shorthair, Chartreux, Egyptian Mau, Japanese Bobtail (shorthaired and longhaired), Korat, Maine Coon Cat, Manx (shorthaired and longhaired), Norwegian Forest Cat, Persian, Russian Blue,

Historical Breeds

Not all attempts at creating a new breed of cat prove viable—or even a good idea. Here are a few that haven't fared so well:

Bristol: A hybrid breed created by crossing domestic cats with Margay wild cats (*Leopardus wiedii*). Cats from this discontinued program were incorporated into the Bengal breed.

California Spangled: A designer spotted cat no longer in existence, developed by a single breeder by crossing individuals from a wide variety of breeds over eleven generations. It had a short period of popularity when kittens from this cattery were offered for sale in the Neiman Marcus Christmas catalog of 1986. However, the breed originator was unable to meet the demand following such a successful marketing campaign and was unable to recruit enough serious breeders for the breed to remain viable. This cat has an important place in feline history, more as successful publicity stunt to draw attention to the plight of endangered wild cats than as a cat breed. Similar to the goals of the Bengal and Savannah breeds, it was hoped that by providing a "wild looking" domestic cat as a pet, admirers would be prevented from attempting to keep wild species in their homes or wearing wild-species pelts as apparel.

Caracat: An accidental hybridization between a domestic cat and a Caracal (*Felis caracal*) occurred in the Moscow Zoo in 1998. Other attempts at the hybridization of a Caracal with Abyssinian cats occurred more recently but did not progress beyond the F1 and F2 generations.

Chinese Harlequin: Cats with high amounts of white spotting are commonly seen in Asian art. This breed was an attempt to replicate the beauty of these cats in the United States in the 1980s through the selective breeding of domestic cats.

Kohana, Hawaiian Hairless: This hairless breed was found in Hawaii in 2002. It was verified to be caused by the same mutation as the Canadian Sphynx. The breed was discontinued due to persistent health and fertility issues, possibly due to excessive inbreeding.

Poodle Cat (Pudelkatze): A curly coated cat with folded ears, developed from a cross between Scottish Folds and Devon Rex.

Safari: These cats are hybrids between domestic cats and the wild Geoffroy's Cat (*Leopardus geoffroyii*). The cats are considered by their breeders to be the most affectionate of the F1 domestic–wild cat hybrid crosses. However, they are difficult to produce due to chromosomal mismatching. These crosses have not progressed beyond the F2 generation, so their future as a true breed is doubtful.

Sumxu/Chinese Lop: Described in literature of the 1800s as a large yellow or black longhaired cat with "pendulous ears," this could have been an early manifestation of the Scottish Fold mutation. A misunderstanding led to the Chinese Lop accidentally being given the name Sumxu (the term for the yellow-throated marten) by European cat fanciers.

Tiffany/Chantilly: A chocolate-colored longhaired cat no longer in development. This breed was inspired by early imports of self-chocolate longhairs from England.

Vienna Woods: A name used for chocolate and silver-colored American Shorthairs. The color variety is no longer in development.

Siamese, Siberian, Singapura, Turkish Angora, and Turkish Van.

Of the many different registries around the world, sometimes including several within a single country, each has its own standards and qualifying criteria. According to the CFA, a cat breed must have at least ten breeders working with it to be considered a bona fide breed and to be accepted for registration within this organization.

The International Cat Association (TICA), the other main registry in the United States, currently recognizes fifty-five breeds. (At least twelve to fifteen experimental breeds may gain full recognition in time, as well.) The difference between the two organizations is that the CFA registration is based on genotype (genetic makeup) rather than physical appearance—that is, the cat is considered a particular breed only if the parents are

▲ Genetics research has revealed that the modern Persian is more closely related to European cats than to her ancient Persian ancestors.

the same breed or there is an allowable outcross. The CFA does not recognize any breeds that are the result of crossbreeding wildcats with domestic breeds, such as the Bengal and the Toyger (see chapter 5, The Breeds). TICA breeds are based on phenotype (visible characteristics) rather than genetic ancestry. A cat is considered to be one of a breed if it meets the standard for that breed; its ancestry may include a wider range of allowable outcrosses or may even include nonpedigree cats who meet the breed standard.

Purebred Genetics

Geneticists say that a breed can be anything the breeder wants it to be. Today, some breeders work hand in hand with geneticists to actually breed certain traits into their litters.

Thus, genetics can also help reveal the history of individual breeds. Geneticists use the terms *lumping* and *splitting* data to refer to how they analyze genetic diversity. *Lumpers* are those who try to explain a lot of disparate data with one theory.

Splitters believe there are lots of theories to explain a particular genetic trait. For example, a lumper might look at a short-legged cat with pointed ears and say it is all one syndrome caused by a single gene; a splitter would state that at least two separate genes were the cause. Both are hypotheses, but in a state-of-the-art laboratory, geneticists have an opportunity to further address these questions.

As part of her research, geneticist Leslie Lyons and her team discovered that although the Persian is perhaps the oldest recognized cat breed originating in Persia, it has undergone so much genetic interaction that the modern Persian cat is more genetically similar to cat breeds found in Western Europe than to those of ancient Persia. Similarly, the bobtail trait found on the Japanese Bobtail isn't actually indigenous to Japan. And geneticists now believe that the Abyssinian, with its hallmark tabby markings, originated in India and not Africa, as previously thought.

Over the years, breeders have often been quick to observe a genetic mutation, such as a folded ear, and breed aggressively for that mutation, declaring cats with the now-hereditary mutation to be part of a new breed and thus introducing a number of the different breeds that exist today. Breeding is a work in progress in the cat fancy, as breeders continue to work with mutations and establish new breeds.

The Feline Genome Project

Although the study of genetics traces the inherited looks and characteristics of humans and animals, it also plays an important role in highlighting inherited medical issues and diseases common to particular species.

The Feline Genome Project is a community endeavor that coordinates research efforts relating to cats around the world. This pooling of knowledge has the universal goal of tackling and one day eradicating conditions that either reduce the quality of life or even cause the death of countless cats.

Researchers have had success in highlighting and working to eradicate polycystic kidney disease in Persian cats. Future work will focus on issues that plague cats in general, such as diabetes, obesity, asthma, hyperthyroidism, and urinary tract diseases. Researchers also hope to understand why many white cats are deaf and what causes feline infectious peritonitis and to eliminate the offending genes. Not only can solving these problems help cats live longer and healthier lives, but it can also help save the lives of many cats who end up in shelters because of undiagnosed disorders. For example, one of the primary reasons cats are surrendered across the country is that they are not using their litter boxes. The heart of this issue often is an undetected urinary-tract health problem, but owners relinquish the cat because they consider her simply delinquent. Therefore, understanding why cats are prone to urinary infections and helping eliminate the cause would make incredible steps toward ensuring the safety and better care of cats everywhere.

Physical Characteristics of Cats

Cats are categorized by body type, coat colors, type of coat, and special markings. The cat fancy also has its own color chart, with interesting names to describe coats of different colors. The following sections summarize all the different physical characteristics used to describe cat breeds.

Body Types

It's very easy for the average dog lover to spot the differences in body type between, say, a Chihuahua and a Poodle, or a Basset Hound and a Great Dane. Although cats also have different body types, they aren't quite as obviously diverse as those of canines. At one point in time, felines were simply categorized as medium-limbed, long-limbed, and short-limbed, but now their body types are described as follows:

Oriental

The Oriental body type includes a long, slender body; long legs and tail; a triangular head; a long nose; large ears; and almond-shaped eyes. Examples of breeds with the Oriental body type include the Siamese, Balinese, Oriental Shorthair, Oriental Longhair, and Cornish Rex.

Foreign

The Foreign type is similar to an Oriental, but more athletic. The tail is also longer and more tapered and the head more triangular (or what's often called a "modified wedge") than that of the Oriental. Examples of breeds with the Foreign body type include the Turkish Angora, Abyssinian, Somali, Japanese Bobtail, Russian Blue, and Nebelung.

Deafness in White Cats

Deafness is a common problem found in both mixed-breed and purebred white cats. It's an inherited disease often found in blue-eyed white cats, as well as in those with two different eye colors.

Semi-Foreign

This is the term used to describe cats of a medium build that are neither slender nor stocky. Such breeds include the American Curl, Devon Rex, Egyptian Mau, Havana Brown, LaPerm, and Snowshoe.

Cobby

This name describes thickset cats with a muscular, compact build; round faces; round eyes; short noses; and small ears. Their shoulders are broad, and their tails are thick and short. Examples of breeds of this type include the Persian, Burmese, Himalayan, and Exotic Shorthair.

Semi-Cobby

These cats have a rounded look without being too stocky. Example breeds include the American Shorthair, British Shorthair, American Wirehair, Korat, Scottish Fold, Singapura, and Selkirk Rex.

Coat and Hair Types

A cat's coat is usually classified simply by its appearance as longhaired, shorthaired, or hairless. A shorthaired cat has a coat that's 1.75 inches (4.5 cm) long; a longhaired cat has a coat that's 6 to 8 inches (15 to 20 cm) long. Shorthaired cats include among their many ranks the American Shorthair and the British Shorthair, as well as the Russian Blue and the Scottish Fold. Longhaired cats include the Angora, Maine Coon, Norwegian Forest Cat, and the Persian, of course. Hairless breeds are less plentiful; the Donskoy and Sphynx are among these rare breeds.

In addition coat length, cat coats can differ a great deal in terms of texture. The majority of cats have straight fur that varies between fine or dense, but some people may be surprised to learn that certain cats have rough, curly coats.

Evolution has designed a cat's fur to deal with extreme weather conditions. Breeds that adapted to cold climates—the British Shorthair, Maine Coon, Norwegian Forest, Siberian, and so on—have dense coats. This dense type of coat is sometimes called a *double coat*, which consists of a combination of an outer coat (made up of guard hairs, literally guarding the cat against the elements) and an undercoat that insulates the cat. In extreme cold, the hair stands away from the body, trapping a layer of air. This can best be equated with the double glazing on a window that traps a wall of air between the cold outside and the warmth of the indoors. (Cats also curl up and cover their faces with their tails to protect themselves from cold air.)

Breeds that live in hot climates shed their insulating inner coats and radiate heat more efficiently. Blood vessels in the skin dilate, speeding up the process of losing body heat. Unlike people, cats don't sweat when overheated; they lick their fur and the evaporating saliva removes body heat. Hairless cats such as the Sphynx have no outer coat. Instead, their bodies are covered with a very fine down, which gives the appearance of hairlessness and feels like chamois to the touch.

The cats who don't fall into these three categories—namely, the rough, curly-coated kind mentioned earlier—include the Cornish Rex and the Devon Rex. The word *Rex* comes from the genetic term *astrex*, which indicates the absence of those insulating guard hairs. The Cornish Rex has a short, crimped coat with no guard hairs and even has crinkled whiskers. The Devon Rex does have guard hairs, but they vary in length, making the fur appear slightly crimped and lumpy. And then there is the unique, somewhat rough coat of the American Wirehair breed.

Cats of Many Colors

Apart from the variety of feline facial features and body types and the array of coat types, the selection becomes even more diverse when coat patterns and a vast assortment of colors are added to the mix. Cats come in black, white, gray, brown, red, orange, blue, golden, cream, and lilac and can be solid, shaded, patched, pointed, bicolored, or tricolored. Some cats' coats are even made up of four or five colors. Keep in mind, however, that the colors given to a cat's coat are not the colors to be found on an artist's palette. A lilac coat, for instance, does not resemble the flower—all of which makes deciphering coat colors more than a bit confusing for beginners.

▼The Cornish Rex is an example of the Oriental body type.

▲The lilac coloration is a diluted form of the same gene that creates a black coloration, demonstrated here by a solid lilac British Shorthair.

Solids

Cat fanciers have some very colorful imagery to describe fur colors and the specialty markings on the muzzle, ears, feet, and tail areas. Interestingly, the feline color chart is based on the colors black and red. When the colors are modified and lightened, the cat fancy uses the term *diluted*. All the various shades of these original colors have their own special names.

Red: *Red* is the proper term to describe what cat lovers commonly call *orange*, *marmalade*, or *ginger*, whereas *cream* is a diluted red gene and sometimes also called *buff*.

Blacks: Mutations of the genes that produce the color black produce colors that are known as *chocolate*, a dark rich brown, and *cinnamon*, which is similar to the color of the spice. The color *fawn* is a diluted form of cinnamon and is similar to a light coffee color, *champagne* is a honey beige shade, *havana* is tobacco-leaf brown, and *sable* is very dark brown. *Seal* refers to dark brown colorations usually found on the ears and tail area, and *bronze* is used to describe a range of browns. Gray is another diluted form of the black gene and is described as *blue* in the cat fancy. It's also sometimes known as *maltese*. *Lilac*, *lavender*, and *frost* are all shades of light or dove gray. Some of these terms are specific to certain breeds.

Tipped

Tipped hairs means that the tip of each hair is a different color from the hair shaft. The amount of tipping on the end of the hair varies. Lightly tipped hair, where only the very end is dark and the rest of the hair shaft is white, is called *chinchilla*. When about a third of the hair shaft is dark, the resulting look is called *shaded*. When nearly two-thirds of the hair is dark, the coat is called *smoked*. For example, *black smoke* is the coat description of a solid black cat with white roots and *blue smoke* is a solid blue (gray) cat with white roots.

Pointed

The darker shadings on the face (muzzle), paws, and tail of Siamese, Birman, and similarly patterned cats are known in the cat world as *points*. Temperature-dependent versions of the albinism gene allow color to develop on the cooler parts of the body (the extremities), while suppressing it on the warmer parts (torso). The Burmese breed is also genetically a pointed cat but with much less contrast between body and points. The third pointed pattern, the Tonkinese "mink" pattern, is intermediate between the high-contrast Siamese-type pattern and the low-contrast Burmese-type pattern.

Tabby Cats

It is believed that most domestic cats have coats that are a variation of the tabby, reminiscent of their wildcat ancestors. Fur striping is the result of a cat having the *agouti* gene in its genetic makeup. This term refers to more than one color distributed along a single hair shaft. This pattern can be bred out through introducing a non-*agouti* recessive gene and results in a cat with a coat that is uniform in color.

There are four tabby coat patterns:

Classic tabby: The classic tabby coat, sometimes called *blotched*, has wide, dark stripes curving over the flanks and the shoulders and three large stripes running from the shoulder blades to the base of the tail.

Mackerel: The mackerel tabby has either continuous or broken stripes running perpendicular to the spine, like a fishbone.

Spotted: The spotted tabby has distinct round spots against a background of lighter fur.

Ticked or agouti: The fourth tabby coat pattern is called ticked or agouti. The coat on the body has almost no stripe. However, the legs, tail, and face sport very thin stripes.

Some breeds have modified tabby patterns. For example, the marbled pattern of Bengal cats is due to the interaction of wild and domestic genes and the naturally occurring marbled tabby pattern of the Sokoke.

The origin of the word *tabby* seems to have an uncertain history. Some claim the name is associated with a type of striped, patterned silk

◄ This LaPerm shows the shaded hair type, in which about a third of each hair shaft is darkly colored.

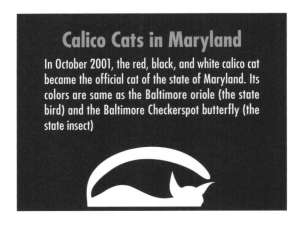

Calico Cats in Maryland

In October 2001, the red, black, and white calico cat became the official cat of the state of Maryland. Its colors are same as the Baltimore oriole (the state bird) and the Baltimore Checkerspot butterfly (the state insect)

called *Atabi* made in Attabiah in the Middle East. Others claim that it comes from the Spanish *tabi*, a kind of cloth with irregular tie-dye-like markings.

Tortoiseshell, Calico, and Bicolored Cats

These names are used to describe coat patterns and colors; they are not types of cat breeds.

Tortoiseshell

A tortoiseshell coat is a combination of red and black or of cream and blue and also exists in the diluted versions of these colors. Some tortoiseshells have distinct patches of each color, whereas *brindled*

tortoiseshells have fur in which the colors mingle and blend and don't form distinct color patches. A tortoiseshell may have significant portions of white, as well, but the remaining colors are blended; this pattern is called a *tortoiseshell and white*. A cat with a mixture of tabby and tortoiseshell markings is called a *torbie* or *patched tabby*.

Calico

Calico cats have a significant amount of white fur and two other colors broken up into distinct patches. The other colors can be red, orange, cream, and black or gray. Sometimes they also have patches of a tabby pattern in their coats that can be very attractive.

Bicolored

Bicolored cats are white and another color such as gray and white, brown and white, or red and white. The *tuxedo cat* is a well-known example of a bicolored cat. Tuxedos are black and white cats with markings that resembled a tuxedo worn with a white bib and spats (an old-fashioned white shoe covering). However, the "tuxedo pattern" can occur in any color and white. Sometimes these white feet on a cat, including on a tuxedo cat, are referred to as *socks*.

▶ No matter what color a cat is, if her pattern is striped she is considered a tabby cat, like this red tabby British Shorthair.

What Is a Moggie?

In the United Kingdom and Australia, nonpedigreed cats are called *moggies*, which may be derived from name "Maggie" (short for Margaret). This was a common name for cows and calves in eighteenth-century England and was also applied to housecats during the Victorian era. In the United States, a nonpedigreed cat is sometimes referred to as a *barn* or *alley* cat, even if it is not a stray. Many owners prefer the term *random-bred*.

Modern-Day Designer Cats

A designer cat is a cross between two existing breeds, combining the traits of both. An example is the Dwelf, which combines the hairlessness of the Sphynx, the swept-back ears of the American Curl, and the short legs of the Munchkin. Some designer cats are developed into new breeds whereas others are crossbreeds aimed at the pet market.

Hybrid cat breeds—in which a domestic cat is deliberately hybridized with a wild felid—date back to a cat show held in Edinburgh, Scotland, in 1875, which included a special class for "wild or hybrid between wild and domestic cats." The first displayed hybrids were based on Scottish Wildcats (*Felis silvestris grampia*) and Caffre Cats (the Egyptian variant of the North African Wildcat, *F. s. lybica*).

The founder of the first cat show, Harrison Weir, also wrote about hybrid cats in his 1889 book, *Our Cats and All About Them:*

> There is a rich-coloured brown tabby hybrid to be seen at the Zoological Society Gardens in Regent's Park, between the wild cat of Bengal and a tabby she-cat. It is handsome, but very wild. These hybrids, I am told, will breed again with tame variety, or with others.

These days, designer cats, along with their canine counterparts—crosses such as the Labradoodle (Labrador and Poodle) and the Puggle (Beagle and Pug)—are very trendy among

▼ Oriental Shorthair showing the ticked or agouti coat coloration.

▼ This cat exhibits tortoiseshell, white, and tabby genes, resulting in a complex and uniquely beautiful coat.

pet owners, but meet with disapproval from many breeders who consider them "mongrels." Breeders started serious work on establishing hybrid breeds such as the Bengal (a cross between a domestic cat and an Asian leopard cat) in the 1960s. Some of the most popular hybrid breeds today include the Cheetoh (Ocicat and Bengal), Savannah (domestic cat and serval), Toyger (domestic cat and Bengal), Serengeti (Oriental cat and Bengal), and Chausie (domestic cat and jungle cat).

Breeders such as Judy Sugden, who is credited for creating the Toyger, have painstakingly selected traits to ensure that resulting litters have the physical characteristics of their big-cat look-alikes—for example, vibrant stripes and facial markings. New breeds continue to evolve, and breeders work closely with geneticists to produce the best and healthiest outcomes.

Household Pet vs. Pedigreed Cat

There are more than 95.6 million owned cats in homes across the United States. Because fewer than 100,000 pedigreed kittens are born each year in the United States, 95–98 percent of owned cats are of unplanned breeding and are categorized as Domestic Shorthair, Domestic Medium Hair (also called the Domestic Semi-Longhair), or Domestic Longhair. Many of the characteristics of pedigreed cats can be found in the domestic cat population, so random-bred cats may have appearances similar to those of the breeds described in the next chapter but are unlikely to share a recent heritage with them. Unlike "mixed breed" dogs, in which the parents or grandparents are often of a recognized breed, "mixed breed" cats are extremely rare, outside of controlled hybrid breed development programs. Many pedigreed cat breeders spay or neuter their kittens prior to placement into pet homes to prevent accidental or unauthorized breeding.

The use of pedigreed cat breed names to describe cats of unknown background is, unfortunately, a common practice. For example, although fewer than 500 pedigreed Russian Blue kittens are born in the United States each year, thousands of blue-colored

▼ Domestic cats were crossed to Asian leopard cats (pictured) in the development of the Bengal and a few other breeds.

domestic shorthaired cats in homes, shelters, and rescues across the country are given this appellation.

That does not mean, of course, that if you have a nonpedigreed cat you have a cat of inferior quality—or even a cat who can't compete in the show ring. Harrison Weir, father of the cat fancy, was concerned that the pursuit of the "fancy cats" would reduce the public's appreciation of the "common cat." He need not have worried: the Household Pet classes at cat shows continue to remain popular with exhibitors and visitors. Any healthy, altered cat over the age of four months that is amenable to handling by strangers, can be bathed, and can have its nails trimmed can be entered in a cat show in this category. Many successful breeders and cat show judges began their careers in the cat fancy by entering their family pet in a local show. Judges base their awards on the condition and temperament of the cat, with wide discretion allowed for personal preference in color, coat length, and conformation. In many registries, these cats compete throughout the show year for similar end-of-year trophies and rosettes as their pedigreed counterparts.

The main advantage to getting a pedigreed cat is that you have a better idea of what the characteristics of your breed are and whether that cat will be a good fit for you and your family's lifestyle.

At present, approximately 5,000 cat breeders in the United States actively register their cats with a major registry, and approximately 75 percent of them breed only one or two litters of kittens a year. Of the pedigreed kittens born in the United States, more than half are Persians (including Himalayans and Exotic Shorthairs). The ten most popular cat breeds in the world, estimated from the number of cats registered by the Cat Fanciers' Association (CFA, United States, Europe, Asia), the International Cat Association (TICA, United States and internationally), the American Cat

▲Attempts to develop the Bristol breed by crossing domestic cats to margays (pictured) met with limited success, and the breed no longer exists.

Fanciers' Association (ACFA, United States), the Governing Council of the Cat Fancy (GCCF, United Kingdom), and Sveriges Kattklubbars Riksförbund—the National Cat Association of Sweden—(SVERAK Sweden), are as follows:

- Persian—including the Himalayan and the Exotic Shorthair
- Bengal
- Maine Coon
- Ragdoll
- British Shorthair
- Siamese and Oriental— including the Balinese, Oriental Longhair/Shorthair, Colorpoint Shorthair, Javanese, and Seychellois
- Birman (Sacred Cat of Burma)
- Norwegian Forest Cat
- Burmese
- Sphynx

In the next chapter, we'll investigate the history, characteristics, and traits of these breeds, as well as of other breeds recognized by cat fanciers.

Chapter 5

The Breeds

By Lorraine Shelton and Sarah Hartwell

Most of the breeds described below are currently accepted for championship competition by one or more cat-registering bodies who are members of the World Cat Congress. This includes the Australian Cat Federation (ACF), Cat Fanciers' Association (CFA), Co-Ordinating Cat Council of Australia (CCC of A), Fédération Internationale Féline (FIFe), Governing Council of the Cat Fancy (GCCF, United Kingdom), New Zealand Cat Fancy (NZCF), Southern African Cat Council (SACC), the International Cat Association (TICA), and World Cat Federation (WCF). Recognition of the breed does not imply recognition of all the variations that may be described. Each registry sets its own limits on what colors or varieties of breeds are allowed to be registered in its studbook records or are permitted to compete for championship titles.

Some breeds that are not yet accepted for championship competition, that are in development, and/or that are only registered with associations that are not members of the World Cat Congress are included for discussion. After all, the recording of cat pedigrees and the competitive exhibition of different varieties of cats to characterize the quality of a selective breeding program is a hobby that is only 140 years old. The cat fancy is in its infancy, and it is likely that many more new and exciting breeds will be recognized in the future.

▶Somali

Abyssinian

Place of origin: England

History: The Abyssinian cat is considered the breed most similar to the first domesticated cats. The cats used to develop the Abyssinian breed are thought to have been brought from the Middle East to England in the mid-1800s. One of the earliest depictions of an Abyssinian cat was in *Cats: Their Points and Characteristics* by Gordon Stables, published in 1874. A color portrait of Zula stated that she belonged to Mrs. Captain Barrett-Lennard and had been brought from Abyssinia (modern-day Ethiopia) at the conclusion of the war in 1868. Some fanciers insisted the cats originated in Chile, not Africa or the Middle East, whereas others suggest the original cats had arrived in Abyssinia as the pets of British army officers and their wives who had previously been stationed in India or Ceylon (Sri Lanka). Sandy-colored, ticked cats were known as Indian cats in the early days of the cat fancy and have more recently been developed into the Celonese breed. Still others believe that the Abyssinian's arrival in Britain was merely coincidental with the end of the Abyssinian war, hence the breed's name.

Harrison Weir wrote that many cats bred in England from ordinary tabbies were almost indistinguishable from the imported Abyssinian in color and pattern. The imported cats, however, were of stouter build than the English cats (which were not as cobby as modern British Shorthairs) and were less heavily marked. At the time, the Abyssinian was considered "most useful" in crossing with other breeds to produce a variety of ticked colors.

In 1889, Harrison Weir's breed standard for the Abyssinian called for a larger cat than we see today. The cats competed in the "Any Other Variety Foreign Cat" class, often against Geoffrey's cats (a species of South American wild cat), Indian cats, and Japanese cats. Abyssinian breeders considered this situation unfair, complaining that they often lost out to wildcats and novelties. In the early days, the Abyssinian was shown under a variety of names including Algerian, Hare Cat, or Bunny Cat; the latter names being derived from its ticked fur.

Around the 1900s, the name Abyssinian was supplanted by "British Tick," and the cats had heavily barred legs and tail from being extensively crossed with British Shorthairs. Although considered "foreign cats," they were not as refined in conformation as modern Abyssinian cats. In the 1920s, a champion Abyssinian called Red Rust was apparently mated to an "Imported African Wild Cat" and the female offspring, Goldtick, was registered and bred as an Abyssinian. An Abyssinian of the 1940s had a Siamese grandparent. This crossbreeding would add to the colors that turned up in later generations. A strain of blue-eyed, creamy-white "albinistic Abyssinians" were bred for a while in England but died out in 1927, and a fawn Abyssinian with a pink tint appeared in a litter bred in Vienna at around the same time. Several Abyssinians bred in the 1930s were solid colored with no ticking but were still used in breeding.

By the 1920s, silver Abyssinians had died out in the United Kingdom having consistently lost out to the usual/ruddy Abyssinian on the show bench. They were not reintroduced until the 1960s, when a usual/ruddy Abyssinian was bred to a silver-spotted British Shorthair. The silver gray Abyssinians also didn't catch on in the United States and have been slower to regain favor there.

Ticked cats occur naturally around the world. The modern Abyssinian may owe more to British ticked tabbies than to cats imported from Africa, but the Abyssinian would not have come into existence without those imported cats to inspire the breed. The term *Abyssinian* is sometimes used to mean any cat with a ticked pattern, regardless of pedigree. The name *Wild Abyssinian* was used to indicate some naturally occurring ticked cats from Singapore, but is not related to the Abyssinian breed.

Physical description: A happily prancing Abyssinian standing on tip-toe is a delight to behold. The perfect specimen is a study of soft flowing contours. The modified wedge head should have no flat planes or drastic changes in the direction of the profile. The large expressive eyes are neither too round nor too slanted. The large ears are cupped forward to give the impression of attentiveness. Neither too long nor too cobby, the body is in proportion to the elegant legs. The fur of the Abyssinian must be long enough to display multiple bands of ticking, consisting of alternating dark and light colors. The coat is dense and resilient, snapping back into place when brushed toward the head.

Colors and varieties: All registries recognize four basic ticked tabby colors: the black-based color is known as ruddy, tawny, or usual; the sorrel or cinnamon color is also known as red (not to be confused with the sex-linked, orange color called "red" in other breeds). Blue and fawn are also recognized. Accepted in some registries as well are the chocolate- and lilac-ticked tabby colors and the above colors in silver-ticked tabby, in which the light band in the ticked pattern is pure white. The blue and fawn colors were developed in England through expansion of the gene pool of the original cats with local domestic cats and imported Siamese and Russian Blue cats. Cats described as "silver" were among those initially brought into the United States to develop the breed, indicating that this color had been present in the breed since its early years.

The color and ticking of an Abyssinian becomes more vivid with age, with color continuing to improve for as long as two years or more. In kittens, breeders look for color development on the paws, around the nose, and at the back of the ears to provide a hint of the adult color.

Ruddy Abyssinian

Red Abyssinian

Silver Abyssinian

Temperament: As one of the most active cat breeds, the Abyssinian makes sure that life is never boring. It is difficult to perform any job in a house with one of these personable, affectionate cats without their paws-on involvement. These intelligent cats learn new tasks easily and eagerly, including leash training and feline agility courses. They should be provided with windows giving visibility to the outdoors, where you may experience insight into their hunting instincts as they make "machine gun" sounds at the birds outside. Many like to play with water, and they may learn how to turn on faucets and open doors, to the surprise of their owners.

Activity level: High

Vocal level: Moderate

Special needs: An occasional bath and a gentle grooming with a soft brush or your moistened hand to remove shed hairs is all that is necessary to keep an Abyssinian's coat in condition. Some Abys are prone to dental disease, so regular dental cleaning and monitoring by your veterinarian is recommended.

Variations: Longhaired Abyssinian kittens had occurred as far back as the early 1900s but appeared to have died out. Longhaired Abyssinian cats have been documented as early as 1936. The name Somali was adopted for this variety in the 1960s

American Bobtail

Place of origin: Western United States

History: Cats with shortened tails appear regularly in feral populations around the world. Among their ranks is the American Bobtail, a true born-in-America breed with a bobcatlike appearance but absolutely no genetic link to its wild namesake or to the short-tailed lynx. Nor is the American Bobtail mutation related to the Manx mutation (see page 121). Researchers believe the bobtail has been around for several generations in the United States. In a 1940 book, zoologist Ida Mellen described the "American Domestic Bobtail Cat of the New England and Middle Atlantic States," although nothing more was said of these cats.

The American Bobtail traces its ancestry to a bobtailed male tabby cat named Yodi, discovered in the 1960s by a couple vacationing in Arizona. The couple took him home and mated him to their sealpoint (Siamese pattern) nonpedigree female, which resulted in short-tailed kittens and a new breed.

At first, breeders mated American Bobtails with colorpoint cats such as Birmans and Himalayans. This led to a myth that the breed resulted from male bobcats mating with female Siamese cats. This original emphasis on a short-tailed, pointed, longhaired cat with white mittens and a white face blaze led to inbreeding and to smaller, less healthy cats. In the 1980s, random-bred bobtailed domestic cats were used to restore the breed's vigor and create a wider variety of colors, as well as both shorthaired and semi-longhaired varieties.

The American Bobtail was recognized by TICA in 1989 and later by the CFA, but remains rare in the United States, having been eclipsed by the Pixiebob. To avoid mixing up different mutations, the American Bobtail is never bred with either the Manx or the Japanese Bobtail.

Physical description: American Bobtails are a sturdy and substantial breed occurring as both shorthairs and as shaggier semi-longhair varieties. A show-quality American Bobtail should have a powder puff tail up to one-third normal length. Kittens with

Sealpoint American Bobtail

much shorter or with longer, kinked tails sometimes occur as a result of using random-bred bobtails to rescue the breed in the 1980s. American Bobtails can have any eye color and any color and pattern of fur, although the modern preference is for a "wild" tabby appearance that gives the impression of a bobcat. A lynxlike ruff, tufted toes, and tufted ears are desirable and add to the wild look.

Colors and varieties: The American Bobtail is recognized in any color and any pattern. The use of random-bred cats has produced a very wide palette of colors. The American Bobtail has been developed in longhaired and shorthaired varieties. Longhaired cats develop "mutton chops" on their cheeks.

Temperament: Playful, sometimes mischievous, American Bobtails make excellent family companions. They are intelligent, gentle cats who are adaptable and amenable to training and are often described as having doglike personalities.

Activity level: Moderate

Vocal level: Moderate; they chirp and "talk" to their family but are not demanding.

Special needs: None

Variations: Sno-Bob is the name given to a color variety of American Bobtail bred to resemble the Alaskan bobcat, being pale in color with darker eartips and a darker bobtail. There are a number of unrelated bobtailed American breeds at various stages of development, including the Alpine Lynx, the Desert Lynx, the Highland Lynx, Owyhee Bob, and the Tennessee Bobtail. The American Ringtail breed is being developed to preserve a trait occasionally found in feral populations, in which the cat carries her tail in a curl over her back.

American Curl

Longhaired American Curl

Place of origin: Los Angeles County, California

History: Curl-eared cats have been reported only a few times: in the United States in 1981, in Australia in 1996, and in western Greece in 2007. Only one in the United States has been developed into a breed. All American Curls trace their ancestry to a black longhaired female cat named

Shorthaired American Curl

The Curl has a moderately long, muscular body and a wedge-shaped head with soft contours and a straight nose. These are medium-sized cats, with the females often being particularly petite.

Colors and varieties: All colors are recognized in both longhaired and shorthaired varieties.

Temperament: American Curls are playful, friendly cats. They are an intelligent breed that adapts well to a household with other pets or children. They enjoy jumping to high places with their athletic bodies and chasing birdlike toys.

Activity level: Medium

Vocal level: Low

Special needs: The American Curl requires no special grooming; even the longhair coat is fairly easy to maintain. However, care should be taken not to handle the ears roughly, especially when cleaning them. Some Curls have narrowed ear canals, so avoid getting water in the ears. Ear mites can be especially serious in this breed, so take steps to avoid infestation (see chapter 9, page 225).

Variations: In recent years, the American Curl has been crossed with other breeds to produce cats such as the Ruffle (recognized by the American Association Cat Enthusiasts) and the Kinkalow (recognized as an experimental breed by TICA).

Shulamith. A couple found Shulamith and another curl-ear cat on their doorstep in 1981 and adopted them. The cats had ears with firmer cartilage than that of typical cats, which caused the ears to curl backward. Although her companion disappeared, Shulamith stayed and produced a litter of kittens in December 1981. When half of the kittens from the litter also had these unique ears, the couple realized that a new mutation had entered the cat world and set about gaining recognition for this new breed. The curl-eared cats attracted attention when exhibited at a cat show in 1983, and the American Curl breed was recognized by TICA in 1985 and by the CFA a year later.

Unlike cats with the Scottish Fold mutation, two cats with the American Curl mutation may be bred together without adverse health consequences in the offspring. Domestic shorthaired and longhaired cats have been used in the development of this breed, and outcrossing to random-bred cats is still permitted to expand the population of this relatively new breed.

Physical description: When Curl kittens are born, their ears are straight, like those of other kittens. The ears start to develop their characteristic curl in the first week of life. Breeders anxiously observe the ears as they change until they reach their final shape at about sixteen weeks of age. Perfect show-quality ears are prominent in size and equally matched, with a smooth curl backward toward a point in the center of the back of the head.

American Shorthair

Place of origin: United States and Europe

History: In the early days of the cat fancy, there was extensive exchange of particularly attractive shorthaired show cats between England, continental Europe, and the United States. These were bred together under the name Shorthair until separate breed standards were established for the American Shorthair, the British Shorthair, the Chartreux, and the Russian Blue. As is often the way, early cat fanciers were more interested in exotic varieties than in the familiar homegrown shorthairs, and the local Domestic (American) Shorthair was overlooked until relatively recently.

In the decades following the establishment of the cat fancy in Britain in the 1870s, British breeders exported a number of champion Shorthairs (it would be a while before they were called British Shorthairs) to their American counterparts to help them found the Shorthair breed across the pond. At that time, what would be the British Shorthair was closer in type to the modern American Shorthair. Two particularly influential sires, sent over in the 1890s, were Mrs. Herring's silver classic tabby Champion Jimmy and Mr. Alfred Park's Champion Silver Mine; many American Shorthairs can claim these as ancestors.

The first Shorthair registered with the CFA in the United States was Champion Belle of Bradford, an orange tabby male born in England in 1900. In fact, many of the early cats registered were imported. Miss Jane R. Cathcart of New Jersey specialized in crossing imported Shorthairs, of both British and French parentage, with carefully selected cats from local farms.

As more breeds appeared, it became necessary to expand the name of the American breed and distinguish domestically bred Shorthairs from the various imported breeds. The shorthaired breed developed in the United States became the Domestic Shorthair, a name intended to reflect its local origins, but the cats were frequently confused with random-bred household domestic pets. As a result, nonpedigree shorthairs were passed off as pedigree Domestic Shorthairs and the breed suffered.

During the late 1930s, small number of dedicated breeders kept the true Domestic (American) Shorthair alive, and the strikingly marked silver tabbies remained the most popular variety. Unfortunately, breeders focused so much on colors and patterns that conformation deteriorated. Some breeders used British Shorthairs and selected American farm lines to restore the looks and vigor of the American Shorthair, in particular broad heads, square muzzles, and strong bodies. From the 1940s onward, the breed gained in interest but continued to be hindered by the confusing name Domestic Shorthair.

In 1961, a group of West Coast breeders formed the American Shorthair Cat Association; in 1966, they convinced American cat registries to rename the breed American Shorthair to reflect its distinct character and to differentiate it from other shorthaired breeds and from random-bred domestic shorthairs.

During this same time, the British Shorthairs were becoming cobbier due to breeding with Persians. The American Shorthairs, however, remained smaller and leaner, yet still powerfully built to reflect their working origins. Hereafter, when British Shorthairs were still allowed to be bred to American Shorthairs, they had to prove they had no Persian ancestry in the last three generations. Such cats tended to be considered pet-quality in Britain, where the standard favored the cobbier type. The last British Shorthairs introduced into American Shorthair lines came from a British cattery in the 1970s that had resisted the move toward the chunkier conformation. Around the same time, a brown mackerel tabby male with an unknown sire was controversially allowed to be registered to contribute to the health of the breed.

Although cats of the American Shorthair type had existed since the 1890s, it was not until the late 1960s and early 1970s that the American Shorthair breed finally took off, becoming viewed as more than just a domestic pet or farm cat and kept distinct from its British cousin. Although it is still not widely known outside of North America, it has become one of the most popular breeds in the United States. When you look at an American Shorthair, you are looking at the type of shorthaired cat who was exhibited at the start of the organized cat fancy.

Torbie and white American Shorthair

Solid black American Shorthair kitten

Physical description: The American Shorthair is "medium" in many ways—medium size, medium boned, and well balanced. This cat has a firm muscular body and a sweet facial expression. The American is smaller than the British Shorthair, with a less cobby body. The American Shorthair has a short, lustrous coat, which developed to be dense enough to protect its working ancestors against the elements but less plush than that of the British Shorthair. Shorthairs are considered low-maintenance cats who are generally healthy. The cat's physical features do not fully mature until the age of three or four years old.

Colors and varieties: The most popular colors associated with the American Shorthair breed are in the classic tabby pattern, with or without white brown: blue, brown, cream, patched (torbie), red, and silver. This pattern is elaborately described in terms that include such accoutrements as vest buttons, bracelets, necklaces, bulls-eyes, and butterflies. The silver classic tabby-patterned American Shorthair cats with bright green eyes are particularly distinctive and popular. There is a wide range of colors and patterns, including mackerel tabbies, shaded silvers, smokes, and solid colors. Chocolate or lilac colors/patterns and the colorpointed pattern are not recognized by the

major registries because these are indicative of crossing with other breeds.

Temperament: The easy-going and adaptable American Shorthair makes a loving, devoted companion that is more outgoing than the British Shorthair. The American Shorthair fits into any household, making a good companion for seniors, as well as fitting into families with children. This cat is intelligent, but does not constantly demand attention. Having developed from working cats, they enjoy playing with preylike toys, such as a toy mouse, or watching outdoor activity from a windowsill. Some American Shorthairs are lap cats, while others just like to be near their people.

Activity level: Moderate

Vocal level: Low

Special needs: Although this breed does not demand any special care, stroking the coat of the American Shorthair with a damp hand or an occasional bath can help remove shed hair and bring out the sparkle of the coat. Like most shorthaired cats, they benefit from being combed once or twice a week.

Variations: The American Wirehair is a coarse-haired relative of the American Shorthair. Chocolate-silver American Shorthairs with brown markings on a pale background have been bred under the name Vienna Woods because the chocolate color was not allowed in the American Shorthair breed. Shorthaired breeds have been developed from domestic cat populations in many countries. The Antipodean, the Celtic Shorthair, and the Mexican Shorthair are other breeds derived from shorthaired populations in other parts of the world.

American Wirehair

Place of origin: New York, United States

History: Wirehaired or broken-coated cats have been reported only a few times around the world. American Wirehairs trace their heritage back to two kittens from barn cat litters born in upstate New York in 1966. The founding father of the breed was a red and white male called Adam, whose coat was dense, harsh, and springy. An experienced Rex breeder noticed Adam's unique fur, acquired him, and bred him to both a related female barn cat and to an unrelated female. Both litters produced wirehaired kittens, thus establishing it as a new dominant gene mutation. Genetic testing determined Adam was indeed a new breed, with no connection to the Cornish or Devon Rex (see pages 95 and 97), two early breeds with wiry coats. Outcrossing to American Shorthair cats helped expand the initial population of cats, and this outcross continues to the present. Select domestic shorthaired cats have also been brought into the breed.

The CFA recognized the American Wirehair in 1977. Unlike that of the earlier Cornish, German,

and Devon Rex breeds, the wirehair of the American breed is due to a dominant gene and therefore does not always breed true. The fur is crinkled and coarse, with hooked or bent hairs, like that of a Fox Terrier dog. This breed does not seem to have attracted the same popularity as the Cornish and Devon Rex and has grown slowly. It has not yet attracted interest outside of North America.

Physical description: The crimped, springy coat is the unique characteristic that defines this breed. The coat is soft to the touch yet has a unique resilience that needs to be felt to be appreciated. The coat texture can take a while to develop in kittens, so breeders may not know until the kittens are many weeks old which ones in a litter will "wire up" and which will have a normal coat. The wired effect is most evident in the whiskers and at the base of the tail. Some cats have extensively wired coats that are so brittle that the hairs are prone to break off, resulting in a sparse coat. Coat texture and appearance varies between individuals, with the most desirable coat being dense, coarse, and wired all over the body. The body and head type of the Wirehair is similar, but not identical, to the solidly built American Shorthair, the breed used to expand the population. This is a medium, well-muscled cat, with large rounded eyes.

Colors and varieties: The American Wirehair occurs in the same colors as the American Shorthair. Tabby colors in brown, silver, patched, and red, both with and without white, are most commonly seen in this breed, although just about every color is accepted, with the exception of chocolate, lilac, and the colorpoint pattern.

Temperament: Like their American Shorthair relatives, Wirehairs are friendly, playful cats who enjoy the caresses of their owners as much as their human family members enjoy the feel of the Wirehairs' unique coats.

Activity level: Moderate

Vocal level: Moderate

Special needs: Because the same abnormality in the hair follicle that causes the hairs to curl or kink also interferes with skin secretions (sebum) moving away from the skin, some Wirehaired cats, like some Rex cats, may need to be bathed frequently and their ears cleaned regularly to prevent these secretions from accumulating in the hair follicles or ear canal and causing dermatological problems.

Variations: Longhaired kittens are occasionally born in American Wirehair litters but are not recognized for competition. An unrelated wirehaired breed called the Bramble has been developed from Bengal and Peterbald cats.

Australian Mist

Place of origin: Australia

History: The Australian Mist breed was developed in the late 1970s by Dr. Truda Straede, who crossed Burmese and Abyssinian cats to tabby domestic shorthairs. As with many breeds, the original mating did not go quite as planned. An Abyssinian female that stopped calling whenever she was driven to her intended beau was mated instead to a neighbor's Burmese male in the hope she would get the idea of what was expected of her. However, the attractive ticked and spotted kittens who resulted were of sufficient interest that a breeding program

commenced. It ultimately produced this unique tabby breed with the sepia pointing pattern of the Burmese and six colors analogous to Burmese colors. The breed originally earned the name Spotted Mist Foreign Shorthair, reflecting the pattern of the early cats.

When the breed standard was amended in 1998 to include the marbled variants that appeared in litters, the breed was also renamed Australian Mist, better reflecting its country of origin. This cat remains rare outside of Australia, although Australian Mist breeding programs now exist in the United Kingdom, and there has been some interest from American breeders. This is the first breed developed in Australia to have gained wider recognition.

Physical description: Australian Mists are neither too cobby nor too long. The head is rounded and broad with large ears set low on the head and cupped slightly forward. These cats have large, expressive, open, almond-shaped eyes ranging from chartreuse green to aquamarine. A broad muzzle contributes to their sweet expression. The coat is short and glossy, yet with enough length to be resilient to the touch and allow expression of the agouti bands that make the tabby pattern appear to float on top of a misty ticked background.

Colors and varieties: The Australian Mist comes in both a spotted pattern and a marbled tabby pattern against a ticked background and in six colors modified by the Burmese gene: blue, brown (sable), chocolate, cinnamon (gold), fawn (peach), and lilac. As in the Burmese breed, the color continues to darken until the cat reaches two years of age.

Temperament: An affectionate lap cat, the Australian Mist is playful without being too busy. These beautiful cats make excellent family companions and are tolerant of children and other family pets. A temperament suited to indoor living was a specific requirement when the breed was developed, and some stud cats are said to be so sociable that they can live in groups without aggression. Australian Mists have been trained to walk on a leash.

Activity level: Moderate

Vocal level: Moderate

Special needs: None; this is a robust, healthy breed with a widely diverse genetic background.

Variations: Longhaired Australian Mists sometimes occur in litters due to recessive genes inherited from Abyssinian and domestic shorthair ancestors. The Australian Mist was slow to gain interest in the United Kingdom because of its similarity to the Asian Shorthair breed.

Balinese

Place of origin: California and New York, United States

History: The semi-longhaired Balinese shares its history with the Siamese cats imported into Britain from Siam (modern-day Thailand) in the 1870s and 1880s. Radically different from the round-headed British Shorthairs and Persians, the Siamese both shocked and beguiled early cat fanciers. Since those early days, occasional longhaired kittens have appeared in Siamese litters. Some people say that it's a recessive trait, claiming that at least one Chinese tapestry depicts pointed longhaired Siamese; the more likely explanation, however, is that the trait was introduced through early crossing with shorthaired domestic cats who carried the recessive longhaired gene. This would have occurred when the Siamese was first imported into the United Kingdom and the United States, and again during wartime to keep breeds going.

After many years of being ignored, a longhaired Siamese was registered with the Cat Fanciers Federation in 1928. However, these longhaired Siamese were not bred in earnest until 1955, when two breeders in California and New York began breeding and showing the longer-haired variety in the United States. Since long hair is a recessive trait, these longhaired Siamese bred true. To keep the new breed separate from the Siamese breed, a new name was required. *Balinese* was chosen to reflect the breed's grace, which was likened to that of Balinese dancers.

In 1961, the Balinese was recognized in the United States and accepted for registration in the same range of colors as the Siamese—blue, chocolate, lilac, and seal. Other colors have been introduced from outcrossing—including cinnamon, cream, fawn, red, silver, smoke, tabby, and tortie. Although other registries accepted all of the colors as Balinese, the US CFA recognized the newer colors under the name *Javanese* because those colors occurred through crossing with the Colorpoint Shorthair (the CFA's name for the red and tabby series Siamese). Not until 2008 did the CFA merge the Javanese under the single heading of Balinese. Bicolor points (colorpoints with white markings, once dismissed as a serious defect) are also recognized by some registries.

The development of the Balinese has paralleled that of the Siamese. In the 1950s, most Siamese and Balinese cats had rounder heads and chunkier conformation than the modern versions. As the more extreme look gained in popularity for the Siamese, its longhaired relative followed suit due to the Balinese's being crossed with the Siamese. Crossing with the Siamese also affected the Balinese cat's long fur so that many Balinese cats resemble Siamese cats with plumy tails rather than semi-longhaired cats. As with the Siamese, a few breeders have continued to breed the older style.

During the 1960s, the Balinese had a competitor in the United States when Siamese cats were crossed to red Turkish Angoras to create a colorpoint, semi-longhair breed called the Singhalese. These were fluffier than the Balinese and lacked the Siamese temperament. The Singhalese was judged to the Balinese standard (with allowances made for its different coat type) but eventually lost out to the Balinese and disappeared.

Physical description: Although this is a medium-sized cat, the terms dainty and graceful are often applied to this breed. Balinese cats may look fragile, but they are surprisingly muscular. Apart from the longer coat, the Balinese is physically similar to the Siamese. The Balinese has a wedge-shaped muzzle, pronounced pointed ears, a long lithe body, and sapphire blue eyes. There is the same sharp delineation between the darker colored points and the light colored body. Selective breeding of show-quality Siamese cats over the decades has created the long, tubular body and exaggerated head type that can also be seen in the Balinese. A "traditional" or "old-style" type of Balinese is also bred by admirers of the less extreme type, and the Balinese's conformation and color range mirror that of the old style of Siamese cat.

Semi-longhaired, rather than longhaired, the Balinese has a silky coat varying from a 1/2-inch to 2 inches (1.25 to 5 cm) in length. The lack of undercoat means the coat does not mat easily and is easy to groom. The Balinese does not have a neck ruff but does have a long plumy tail with fur up to 5 inches (13 cm) long.

Colors and varieties: The Balinese occurs in the same colorpoint range as the Siamese. The original

Traditional or old-style Balinese

Red and tabby Balinese formerly were considered a separate breed, the Javanese

colors were blue point, chocolate point, lilac point (also called lavender point or frost point), and sealpoint. This has been expanded in parallel with the Siamese breed to include cream, red, tortie, and tabby points, and, lately, bicolor points. As with any internationally recognized breed, not all registries recognize the same range of colors. The name Javanese, used by the CFA to separate out the red and tabby series Balinese, has become redundant in the United States.

Temperament: Intelligent, affectionate, inquisitive, and mischievous, the Balinese have inherited the extrovert personality of their Siamese parents. They are highly social cats who appreciate the companionship of other cats. Balinese are very people-oriented and bond closely with their families. They are playful, turning almost anything into a toy, and want to be involved in all family activities. Balinese have a highly vocal nature and will chat with their humans—they don't like to be left out of anything. This high-energy and conversational temperament means the Balinese is not for everyone.

Activity level: High

Vocal level: High, but usually has a quieter and less insistent voice than that of the Siamese. Owners of Balinese enjoy talking to their cats, and their cats enjoy talking back to them.

Special needs: As with some lines of Siamese, some Balinese may have sensitive digestive systems that require special dietary considerations.

Variations: Confusingly, outside of the United States, Javanese referred to the noncolorpoint relatives of the Balinese. In various parts of the world, the names Oriental Longhair, Foreign Longhair, and Mandarin are used for noncolorpoint Balinese-type cats. These breeds differ from the Balinese only in color.

Bengal

Place of origin: Riverside County, California, and various other locations

History: Since the first cat shows in England, small wildcats and crosses between domestic cats and wild cats have been bred and exhibited. No crosses, however, have been more successful that those between the Asian leopard cat (ALC, *Prionailurus bengalensis*) and domestic cats (including Egyptian Maus, Indian Maus, and Abyssinians) that formed the foundation of the modern Bengal breed.

In 1889, Harrison Weir described a rich-colored brown tabby that was purportedly a hybrid between the "wild cat of Bengal" and a female tabby cat; this animal was exhibited at the Zoological Society Gardens in London. In 1934, an ALC–domestic hybrid was documented in a Belgian scientific journal, and in 1941 a Japanese cat publication printed an article about a pet ALC–domestic hybrid. In 1946, Jean Sugden, who would later be considered the founder of the Bengal breed, submitted a term paper about hybrids for her genetics class at the University of California, Davis.

The ownership of small wild species of cats was popular throughout the world at one time, especially in the United States from 1940s through 1960s. Retail stores commonly offered both wild-caught and domestically bred ALC, ocelot, margay, and other such species as pets. There were numerous attempts to hybridize these with domestic cats to improve their temperaments and suitability as pets; the sterility of the male hybrids proved an obstacle.

In 1963, Jean Sugden (now) Mills bred her first ALC–domestic hybrid and proved that a female hybrid could be successfully bred back to a domestic male cat. She was not alone in breeding ALC–domestic hybrids at this time: five were born at a zoo in Tallinn, Estonia that same year; the Long Island Ocelot Club reported ALCs being bred to Siamese and Burmese cats in 1968; and by 1972 Bill Engler had crossed ALCs to American Shorthairs to produce what he would officially call the Bengal. His cats came in a wide variety of colors, including red and tortoiseshell. Engler's cats came in for much criticism because the first- and second-generation hybrids proved too wild to make good family pets.

Although various owners of wild cats had produced hybrids, none had gone on to develop a domestic breed from them. Hence, the credit for the modern Bengal breed is given to Jean Mill, who went on to develop the breed in the following decades. The initial hybrid cats she used to create the Bengal breed had been part of two university research projects. Once these cats had donated their blood for research, they were placed with breeders who proceeded to develop these unique cats into a breed in the 1980s.

Around 1982, Jean Mills and her husband visited India, where a zoo curator showed them a rosetted feral "Indian Mau" living in one of the enclosures. Named Millwood Tory of Delhi, he is credited with introducing the glittered effect into the breed. The modern Bengal breed is derived from crossing ALCs with a variety of domestic breeds: Abyssinian, American Shorthair, Burmese, Egyptian Mau, and some nonpedigree cats.

Research into mapping the feline genome has also been performed by evaluating the genetic results of mating the ALC to domestic cats. Other breeders around the world created new lines of ALC crosses that were used to expand the gene pool. Purported margay or ocelot crosses (called Bristol Cats) have also been incorporated into the Bengal breed. The Bristol was purportedly derived from margay–domestic hybrids, but only ever numbered a few individuals before dying out due to poor fertility. In 1991, the last fertile Bristol females were absorbed into Bengal breeding programs. Those Bengals bearing Bristol blood inherited a more robust type, small ears, and superior rosetted markings.

The Bengal gained recognition in 1986 and rapidly became one of the most popular breeds in the United States. Although the Bengal breed is also popular around the world, recognition—and even legality of ownership—in some countries has been hampered by its hybrid origins. The Bengal must be a least the fourth-generation descendant (F4) of a crossing between the wild ALC and a domestic cat. The first three foundation crosses are the F1s, F2s, and F3s.

Snow marbled Bengal

Physical description: The wild appearance is emphasized in these cats by selective breeding toward large, rounded, "nocturnal" eyes; a straight nose; small ears set far back on the head; prominent whisker pads; a long neck; and a muscular body. Bengals are medium to large cats, with females usually weighing from 6 to 12 pounds (3–5 kg), males 10 to 18 (4.5–8 kg).

The coat is soft and dense, often described as a "pelt". What really sets the Bengal apart from any other breed, however, is its coat color pattern. In the spotted pattern, the spots may have the appearance of open rosettes with different shades of color. They are aligned in neither a vertical pattern nor a circular pattern, but rather in a random pattern that flows horizontally across the cat's body. The marble pattern is a modification of the common classic tabby pattern: instead of "bulls-eye" circular stripes, the pattern is stretched horizontally into a unique multishaded pattern not seen in any other breed of cat.

Colors and varieties: To prevent it from becoming "just another tabby breed," the Bengal is currently recognized in brown/black, spotted (including rosetted), and marbled colors only. The background color varies from gray to golden red, with deep brown to jet-black markings. The underside may be nearly white. This may be modified by the albino series of genes inherited from Siamese and Burmese ancestors, resulting in pointed (snow), sepia, and intermediate (mink) varieties, which have paler coat colors and blue or aqua eyes. The increasingly popular silver and silver smoke Bengals have nearly white backgrounds with black or dark gray markings. All of these colors occur in spotted and marbled patterns. Some Bengals have a high degree of glitter (a metallic sheen) in the coat, complementing the background color.

Temperament: The Bengal breed was developed for those who might have otherwise considered bringing a species of wild cat into their homes, so this breed is definitely not for those looking for a mellow lap sitter. Breeders are careful to well socialize their kittens at an early age to keep in check their natural tendencies toward stubbornness and overly aggressive play. These can be headstrong cats who need a firm owner to give them guidance on the rules of the house. Their agility and intelligence make them excellent candidates for feline agility competitions and learning to walk on a leash. They are as serious about their displays of affection as they are about their playful pursuit and destruction of their favorite toys.

Activity level: High

Vocal level: High

Special needs: Although most Bengal breeding programs have progressed many generations beyond the initial crosses to ALCs, some programs continue to use "early generation" breeding cats. Cats from these programs may have some undesirable characteristics from their wild cat ancestors, including aggressive behavior or poor litter box habits. In addition, males from these matings may be sterile.

Variations: The Bengal's wide gene pool means a number of variations occur naturally due to recessive genes. Blue-based colors may appear from time to time, recessive to the black-based colors, and cats of these colors have been exhibited toward possible eventual recognition. Solid black Bengals are being used in developing the Pantherette, which is still in the early stages of development and is meant to resemble a panther. The Toyger is a mackerel-striped version being developed to resemble a miniature tiger. Pardino and Cashmere are names that have been proposed for longhaired Bengals, although these are not currently recognized by any registry. Bramble is the name used for a variant in development as a wire-coated Bengal. The Bengal has been crossed with a number of other hybrid breeds and with a number of small wildcat species in the hope of creating additional hybrid breeds.

Birman

Place of origin: Thailand; France

History: Legend claims that the golden, blue-eyed goddess Tsun Kyan-Kse blessed these equally golden, blue-eyed cats to carry the souls of Buddhist priests to Paradise, making the Birmans sacred temple companions. According to the legend, a white cat gained the colorpoint markings when protecting the body of a murdered priest. Only the cat's feet remained white. This charming legend may allude to the fact that colorpoint kittens are born white and develop their point color in the first few weeks of life. On a purely pragmatic note, the temple residents undoubtedly valued their cats as small warriors who protected sacred writings against the ravages of gnawing rodent teeth.

Although the exact origins of the Birman, also called the Sacred Cat of Burma, cannot be known, late-nineteenth and early twentieth-century European travelers in Siam and Burma wrote about seeing longhaired cats with the coloration of the Siamese. So how and when did Birmans make their way from the Far East to Europe? According to some sources, the breed arrived as a thank-you gift. In 1916, the story goes, two Englishmen helped a group of priests save a temple in Tibet, and in 1919, when the Englishmen established residence in France, the priests expressed their gratitude by presenting the men with a pair of the beloved temple cats. Unfortunately, only the pregnant female survived the journey. With no Birman male available for further mating, the cat and her female offspring were then crossed to Siamese, Himalayan (colorpoint Persian), and white longhaired cats. Subsequently, it is said, more Birman cats were smuggled out of the temples of Burma and brought to France. The cats were said to be very difficult to rear, with only about one in ten surviving.

Birman

Uncertainty about the breed extends to its naming as well. In the early days, the cats were variously known as Birmans, Sacred Cats of Burma, Tibetan Temple Cats, and Khmers. In 1927, a Paris Cat Show judge described the Birmans as resembling poorly bred Persians with coloring exactly like that of Siamese, but sometimes having feet with white toes. Photos of the Khmer in the French magazine *La Vie a Campagne* in the late 1920s show a Birman-type cat lacking the now-characteristic white bootees. In *Sa Majeste, Le Chat* (1932) there was a picture of a Birman-type cat described as "half-Persian, half-Siamese."

As with many breeds, the Second World War took its toll on the Birmans. Records indicate that all modern Birmans descend from the only two breeding cats who remained in France after the war. These cats were outcrossed with Siamese and black, or black-and-white, longhairs to recreate the breed. Himalayans (colorpoint longhairs) were used to expand the gene pool, introducing new colors into the breed. (The Khmer name was dropped in 1955, when Himalayans appeared on the scene.) As a result of the Birman's early near loss and recreation, although some say the Birman traces its ancestry

Tortoiseshell Birman

to temples in Burma, others claim the breed was entirely manufactured in France.

The first Birmans arrived in the United States from France in 1959 and in Britain a year later. In 1960, a pair of "Tibetan Temple kittens" was given to a North American cat lover; although these came from Cambodia, they traced their ancestry to French lines and were identical to the Birman cats being bred in Europe and the United States.

When Birmans were first exhibited in the United States, at a cat show at Madison Square Garden in 1967, the same year the CFA recognized the breed, the airline arranged to have photographers cover the arrival of these rare cats, which had been insured for $10,000 apiece for their trip from Florida.

Physical description: The Birman is a substantial, medium-sized cat, with a body that is neither cobby nor elongated. The profile exhibits a distinctive Roman nose, displaying a downward curve from a point slightly below the level of the eyes. The ears are medium in size and placed at the corners of the modified wedge-shape head. The blue eyes are nearly round. The long coat is silky, and the fur around the neck forms a ruff that frames the face.

Colors and varieties: Initially, Birmans were recognized only in the colors sealpoint and blue point, but crossing with Himalayans during the expansion of the breed introduced other pointed colors, including chocolate, cream, lilac, red, tabby (lynx), and tortoiseshell. Eyes are always blue. The four matching white gloves are an essential component of the show standard. The gloves extend in an upside-down V-shape to the hocks of the back legs in a pattern known as laces. No other white is permitted on the face or body. A warm beige color on the back, called the golden mist, is desirable and develops as the cat matures.

Temperament: These cats seem almost cognizant of their historic link to the exotic temples of the Far East, having about them an air of self-assuredness even more pronounced than that possessed by most cats. They are gentle, affectionate cats, tolerant of children and other pets in the household. They are wonderful lap cats who often enjoy being petted and groomed.

Activity level: Low

Vocal level: Low, although Birmans can become quite conversational with owners who talk to them. They have a unique "huff" sound that they sometimes use to express discontent or excitement.

Special needs: Although the coat is relatively nonmatting, regular bathing and combing is required to keep the fur in top condition.

Variations: The name Templecat (also Tsuncat) has been adopted to describe a shorthaired variety of the Birman; it was developed in New Zealand in 1995 by outcrossing Birmans to a cinnamon spotted tabby Oriental and was originally called the Birman Shorthair. The term Tibetan has been used to describe nonpointed color varieties of the Birman cat, created through outcrossing this breed to nonpointed longhaired cats. Booteeless Birman variants are known as the Khmer. The Birman has been used in developing the Ragdoll breed (see page 140).

Bombay and Asian Shorthair

Origins: Thailand, France

History: The development of the original Bombay breed began in the United States in the 1950s, although the present Bombay look was not achieved until 1965. The breed was developed using black American Shorthairs and American Burmese with the specific aim of recreating the appearance of a black leopard in miniature (hence one of its nicknames the parlor panther). The breed name alludes to India, where black leopards (black panthers) are not uncommon. Breed creator Nikki Horner wanted to create a cat with the sleek coat and muscular conformation of the Burmese, the inky color of a black American Shorthair, and bright copper eyes that are often likened to new pennies.

Although recognized by the CFA in the 1976 and by TICA in 1979, the Bombay remains rare.

Because the American Burmese differs greatly in conformation from the European Burmese recognized in Europe and Australasia, outside of North America, the Bombay has been recreated to conform to European Burmese standards. In the United Kingdom, the Bombay forms part of the Asian Self grouping, which encompasses cats of the European Burmese type, but with solid coloration rather than the sepia-pointed pattern of the Burmese.

In the United Kingdom, the Bombay (or European Bombay) arose in two ways. Solid black Burmese occurred in Burmese litters in England as far back as the 1960s. Although they attracted interest at shows, they did not go forward as a breed. The modern European Bombay began in the 1980s, when Burmese breeders decided that non-sepia-pointed Burmese, including the solid black color, would make an attractive addition to the show bench. Because American Burmese are not recognized in the United Kingdom and are not allowed to be crossed to European Burmese, UK breeders had to start from scratch. The new breed was registered as the Asian Self, and the black Asian Self is also known as the Bombay. This Bombay breed was recognized in the United Kingdom in 1990, with other solid colors being recognized in 1994.

Although the Bombay in the United Kingdom is part of a wider group of breeds that began with the Burmilla, in the United States, there has been no attempt to breed other solid-color or nonsepia Burmese. Kittens with Burmese color restriction still occur in Asian Self and American Bombay litters due to recessive genes and are registered as Asian Variants.

In continental Europe, Australia, and New Zealand, new lines of Bombay, meeting the European Burmese conformation, were developed from local lines of European Burmese and black shorthairs. American Bombays have been imported into a few parts of Europe by those who consider the black self Asian Shorthairs to be pretenders to the Bombay name. In New Zealand, the Asian Shorthair group is called the *Mandalay*, with the black self Mandalay being analogous to the Bombay. The Mandalay began with accidental matings between Burmese and other domestic cats in the 1980s and were recognized in 1990. British-bred Bombays have also been used in some Mandalay bloodlines.

Physical description: In the United States, the Bombay, except for its solid color, conforms to the American Burmese standard. This means a robustly built, muscular, and medium-sized cat with a rounded head; large eyes, set wide apart; and ears set wide apart. Outside of the United States, the Bombay conforms to the more Oriental (foreign) type of the European Burmese: the body is lighter in build and the head forms a short wedge, slightly rounded at the top and with a longer muzzle than that of the breed's American counterpart. To ensure

Blue Self (above) and Black Smoke (below) Asian Shorthairs.

the coat and conformation remains close to the Burmese, the Bombay is crossed to the Burmese in the United States and to the European Burmese and Asian elsewhere. Those differences aside, the Bombay resembles a miniature black panther.

Colors and varieties: The signature color of the Bombay is the deepest, densest, inkiest black imaginable, with eyes ranging from deep gold to copper. The black coat should shine like patent leather. In the United States, only the Bombay is recognized. In Britain and continental Europe, "Bombay" is a synonym for the black self Asian Shorthair. In New Zealand, the black self Mandalay is analogous to the European-style Bombay.

Temperament: The Bombay's temperament reflects its origin. This cat combines the easy-going nature of the American Shorthair (or British/European Shorthair outside of the United States) with the adaptable, inquisitive, social nature of the Burmese. Bombays are intelligent cats who enjoy interaction with their humans and enjoy playing games. Their playfulness and intelligence mean they can often be trained to walk on a leash or to do agility activities. Many Bombays will helpfully retrieve toys thrown by their owners. Like Burmese, Bombays enjoy snuggling up to their owners, whether on a lap or under the bedcovers. Their sociability and playfulness mean they need company and interaction during the day, either with humans or with other similarly active cats.

Activity level: Moderate

Vocal level: Moderate; like their Burmese ancestors, Bombays have a distinctive voice, although some Bombays are much more talkative than others.

Special needs: The short, sleek coat needs little maintenance. Loose hairs can be removed with a quick rubdown with a rubber brush. The coat benefits from being stroked with the palm of your hand to maintain its sheen—something the affectionate Bombay will enjoy as much as her owner.

Variations: In addition to the Bombay, there are other Burmese-type cats without the form of partial albinism that results in the unique color of the Burmese breed. These include New Zealand's Mandalay, which are bred in solid colors and in tabby and tortie patterns; and the Asian Shorthair group in Europe, which includes tabbies, torties, smokes, and shaded and tipped varieties. The tipped Asian Shorthair is recognized under the name Burmilla. Semi-longhaired varieties are recognized in Europe as the Asian Longhair group, also known as the Tiffanie (not to be confused with the Australian Tiffanie or the American Chantilly/Tiffany).

British Shorthair

Place of origin: Britain

History: British Shorthairs trace their ancestry back to domestic cats imported during the Roman occupation of Britain in the second century AD (see chapter 1). With increasing urbanization, domestic shorthairs moved into towns as pets and as alley cats. According to Charles Darwin in 1859, developing distinct cat breeds was not particularly successful, and he implied that it was largely a woman's hobby. Only a few decades later, Britain would have a flourishing cat fancy—founded by a man (see chapter 4).

British Shorthair kitten

Cream British Shorthair

The British Shorthair is one of the oldest recognized breeds in the organized cat fancy but has changed greatly from the cats exhibited during the 1870s and 1880s. Known simply as the Shorthair, the early British Shorthairs would have been more reminiscent of modern American Shorthairs. It was recognized in the naturally occurring colors of black, blue-eyed white, blue, red, tortoiseshell, blue-cream, brown (black) tabby (in both classic and spotted pattern), and silver tabby. Most of those colors and patterns were also accepted with white markings.

Early reds tended to be a sandier color than the rich reds we see today and were often known as "yellow." The Blue Shorthairs, or Maltese, were crossed with Blue Persians, Russian Blues, and the French Chartreux so that the color varied from silver gray and bluish lilac to deep slate blue, with the lightest color cats probably being lilac Shorthairs. The brown tabby Shorthair occurred in two distinct colors: the original brown (black) tabby and the more golden-hued sable tabby. In The Book of the Cat (1903), Frances Simpson describes a number of colors that were not recognized at the time but which modern cat fanciers would recognize as golden tabby (a relative of the silver tabby), chocolate tabby, solid lilac, blue-silver tabby, tipped and shaded silvers, and black smokes. A color that early fanciers called biscuit would later be recognized as cream.

British Shorthairs were so greatly outnumbered by Persians at the early cat shows that special prizes had to be offered just to attract entries in the Shorthair classes. The "Britisher" was similarly slow to take off in the United States. Early breeders developed the breed by selecting for a cobbier type and plusher coat to set it apart from its humble alley-cat ancestors. During the First World War, valuable bloodlines were lost, and the British Shorthair had to be restored by crossing to other breeds, most notably the Persian longhair (which had not developed the extremely short face of modern Persians). In 1926, *Cat Gossip* magazine editor H. C. Brooke wondered how "Short-hair Persians" (later to become Exotic Shorthairs), shown at a cat show in Lille, France, were distinguished from ordinary Shorthairs!

Breeders of the British Shorthair suffered a second serious setback during the Second World War and were obliged to cross their cats to nonpedigree shorthairs and to other breeds such as the Russian Blue simply to preserve bloodlines, losing the sturdy conformation and gaining a more "foreign" look. Breeders turned again to crossing the British Shorthair with Persians to restore the breed's looks, but writer P. M. Soderberg still had cause to complain about the lack of first-rate British Shorthairs into the 1950s.

The main British registry, the GCCF, eventually ruled that British Shorthairs must not have any Persian ancestry in last three generations, but by the 1970s, the influence of the Persian on the British Shorthair meant breeders and judges favored the rounder-headed, cobbier conformation. As a result, the last cattery in the United Kingdom breeding "pure" British Shorthair cats without any Persian ancestry exported its remaining cats to the United States to become part of the American Shorthair breed.

The British Shorthair could be found in a wide range of colors. From the end of the nineteenth century, prizewinning (British) Shorthairs, in particular the silver classic tabbies, were exported to the United States where they influenced the development of the American Shorthair breed. They were registered as Domestic Shorthairs until the 1950s, when the most popular color was recognized in its own right as the British Blue. During the 1950s and 1960s, the Domestic Shorthair breed included both the British—in the solid colors except for blue—and the American Shorthairs, but because these differed in conformation it became necessary to properly distinguish between the two shorthaired breeds. The chunkier British Shorthair, in its various colors, gained acceptance in 1979.

Physical description: Unlike its American cousin, the British Shorthair coat is not only resilient but also quite plush. The British Shorthair does match the American Shorthair in having a compact, well-balanced muscular physique. The breed standard describes the body as "semi-cobby, wide, and firm." Like the American also, the British has a broad head, powerful jaws, and a powerful chest.

Colors and varieties: Although the British Shorthair is accepted in most colors, the most popular is the blue, a reflection of the popularity of the related blue Longhairs (Persians) in Victorian times.

Colorpoint British Shorthairs, developed in the 1980s by crossing the British with the Himalayan (colorpoint Persian), are popular in the United Kingdom. Mink British Shorthairs (the Tonkinese pattern resulting from a mix of Siamese and Burmese ancestry) are bred in France, the Burmese sepia gene having been introduced at some point. Although ticked shorthaired cats were among the early Shorthairs, they formed part of the Abyssinian breed, and ticked British Shorthairs are not currently bred. Chocolate, lilac, and pointed colored British Shorthairs are popular in England but are not currently recognized by all registries in the United States.

Temperament: Like the American Shorthair, the British Shorthair makes a loving, devoted companion, but like her countrymen, the British is a bit more reserved in her affections than the American. The British Shorthair is a working breed that enjoys the pursuit of prey, even if the prey must be in the form of a toy mouse.

Activity level: Low

Vocal level: Low

Special needs: The plush coat of the British Shorthair should be brushed occasionally to remove shed hair.

Variations: The British Longhair has been recently recognized as a championship breed in some registries, as a way to preserve the "old-style" Longhairs of England prior to the advent of extreme brachycephaly in the Persian breed. The Antipodean, Celtic Shorthair, and Mexican Shorthair are other breeds derived from native shorthaired populations in other parts of the world.

Burmese

Place of origin: Thailand

History: The temple cats of Burma have been cherished by priests there for centuries, and they exist in many different colors and varieties. In the late nineteenth century, cats described as "chocolate Siamese" were imported into England but did not find favor with cat fanciers at that time. Dun-colored cats with dark extremities were considered "Royal Siamese," whereas the chocolate cats were considered "Temple cats" or "Rajah type." A photograph of a cat taken back to England as a "Burmese cat" shows an Oriental ticked tabby.

In 1903, Frances Simpson's The Book of the Cat mentioned the legend about the Siamese and Burmese cats: the light-colored cats with blue eyes represent silver, whereas the dark cats with yellow eyes represented gold; according to legend, anyone possessing both cats would have plenty of silver and gold. Early fanciers also encountered imported Siamese with "coats of burnished chestnut with greeny-blue eyes" (suggestive of the modern Tonkinese) and "chocolate colored Siamese with the same color all over." Simpson's book stated that it was a great mistake to mix the two varieties because the result was a blurring of the markings and a patchy coat. The *Encyclopaedia Britannica* (eleventh edition) referred to a "wholly chocolate–colored strain of Siamese" that was exhibited in 1894 under the name Swiss Mountain Cats. The standard of points for the chocolate Siamese were the same as for the Royal Siamese, with the exception of the dark, rich brown body color, which made the markings less noticeable—this strongly suggests the Burmese sepia color. However, those chocolate colored cats vanished in the 1920s, when the Siamese Cat Club ruled that only blue-eyed Siamese were acceptable.

With so many years elapsed and so few photos, it is impossible to say with certainty whether the chocolate-brown Siamese were equivalent to Burmese, to Tonkinese, or to modern Havanas (chestnut-brown Orientals). In any case, the modern breeds with those names are Western refinements, especially in terms of physical conformation, of varieties first imported from

European Burmese

Lilac Burmese

Thailand and neighboring countries in the late 1800s and early 1900s.

The chocolate-brown Siamese having died out in the United Kingdom during the 1920s, today's Burmese breed traces its ancestry back to a single "copper cat" (called by the Thai people *Thong Daeng*—literally "red gold") named Wong Mau; she was taken to the United States in 1930, where she caused a sensation in the cat fancy. As was common in Thailand, Wong Mau was mated to a sealpoint Siamese cat, resulting in kittens of both Siamese coloration and those colored like their dam. This means Wong Mau was equivalent to a modern mink-patterned Tonkinese cat. When one of the male kittens was bred back to his mother, it resulted in sable brown kittens who were darker than either parent. When these brown offspring were mated to each other, they produced only brown kittens—the Burmese breed had been born.

It took skillful management by the initial breeders to create a unique breed from a single cat and a limited gene pool. Early breeders continued to cross to Siamese to avoid inbreeding, with the result that the American Siamese cat clubs of the early twentieth century initially fought the acceptance of the new breed into the cat fancy, and Burmese were removed from the show bench in 1947. Breeding with Siamese also created a more foreign-looking cat, and regaining the rounded head type and cobby body of the breed remained a challenge for many years.

Additional imports were later added to strengthen the gene pool. Once the breed was established enough to meet the requirements of three generations of pure breeding, the Burmese breed was reaccepted for recognition in 1957. In the United States, blue, champagne, and platinum were registered as Malayan in 1979, but became part of the Burmese breed five years later. These occurred in Burmese litters as a result of recessive genes carried either by Wong Mau or by the Siamese she was bred to.

The Burmese was recognized in the United Kingdom in 1952. The breed was based on a small number of cats imported from the United States from 1949 to 1956, although cats resembling Wong Mau had been brought back by soldiers stationed in the Far East during the late 1940s. Continental Europe and the Commonwealth countries (countries once under British rule) have based their Burmese breeding programs on cats from the United Kingdom so that the more foreign-looking European Burmese has become the prevalent type worldwide.

The first blue Burmese appeared in England in 1955. Although blue, champagne (chocolate in the United Kingdom), and platinum (lilac in the United Kingdom) had appeared in litters bred in the United States, breeders chose to concentrate on the original sable color. The red, cream, and tortie Burmese were developed by British breeders. In 1964, a blue Burmese female escaped and mated with a red tabby shorthair. A deliberate mating was made between a brown Burmese to a red point Siamese. A third mating was between a brown Burmese male and a calico farm cat who had Siamese ancestry.

The resulting Burmese colors gained recognition in the United Kingdom between 1973 and 1977. Cinnamon Burmese were developed in Europe and New Zealand in the late 1980s and the 1990s. In North America, these colors are only recognized in the European Burmese.

Physical description: The Burmese has diverged in type between the United States and United Kingdom/Europe, with the result that they are effectively two different breeds. The relatively round-headed American Burmese is not recognized, even as an outcross, in Europe because of a lethal gene mutation carried by some lines. The more Oriental-looking Burmese cat of Britain and Europe is bred under the name European Burmese (or Foreign Burmese) in the United States.

The American sable Burmese can be summed up as "round and brown" with a rounded head, relatively short nose, rounded eyes, and a cobby body. The large, round gold eyes contrasting with the glossy, close-lying coat gives the breed a unique appearance. Its broad and sturdy chest, cobby body, short neck, and thick tail result in a cat who is surprisingly heavy for her compact size and sometimes likened to a feline bulldog. This style of Burmese is largely restricted to North America.

The European Burmese has become the more prevalent type around the world (the "European" prefix is used only in North America) and is described as an elegant cat of a foreign type with the head forming a short wedge and only slightly rounded. The top line of its eyes has a slight slant.

Caramel Burmilla

Chocolate Burmilla

The neck is medium length, rather than short. In general, it is more slender and more angular than its American Burmese cousin, but still a muscular cat.

Colors and varieties: Although initially recognized only in the sable brown or dark walnut color that inspired the breed, the Burmese is now accepted worldwide in three additional colors: blue, lilac (also called platinum), and chocolate (also called champagne). In the American Burmese breed, these additional colors were originally registered as a separate breed, the Malayan. In the United Kingdom and Europe, no such distinction was made. Crossing performed to establish a wide gene pool in Europe and Australia introduced additional colors, including red, cream, and the tortoiseshell, silver, and tabby varieties of the four basic colors. In Europe, the silver and tabby varieties form the Asian Shorthair breed group. Some are recognized under individual breed names, such as the Bombay (a black self Burmese) and the Burmilla (a tipped silver Burmese).

Temperament: Burmese cats bond very closely with their owners and can be territorial toward other cats. They are very affectionate and enjoy crawling under the bedcovers with their favorite family members. These playful cats enjoy games of fetch and chasing after toys. Females can be quite headstrong and are usually the dominant cat in the household, whereas males are more laid-back and willing to please. Burmese are very social cats and thrive on company—if you are away from home for long periods, it is usually better to have two Burmese so they can keep each other company.

Activity level: Moderate

Vocal level: Moderate

Special needs: Burmese are a healthy and long-lived breed that requires little maintenance beyond a regular grooming with a rubber brush to remove shed hair and a polish with a chamois cloth to bring out the natural sheen in the coat. Breeders of the

American Burmese need to be aware of the Burmese craniofacial defect that results in lethal skull malformations and stillborn kittens (see Burmese Craniofacial Defect, page 322). This gene mutation is not present in the European Burmese.

Variations: Burmese conformation cats have been bred that lack the partial albinism that results in the unique color of the Burmese breed. These result from crossing the Burmese with American Shorthairs or other shorthaired cats. These breeds are known as the Bombay (with its black, shiny, patent leather appearing coat), Asian Shorthair, and New Zealand's Mandalay (the other solid colors). Because these breeds do not express the partial albinism gene, the eye color of the Bombay and Mandalay tends toward deeper shades of gold and copper. Several outdated names are sometimes still heard: Cornelian (red self Asian Shorthair), Burmoire (smoke Asian Shorthair), and Burmali (ticked tabby Asian Shorthair).

The Burmilla, which has both shorthaired and semi-longhaired versions, originated in the United Kingdom in 1981 with an accidental cross between a Chinchilla Persian and lilac Burmese. As a result of the crosses with silver Persians that were performed to develop the Burmilla, longhaired Burmese have been developed as the Tiffanie and Asian Longhair. The separate Australian Tiffanie is a cobbier cat with a greater amount of Chinchilla Persian blood than the European Tiffanie.

Chartreux

Place of origin: France

History: The origins of the Chartreux (or Carthusians) and their name, like those of many breeds, are shrouded in time and conflicting stories. The best known claims that the cats journeyed from South Africa to France with a group of Carthusian monks who carried their companions home to live in the order's head monastery, the Grande Chartreuse, in the Chartreuse Mountains. Another tale says that the ancestors of the Chartreux were feral mountain cats from Syria who traveled to France courtesy of returning thirteenth-century Crusaders, many of whom later entered the Carthusian monastic order with their felines. The connection between the order and the cats was challenged in 1972, however, when the prior of the Grande Chartreuse stated that its archives held no records of the monks' having kept cats resembling the Chartreux.

Whatever the monastery's archival records might or might not say, the "little gray cat" of France appears in the country's literature as early at the sixteenth century and by the eighteenth century is referenced by the name Chartreux. A more prosaic explanation for the breed's name claims that it is derived from the name of a luxurious eighteenth-century Spanish wool, *pile de Chartreux*. The cat's wooly coat, developed from generations of cats surviving outdoors in often harsh conditions, resembled the Spanish wool. In the eighteenth century, the dense coat of the Chartreux was prized by furriers because it could be dyed and sold as otter fur.

Some of the early texts describe the Chartreux as having longer fur, akin to the Persian or Angora of that time. In the eighteenth century, naturalist Georges Louis Leclerc, Comte of Buffon, considered the Chartreux familiar enough that he described a blue Persian by likening its color to that of the Chartreux. He believed the Persian, the Angora, and the Chartreux to be related. Buffon wrote that a comparison of the wild cat with the Chartreux cat found that they differed only in the grayish-brown color of the wild cat being changed to ash-colored gray in the Chartreux. German writer Jean Bungartz described the Carthusian (the Chartreux's other

name) in An Illustrated Book of Cats (1896) as a self-colored blue variety with long fine hair, black lips, and black soles, and being somewhat phlegmatic, like the Angora and the Persian.

In his 1926 book Les Races des Chats (The Breeds of Cats), Philippe Jumaud likened the Carthusian or Chartreuse cat to the "Maltese cat" known in the United States, describing its large head, large, full eyes, short nose, and small erect ears. Its coat, he wrote, was "half long and woolly" and the color was bluish gray. A year later, an English cat show judge visiting the Paris Cat Show saw a class for "Chats de Chartreux." As the breed was unknown in the United Kingdom, she asked for more information and came away little the wiser for being told by different parties that they were "the American cat" and the Maltese!

Natural colonies of these blue-gray cats existed in parts of France up until the early twentieth century. The modern Chartreux trace their ancestry to a few individuals from small, isolated colonies of domestic cats in France collected by breeders interested in preserving this ancient breed. The breed was largely preserved by two sisters, Christine and Suzanne Leger, who selectively bred the Chartreux from feral blue cats from isolated colonies crossed to British Blue Shorthairs. The early breeders based their breed standard on eighteenth-century naturalist descriptions; Chartreux from those breeding programs were exhibited in France in 1928.

In common with cat breeds across continental Europe, the Chartreux breed was greatly diminished during the Second World War. There were no known natural colonies of these robust blue cats left in France. Only the determination of European breeders kept the Chartreux from extinction; breeders crossed the remaining cats to British Blue Shorthairs and blue-cream shorthairs, to Russian Blues and to blue Persians. These efforts helped, but the breed remained rare even in its home country.

In the 1950s, French cat fancier Fernand Mery wrote that the Chartreux was not to be confused with the British Blue, calling this a cat of rural France with a stockier body than the British Blue, standing solidly on comparatively short, well-muscled legs. He described the head as being round and full cheeked, on a thick-set neck. The powerful jaw made Chartreux "temptingly reminiscent" of the European wild cat. The fur was described as woolly and any shade of grayish blue, although paler hues were preferred. In contrast, British cat fancier Rose Tenent did not distinguish between the British Blue and Chartreux when she wrote, "On the Continent, too, this cat [the British Blue] is becoming increasingly popular, and there its name is the Chartreuse," whereas British breeder and judge Grace Pond described the Chartreux as confusingly similar to the British Blue.

Although the two breeds differ in temperament and physique, the Chartreux breed is not recognized as a separate breed in the United Kingdom because it is considered too similar to the British Blue Shorthair. Early cat fanciers greatly favored blue cats but did not distinguish between breeds until later, so any imported blue French cats would have been interbred with British Shorthairs.

By 1970, the FIFe (the major European cat registry) had assimilated the Chartreux and the British Blue under the more attractive breed name Chartreux but with the breed standard of the more populous but less interestingly named British Blue Shorthair. Breeders of the pure Chartreux objected, and the move was reversed in 1977, so that the Chartreux and British Blue Shorthair could be maintained as separate breeds, and crossbreeding was discouraged. Some European cat clubs that were not affiliated with FIFe continued to use the name Chartreux for the British Blue Shorthair, for European Blue Shorthair, or for crosses between one of these shorthairs and the genuine French Chartreux (this may change under the growing influences of TICA and of the WCF). This tended to occur in countries where the genuine Chartreux was rarely, if ever, found and has resulted in Chartreux longhairs and blue-cream Chartreux. Although the Chartreux longhairs and blue-cream Chartreux are attractive in their own right, breeders of the genuine Chartreux are careful not to introduce these into their breeding programs.

The first Chartreux were taken to the United States in 1971, and in 1987 the breed gained formal recognition; however, it remains relatively rare. Unlike many breeds with a long history, the Chartreux has remained almost unchanged in looks since the 1930s. Some of the purest Chartreux bloodlines are now to be found in the United States.

Traditionally, the first letter of the official name of a Chartreux cat relates to the year of its birth; all Chartreux born in the same year have official names beginning with the same letter. The code letters rotate through the alphabet each year, omitting the letters K, Q, W, X, Y, and Z.

Physical description: The Chartreux is a study in contrasts. The medium-size, upright ears and small, narrow muzzle seem out of place on the broad head attached to a thick powerful neck. The shape of Chartreux's head and muzzle give this cat a sweet-looking expression, and the Chartreux is often described as smiling. The substantial, robust body seems to overpower the fine-boned legs and delicate, compact feet. This has earned the Chartreux the rather unflattering nickname of "potato on matchsticks." But when these discordant parts come together, the overall impression is that of a uniquely beautiful cat. This is an extraordinarily slow-maturing breed, with the dense coat reaching its full maturity after three years of age.

The dense coat is medium short and slightly woolly in texture with a resilient undercoat. It often parts like sheepskin at the neck and flanks. The coat develops as the cat matures, being silkier on younger cats and woollier on mature cats. The cat's orange- or copper-colored eyes contrast with the blue-gray coat. Mature cats usually weigh from 12 to 16 pounds (5–7 kg).

Colors and varieties: This breed exists only in the color blue, ranging from ash gray to a deep slate blue. The tips of the fur give the coat a silvery sheen.

Temperament: Loyal to their owners, these sweet-natured, quiet cats are adaptable. They do well as solitary cats and in homes where their owners may be gone for most of the day. Although tolerant of children and other animals, they prefer a quiet home and are an excellent breed for senior citizens. They often bond closely with one person, although not to the exclusion of other family members. They like to sleep with, or preferably on, their owners. Despite their sedentary nature, they are intelligent and observant, sometimes learning to unlatch doors. They retain their hunting instincts and enjoy chasing and "killing" a toy; some will also retrieve a toy so it can be thrown for them to "kill" until they tire of the game.

Activity level: Low

Vocal level: Low; many Chartreux will never vocalize.

Special needs: Grooming with a brush, especially during the springtime shedding season, will help keep the coat in good condition. This sedentary breed can be prone to obesity if overfed.

Variations: Benedictine is a term used to describe a breeding program of longhaired Chartreux. Some European cats known as Chartreux have mixed heritage resulting in blue-cream variants and longhairs.

Chartreux kitten

Cornish Rex

Place of origin: Cornwall, England

History: The term rex was originally used for curly furred rabbits. The first formally recognized Rex cat arose in 1950, in a litter of farm cats in Bodmin, Cornwall, England. A calico female was believed to have mated with her red tabby brother. One cream-colored kitten in the resulting litter had short curly fur; named Kallibunker, he was to become the founding father of the Cornish Rex breed. Kallibunker was mated back to his mother, which resulted in two more curly-coated kittens. The effects of excessive inbreeding hampered the first ten years of breed development, however, and it was almost abandoned.

Kallibunker's son Poldhu sired a blue female called Lamorna Cove. The breeder exported Lamorna, already pregnant by Poldhu, to the United States. Unfortunately, Poldhu never again sired kittens. He was sent to the veterinarian for testing because of his unusual blue cream and white coloring. Blue cream (dilute tortoiseshell) is a genetic anomaly in males, so the veterinarian took tissue samples from him. Being a fertile tortie male, Poldhu was probably a chimera, the result of two embryos fusing in the womb. However, something happened, and Poldhu could no longer breed.

That left only one fertile male Cornish Rex in Britain, another of Kallibunker's sons, a cream and white bicolor. In a last attempt to establish the Cornish Rex as a breed, he was mated to domestic shorthair females and Burmese females. This proved successful, reinvigorating the breed.

In the United States, the California breeder who had imported the pregnant Cornish Rex female Lamorna Cove expanded the breed's gene pool using Siamese and domestic shorthair cats. A red tabby Cornish Rex male exported with Lamorna Cove appears to have been infertile. The genetically compatible German Rex was also bred to Cornish Rex in the United States.

In 1960, on the tenth anniversary of the first appearance of the Cornish Rex, a story in *The Daily Mirror* newspaper claimed them to be the only curly-haired cats in Britain. A cat lover in Devon wrote back to say she had a curly-coated cat named Kirlee. Kirlee was mated with Cornish Rex but proved to have an entirely different mutation and went on to become the founder of the Devon Rex breed. The spontaneous appearance of Rex cats in neighboring counties attracted the belief that radiation from local tin mines was causing mutations in the local cat population.

The Cornish Rex breed was recognized in the United States in 1964 and in the United Kingdom in 1965. To prevent inbreeding, Cornish Rex are still outcrossed to a small number of other breeds. The kittens from outcrossing will be straight-coated, but when mated to a Cornish Rex some will have the Rex coat. Careful breeding has ensured that modern Cornish Rex closely resemble the original cats of the 1950s. However, the American Cornish Rex has diverged from the British/European Cornish Rex. As well as a different look, the American Cornish Rex has a different genetic history, having been crossed with German Rex and Siamese/Oriental Shorthairs.

Although most cats have three distinct types of hair in their coat—longer *outer guard hairs,* a middle layer of *awn hairs,* and the undercoat or *down hair*—the Cornish Rex has only a fine, curled coat. The guard hairs, if present, are highly modified and indistinguishable. It is a common misconception that the Cornish Rex's short, soft hair makes it

hypoallergenic. Cat allergy is almost always due to the Fel d1 protein present in the saliva and deposited on the fur through grooming. Cornish Rex groom themselves as much as any other cat and are equally likely to trigger an allergic reaction in susceptible individuals.

Physical description: The soft, velvety coat of the Cornish Rex comprises tight curls forming a wavy pattern called a Marcel wave (named after nineteenth-century French hairdresser François Marcel, who invented a hot curling iron hair styling process that became popular with women in the early twentieth century). The fur forms ripples,

Cornish Rex. Note the crinkled whiskers.

Sealpoint Cornish Rex

especially on the back, sides, tail, and anywhere else it is long enough to form waves. Even the whiskers and eyebrows are crinkled.

The British/European Cornish Rex has a medium length, slender but muscular body on long straight legs. The body is "tucked up" behind the rib cage, and the tail is long and tapering. It has a medium wedge-shaped head with high cheekbones and large expressive ears.

The American Cornish Rex is more delicate and longer legged than its British cousin. It has a fine-boned, long-legged body with a "tuck up" reminiscent of a Greyhound. The head is an oval egg shape, with a Roman profile and a slight hint of constriction at the whisker pads. The strikingly large ears are set upright on the head. The tail is frequently described as "whiplike."

Colors and varieties: The Cornish Rex is accepted in a rainbow of colors, including solids, bicolors, tabbies, torties, silvers, and smokes. In the United States, the colorpointed varieties may be separately recognized as the Si-Rex, while elsewhere these are a color variety of Cornish Rex.

Temperament: One of the most active cats in the cat fancy, Cornish Rex busily engage themselves in every household activity. Skillful with their monkeylike paws, they almost seem to have opposable thumbs at times. Life with this breed is never without excitement, and owners must take care to catproof a house before introducing this mischievous breed. These cats are as enthusiastic with their affection as they are about their playtime.

Cornish Rex are generally healthy, active cats who stay playful and kittenish into adulthood; some enjoy retrieving small toys for their owners to throw again and again. They are affectionate, curious, intelligent, and adaptable. The extrovert traits may be more pronounced in the American Cornish Rex due to their Siamese ancestry.

Activity level: High

Vocal level: Moderate

Special needs: The abnormality in the hair follicle that causes the hairs to curl or kink also interferes with skin secretions (sebum) being pulled away from the skin. Some Rex Wirehaired cats may need to be bathed frequently and have their ears cleaned regularly to prevent these secretions from accumulating in the hair follicles or ear canal and causing skin problems.

Variations: Semi-longhaired Cornish Rex sometimes occur due to recessive genes in the breed. Curly-haired cats can appear, seemingly out of nowhere, due to hidden recessive genes or new mutations. They have been reported from all over the world—from Europe, to North America, to Australia. Many turn out to have mutations identical to the established Rex breeds and may result from unneutered pedigree pets mating with free-ranging cats, but occasionally completely new Rex mutations occur.

Devon Rex

Place of origin: Devon, England

History: The second curly-coated breed to be formally recognized was the Devon Rex, originally known as the Butterfly Rex because of its large ears. In 1960, a curly-coated grayish kitten was discovered in Buckfastleigh, Devon, England, in a litter born to a tortie female. Named Kirlee and later identified as black smoke in color, he was to become the father of the Devon Rex breed.

Kirlee's finder recalled seeing, around a local tin mine, a large black cat with tight curls on his body and ringlets hanging from his tail; this was probably the kitten's father. Although Kirlee was shorthaired, he turned out to carry the recessive mutation for long hair.

In fact, a local variety nicknamed the "Buckfast Blue" had been a familiar sight in the area of Buckfast Abbey, Devon, since the 1950s. These were wavy-coated gray-blue stray and feral cats who were considered nothing more than an attractive curiosity by locals and eventually died out.

Around the time Kirlee was born, the Cornish Rex was getting publicity. Kirlee was initially assumed to be another Cornish Rex because Cornwall and Devon are neighboring counties. When Kirlee was mated to a female Cornish Rex, however, only straight-haired kittens were born. This meant Kirlee had a different genetic mutation. From then on, the two Rex breeds were developed independently of each other, and the Devon Rex was recognized as its own breed in 1967.

The straight-coated kittens from early test matings with Cornish Rex were used in developing the Devon Rex breed. As a result, Devon Rex share their ancestry with the Cornish Rex, and "Double Rex" kittens are sometimes born. As well as altering the fur, the Devon Rex mutation produced a longer, but still muscular, body type with long hind legs and a distinctive head shape. Selective breeding has exaggerated the head and

ear conformation, but the Devon Rex varies little in conformation around the world.

The first breeding Devon Rex were exported to North America in 1968 and recognized by the American Cat Fanciers Association (ACFA) as a breed in 1972. The CFA, however, classified the Devon and Cornish Rex together until 1979, despite their being genetically different.

The Devon Rex came from very inbred stock and is outcrossed to approved breeds to keep the gene pool healthy. Abyssinians, American Shorthairs, British Shorthairs, Burmese, and Korats have all been used to expand the gene pool. So far, no other Rex mutation has been found to be compatible with Devon Rex. Genetic investigation of the Devon Rex and Sphynx breeds, however, have found these to be mutations of the same gene, which may account for the varying degrees of baldness found in Devon Rex. Sparse-coated Devon Rex have been used in developing the hairless Sphynx breed. Devon Rex with Sphynx ancestry may not be registered as Devon Rex or used in Devon Rex breeding programs.

Along with the Cornish Rex, the Devon Rex is sometime reputed to be hypoallergenic. However, most cat allergies are caused by the Fel d1 protein in the saliva, not by the fur itself. This protein is deposited on the fur when the cat grooms herself,

Devon Rex

One-month-old Devon Rex kitten

which means the Devon Rex will still cause allergic reactions in susceptible people.

Physical description: The breed was developed in a style very distinct from the Cornish Rex. The Devon Rex is an athletic, small- to medium-sized cat. The body is slender, with a broad chest, long legs, and a long, fine, tapering tail. The cat has a distinctive pixielike expression: short muzzle, prominent cheekbones, and large bell-shaped ears set low on a short wide head. This distinctive face earned the Devon Rex the early name Butterfly Rex, while her personality earned her the nickname of "monkey cat."

Cats normally have three types of hair in the coat: guard hairs, awn hairs, and undercoat or down hair. The Devon Rex has randomly arranged soft curls ranging from velvety to slightly harsh, depending on the number of guard hairs present. The hair is evenly waved on the bodies; these waves may extend down the legs and along the tail. Many Devon Rex have a sparse coat on the underparts, and some are born almost bald, their coats not developing fully until the second or even third, year. The coat varies throughout the seasons, with some cats molting imperceptibly and others becoming noticeably sparse-coated before their new coat grows in. The whiskers are short, curly, and easily broken.

The recessive longhair gene has been in the breed from the beginning. To expand a highly inbred gene pool, outcrosses have been made to both shorthaired and semi-longhaired cats. As a result, semi-longhaired versions appear, some of which have long wavy or ringleted ruffs and britches and plumed tails. Although the longhaired Devon Rex is not recognized for exhibition, some people consider its thicker coat to be more attractive than the sometimes sparse coat of the traditional shorthaired Devon Rex.

Colors and varieties: The Devon Rex comes in all colors of the domestic cat: solids, bicolors, tabbies, silvers, smokes, and both the Burmese and Siamese pointed patterns. Kirlee was a black

smoke, and this remains a popular color in the breed. Some Devon Rex carry the recessive gene for long hair, which results in semi-longhaired "Angora Devon Rex" occasionally appearing

Temperament: An active, playful cat, the Devon Rex is particular fond of perching on high places, including the shoulders of their owners. The short coat makes the breed fond of seeking out warm places, such as under the bedcovers and on top of warm household appliances. These are active, intelligent, playful, people-oriented cats. They often bond closely with a particular family member. The Devon Rex's mischievous personality is often described as part cat, part dog, and part monkey.

Activity level: Moderate

Vocal level: Moderate; they chirp rather than demand.

Special needs: Hand grooming is usually sufficient for the shortest-haired Devon Rex. Those with longer or fuller fur benefit from brushing with a soft bristle brush. Because the abnormality in the hair follicle that causes the hairs to curl or kink also interferes with skin secretions (sebum) being pulled away from the skin, some Rex and wirehaired cats may need to be bathed frequently and their ears cleaned regularly to prevent these secretions from accumulating in the hair follicles or ear canal and causing dermatological problems. Breeders are working to eliminate spasticity (a genetically inherited problem) from some lines of Devon Rex.

Variations: Semi-longhaired variants are shaggier and often develop ringlets. Straight-haired kittens from crossing to other breeds are known as Devon Rex Variants and used in keeping the gene pool healthy. Crossing between the Scottish Fold and Devon Rex produced the Poodlecat (Pudelkatze) in Germany. The Poodlecat has a chunkier build and denser coat and is not widely known.

Donskoy

Place of origin: Russia

History: For many years, the Canadian-bred Sphynx was unopposed on the show bench as the sole hairless cat breed. Other hairless cats had appeared but had either become foundation cats for the Sphynx or had not been bred. This changed in 1987 with the Donskoy, which originated in the small Russian town of Rostov-on-Don. The foundation cat was a blue-cream tortoiseshell female rescue named Varvara (or Varya). At first, it was believed Varvara was hairless due to illness or a skin condition, but as time went on Varvara was found to healthy. Around 1989, Varvara was bred to a neighboring tomcat and produced several hairless kittens, demonstrating the mutation to be a dominant gene. The progeny were bred to European Shorthairs and Domestic Shorthairs and became the foundation cats of the Donskoy Sphynx breed.

Unlike the recessive hairless mutation that created the Sphynx breed, the Russian hairless mutation is a dominant "hair loss" gene, meaning that only one parent needs to have the gene for hairless kittens to be produced. Some kittens born from mating a Donskoy to a fully furred outcross can have a residual curly or fine coat at birth. This fur is shed between two months and two years of age. Other kittens from matings between Donskoy and furred cats retain a curly coat throughout their life and are known as *brush* coated. When this first generation of offspring are bred among themselves, kittens who are hairless at birth appear in the litters.

Physical description: The Donskoy is a solid, medium-sized cat with a short wedge-shaped head with prominent cheekbones; large, upright ears; and wrinkles on the face, forehead, and jowls resulting in an "old man" expression. Some Donskoy have whiskers, others don't. Young cats may have curly whiskers and short fur on the muzzle, on the cheeks, and at the base of the ears.

Donskoy have endearing, almond-shaped eyes and paws that look almost like human hands. These cats may grow a fine coat of fur in the winter.

Colors and varieties: These cats are recognized in all colors. Because hairlessness in these breeds is a dominant trait, expression of the hairlessness trait varies more widely than in the recessive Sphynx.

Peterbald

Cats with one copy of the gene may have a different feel to their skin than cats with two copies of the gene. Variations include complete hairlessness on the body, resulting in a rubbery feel to the skin that resembles vinyl; a soft, velour coat of short hairs that feels like crushed velvet; and a curly, coarse, brushlike coat. The amount of hair may change with the seasons, becoming denser in the cooler months.

Temperament: The Donskoy is an affectionate and sociable cat who enjoys the comforts of an available lap.

Activity level: High

Vocal level: Moderate

Special needs: Because hair growth does not pull skin secretions (sebum) from the skin, hairless cats need to be bathed and their ears cleaned regularly to prevent these secretions from accumulating on the skin and in the hair follicles. They should also be provided with warm areas to crawl into and should be protected from excessive cold or unfiltered sunlight, as they may sunburn. Because they do not have fur to protect their skin, their nails should be kept well groomed, and they should be kept from exposure to sharp objects in their environment to prevent scratches. Rough play with other pets in the household can lead to skin injuries as well.

Variations: In 1993, some Donskoy cats were mated to Oriental/Siamese in St. Petersburg and Moscow in 1993, resulting in an Oriental conformation hairless cat known as the Peterbald. In 2005, the Ukrainian Levkoy Cat was created using the Donskoy and Scottish Fold. The Ukrainian Levkoy has a wider, rounder face than the Donskoy. The ears do not fold tightly to the skull, as in the Scottish Fold, but stand out from the head and fold near the ear tips. This variation also occurs in the various coat types of the Donskoy and in a prick-eared form due to recessive genes.

Egyptian Mau

Place of origin: Egypt

History: Although regarded as one of the initial ancient cat breeds, the modern Egyptian Mau was developed in Europe from spotted cats imported from the Middle East. The breed name is derived from the Middle Egyptian word mau (an onomatopoeic word that means "cat"). Along with the rare Bahraini Dilmun Cat, the Egyptian Mau is one of very few naturally occurring spotted breeds of cat recognized by cat registries. To add to the romance of the breed, it was saved from possible extinction by an exiled Russian princess.

Cats resembling Egyptian Maus are depicted in Egyptian artwork more than 3,000 years old. The ancient Egyptians are said to have trained their Mau-like cats to hunt and retrieve birds. They are known to have worshipped cats and mourned their death and said to punish those who harmed a cat with death. Ironically, cats were also bred en masse by temples in order to be sacrificed and mummified.

During the Second World War, like many breeds, the Egyptian Mau faced extinction. Already, the native spotted domestic cats were becoming increasingly mongrelized with stray pets, losing the distinctive look of their ancestors. According to some accounts, the modern Egyptian Mau

The Breeds

began when an exiled Russian princess, Nathalie Troubetskoy, met a cat belonging to the Egyptian ambassador to Italy, where she was living. Intrigued by the cat's looks, she persuaded the ambassador to import several more of the Egyptian cats for her. According to other accounts, she was given a silver-spotted Mau kitten by a boy who had received it from a diplomat working in the Middle East, and she persuaded the Syrian Embassy to obtain more cats from Egypt. Still other accounts will tell you that Troubetskoy was so impressed by the spotted markings of street cats in Cairo that she imported a female to Italy to mate with a local tom. Whatever the case, the cats she imported from Egypt became the basis of a breeding program, and in 1956, Troubetskoy immigrated to the United States, taking three Egyptian Maus with her.

Three cats made inbreeding inevitable, so it is likely Troubetskoy outcrossed her purebred Maus to other cats to keep the gene pool healthy. Early pedigrees show only silver, bronze, and smoke-colored cats, but where there are smokes there also had to be solid black cats, even if these were not recorded or bred from. Outcrossing may have introduced the classic tabby pattern and the blue colors that occur in the modern Egyptian Mau.

In 1980, Bengal cat breeder Jean Mill imported a bronze rosetted stray male cat from New Delhi, India, for her own breeding program. Along with a bronze female, these two cats created the "Indian Mau" breed line that was incorporated into the Egyptian Mau. This controversial move opened the door to further imports of cats from Egypt in the 1980s and 1990s. The new "Egyptian Lines" tended to be larger and more vigorous than the now inbred original breeding lines.

These cats are not accepted for registration as Egyptian Maus by cat fancies unless they meet an exacting standard. In the CFA, the imported cats are known as "Native Maus." The second and third generations are "Domestic Maus." The fourth-generation cats can be considered for registration as Egyptian Maus as long as they meet the breed standard. However such imports are essential to expand the gene pool, especially because the

Egyptian Mau may not be outcrossed to any other breeds. The Egyptian Mau Rescue Organization is an adoption agency for Egyptian and Arabian street cats of unknown pedigree.

The Egyptian Mau was recognized as early as 1968 by some organizations and by TICA in 1979. Maus first arrived in the United Kingdom from the United States in late 1998 and achieved recognition in 2004. However, they remain rare in the United Kingdom and in continental Europe. They have also achieved recognition in Australasia.

Physical description: The show bench Egyptian Mau has a randomly spotted pattern on a silky, resilient coat. The coat of the smoke variety tends to be somewhat softer. This spotted pattern is showcased on a strong, slim, but muscular body held by elegant, long legs. This is a medium-size, well-balanced cat of moderately foreign conformation. Females range from 6 to 8 pounds (2.75–3.5 kg), while males can weigh up to 12 pounds (5 kg).

The Egyptian Mau has a distinctive flap of skin hanging from the belly extending from the flank to the hind knee. This is called a primordial flap or greater omentum and is seen only in the Egyptian Mau and the American Keuda (a breed that is in development), whereas all other domestic breeds should have a tucked-up belly. Its purpose is to allow the cat to run very fast by hyperextending her longer hind legs and may be evidence of the breed's antiquity.

Overall, the Mau is an elegant cat who manages to combine a regal bearing and alert appearance with a unique "worried" expression caused by the brow line and set of the eyes. This cat appears to be standing on tiptoes. It has a gently concave profile from nose to forehead, large upright ears, and characteristic gooseberry green eyes.

Colors and varieties: As a result of the limited gene pool and careful selective breeding, Egyptian Maus occur in five colors. From most to least common these colors are silver spotted, bronze spotted, smoke (with ghost spotting), solid black, and blue/pewter (spotted, smoke, and solid). Classic tabby Maus also sometimes occur due to recessive genes. Although the solid colors, classic tabbies, and blue varieties cannot be exhibited except as household pets, they inherit the same conformation and temperament as the recognized colors and are equally good pets for anyone wanting an Egyptian Mau.

The show bench Egyptian Mau has been developed in three black-based colors in the spotted pattern: bronze, silver, and smoke. Other colors occur, but are not recognized for exhibition except as household pets. All Maus will either have a scarab beetle or M marking on their foreheads. The legs, tail, neck, and upper chest are striped, while the haunches and shoulders show a transition between spots and stripes; there is a dorsal stripe along the length of the spine.

The smoke Mau is genetically a solid-colored

Egyptian Mau

Black Smoke Egyptian Mau

cat. It has "ghost" spotting resulting from selective breeding toward high contrast in the underlying tabby pattern (solid colors simply mask out the tabby pattern). This results in subtle black spots on a charcoal gray color, with silver undercoat, unique to the breed. Genetically, the bronze Mau is a brown (black) spotted tabby and the silver Mau is genetically a black silver spotted tabby. Due to recessive genes, all of these patterns also occur in blue (pewter). Solid-color and classic (blotched) tabby Maus also occur.

Temperament: Affectionate and sensitive cats, Egyptian Maus can be slow to accept strangers and change in their environments. This can make them seem aloof and shy; however, they forms loyal and close bonds with their people and can be very demanding of their attention. Their extremely alert nature means they tend not to be lap cats. Maus are intelligent cats who retain their ancestors' good hunting instinct, and they need toys or interactive play with their owners. Their intelligence means they can be trained for tricks and walking on a leash, and they seem to have a penchant for getting into mechanical mischief, such as learning how to turn on faucets or open doors.

Activity level: Moderate

Vocal level: Low; although Egyptian Maus will chirp or chortle when they feel it necessary.

Special needs: Kittens mature slowly and may need to stay with their queens for a longer period of time than other breeds. Egyptian Maus appear to be more sensitive to anesthetics, vaccines, and pesticides than many other breeds. Breeding females may also have longer pregnancies than other breeds. The short Mau coat is nearly maintenance free, but owners need to comb the coat to reduce shedding. Don't brush vigorously; doing so can strip away the spots formed by the ticking at the end of the hair shaft.

Variations: Another naturally occurring spotted cat

is the Bahraini Dilmun Cat, which only recently has been developed as a breed and has not received widespread recognition.

Exotic Shorthair

Place of origin: United States

History: An early breeder described the origins of the Exotic Shorthair breed in the United States as "making saints out of sinners." Although not strictly in accordance with the rules of American cat registries at the time, in the late 1950s and early 1960s, American Shorthair breeders would introduce new colors into their breed to create more successful, winning show cats by breeding their shorthairs to Persians, British Shorthairs, and Russian Blues. In a similarly controversial practice, breeders crossed Burmese with American Shorthairs, resulting in a cat distinctly different from the "common" American Shorthair. To accommodate the popular Persian and Burmese crossbreeds, without endangering the original American Shorthair type, a new breed was born, the Exotic Shorthair. American Shorthair breeders had the choice of registering their kittens as either American Shorthairs or as Exotic Shorthairs. Once registered as Exotics they, and their progeny, could not change back to being American Shorthairs. Since the late 1980s, the only permitted outcross for the Exotic is to the Persian, in order to maintain the Exotic Shorthair's conformation.

The initial standard was identical to the standard for the Persian standard, with the exception of coat length and the description of the nose break. That was removed to prevent some of the health issues associated with extreme brachycephaly (short-face) that began appearing in the Persian breed. However, despite these initial intentions, breeders selectively bred cats to be closer and closer in type to the Persian so the nose break was later incorporated into the standard. Thus, Exotic Shorthair became "the lazy man's Persian."

Across the Atlantic, cat fanciers had been crossing British Shorthairs with Persians for decades. This added new colors to the Persian breed and "improved" the British Shorthair conformation by making it a cobbier, denser-furred cat than the original Shorthairs. Those matings produced kittens who were too close to the Persian in type, or whose coat was too long and soft for them to be exhibited as British Shorthairs. Some breeders found these different-looking cats attractive enough to be developed in their own right and pursued an Exotic Shorthair breeding program in the United Kingdom. Meanwhile, Australian breeders had become aware of the Exotic Shorthair in the United States and they also began to develop Exotic Shorthairs, crossing Persians with domestic shorthairs, British Shorthairs, and Scottish Folds.

Despite the different foundation cats used in different countries, the end result was a shorthaired cat with the conformation, temperament, and color palette of the Persian. The Exotic Shorthair was recognized in the United States in the late 1960s and in Britain and Continental Europe in 1986.

Physical appearance: The Exotic Shorthair has a compact, rounded, and powerfully built body with a wide chest, relatively short legs, and a short, thick neck. A large head, large round eyes, small ears, and a short snub nose give this cat a sweet facial expression. This breed is slow to mature, not reaching full physical maturity until around two years of age. Although a shorthaired breed, this cat has fur that is denser and slightly longer than that of other shorthaired breeds. The look differs slightly

Exotic Shorthair

around the world, with Exotic Shorthairs (and Persians) in the United States tending to have more extreme facial conformation.

Colors and varieties: The Exotic Shorthair is recognized in all colors found in the Persian, including colorpoints. In North America, where the Burmese was used in the breed's development, it is also recognized in the sepia (Burmese) and mink colors.

Temperament: The Exotic Shorthair has inherited the calm personality of the Persian but is a more active cat. The Exotic Shorthairs have also inherited the inquisitive and playful nature of their American and British Shorthair ancestors, including a hunting instinct, although that is more often exercised on toys than on real prey. They are affectionate and loyal pets who like to be with their owners, enjoy attention, and are suited to being lap cats. If you are attracted to the Persian's personality, but are deterred by their high-maintenance coat, this "Persian in petticoats" may be the cat for you.

Activity level: Low

Vocal level: Low

Special needs: Although not as high maintenance as the Persian, the Exotic Shorthair has a soft, dense coat that is prone to matting. Combing or brushing will remove shed hair and prevent mats. Due to the flattened face and the folds of skin around the muzzle, the Exotic's tears are prone to overflow and stain the cheeks. This should be wiped away with a moistened cloth.

Exotic Shorthairs, along with Persians, are at increased risk of inheriting polycystic kidney disease (PKD). DNA screening is advised if you intend breeding Exotic Shorthairs; cats carrying the PKD gene should not be bred.

Variations: Some breeding programs have maintained a less extreme skull structure, with a longer muzzle, and refer to their cats as "traditional" or "old style." Because Exotic Shorthairs were developed using Persians and are still outcrossed to Persians, some of them carry the recessive longhair gene. When two carriers are bred together, they can produce longhaired offspring. Most registries allow these to be registered as Persians. Some, such as the CFA, register them as Exotic Longhairs based on their shorthaired parentage. In Australia, the longhaired progeny of Exotic Shorthairs may be registered as Persian Variants. The Exotic Longhair meets the standard for the Exotic Shorthair except for coat length. The Exotic Longhair's coat tends to be less long and full than that of a Persian.

German Longhair

Place of origin: Germany

History: In the early twentieth century, longhaired cats in Germany were generically called Angoras and bred for color rather than consistent conformation. Professor Friedrich Schwangart found the German cats to be different from British-bred Persians, so he created a separate German Longhair breed standard in 1929. Breeders of the German Angoras had to decide whether to breed British-type Persians or the more natural-looking, silky-haired German Longhairs. The German Longhair was first exhibited and recognized in Berlin in 1930, and Schwangart continued to champion the breed until the 1950s. The German Longhair continued to be exhibited until the Second World War.

Schwangart believed the cat resembled the European Wildcat (*Felis silvestris*) in conformation. In his last description of it in 1954, he noted that there was variability in conformation, especially among the different colors. By the 1950s, it was considered to be extinct as breeders concentrated on the Persian. In 1979, some German Longhairs traceable to original bloodlines were located and were used to reestablish the breed. Further foundation cats, matching Schwangart's breed standard, were found among free-ranging farm cats.

The modern German Longhair standard was registered with the World Cat Federation in 2008 and is based on Schwangart's original breed standard. It is considered the longhaired relative of the European Shorthair breed, which it resembles in general conformation.

The related German Angora has been bred since 2000, but is not recognized by any cat association, either nationally or internationally. It was founded by breeders who considered the genuine German Longhair to be extinct. The German Angora is described as a naturally occurring longhair akin to the Siberian and Norwegian Forest Cats. Until 2007, when the German Longhair was recognized, the names German Angora and German Longhair were used interchangeably. Following a dispute over the authenticity of the modern German Longhair, the German Angora became a trademarked breed and can only be bred by the German Angora Cat Club.

Both the German Longhair and the German Angora have been crossed to old-style Persians to improve the conformation and coat and to maintain a healthy gene pool. The longhair gene is found in the gene pool of random-bred cats, and foundation cats of the correct conformation are still used in reestablishing the German Longhair breed.

Physical appearance: The German Longhair is a medium-sized cat with a long, robust body, sturdy short-to-medium length legs, deep chest, and medium-length, tapering bushy tail. The rounded head is longer than it is broad with a sloping nose, strong chin, and medium-sized upright ears. The coat is medium long with distinct ruff and britches, but is not as dense or woolly as the Persian's coat.

Colors and varieties: All colors are accepted in the German Longhair except chocolate, cinnamon, and their dilutes, lilac and fawn (in both solids and in patterned cats). The colors/patterns otherwise include self/solid, bicolor, tortoiseshell, tortie and white, tipped, smokes, silvers, and both mackerel and classic tabbies.

Temperament: The German Longhair is an intelligent and people-oriented cat. Being partly derived from free-ranging farm cats, they may retain a hunting instinct that can manifest in a playful streak.

Special needs: All longhaired cats benefit from being regularly combed to remove dead hairs and prevent matting. The silky coat of the German Longhair is more "wash and wear" than that of the Persian.

Variations: None

German Rex

Place of origin: Germany

History: In 1951, a curly-coated stray known as Laemmchen (Lambkin) was found in the grounds of a Berlin hospital, although she was believed to have lived there since 1946. (It is unclear whether she was related to Kater Munk, the Prussian Rex.) In 1956, Laemmchen mated with one of her own sons, producing more Rex-coated cats. By then, the Cornish Rex was being established, and test mating between German and Cornish cats found them to have the same genetic mutation.

In 1961, German Rex were exported to the United States and attracted much interest. However, breeding of German Rex ceased in the States in 1970; instead, they were used to expand the gene pool of the Cornish Rex. The German Rex was almost lost in their own country as well. Laemmchen bore her final litter in 1962, and by 1968, only three of her direct descendants were known, all in East Berlin, where the breed was maintained using European Shorthairs as outcrosses.

Although the FIFe recognized the German Rex in 1982, by 1999 only two breeding females were known to exist. Then a Swiss breeder managed to locate a male and a female in 2000, when a former breeder closed his breeding cattery. Unfortunately, the male panicked and fatally injured himself while the pregnant female miscarried and had to be spayed. The remaining few cats were sickly and almost feral. To make matters worse, one of the two remaining breeding females developed a womb infection as a result of not being bred. To save the breed, she was mated to an Abyssinian male, and one of the offspring was bred to the remaining German Rex female. By chance, in 2005, more German Rex were located in northeast Germany and turned out to come from known breeding lines. Since then, the German Rex has been developed using European Shorthairs.

Physical appearance: The German Rex is muscular, but medium in size and conformation, with a medium-length tail that tapers to a rounded tip. Its head is rounded like that of the European Shorthair, and the ears are medium in size. The short, curly coat has a velvety texture and either lacks guard hairs or they are highly modified and indistinguishable. The whiskers are also curly. Today's German Rex has a thicker coat and more moderate conformation than the Cornish Rex.

Temperament: The German Rex is a friendly, lively, and intelligent cat. It bonds closely with its owner.

Activity level: Moderate.

Vocal level: Low. Although it shares a coat-type mutation with the Cornish Rex, it does not share any Siamese ancestry and has a softer voice.

Special needs: The abnormality in the hair follicle that causes the hairs to curl or kink also interferes with skin secretions (sebum) being pulled away from the skin. Some Rex cats may need to be bathed frequently and their ears cleaned regularly to prevent these secretions from accumulating in the hair follicles or ear canal and causing skin problems.

Variations: Semi-longhaired German Rex can occur due to recessive genes. The Angora German Rex remains an important part of German Rex breeding programs.

Havana Brown

Place of origin: Britain and United States

History: Solid brown cats were among the varieties described in *The Cat Book Poems* (*Tamra Maew*) compiled in Siam (modern-day Thailand; 1350–1767). These cats, along with the royal Siamese, eventually found their way to the emerging cat fancy in Britain. During the 1890s, solid brown cats from Southeast Asia were exhibited in the United Kingdom, having been imported alongside the sealpoint Siamese. These chocolate colored cats were known as Swiss Mountain Cats and mentioned in Frances Simpson's Book of the Cat (1903) and the Encyclopedia Britannica (eleventh edition). They were described as "Siamese with coats of burnished chestnut with greeny-blue eyes." One of these solid brown cats, Granny Grumps, was bred with Siamese and produced many Siamese-patterned kittens, which means she carried the colorpoint gene. These cats may represent early examples of the Havana Brown and chocolate Oriental Shorthair. The breeding of solid-color Siamese was abandoned in the 1920s, however, after the Siamese Cat Club of Britain discouraged the breeding of any but blue-eyed, colorpointed Siamese.

There was renewed interest in solid-color Siamese-type cats following the Second World War. The breeding of pedigree cats had suffered during the war, and breeders resorted to crossing Siamese, Burmese, and Russian Blues just to keep bloodlines going. In the 1950s, British breeders produced chocolate-colored (chestnut) kittens through mating a black shorthair and a chocolate point Siamese. It is perhaps fitting that the first of the solid-color Siamese-type cats to be developed was the "Chestnut Foreign Shorthair," abandoned before the war and recognized by the GCCF in 1958. The GCCF accepted the name "Havana" in 1971, although English Havanas are not the same as American Havana Browns. In FIFe, the major European Registry, the English Havana is termed a "Chocolate Oriental Shorthair."

US breeders imported some of these cats from England in the mid-1950s and then bred them to be significantly different from the Oriental Shorthair

Havana Browns sometimes give birth to lilac-coated kittens due to recessive genes.

in the United Kingdom. The breed would be given the name Havana Brown—some say because of the similarity of its color to a Havana cigar or to a Havana rabbit.

The standard for a Havana Brown is different than that for a Siamese and an Oriental, making it a distinct breed. Although British breeders developed their cats to reflect the Siamese/Oriental conformation, US breeders developed the Havana Browns to have a boxy muzzle and the overall impression of a cat who is "looking down its nose." This is believed to reflect the look of the original foundation cats imported into the United States. The Havana Brown, in this form, is not recognized in Britain or Continental Europe, making this an entirely American breed of cat.

Although recognized in the United States since 1959 (by the CFA), the Havana Brown still remains a rare breed with a small gene pool. To counter a harmful degree of inbreeding, some registries have allowed Havana Browns to be outcrossed to Oriental Shorthairs (excepting colorpointed, fawn, or chocolate varieties) and to solid black and solid blue domestic shorthairs. Some North American breeders outcrossed to Russian Blues and Siamese, a practice that was brought to an end in 1974. As a result, lavender (lilac) Havanas with pinkish-gray coats are sometimes produced and are accepted as variants by certain registries. In 1983, TICA reflected this by changing the breed name from Havana Brown to Havana; CFA maintains the breed name Havana Brown. Moves to merge the Havana Brown into the Oriental Shorthair group have been resisted by breeders because it risks losing the breed's distinctive look.

Physical description: The Havana Brown is a muscular but elegant, medium-sized cat. The body is described as "semi-foreign," being less elongated or extreme in type than that of the modern Siamese. Havana Browns stand relatively high on their legs. Large forward tilted ears give the Havana Brown an alert appearance, especially as they are in frequent motion, reflecting this cat's curiosity about everything.

The lustrous shorthaired coat and whiskers are a solid mahogany brown. The eyes should be brilliant green, which contrasts with the reddish brown of the coat. The head is slightly longer than it is wide, and the nose has a distinct break on both sides behind the whisker pads, which differentiates the Havana Brown from the Oriental. There is also a distinct "stop" (change in direction) at the eyes. A well-developed chin gives the muzzle an almost square appearance that is sometimes referred to as a corncob.

Temperament: These are affectionate, sociable cats who thrive on attention and need human companionship. They are curious and even tempered, sometimes described as unflappable, and adapt equally to living with seniors or in households with children. They are intelligent cats with a sometimes doglike willingness to please their owners. Even adult Havana Browns retain a kittenish playfulness. Many enjoy playing fetch with small toys and can often be seen carrying a toy around with them in the hope of starting some sort of game with their humans. Their intelligence and desire to join in with human activities makes them good candidates for leash training.

A frequently mentioned characteristic of the breed is their fondness for using their paws. They use them to investigate things, manipulate small objects, and attract attention by tapping their owners.

Activity level: Moderate

Vocal level: Low. Despite its Oriental ancestry, the Havana Brown has a softer voice than do Siamese or Oriental Shorthairs.

Special needs: None

Variations: Due to recessive genes, Havana Brown litters sometimes include kittens with pinkish gray or lilac coats. Seen as evidence of outcrossing by some registries, these are accepted in their own right by others. They have the same brilliant green eyes, conformation, and temperament as their tobacco-colored counterparts. The English Havana conforms to standards for Oriental cats, being a more active and vocal breed.

Himalayan

Places of Origin: Canada, United Kingdom, United States

History: The Himalayan is a colorpoint variety of the Persian. Its Persian progenitor was developed by mid-nineteenth-century cat fanciers in Britain using longhaired cats imported from Russia, northern Europe, and Turkey bred to domestic cats in England. Selective breeding created a cobby, profusely coated cat with a distinctive shortened muzzle. With the Persian and the Siamese—opposites in terms of conformation—being the most popular breeds on the show bench, it was perhaps inevitable that breeders would combine the Persian's conformation with the Siamese colorpoints.

The first recorded breeding of Siamese with Persian cats was by Swedish geneticist K. Tjebbes, who published "Crosses with Siamese Cats" in the *Journal of Genetics* in 1924. Tjebbes—whose interest was in genetics, not in creating a new breed—had bred a white Persian female to a Siamese male, which resulted in seven white kittens and three colored ones and a predominance of shorthaired kittens. Breeding the kittens back to their parents gave 50 percent white, so Tjebbes concluded that Siamese coloring and short hair dominated.

In 1931 in the United States, Virginia Cobb (Newton Cattery) and Dr. Clyde E. Keeler (Harvard Medical School) began their experimental breeding program to study the genetics involved in producing a colorpoint longhaired cat. Unlike Tjebbes, they used black Persians. Using only pedigree cats, they selected the most perfect kittens from each litter to create the next generation. When a black Persian male was mated to a Siamese female or a Siamese male was mated to a black Persian female, they got only black shorthaired kittens. Yet when these kittens were bred to each other and to their parents, the results included "Siamese-Persian kittens" with the long hair of the Persian and the markings, blue eyes, and distinctive voice of the Siamese. In 1936, they published a paper about colorpoint inheritance, "Siamese-Persian Cats," in the *American Journal of Heredity*, demonstrating that both colorpoint and longhair are recessive genes. Having achieved their aim, they ended the breeding program. Although what they had produced was a "longhair Siamese" (equivalent to the modern Balinese), they had provided the formula for breeders to use in creating the Himalayan.

In Britain, in 1947, Siamese cat breeder Brian Stirling-Webb was approached by a cat owner who wanted to mate her "long-haired Siamese queen," a stray of unknown parentage, to one of his Siamese stud cats to create a new breed. Stirling-Webb was aware of Keeler and Cobb's experiments and strongly disapproved of longhaired Siamese so he recommended mating the longhaired Siamese cat to a black Persian instead and then mating the offspring together. However, when he saw the "long-haired Siamese" cat, he found her to be Persian in type and became enthusiastic about creating colorpoint Persians. Along with other breeders, he repeated Cobb and Keeler's "formula" and also used a black longhaired male who had one Siamese grandparent. In 1955, the cats achieved breed recognition. To expand the gene pool, British breeders outcrossed their colorpoint longhairs to "bad" Siamese (that is, round-headed Siamese). From the outset, colorpoint longhairs were considered a variety of longhair (Persian) and, as a side effect, produced the self-chocolate longhair and self-lilac longhair.

In the 1940s and 1950s, cattle ranchers and Siamese cat lovers Ben and Ann Borrett of Chestermere Ranch (western Canada) became aware of Stirling-Webb's experimental breeding program and traveled to England to buy several of his cats for their own breeding program. They also developed several new bloodlines. In 1957, the Borretts exhibited two of the imported cats at an ACFA show in Calgary, Alberta, Canada, and were asked to produce a "Himalayan" breed standard, *Himalayan* being the name used for colorpoint rabbits and goats from the Himalayan region.

Around the same time, California artist and cat breeder Marguerita Goforth (Goforth Cattery) was looking after a friend's sealpoint longhair adopted from the San Diego Humane Society. Goforth gained permission to breed the cat to create a Persian-type cat with Siamese coloring based on the Borretts' breed standard. The British and North American breeding programs were combined, resulting in a breed (or, in some associations, a color division of the Persian breed) known as Colorpoint Longhair in England and as Himalayan in the United States.

In the 1950s, the Himalayan was recognized in the original four Siamese colors: sealpoint, chocolate point, blue point, and lilac point. Red (flame) point and tortie point were recognized in the United

States in 1964 and were later joined by blue-cream point, cream point, lynx (tabby) point, and tortie point; the last two having been introduced through outcrossing of Himalayans to tabby or silver Persians in the 1970s. While the Himalayans were recognized separately from Persians, the two breeds began to diverge in type, with the Himalayan becoming a longer-nosed colorpoint longhair. During the 1970s, American breeders reversed this trend by outcrossing regularly to Persians, and in 1984, the CFA made the Himalayan a division of the Persian breed.

In the 1960s, French writer Fernand Mery described the Colorpoint Longhair, still a newcomer on the show bench, as being "remarkably like a breed recognized in France, the Khmer, which has its own standard in that country, though it is not recognized by La Federation Internationale Feline d'Europe." The Khmer dated back to the 1920s and would eventually become the Birman.

A few Himalayan breeders breed bicolor point Himalayans, using bicolor Persians to introduce the white spotting pattern. Others have been working with the cinnamon gene in Himalayans; although cinnamon was probably present in early Siamese outcrosses, it does not seem to be in the modern Himalayan gene pool, although it is found in some Persian lines.

In the United Kingdom, this breed is known as the Colorpoint Longhair (or Colorpoint Persian). In the United States, Himalayans with tabby or tortie points may be called Colorpoint Longhairs in some registries.

Physical description: The Himalayan is a Persian in a colorpoint coat and with blue eyes. Like the Persian, the Himalayan is a solid-looking, medium to large cat with a short, cobby, broad body and a relatively short tail. The head is large, broad, and round; the chin is strong. The large eyes, set wide apart, create a sweet, almost childlike expression. The nose is short with a break between the eyes. To prevent excessively extreme typing, some registries dictate that the upper edge of the nose must be no higher than the lower rim of the eye. The Himalayan's coat is long and full and requires daily

Cream Himalayan

Blue Point Himalayan

Tortoiseshell Himalayan

grooming to prevent matting. Color is restricted to the face, ears, legs, and tail, with a distinct contrast between the body color and the points.

As with the Persian, the Himalayan has diverged into two types: the "traditional" or "old-fashioned" style and the flatter-faced "ultra" style (sometimes incorrectly called a Peke-face).

Colors and varieties: Accepted pointed colors in the Himalayan include seal, blue, lilac, chocolate, red (also called flame), cream, and the tortoiseshell and tabby versions of these colors. Cinnamon-, fawn-, and bicolor-pointed Himalayans remain a rarity and are not widely recognized. All Himalayans have blue eyes.

Temperament: The Himalayan is a people-oriented cat, with the peaceful temperament of the Persian. This is a sedate, affectionate, and intelligent cat who enjoys playing with toys. Some owners contend that these colorpointed longhairs inherit a little of the Siamese's more active personality and may be more talkative and more playful than other Persians. They need owners willing to devote time to them. They won't enjoy noisy, busy households, but they get along well with older or quieter children.

Activity level: Low

Vocal level: Low

Special needs: Being part of the Persian family, Himalayans need daily combing or brushing with a metal pin brush (as opposed to a bristle brush) to remove shed hair and prevent mats. Monthly bathing will also remove oils from the coat that can contribute to matting. Owners unable to maintain the long coat of a Himalayan or a Persian should consider the shorthaired equivalent, the Exotic Shorthair. In hot climates, some owners opt for a "lion cut" (by an experienced groomer) for their Himalayan/Persian cats, although such drastic grooming is not considered acceptable in all countries. Shaving of the coat is a more humane way to deal with a matted coat than tugging at the cat's skin with a comb or attempting to cut out mats with scissors.

The cranial anatomy of this breed brings some special considerations. The face should be washed or wiped regularly to prevent the accumulation of debris around the eyes and in the facial folds. Cats with more extreme-type faces may suffer from blocked or misrouted tear drainage ducts resulting in running eyes or in dental or nasal problems that require veterinary attention.

Variations: A side effect of crossing Persians with Siamese was the introduction of solid chocolate and lilac colors into the Persian breed. Although most registries consider these Persians, others term them Kashmirs to reflect their outcrossed ancestry.

Japanese Bobtail

Place of origin: Japan and throughout eastern Asia

History: In the Far East, cats with various degrees of kinked tails are frequently found. Bobtail cats were known in China in the twelfth century, and illustrations of primarily white cats with pom-pom tails are seen repeatedly in Asian art dating back centuries. They are believed to have come to Japan from China more than a millennium ago. "Kimono cats," white cats with a black spot on their back resembling a woman in a Kimono, were historically presented to Japanese temples as the embodiment of the soul of a family's ancestor. Calicos, known as Mi-Ke, are depicted in both Japan and China as "beckoning cats," welcoming a person into a temple or household.

The name "Malay cat" was attributed to these cats by early naturalists. In 1783, William Marsden, fellow of the Royal Society, described the bobtailed Malay cat in his History of Sumatra: "All their tails imperfect and knobbed at the end." Other travelers to the Malayan Archipelago corroborated his report. Bobtailed cats were sighted in Portugal in the 1870s, and the trait attributed to a supposed Portuguese custom of pinching or breaking the tails of newborn kittens. Most likely, these cats were descended from cats brought back by Portuguese traders in the Far East. In the 1880s, some of these Malay cats were exhibited as curiosities in the Netherlands and in the Jardin d'Acclimatation in Paris.

Bobtailed mutations have occurred independently in various geographic areas, especially on islands due to inbreeding caused by the closed gene pool. Colonies of bobtailed cats exist on some Greek islands and on Spain's Canary Islands.

In many breeds, achieving a perfectly straight tail without any abnormalities can be a challenging aspect of breeding a perfect show cat. However, in the Japanese Bobtail, a tail that is foreshortened due to kinking of the vertebrae is a cherished trait. The tails of these cats are not docked by breeders (as occurs in some dog breeds) nor are they missing vertebrae (as is seen in the Manx cat).

Because Japanese Bobtails have been around in Japan for centuries, Japanese cat fanciers did not take a lot of interest in them, preferring to focus on imported breeds. This mirrors the development of the cat fancy in Britain and the United Stated, where local shorthairs tended to be overlooked in favor of more exotic-looking imported varieties. Little regarded in Japan, these bobtailed felines attracted the interest of American breeders, who gained recognition for the breed in the United States in 1978. Hence the development of the Japanese Bobtail as an exhibition breed was primarily performed outside of its native country. Since then, however, pedigree Japanese Bobtails have gone full circle back to Japan. The semi-longhaired version has always existed in Japan (long hair is due to a recessive gene) but was not given breed status until 1991.

Genetic studies have found the Japanese Bobtail breed to be more closely related to Western cats than to Asian cats, although the breed shows some Asian genetic influence. This may be because the exhibition Japanese Bobtail was developed as a breed in the United States beginning in 1968, when the first cats were imported, and the gene pool is more greatly influenced by European and American cats than by Asian cats.

Physical description: The Japanese Bobtail is an elegant cat with long, fine-boned legs and a semi-long body. The head is triangular in shape with distinctive high cheekbones, large expressive eyes, and upright ears. No two bobbed tails are exactly alike, varying in length and pattern of kinks. The cats are often able to wiggle their tails when excited. The coat is fine-textured, without a wooly undercoat, even in the longhaired variety.

This breed's defining feature is its bobbed tail. The normal feline tail ranges from 8 to 12 inches (20–30 cm), depending on breed. If fully extended, the Japanese Bobtail's tail would be 4.5 to 5.25 inches (10–13 cm) long, but due to the variable kinked structure of the tail, it appears only 1.5 to 3 inches (4–7 cm) long. It is often possible to feel a bony knot inside the kink where vertebrae have fused, which also means the tail cannot be straightened. Adding to the effect, the tail hair often grows straight out in all directions, producing a rabbitlike scut or pom-pom appearance.

Colors and varieties: Although the Japanese Bobtail is accepted in almost all colors, the most popular is that of a primarily white cat with vivid, dramatic markings of black and/or red. The tricolor female cat is known as a Mi-Ke. This breed is accepted in both short- and longhaired varieties. In Japan,

Japanese Bobtail

Kurilian Bobtail

bobtails are found in all colors, including ticked tabby (Abyssinian pattern) and colorpoint, although these are not accepted in the Western fancy.

Temperament: One of the most active of the cat breeds, this highly intelligent breed will wrap you around its paw in short order. This is not a breed that does well left alone in a household for a long period of time. It does best with children or other pets to provide continuous stimulation and amusement. Japanese Bobtails need to be in the middle of household activities, contributing a helpful paw. They are highly devoted to their owners.

Activity level: High

Vocal level: Moderate

Special needs: The Japanese Bobtail, due to an extensive gene pool from a large natural population, is a healthy, long-lived breed that requires little grooming or special care. The tail should be handled gently.

Variations: The bobtail trait is widespread in Asia and parts of Russia. The Karel Bobtail (Karelian) from the coasts and islands of Lake Ladoga and the Kurilian Bobtail (Curilsk) from the Russian Island of Sakhalin and the Kuril Islands are natural breeds undoubtedly closely related to the Japanese Bobtail. The Karel Bobtail is a svelte cat with a

pompom tail, while the Kurilian Bobtail is smaller and cobbier. Both occur in shorthaired and semi-longhaired forms and are sturdier and larger than the Japanese Bobtail.

Other Asian bobtailed breeds that are being developed include the Mekong Bobtail and Thai Bobtail (confusingly, the latter name is given to two different breeds). The Mekong Bobtail is a colorpointed bobtailed cat of moderate conformation. The Malaysian Thai Bobtail is a naturally occurring bobtailed variety, most often colorpointed, of Oriental/Burmese type found in Thailand and Malaysia. The Russian Thai Bobtail resembles a round-headed Siamese with a bobbed tail, whereas the Toy-Bob or Toy Bobtail is a miniature version.

The Malay cat, widely reported in the nineteenth and early twentieth century, is similar to the Japanese Bobtail but has not been adopted as a formal breed. Naturally occurring colorpointed cats of Japanese Bobtail type are sometimes referred to as Si-Bobs or Si-Bobtails. In 1988, the Cat Association of Britain finalized the standard for the "Oriental Bobtail"—a cat of oriental (or foreign) conformation and coat, but with a bobbed tail. Since then, little has been heard of this breed.

Korat

Place of origin: Thailand

History: Called Korat after the unofficial name of Thailand's former capital, the cat known to the Thai people as the Si-Sawat Maiow was first introduced to the British cat fancy in 1896 as a "Blue Siamese." This breed would not achieve recognition in its own right for more than half a century. A significant reason for this may have been that breeding stock was difficult to come by.

Highly valued among the Thai, the Korats could not be purchased. They were given as gifts to Thai government representatives or nobility or presented to representatives of foreign governments as an expression of highest honor, bestowing health and fortune to the recipient. Known also as the "cloud-colored Cat" with eyes the color of young rice, Korats were supposed to bring a good harvest. They played a role in rainmaking ceremonies at the end of the dry season and were carried in procession to have water sprinkled on their cloud-colored fur. Traditionally, a pair of Korats was given to a bride on her wedding day to ensure prosperity in the years ahead. The silvery sheen on their coats symbolized a gift of silver. They also played a much different role in wartime, according to legend, when male Korats were taken into battle on the shoulders of warriors and would launch themselves fiercely at the enemy.

Being valued so highly, Korats were never sold and could only be given as gifts, occasionally being presented to honor a Western dignitary. This explains why so few "Blue Siamese" reached early cat fanciers and why nineteenth-century enthusiasts had such problems obtaining breeding stock.

Another problem in developing the Korat breed was Western confusion over the breed itself. To Europeans at the turn of the twentieth century, there was only one true cat from Siam (Thailand), the royal Siamese. Yet Bangkok's National Museum holds the *Smud Khoi*, the Thai *Book of the Cat* (circa 1868–1910), which describes cats of different types and colors. As well as the Vichien Mas (Siamese) and Thong Daeng (Thai Copper), there is a description of Doklao or Si-Sawat Korat. (Both of those names refer to the silvery hue of the Korat, making it clear that only cats

All Korats have green eyes.

with this coat color were considered true Korats.) All of these are authentic Thai cats, but only one variety was given the name Siamese by nineteenth-century cat fanciers in the West. The other varieties were rejected by judges who declared only the "royal" sealpointed Siamese to be the legitimate Siamese cat.

In 1896, a Blue Siamese called Nam Noi was exhibited at Holland House, London. Reports of the time variously describe the cat as a Siamese or a Russian Blue, the Korat not being a recognized breed at the time. Nam Noi was registered with the National Cat Club as a male Siamese of unknown parentage. He caused much discussion, but there was no doubt that he was a Siamese in every detail apart from his color. He was disqualified from the Siamese class, however, because he was not the accepted dun with black points. He was awarded first prize in the "Russian or Any Other Blue Cat" class. According to W. R. Hawkins in the July edition of *Around the Pens*: "Nam Noi, a Blue, was entered as a Siamese, and very possibly came from Siam; but that does not make him a Siamese any more than an English cat coming from Persia would be a Persian. To my thinking, Nam Noi was an undoubted Russian. . . . In Russians Nam Noi in its right class won." With no knowledge of the variety of cats to be found in Asia, Western cat fanciers had decided that a blue cat from Siam could only be a Russian Blue.

Despite the disagreements on classification, from a very few imports, the gene pool for the Korat breed was developed in the 1920s through crossing to imported, rather than domestically bred, Siamese cats. Due to the presence of breeding programs in Thailand, more imports followed in subsequent years.

In 1959, the Korat arrived in the West as a breed in its own right when two cats were presented to the American ambassador to Thailand. These were sent from Bangkok to Mrs. Jean Johnson in the United States. She had been attracted to these cats during a visit in 1947 but had not been able to obtain any. More were imported into the United States during the 1960s. To be considered authentic Korats, they had to have a pedigree traceable to cats in Thailand. In 1966, the breed gained recognition. The Thai spelling, *Koraj* (the province these cats came from) was changed to *Korat* by European breeders to reflect the word's pronunciation (at least to Western ears). Korats didn't return to Britain until 1972, and didn't achieve recognition there until 1984.

Adhering to the Thai definition of the Korat, cat fanciers stipulated the blue-gray color in the breed standard. However, the Korat naturally produced other color variants right back to its arrival in the United States when lilac-pointed (lavender-pointed) kittens sometimes occurred. Most breeders considered the naturally occurring colorpointed kittens to be a defect or signs that their bloodlines were impure. Then, in 1989, two Korats in the United Kingdom produced a "pink" kitten. During the 1990s, other Korats in Britain produced white kittens (who developed into blue-pointed cats) and "pink" kittens. In fact, old Thai writings mention the *Ratana Kampon*, a cat "pink like the inside of a conch shell," so it was evident that these unexpected colors were due to recessive genes that had long existed in Korats in their native country.

Physical description: The Korat is a small to medium-sized (4–10 pounds [2–4.5 kg]) but substantial cat, with a broad chest. The face is heart-shaped; the ears are round-tipped and set high. The Korat has large, round, luminous peridot-green eyes. There should be a lionlike slope to the nose. The close-lying short coat is glossy and fine in texture. The hairs are delicately tipped in silver, known in its homeland as "sea-foam." The Thai Lilac and Thai Blue Pointed have the same physical conformation as the Korat.

Colors and varieties: The Korat has a coat with roots like clouds and tips like silver. Any color other than silver blue is not a Korat. Their breeders have been very effective in protecting the breed against the development of any other varieties.

Temperament: Intelligent, inquisitive, and sensitive to her owners, the Korat is a delightful and entertaining companion. The Korat is a gentle, but active and playful cat and will often retrieve tossed toys for her owner. Being family-oriented, the males are said to be good fathers if left with their kittens. In the home, Korats are sweet-natured and mild. They form strong bonds with their owners. Because of an acute sense of hearing, Korats are extremely sensitive to events taking place around them.

Activity level: Moderate

Vocal level: Moderate; although vocal, the Korat has a soft voice.

Special needs: Regular grooming with a rubber brush to remove shed hair and a polish with a chamois cloth will bring out the shine in a Korat's coat.

Variations: Due to recessive genes, blue-pointed and solid-lilac kittens sometimes occur in Korat litters. In the United Kingdom, these variant colors are accepted as being naturally occurring in Korat lines and separately registered under the names Thai Blue Pointed and Thai Lilac respectively. These gained recognition from the GCCF in 2002. The Thai Lilac is a warm pinky-beige color, tipped with silver and having the characteristic green eyes. The Thai Blue Pointed differs from the Korat only in the eye color and coat pattern; its blue points have the characteristic silver tipping.

LaPerm

Place of origin: Oregon, United States

History: The first LaPerm occurred as a spontaneous mutation among random-bred farm cats at a cherry farm in The Dalles, Oregon. In 1982, a straight-coated brown tabby shorthair called Speedy gave birth to a bald female kitten who later grew a soft curly coat. She was named (naturally) Curly. Curly, like the farm's other felines, was a working cat, protecting the farm from rodents and roaming freely. She later produced five bald male kittens who also grew curly coats and bred freely. As a result, the farm's feline colony soon included a large number of Rex-coated cats in a wide range of colors and patterns and in both long- and shorthaired forms. Colorpointed cats were included as well, thanks to a local cat of Siamese ancestry.

The farm's owner took six of these unique cats to a local cat show to display them to the exhibitors and judges present. Cat fanciers there and elsewhere enthusiastically embraced the ringleted cats, which attracted sufficient interest to be pursued as a breed in North America. Foundation cats were later exported to breeders around the world. Early on, most of the kittens were born bald and developed their curly coat within three to four months. A small number of kittens were born straight-coated due to recessive genes and remained this way. A few kittens were born

straight-coated and shed this coat, becoming almost bald until a new—and curly—coat grew in.

Originally known as the Dalles LaPerm, the breed name evokes both the shaggy coat and adopts the local Chinook tradition of adopting French words, complete with the definite article (*la* or *le*), into their language. It was recognized as a breed by TICA in 1995 and has since gained breed recognition in a number of countries.

TICA and the CFA currently allow outcrossing of LaPerms to nonpedigree cats of suitable conformation with coats that are not excessively thick. In the United Kingdom, the Trades Description Act 1968 legally defines a pedigree cat as one with a fully recorded three-generation pedigree. This means LaPerms can only be outcrossed to other pedigree breeds, otherwise the next three generations are not pedigree cats. Similar legislation applies in other European and Commonwealth countries, so breed registries define an "approved outcross" list, typically listing Abyssinians, Somalis, Ocicats, Asian Shorthairs, Tiffanies (Asian Longhairs), European Burmese, and Tonkinese (plus Turkish Angora in some countries) as approved outcrosses for the LaPerm breed.

Like other Rex-coated breeds, LaPerms have attracted the reputation of being hypoallergenic. Cat allergy is caused not by the fur, but by the Fel d1 protein secreted in feline saliva. This means the LaPerm is just as likely to trigger an allergic reaction in those susceptible individuals.

Physical description: The LaPerm's working cat background has produced a lean muscular cat with no exaggerated features. These are medium-size, athletic cats with a moderately long (semi-foreign) body supported by medium-long legs. This breed has a modified wedge head extending from a long, elegant neck. The ears are flared, and the eyes are an expressive open-almond shape.

The tousled coat, with its loose shaggy curls, is the most dramatic feature. The curly outer guard hairs may form a "halo" above the more tightly curled undercoat, creating an appearance unique from the other Rex breeds. It has an artfully unkempt appearance and there may be a natural parting

Silver tortie tabby LaPerm

along the back. In longhaired LaPerms, the coat forms longer ringlets in the ruff and tail. Even the whiskers and the hairs inside the ears are curly. The tail of the shorthaired LaPerm may resemble a bottlebrush.

Colors and varieties: LaPerm cats exist in all possible coat colors, in both longhaired and shorthaired varieties. Tabbies, reds, and torties are common, reflecting the cats' random-bred origins. Colorpoints are also popular. Newer varieties include ticked tabbies and silvers/smokes.

Temperament: Affectionate, active, and outgoing, these fun-loving cats inherit the attentive hunting instincts of their farm cat ancestors, even though their prey may be no more than a furry toy. Coming from farm cat stock, the LaPerm is clever, inquisitive, and mischievous. They also get on well with children and with other pets.

Activity level: Moderate

Vocal level: Moderate

Special needs: Light combing with a long-toothed comb will remove loose hair. Because the abnormality in the hair follicle that causes the hairs to curl or kink also interferes with skin secretions (sebum) being pulled away from the skin, some Rex and Wirehaired cats may need to be bathed frequently and their ears

cleaned regularly to prevent these secretions from accumulating in the hair follicles or ear canal and causing dermatological problems. Towel dry rather than blow dry your LaPerm because blow drying will make the coat frizz.

Variations: None

Maine Coon

Place of origin: New England, United States

History: There are a plethora of folktales about the Maine Coon's origin. The breed's modern name reflects folklore that the breed resulted from crossing raccoons to cats, something that is genetically impossible. Then there are the stories that claim Maine Coons, as evidenced by their tufted ears and large size, are hybrids between domestic cats and bobcats or lynxes. Other tales speak of Vikings, in the tenth century, taking Skogkatts (Norwegian Forest Cats) to North America, where the cats bred with small native cats. However there were no small native cats in North America, and recent genetic studies have found that the Maine Coon and Norwegian Forest Cat are not closely related.

Another story is that sailors from New England

returned home with Angora cats from Turkey in the late seventeenth century or that the doomed Marie Antoinette sent her Turkish Angora cats to safety in the United States in 1793 and that they interbred with the local shorthaired domestic cats. Slightly more plausible is the story of Captain Charles Coon whose preference for longhaired ship's cats led to longhaired "Coon's Cats" appearing in dockyard feral populations up and down the East Coast.

The prosaic truth is the that "Maine Cat" is descended from longhaired and shorthaired cats who arrived in New England with Western European explorers and as ratters on trading ships between the Old and New Worlds. This is upheld by recent genetic studies that found the Maine Coon to be related to British Shorthairs. The rugged longhaired cats of Scotland, Norway, and Russia may have contributed to its ancestry, with the later addition of Persians and Angoras, which interbred with the local cat population. Several early cat fanciers in North America mentioned the arrival of blue-eyed white longhaired cats during the nineteenth century; these arrived at East Coast seaports on ships from Europe and either jumped ship or were traded with local cat lovers.

This was a "working breed" of cat who survived for generations outdoors in the harsh New England winters. Over the years, the cats were known by a variety of names, most alluding to their raccoonlike appearance or to their heavy, weather-resistant coat: Coon Cat, Maine Trick Cat, American Shag, American Snughead, and American Forest Cat.

By the 1880s, Maine Coons were being regularly exhibited in local cat shows, with some winning cats tipping the scales at 20 pounds (9 kg), and Maine was becoming well-known to cat fanciers for its brown tabby longhairs. Silvers, smokes, and chinchillas were then rare in the Maine Coon. A brown tabby female named Cosie won Best Cat at the Madison Square Garden Show in New York in 1895. Many of the prize-winning cats of the 1890s resembled the early Persian in conformation.

Even early cat fanciers in Britain were aware of the "Maine Cat," although the breed wouldn't arrive on British shores for another century. They

Maine Coons are big cats!

Black Maine Coon kitten

Maine Coon

were first recorded in American cat literature in 1861. In 1889, Harrison Weir (or rather one of his American correspondents) described Maine Cats in his book *Our Cats and All About Them* as "neither Persian, Angora, nor Indian. They are called here 'Coon' Cats, and it is vulgarly supposed to be a cross between a common Cat and a 'Coon.'"

Photographs sent to Weir showed a cat with unusually large ears, large legs, and large feet. They had very bushy tails and a fine neck ruff. Colors included solids, bicolors, and tabbies; yellow was a popular color. There were no tufts between the toes and a considerable frill at the neck. The eyes had a wild, staring expression, and the tail was long and like a fox's brush. Weir considered the breed worthy of attention, although no one seemed interested enough to import these cats into Britain.

Maine Coons warranted a section in English writer Frances Simpson's *Book of the Cat* in 1903, but three years before American cat writer Helen Winslow had given only a brief nod to the handsome "coon cat" in *Concerning Cats*—just enough to mention the cat's size, thick woolly fur, and bushy tail. She said these Maine cats were so fond of outdoor life that they became savage and disagreeable if confined indoors. When allowed their freedom, however, they were affectionate and intelligent. The problem was that Maine Coons were so commonplace in their own region that they had not aroused any great enthusiasm until the craze for longhaired cats struck.

However, the breed's popularity as a show cat declined when Persians from Britain and Europe arrived in the United States. Overshadowed by imported Persians, the homegrown Maine Coon found itself largely relegated to the role of pet. As a result, the Maine Coon had almost vanished from cat shows after 1910, and its decline within the cat fancy was so serious that, by the 1950s, the breed was considered extinct.

Luckily, the breed was down but not out, and there were still Maine Coons around when cat fanciers began to take a serious interest in the breed in the 1950s. Breeders started to record pedigrees for these homegrown cats, accepting foundation cats based on appearance. In 1965, the first breed standard was created, and the Maine Coon was promoted as a respected pedigree breed. The cat first achieved breed recognition in 1967, and by 1980, all major American registries recognized the Maine Coon breed. In addition to registry recognition, the Maine Coon became the state cat of Maine in 1985.

In 1953 or 1954, a pregnant female Maine Coon was imported into Austria. These cats were originally known in Europe as American Forest Cats. The first Maine Coons were imported into Britain in 1984, and the breed was recognized by the GCCF in 1988. Their gentle disposition, large size, and adaptability resulted in exploding popularity overseas as well, making them the second most popular breed in the world—a far cry from the breed being considered extinct. When self-proclaimed "dog people" are unwillingly dragged into cat show halls by their cat-loving family members, they are frequently drawn to the big, friendly Maine Coons on display.

Physical description: The size of this breed is its most striking trait. The long fur adds to the perception of the immense size of a tall, muscular, big-boned cat with large, long bodies. Males commonly reach 13 to 20 pounds (6–9 kg), with females normally weighing about 9 to 12 pounds (4–5.5 kg). This is a slow developing breed, and individuals may not reach their full size until three to five years old.

The Maine Coon's shaggy, water-resistant coat is unique to the breed and evolved naturally to withstand the challenges of a cold environment. Big, round, tufted feet act as natural snowshoes. The long hair around the neck, stomach, and britches protect the cat against rain and snow, and the shorter fur on the back and top of the neck guards against tangling in the underbrush. The cat buries her nose into her long, bushy tail during the chill of winter to protect her respiratory system from cold, dry air.

The head is slightly longer than it is wide, presenting a gently concave profile with high cheekbones and ears that are large, wide at the base, moderately pointed, and well tufted inside. They are set well up on the head, approximately an ear's width apart. The ears are heavily furnished (referring to the presence of fur inside the ear), and the tips of the ears may have long fur, known as "lynx tips." Their large, oval eyes are set at a slightly oblique angle and give these cats a unique expression. The relatively long, rectangular, strong muzzle is perfectly designed for hunting.

Colors and varieties: Maine Coons are registered in all almost colors and patterns, including silvers. Brown tabby is perhaps the most iconic of the Maine Coon colors. Colorpoints, sepia, and mink patterns are not recognized because these indicate crossing to other breeds. Likewise, chocolate, lavender, and ticked tabby are not allowed. Eye color ranges from green to gold. Blue eyes and odd eyes (one blue and one gold or green eye) are allowed in white and "with white" colored cats.

Temperament: Maine Coons are friendly, relaxed, people-oriented cats, but they do not constantly demand attention of their owners. They tend to prefer being next to, rather than on the laps of, their owners. They are excellent companions, tolerant of other pets, and known for being especially patient with children. Many Maine Coons love exploring water, such as a running faucet.

They maintain a playful, kittenish attitude throughout their lives. Males especially tend to be clownish at times, while females try to maintain an air of dignity. They are intelligent and athletic cats. Many Maine Coons enjoy playing "fetch" or learning to walk on a leash. They keep a watchful eye on all the activities of the house and like to be involved in these activities. They prefer ground-based toys that remind them of their breed's renowned prowess as mousers.

Activity level: Low to moderate

Vocal level: Very low; the quiet trill of the Maine Coon's voice is an amusing contrast to their large size.

Special needs: The coat is almost maintenance free; a weekly combing is all that is usually required to keep it in top condition. This coat varies according to season, being thicker during the winter months. Middle-aged cats may develop weight problems, which can usually be controlled by feeding a primarily wet-food diet. Maintaining a healthy weight is essential to avoid the risk of hip dysplasia. When these cats are carried, they must be well supported by the chest and hips due to their large size.

Variations: The Maine Waves was a naturally occurring Rex-coated version of the Maine Coon. It arose by mutation in Britain in the 1990s, causing controversy among Maine Coon breeders. The cat fancy in the United Kingdom lacked the mechanism to register such mutations in existing breeds, and this attractive variety appears to have died out. Colorpointed Maine Coons occurred in Europe in the late 1970s; how the gene got into the breed has not been proven. Although controversial, they are attractive cats, hence Maine Coon Colorpoints are now being bred in France. Some breeders in the United States and elsewhere are working with the polydactyl trait (cats with more toes than normal) in this breed. This trait is commonly found in the native longhaired cat population.

Manx

Place of origin: Isle of Man, British Isles

History: Tailless cats have occurred naturally in various parts of the world as a result of spontaneous mutation. In 1809, for example, a female cat in Edinburgh produced several litters of tailless kittens. In the mid-nineteenth century, a breed of tailless cats existed in parts of Cornwall, Dorset, and on the Isle of Man. The breed was known variously as the Cornwall cat or the Manx cat until the early 1900s, when the Cornish and Dorset strains died out and only the Isle of Man cats remained. On the Isle of Man, geographic and genetic isolation from tailed cats allowed the tailless trait to become widespread.

Numerous folktales were spun to explain the tailless (or near tailless) state of the Manx cats. According to one, the Manx were slow in boarding the Ark and their tails were cut off when Noah slammed the Ark doors shut; according to another, the defenders of the Isle of Man trimmed their war helmets with long fluffy cat tails. A variation on this mentions quick-thinking mother cats biting the tails off their own kittens to save them from becoming trophies; after many generations of this treatment, Manx kittens were born tailless. The Manx began to be mentioned in print in the early 1800s, when visitors to the isle saw them. In 1845, Joseph Train, who was supposedly not writing folktales, described the Manx cats in *An Historical and Statistical Account of the Isle of Man* but thought they were the result of female cats mating with buck rabbits.

As visitors to the isle brought Manx cats back to England, cat fanciers began to develop the breed. They crossed the Manx to domestic cats, British Shorthairs, and even Persians. Crossing a Manx cat to a tailed cat resulted in mostly tailless or part-tailed offspring. As breeders discovered, Manx taillessness ranges from the *rumpy* (no tailed), which may have a dimple at the base of the spine, to the *rumpy-riser* (one or two vertebrae), to the *stumpy* (a bit longer and often knobbly), and to the rare *longy* (full tailed, although this is often shorter than that of a non-Manx).

Harrison Weir, who penned the early breed standards, wrote that wholly tailless cats were preferred. He noted that some Manx cat exhibited at the Crystal Palace and other early cat shows had small stumps of tails, which some people took for signs of fakery. One of the earliest studies into Manx inheritance appeared in a German paper in

1900, and it was found that Manx cats produced both Manx and tailed offspring.

Weir also wrote that Manx's the hind legs should be thicker and rather longer so that the cat ran more like a hare than a cat. In 1902, six types of Manx were described. The commonest, and worst, type was the long straight-backed cat. The short-backed cat with high hindquarters was considered the "correct" type and became the show-quality Manx. The remaining types were the long roach-backed cat, the long straight-backed cat with high hindquarters, the short straight-backed cat, and the short roach-backed cat. In all cases, only the "rumpy" or "stumpy" tail types were recognized as true Manx.

Many of the Manx up until the early 1900s had no pedigree, and some were strays, believed to have been stolen from the Isle of Man by tourists. They were what modern breeders would term

Manx

Manx

foundation cats—having the correct conformation to be declared Manx cats by judges. A few were fakes, manufactured by unscrupulous exhibitors. There was also confusion between the Manx and imported bobtailed cats. In 1900, a "stumpy" Manx won the Manx class, but was later exhibited—and won—as a Japanese cat because some "connoisseurs of foreign cats" declared the cat to be Japanese purely because there was a kink in the tail.

The Manx seems to have reached North America as early as 1820, when the seafaring Hurley family of New Jersey brought back tailless cats from the Isle of Man. The cats were described as doglike and fierce hunters, and descendents of these cats were being bred many decades later. The pedigree Manx was recognized in North America in the 1920s and early 1930s.

Historically, a rabbitlike (or even kangaroolike) hopping gait was an essential part of the Manx breed standard. This is now considered a fault but has already helped perpetuate the urban legend of a "cabbit"—a genetically impossible hybrid between a cat and a rabbit. To keep the breed genetically healthy, many registries allow outcrossing to the related British Shorthair, and some also permit outcrossing to the Persian and to nonpedigree tailless cats indigenous to the Isle of Man.

The Manx gene is known as a sublethal gene. Embryos that inherit two copies of the gene generally die at an early stage of development or result in stillborn kittens. Hence, all surviving Manx kittens have the recessive gene for a full tail. The Manx mutation is also an "incomplete dominant" trait, meaning that it interacts with other genes to produce the variety of tail lengths. Embryos that inherit two copies of the Manx gene are often reabsorbed during pregnancy so that Manx litters tend to have fewer kittens than many other breeds. Stillborn kittens, and those who die early on, have been found to have a greater number of skeletal and organ abnormalities than those who survive beyond twelve months.

The Manx gene affects the entire spine and can cause shortened, missing, malformed, or fused vertebrae. The pelvic opening may also be unusually narrow. In some Manx cats, the spinal cord does not extend the whole length of the backbone; this affects bowel and bladder control and control of the hind legs (sometimes resulting in a hopping gait). This is called the Manx Syndrome. Responsible breeders avoid breeding from any cats with obvious spinal defects, and the number of abnormalities has dropped considerably in the breed since the syndrome was first recognized. In 1968, the GCCF removed the "hoppity gait"—once a defining characteristic of the breed, but eventually recognized as symptomatic of a spinal defect— from the breed standard.

The Council of Europe's Convention for the Protection of Pet Animals legislation effectively prohibits the Manx breed in those member nations that have signed the convention. This legislation aims to eliminate certain characteristics or potential genetic abnormalities—where necessary by discontinuing the breeding of animals in which the defining trait is a physical abnormality or the gene involved causes the death of some offspring. The legislation recommends a total ban on breeding Manx cats since offspring are likely to have pain, disease, defects (pelvic abnormalities, spina bifida), and/or locomotor problems and are deprived of a means of social communication. In Britain, the GCCF accepts the Manx (one of the earliest recognized breeds in the country) but will not recognize new breeds based on structural anomalies in the future. In Victoria, Australia, the Animals Legislation (Animal Care) Bill prohibits the breeding or selling of animals with heritable defects, but the list of defects does not include Manx taillessness. There is no comparable legislation in the United States.

Physical description: A medium-size, compact, muscular cat, similar in type to the British Shorthair and described by FIFe as "chubby." The Manx has the cobbiest body of all breeds, with a depth of flank and well-padded feel that adds to the impression of a substantial build. Males usually weigh range from 10 to 12 pounds (4.5–5.5 kg), females from 8 to 10 pounds (3.5–4.5 kg). The head is round, set on a short neck, with a short muzzle. The ears have a unique, slightly outward turning set that is described as being the shape of the rocker on a cradle. The rounded eyes give the Manx a sweet expression.

The short back forms a continuous arch to the rounded rump. The hind legs are longer than the front legs, and the rump stands higher than the shoulders. The most prominent feature is the taillessness, which in top show specimens does not stop a hand as it proceeds down the back and around the rump. Manx can take up to five years to reach full maturity.

The shorthaired Manx has a thick double coat that tends to obscure the dimple of a rumpy or stub tail of the rumpy-riser. Although only tailless (rumpy) Manx are considered exhibition quality, they are categorized into four tail lengths: rumpy, rumpy-riser, stumpy, and longy.

Colors and varieties: The Manx is accepted in all solid, tortoiseshell, particolor, and tabby colors, including silvers and smoke varieties. Not all registries recognize chocolate, and lilac (lavender) is not accepted because this color originally came from colorpointed cats; they may be found in Manx cats registered with organizations that permit outcrossing to Persians or British Shorthairs. Colorpoint Manx have occurred in Australia.

Temperament: Once reputed to be fierce hunters, the modern Manx is calm, even-tempered, and lovable. These cats enjoy the quiet comforts of a lap, but can be quite playful when the mood strikes them. The powerful hindquarters make Manx surprisingly good jumpers and give them fast acceleration (so good that when a British pub organized indoor cat racing, they banned the Manx from competing). They are intelligent cats and some enjoy games of fetch or can be trained to walk on a leash. Some like to bury their toys. Although some of them form a close bond with just one person, others give and receive attention from any available humans. Being people-oriented, they are tolerant of children.

Activity level: Low

Vocal level: Low

Special needs: Although some cat fanciers dispute the existence of Manx Syndrome, it is well documented in veterinary and heredity journals, and the appearance of spinal abnormalities in the breed has led to Manx-type cats being used in biomedical research into human spina bifida and other neural tube defects. Some completely tailless Manx may have elimination issues due to a disruption in the normal enervation of the bowel or bladder. Dietary management under the guidance of your veterinarian can help with bowel issues. Care should be taken when handling the rump because pressure where the tail should be can cause pain due to unprotected nerve endings.

Ethical Manx breeders use tailed cats (Manx variants) in breeding programs and do not allow kittens to leave home until they have reached four months of age with no signs of abnormality. This ensures that the kittens they place in pet homes do not have any health issues resulting from the Manx gene. Breeders in the United States may dock kittens' tails at four to six days old to avoid another effect of the deferred lethal mutation. The tail vertebrae may become painfully ossified and arthritic, necessitating amputation. Tail docking is not allowed in all countries.

Variations: Only cats descended from Isle of Man stock can be called Manx cats; random-bred tailless cats are domestic tailless because they cannot prove Manx ancestry. Longhaired Manx are known in some registries as Cymrics. The Tasman Manx is a curly-coated Manx that has appeared in Australia and New Zealand; it gets the curly coat from outcrossing to Persian cats who carried a recessive Rex gene. Because of anatomical problems that accompany the Manx mutation, breeders are discouraged from creating new tailless breeds. A line of tailless cats in Denmark is believed to be Manx in origin, probably from ship's cats. A similar colony of tailless cats occurs at the south end of

Cymric

Cape Breton, Nova Scotia, where they are known as Cape Breton Bobtails. In Australia, a wandering Siamese stud and a Manx female were responsible for the arrival of a "Si-Manx." Phyllis Lauder (1981) wrote of news from Australia regarding the crossing of Manx with Scottish Folds. This was inadvisable considering the potential health problems associated with those breeds.

Munchkin

Place of origin: Louisiana, United States

History: Although the Munchkin is the first short-legged breed to be recognized, short-legged mutations in cats have been reported and studied since the 1930s, when the mutation was observed among feral cats. In 1944, a dynasty of four generations of short-legged cats in England was described by Dr. H. E. Williams-Jones. Healthy and thriving, the cats had short and somewhat bowed forelegs and hind legs of normal proportions. The cats moved like ferrets and sat upright on their rumps like meerkats. The bloodline died out during the Second World War because the few remaining cats had been neutered. A similar colony was found in the neighborhood of Flatbush, Brooklyn, New York, in the 1950s, when a short-legged female stray gave rise to several generations of similar-looking cats. The bloodline died out as the area was redeveloped.

Short-legged cats turned up in New England in the 1970s, but it was not until a short-limbed stray turned up in Louisiana in 1983 that the trait was established as a breed. Since the publicity surrounding the controversial Munchkin, short-legged cats have been reported in various locations around the world as spontaneous mutations born to long-legged parents. Some, such as the Munchkin, had all four limbs affected, whereas others, such as the prewar British cats, had only the forelegs affected.

The Munchkin breed derives from a pregnant short-legged stray found in 1983 under a truck in Rayville, Louisiana. Two short-legged and pregnant female cats, one gray and one black, had been chased under the truck by a dog. Their rescuer, who dubbed them "Munchkins" after the small folk in *The Wizard of Oz*, rehomed the gray female and kept the black one, which she called Blackberry. When Blackberry's kittens arrived, almost half had short legs and a ferretlike gait. One of these, a male named Toulouse, founded a free-ranging colony at a Louisiana plantation (earning the breed's alternative name, now discarded, Louisiana Creole Cat). Meanwhile, Blackberry had several more litters of both short- and long-legged kittens before she disappeared.

Similar unrelated short-legged cats were accepted by TICA as foundation cats for the new breed. About thirty such cats were found across the United States, some of which have been used in breeding. Thus, the Munchkin is a natural breed with a diverse gene pool. The gene is dominant, meaning that only one parent must have shortened legs for offspring to inherit the trait. The most common condition that causes short limbs is *achondroplasia*, which shortens the long bones of the limbs while leaving the trunk unchanged; however, this is associated with an enlarged and abnormally shaped head. Because the Munchkin's head is normally proportioned, *hypochondroplasia* is a more likely candidate for this breed's condition.

Munchkins are bred to other Munchkins and also to long-legged domestic cats to ensure a wide, healthy gene pool. Unfounded fears about back and joint problems were based on the visual similarity of the Munchkin to short-legged dog breeds (which have those problems). However, the cat's more flexible spine makes the breed more comparable to a ferret than to a Dachshund. Although there remained concerns about the mutation, the breed was recognized by TICA in the United States in 1994.

The FIFe in Europe and the GCCF in the United Kingdom refuse to recognize breeds, such as the Munchkin, that are based on structural abnormalities. The Council of Europe's Convention for the Protection of Pet Animals legislation prohibits the breeding of cats with dwarfing conditions, including Munchkins, considering it to be a structural defect affecting function and preventing normal feline behavior/locomotion. Munchkins are therefore banned by law, regardless of recognition by cat registries in the countries that have signed this convention. In Victoria, Australia, the Animals Legislation (Animal Care) Bill prohibits the breeding or sale of animals with heritable defects and lists the Munchkin's short-legged condition as one of the prohibited traits. There is currently no comparable legislation in the United States.

Physical description: The defining characteristic of the Munchkin is the short legs, similar to the phenomenon seen in Dachshund, Corgi, and Basset Hound dog breeds. The trait is dominant and heterozygous in these cats, meaning that long-legged variants can be born in Munchkin litters. Because of their low-to-the-ground build, Munchkins corner well, and they run and climb

Munchkin kitten

Longhaired Munchkin

without problem. Contrary to many reports, Munchkins can jump, but their short legs mean they don't jump quite as high as many long-legged breeds. Many like to sit upright like prairie dogs.

Colors and varieties: Being derived from a wide gene pool, the Munchkin is bred in both shorthaired and semi-longhaired varieties and in all colors and patterns. A number of derivative breeds exist and include Munchkin-type cats with additional traits such as curly-fur, hairlessness, and curled ears. Because the gene controlling the trait is dominant, Munchkin-to-Munchkin breedings can produce "nonstandard Munchkins" with long legs.

Temperament: Because these cats are still outcrossed to random-bred domestic shorthaired and longhaired cats, they can have a wide variety of personalities.

Their short legs do not appear to slow these active cats down, and they have jumping and running abilities that match that of many other cats. Many are reported to have magpie tendencies and to steal and hide toys and trinkets, often underneath furniture.

Activity level: Moderate

Vocal level: Moderate to low

Special needs: Unlike cats whose forelimbs are shortened to a crippling degree by radial hypoplasia (underdeveloped long bones), Munchkins are healthy and agile cats with a good quality of life and no locomotor problems except for the inability to jump to the same heights as longer legged cats. They do not have the health issues (especially back pain) that can occur in some short-legged breeds of dog. Some Munchkins may develop bowing of the legs that can impair normal mobility, lordosis of the spine, or pectus affecting the chest and ribcage (these two conditions are not unique to the Munchkin). Breeders carefully select for straight leg and back conformation in their breeding cats to minimize the incidence of these faults. Munchkin litter sizes also tend to be smaller than average, suggesting that embryos inheriting two copies of the Munchkin mutation do not develop.

Variations: The Munchkin has been crossed with a number of other short-legged breeds. In theory, the short-legged trait could be combined with almost anything, but in practice some combinations are best avoided due to the risk of skeletal problems. It remains to be seen which of these breeds will reach championship status with registries and which will fall by the wayside.

The Minskin is a semi-cobby cat combining the Munchkin's short legs with the Canadian Sphynx's near-hairlessness, but with furred points. The Bambino is a cross between the same two breeds but has a wedge-shaped head and medium-boning. Munchkins were crossed with LaPerms to create the curly-haired Skookum, and with the Selkirk Rex to create the more densely coated curly-furred Lambkin (also called the Nanus Rex). Crosses with Persians and Exotic Shorthairs created the cobby, round-headed Napoleon (see page TK). Other short-legged varieties include the Dwelf/ Elf (hairless with curled ears), Kinkalow (curled ears), Jaguarundi Curl (curled ears, selectively bred to resemble a wild jaguarundi), Genetta (Bengal crossbred to resemble the wild genet), and Meerkat (selectively bred to resemble the African meerkat).

TICA have since clamped down on what it considers mix-and-match breeding. To accommodate and foster a responsible approach to experimental breeds, the Designer Cat Association (TDCA) was founded; however, this does not deter unregistered breeders from creating "Munchkin-ized" novelties for the pet market.

Norwegian Forest Cat

Place of origin: Norway

History: A natural breed of northern Europe, with long, profuse coats evolved to protect them against the harsh winter clime, these hardy cats were used in the development of the Persian breed in Europe and contributed to the ancestry of America's Maine Coon. The Skogkatt, or "Forest Cat" as it is known it homeland, is considered the official cat of Norway.

Longhaired cats can be found throughout Norse mythology and Norwegian fairy tales. Two large cats, gifts of her husband, Thor, draw the chariot of the goddess Freya across the heavens. The cats are described in various legends as silver, blue, black, or white—good indications of the colors found in the ancestors of Norwegian Forest Cats. In Norwegian folk tales, there are wood—or forest—cats with thick bushy tails called *Huldrekat* or "Fairy Cat."

The exact origins of the Norwegian Forest Cat are not known. Some believe Vikings took cats from Britain home to Scandinavia, where they bred with local farm cats. The Norwegian Forest Cat "type" appears to have been documented as far back as 1599. However they originally reached Norway, these cats became well adapted to living in a cold, wet climate. Generations of natural selection have produced a cat with a heavy, weather-resistant coat comprising a long, coarse glossy outer coat; a warm woolly undercoat; a thick ruff; and a long flowing tail. True to its forest cat name, it is an excellent climber and still retains a love of surveying the world—or supervising the household— from upon high. Norwegian Forest Cats are also is known to be accomplished anglers, plucking fish from streams and lakes.

The resemblance to the Maine Coon has led some to suggest that Vikings originally took Norwegian Forest Cats to North America. However, the absence of domestic cats in North America when European colonists arrived rules this out. Nor is the Norwegian Forest Cat a hybrid with European wildcats or European lynxes.

The Norwegian Forest Cat appeared in its first official cat show in the 1938, the same year that the first Norwegian Forest Cat Club was formed. The breed had grown scarce over the centuries, and club members were taking the first steps to preserve the breeding. Breeders of the pedigree Norwegian Forest Cat used semi-wild outdoor cats and farm cats to strengthen the Forest Cat, but their work was interrupted by the Second World

Norwegian Forest Cat

War. By the end of the war, the breed was in danger of slipping into obscurity. Breeders took up the task of again reviving the Skogkatt.

Many of the foundation cats came from near the Swedish border. Swedish cat breeders declared that the breed belonged to Sweden as much as to Norway. Norwegian breeders disputed this. Finally, it was agreed that foundation cats must come "straight from the Norwegian forests." It was also determined that while the Norwegian breeding program was under way and breeders were waiting for the Skogkatts to be recognized, no unneutered registered Forest Cats would be allowed out of Norway.

In 1963, the breed was shown under the name *Skogkatt* but did not undergo a serious revival of fortune until the early 1970s. In 1972, the Norwegian Forest Cat gained formal breed recognition in its home country. The breed could then to be exported and was recognized by the FIFe in Europe in 1977, by TICA in the United States in 1984, and by the GCCF in Britain in 1987. The cat's popularity has soared since the 1970s. As well as cat fancy recognition, this breed received royal recognition when the late King Olaf made it the official cat of Norway.

Physical description: The Norwegian Forest Cat is a strikingly large breed; mature males may reach 12 to 15 pounds (5.5–7 kg) or more. With their lionlike winter ruff, mature cats have a regal appearance. A slow developing breed, the Norwegian Forest Cat can take three to five years to reach full size and maturity and attain a truly spectacular winter coat. The long, dense, water-resistant fur adds to the impression of massive size. The back legs are slightly longer than the front legs, giving a rise to the back and rump. The tail is spectacular both for its length and bushy fur.

The triangular-shaped head, with a straight profile, large almond-shaped eyes, and medium to large ears, gives the breed a unique and engaging expression. The breed standard was clarified at the end of the 1990s to ensure the head also has depth. A show-quality cat will have lynx tips on the ears and tufts between the toes.

Colors and varieties: Although most commonly seen in brown, blue, patched, and red tabby patterns with and without white, this breed occurs in many other colors as well. Eye color is green or gold except in white cats, who may have blue or odd eyes.

Some purebred Norwegian Forest Cats in Europe produce what appears to be chocolate/lilac and cinnamon/fawn offspring—colors that do not officially exist in the breed's gene pool. This is the "amber" mutation believed to be unique to the Norwegian Forest Cat. It is caused by the Extension gene, which brightens black pigment to reddish brown. Black kittens with this mutation eventually turn a cinnamon color called *amber*. Blue kittens with the mutation turn a pale beige color called *light amber*. Amber/light amber replaces black/blue in tabby and tortoiseshell cats who inherit the gene.

Temperament: These cats tend to be intensely loyal to their favorite family members but are also friendly toward other pets, children, and strangers. They are intelligent, alert, and adaptable to new environments.

True to their name, they enjoy looking at the world from a high perch and should be provided with a sturdy indoor "tree" to climb. Some owners report these cats to have a liking for water and to enjoy resting on something cool. They enjoy attention, but in regions where they have outdoor access, they may be independent and resourceful hunters. They are mild-mannered cats who like to interact with family members and enjoy playing.

Activity level: Moderate

Vocal level: Low

Special needs: The coat of this breed is startlingly seasonal, and spring brings an explosion of shedding as the coat transitions to its much shorter summer presentation. During this period, daily combing is essential to remove the shed fur from the coat.

Variations: The Skogkatt has cousins in the Swedish Rugkatte and the Siberian Forest Cat and no doubt in unrecognized longhaired strains of cat in Scandinavia and northern Europe. All of these Scandinavian varieties adapted to a harsh environment to become excellent hunters with weather-resistant coats. Often, people cite the so-called Danish Racekatte as a similar breed. According to Danish cat fanciers, however, there is no such breed: racekatte simply means "pedigree cat."

Ocicat

Black and silver Ocicat

Place of origin: United States

History: As knowledge about the genetics of cat coloration grew in the mid-twentieth century, experimentation with crossing breeds became an increasingly popular activity with cat breeders. In 1964, a Siamese breeder crossed a large female sealpoint Siamese to a ruddy (usual) Abyssinian male toward the goal of creating an "Abyssinian Pointed Siamese." The first generation resulted in kittens who all resembled their Abyssinian sire, but when a female kitten from that breeding was bred to a Siamese male, in addition to producing the desired ticked-tabby pointed Siamese kitten, a striking cinnamon-spotted kitten, named Tonga, was produced. Tonga is described as being ivory colored with golden spots. The breeder's daughter nicknamed him an Ocicat because his pattern reminded her of a wild ocelot; the nickname name stuck and would later become the breed's official name.

At the time, there had been no intention of creating a new breed, and the possibility of creating ticked-tabby pointed Siamese had been demonstrated, so Tonga was neutered and homed as a pet. Geneticist Clyde Keeler became interested in Tonga after this unique cat was featured in a newspaper. He wanted to recreate a cat with the look of the extinct Egyptian spotted fishing cat and suggested Tonga be mated with his mother. By then, Tonga had been neutered so the mating of Siamese and Abyssinian was repeated and a tawny spotted male kitten was born.

Ruddy Ocicat

Having produced more of these attractive "dotted" kittens (as the founder preferred to call them), the breed expanded through the use of additional Siamese, Abyssinian, and American Shorthair cats. The American Shorthair created a more robust build and introduced silver colors into the mix. The CFA recognized the Ocicat in 1966, but personal issues meant the original breeding program was put on hold between 1966 and the early 1980s. Other cat fanciers became interested in these spotted cats and developed new lines. In 1986, TICA recognized the Ocicat. Two years later, the cat arrived in the United Kingdom in 1988 and was recognized there in 1997.

Although the breed's name alludes to an ocelotlike appearance, the Ocicat has a wholly domestic ancestry. Some people have also called this breed the *Acci*cat—for the happy accident that led to its creation. At the time the Ocicat appeared, breeders believed that the spotted pattern was separate from the ticked, mackerel, and classic tabby patterns. It became evident that the spotted pattern in the breed was due to the tabby markings being broken up. Mackerel tabbies, with their narrow stripes, were removed from the gene pool early on so that Ocicats would have larger, more dramatic spots. Classic tabbies therefore still occur in the breed.

Physical description: The Ocicat is a large, muscular, athletic cat; males weigh between 9 and 14 pounds (4–6 kg), females 6 and 9 pounds (3–4 kg). The conformation is semi-foreign on medium-length legs. The head is an elongated egg shape (a modified wedge), with large almond eyes, and the cat has a well-defined muzzle with a slight suggestion of squareness, resulting in a pleasant, but slightly wild, expression. The short and glossy coat has a bold pattern of thumb-size spots against a ticked background. The powerful looking Ocicat is the perfect choice of cat for an owner who wishes to have an exotic-looking pet with a completely domestic temperament, without any recent wild cat ancestors.

Colors and varieties: The Ocicat comes in six basic spotted tabby colors: black (tawny or ruddy), blue, chocolate, lavender (lilac), cinnamon, and fawn in both silver and nonsilver varieties. The black silver variety is also known as ebony silver. The spots are aligned in a circular pattern, indicating the underlying classic tabby pattern of these cats. As a result, ticked tabby and classic tabby-patterned kittens can be born to spotted parents. Tabby Ocicat variants are not recognized for competition in North America, but the variety is recognized under the name Jungala in New Zealand and Ocicat Classic in Britain. The classic tabby pattern is most striking in the silver tabbies. Reds, creams, and tortoiseshells are not permitted in either breed.

The Ocicat and Jungala can be mated and progeny can be registered according to their pattern. Mating two spotted Ocicats together produces smaller spots, while mating a spotted Ocicat to a classic tabby Jungala can produce larger spots. The Jungala's name comes from the Sanskrit word for "jungle"; the Jungala is also known as the Classicat.

Temperament: The friendly and adaptable Ocicat breed combines the best attributes of its component breeds: the intelligence of the Abyssinian, the talkative and friendly nature of the Siamese, and the stable temperament of the American Shorthair. Ocicats are intelligent and playful companions who become devoted to their human families. There are a few cat breeds that seem to especially attract male owners in this female-dominated hobby, and the Ocicat is one of them. People who share their lives with Ocicats often compare them to dogs: they love to fetch, are toy-oriented, interact with other human and nonhuman family members, and go for walks on a leash. They are excellent (although sometime a bit noisy) travel companions, and they adapt well to change and to busy households.

Activity level: Moderate

Vocal level: High

Special needs: Use of a rubber brush to remove shed hair can help bring out the shine of the coat.

Variations: None

Oriental Shorthair

Place of origin: Britain; United States

History: The Oriental Shorthair is the nonpointed sister breed to the Siamese. Cats equivalent to the Oriental Shorthair are described in the Thai book *Cat Book Poems* (compiled 1350–1767). As well as depicting colorpoints, this book depicted native cats who were black, black-and-white, brown, and blue. The Siamese was one of the earliest breeds in the cat fancy, having been brought to the West

Oriental Shorthair

Oriental Shorthair

by explorers and colonists during the nineteenth century. Although nonpointed Siamese-type cats reached Britain, they did not find the same kind of favor on the show bench and, in the 1920s, the Siamese Cat Club in Britain began discouraging the breeding of nonpointed Siamese cats.

So, although cats equivalent to black and blue Orientals existed in Germany before the Second World War, not until after the war did Oriental Shorthairs develop in England. Their development was more a by-product, rather than an initial goal, of postwar breeding efforts. With so many bloodlines lost and the number of pedigree cats severely reduced, it became necessary to cross different breeds to increase numbers and to avoid unhealthy inbreeding. Siamese cats were crossed to Russian Blues, British Shorthairs, and Abyssinians, resulting in nonpointed offspring. The nonpointed

cats were bred back to their Siamese parents to produce colorpointed cats. Continued backcrossing to Siamese cats soon restored the elegant type of the parent breed (see page 153 for development of Siamese). A side effect of crossing to other breeds was the emergence of nonpointed cats who were identical to the Siamese in body type. Breeders found these new cats interesting enough that they developed them into breeds in their own right. One British breeder with a special interest in chocolate (chestnut) and lavender (lilac) colors crossed Russian Blue, Abyssinian, and Siamese, which resulted in the Ebony (Foreign Black) and Chestnut Foreign Shorthair (Chocolate Oriental/British Havana), registered as Foreign Cats with the GCCF in 1958.

As knowledge about feline genetics grew in the mid- to late twentieth century, there was further experimentation with cat color varieties. By crossing Siamese cats with shorthairs, more and more colors arose in both pointed and nonpointed forms.

The GCCF has a tradition of recognizing colors as separate breed numbers, so the solid white Siamese-type cats became Foreign Whites, the chocolate became the Havana, and the spotted form became the Oriental Spotted Tabby. In general, the solid colors became Foreign Shorthairs, while the tabby-patterned cats became Oriental Shorthairs. This system proved unwieldy with so many possible permutations of color and pattern, so the nonpointed cats were grouped together as Oriental Shorthairs while the longhaired version became the (British) Angora.

Oriental Shorthairs were imported into North America in the 1970s, and further bloodlines were developed there using American Shorthairs and Siamese. The British Havana was developed into a separate breed called the Havana Brown (see page TK). In 1977, the CFA recognized the Oriental Shorthair for championship status; in 1995, the CFA accepted bicolor Oriental Shorthairs. In Europe, the Oriental Bicolor is recognized separately from the Oriental Shorthair/Longhair. This is to prevent white spotting from entering the Siamese and Balinese breeds. The Seychellois, or bicolor Oriental, is essentially a bicolor-pointed form of Siamese developed in Britain in the 1980s through crossing a tortoiseshell and white Persian to a Siamese (see Seychellois, pages 157 and 164). The white Oriental Shorthair is due to the white masking gene

In the late 1960s and early 1970s, a British breeder crossed a sorrel (red) Abyssinian and a sealpoint Siamese. When two of their offspring were mated together, the Oriental Cinnamon Shorthair was created in 1971. However, the Abyssinian sire carried the gene for long hair and, in 1973, a "Longhaired Havana" was born. The British Angora breed arose from these cats and was recognized by the GCCF in 1998. This Angora was developed to resemble the longhaired cats imported into Britain in the late nineteenth century and lost from the show bench when the cobby-bodied Persian became the preferred type. At the time of the British Angora's recognition, the Turkish Angora had not been recognized in the United Kingdom. In June 2003, the name was formally changed to Oriental Longhair, bringing the British breed into line with the breed name used in the United States. Other cat registries recognize this breed as Mandarin or Javanese. The solid colors have also been called Foreign Longhairs.

In the United States, the Oriental Longhair originated independently from the British breed and was the result of an accidental mating of an Oriental Shorthair and a Balinese in the late 1970s; it was recognized as a breed in 1985.

Because the colorpointing gene is recessive, it can be carried by Oriental Longhairs and Oriental Shorthairs. Some registries class colorpointed cats born to Oriental Shorthair parents as "Any Other Variety" (AOV) or Colorpoint Shorthair, whereas others class them as Siamese. Many registries allow the intermating of Oriental Longhairs, Oriental Shorthairs, Siamese, and Balinese and register the offspring based on appearance (long or short fur, colorpoint or noncolorpoint). Other registries are less flexible and do not allow "variants" (e.g., colorpoint offspring born to solid color parents) to be registered or exhibited in a different class. Crossing the breeds maintains their identical conformation and temperament, allows new bloodlines to be created, and ensures genetic diversity.

Physical description: Oriental Shorthairs and Longhairs have the long, elegant, but muscular bodies of their Siamese ancestor, with an elongated wedge-shaped head, large ears, and almond-shaped eyes. The tail is long and tapered. Although they appear fine-boned, they are surprisingly solid cats.

The Oriental Shorthair has a short, glossy, close-lying coat while the Oriental Longhair has a semi-longhaired coat and plumy tail due to inheriting two copies of the recessive gene for long hair. The Oriental Longhair's coat is silky and flowing, as opposed to the dense, profuse coat of many other longhaired breeds.

As with the Siamese and Balinese breeds, the Oriental can be found in both the extreme version and in a more moderate "old" or "traditional" style. The former is favored on the show bench, while the latter is popular with those pet owners who find show-quality cats too extreme for their tastes.

Colors and varieties: More than 300 color and pattern combinations are possible in the Oriental group. The solid colors are white, red, cream, black (ebony), chocolate (chestnut), cinnamon, fawn, blue, lavender (lilac/frost), caramel, and apricot. Tortoiseshells, known as particolors in some registries also occur. All of these can occur with white to give bicolor cats. These can be combined with silver to give smoke, shaded, tipped, and silver tabbies. The tabby patterns are mackerel, classic, spotted, and ticked.

Registries differ as to which colors they recognize. Not all recognize chocolate, lavender (lilac), caramel, apricot, or tortie-tabby (torbie) Orientals. Some registries recognize bicolors as a color division of the Oriental Shorthair/Longhair breeds, while others recognize them as separate breeds. The sepia (Burmese) and mink (Tonkinese) patterns are not currently recognized in Orientals.

Temperament: Intelligent, affectionate, inquisitive, and mischievous, the Oriental group inherits the personality of its Siamese parent, but wrapped in a wide variety of colors and patterns. These are highly social cats who appreciate the companionship of other cats and may form communal "sleep heaps" in a single small cat bed. They are very people-oriented cats, and their vocal nature only seems to further connect them with their equally loyal owners.

Being intelligent and athletic, many Orientals enjoy games of "fetch" and often have a favorite toy that will be played with—either on their own or with a human—until worn out. They can often be trained to walk on a leash or perform in agility trials. They are very people-oriented, and a confident Oriental is quite the social butterfly, moving from one person to another.

Activity level: High

Vocal level: High; these cats will hold long conversations with their owners and will make sure their presence is not ignored.

Special needs: Their diverse genetic origins mean an Oriental, in any of its forms, is a generally healthy cat. In common with the Siamese, some Orientals cat may inherit sensitive digestive systems that require special dietary considerations. Oriental Longhairs will benefit from combing to remove dead hair.

Variations: None

Persian

Place of origin: England

History: The profusely coated, sturdy-bodied Persian longhaired cat was the first coveted show cat of the cat fancy, starting in the mid-nineteenth century. Despite its name, the modern Persian is a man-made breed created through crossing a variety of early longhaired cats, including Turkish Angoras and Russian longhairs, with English longhaired domestic cats. Long hair in domestic cats is a recessive mutation and appears to be an adaptation to a cold, rather than desert, climate; DNA studies found that the Persian is more closely related to random-bred cats in Western Europe/America than to random-bred cats of the Near East. Early naturalists even speculated that Persians arose through hybridization with the Pallas's Cat. Generations of selective breeding for neotenic traits (those similar to baby animals) produced a cat with a rounder head, larger eyes, shorter legs and tail, and shorter muzzle. It remains the most popular breed by an overwhelming margin.

Longhaired cats purportedly from Angora (modern-day Ankhara in Turkey) arrived in Italy as early as 1521 and in France a little later. Pietro della Valle imported the ancestors of the Persian breed from Persia (modern-day Iran) into Italy in 1620, and Nicholas-Claude Fabri de Peiresc did so from Turkey into France at around the same time. Eventually, through France, Persian and Turkish cats reached Britain, where they were interbred. They were variously known as Angoras or French cats, the latter mostly being white. Confusion over their exact origins meant they were also known as Chinese (some were imported from China), Russian (some imported Russian longhairs/Russian Angoras), and Indian cats (apparently taken there by Portuguese travelers).

By the late eighteenth century, longhaired cats were arriving in Britain from various countries. Those from Turkey were mostly whites with a short, soft, silky top coat and little undercoat. Those from Russia, Afghanistan, and Persia were mostly black or gray with coarser, woollier fur and a more thick-set conformation. In the 1880s, the Russian

Longhair was described as having a larger body and shorter legs than the Angoras and Persians, woollier fur with a coarser top coat, and a very profuse mane. The Tobolsk variety was a large cobby cat with a large head, large eyes, short nose, and small erect ears. The cat had long, woolly fur and occurred only in the red color.

In 1889, Harrison Weir described several types of longhaired cats: the Russian, the Angora, the Persian, and the Indian. In 1896, the Persian warranted only a footnote in Jean Bungartz's book Illustriertes Katzenbuch (An Illustrated Book of Cats): "The Khorassan or Persian cat seems to be a modification of the Angora cat, their hair is somewhat more woollier and curlier, but nevertheless still especially long. The color is dark bluish gray." The terms Angora and Persian were being used interchangeably to mean any longhaired cat, but by the early 1900s, only the Persian would remain. In 1907, the naturalist Pocock described the Persian as having a shorter, wider face than the Angora, although those early Persians were considerably less cobby than those seen on the modern show bench. In the 1920s, London's Natural History Museum displayed a large "Russo-Persian" cat with an immense coat.

Early Persians were bred in white, black, blue (gray), orange, fawn or biscuit (cream), tortoiseshell, blue cream, black (brown) classic tabby, spotted, red tabby, sable tabby (either golden tabby or shaded golden), silver tabby, black smoke, and chinchilla. The solid colors and tortoiseshells were also permitted "with white." Other colors, now familiar on the show bench, turned up in those early days but were not recognized for exhibition. By the early 1900s, Persian Longhairs outnumbered British Shorthairs almost four to one at cat shows.

The blue-eyed white Persian was especially popular, despite the problem of deafness, and was preferred over the yellow-eyed white Persian on the show bench. Green-eyed white Persians were considered to have Russian Longhair ancestry. Blue Persians and black smokes were also especially popular.

Pietro della Valle had written of silver-gray longhaired cats whose color was darker on the back and head and almost white on the underparts; this description indicates that the silver gene was present in the ancestors of the Persian cat. The spectacular silver-gray color known as chinchilla can be traced to cats born in 1882 and is the only Persian variety with green to blue-green-colored eyes. Chinchilla is caused by the same gene that produces silver tabby and smoke, two colors that were already recognized in early Persians, but the early chinchillas were either disqualified or were judged to be "very light blue" or "light smoke." The chinchilla variety was recognized as a breed in 1894, and these cats traced their ancestry to a female called Chinnie and a silver tabby male called Fluffy I. Their descendents included chinchillas, silver tabbies, black smokes, and shaded silvers, which were considered "spoilt tabbies" at the time. From the start, blue chinchillas, blue-silver tabbies, and blue smokes occurred in litters but were disregarded. The orange-eyed chinchillas/shaded silvers, known as pewters, also fell out of favor in the 1890s.

Silver chinchillas have a pure white undercoat tipped with a darker color, while the rarer golden chinchillas have a pale honey to bright apricot undercoat tipped with color. Red and cream chinchillas are also known as *shell*, and red-shaded silvers are also known as *cameo*. The more heavily tipped versions are known as *shaded silver* and *shaded golden*. Shaded-silver Persians with dark faces were known as *masked silvers* but are not recognized by major registries. The chinchilla's equivalent in nonagouti cats (those lacking the tabby gene) are known as smokes.

In Britain, the cats officially became known as Longhairs (there being no other longhaired breeds at that time), although many refer to them as Persians/Persian Longhairs to distinguish them from more recently recognized longhaired breeds. In the United States, Persian is the breed name although some registries did not originally recognize the chocolate or lavender solid (lilac self) colors introduced from crossing Persians to colorpointed cats to create the Himalayan (Colorpoint Longhair). Consequently, chocolate and lavender Persians were variously known as Kashmirs, Self Himalayans, or Himalayan Reflections in those registries.

In Britain, the GCCF regards each color variety of Longhair as a separate breed with its own breed number. This meant some colors succumbed less quickly to the trend of extreme typing. In the 1960s, French writer Fernand Mery wrote that the development of longhairs into extremely cobby cats was due to either the British climate or was a British preoccupation with breeding cobby animals!

During the mid-1970s and early 1980s, American Persians changed dramatically. The pre-1980s look had heavy brows, an "open expression," and flat-topped rather than domed heads. Selective breeding shortened the nose, moved the nose leather higher, and moved the nose break above the eyes. The round eyes became more teardrop shaped. The new look was deemed an exciting development and open-ended wording in breed standards favored these cats on the show bench. During the 1990s, both "open-face" and "extreme Persian pigs" were advertised, but health concerns and public opinion is once more favoring less extreme head conformation. Extreme typing occurred later in Britain, causing sufficient concern among breeders and fanciers that breed standards were revised to ensure the top of the nose leather remained below the lower eyelid.

True Peke-faced Persians, found only in solid red and red tabby, was a mutation that was selectively bred between 1958 and 1993. These had higher ears and a different skull structure that resulted in a very round head with a strong chin and very wide-set eyes. The nose was depressed and indented between the eyes. The muzzle was wrinkled, and there was a second horizontal break located between the usual nose break and the top dome of the head. This second break created half-moon boning above the eyes and an additional horizontal indentation in the center of the forehead. The standard for the peke-face called for a browridge, dimple, and a double dome. This mutation practically eliminated the muzzle and was associated with breathing problems, tear duct problems, a high palate (making suckling difficult), and birthing problems due to kittens' having outsized heads. The peke-faced Persian has

since died out, although the term is often incorrectly used to describe extreme-type Persians.

In Europe and North America, a minority of breeders still breed the traditional or old-style of Persian. Although not competitive on the show bench, these are preferred by many who want a Persian as a pet. During the 1990s in the United States, there was an attempt to establish the older style of chinchilla, shaded-silver, and shaded-golden Persians under the breed name Sterling.

To further confuse the Persian story, longhaired individuals are sometimes born to Exotic Shorthair parents due to the recessive nature of the gene for long hair. Not all registries accept these as Persians due to their non-Persian parentage and their relatively poor coat compared with the coat of Persians born of Persian parents. Some registries accept these as Exotic Longhairs.

The highly modified head shape of Persians and Exotics is not without its problems, and papers about "brachycephalic syndrome" have been published in veterinary journals. A severely flattened face is associated with blocked or misrouted tear ducts, excessive folds of skin around the nose that may rub the eyeball, and shallow eye sockets. The teeth may be crowded or uneven, and the muzzle so short that cats must use their tongues to flip food upward into the mouth, and cannot use their carnassials (cheek teeth) effectively or groom themselves. Blocked nostrils and long or high palate can obstruct the airways and cause noisy breathing. Researchers express concern that a condition called *syringomyelia* (seen in some short-faced dog breeds) may occur in Persians and Exotics due to the brain being crowded into the wrong-size skull. Although the studies were based on magnetic resonance imaging (MRI) scans, X-rays, and necropsies, some breeders argued that the criticism of the Persian was unfair.

The Council of Europe's Convention for the Protection of Pet Animals legislation potentially bans the breeding of cats with facial defects such as brachycephaly and brachygnathia (short muzzle) and any cats with misaligned jaws, underbite, or overbite. In those member states that have signed the convention, this legislation overrides breed standards written by registries. It bans the breeding of extremely short-nosed cats in which the upper edge of the muzzle is higher than the edge of the lower eyelid and requires health screening to detect breathing problems, tear duct problems, shortened upper jaw, and dental problems, and it bans the breeding of individuals showing any of these problems. The legislation recommends modification of breed standards to avoid extreme brachycephaly and/or brachygnathia and to give preference to cats with longer facial bone structure. In Germany, extremely brachycephalic cats in which the tip of the nose is higher than the level of the lower eyelid and/or which show other anomalies of the facial bones detrimental to health may not be bred.

In Victoria, Australia, the Animals Legislation (Animal Care) Bill (2007) would effectively outlaw a number of cat breeds due to health issues but does not mention brachycephaly or brachygnathia. American cat breeders have expressed concern that they might face similar legislation. Some humane societies, veterinary associations, and animal rights groups would like to see comparable legislation on certain breeding practices. At present, breeding ethics remain the province of breeders and breed societies and are jealously guarded from interference.

Physical description: The Persian is a medium to large cat with substantial boning that appears round from every angle, including a round body, a round head with an extremely short muzzle, and large round eyes. Persians have small ears that do not protrude enough to distract from the roundness of the head and short legs and tail that do not distract from the roundness of the body.

Persians should have open sweet expressions. American, Australian, and New Zealand standards call for a snub nose right between the eyes and a domed head as high above the nose break as the round chin is below the nose break. The GCCF in Britain disqualifies cats in which the upper edge of the nose leather is above the lower rim of the eye. The European FIFe calls for a short, broad nose, but not snub, and the stop to be between the eyes.

Black Smoke Persian

Red and White Persian

Cream Persian

As a result, Persian Longhairs bred in Europe are generally less extreme in head shape.

The profuse, fine coat adds to the picture of roundness and softness. The coat should be long and luxuriant, with a heavy ruff or frill and a thick, flowing, plumy tail. In prize-winning show cats, the coat reaches to the floor. The color of the coat affects the structure and texture of the fur: silkier, shinier, and more resilient with the nondilute colors, and softer with the dilute colors. Because the white masking gene obscures the underlying color, white Persians can have either coat type.

Colors and varieties: As the most popular breed worldwide since the inception of the cat fancy, the array of colors and patterns in this breed are extensive, with breeders often specializing in perfecting a particular color variety. "Colorbred" breeding programs focusing on exclusively blue or silver color, for example, were popular in the first half of twentieth century, but most breeders now include a variety of colors in their catteries. Almost all colors and patterns are recognized, either in the Persian or in derivative breeds. Not all registries recognize sepia, mink, ticked tabby, or tortoiseshell-tabby.

Temperament: The quintessential lap cats of the fancy, the lovable, sweet Persians bring out the nurturing instincts of their owners. Since these cats must be bathed and combed regularly, breeders start kittens early with the grooming routine so that the cats become accustomed to the attention long before they go to their new home. Some breeders feel that different colors of Persians have distinct personalities: gentle blues and creams, lovable blacks, playful tabbies, sensitive silvers, and mischievous tortoiseshells, for example.

Activity level: Low

Vocal level: Low

Special needs: Persian cats need regular grooming because the soft, dense coat is prone to matting. Combing or brushing with a metal pin brush (as opposed to a bristle brush) is the most effective way to remove shed hair and prevent mats. Monthly bathing will also remove oils from the coat that can contribute to matting. The face should be washed regularly to prevent the accumulation of debris around the eyes and in the facial folds. Owners unable to maintain the long coat of a Persian should consider an Exotic Shorthair as an alternative (see Exotic Shorthair, page 104). In North America, professional groomers offer a "lion cut" because shaving and trimming the coat prevents mats and avoids the trauma of tugging at matted fur or attempting to cut out mats with scissors. In Britain,

where there are few professional cat groomers, shaving cats is generally only undertaken at a vet clinic with the cat sedated and usually after mats have formed. Lion cuts are also a way of keeping Persians from overheating in hotter climates.

Variations: Some breeding programs have maintained a less extreme skull structure and refer to their cats as "traditional" or "doll-faced." The shorthaired equivalent of the Persian is the Exotic Shorthair, which has the same conformation but a short, dense coat. In some registries, the colorpoint longhair or colorpoint Persian is known as the Himalayan.

Sepia (Burmese color), mink (Tonkinese pattern), and ticked (Abyssinian pattern) Persians have all been produced but are not recognized by all registries. The longhaired Napoleon cat is a short-legged cobby longhaired cat bred through outcrossing Persians to Munchkins. In North America, a number of individual breeders have produced diminutive Persians variously known as *toy, teacup, pocket, mini,* and *pixie* Persians. Some result from spontaneous mutations, whereas others result from selective breeding (progressive downsizing). None of these miniature Persians is recognized as breeds by major registries. Currently, individual breeders set their own standards for size. There is also no guarantee that miniature Persians will not exceed the estimated size.

Pixiebob

Place of origin: Pacific Northwest, United States

History: Cats with shortened tails appear regularly in feral populations around the world. In the United States, they are often inaccurately attributed to crosses between domestic cats and the wild bobcat. A number of breeds have been developed with the intention of capturing the appearance of this wild cat through selective breeding, as opposed to hybridization. Due to early divisiveness among breeders, two separate but equally successful programs came out from this vision: the Pixiebob, which was developed in a single color, similar to that of the wild bobcat, and the American Bobtail, which is bred in a range of colors, including pointed varieties.

The Pixiebob breed began in 1985 and 1986 with two male cats—one a spotted polydactyl acquired in the Cascade Range of Washington State and the other a very large bobtailed classic tabby male reputedly sired by a bobcat. In 1986, the bobtailed male sired bobtailed kittens on a wild-looking brown-spotted female. One of the kittens was a female named Pixie who became a foundation cat in the Pixiebob breed. There was a belief in the region that bobcats and domestic cats sometimes interbred, and a number of bobcatty-looking cats from the Cascade Mountains were added to the breeding program. These purported hybrids became known as Legend Cats. DNA testing has since proven that Pixiebobs are not genetically related to bobcat.

Around the same time, other breeders were also producing bobcatty-looking cats, and some of these became part of the developing Pixiebob breed. In 1993, TICA recognized the Pixiebob, which was considered a naturally occurring breed. To expand and diversify the gene pool, TICA had an open registry that allowed similar-looking cats to be registered as foundation cats. These included American Bobtail, Japanese Bobtail, Maine Coon, Manx, and spotted Chausie variants (Jungle Cat hybrids). All TICA Pixiebobs must be able to trace their ancestry back to Pixie through at least one parent. Currently, the Pixiebob is the only fully recognized breed in the United States that is permitted to have multiple toes.

Pixiebobs

France first imported the Pixiebob in 2001, Britain in 2004. In Europe, Pixiebobs are registered with bodies affiliated with TICA. The Council of Europe's Convention for the Protection of Pet Animals legislation affects the Pixiebob. Bobtailed and kink-tailed cats, regardless of breed, must be examined by a veterinarian for both increased sensitivity to pain in the tail area and possible fused vertebrae before being allowed to breed. Polydactyly is described in the legislation as a semi-lethal gene (deferred lethal), and the legislation recommends entirely banning the breeding of polydactylous cats. The legislation does not distinguish between the benign "mitten foot"/"thumb cat" form and the potentially disabling radial hypoplasia form and thus bans all forms of polydactyly. In the United Kingdom, the GCCF currently bans polydactyly as a genetic defect.

Physical description: Pixiebobs are medium to large cats, with some males reaching 17 pounds (8 kg). Like many of the larger cat breeds, the Pixiebob matures slowly; some cats take three years to reach their full adult appearance. The breed has been developed in longhaired and shorthaired varieties and with polydactyly. A maximum of seven toes on a paw is permitted in the breed.

The Pixiebob is a brown spotted tabby cat, with muted markings of small- to medium-sized spots and is selectively bred to resemble the North American bobcat. The heavy-browed, inverted pear-shaped head and bobbed tail are, therefore, considered the most important characteristics. The deep-set golden-brown or gooseberry-green eyes, lynx-tufted ears, and muttonchops (especially in the longhair) all contribute to the wild appearance of this wholly domestic breed.

The tail length varies from no tailed (equivalent to the Manx rumpy) through to long tailed, although TICA breed standards call for a bobbed tail 2-4 inches long, that is, no more than hock length. Pixiebob tails may contain knots or kinks. In the United States, long-tailed variants may have their tails docked to achieve the bobtailed look for pet owners. A naturally bobbed tail generally has a black tip and at least one black ring near the tip, whereas a docked tail lacks these features. Docked tails are not permitted in exhibited cats. In Britain and Europe, cosmetic tail docking is illegal.

Colors and varieties: Brown spotted tabby comes in both longhaired and shorthaired versions. Warm-toned Pixiebobs have reddish hues in their coats, while cool-toned Pixiebobs have grayish hues. Because of their diverse foundations and recessive genes, Pixiebob variants who are solid color, melanistic, striped, classic tabby, marbled, or rosetted can appear.

Temperament: Playful, generally confident, and sometimes mischievous, Pixiebobs make excellent family companions. They are intelligent, gentle cats who are adaptable and amenable to training. This is another breed that is described as doglike due to the cat's tendency to follow her favorite family member around the house.

Activity level: Moderate

Vocal level: Moderate; they tend to chirp rather than meow.

Special needs: The tail should be handled gently.

Variations: Other breeding programs that promote a "bobcatty look" include the American Lynx,

Desert Lynx, Highland Lynx, and Alpine Lynx. In the early days, the "lynx" breeds were advertised as having bobcat blood, but DNA testing has not supported those claims. The Highlander is a curl-eared, bobtailed, polydactylous breed. Under European legislation, polydactyly is considered a potentially harmful mutation. Registries in Australia and New Zealand appear the most liberal in accepting polydactylous breeds and some (although not all) accept the Polycoon (Polydactyl Maine Coon), Nepalayan, and Clippercat.

There is always the risk of "look-alikes" when a breed becomes popular, and to the dismay of ethical Pixiebob breeders, random-bred polydactyl bobtailed cats have been sold as Poly-Bobs. Such cats are not recognized by any registry, and some were found to have the radial hypoplasia mutation that causes disabling forelimb defects, instead of the benign cosmetic form of polydactyly found in the Pixiebob breed.

Ragdoll

Place of origin: California, United States

History: The Ragdoll originated in California in the early 1960s and courted controversy through the claims made by the breed founder and her marketing of the breed through franchising. The breeding program was founded by Ann Baker, who produced a longhaired, pointed, "designer cat" that she planned to market in a controlled manner. The sale of breeding franchises to breeders and the royalties from each kitten sold was supposed to provide an income to their originator. The provision of breeding cats and the rules governing breeding of them was supposed to keep the Ragdoll under the originator's control.

Although Ragdoll cats became overnight sensations, thanks in part to the implausible stories of their origin and an expertly designed promotional campaign, very few cat breeders successfully make money out of their breed, and the Ragdoll was no exception. The popularity of the breed quickly grew beyond its originator's ability to keep the "franchisees" under control, and dedicated breeders worked hard to gain credibility for this breed. Recognition was held back due to the skepticism of the major cat associations over the tales, misconceptions, and even publicity stunts surrounding the breed.

The breed began with a semi-feral white domestic longhaired cat called Josephine whose kittens were, quite normally, as wild as their mother. Following a car accident and intensive nursing, Josephine became tamer, and her subsequent kittens were also tamer. Josephine's later suitors were most likely Burmese and Birman males. The greater docility of her kittens is attributable both to better socialization and to the genetic influence of their fathers. However, the publicity for the Ragdoll breed claimed it to be due to changes in Josephine herself caused by the car accident. This was elaborated into claims that Josephine was experimentally treated for her injuries and had been infused with genes from skunks, raccoons, or even humans. Ragdolls tend to be very tolerant, relaxed, and quiet-voiced cats, and this resulted in the claim that they were immune to pain and that they went limp when handled.

The foundation cats included a Burmese-type cat and one of Josephine's progeny that resembled a Birman. Unfortunately, breed matriarch Josephine and a subsequent litter of kittens were destroyed by the owner after the protective cat fought with the family dog. Baker produced a book of rules that dictated how the two breed lines were to be bred together to produce Ragdolls. Breeders had to line breed for seven generations, backcrossing each generation to the male sold to them as part of the franchise. After the seventh generation, the breeder had to buy another direct male descendent of Josephine, at which point they could use this male to breed "authentic" Ragdolls.

Baker believed that by the seventh generation, the bicolor and colorpoint Ragdolls would be eliminated, leaving only the desired mitted pattern. Due to the way the white spotting gene works, this did not happen. She had named these patterns mitted, black-legs (now called pointed), and white-legs (now called bicolor), although these were not terms recognized by mainstream registries. After only a few years, some breeders were becoming frustrated that registries would not recognize Ragdolls due to the breeding policies. They broke away from the franchise agreement and started to get the breed onto a sound genetic footing.

In the late 1960s (accounts conflict as to the exact year), the version of Ragdoll bred by these breakaway breeders was recognized. That meant there were two breeds using the name "Ragdoll" that were bred in very different ways. In 1971, Baker created the International Ragdoll Cat Association (IRCA) for her lines of Ragdolls and derivative breeds. In 1975, Baker trademarked the Ragdoll so that only IRCA breeders could use the name. This restriction came too late to be applied to the non-IRCA cats who were already recognized under the Ragdoll name and were becoming increasingly popular. By 1981, Ragdolls were being exported overseas, although the myth of a limp cat impervious to pain would travel with them and hamper progress in registries outside of North America. Baker died in 1997 and the trademark expired in 2005, by which time the few remaining IRCA breeders appeared ready to join the mainstream cat fancy.

When the IRCA Ragdolls appeared on British TV in the early 1990s, animal welfare groups were

Ragdoll

Sealpoint Mitted Ragdoll

Physical description: The Ragdoll is a large, sturdily built cat, with a moderately long body, strong muscular legs, and a soft, rabbitlike semi-longhaired coat. The blue eyes are large and oval shaped, set at a slight slant to follow the shape of the broad, wedge-shaped head. There is nothing extreme about its conformation. The wide-set ears are slightly tilted forward.

The Ragdoll is one of the largest recognized breeds with some reaching 20 pounds (9 kg) in weight. In common with other large breeds, it is slow to mature. Some take up to four years to reach full maturity.

Colors and varieties: Ragdolls have blue eyes and come in pointed colors including seal, blue, lilac, chocolate, red, cream, and the tortoiseshell and tabby varieties of these colors. Three varieties are recognized for exhibition: pointed (colorpoint with no white markings), mitted (colorpoint with white mittens and boots), and bicolor (colorpoint with extensive white markings on the feet and face).

The variability of the white spotting gene means there are three further patterns that are not recognized for exhibition: "high mitted," where the mitts extend up legs; "mid-high white," which is a Bicolor with additional white in the "saddle" area; and "high white," which is a Bicolor with an even greater degree of white where the darker "saddle" may be absent (equivalent to Van pattern). Ragdolls also produce pet-quality variants that deviate from the show standard by having a few white toes on colorpoint Ragdolls, a few dark toes on mitted Ragdolls, undesirable white markings appearing in dark areas, or undesirable dark markings in light areas. All of these inherit the Ragdoll's temperament and conformation.

Temperament: As their name implies, these cats are known for their loving, placid, and docile dispositions. They are tolerant of children and other pets and adaptable to a variety of home environments. However, they also enjoy their playtime and chasing after toys, especially cherishing interactive games with their owners.

concerned that these apparently fear-free, limp cats could be tossed around like cushions. A show judge assessed them and declared them to be perfectly normal and "not in the least limp," while British veterinarians dismissed the claims of immunity to pain. Initially, they were exhibited under the auspices of the now defunct Cat Association. They were recognized by the GCCF in 1990. In Britain, the GCCF allowed the gene pool to be expanded using certain colors of Siamese and Persians as outcross cats up until 2004.

This cat is relaxed, rather than floppy or limp. The easy-going Ragdoll often allows itself to be carried around like a baby, even by children, or even dressed up! Younger Ragdolls tend to be more active and playful, before mellowing into very laid-back adults.

Activity level: Low

Vocal level: Low

Special needs: Although the fine coat does not mat to the same degree as the coat of a Persian, regular combing or brushing with a wire (not a bristle) brush can help free shed hair from the coat and keep it in good condition. Tangles can occur when the cat is shedding.

Variations: Some pet-quality Ragdolls, described as "high white" have a greater amount of white than permitted in the show standard. The RagaMuffin is a nonpointed cousin of the Ragdoll. Following the death of the breed founder, the dwindling number of IRCA breeders also sought recognition from major registries. Their cats formed the foundation of the RagaMuffin (with an all-important capital "M" in the name), a nonpointed cousin of the now widely recognized (non-IRCA) Ragdoll. Cherubims, Honey Bear, and Miracle Ragdoll were names previously used to describe various lines of cats descending from the originator's cattery. Prior to her death, the originator was planning to create two further breeds, Little Americans and Catenoids.

RagaMuffin

Russian Blue

Place of origin: Archangel Islands, Russia; United Kingdom; and Scandinavia

History: The Russian Blue is one of the first official breeds of the cat fancy. Purportedly, sailors from the Archangel Isles brought these cats to England and Scandinavia in the 1860s. They were first exhibited in 1875, at the Crystal Palace in England as the Archangel Cat. Early cat fancy records show the foundation cats of the Russian Blue breed included imported solid blues, solid whites, lavender-blues, blue-and-whites, blue tabbies, and solid blue "Siamese" (these last being the unrecognized Korat breed). These were bred to black British Shorthairs in the hope of improving the fur color and to Persians to improve the eye color. Although claimed to be a naturally occurring breed and favored pets of the Russian Tsars, the Russian Blue was developed in Britain using a variety of random-bred and pedigree cats and is more accurately a man-made breed.

According to Harrison Weir (1889), imported blue cats were exhibited under a variety of names: Archangel Cat, Russian Blue, Spanish Blue, Chartreuse Blue, and American Blue. The names reflected the different origins, real or supposed, of imported gray cats. These were judged in a single class, based mostly on the bluish-lilac color; however, the Archangel (Russian Blue) was distinguishable from British cats due to its more foreign appearance: larger ears and eyes, longer heads and legs, and bright glossy fur.

Frances Simpson (1903) wrote that judges considered Russian Blues to be part of the short-haired Blue judging class, and they were judged against the English cats despite their obviously different conformation. One of the foremost breeders of Russian Blues was Mrs. Constance Carew-Cox who had been breeding them since 1890. Modern Russian Blues have green eyes, but in the late nineteenth-century they were crossed with Persians to get the preferred deep orange eye color, which ruined the conformation and would result in longhaired "sports" in later generations. Imported Russian Blues varied in type, with some having long, lean, pointed heads and large ears, while others had rounder heads, small ears, and wide-set eyes. The coat was short, close, glossy, and silvery but sometimes rather woolly due to the severity of their native climates, and the color varied from lavender-blue to darker shades. The best Russian Blues were considered to be those imported from Archangel.

Carew-Cox also owned cats of "Canon Girdlestone's breed"—blue tabbies imported from Norway, although these appear to have been sickly and died without being bred. In 1896, a Blue Siamese was transferred from the Siamese class (on account of not being sealpointed) and placed in the "Russian or Any Other Blue Cat" class, which he won. Up until 1912, the Russian Blue competed in a class including all other blue cats, often a class for "Blue, With or Without White." Because the longer, leaner, leggier Russian Blue was judged to the British Blue standard—which it could not hope to meet—numbers declined, and dedicated Russian Blue breeders protested. In 1912, it was given its own class under the name "Foreign Blue."

Right from the start, Russian whites and Russian bicolors were also imported. Registrations in 1898 and 1899 recorded an unnamed white Russian female imported by a Mr. Brooks; another white Russian registered as "Granny," and "Olga," a Russian Blue with a white spot. Carew-Cox imported a blue-and-white Russians called Kola.

Russian Blue

Russian White

In the United States, in 1900, Helen Winslow mentioned fine short-haired cats from Russia who were usually solid blue, although a cat fancier in Chicago owned a very handsome blue-and-white Russian. Ultimately, it was the solid blues that found favor with early fanciers and only recently have the "lost" colors of the Russian Shorthair been recreated and recognized by some registries.

Many breeds suffered a loss of purebred cats during the Second World War. In Britain, some breeders crossed their Russian Blues to the Siamese in order to preserve the foreign conformation. This introduced the recessive gene for colorpoints into the Russian. Others crossed to the British Blue to preserve the color. The original conformation has largely been restored, but some European lines still carry the gene for colorpoint. Except for their pattern, Russian colorpoints are identical to the

Russian Blue. Scandinavian breeders crossed their Russian Blues to Siamese to a blue cat from Finland, preserving both the short coat and the green eyes. Although Russian Blue had arrived in the United States in the early 1900s, serious breeding did not begin until after the Second World War. American breeders used cats imported from Scandinavia and Britain and worked to eliminate any Siamese traits. As a result, the Russian Blue recognized in North America is not identical to Russian Blues in Britain, Europe, and Australasia.

The Russian White program started with a genuine white Siberian domestic cat owned by an official at the Thai Embassy in Australia. Mated to a Russian Blue, she produced two white kittens and the green-eyed white Russian was born. The kittens had the conformation and temperament of Russian Blues, but a white coat. The fourth generation of Russian Whites achieved full recognition from the Royal Agricultural Society Cat Club (RASCC) of New South Wales in November 1975. There is now a Russian White at stud in the United States.

The Russian Shorthair group comprises cats of Russian Blue type, but of a wider variety of colors. Currently, those with varying degrees of recognition are Blue (the first color recognized), White, and Black. The Russian White breed program also gave rise to the Russian Black, Black (Brown) Tabby, and Blue Tabby. Russian Colorpoints have also occurred. Peach Russians, possibly lilac variants, occurred in the United States in the 1990s, possibly due to recessive genes from wartime outcrossing.

Physical description: The Russian Shorthair is a graceful, medium-size, muscular cat with a foreign conformation and an aristocratic bearing. The conformation is not as exaggerated as the Oriental/Siamese. The dense, plush, "double coat" of these cats is tipped in silver, giving them a radiant sheen. Their large, emerald-green almond-shaped eyes are set at an angle following the contours of their wedge-shaped heads. Their ears are large and continue the triangular shape of the head. They have a sweet smile formed by the blunt tip and prominent whisker pads of their straight-nosed muzzle. They have elegant, long-legged bodies with delicate feet. Dull stripes may be discerned on the tail in some lighting conditions.

Colors and varieties: The most widely recognized member of the Russian Shorthair group is the Russian Blue. It is accepted for competition worldwide in the distinctive silvery gray color that defines the breed. Due to the presence of the recessive pointed gene in some lines from the Siamese crosses used in the breed's development, occasional blue point or lilac kittens are born. Russian Whites and Russian Blacks are fully recognized in Australia, New Zealand, and South Africa and exist in various stages of recognition in the United Kingdom, Europe, and the United States.

Temperament: Russian Blues are very sensitive cats who tend to bond very closely to a favorite family member. They can be shy and cautious with strangers, but playful and affectionate when settled into familiar surroundings. Intelligent cats, they pay close attention to the activities of others and can learn mischievous "tricks" quickly, such as opening doors and turning on faucets. They enjoy a variety of toys, and some enjoy playing games of fetch and retrieving thrown toys.

They are generally quiet cats, but if you talk to them they will respond and may develop a large vocabulary. They get along well with children and other pets and are excellent pets for a modern family, being content with their own company, but enjoying both play-time and lap-time when their people are at home.

Nebelung

Activity level: Moderate

Vocal level: Low

Special needs: The Russian Blue has no special needs. The coat requires little care beyond grooming away shed hair during the warmer months.

Variations: Crossing to other shorthairs in Australia and Europe has recreated the Russian White (originally seen in 1898 and 1899) and added Russians Black. Apart from their color, these are bred to the standard of the Russian Blue and are becoming more recognized as part of the Russian Shorthair group, although not by the CFA or TICA in the United States. Some fanciers and registries dismiss these colors as indicative of mongrelization, even though the Russian Blue itself was originally developed using a variety of breeds. The Nebelung is a blue-gray semi-longhaired breed of cat created through the crossing of domestic longhaired cats with Russian Blues.

Savannah

Place of origin: Pennsylvania, United States

History: This popular hybrid breed is created through crossing the African serval (Leptailurus serval) with female domestic cats to produce a domestic cat resembling the serval. Early-generation cats are much tamer than similar generations of Bengals and are particularly popular as pets because of their unusually large size and wild look.

Despite rumors of earlier hybrids, the first documented serval–domestic hybrid was in 1986 when a sealpoint Siamese gave birth to a kitten fathered by a captive-bred pet male serval. Named Savannah, she inherited the serval's rangy body conformation, shortened tail, and black spotting, but on a grayish-brown background. Savannah was bred to a Turkish Angora male (male hybrids being infertile) and produced the F2 generation. A breed standard was created, and TICA recognized the Savannah breed in 2001.

Early breeders used the Bengal and Egyptian Mau to develop the breed. TICA permits outcrossing to the Egyptian Mau, Ocicat, Oriental Shorthair, and domestic shorthair. Some breeders have also used Maine Coons for size, introducing the recessive longhair gene by doing so. The serval has three color forms: melanistic, brown (usual), and white (with pale lilac spots), and some Savannah breeders have mimicked these by producing solid black and colorpointed Savannahs.

From F4 onward, Savannahs are considered domestic cats. Laws governing ownership of early-generation Savannahs in the United States vary, with some states and cities restricting the ownership of hybrid cats. In some Canadian provinces, the F1–F3 generation Savannahs cannot be owned as pets, and only TICA-registered Savannahs may be imported. The Savannah is prohibited in Australia where a risk assessment by the Invasive Animals Cooperative Research Centre and DEWHA (the Australian government's environmental authority) class it as a risk to Australia's fragile environment.

In the United Kingdom, the keeping of F1 and F2 Savannahs is restricted under the Dangerous Wild Animals Act. The Department of Farming and Rural Affairs (DEFRA) advises that F1–F4 hybrids require CITES paperwork for them to be imported. The GCCF will not recognize the Savannah because of its hybrid origins. In Continental Europe, imported early-generation Savannahs lacking appropriate paperwork have been seized by Customs officials.

A separate breeding program also aimed to replicate the look of the serval, but without hybridization. In the United States, the Serengeti was developed in 1994 by crossing Bengals and Oriental Shorthairs to produce a spotted cat with long legs and tall ears. TICA recognizes the Serengeti in spotted tabby (black spots on a tawny or golden background, known in the United Kingdom as leopard spotted), ebony silver, ebony smoke and solid black. Meanwhile, in the United Kingdom, breeders crossed Bengals to both Siamese and Oriental Shorthairs, originally calling their serval-inspired cats "Savannahs." This name was changed to harmonize with the American-bred Serengeti and to avoid a clash with the Savannah hybrid. The British-bred Serengeti additionally has the "Snow Leopard" pattern resulting from Siamese parentage; this is not yet recognized by TICA. The American-bred Serengeti has larger ears due to the larger ears found in American Oriental Shorthairs.

Physical appearance: The Savannah is tall, lean, and graceful—often described as rangy—with exceptionally long legs, long neck, and tall ears and a medium-length tail. Hooded eyes add to the exotic appearance. Its striking spotted markings resemble a wild African serval.

Savannahs are a large domestic breed, and their long legs and neck give the impression of even greater size and weight. The F1 and F2 hybrids are larger and wilder-looking than the later generations, with hindquarters standing higher than their prominent shoulders and a relatively small head. Early generations are more likely than later generations to have ocelli (white spots) on the backs of the ears and dark "tear marks" from the corner of the eyes down the sides of the nose.

Colors and varieties: The TICA standard permits brown spotted tabby (black/dark brown markings on a tawny or gold background), silver spotted tabby (black/charcoal spots on a silver background), black/melanistic (with ghost spotting), and black smoke (black spots on black-tipped silver background) only. These spotted patterns have dorsal stripes. Recessive

Savannah

The Savannah breed was created by crossing domestic cats with African servals, such as the one shown here in Kenya's Masai Mara Park.

genes means the Savannah variants occur in classic tabby and marble patterns, snow (colorpoint), and blue (blue spots on a paler blue-gray background). Although most breeders eliminated these from their breeding program, a few are selectively breeding Snow Savannahs because these resemble a rare natural mutation in the serval.

Temperament: The Savannah is a curious, assertive, and active cat who requires a lot of interaction from her owner. She is very loyal to her owners, often following her preferred person around, and is very affectionate although not a lap cat. Savannahs are sociable, playful, and often learn to play fetch with a favorite toy. Their inquisitive nature may mean catproofing parts of the house. They are also noted for their jumping ability. Many Savannahs enjoy playing in water, and some will join their owners in the shower! Savannahs can often be trained to walk on a leash.

Vocal level: Savannahs have a variety of vocalizations including chirps (like the serval) and sounds that are a mix of serval and domestic vocalizations. Their serval-like hiss is different from the domestic cat's hiss.

Activity level: Moderate to High

Special needs: Anecdotally, Savannahs may be sensitive to some types of medication, and some breeders state that ketamine is to be avoided in anesthesia and that only killed virus vaccines be used. Savannahs may require more taurine in the diet than other domestic breeds.

For those interested in breeding Savannahs, fertility appears to be a continuing challenge, even in later generations. Typical domestic cats rarely reach 20 pounds (9 kg), whereas servals are in the 30 to 40 pound (13.5–18 kg) range. Domestic female are sometimes killed accidentally as the serval male grips her neck during mating. A domestic cat pregnancy averages sixty-three days, but a serval pregnancy averages seventy-four days. Hybrid kittens are usually larger than pure domestic kittens. If born at sixty-three days, they are premature by serval standards and may need to be hand-reared.

Scottish Fold

Place of origin: Scotland

History: Cats with folded ears have been reported in the Hebrides, England, Germany, Belgium, and the Greek Islands, but have been regarded as curiosities and not bred. However, all Scottish Folds trace their heritage back to a white barn cat named Susie, living near Coupar Angus, Perthshire, Scotland in 1961. Susie produced a number of fold-eared kittens, but was killed by a car in 1963. One of her female offspring, Snooks, became the foundation for the Scottish Fold breed (alternatively known as the Scottish Lop). Snooks' son, Snowball (sired by an unnamed red tabby male) became the first Scottish Fold stud and was mated to a British Shorthair. A number of other Folds were given away as pets and neutered by their new owners. Novel mutations often attract adverse attention, and Susie's owners were accused of breeding deformed cats for profit.

Initially, the Scottish Fold was registered with the GCCF in the United Kingdom in 1966, and by 1967 numerous "Scottish Lops" had been born. However, the breed was not accepted by European registries, and the GCCF stopped recognizing it in 1971. By then it had become evident that the gene causing the cartilage of the ears to fold also caused limb and tail deformities. There were additional concerns about ear problems, such deafness and greater risk of ear mites or ear infections.

Interest in Scottish Folds in the United States led to almost all the breeding cats being exported there and to the Scottish Fold being developed in the United States. Geneticists had determined that the gene responsible for this trait was an incomplete dominant and that breeding two folded ear cats together risked producing offspring with severe joint abnormalities. Therefore, folded ear cats must only be bred to straight-eared cats. British and American Shorthairs were used to expand the population of this breed, and Persians, Exotic Shorthairs, and Burmese were used early in the breed's history.

In the United States, the Scottish Fold was recognized as a breed in 1973 and gained championship status with the CFA in 1978. Longhaired cats were present in the breed right from the start, but the shorthaired variety was initially preferred because the ear shape was more visible. Early Scottish Folds had one fold in their ears; selective breeding has resulted in a double or triple crease so that the ear folds forward and downward, lying completely flat against the head. The Longhair Scottish Fold has been called the Highland Fold in the United States. In the United Kingdom, the Longhair Fold is known as the Coupari, reflecting the cat's origin in Coupar Angus (which is in a lowland region of Scotland, not in the Highlands).

Scottish Folds eventually returned to the United Kingdom in 1982. In 1983, the now defunct Cat Association recognized the Scottish Fold (shorthair) and recognized the Coupari (longhaired Fold) in 1986. The GCCF still does not recognize the Scottish Fold and has no plans to do so. In Europe, it is not accepted by FIFe and is impacted by animal welfare legislation; however, it has been shown in FIFe shows as an unrecognized breed under FIFe's "open doors" policy.

In 1986, a folded-ear "Hebridean Cat" appeared in a British cat magazine. The tabby shorthair had small, folded ears that the owner claimed to be a feature of random-bred Hebridean cats. However, nothing further was heard of the variety. It is tempting to think that one of Snooks' descendents may have been taken to the Hebrides and founded a branch of the Scottish Fold dynasty there, just as the barn cat Susie founded the breed now seen around the world.

Scottish Fold kittens start off straight-eared and start to develop the folding at around 4 weeks of age. The fold is fully developed at around three months of age. Because the fold-ear gene is dominant and because ethical breeders do not breed Fold to Fold, straight-eared kittens appear in Scottish Fold litters. On average, only one-quarter of the kittens in a litter develop folded ears. This means demand for these popular cats outstrips supply.

In Australia, Straight-eared Scottish Folds have given rise to the Scottish Shorthair, which has longer legs and tail and a different coat texture than the British Shorthair. The Scottish Shorthair

Scottish Fold

Scottish Fold kittens

was recognized as a breed by the Queensland Independent Cat Council (QICC) in the 1980s. It may only be bred to other Scottish Shorthairs or to Scottish Folds and not outcrossed to British Shorthairs. There is also a Scottish Longhair awaiting recognition.

In Europe, the straight-eared variants are recognized for exhibition as Scottish Straight (shorthair) and Highland Straight (longhair). They meet the same standard as the Scottish/Highland Fold except for the ear conformation.

Scottish Folds fall foul of the Council of Europe's Convention for the Protection of Pet Animals legislation, which imposes a total breeding ban because of cartilage and bone defects, especially in

Longhaired Scottish Folds are often called Highland Folds or Couparis.

Colorpoint Scottish Folds are not officially recognized.

cats who inherit two copies of the gene. In addition to locomotor problems and pain, the ears serve as a signal system in establishing social contacts, a function lost in fold-eared cats. This legislation overrides any breed standards in member countries. In Victoria, Australia, the Animals Legislation (Animal Care) Bill prohibits the breeding or sale of animals with heritable defects. This includes the Scottish Fold.

No account of the Scottish Fold would be complete without a mention of the almost mythical Chinese Lop-Eared Cat. Martino Martini visited the Peking province of China in the 1650s and described cats who resemble the Maltese dog in having long white fur and long ears. These cats were indolent and did not hunt mice, but were favored as lap-cats by ladies and fed delicacies. Over the centuries, a series of mistranslations of explorers' texts confused this white lop-eared cat with the Sumxu, a sable-and-yellow marten found in southern China and tamed as a pet and to hunt rats. A series of assumptions and mistranslations led to the name "Sumxu" becoming attached to the cat instead of to the yellow-throated marten. Later writers suggested the Chinese Lop-Eared Cat was kept in cages and fattened up to be eaten as a delicacy.

In 1796, a droop-eared cat was brought back to Hamburg from China and was later taxidermized. It was similar in appearance to an Angora, but a dirty white-yellow in color, and it had pendulous ears. The British breeder H. C. Brooke saw this specimen in 1882 and thought it might be a fake or have ears deformed by canker. Despite several searches by nineteenth-century naturalists and collectors, the Chinese Lop-Eared Cat was not found again. Not even Hagenbeck, a noted animal importer and dealer, was able to locate it. The last reported sighting of the Chinese Lop seems to have been in 1938, when a second droop-eared cat was imported from China.

Physical description: The Scottish Fold is a sturdy and solid cat. The round head and short muzzle, with large eyes resulting in an owl-like expression, is accentuated by the folded, capped ears. This results in a cat who epitomizes the definition of "cute." The extent to which the ears are folded varies between individuals and may even change with the age or hormonal state of the cat. Almost everything about the Scottish Fold is rounded. A short neck, well-padded body, and plush coat add to the impression of an adorable, cuddly companion.

The degree of folding is variable. An exhibition-quality Scottish Fold has ears that form a close-lying cap. Smaller, tightly folded ears are preferred over a loose fold and larger ear. Scottish Folds can still swivel their ears to track sound, lay them back to express anger, and prick them up (but not unfold them) to express interest.

Colors and varieties: This breed is recognized in a wide variety of colors, including solids, bicolors, torties/tricolors, tabbies, silver tabbies, tipped, and smoke. Colorpoints, chocolate, and lavender are not generally recognized. Longhaired Scottish Folds are sometimes referred to as Highland Folds or Couparis. Some registries recognize the straight-eared offspring of Scottish Folds as Scottish Straight or Scottish Shorthair/Scottish Longhair.

Temperament: These cats share the laid-back, tolerant nature of the British Shorthair and American Shorthair cats who continue to be crossed into this breed. Very people-oriented, these soft-spoken cats are known to be excellent lap-cats. Scottish Folds are affectionate, intelligent, and loyal and get along well with children and with other pets. They are also playful and adaptable. An especially endearing trait of the breed is "the Buddha sit"—a Scottish Fold sitting with hind legs outstretched and front paws resting on its belly as though lounging in an armchair. The straight-eared variants of this breed have the same sweet temperament.

Activity level: Low

Vocal level: Low

Special needs: It is a myth that folded ear cats are more susceptible to deafness or ear mites, but infection with these parasites must be prevented, as with any breed of cat. Due to the nature of the cartilage defect that causes the ears to fold, some Scottish Folds, even from the most conscientious breeding program, may develop symptoms of arthritis that range from mild to crippling (osteochondrodysplasia). These problems include a thickened tail caused by tail vertebrae fusing and thickened legs with swollen feet due to overgrowth of cartilage around the paw. Cats who inherit two copies of the folded ear gene are worst affected, hence unaffected straight-eared variants are important in Fold breeding programs.

Variations: A Rex-coated variety called the Poodlecat (Pudelkatze) combines the Scottish Fold conformation and ears with the curly coat of the Devon Rex. Outcrossing to Siamese to create colorpoint folds resulted in Oriental Folds, with larger ears and more foreign conformation. The Hemingway Fold has folded ears and extra toes. The Foldex or Exotic Fold combines the cobby Exotic Shorthair conformation with folded ears and is described as resembling "a little furry owl." The Ukrainian Levkoy Cat, a hairless fold-eared cat, was created in 2005 by crossing the Donskoy to the Scottish Fold. The Ukrainian Levkoy's ears do not fold tightly to the skull as in the Scottish Fold, but stand out from the head and fold closer to the tips.

These derivatives are prone to the same cartilage problems as the Scottish Fold and produce straight-eared variants. Crossing Scottish Folds with breeds having other physical mutations (e.g., Manx, Munchkin) is discouraged by most registries due to the potentially crippling interaction of genes.

Selkirk Rex

Longhaired Selkirk Rex

Place of origin: Montana, United States

History: In 1987, in a litter of kittens born to a female rescue cat who had lost her foot in a trap was a single curly-coated kitten. "Curly-Q" was placed in a pet home at a very young age, but her initial adopter returned her to the rescue group because she demanded too much attention. She was then given to a Persian breeder who had an interest in feline genetics and wanted to determine if this funny-looking shorthaired calico cat represented a new Rex mutation. The breeder renamed the cat "Miss DePesto," after a curly-haired character on the television show Moonlighting and the cat's own reputation as a "pest." When she matured, Miss DePesto was bred to a black Persian, and three of the six kittens were born with curly coats.

This demonstrated that a dominant mutation was at work, unlike the previously established Rex mutations that had a recessive mode of inheritance. Inspired by the attractive appearance of these Persian-cross kittens, the original breeder and others expanded the initial gene pool using American Shorthairs, British Shorthairs, Exotic Shorthairs, and Persians/Himalayans to develop for this breed. The originator named her new breed of cats Selkirk Rex in honor of her stepfather. It was recognized by TICA in 1992 and in the United Kingdom by the GCCF in 2009. The breed is now found in most cat fancying countries around the world.

Physical description: The living embodiment of a soft, plush teddy bear, the Selkirk Rex has a round head, large rounded eyes, and a sturdy body, all of which adds to the appeal of its curly coat. The muzzle is short, but more reminiscent of a British Shorthair than a Persian. The longhaired version displays a cascade of loose ringlets, while the shorthaired version has random loose curls. The curls are most evident on the underside of the cat, around the neck, and on the britches of the back legs. Kittens and young cats may appear to have relatively little curl compared with adult cats. Males tend to be curlier than females. Because the mutation that causes the curly coat is dominant, breeders produce noncurly kittens in their breeding programs that make delightful pets, with coats that have all the soft plushness of their littermates, but without the curls.

Colors and varieties: The Selkirk Rex comes in all colors of the domestic cat, including the Burmese- and Siamese-derived semi-albinism colors. The longhaired and shorthaired varieties exist in both curly and noncurly versions.

Temperament: Selkirk Rex seem to have inherited the mischievously affectionate nature that gave their ancestor "Pest" her nickname. Easy-going, somewhat goofy cats, they take advantage of the fact that their soft, plush coats make it easy to elicit cuddles and strokes from their owners. Surprisingly playful at times, but never overly busy, they are very tolerant of children and other pets.

Activity level: Low

Vocal level: Low

Special needs: Because the abnormality in the hair follicle that causes the hairs to curl or kink also interferes with skin secretions (sebum) being pulled away from the skin, some Rex and Wirehaired cats may need to be bathed frequently and their ears cleaned regularly to prevent these secretions from accumulating in the hair follicles or ear canal and causing dermatological problems.

Variations: None

Siamese

Place of origin: Southeast Asia

History: One of the earliest breeds recognized by the organized cat fancy, the Siamese is surrounded by legend and whole books have been devoted to the fact and fiction surrounding the breed. It is probably the most recognizable breed, even to noncat-fanciers. The kinked tail (a widespread genetic mutation in Asia) seen in the early imports was attributed to a princess putting her rings on her cat's tail while she bathed; supposedly, the young lady tied a knot in the cat's tail to prevent the rings from falling off. Others wrote that the Siamese cat resulted from crossing the sacred cats of Burma and the Annamite cats when the Siamese and the Annamese conquered the Khmer empire.

Colorpointed cats were among the varieties described and illustrated in manuscripts called *Tamra Maew* (*Cat Poems*), written between the fourteenth and eighteenth centuries. One of these manuscripts, dating from 1350, pictures a pale-coated cat with a black mask, tail, feet, and ears. Early descriptions of the sealpoint Siamese in 1676 call it *Vichien Mas* (or *Wichien-Maat*). Over the years, other names for cats considered ancestral to the Siamese include Singhasep, Annamese, Laotian Lynx, and Gould's Cat.

The enigmatic and elegant Siamese continued to attract myths into the twentieth century. Due to its distinctive appearances and voice, as late as the 1920s, some fanciers claimed the Siamese to be the product of a mating between domestic cats and, variously, the Indian (yellow-throated) marten,

the civet, the Bay Cat, or Temminck's Golden Cat (Asian Golden Cat). Siamese cat fancier Lilian J. Veley (1926) remained adamant that the Siamese had traits inherited from some type of viverrine, possibly one unknown to science, that lived in its native country.

During the British exploration and colonization of Asia in the 1800s, it became common to bring back treasures and curiosities. One of those curiosities was a cat who was described by the father of the modern cat fancy, Harrison Weir, as "the nightmare cat." Its unusual color and type shocked a cat fancy that was accustomed to the round-headed and heavily built Persians and British Shorthairs.

Two Siamese cats were exhibited at the Crystal Palace Cat Show in 1871, where they were considered "ugly" and "frightening" by many, but attracted enough attention that another Siamese was exhibited at the 1872 Cat Show. It appears that these early imports were not used for breeding, but were exhibited as curiosities. In 1878, the wife of American President Rutherford B. Hayes received a Siamese cat as a gift from the American Consul in Bangkok; this is the first documented Siamese in the United States, but again was not used for breeding. In 1879, a writer for the (London) *Daily Telegraph* was unimpressed by the unfamiliar Siamese, referring to them as having "black muzzles, ears, feet and tail setting off a close, yellowish drab coat and completing the resemblance of the little brutes to a pair of pug puppies."

The first breeding imports were a pair of sealpointed Siamese in 1884. These were exhibited at the Crystal Palace in 1885 and attracted enough attention that more were imported. It is likely that other Siamese cats did not survive the long journey to England, whereas those who did were considered delicate in health. Blue-pointed Siamese occurred naturally in litters due to recessive genes and appeared in England in 1894, but early breeders did not consider them worth retaining. In 1896, Louis Wain, another founding father of the cat fancy, refused to judge a Siamese on grounds that it was blue rather than seal. Chocolate point Siamese were initially considered badly colored Sealpoints and appear traceable to a cat called Prince of Siam imported in 1897. These other colors could only be shown in "Any Other Variety" classes. Many Siamese fanciers dismissed "any other color" Siamese as freakish crossbreeds.

Right from the start, these cats were described as highly intelligent and doglike in their affection and devotion to their owners. They were also found to be formidable fighters, great hunters, and to have a cry like a human infant. Although Siamese cats were reportedly prolific breeders in their home country, a high kitten mortality rate was reported by early breeders in the United Kingdom.

Although Harrison Weir encountered both the colorpointed and the chocolate variety (which later became the Burmese), he favored the "Royal Siamese," which were described as light gray, fawn, or dun with black or dark chocolate points and blue eyes, and it was this type that early breeders concentrated their efforts on, forming the first Siamese cat club in 1902.

Cat fanciers were also fascinated by claims that the only pure Siamese cats were kept at the King of Siam's palace and were very difficult to obtain, especially male cats, because the King did not want the Royal cats to be bred outside of his palace. Supposedly to gain a cat, these travelers either had to do some favor for the king or steal a cat from the palace. An early champion, Wankee, bred in Hong Kong in 1895 was allegedly the offspring of a female kitten stolen from the palace.

Early descriptions indicate different conformations ranging from slight to substantial. Some were described as delicately made cats with a curiously elongated "wedge-shaped" or "martenlike" face. Part of this delicacy, both in conformation and health, can be attributed to inbreeding during the late 1890s; this was overcome by further imports and crossing to other shorthairs. In 1903, Frances Simpson mentioned crossing Siamese to a blue-eyed white cat. On the other hand, one male Siamese was described as "massive." All that can be said for sure is that early Siamese cats varied in body type and that the exaggerated long, lithe look was not set until the twentieth century.

In 1903, Frances Simpson's *The Book of the Cat* had stated the tail kink to be a peculiarity of the breed and therefore desirable, not a defect. By the 1930s, American breeders declared the kinked tail to be a fault, insisting that true Royal Siamese cats did not have kinked tails—any kink-tailed Siamese in the United States were therefore the result of sailors picking up common street cats! Dr. Hugh M. Smith, Adviser in Fisheries to His Siamese Majesty's Government between 1923 and 1934, wrote that there were no "palace" or "royal" cats in Siam— colorpointed cats could be owned by anyone as a household pet. A Siamese prince visiting London was apparently interviewed by a Siamese cat fancier and replied that there were more Siamese cats in London than in all Siam. In 1939, the American authority on cats Ida M. Mellen reiterated this as "any Royal Palace can have stray cats."

Siamese cats were continually imported into the United States and United Kingdom throughout the early and mid-twentieth century, and show halls, homes, and popular culture quickly became filled with these elegant blue-eyed beauties. The move toward the extreme type began in earnest during the early 1960s. Although pet owners often preferred a moderate cat, breeders and exhibitors preferred an extremely slender cat with a very long head, almond-shaped eyes, and flaring ears. A cat of this type, called Fan Tee Cee, greatly impressed show judges, and his name appears many times in some pedigrees, changing the look (and breed standard) of the Siamese cat into the breed we now see.

By the 1930s, the four original colors—sealpoint, chocolate point, blue point, and "frost point" (lilac, or lavender, point)—were well established in the breed in the United Kingdom and United States. Breeders started to imagine the Siamese in an even wider variety of colors. Breeders introduced these colors by crossing Siamese to Abyssinians, American Shorthairs, and red domestic shorthairs.

The first "new" color to be pursued was the red point (and the associated, but considered less desirable at the time, tortoiseshell point), originally called the "Red Concha." These new colors were declared "heretical" by more conservative Siamese breeders who refused to allow them to be recognized as Siamese. The name Colorpoint Shorthair was adopted for the new colors in the United States; these included the Red (or Flame) and Cream Points, the Tortoiseshell Points, and the Tabby (or Lynx) Points. After almost half a century of breeding only to Siamese cats, only one registry in the world does not currently recognize these cats as Siamese, and they must be registered separately as Colorpoint Shorthairs. Meanwhile, Tabby Point Siamese had been mentioned as early as 1902 and were being were bred in Scotland as Silverpoint Siamese in the 1940s.

In the United States, the CFA is a "genotypical registry" (or pedigree-based registry), accepting cats based on their genetic make-up rather than their appearance. Only cats bred from eight generations of registered Siamese, and in the original four colors, can be registered as Siamese. The CFA considers all other colors and patterns to be evidence of hybridization because they were not present in original imports (although such colors and patterns occur naturally in Thailand and neighboring countries), and they can only be registered as Colorpoint Shorthairs. All other registries consider them a single breed—the Siamese—although not all registries recognize all colors or patterns.

Physical description: The original conformation of the Siamese is a frequent bone of contention. Original imports included small, delicate Siamese, long, lithe Siamese, and even a Siamese male who early fanciers referred to as massive. The wedge-shaped muzzle, pronounced pointed ears, and lithe body have been traits of the Siamese breed since the first imports. However, selective breeding has made the modern exhibition Siamese much more extreme in type, with an exaggerated wedge-shaped head, large ears, and long tubular body. Nothing about the modern Siamese is round—it is angular in every way. Once common traits such as cross-eyes (resulting from crossed optic nerves), kinked tail, and white toes have largely been bred out.

Sharp delineation between the dark colored points and a light colored body is an important focus of the breed standard. The semi-albinism that produces

Seal Tabby Siamese

Brown Siamese

this color is temperature-related and affected by environment and age. The color develops on the cooler extremities of the body. Kittens are born white, gaining their point color in the first two weeks of life, and older cats tend to have a darker body. The coat is very short, sleek, and glossy.

Admirers of the less-extreme type of the original imports may call their cats "traditional" or "old-style" Siamese, although the recent acceptance of the "Thai" breed by some registries has given these cats recognition in their own right. Cats referred to as "apple-headed Siamese" were created by crossing imported cats with domestic shorthairs in order to meet increasing public demand for these cats as pets, especially in the 1980s. For a while, colorpointed cats with the American Shorthair conformation were known as the Opal, whereas in the United Kingdom, the Colorpoint British Shorthair combined the British Shorthair conformation with the pointed pattern of the Siamese cat. The Tonkinese, derived from Siamese-Burmese crosses in the cat fancy, also appeals to lovers of the "older style."

Colors and varieties: Originally accepted by the cat fancy only in the "Royal" color of sealpoint, Siamese of other colors soon emerged, including blue point, chocolate point, and lilac (frost) point. Crossing with other shorthaired cats expanded the palette to include pointed colors of red, cream, tortoiseshell, tabby, silver-tabby, smoke, and even bicolor points. Other colors, such as fawn, caramel, apricot, and cinnamon may not be recognized by all registries.

Temperament: Intelligent, affectionate, and mischievous, the personality of the Siamese is as unique as its coloration. These are highly social cats who appreciate the companionship of other cats to the extent that pictures of large numbers of these cats intertwined with each other in a single small cat bed are legendary. They are very people-oriented cats, and their vocal nature only seems to further connect them with their equally loyal owners. Many are extroverts, while others are more nervous and sensitive and bond closely with a single person.

They are good with children and other pets. Although a Siamese can entertain itself, many owners consider it better to have two so they can entertain each other whenever the owner is out. Many Siamese are natural retrievers and will play "fetch" with the owner. They can often be trained to walk on a leash and have been popular in films due to their distinctive looks and trainable nature.

Activity level: High

Vocal level: High; Siamese are generally extremely vocal, with a loud, low-pitched voice that is sometimes mistaken for the cry of a human baby. Owners of Siamese enjoy talking to their cats, who obligingly talk right back to them.

Special needs: The coat needs occasional brushing with the short side of a small rubber brush to remove loose hair. The coat can be smoothed using a chamois cloth. Some lines of Siamese may have sensitive digestive systems that require special dietary considerations. There also appears to be a higher incidence of cancer in Siamese than in other breeds.

Blue Point Siamese

Lavender Siamese

Variations: The Siamese has been very influential in the cat fancy. In addition to its Colorpoint Shorthair cousin, it has been used in developing an array of other breeds, the most popular of which have separate entries in this book.

Semi-longhaired kittens have appeared in Siamese litters since the early days and are recognized as the Balinese breed. The semi-longhair form of the Colorpoint Shorthair is known as the Javanese by the CFA in the United States (the term Javanese is used in Europe and New Zealand for nonpointed Oriental-type cats).

The pointed color of the Siamese breed is caused by a recessive mutation for semi-albinism; however, some carry a recessive mutation for full albinism. Albino Siamese have no pigmentation at all. They have white fur and pinkish-blue eyes instead of the normal blue color of the pointed Siamese. These albino Siamese are photosensitive and `avoid bright light.

The albino Siamese is not to be confused with the Foreign White or white Oriental Shorthair, which have the dominant-white color mutation.

Crossing Siamese to American Shorthairs produced the bicolor-pointed Snowshoe in the 1960s and the Opal (Colorpointed American Shorthair) in the 1990s.

In the early days, some Siamese cats had white toes; this was considered a serious fault that breeders worked hard to eliminate. When Bicolor-Pointed Siamese were developed, some European registries declared that Siamese cats with color-and-white points could not be called Siamese in case they reintroduced the problematical white toes. These were recognized under the name Seychellois by some registries, whereas others recognize them as Bicolor Oriental Shorthairs or Bicolor-Point Siamese. A few breeders prefer the name Snowshoe Siamese. Confusingly, the Seychellois name has also been used for noncolorpointed Van-pattern Oriental Shorthairs!

The original imports of Siamese were more moderate in type than the modern exhibition Siamese. Breeders in England, continental Europe, and North America returned to Thailand in recent years and imported Thai cats in an effort to preserve the Wichien-Maat (or Vichien Mas) cat in its original form. Modern Siamese have been used as outcrosses to develop the population of these cats, but the standard for the "Thai" (or "Thai Siamese") breed recaptures the style of the early imports that captivated, or horrified, fanciers in the late 1800s. However, some registries use the name "Thai" to refer to the naturally occurring pointed or lilac offspring of Korat cats. Thai Bobtails, combining the colorpointed pattern with the bobtailed trait common throughout Asia, have also been bred.

The colorpoint pattern has been introduced into a number of breeds by crossing with the Siamese. Some, such as the Snowshoe and Colorpoint Persian (Himalayan), are formally recognized whereas others, such as the Si-Manx are not. It should be warned that less scrupulous cat owners sometimes advertise for sale Siamese crossbreeds or random-bred colorpoints as Si-something or Something-amese to give the impression of a controlled breeding program or rare variety.

Siberian

Place of origin: Russia

History: The Siberian Forest Cat has been present in Russia for centuries and was first recorded around 1000 AD. It is believed to have originated in the Siberian Taiga, where domestic cats mated with wild cats; this naturally occurring breed is described in one of the USSR's Red Books. "Russian Longhairs" or "Russian Angoras" were documented in nineteenth-century cat fancy literature and used to develop the Persian breed. Although sometimes claimed as equivalents to the modern Nebelung, those Russian Longhairs were large, tabby cats with shorter and heavier boned legs than the (Turkish or French) Angora and with a massive coat and ruff that is consistent with the modern Siberian breed.

According to Harrison Weir (1889), the Russian Longhair differed from the Angora/Persian in having a larger body, shorter legs, a short thickly furred tail, and a thicker, woollier, and longer mane with coarse hairs in it. The Russian Longhairs seen by Weir were mostly dark brown tabbies with indistinct markings or solid black. Weir described a "Siberian cat" separately based on a slate blue female who also had a rather short body, legs, and tail.

The modern Siberian breed began after the Second World War using free-ranging cats from Leningrad (St. Petersburg) and Moscow. By the 1960s, breeding was still small-scale, and the cats were unknown outside of Russia until borders with Western Europe opened up. During the 1980s, Russia developed its own cat fancy, and the Siberian standard was recognized by the Kotofei Cat Club in Moscow in 1987. The colorpointed variety is believed to have originated during the 1960s through matings with colorpointed feral cats in the Neva River region near Leningrad.

Siberians reached the United States in 1990. The separately recognized Neva Masquerade arrived in the United States in 1997. Siberians were recognized by the FIFe in Europe in 1997. They were exported from Russia to South Africa in 2000, Australia in 2001, and the United Kingdom in 2002.

There are claims that the Siberian breed is hypoallergenic due to producing less of the Fel d1 allergen in its saliva. Scientific studies between 1999 and 2010 found that only around half of the Siberians surveyed produced less Fel d1 allergen than other breeds, whereas other Siberian cats produced high levels of the allergen. There is great variation between individual cats, and they are not allergen-free.

Siberian

Physical description: Siberians are strong, stocky, powerfully built cats and agile jumpers. They are large, heavy-boned, and imposing. The dense, triple coat is not shaggy, like that of the Maine Coon, but the same length all over the body. The coat varies with the season, being thicker and coarser with an abundant ruff in the winter, but less dense in the summer. The tail is medium-long, rather thick, and tapers to a blunt tip. The large head is a modified wedge with rounded contours. The body is shorter than the Maine Coon or Norwegian Forest Cat, but less cobby than the Persian. With its protective coat and no extremes of conformation, this is a cat who evolved to survive in a harsh climate. They can take up to five years to reach their full magnificence, and females may be considerably smaller than males.

Colors and varieties: Almost all colors and patterns are found, including naturally occurring colorpointed varieties. Some registries recognize the colorpointed cats separately as Neva Masquerade (alluding to masked cats from near the Neva River). The brown and silver tabbies are the most popular colors. The shade of brown tabby can be unique in some individuals, and they often referred to by their breeders as "golden." Chocolate, cinnamon, caramel, lilac (lavender), fawn apricot, and the Burmese or Tonkinese patterns are not accepted.

Temperament: The Siberian is friendly, intelligent, loyal, and affectionate toward her owners. They are playful and adaptable cats and sometimes described as doglike in character. They get along well with children and other pets and, being sociable, are better kept in pairs. They can be talkative, using soft mews to comment on anything they find interesting and when asking their people to open doors and the like. True to their origins, Siberians often like being in sheltered places outdoors, even in cold snowy weather. They also seem to have a fascination with water. In Russia, these easily trained cats sometimes perform in circuses and on stage.

Although they may take four to five years to mature physically, Siberians reach sexual maturity relatively early. Siberian females often bond closely to only a single mate. Siberian males, unusually in cats, may take an interest in rearing the kittens.

Activity level: Low

Vocal level: Low

Special needs: The profuse, glossy coat needs regular combing to keep it in good condition and ensure that mats do not form. This is generally a very healthy breed, but lines of "golden" Siberians may be prone to hypertrophic cardiomyopathy due to inbreeding of the limited foundation stock during the 1990s.

Variations: The pointed colors are called Neva Masquerade and recognized as a separate breed in some associations, with a slightly different standard from the Siberian.

Singapura

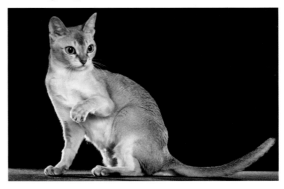

Place of origin: Texas, United States; Singapore

History: Even this recently established breed has attracted myths about its origins. When three brown-ticked cats were imported into the United States in 1975, they were claimed to be native Singaporean "drain cats," and their small stature was supposedly due to generations of living in storm drains. It was some years before the true origins of the breed were uncovered. It was later revealed that the military family of an established Abyssinian and Burmese breeder had been relocated to Singapore in 1974, taking five of their cats with them. Quarantine papers described the five cats as two Burmese and three brown Abyssinians, although it is claimed the latter merely described their brown-ticked appearance and was not a reference to their breed.

When the breeders returned to the United States in 1975, they began promoting a new breed they called the Singapura, which exhibited the ticked tabby pattern of the Abyssinian cat and the semi-albinistic color and body type of the Burmese cat. These cats are widely believed to be Burmese-Abyssinian crosses, although they are also claimed to be the descendents of three ticked cats sent home from a previous (and apparently secret) spell in Singapore.

The Singapura breed was established from those three brown-ticked cats plus a Singaporean cat discovered in 1981 that fitted the breed standard apart from being part-tailed. This gave the Singapura breed a legitimate claim to being partly Singaporean in origin. During the 1980s

Singapura

and 1990s, American breeders sought further Singapuras in Singapore, with minimal success. In 1987, a Singapura breeder visited Singapore looking for street cats fitting the description of the Singapura breed to take back to the United States as foundation cats. He spoke to local people, only to find they were unfamiliar with the type of cat known in the United States as a Singapura!

When asked to explain how Burmese and brown Abyssinians exported to Singapore in 1974 had somehow become Singapuras in 1975, the breeder claimed the three ticked brown cats were in fact descendents of Singaporean cats brought back from an earlier stay in Singapore in 1971. Because that trip that was related to a sensitive military mission, this fact had originally been withheld as part of the breed's history. This explanation was accepted by the CFA, and the breed is still classed as a naturally occurring one. Feline DNA studies in 2007 found very few genetic differences between the Singapura and Burmese, reinforcing the likelihood of a man-made breed.

TICA recognized the Singapura in 1979 and the CFA in 1982. Singapuras arrived in the United Kingdom in 1988 and were recognized by the GCCF in 1997. They are now also bred Australia, South Africa, and other parts of Europe.

Careful selection to establish the color to "breed true" created a very small gene pool of original cats, which contributes genetically to its position as the smallest of the recognized cat breeds (only the unrecognized Teacup Persians are smaller). Solid-color brown kittens occurred in early litters due to a recessive gene inherited from two of the original foundation cats. Singapura litter sizes tend to be small, a characteristic associated with inbreeding.

A number of experimental Burmese-Abyssinian crosses have closely resembled the Singapura in color and type. In Continental Europe, some Abyssinians have so closely resembled the Singapura in color that judges suggested they be registered as Singapura foundation cats to expand the gene pool. The Singapura is genetically very uniform. Although this ensures consistent conformation and color, it can result in health issues due to inbreeding depression. Most registries and breeders are not receptive to the idea of crossing to other breeds, in order to maintain the integrity of the Singapura. However, careful outcrossing may become unavoidable in the future due to the inevitable inbreeding caused by the very small foundation stock.

Despite the lack of Singapura-type cats in their alleged native country, the Singapore Tourist and Promotion Board (now Singapore Tourism Board) made the Singapura a tourist emblem in the guise of "Kucinta—The Love Cat of Singapore." Statues of the cat can be found alongside the Singapore River. This appeals mainly to Western tourists because the official emblem of Singapore is the lion.

Although most feline historians, including cat fanciers of that country, remain highly skeptical of the breed's purported origins as a "street cat of Singapore," it cannot be denied that these two genetic traits may be naturally found in this part of the world. A few ticked cats have been found by American fanciers; dubbed the "Wild Abyssinian," they resembled a dark Abyssinian-type cat and can still be found among street cats in Singapore today. A red-ticked cat was referred to as the "Limau Kohlum." However, the majority of Singaporean street cats are bobtails, and they are generally mackerel tabbies, tortoiseshells, and bicolors.

Physical description: A small, dainty-looking breed with a rounded head, large expressive eyes, and deeply cupped, large ears, the Singapura is an athletic cat who only looks delicate. Although compact, they are well-muscled, with medium boning and strong, legs that are long relative to their size. The tail is slender, but not "whippy" and has a blunt tip. Singapuras do not develop to their full size until they are almost two years old, with males weighing 6 to 8 pounds (2.75–3.5 kg) and females weighing slightly less.

The Singapura has an angelic face, with the impression of "high cheekbones" below its large eyes giving it an expression of innocence. Deep eye colors range from celadon (pale jade) green through hazel or gold to copper. The fine-textured coat is a distinctive sepia-shaded brown ticked tabby in color. Its muzzle is medium-short and broad with a blunt nose.

Colors and varieties: This breed exists only in the color sepia (Burmese brown) ticked tabby. This produces a rich, warm, sable brown ticking against an "old ivory" hued background, often with yellow tones. The color is darkest along the back and fades to sepia on the undersides. Residual tabby barring is present on the forehead and lower legs. Solid brown cats appeared early in the breed's history, but test matings appear to have eliminated cats carrying the solid color.

Temperament: These active, intelligent cats are mischievous, lovable family members. They get on well with children and are content to be indoor cats, but they need the company of people or of other cats. They are also gentle and sociable with other cats and nonconfrontational. They love to be up high, surveying the world. They also enjoy shoulder-riding and snuggling with their humans.

Activity level: Moderate

Vocal level: Moderate

Special needs: The short, sleek coat of the Singapura requires only a weekly grooming to keep it in good conditions. One of the foundation cats had the heritable condition of uterine inertia (weak uterine muscles that cannot push a kitten from the womb), and because of inbreeding, this is found in some Singapura females. If you are interested in breeding

Singapuras, it should be noted that affected females may require caesarian sections.

Variations: None

Snowshoe

Place of origin: Pennsylvania, United States

History: Another early "designer breed," the Snowshoe was inspired by kittens born of an accidental breeding in the 1960s of a Siamese queen with an unknown male bicolor cat who must have been carrying the recessive colorpointing gene. Three of the kittens were colorpointed with white feet, similar to the pattern of the Birman. The Snowshoe breed was developed during the 1960s through crosses of Siamese with bicolor American Shorthairs. The aim was a cat with unique conformation, rather than Siamese type, but with the specific color pattern of white spots on a Siamese colored cat.

Much of the detailed early history of the Snowshoe has been lost due to poor recordkeeping. The breeder used sealpoint Siamese with "tuxedo pattern" bicolor American Shorthairs to breed more of these attractive cats. The first generation offspring lacked the recessive Siamese colorpoints because they inherited only one gene for this trait. By breeding these offspring to Siamese cats, the desired colorpoints with white feet were produced. These white feet gave rise to the breed's name, and they were exhibited at local cat shows, but not recognized by any registry.

The Snowshoe was initially recognized in 1974 by both the Cat Fanciers Federation (CFF) and the American Cat Association's (ACA), but by 1977 there was only one breeder keeping the Snowshoe breed alive in the United States. The original pattern restrictions discouraged existing and prospective breeders because of the difficulty of breeding cats whose markings met the breed standard. Luckily, more breeders came forward to work with the Snowshoe, and it was recognized by TICA in 1993. The breed has not attained sufficient numbers to be recognized by the CFA.

The Snowshoe breed remains rare despite having existed for almost fifty years. Although the colorpoint gene is recessive and breeds true, the dominant white spotting (piebald) gene has very variable expression, making it difficult to consistently produce Showshoes with the preferred patterns. Cats with only one copy of the white spotting gene may have as little as a locket and white tail tip, but lack the desired white feet, whereas cats with two copies may be almost completely white with colored markings on the head and tail. All degrees of white spotting between these two extremes can be produced, making it difficult to predict the appearance of offspring even though both parents may have the correct pattern.

The gene that produces the inverted "V" on the face appears to be incompletely dominant. A cat inheriting two such genes usually has an undesirably large amount of white on the face. The white gloves and boots are due either to the white spotting (piebald) gene or to a related "gloving" gene. Variant (nonstandard) Snowshoes have white that extends too far up the legs, white that does not extend far enough, or asymmetrical markings. Cats with too much or too little white, or with colored toes, still have the Snowshoe temperament and make excellent pets. This variability makes every Snowshoe, whether exhibition or pet quality, a unique individual.

Although visually similar in pattern, the American lines of Snowshoe are not related to the longer-haired Birman or Ragdoll. However, in the United Kingdom and Europe, new bloodlines were founded using Ragdolls as outcrosses due to the impossibility of importing American-bred Snowshoes. To expand the gene pool, some American registries permit outcrossing to the Siamese and American Shorthair. The American Shorthair is not recognized in the United Kingdom or Europe, necessitating the use of other outcross breeds instead.

The Snowshoe arrived in the United Kingdom in 1980, and a dedicated breeding program began in 1986, but by 1998 only one breeder and five cats remained. Its progress was also hampered by a misconception that it was a "Shorthaired Birman." In 2002, cats from Germany were imported to reinvigorate the breed. It proved impossible to obtain Snowshoes from the United States, and American Shorthairs are not found in the United Kingdom, so British breeders outcrossed Snowshoes to Ragdoll/Oriental-mix females, a Snowshoe-patterned rescue kitten of unknown ancestry, a bicolor-pointed British Shorthair, and a sealpoint Ragdoll male. Descendents of these cats can now be found in Snowshoes all over Europe.

In Europe, Snowshoes have been recognized by the FIFe since 2004. In the United Kingdom, they have preliminary recognition with the GCCF.

The Snowshoe is sometimes likened to a snowflake or to "pebbles on a beach"—no two are alike, either in pattern or in personality.

Physical description: As the name suggests, the outstanding feature of the Snowshoe breed is its four white feet. The Snowshoe also has striking splashes of white on the muzzle and chest. The body is semi-foreign in conformation, neither oriental nor cobby, but is intermediate between the American Shorthair and the Siamese. The long legs are muscular and in proportion with the medium-length, strong body, resulting in an athletic and deceptively powerful cat. These are not delicate cats; it is often remarked that they have surprising heft when lifted.

The head type is that of a moderate, early-style Siamese, with medium to medium-large ears that continue the line of the modified triangular head with gentle contours. The blue, oval-shaped eyes give a sweet expression to the face. The Snowshoe should have a smooth, short coat without noticeable undercoat.

Colors and varieties: Snowshoe point colors are seal, chocolate, fawn, blue lilac (lavender), and tabby (lynx). The FIFe also recognizes the red series of colors (red, cream, and tortoiseshell, and the tabby versions of these colors), and TICA recognizes all possible pointed colors including silver and smoke varieties. The colored points should be clearly defined and contrast with the paler body color. There is less contrast in the paler colors such as red, cream, and fawn. In common with other colorpointed cats, the body is darker along the back and paler on the chest and underside, and older cats tend to have darker bodies. Snowshoe kittens are born white, developing colored points in the first three weeks of life, and it may take up to two years for a Snowshoe to develop its full color, especially in the dilute colors.

Mitted Snowshoes have the white limited to the paws, hind legs, chest, and chin; typically, one quarter of the body is white. Bicolor Snowshoes have the addition of the white facial pattern and other white markings on the body (which may be difficult to discern against the pale body color). The body may be one-quarter to one-half white ("high white"), although less white is preferred for exhibition cats. Unrecognized Snowshoe patterns (variant or "nonstandard" Snowshoes) are harlequin (mostly white with colored patches) and colorpointed-without-white.

Temperament: An active, friendly, and playful cat, this breed makes an excellent family pet because little seems to faze them. They are attentive to family members and get along well with children

Snowshoe kitten

and with other pets. Some Snowshoes are shy, while others are more extrovert and assertive. Some seem to adopt the role of feline nursemaid to their chosen human. They do not like to be left alone for long periods of time.

Snowshoes quickly learn how to play "fetch" and enjoy climbing frames, especially those with tunnels and resting platforms, because they enjoy surveying the household from a high place. They are very intelligent and can learn to open doors or do tricks. Some Snowshoes enjoy playing with water and may even try to join their owners in the bath or shower.

Activity level: High

Vocal level: Moderate; some Snowshoes are very chatty, although their voices are not as loud or strident as the breed's Siamese ancestors.

Special needs: None; their short coat is easy to keep in condition. The mix of American Shorthair and Siamese (and other breeds in Europe) means Snowshoes are generally healthy cats. Buyers should be wary of Snowshoes sold as "CFA registered" because this breed is not yet recognized by the CFA.

Variations: Due to outcrossing, some European lines of Snowshoe may carry the recessive gene for long hair and may produce semi-longhair variants. Other well-known breeds with a mitted colorpoint pattern include Birmans and Ragdolls. Lesser-known breeds with this pattern include:

- Piawaian Kucing Malaysia (Malaysian Piawaian Cat): similar to the Tonkinese in conformation and to the Ragdoll in pattern; this homegrown Malaysian breed generally resembles the Snowshoe.
- Seychellois: bicolor-pointed Siamese, bred and recognized in Europe; like the Snowshoe Siamese, these have the extreme Oriental conformation.
- Snowshoe Siamese: Siamese with white feet; these differ from mitted Snowshoes in having the extreme Siamese conformation. Despite the similarity of name, this should not be confused with the Snowshoe.
- Snow-Toes: Himalayans with white feet, bred in the 1960s from crossing Himalayans to Birmans.
- Tibetan (Nepalese, Nepalayan): mitted colorpoint polydactylous breed with the cobby, short-faced conformation of Persian Longhairs and Exotic Shorthairs, developed in New Zealand.

Sokoke

Place of origin: Denmark; Kenya

History: The Sokoke was developed in Denmark from cats found in greater Arabuko-Sokoke Forest Preserve, in the coastal region of Kenya. It was previously known as the African Shorthair, but is only native to this one region within Kenya. The Sokoke had already become a natural breed when discovered by cat fanciers and lived among Giriama tribal elders, who called it Khadzonzo, literally "looks like tree bark," because of the pattern of the coat.

Theories abound as to the origins of cats in the Sokoke region: independent evolution from a local strain of African Wild Cat or descended from domestic cats introduced by Portuguese sailors or from British settlers. DNA testing as part of the Cat Genome Project found it to be related to the Asian group of breeds and related to the Arabian wild cat (with which domestic cats can interbreed).

In 1978, a British/Kenyan woman found some feral Sokoke kittens on a coconut plantation. She allowed them to breed and showed them to a Danish friend who imported a pair into Denmark in 1984. More followed in 1991, and these formed the "Old Line" foundation for the Sokoke (or Afro-Danish Sokoke) breed recognized by the FIFe soon after. When inbreeding became a problem, progressive breeders proposed outcrossing to Oriental and Russian Shorthairs while more conservative breeders sought foundation Sokoke cats imported from Kenya.

Luckily, in 2000, a British/Kenyan resident in the region obtained several Sokokes from near the Arabuko-Sokoke Preserve through her native gardener. These became the "New Line" and were registered with the FIFe in Europe in 2003 and with TICA in the United States in 2004. Outcrossing is no longer allowed, but Sokoke cats may still be imported from Kenya as foundation cats. The breed is becoming increasingly rare in its homeland due to mongrelization with street cats.

Physical description: The Sokoke has a modified wedge-shaped head with medium-large tufted ears and almond shaped amber to light green eyes. The head looks small compared to the body. It has a medium-long, slender body and medium boning, but is surprisingly muscular. The hind legs are longer than the forelegs and are well angled; this is another distinctive breed characteristic—the cats have a tip-toe gait, but the back remains level (leading to comparisons with the wild cheetah).

These cats tend to feel rigid when alert. The coat is very short and glossy, with a rather hard texture and minimal undercoat.

Sokoke cats are found in two types that can occur in the same litter. The first type is leggier and more svelte, whereas the second type has a rounder head and heavier boning. These differences are more obvious in young cats than in adults. Males may be considerably larger than females. Old Line Sokokes tend to have a hard, thin, stiff-feeling tail. New Line cats lack the hard tail, although the Old and New Lines are being interbred to preserve the trait.

The Sokoke differs from other domestic purebreds due to its behavior and its color and pattern. The "see-through tabby" pattern is akin to the "marble" pattern of the Bengal and is also sometimes seen in random-bred cats.

Colors and varieties: The only recognized color is black tabby in a modified classic tabby pattern. Agouti regions are present within the black markings, giving a modified tabby, marbled, or clouded pattern sometimes called "see-through tabby." Sokokes sometimes produce tabby colorpoint kittens (Snow Sokokes), solid blacks, blue solid/tabby, and semi-longhairs probably inherited from outcross cats.

Temperament: The Sokoke is intelligent, active, and nonaggressive. It is playful and family-oriented and forms close bonds with other cats and with its human family. This bonding means Sokokes may take longer to settle into new homes. It is also a very interactive cat, demanding attentions from its family. Although a Sokoke loves to be near its humans, it prefers to be high up rather than on a lap. Sokokes can keep themselves and each other amused for hours with small toys, and they are prone to hiding a toy and then retrieving it at a later date. They often enjoy playing with water.

Activity level: Moderate to high

Vocal level: Moderate to high; Sokokes have a rather strong voice and can be talkative.

Special needs: Due to its geographic origins, the Sokoke appears to have limited resistance to common New World cat illnesses and to be less well adapted to cold climates. Their short coat needs little additional care. Many owners report their Sokokes to enjoy sand-bathing.

Sphynx

Place of origin: Ontario, Canada; Minnesota, United States

History: Hairless cat have been reported from around the world throughout history. The most famous of these historical hairless cats were Dick and Nellie, a brother and sister pair of Mexican Hairless cats obtained by a New Mexico couple from local Pueblo Indians in 1902. Unlike the modern Sphynx, the extinct Mexican Hairless grew fur along their backs in winter.

Hairless cats born in France in 1930 died without reproducing. In 1936, several hairless kittens were born to a pet cat in North Carolina. In 1938 and in 1950, hairless kittens were born to Siamese cats in Paris, France. These were bred among themselves as a genetics study, resulting in hairless offspring but were not developed as a breed. Cat lovers at the time considered hairless cats unaesthetic.

The history of the modern Sphynx (Canadian Hairless) began in the 1966 when a hairless kitten called Prune was born to a domestic cat in Toronto, Canada. He was mated to his mother, resulting in further hairless kittens, and it was established that the trait was due to a recessive gene. Prune's bloodline was bred, successfully at first, but the breeding was discontinued in the late 1970s due to poor fertility and serious health problems. The Sphynx breed was initially recognized by the CFA in 1970, but recognition later lapsed.

In 1978, the last two cats from Prune's bloodline, a brother and sister, went to the Netherlands. The male was uninterested in mating and the pair's only litter did not survive. In 1978 and 1980, further hairless kittens were discovered among street cats in Toronto. Two hairless females born in 1980 were sent to the Netherlands to join the last of the original bloodline. Although one female conceived, she lost the litter and, by then, Prune's last male descendent had been neutered. No modern Sphynx are traceable to Prune.

The only recourse was to outcross the hairless cats to other breeds. Although the offspring would be furred, they would carry the hairlessness gene. Doing so would also combat the problems caused by inbreeding. The Sphynx was crossed to sparse-furred Devon Rex variants (DNA analysis in 2010 has since shown that Devon Rex and Sphynx are variants of the same gene) and also to Siamese, American Shorthairs, and domestic shorthairs to expand the gene pool. Hairless cats from domestic cat litters were located in North America and test-mated to the Sphynx; those who were genetically compatible also expanded the gene pool. The best known of these were two hairless female kittens (Epidermis and Dermis) born to barn cats in Minnesota in 1975 and 1976.

Hairless cats found in domestic cat litters are still used to expand the Sphynx gene pool. These include hairless cats found in Texas, Arkansas, and Indiana. Some of these produce extremely hairless offspring due to interacting genes, but others have left no recorded descendents. Some proved genetically incompatible with the Sphynx. In one case, the

owners were unwilling to allow the cats to be used for breeding. In Europe, the Sphynx has also been outcrossed to Cornish and German Rex. Careful selective breeding and outcrossing has ensured the Sphynx is a healthy breed.

Although the Sphynx was initially developed as a potentially hypoallergenic breed, studies have demonstrated that hairlessness did not prevent an allergic response in many owners. This is because cat allergy is not caused by the fur itself, but is caused by the Fel d1 protein secreted in feline saliva

Sphynx

The Elf is a curl-eared Sphynx.

and deposited during grooming. Because there is less surface area for saliva to dry on, some allergy sufferers find they are better able to tolerate Sphynx than haired breeds.

TICA recognized the Sphynx for championship competition in 1986, with several other North American cat associations following suit during the 1990s. In 1998, the CFA once again recognized the Sphynx. The Sphynx arrived in the United Kingdom in 1988. In 1990, the GCCF refused to recognize the breed on the basis that it was not viable in a normal pet. Although unable to exhibit Sphynxes at GCCF shows, breeders were undeterred, and the GCCF eventually recognized the Sphynx in 2006.

Although the Sphynx is recognized in Europe by the FIFe, the Council of Europe's Convention for the Protection of Pet Animals (1995) legislation impacts the breeding of Sphynx in member states that have signed the convention. The legislation recommends a total ban on breeding cats who have curled (useless), shortened, or absent vibrissae (whiskers and other tactile hairs) on the basis that these are an essential sensory organ important for orientation in the dark, in predation, in examination of objects, and in social behavior.

Physical description: The Sphynx is not completely hairless. Rather, the cat is covered in a soft downy fur that is especially evident on the face, tail, outer edges of the ears, and feet. This gives a soft, chamois-like feel to the cat. The skin wrinkles around the face, between the ears, and on the shoulders. Whiskers and eyebrows are either absent or broken. The head features prominent cheekbones, large ears that are wide at the base, and a definite whisker break that accentuates the muzzle. The eyes are large and lemon-shaped. The body is hard and muscular, with a rounded chest and rump and a full, round abdomen. Observing a Sphynx in motion provides a unique opportunity to study feline anatomy in detail.

Colors and varieties: All colors are possible, with the pigmentation of the skin reflecting the cat's color.

Temperament: These gremlinlike cats love to be on laps and to crawl under the bedcovers with you, both as a sign of affection and as a mechanism for keeping warm. They can often be found in other warm spots, such as sunny windowsills and on top of computer monitors and TV sets. Inquisitive, intelligent, and playful, these friendly cats never fail to amuse their owners. They are highly active cats who can entertain themselves for hours and many learn to play "fetch" with small toys. They enjoy the company of other cats and pets, and their friendly, outgoing nature means they readily accept new people in their lives.

Activity level: High

Vocal level: Medium

Special needs: Because hair growth does not pull skin secretions (sebum) from the skin, all Sphynx cats need to be bathed with a suitable cat shampoo and their ears cleaned with a moist cloth regularly to prevent these secretions from accumulating on the skin and in the hair follicles. Sphynx should be provided with warm areas to crawl into and should be protected from excessive cold or unfiltered sunlight, as they may sunburn. Because they do not have fur to protect their skin, their nails should be kept well groomed, and they should be kept from exposure to sharp objects in their environment to prevent scratches. Rough play with other pets in the household can lead to skin injuries as well.

Variations: Until 1987, the Canadian-bred Sphynx was the sole hairless breed in the cat fancy. Although incompatible hairlessness mutations were found during development of the Sphynx, these were not perpetuated. An unrelated mutation in Russia resulted in the Donskoy (1987) and its derivative breeds, the Peterbald (1993) and the Ukrainian Levkoy (2005).

In 2002, the Hawaiian Hairless (Kohana) appeared among feral cats in Hawaii. They were claimed to be the only completely hairless cats as they lacked hair follicles and had a skin texture like rubber. Early reports suggested it was the result of mating a Donskoy to a Canadian Sphynx and the interaction of the two different genes, but in 2010, DNA analysis confirmed the Kohana to have the same hairlessness mutation as the Sphynx, with the other effects being due to interactions with other genes. The Kohana appears to have died out due to reproductive problems and other health issues, again possibly associated with inbreeding.

In 2004, the Cheops was derived from Canadian lines of the American Cornish Rex. It has a very short, fine coat, approximately over the head, neck, back, and sides and a slightly longer coat on the chest and hips, however this residual coat lacks the waviness of the Cornish Rex. The tail may have a tuft at the tip.

The Canadian Sphynx has been used to found several hairless "designer cats" such as the short-legged Minskin and Bambino breeds, the Elf (curl-eared Sphynx) and Dwelf (curl-eared, short-legged Sphynx), and the polydactylous Hemingway Sphynx.

Genetic mutation is no respecter of pedigree— hairlessness has also occurred as a spontaneous mutation in longhaired breeds such as Persians and Birmans.

Finally, two fictional hairless "breeds" are the Egyptian Hairless Cat (a hypoallergenic cat invented by the TV show *Friends*) and the Chinese Hairless Cat (based on claims made by a French breeder of Sphynx). The "Longhair Sphynx," claimed to be the powder-puff version of the breed, was a *Cat Fancy* April Fool's joke, although several cats later turned up in the United States that had long fine fur on the chest, but were otherwise almost hairless.

Tonkinese

Place of origin: Thailand

History: According to Thai legend, the pointed Siamese cat represents royalty and power, whereas the Burmese cat represents holiness and spirituality. The interbreeding of these two color forms of the native Thai cat is not uncommon in their native country, providing the historic foundation of what much later became known as the Tonkinese breed. Before the selective breeding programs of twentieth-century cat fanciers, the Siamese, Tonkinese, and Burmese might have been mistaken for three coat patterns of a single breed (the conformation of the Siamese and Burmese did not properly diverge until the 1970s).

Nineteenth-century descriptions demonstrate that all three varieties, with their different eye colors, along with early Korats, were imported and termed *Siamese*. Both Harrison Weir (1889) and Frances Simpson (1903) described "Chocolate Siamese" (not to be confused with chocolate point Siamese!) whose pattern matches the "natural mink" pattern (also called sable or brown mink).

The foundation cat of the Burmese breed, the walnut-brown cat Wong Mau, along with those other early "Chocolate Siamese" imports, were genetically natural (brown) mink. In the 1930s, Wong Mau produced both pointed and mink pattern offspring when mated to a sealpoint Siamese. To do so, she had to carry genes for both the Siamese and Burmese pointing patterns, meaning that she was effectively a naturally occurring Tonkinese.

The popularity of these "in-between" patterned cats with pet lovers between the 1930s and 1950s was an obstacle to the development and acceptance of a "pure" Burmese breed because some breeders (realizing their commercial appeal) continued to use mink pattern cats in their breeding programs rather than create sufficient numbers of pure-breeding Burmese.

In the 1950s, a New York pet shop owner bred Sealpoint Siamese with Sable Burmese for several generations, calling these "Golden Siamese" and selling them as pets. He had seen several cats with rich brown bodies and darker points that were intermediate between the Siamese and Burmese. These were destroyed by many Burmese breeders because they did not breed true. His Golden Siamese proved popular pets during the 1950s and 1960s, but he discontinued breeding, having apparently proven that they could breed true.

In the mid-1960s, a breeder in New Jersey and another in Canada independently crossed Burmese to Siamese cats. Both produced a line of brown cats with darker points and aquamarine eyes, later combining their breeding programs and writing the "Tonkanese" breed standard. They called the brown pattern "natural mink" because it resembled an undyed mink pelt, and it was later joined by blue and honey varieties. The "Tonkanese" was recognized by the Canadian Cat Association (CCA) in 1965; in 1971, the breed was renamed Tonkinese. It was recognized by the CFF in 1975 and the CFA in 1978.

In the United Kingdom, it was first recognized by the Cat Association of Great Britain. It was recognized in 1991 by the GCCF a year later. In Europe, the FIFe does not yet recognize the Tonkinese, so European breeders register their cats with TICA instead. It was recognized by the South African Cat Association in 2000 and is also recognized in Australia and New Zealand. In Australia, the Tonkinese faced opposition from Siamese and Burmese fanciers because it was a "crossbreed" and did not breed true.

Since the 1980s, these cats have a sufficiently large established gene pool that crossing to their parental breeds is no longer strictly necessary. To keep the gene pool diverse, many registries permit outcrossing to Siamese, American Burmese, and/or European Burmese. Tonkinese bred in associations that do not permit outcrossing may have smaller litters due to higher levels of inbreeding. The Tonkinese is believed to be clear of the lethal head defect gene carried by some lines of Burmese in the United States.

In the early days, the name was spelled "Tonkanese," alluding to the residents of a fictional island in the musical South Pacific where "half-breeds" suffered

no discrimination. The modern spelling, Tonkinese, suggests the Tonkin region of Indochina, not far from its Siamese and Burmese sister breeds.

The mink-patterned Tonkinese inherits one gene for Siamese color restriction and one gene for Burmese color restriction. As a result, it exhibits an intermediate pattern. By definition, a Tonkinese is heterozygous; that is, the pattern is produced by inheriting one of each gene. When bred together, mink Tonkinese also produce colorpointed variants and Burmese-patterned variants as well as mink pattern cats; however, these do not have the conformation of either the Siamese or Burmese and are registered as variant or nonstandard Tonkinese.

Once dismissed as a "poor quality Siamese," the mink and pointed Tonkinese continue to appeal to cat lovers seeking the older, less extreme style of Siamese. The solid Tonkinese variant resembles the early Burmese, being more foreign in conformation. Tonkinese are not simply Siamese–Burmese crosses; after several generations, these cats have a look and character all their own. To its aficionados, it is a modern recreation of an ancient variety.

Physical description: A "medium" cat in every way, breeders strive for the elusive perfect middle point between the elegance and length of the Siamese and the more rounded conformation of the Burmese. North American standards call for substantially built, strong cats. European standards call for medium build and foreign type. These differences result from the more foreign conformation of the

Tonkinese

European Burmese used in European Tonkinese development compared to the cobby, rounder-headed American Burmese (which is not recognized in Europe). Tonkinese are muscular and surprisingly hefty cats. Males weigh from 8 to 12 pounds (3.5–5.5 kg) females 6 to 8 pounds (3–3.5 kg).

In the United States, the head is a modified, rounded wedge with open, almond-shaped eyes and medium-sized, wide-set ears. European standards call for a moderately proportioned wedge, more foreign in type than American lines. In Australia, breeders have combined Australian, New Zealand, North American, and British/European bloodlines, which they have outcrossed to American Burmese to create their own, subtly different, "Australian Tonkinese" look. The short coat is close-lying with a glossy sheen. Tonkinese can be late developers, coming into their best around two years old.

Colors and varieties: The three Tonkinese patterns are mink, solid (Burmese pattern), and pointed (Siamese pattern). Mink Tonkinese have shaded "points" that are a darker version of their body color. Mink is intermediate between Burmese and Siamese, with less contrast between body and legs than Siamese, but more contrast than Burmese. Mink is the preferred pattern for show-quality Tonkinese. Just like the Siamese, the torso of the pointed and mink Tonkinese tends to darken with age; those living in cooler climates also tend to be darker.

In North America, only the four basic colors—seal (also called natural), chocolate (champagne), lilac (platinum), and blue—are recognized. Elsewhere (and depending on the registering body), the Tonkinese is recognized in brown, blue, chocolate, cinnamon, lilac, red, cream, blue-based caramel, lilac-based caramel, apricot, and in the tortoiseshell, tabby, and tortie-tabby (torbie) versions of those colors. This wider palette is due to the wider range of colors inherited from the European Burmese.

Eye color is linked to coat color: solid Tonkinese having gold or golden-green eyes; minks having aqua eyes; and pointed Tonkinese having shades of blue.

On average, mink-to-mink matings produce 50 percent mink kittens, 25 percent pointed and 25 percent solid. Solid-to-pointed matings produce only mink kittens. Mink-to-solid produces 50 percent mink and 50 percent solid. Mink-to-pointed produces 50 percent mink and 50 percent pointed. Although considered pet quality by most registries, the pointed and solid Tonkinese variants inherit the same conformation and charming personality as their mink pattern brethren.

Temperament: Friendly, active, affectionate, and companionable, these cats love to play. The game of "fetch" seems to come naturally to them. Curious and intelligent, the Tonkinese loves to be involved in household activities and enjoy interactive play as well as lap time and shoulder-riding. They are gregarious and get on well with children, dogs, and other pets.

The Tonkinese combines traits from both parent breeds. Although active and chatty, its voice is less strident, and it is less highly strung or demanding, than the Siamese. However, a bored or lonely Tonkinese can become mischievous. Some enthusiasts claim that pointed variants inherit more personality traits from the Siamese, whereas solid variants are more similar in character to Burmese.

This breed has a wonderful reputation in the animal therapy community due to their tolerant nature, willingness to please, and trainability.

Activity level: High

Vocal level: High

Special needs: The Tonkinese is a robust cat who is easy to care for. An occasional grooming with a rubber brush to remove shed hair, followed by stroking the coat with a chamois cloth, will keep coat sleek and in top condition.

Variations: Over the decades, several names have been proposed for semi-longhaired Tonkinese and mink pattern Persian Longhairs, bred by crossing Tonkinese or Burmese to Himalayans (Colorpoint Persian Longhairs). The names proposed have included Burmalayan, Himbur, Iranese, Layanese, Silkanese, Tibetane (Tibetaan in Dutch), and Tonkalayan. Thus far, only the Tibetaan and Tonkinese Longhair appear to have any form of recognition.

Toyger

Place of origin: California, United States

History: In the late 1980s, the daughter of the Bengal breed founder noticed that one of her Bengal cats had two spots of tabby markings on its temples, unusual in domestic tabbies and reminiscent of the circular pattern on a tiger's head. Instead of developing this as part of the Bengal breed, she envisaged a cat who would resemble a miniature baby tiger, both in color and type.

The foundation cats were a mackerel tabby domestic shorthair, a Bengal, and a street cat from Kashmir, India, imported in 1993. This Indian cat had spots between his ears rather than the usual striped pattern. The goal was a large, long-bodied cat with bold, vertical "candle-flame" (braided) pattern and facial markings akin to those of a tiger and a laid-back temperament. Hybridization with the Asian leopard cat in the Bengal breed had resulted in a unique expression of the mackerel tabby pattern.

During the early stages of its development, the Toyger was conceptualized using computer graphics to give a clear idea of the aims of the breeding program. This "toy tiger" received an overwhelmingly positive reaction from both the cat fancy and the pet-owning public. TICA recognized the Toyger in 1993 and awarded it championship status in 2007. They were imported into the United Kingdom in 2004.

A newly noted recessive mutation causing unusually short, rounded ears (from a cat born in Italy named Faan) is in the initial stages of being incorporated into this breed to distinguish it even further from the Bengal. Breeders are also aiming for a more tigerlike body color and facial conformation.

Scaled-down versions of big cats are currently very popular. The Cheetoh is another Bengal-derivative resembling a wild species. It derives from crossing Bengals and Ocicats to produce a large, long-legged, spotted breed with a low-shouldered, prowling gait reminiscent of a wild cheetah. The six recognized colors are the Black/Brown Spotted Sienna (tawny hues), the Black/Brown Spotted Tan (gray-brown hues), the Black Spotted Smoke, the Black Spotted Silver, and the Lynx Pointed Gold Spotted Snow (colorpointed with gray-brown or buff extremities). It is intelligent, trainable, curious, highly energetic, and loyal to its owner. The Cheetoh currently has experimental status with TICA.

Physical description: The Toyger is a medium-sized, muscular, and long-bodied cat with bold, vertical "candle-flame" (or "braided tabby") markings akin to those of a tiger. Its eyes are small to medium size, circular, and slightly hooded. Like a wild tiger, the tail should be long and blunt tipped, set and carried low. The overall impression is a low-slung, powerful look with big bones, high shoulders, and a tigerlike gait.

Perhaps the first breed to be conceptualized on the computer as a graphic image in its earliest stages of development, the Toyger has only just begun to realize the vision of its founder. However, the overwhelmingly positive reaction of the cat fancy and the public to this new breed has led to its rapid advancement to championship status in a major US cat association, the International Cat Association.

Colors and varieties: This breed is only recognized in the black braided tabby pattern on a highly rufoused background. The horizontally distorted pattern, resembling the braided stripes of the tiger, are unique to this breed and resemble randomly placed vertically stretched rosettes, often broken or branched. It should have facial markings circularly aligned around the face, pale or white "spectacles," and pale ocelli ("thumb prints") on the backs of the ears. The belly, chest, throat, cheeks, and inside of legs should be pale or white. Like the Bengal, a glittered pelt is desirable as long as it does not obscure the contrast of the markings.

Temperament: Even further removed from its wild cat roots than other hybrid breeds, these cats are sweet-natured and affectionate. Very playful and outgoing, but occasionally head-strong, these "baby tigers" need firm, loving guidance in their raising. They get on well with other pets. Their intelligence means they are easy to train, and they can be taught to walk on a leash or play "fetch."

Activity level: High

Vocal level: High

Special needs: None

Variations: None

Turkish Angora

Place of origin: Turkey

History: One of the original breeds in the early days of the organized cat fancy, the Turkish Angora

(Ankara Kedisi) was quickly overtaken in popularity by the Persian Longhair in the early twentieth century. These longhaired cats of the Middle East share the name "Angora" with other longhaired animals, such as the Angora goat and Angora rabbit, although some books of the mid-nineteenth century also refer to these cats as Angora Cats or Asiatic Cats. Hence, the name refers as much to the long, silky fur as to the breed's purported origins in the Ankara Province of Turkey.

Much of the early history of the Turkish Angora is shared with the Persian Longhair. In the 1800s, the naturalist Pallas suggested that the Angora was descended from the Pallas's Cat (*Felis manul*) of middle Asia, but this was refuted in 1907 by the Royal Zoological Society based on differences in the skulls of the domestic cat and Pallas's Cat and the lack of viable hybrids between domestic cats and Pallas's Cat. Later DNA studies found no link to the Pallas's Cat, and the long hair is due to a recessive gene mutation that adapted domestic cats to Ankara's cold, snowy winters. During the nineteenth century, Angora (a generic term for longhaired) cats were reported, and imported, from Russia, Persia (Iran), and Turkey.

Angora cats arrived in Italy and France during the early 1500s and were named after the Turkish city of Angora (Ankhara). Further longhairs were imported in the early 1600s from Persia into Italy by Pietro della Valle, and from Turkey into France by Nicholas-Claude Fabri de Peiresc at around the same time. An Angora cat is depicted in Buffon's "Natural History" (1756), and Buffon described "*Catus Angorensis*" as belonging to the province of Chorazan and having long, silky, gray hair that was darker on the head and back and almost white on the belly (quite probably the color now known as Black Smoke). The most beautiful aspect of these cats was their plumy tail with hair five or six inches long. He did not distinguish between the Angora and Persian cats.

Turkish Angora cats, in particular the solid white variety, reached Britain from France, but were interbred with Persian and Russian Longhairs, with the result that the Turkish Angora vanished from the cat fancy relatively early on, replaced by the thicker set Persian with its woollier coat. The breed standards written in the nineteenth century favored the more popular round-headed and cobby-bodied cats, although the terms *Persian* and *Angora* were often used interchangeably by early breeders. French cat writer Fernand Mery would later comment that this preference for cobby animals was an English peculiarity.

In 1896, Jean Bungartz referred to the Angora as *Felis maniculata domesticus angorensis* in his *Illustrated Book of Cats* and called it the most beautiful and best known of the foreign cats, with a calm and aristocratic nature. He wrote that outwardly it resembled a lion because of the full mane hanging from its face, neck, and chest. Angora cats seemed, to him, to be conscious their beauty.

Harrison Weir described Angora cats in *Our Cats and All About Them* (1889). He believed them to be great favorites with the Turks and Armenians (other writers of the time suggested the exact opposite, believing they helped spread plague), with the blue-eyed white variety being the most valued. The slate colors, light fawns, deep reds, and mottled gray apparently blended well with Eastern (i.e., Turkish) furniture and other surroundings. He particularly mentioned the silver and smoke colors, but had never seen imported strong-colored tabbies and did not believe they existed in the true Angora breed. They had a small head (in comparison to British Shorthair cats) and rather large ears with tufted tips. Their coat differed from both the Persian and the Russian Longhair in being long and silky without a woolly undercoat.

Helen Winslow, an American cat lover who wrote *Concerning Cats* in 1900, added that the body was longer than that of the ordinary cat in proportion to its size and that the Angora was extremely graceful and covered with long, silky, crinkly hair. She likened its tail to an ostrich plume. The suppleness of the Angora's tail was considered a sign of fine breeding. A high-bred (i.e., pedigree) Angora allowed its tail to be doubled or twisted without the cat noticing! Unlike Weir, Winslow mentioned tabby Angoras.

Despite these glowing descriptions from the United States and Britain, the Turkish Angora was

Turkish Angora

primarily used to improve the Persian Longhair breed. It was crossed indiscriminately with the other longhaired imports and with the more robust-bodied British Shorthairs, so that by 1903 the Persian had supplanted the Angora on the show bench and the Turkish Angora vanished from the Western cat fancy.

The Angora breed remained extinct in outside of Turkey until after the Second World War. Turkey, however, considered these graceful cats a national treasure, and a breeding program was established at Ankara Zoo to preserve it. Ankara Zoo concentrated on solid white cats with blue eyes, orange eyes, and the highly valued odd eyes, as well as on genetic soundness. They kept detailed records of the breeding program but were reluctant to allow any cats to be exported. In the 1950s, visiting American servicemen discovered these cats at Ankara Zoo and sent news of them back to the United States. The first recorded imports into the United States were in 1954. In 1962, a pair of solid white Turkish Angoras was imported into the United States to found a breeding program there. More cats followed during the 1960s and 1970s, allowing the Turkish Angora breed to become established breed in North America. Meanwhile, other Turkish cat were exported to Britain and Sweden, although only the Turkish Van, once thought to be a "true-breeding color variety" of Turkish Angora, achieved breed recognition in Britain.

In the mid-1960s, Turkish Angoras in the United States reached sufficient numbers to be recognized by the CFA. Initially, only the solid white Turkish Angoras were recognized as a breed in 1970. The other colors had to wait until 1978 for recognition as part of the Turkish Angora breed. All Turkish Angoras registered by the CFA must be able to trace their ancestry back to Turkey. Although solid whites remain popular, breeders began to focus on the other colors that had been hidden by the dominant white gene.

In Britain, an unrelated breed was known as the Angora until 2003, when it became the Oriental Longhair (also called Javanese or Mandarin in some parts of Europe). This British Angora had been developed to recreate the look of the Angora ancestors of the Persian Longhair and was more foreign in type, with a longer, narrower head and larger ears than the Turkish Angora. The possibility of importing Turkish Angoras was considered, but a British preoccupation with bureaucracy apparently prevailed—the GCCF was apparently unwilling to accept the documentary evidence (verification of breed) supplied by the Ankhara Zoo. The alternative was to import cats from North American lines, but this would have meant a six-month stay in a quarantine facility. Although the Turkish Angora is now bred in Britain, the GCCF does not yet recognize it as a breed so it must be registered and exhibited with the FIFe or TICA.

Intriguingly, DNA studies during 2007 found the Turkish Angora to be related to random-bred cats from Tunisia and Turkey, but more distantly related to the Turkish Van, despite their geographical proximity. A naturally occurring variety called the Anatolian (Anadolu Kedisi, Turkish Shorthair), which has been interbred with both the Turkish Angora and Turkish Van, has also been exported from Turkey. Anatolians can produce longhaired offspring due to recessive genes, and some of those are believed to have been registered as Turkish Angoras.

The term *Angora* is used among animal breeders to refer to a long, silky coat regardless of a breed's geographical origin. In addition to the Turkish Angora there is a German Angora and an Angora German Rex. Historically, there have been Russian Angoras and British Angoras

Physical description: The Turkish Angora is sometimes called the ballerina of the cat fancy.

Turkish Angora kitten

Turkish Angoras with differently colored eyes are particularly desirable.

It is medium-sized, finely boned, and graceful, but its delicate looks are deceptive because it is a surprisingly muscular and athletic breed. The long, elegant body and neck sets off the distinctive, smallish, modified wedge-shaped head with its two-plane profile, large walnut- or almond-shaped eyes, and large, upright ears set high on the head.

The Angora does not have a wooly coat, but a fine, silky coat that has been compared to cornsilk. The long tail is not bushy, but rather has the appearance of a long, elegant ostrich plume. The tail is often carried low, but not trailing the ground; when the cat is happy, it is carried upright or even brought forward, so much so that the tip may appear to almost touch the head.

The distinctive ruff around the neck has been called the "Queen Elizabeth ruffle." The ruff, britches, tail, and belly fur have a tendency to crinkle. A full winter coat has medium length, fine, silky hair with a mane, britches, and fully plumed tail. The coat may take two years to reach its full glory.

Colors and varieties: The most popular color is

white, with amber, gold, green, or blue eyes. Odd-eyed cats are particularly desirable, with one eye blue and the other amber, gold, or green. The breed has also been developed in a wide variety of solid, bicolor, tabby, silver, and tortoiseshell coat colors. It is recognized in every color except for colorpointed, lavender (lilac), and cinnamon, all of which would indicate outcrossing to Siamese.

Temperament: The Turkish Angora is a sensitive, highly intelligent cat who is affectionate toward her human family. These cats crave attention and demand to participate in activities around the home. This can result in attention-getting behavior and mischief if they feel ignored.

They are graceful, energetic, and outgoing. Their extraordinary leaping ability makes them exciting cats to play with, with imitation bird toys being particularly popular. It also means they can be found on high shelves and the tops of doors, supervising the household from on high.

Activity level: High

Vocal level: Moderate

Special needs: Their long coats require less attention than many other longhaired breeds, although a regular combing with a fine-tooth comb or slicker brush will remove shed hairs and prevent mats from forming. Some owners like to follow this by bathing their Turkish Angora.

A significant portion of white cats (of any breed) are deaf, and because white is the most popular color of this breed, deaf Turkish Angoras are relatively common, especially those who have unilaterally or bilaterally blue eyes. Deaf cats adapt very easily to their sensory deficit, and many owners aren't even aware that their cats are deaf. If a cat is deaf, care should be taken to not startle her; for instance, before touching the cat, alert her to your presence by touching the surface the cat is resting on to create a vibration.

Variations: None

Turkish Van

Place of origin: Van Lake Basin, Eastern Turkey; Western Armenia

History: This ancient breed has existed for centuries in Eastern Anatolia, but only came to the notice of the cat fancy in 1955 when two British tourists brought back a male and a female cat who were primarily white in color, with an auburn (red) tail and auburn markings on the head. Three more cats were imported in the 1950s and 1970s. When bred together, these cats produced kittens with very similar markings.

The Van (or Seychelles) pattern is caused by the white spotting gene common to many cat breeds and was previously known as "harlequin." Expression of this gene varies from white lockets (Grade 1 to 2) to solid white (Grade 10); cats with two copies of the gene having higher degrees of white on their bodies. The exhibition-quality Turkish Van (Grade 8 to 9) has colors restricted to the head and the tail. The consistency of the Turkish Van's markings leads some to suggest it is a mutation of the white spotting gene, but the occurrence of nonstandard Vans, either solid white or with additional color patches, tends to contradict this.

Adaptation to the seasonal extremes of the Eastern Anatolian region has produced a cat who is semi-longhaired, with a mane in winter, but much shorter coated in summer. It was once considered a true-breeding color form of the Turkish Angora, but DNA studies in 2007 found the Turkish Van to be closely related to Egyptian cats, but a more distant relation of the Turkish Angora.

Although the preferred variety in Turkey is a solid white cat with blue, gold, or odd eyes, it was the auburn-and-white variety that became known as Turkish Van in the cat fancy. It was recognized as the "Turkish" by the GCCF in 1969, with "Van" being the breeder's prefix. In 1985, the breeder retired and her prefix lapsed, allowing the GCCF to rename the breed "Turkish Van." Initially, the GCCF only recognized the amber-eyed auburn variety. Naturally occurring cream-and-white Vans (due to recessive genes) were not recognized until 1986. In 1988, blue eyes and odd eyes were allowed. Not until 2000 were other patch colors permitted; these resulted from Vans imported from Turkey into the Netherlands to expand the gene pool during the 1980s.

The auburn-and-white Turkish Van was recognized by the FIFe in 1971, followed by cream-and-white in 1986 and the other colors in 1997. TICA recognized the different colors right from the start in 1979. Although Turkish Vans had reached the United States in the 1970s, the first breeding cats were imported from France and the Netherlands in 1983.

Some patterned Turkish Vans have a small mark between the shoulder blades. Kurdish folklore calls this "the thumbprint of God's right hand" and considers it lucky. Another local legend says the red Van pattern is where God blessed these cats as they left Noah's Ark, having kept its rat population under control.

The Turkish Van is also known as the "Kurdish Cat" or "Kurdish Van" and is used as a symbol of Kurdistan by some Kurdish nationalists. Armenians consider the breed to be an Armenian one and call it "Vana Katu." Both consider the name "Turkish" to be an attempt to suppress their cultures, although the Van predates these ethnic groups. The Van cat preferred by the Turks is solid white, whereas the Kurdish Van has the now familiar auburn markings.

In Turkey, the true Van Kedisi (Van Cat) is solid white cat, either longhaired or shorthaired, and preferably with one blue and one gold eye.

Within the cat fancy, some registries use the name Turkish Vankedisi as an umbrella term for both the patterned and solid white versions, these being interbred and the offspring registered according to pattern. Solid white Vankedisi can have different genotypes: some are due to Grade 10 expression of the white spotting gene and others are due to the dominant "white masking" gene that obscures any underlying color and pattern. Offspring of solid white Vans that do not inherit the white masking gene from either parent may be solid, bicolor, or patterned, including Van-patterned.

Due to restrictions placed on the export of the odd-eyed white Vans, few have been allowed to leave Turkey, where it is conserved due to declining numbers. In the early 1990s, Turkish authorities permitted an odd-eyed white female to be exported to the United Kingdom. This solid white variety was recognized by the GCCF in 2006 (as Turkish Vankedisi) and by TICA in 2007 (as a variety of Turkish Van). The CFA, WCF, and FIFe recognize only the Van-patterned cats.

It is claimed that the fine fur of the Turkish Van/Vankedisi holds less dander makes them less likely to cause allergies. They may be easier to bathe than other breeds, helping to reduce the amount of the allergen Fel d1 on their fur.

The Anatolian (Turkish Shorthair, Anadolu Kedisi) is the shorthaired equivalent of the Turkish Van/Vankedisi and has interbred with both the Turkish Van and Turkish Angora. It occurs in all natural colors, including Van-patterned and is said to like water even more than does the Turkish Van. Because of interbreeding with the other Turkish breeds, some Anatolians carry the recessive longhair gene and produce longhaired offspring, some of whom have been exported as Turkish Vans and Turkish Angoras. Dutch and German cat fanciers are now developing the Anatolian as a separately recognized breed.

Physical description: In contrast to the Turkish Angora, the Turkish Van/Vankedisi is a substantial cat, with a strong chest, medium long body, and muscular legs. Males are particularly imposing, their shoulders and chest being so broad it is said that they are the only domestic cats who cannot follow their heads through a gap! The medium-to-large head is a modified wedge with rounded contours and large, walnut-shape eyes. The moderately large ears are set high and wide apart and have rounded tips.

The semi-long coat is very fine and soft; the lack of woolly undercoat makes it less likely to mat than some other longhairs. The texture is often likened to cashmere and helps to make these cats waterproof. In summer, only the fox-brush tail and britches show the Turkish Van to be a semi-longhair. There is some difference between the coat of the Van cats from English/American and Dutch breeding programs, most noticeably in young cats. The Turkish Van/Vankedisi can take three to five years to reach full maturity and splendor.

The shorthaired Anatolian is similar in conformation and color except for coat length.

Colors and varieties: The Turkish Van was initially recognized only as a chalky-white cat with auburn (red or red tabby) markings. It is now recognized for competition in a wider variety of solid colors, tortoiseshell, tabby, and silver and smoke colors. Up to 20 percent of the coat (including head and tail) may be colored. This includes color extending onto the face, color extending onto the rump, and some random spotting as long as it does not detract from the Van pattern. There may be a thumbprint on left shoulder. The head markings have a white "blaze" running from the forehead to the back of the head.

The eyes may be amber, blue, or odd-eyed (one of each color). In Turkey, an odd-eyed, solid white cat is preferred, but the foundation cats imported into the United Kingdom were amber-eyed. Green-eyed Turkish Vans sometimes appear.

TICA recognizes Turkish Vans in solid white and in Van-patterned varieties. Other associations may recognize the all-white Turkish Van (Van Kedi or Vankedisi) as a separate breed or not at all.

Temperament: The most famous characteristic of this breed is its love of water. Many Vans,

Anatolian

Vankedisis, and Anatolians enjoy playing with water and some enjoy a swim when presented with the opportunity. Turkish Vans are loyal, loving, active, and highly intelligent. This means a bored or ignored cat will find ways of getting into mischief. They are great jumpers and climbers and enjoy observing the household from high vantage points. They may learn to play games of fetch with their favorite toys. They also get on well with dogs, just so long as the cat is the boss!

Turkish Vans are affectionate with their chosen special person. They tend to express this with head bumps and gentle nibbles. Although not a breed that enjoys being picked up and cuddled for long periods, they enjoy lap-time when they want it.

Activity level: Moderate

Vocal level: Low

Special needs: The coat does not require a great deal of grooming, due to the lack of undercoat. However, regular combing, especially during the spring shedding season, is recommended. Like other cats with white ears, nontoxic sun block on the ears of indoor–outdoor cats will help to avoid sunburn or skin cancer.

Variations: In its native Turkey, the Van Kedi is also recognized as a shorthaired cat, now known to the cat fancy as the Anatolian.

Chapter 6

Is a Cat Right for You?

I love cats because I enjoy my home; and little by little, they become its visible soul.

— Jean Cocteau

Before you consider whether you want a specific breed of pedigreed cat, are interested in adopting a cat from a shelter or a rescue, or will take in the stray that's been hanging around graciously indicating she would be willing to live with you, you need to take stock of your life. Ask yourself: Is a cat right for me?

To get the big picture, it's often a good idea to write down all the issues involved in owning a cat and see how you stack up. That way, you can properly evaluate your emotional wants and needs, your expectations and shortcomings, and the expectations of a feline friend. If you answer honestly, it will be abundantly clear whether you are ready to bring a feline into your life. Always remember the old adage: when in doubt, don't!

Time, Family, Space,

There are certain basic questions you need to ask yourself when determining whether getting a cat is the right thing to do. Do I have the time and resources to take proper care of a pet? Will everyone else in my family accept a cat? Can I offer a cat the kind of home where she will be happy and healthy?

▶ Before you acquire a feline friend, make sure you have the time to provide her with proper care and plenty of attention.

Do You Have the Time?

If you are looking for a feline companion, then you need to ensure that you have time in your schedule to attend not only to her daily needs but also to her mental and physical stimulation. You can't merely shake out some kibble, top up the water bowl, scoop the poop, and trot off for the rest of the day. There has to be lots of time for interaction and play. Cats need to spend time with their people. Cats don't sleep all day by choice; it's a sign of boredom. And, if left alone for excessively long spells on a regular basis, they can suffer from separation anxiety.

Cats thrive on company. A lot of them are lap kitties who give you seconds to settle before taking up residence in your lap and making it clear that you're not moving for the next hour. Then there is time for grooming. Sure, cats tend to be tidy and meticulous self-cleaners, but they still need to be groomed—some more than others. Certain longhaired breeds need to be brushed on a daily basis. Maybe not a hundred strokes, but daily grooming can be very time-consuming. And don't forget the nail care.

Do you have time to learn about nutrition and health care for your cat, to socialize with and groom her, as well as train her to keep off counters, if that is your preference? Not to mention teaching her not to scratch your favorite chair? If you work all week and are out socializing on weekends, or if you spend large chunks of your day car-pooling your kids to various extramural activities and supervising homework, then this may not be the time to commit to the responsibility of a cat.

Is Your Family Ready?

If you are in a committed relationship, does your partner like cats or merely tolerate them? This is very important, and you have to be truthful with yourself.

And, although it's wonderful to bring up kids with pets, in a household filled with small children, do you have the time to devote to an animal and also teach children to respect a feline friend? Both children and feline will need to be taught and protected.

Furthermore, it's important to determine beforehand who in the household is going to be head of the Department of Feline Affairs. This is the person ultimately responsible for the cat. *Never* designate a child who is keen to have a pet as that pet's sole caretaker. Children cannot be responsible for visits to the veterinarian or for keeping track

▼There is no guarantee a new cat will get along with your dog or other pets you may already have.

Ownership vs. Guardianship

Under American law (as under the law of many other countries), cats, like all domestic animals, are considered property when they clearly belong to someone. It follows, then, that if cats are *property*, from a legal standpoint, people are *owners*. This terminology, however, has long sparked heated debate among animal lovers, animal-related organizations, animal-rights groups, and lawmakers.

The country's current legal standpoint maintains that keeping pets classified as property is the best way to protect them and that changing the *property* classification would be problematic. For example, in order to change it, animals would have to be able to sue for an injury or harm done, and thus the issue is further exacerbated by the question of who will represent the animal in court and who will have the right to bring suit on behalf of the animal.

In 1999, an organization called In Defense of Animals (IDA) launched a campaign called *They Are Not Our Property—We Are Not Their Owners*, which, as the name clearly states, opposed the concept of animals as property. The IDA organization wanted to have the term *pet owner* legally replaced by the term *guardian* and ultimately "reconstruct the social and legal relationship between humans and animals."

The IDA organization, which continues to advocate for this changes, believes this change in terminology will help alter how individuals and society in general perceive and treat other species. The group's viewpoint is that the concept of *guardianship* promotes a much more respectful and responsible relationship. According to the IDA:

> By disavowing the concept and accompanying language of animal ownership, we can reconstruct the social and legal relationship between humans and animals. As our societal perceptions of animals change, the legislatures and courts will recognize our obligation to protect animals, not as someone's personal property, but as conscious being[s] with feelings and interests of their own.

In 2000, Boulder, Colorado, became the first city to amend its animal ordinance to include the *guardian* term. In 2001, Rhode Island added *guardian* to its state statutes concerning animals. Berkeley, San Francisco, Beverly Hills, and West Hollywood in California; Sherwood, Arkansas; Amherst, Massachusetts; Menomonee Falls, Wisconsin; and several other jurisdictions subsequently passed ordinances that allowed animal owners to be called pet guardians.

Not everyone agrees that this would be a change for the better. The Cat Fanciers' Association (CFA), International Cat Association, American Veterinary Medical Association, American Kennel Club, Pet Industry Joint Advisory Council, National Animal Interest Alliance, American Dog Owners Association, Responsible Pet Owners Alliance (Texas), California Veterinary Medical Association, and the office of the Los Angeles City Attorney have all at one time or another issued public statements opposing the *guardian* term or its use in laws. The CFA's statement in 2003 summed up the general consensus of this opinion:

> The Cat Fanciers' Association, Inc. strongly supports caring and responsible pet ownership. CFA upholds the traditional property rights of animal owners that provide the basis for their ability to make decisions about their animals' well-being, including health, reproduction and transfer to a new owner. Owned cats are valued family members. As legal property, they cannot be taken away from us except by constitutional due process. The term "guardian," whether inserted into animal laws or in common usage, contradicts this critical protective and personal relationship. CFA rejects the concept of animal "guardianship," which can be challenged or revoked, because of the potential legal and social ramifications that would negatively impact veterinarians, animal rescuers, breeders and sellers of animals as well as pet owners.

In the past decade, many cat owners have taken to calling themselves *pet parents* and their feline companions *fur kids*. Many of those who support the *owner* label say that such terms of endearment are fine in a domestic setting. But it's different when dealing with the law because the term *owner* is the one that best looks after the interest of the pet concerned.

The IDA continues to fight for *guardianship* to be nationally accepted. (Currently thirty American cities recognize the term *animal guardian*.) Others vigorously defend the value of *pet ownership*. Those on both sides of this controversial issue have similar goals: to ensure that animals kept as pets are respected and protected from neglect or abuse.

▲ Statistically, cats live healthier and longer lives when kept indoors all the time.

of medical records and vaccinations. And, as much as your child may promise to take care of a cat's grooming needs, in reality, the novelty often wears off and the cat gets neglected.

Will Your Other Pets Be OK?

If you already have pets in the household, it's very important to take them into consideration, too. Some dogs love cats. For others, the mere sight of a fluffy tail revs up their prey drive. Remember that two cats who come into the home at different times may not get along either. It can cause anxiety and stress for both felines, resulting in behavioral issues such as going outside of the litter box. Veterinarians liken a household situation in which cats do not get along to an office scenario in which you simply can't stand the person sharing your cubicle. Such a situation can be very stressful and, if you have ever been in such a predicament, it's easy to empathize. When cats in a household do not get along, they will do things such as block one another from using litter boxes and passageways, which ultimately puts a strain on the entire household. The antagonistic situation may resolve itself over time or at least become tolerable for the felines concerned. You need to ask yourself

if you have the time and patience to wait for that to happen, or if you will be willing to actively help resolve such a situation, which may include consulting an animal behaviorist. It may also involve dividing up the home so that certain cats are downstairs and others upstairs. Is this something you can live with long term? It's a decision that has to be made before you introduce another pet.

You should consider that an elderly cat or dog may feel threatened by a rambunctious kitten. And what if you have birds that you let fly freely around the house or a hamster that enjoys rolling around in a hamster ball? Every creature in the household has to be taken into account. Simply wanting a cat or a second cat shouldn't be your prime motivation. The basic questions you need to answer are: Is there a safe and secure place for a cat in my home? And will my other animals be safe and secure?

Do You Have Enough Living Space?

Cats don't require a large apartment or house. But all animals need their space, and you will need to ensure that a cat will have some place in the home to call her own, such as a cat tree or a kitty condo, for some feline privacy.

Part of the process of domesticating the *Felis catus* has been the recognition that cats are in fact much safer if they are kept indoors. Whether you live in the country or enjoy an urban lifestyle, cats who are allowed to roam freely are more likely to be in contact with fleas, ticks, and other parasites. They stand the chance of being attacked by predators, becoming the victims of animal cruelty, and suffering injury or death from traffic.

Consequently, these days, most cat activists, breeders, and welfare organizations promote an indoor lifestyle, but can *you* live with the idea? If not, does your current living arrangement allow you to have a safe outdoor cat enclosure that your cat can access? And will everyone in the household be responsible about ensuring the cat doesn't escape?

Will You Relocate with Your Cat?

Whether you own your own home or are renting is another deciding factor. Owning your own home means that you are in charge of your domestic destiny. But a rental situation can be precarious. A lot of places are not pet friendly. And, even if you are lucky enough to find one that is, circumstances can change, and, at any time, you could find yourself being given notice by a landlord that you must vacate the premises or that your cat is no longer welcome. Then what happens to your cat? If you are in a rental situation, it's important to have a Plan B in place before you become a cat owner.

It's important to assess your job situation, too. Are you likely to remain in one place, or is there the possibility of relocation? And, if so, are you prepared to relocate with your cat? Far too many cats end up in shelters simply because their owners consider it too much trouble to relocate them and further ensure that they settle down well in the new environment.

Do You Have Health or Financial Issues?

You need to take your personal health and that of any close family members into account, too. That includes elderly relatives who may visit regularly. Does anyone have allergies? Many people are allergic to cat hair and dander and don't even know it. So it's a good idea to spend time around cats beforehand to ensure that you and your immediate family members don't suffer from itchy eyes, a blocked nose, or a wheezy chest whenever a cat enters the room.

Can you afford to keep a pet? Apart from the basic expenses of preparing your home for a cat, such as buying a bed and food and water bowls, you could incur such costs as having to replace door and window screens to ensure your home is a safe environment. Then there are the ongoing costs of good-quality food, toys, and regular veterinary check-ups—not to mention the unknown medical costs that could arise in the future.

How Many Cats?

One cat or two? According to the 2013–2014 National Pet Owners Survey (an NPO survey is published every two years by the American Pet Products Manufacturers, APPA), nearly three-quarters of all the cats living in American households reside in multicat homes, and the national average is 2.11 cats per household. It's important to weigh up the advantages of a multicat household against the disadvantages. Although you are doubling your financial costs, there's a lot to be said for adopting two cats at the same time, allowing them to grow up together and provide companionship for each other. In fact, some adoption agencies insist on two cats being adopted at once for this very reason. Before you adopt is the right time to make this decision because if you bring in a second cat later on, the cats may not bond.

Nuisance Laws

Cats can cause problems in neighborhoods, such as noise, attacks on other cats, defecating in gardens and on lawns, and spreading diseases. Although there are no state-specific nuisance laws pertaining solely to cats, municipalities and cities often create limitations on the number of pets per household. Some laws specify the number of same-species pets allowed. Very often, even though such laws exist, they are not usually acted on unless a complaint is filed.

Cats and Kids

If you are willing to put in the time socializing your kitten in her new home and teaching your children how to safely interact with her, the fact that there are children in your home does not preclude you from getting a new cat. In fact, the same NPO survey also points out that in households of three or more children, the average number of cats owned increases.

Kittens are, of course, very cute and playful bundles of fur. But suddenly during exuberant play, and for no apparent reason, they can inflict painful bites and scratches. Often, if not taught proper manners, they continue to do this in adulthood. Such behavior has been known to give parents second thoughts about having a cat in a household with children or the elderly. However, once this rough play is put into perspective, understood, and controlled, people can see that having children in the home is no reason to have second thoughts about adopting a cat, and it is certainly not a reason to give away the cat.

Understanding Feline Play

Felines have a natural prey drive and instinctively tend to play rough attack-and-retreat games with each other and with the people in their lives. This characteristic usually becomes evident in kittens when they are around three months old and is a normal part of a kitten's development. Kittens

▲ Two cats provide each other with companionship, so you may want to consider adopting two at the same time.

pounce on each other, wrestling and tumbling about, and even latching on to one another with their teeth. It looks serious and can be noisy, but it's nothing more than their natural instincts at play. They also get into chasing mode, where they will crouch down, almost flat on the floor, then stealthily creep up on their "prey" and spring.

Of course, if the "prey" happens to be your hand, this can be disconcerting and a little painful, especially if the kitten sinks her tiny teeth into your skin and adds some kicks with her back feet. Such behavior can be truly frightening to a small child.

Children should be taught never to shout and scream or lash out and hit. Instead, they should be taught to stay out of such games completely. When rough feline play starts up, children must know to leave the cat or kitten alone and retreat, seeking out a parent instead.

Once you learn to read the signals that an "attack" may be imminent, you can keep it from happening. Signals to watch for are a flicking tail and a wild look in the eyes. Simply stop petting, don't initiate any more games, and move away. Children must be taught to do the same.

One way of allowing a child and a young cat to play without the danger of a scratch or a bite is to teach the child to interact with the cat using a

Time to Stop Play

Teach children to watch for the early warning signs that feline fun and games are about to get rough so that they can stop play before a time-out is needed. It's also a good idea to ensure that your cat has somewhere to retreat for a little privacy and feline alone time, such as a nice tall cat tree or kitty condo.

Toxoplasmosis and Pregnant Women

One of the biggest concerns for pregnant women is contracting toxoplasmosis from cleaning cat feces in litter boxes. Toxoplasmosis is caused by a parasite found in cats who have eaten infected meat. According to the Center for Disease Control and Prevention (CDC), women who test positive for toxoplasmosis don't pass it on to the fetus because they have the necessary antibodies in their systems to fight the condition. Thus, the hysteria regarding pregnant women is overblown.

There's no reason to get rid of a cat because of a pregnancy. Instead, women should avoid direct contact with feline feces by getting someone else to clean the litter box. The alternative is to wear gloves and disinfect the box every time you change the litter.

Although toxoplasmosis is associated with feline feces, it is also very easy to pick up the parasite by eating raw or partly cooked meat, especially pork, lamb, or venison, or by touching your hands to your mouth after contact with raw or undercooked meat in the kitchen. Consequently, cats often are blamed unnecessarily.

People infected with toxoplasmosis are often unaware of having this disease because typical symptoms are similar to muscle aches and pains associated with the flu.

wand-type toy. The wand directs the cat's prey drive away from the child to the toy. Once again, though, it's important to teach children to watch for signs the play is getting out of hand, such as a flicking tail. In this way, it's possible to put an end to the game before it gets too rough and you have to call for a time-out.

Kids and Feline House Rules

Children need to be taught the following simple rules to establish a loving kid–cat relationship:

- A cat is not a toy. Small children should not be allowed to carry a cat around. Instead teach them to sit next to their pet and stroke her gently.
- Learn to read basic cat body language that indicates annoyance, anger, or fear, such as a flicking tail and flattened ears.
- Learn to recognize that the cat has had enough and wants to be left alone.
- Never hold a cat against her will or back her into a corner so that she is unable to escape.
- Never bother a cat when she's sleeping, eating, or using the litter box.
- Loud boisterous screaming can frighten even the mildest tempered feline.

It's important to invest time into developing the bond between your child and your pet. Give

children treats to give to the cat because this helps to establish a positive relationship.

From the age of about five years old, encourage children to be involved with the cat's daily care. A simple task such as making sure that the water bowl is always full and that there's food in the dish will teach responsibility in caring for a pet.

▶ Cats and kids can become great friends, but their interactions should be supervised by an adult to make sure they both are having a good time.

▲ If you have a newborn on the way, it's a good idea to let the cat get used to the crib and other baby items before the big day.

in a household with a newborn baby (or a household preparing for a newborn) is nothing more than anxiety, a reaction to all the new activity in the household.

Cats are curious. If you deliberately exclude them from a certain room in the house—one you're preparing for the baby—they will make a concerted effort to gain access on their own. Instead of completely barring them, allow them inside a new baby's room under controlled supervision, especially when you are preparing it for the baby's arrival. Let them lie around while you decorate and set things up. It's a good idea to even play with them in this environment so that they feel comfortable in this territory.

If friends with babies visit, keep your cat around to get used to the sounds of crying and gurgling. In fact, take a recorder on a visit to the OB/GYN's office; there's bound to be a crying baby you can record. Replay at home, especially when you are working in the nursery and in the room in which you intend to feed and entertain the baby. Play with musical toys, too.

Because scents are very important to animals, it's a good idea for the mother-to-be to start wearing baby powder, lotion, and any other baby-related products before the baby's arrival.

While you are out shopping for baby, shop for kitty, too. Buy new cat toys, even a new kitty condo. But keep these items hidden and only bring them out when the baby actually arrives home, to create a diversion.

Over the years, various studies done around small children and pets have shown that children who are attached to a pet and possibly even involved with its care often have high IQ test scores and are better able to understand and communicate with their peers. There's no doubt that a loving relationship with a pet will impact on a child's life and teach him or her to love and respect animals.

Of course, the success of a toddler–cat relationship depends a lot on the demeanor of the cat, too.

Cats and Newborns

So what happens if the situation is reversed? That is, what happens if the newcomer is a human baby and the established resident is a cat? Some people mistakenly believe that cats and newborns don't mix and that cats can even pose a danger to a newborn.

This is simply not true. If you already have a cat, you don't have to find your cat another home. Cats are very intuitive creatures, and cat owners often say that their felines "know" about the impending arrival of a baby and that it brings out their nurturing instincts. I have experienced this personally!

Preparing Your Cat

According to popular belief, cats are extremely jealous of babies. In fact, usually the behavior a cat exhibits

Keeping the Cat Out

Parents who would prefer to keep the family cat out of the baby's room both before and after the baby's arrival should invest in a special motion detector device that is triggered by the presence of an animal. Numerous models are available that either beep or making a hissing sound. Others spray water or a harmless citronella spray. Even a can of compressed air used to clean a computer keyboard will do the trick! Cats are fast learners!

▲ Allow your cat to meet your new baby as soon as possible. This is a good time to break out new toys and treats, so she views your newborn positively.

It's the same thing you would do if there were older children in the house who may be apprehensive of a new arrival in their midst.

Preparing for the Baby's Arrival

If you're the main cat caretaker of the household and the one who'll be giving birth, it's a good idea to let your spouse (or whoever will be cat sitting) take over feeding duties at least a month before the baby's arrival. Let the same person be the dispenser of treats, too. This is an excellent way of helping the cat become comfortable with her temporary caregiver during the time immediately after the baby's arrival. When it's time to go into the hospital, leave worn items of your clothing around, especially where the cat sleeps. Make sure that feline feeding times and any other routines don't change. Make the same preparations if you are planning on giving birth at home; even though you'll be in the house, you'll be in a separate space.

Introducing Cat to Baby

Cat behaviorists believe that it's a good idea to introduce a cat to a baby under controlled circumstances very soon after bringing the baby home or as soon after the home birth as possible. If you include the cat by stroking and petting her when she's in close proximity to an infant, she will automatically associate the baby with behaviors that feel good.

When the baby actually arrives, this is the time to take out the new kitty toys. In addition, if an increase of visitors into your home makes your cat anxious, spray special feline pheromone sprays around to soothe feline nerves. They are widely available from pet supermarkets and veterinarian offices. There are also soothing pheromone collars made from all-natural, safe ingredients. To be effective, they should be replaced monthly.

Allow the cat and the baby to "meet" one another. If anyone in the household is tense and worried, the cat is likely to pick up on these feelings. So remain calm and let them get to know each other, particularly during feeding and changing routines. And give your cat space—make sure there is somewhere she can go and chill out when the noise and the crying all become too much!

Is a Cat Right for You?

Chapter 7

Finding the Right Cat

There are no ordinary cats.

— Sidonie-Gabrielle Colette

As discussed in chapter 4, Breed Development and Characteristics, there are in total about eighty distinctive breeds recognized by the world's cat breed associations. That means there are a myriad of different kinds of cats with distinctive looks, characteristics, and personality traits from which to choose. It's important to carefully research their different individual qualities to ensure that you choose the perfect companion to match both your personality and your lifestyle.

Start by reading over the breed profiles in chapter 5 to learn about the specific qualities of the breed or breeds you're interested in; then expand your research by talking with your cat-owning family members and friends, breed clubs, and breeders. Next, visit breeders to meet individual cats or go to the local animal shelter and visit with all of the cats there. With all those different body shapes, sizes, and coats in a variety of colors and "styles" (shorthaired, longhaired, curly, and even, as in the Sphynx, hairless), somewhere out there is the perfect cat—or cats—for you.

There are many different ways to acquire a cat. The 2013–2014 American Pet Products Association (APPA) National Pet Owners Survey listed the following sources where cats are obtained:

- 32 percent obtain a cat from a friend or family member.
- 26 percent obtain kittens and cats from an animal shelter or humane society.
- 35 percent of all cats are strays who adopted their owners.
- 8 percent obtained a kitten born to a cat they already own.

▶ Many people obtain cats because a stray shows up at their door and decides to stay.

▲ As a rule of thumb, longhaired breeds, such as the Persian, are mellower and less demanding than the shorthaired breeds.

- 8 percent obtain cats and kittens privately or from a newspaper advertisement.
- 2 percent obtain from a variety of other sources, such as from their veterinarian or from a breeder.

Cats from a Breeder

If you are looking to acquire a pedigreed kitten, it's best to purchase directly from a breeder. With a breeder, you can verify pedigree and know that if you're looking for, say, a Bengal, you will be getting a Bengal. A breeder will be able to confirm what you have learned from your research with regard to specific breed character traits, as well as the type of grooming routine you must be prepared to undertake. Breeders can also point out any inherent medical issues pertaining to that specific breed and how they may relate to their own breeding cats.

Many cat breeders say that a kitten's father has the biggest influence on the kitten's personality and behavior even if he has had little or no contact with the litter. So be sure to ask about the kitten's

parents and, if possible, ask to meet both the mother and the father so you can get an idea of what kind of cat your kitten might grow up to be in terms of both looks and personality. It will give you an idea whether the kitten you are interested in will grow up to be outwardly friendly or very shy. Remember to brush up your knowledge of general trait information from the breed profiles in chapter 5.

Generally speaking, longhaired or semi-longhaired cats are more placid and less vocal and demanding than shorthaired felines, which are often very energetic and lively.

The following popular breeds are examples of different feline personalities:

- Abyssinian: gentle and loyal, very active, and playful
- American Shorthair: sociable and laid back
- Asian Shorthair: curious, intelligent, and not very demanding
- Birman: a sweet devoted personality, intelligent, and quiet
- Bengal: very athletic and playful

- British Shorthair: friendly and affectionate
- Burmese: outgoing and energetic; enjoys lots of attention
- Devon and Cornish Rex: playful and intelligent
- Egyptian Mau: playful and loving
- Exotic Shorthair: gentle and undemanding
- Korat: quiet, sweet-natured, playful, and intelligent
- Maine Coon: sweet, intelligent, and easy to train to do tricks
- Norwegian Forest Cat: very gentle and loving
- Persian: sweet, devoted, docile, affectionate, and laid-back
- Ragdoll: gentle and affectionate; enjoys being handled by everyone
- Russian Blue: affectionate, quiet, and gentle
- Siamese: very vocal, intelligent, and demanding
- Scottish Fold: mellow and sweet-tempered
- Sphynx: lively, devoted, and loyal
- Tonkinese: people-oriented and affectionate; loves to play
- Toyger: highly intelligent, active, and friendly

Meeting the Breeds

If you have decided on a pedigreed cat, it's very important to do your homework about the breed (see chapter 5). It's also important to meet the breeds that appeal to you, and there's no better way to do that than to attend a cat show.

Breeders love to share information with cat lovers and will happily chat if they are not grooming and getting ready for the show ring. It's a good idea to take a business card with their information and contact them afterward, when they have more time to talk. This is also an excellent opportunity to find breeders in your area so that you can visit them at home, too.

Breed showcases and information workshops are a popular feature at many cat shows and are an excellent way to learn from the experts and educate yourself about personality and breed temperament.

The best way to find out about cat shows in your area is to consult local newspapers or specialist magazines such as *Cat Fancy*. Notice boards in both pet stores and veterinary offices are another excellent

source of information. Both the Cat Fanciers Association (CFA) and the International Cat Association (TICA) post events on their respective websites, www.CFA.org and www.TICA.org.

Apart from listing information about cat shows, magazines such as *Cat Fancy* also list bona fide breeders in every issue. Furthermore, CFA and TICA are willing to help first-time purebred cat buyers by giving them information about those certified breeders who are members of their respective organizations.

It's important to remember that responsible breeders do not over-breed, and you may find that you have to put your name on a waiting list. Depending on the breed, the wait could be a long one. But then, looking after a cat is a lifetime commitment and thus acquiring a cat should

Crossbreed Cats

A crossbreed cat is the offspring of pedigreed parents but of different breeds. The kittens could resemble either parent or be a cross between the two. Their coats can vary, too, from longhaired to shorthaired to semi-longhaired.

If you know what the parents' looks, personalities, and character traits are, you have a reasonable idea what to expect in the long run.

Deliberate crossbreeding is how some of the newer "hybrid" breeds, such as the Bengal and the Toyger, came into being in the first place. However, kittens born of two different-breed parents who have been casually bred (in other words, not as part of a specific program to create a new breed) are also known crossbreeds.

In this instance, crossbred kittens and fully grown cats are much easier to obtain and less expensive than purebred pedigree cats. Breeders often know about crossbred litters. Notice boards at veterinary offices are another good source of information.

never be "an impulse buy." If you're not prepared to wait for what you want, then you may not really want a cat at all.

Working with a Breeder

Once you've found a breeder with whom you would like to work, it's important to build up a rapport, preferably in person, but if that's not possible, by telephone or e-mail. Many breeders have websites and post daily photographs to give you an inside look at life in their catteries if you are unable to visit.

Often, breeders like to raise their kittens "underfoot," which means they have both the mom and the litter in their homes rather than in a cattery environment. This doesn't mean it's a backyard operation. In fact, kittens who are raised in the family home are usually very well socialized because they have so much contact with people. Nevertheless, it's still important to learn about the hygienic conditions of the home and make sure everything is well run and clean.

Don't be afraid to ask questions about the environment, the breeder's background, the kittens, and so on. Breeders like it when prospective cat owners ask questions because it shows that these people are committed to raising a healthy pet in a healthy home.

Ask how many litters they raise per year. A queen should not be bred more than once a year. Find out if the mother has been under veterinary care throughout the pregnancy, whether a veterinarian has examined the kittens since birth, and if they have subsequently received their first vaccinations.

Ask if the cattery screens regularly for feline leukemia (FeLV) and feline AIDS (FIV). It's important to have some knowledge of the breed you are interested in so that you can inquire about any health issues associated with the breed and find out whether the breeder screens for those specific issues. For example, Maine Coons are prone to hip dysplasia whereas breeds such as the Persian, Ragdoll, and Maine Coon have been known to

▲ Attending a cat show is an excellent way to see a number of different breeds and learn about them up close.

suffer from a heart disease called hypertrophic cardiomyopathy (see chapter 14, page 326-327), characterized by a thickening of the left ventricle of the heart, which pumps the blood to circulate it throughout the body. The condition can be mild to life-threatening. Be sure to inquire whether the breeder will give a written guarantee outlining any genetic or health problems.

If you are considering a life in the show ring for your kitten, be sure to ask if the kitten has been registered and with which organizations, and be sure to confirm that such registrations do exist. All pedigreed kittens should be sold with their pedigree as well as their registration papers, even if the buyer is not planning to breed or show.

If you are able to schedule a visit to the breeder, be sure (as mentioned earlier) to ask to see both the mother and the father. This will give you an excellent idea of what your kitten is going to grow up to look like. Often, breeders use a stud service, and the father isn't on the premises. If this is the case, ask to see a photograph.

If a breeder is reluctant to answer your questions or allow you to tour his or her home or cattery, consider it a red flag and go elsewhere.

Designer Breed Bans

In recent years, designer cat breeds, such as Bengals (a cross between a domestic feline and an Asian leopard cat), Savannahs (a cross between a domestic feline and a serval), Chausies (a cross between a domestic feline and a jungle cat), and Toygers (a cross between a striped domestic feline and a Bengal), carefully bred to resemble wild cats such as leopards, jungle cats, and tigers, have become increasingly popular.

However, there are restrictions to owning a hybrid breed, and these laws vary across America. They are banned outright in Hawaii. States such as Connecticut and Massachusetts have laws that require breeders to register their cats with the Department of Agriculture since 1996. This means that the original parents of today's cats had to be officially registered, thus making their offspring legal. It also means that Bengals, Savannahs, and other domestic and wild-crossed hybrids cannot be legally brought into those states. Effectively, this means that no new crossbreeding programs are officially allowed in these states.

These states also require owners of hybrid cats to register them with a cat registry such as TICA to prove that the cat has had no wild lineage for the past four generations. Hybrid cats such as Bengals, Chausies, Savannah, and Toygers are subject to a filial generation labeling system. The term *filial* is based on the Latin word *filius*, which means "son" and relates to the number of generations away the cat is from a nondomestic ancestor.

- An F1 cat has a parent who is of a nondomestic species.
- An F2 cat has a grandparent who of a nondomestic species.
- An F3 cat has great-grandparent who is of a nondomestic species.
- (All F1, F2, and F3 cats are also often referred to as early-generation or EG cats.)
- An F4 cat has a great-great grandparent who is of a nondomestic species.

All cats who are F4 or greater (F5, F6, and so on) are also referred to as stud book tradition (SBT) cats. This is based on a complicated coding system that guarantees that the cat in question has no cats of unknown, unregistered, or of another breed group in her genetic background within a standard three-generation pedigree.

One of the main reasons why such an influential registry such as TICA recognizes hybrid cats as fully domesticated only starting with the fourth generation (F4) is because the first three generations of males are sterile, and the organization's rules require both males and females of any breed to be able to reproduce.

Hybrid breeds are partially banned in some states like Georgia, Alaska, and New York. This means that early-generation cats (F1, F2, and F3) are banned but not later generation cats (F4, F5, and onward). However, some places, such as New York City, despite the state's partial ban, still uphold an outright ban in the city itself.

Furthermore, although breed bans may officially still exist on some state or city law books, they are not enforced. And because the situation is constantly changing, it's important to check for up-to-date information on a website such as www.hybridlaw.com

Another red flag is a breeder who is keen to let kittens go too young. Kittens need to be with their mothers until they are at least twelve weeks old. Some breeders like to wait until the kitten is sixteen weeks old before allowing her to go to a new home. So beware of anyone who is keen to let kittens go at six to eight weeks of age. Extra time spent with the mother is vital to both kittens' physical development and the strengthening of their immune system, as well as to their socialization. Besides, there's a lot for their mothers to teach them, too.

It is also reasonable to ask for references and contact people to learn of their experiences with a particular breeder.

▲ Research your breeder and breed thoroughly and don't be afraid to ask any questions you have before you commit to buying a cat.

Answering a Breeder's Questions

A responsible breeder wants to ensure that every one of her kittens goes to a good home, and you must expect to be quizzed about your home and lifestyle, too. Expect to be asked what will happen if you decide not to keep the kitten. Some breeders will insist on the kitten or the fully grown cat coming back to them.

Expect questions about other animals and children in the home and your views on spaying, neutering, and declawing. They will want to know what arrangements you plan to make if you travel and whether the cat is going to be home alone for long periods of time. They may also want to know how much you know about the breed in general and what type of research you have done to ensure that you are making the right choice.

Signing the Sales Contract

There will always be a sales contract to sign when purchasing a kitten from a breeder. The contract will vary from breeder to breeder, but essentially they all cover the same ground, with clauses relating to the daily care of the cat, declawing, and spaying or neutering. Insistence on spaying or neutering is a common practice when owners simply want a cat as a pet because it gives the breeder the assurance that the cat will not be bred indiscriminately and add to the problem of pet overpopulation.

There may be a clause ensuring that the breeder will be given the first option to buy the cat back and also clauses prohibiting the cat from being sold or given to a pet shop or to a research laboratory.

All contracts are open to reasonable negotiation. Once signed, however, they are binding on both parties. So read the fine print!

Cats from a Breed Rescue Group

If you are not planning a career in the show ring for your cat but are intent on bringing a certain breed of cat into your home, consider adopting from a breed rescue group. It's a sad reality that pedigreed cats also lose their homes for a variety of reasons. Breed rescues groups are usually run by volunteers who are familiar with a particular cat breed (many of them breeders themselves) and collectively they work to re-home pedigreed cats.

The cats are usually kept in foster care in a home environment, although they may also be housed at a specific group rescue shelter. There are breed rescue groups for almost all pedigreed cats.

Although cats of all ages can be found through a breed rescue group, most are fully grown, not kittens. Very often these cats have all their pedigree and registry papers, too. Purchasing a cat directly from a breeder can be quite expensive, and breed rescue is definitely a much cheaper option because you will ultimately only be paying an adoption fee that includes the cost of spaying or neutering if it hasn't already been done. Adopting from a breed shelter, however, is more expensive than obtaining a cat from a standard shelter because the costs of keeping these pets in a home environment are greater.

Most breeders, even if they are not personally involved in a rescue group, have knowledge of such groups in their area and are a good source of information. Very often, breed rescue groups take booths at regular cat shows to try to find their charges new forever homes. Local cat organizations are another good source of information.

If you are planning to adopt from a breed rescue group, be prepared to be asked a lot of questions similar to those asked by a breeder because rescue group volunteers work hard to re-home their charges

and ensure that each cat goes to a loving and a forever home. Be prepared for a home inspection visit, too.

Cats from an Animal Shelter

The majority of cats in the world are nonpedigreed animals, born of mixed parentage, and thus are generally referred to as mixed-breed. Over the years, they've had a variety of nicknames from "pavement specials" (being born to feral cats) to "moggies." The latter is derived from name Maggie, short for Margaret, reputed to have been a common name for cows and calves in eighteenth-century England and later applied to housecats during the Victorian era. In the United States, a nonpedigreed cat is also sometimes referred to as a "barn cat" or "alley cat," even if it is not a stray.

Very often litters of nonpedigreed kittens are born to domestic cats, and the owners, unable to raise the kittens, take them to a nonprofit rescue shelter or municipal pound. Because so many city-run shelters still euthanize the animals in their care, nonprofit animal rescue groups will often rescue cats and kittens from these places and undertake to care for them until they find them homes.

The staff at a shelter or an adoption event should be forthcoming with answers to your questions. You are entitled to whatever information they have to offer about the background of any kitten or cat in their care, her age, and her state of health. Also try to ascertain whether she was a stray or a cat who was relinquished by a previous owner and how long she's been in the shelter. Finally, it's important to find out about the shelter's return policy in case the adoption does not work out.

Whether you're adopting from a city shelter or a rescue organization, all cats and kittens will be spayed or neutered before being allowed to go to a new home. Consequently, as with a specific breed rescue group, you will also be charged an adoption fee, which varies from shelter to shelter. You can also expect to fill out comprehensive paperwork. If you are dealing with an animal rescue group, more than

◄ Most breeders will ask a prospective buyer questions, such whether he or she plans on letting the cat go outside.

Not a Mill Kitty

In recent years, a number of pet stores around the country have been prosecuted for selling unhealthy kittens and cats who have been bred in illegal kitten mill operations. Furthermore, dishonest storeowners have lied to prospective purchasers about the backgrounds of such cats in their stores. If you are looking to purchase a purebred cat, it's best to make such a purchase directly with a registered breeder. Genuine cat breeders who love and support their breed never sell their kittens to a store. They have a very responsible attitude when it comes to placing one of their kittens in a new home, and many are keen to meet prospective owners and question them to ensure that the kitten is going to a loving home.

likely they will insist on a home inspection before the animal is released into your care.

Rescue groups often have an arrangement with pet boutiques and supermarkets to hold in-store adoption events. Some even have a permanent in-store arrangement and rotate the cats and kittens between the store and their off-site shelter to give the animals a better chance of being adopted. This is a very acceptable manner in which to adopt a cat or a kitten and should not be confused with pet stores that sell cats and kittens that they have obtained from a kitten mill. But be sure to ask!

It's important to bear in mind that whether you are adopting from an animal shelter or from an adoption clinic run by a volunteer organization within a pet store, any animal in this environment may appear timid. Ask if there is safe area where you can possibly have some one-on-one interaction with the kitten or cat you are interested in adopting. A store situation is stressful for a small animal. Often, a kitten or cat will only really begin to blossom once she is in a home environment—with you.

Cats from Other Sources

There are other sources to tap when you go looking for your cat, including online sources (check these out carefully), family or friends, and even your back doorstep, when the cat who has been hanging around—and who you have been kind-heartedly giving food and water—decides to adopt you permanently.

Online

In 1995, two computer-savvy animal lovers named Betsy and Jared Saul launched a website called Petfinder.com that has become a leading platform for pet adoptions in the United States. The site posts information about pets for adoption from more than 13,966 shelters and, with a simple click of a computer mouse, links them with millions of people around the country looking to adopt at any given time. It's a free service for shelters and rescue groups to use, as well as for potential adopters. Since its inception, Petfinder.com has helped to find homes for more than 13 million pets, and the numbers continue to grow daily.

In 2006, Discovery Channel bought the website. This takeover gave the company the opportunity to use its network of TV stations to further promote the site and the concept of pet adoptions. In the past decade, the idea of looking online for an animal companion has spawned numerous competitive sites and also prompted small rescue groups to

▼ Adopting a cat from a shelter or rescue group is a wonderful way to give a second chance to a homeless kitty.

▲ Many people adopt a cat after a friend's or neighbor's cat has kittens.

maintain their own websites that are updated daily. Collectively, it's all for the greater good of finding unwanted pets homes. In July 2013, the site was bought by Nestle Purina PetCare.

It's important to verify that any website you visit is bone fide and not a smokescreen for a kitten mill.

Family and Friends

Cat lovers who have not had their cats spayed or neutered often find themselves with unwanted litters and are willing to offer the kittens to family and friends for free. This is a good option because you can usually get to see the kittens interacting with their mother and check out the hygienic state of their environment. According to the 2013–2014 American Pet Products Association National Pet Owners Survey, more than 32 percent of Americans find a cat this way.

Cats Who Adopt People

It's a sad fact that, all too often, people who don't take the responsibility of pet ownership seriously simply move to a new location and leave their cats behind to fend for themselves. To survive, these cats turn feral. If given a chance, however, they still gravitate to people in the neighborhood, and, if given the opportunity, will adopt a new caregiver for themselves. Because such cats are in need of human affection, they usually make great companions. I have been adopted twice!

Assessing the Prospects

No matter how you are planning to adopt, whether it's directly from a shelter, at an organized adoption event, or from a private home, take your time. This is an important decision that's going to affect your life and the lives of those around you for many years to come.

When confronted by numerous bouncing kittens, it can be difficult to choose. They are all cute. Obviously, if you have a penchant for a particular coloring, that may help to narrow the field.

Picking up a Cat

The best way to pick up a cat so that she feels secure is to lift her from the front, with one arm under her front legs and the other gently supporting her back legs. Never take young children with you to an animal shelter or an adoption event. They can unnerve a kitten or cat and distract you, too!]

Here are some pointers to help with your assessment:

- When you walk past the cage, does a particular kitten stand and try to attract your attention?
- Are her eyes clear and bright?
- Does she appear to be alert and curious, even if she's shy?
- Check for any nasal discharge or smelly ears.
- Jingle keys to check her hearing ability.
- Check how she moves and walks and look for any signs of awkwardness.
- How does a particular kitten that's caught your attention interact with other kittens in the cage?
- How does she respond if you wiggle your fingers and invite play?
- Does the kitten relax in your arms? Does she show signs of contentment? Remember, some cats don't purr!
- Check her mouth. The gums should be pink and the teeth aligned.

Special-Needs Cats

Often, among the bouncier kittens there may be one who is smaller and weaker than the rest, and she may possibly even have some kind of deformity. Such kittens are known as the runts of the litter. Adopting a special-needs kitten can be a very rewarding experience. But before you consider such an undertaking, it's important to get an opinion detailing exactly what the kitten's special needs may be. Very often, shelter personnel are not trained to give the answers you need, and you are going to have to seek an expert veterinary opinion and, furthermore, inquire what kind of ongoing medical treatment may be needed and a guesstimate of the costs involved.

Older Cats

Sadly, adult cats often lose their homes for a variety of reasons and find themselves in shelter situations. It's very stressful for a cat to suddenly lose her family and familiar surroundings, and these cats often cower at the rear of a cage, shy and unable to project their true personalities.

Most shelters have a visitor's room where you can spend some quality time together with a prospective adoptee and try to get to know each other. Be sure to ask. It is often a good idea to visit several times, to give the cat an opportunity to warm to your attention.

You are quite entitled to ask questions relating to a

We Choose Her!

Lori Van Hove knows exactly what it's like to be adopted by a cat—in triplicate.

During a November rainstorm, I came home to find two wet cats, a small black female with white marking on her face and a pink nose and a teeny black kitten, sheltering under the overhang of my front door. I saw them, they saw me—it was mutual adoption at first sight, and they immediately moved into the house. I named the cat Mamma Starr because the white on her face resembled a star and the kitten Midnight.

The third cat to adopt me, a tabby named Tigre, had been an outside cat in the neighborhood and a buddy for years. Until Mamma Starr and Midnight's arrival, Tigre had come and gone, in and out of my house pretty much as he pleased. Now with two cats permanently at home, I couldn't let him just wander in, so I tried to keep him outside. When he finally begged to be allowed back in one day, I told him to be careful what he asked for . . . but he darted through the open door the second it was wide enough. Fortunately, he fit right in with Mamma Starr and Midnight. The three of them had been strangers (as far as I knew), yet they all got along well and were sharing a litter box from the first day.

People told me that trying to change Tigre from an outdoor cat to an indoor-only cat wouldn't work. They said he would be trying to get out every chance he could. They even said I was cruel not to let him be free. Tigre, of course, didn't care what anybody said. He accepted indoor life from the first and never seemed to want to go out again. He knew a good thing when he saw it.

Lemon Laws Relating to Breeders

The sale of cats is subject to consumer protection, known as the Pet Lemon Law. This law applies after the fact—after a buyer gets home and learns that he or she has purchased a "poor-quality, unhealthy" pet from a commercial pet store or breeder. The law entitles them to a refund, an exchange, or reimbursement of veterinary costs within 14 days of the sale or receipt of the written consumer rights notice from the seller, whichever occurs later.

Sixteen states (Arizona, California, Connecticut, Delaware, Florida, Maine, Massachusetts, Minnesota, Nevada, New Hampshire, New Jersey, New York, Pennsylvania, South Carolina, Vermont, and Virginia) have enacted lemon laws offering consumer protection measures solely geared to provide specific recourse to members of the public who purchase sick or diseased animals from pet shops.

In states where there is no lemon law, the state attorney general's office, the state department of consumer affairs, or the Better Business Bureau may have jurisdiction to address consumer disputes with a particular pet shop. These states also require pet shops to disclose particular information to purchasers and prospective purchasers; this may include the name and contact information of the breeder, any veterinary care provided to the animal prior to sale, a guarantee of good health, the animal's vaccination history, recommendations for spay/neuter, and/or species-specific care guidelines.

The following states have lemon laws relating to breeders: Arkansas, California, Connecticut, Florida, Minnesota, Massachusetts, New Jersey, New York, Pennsylvania, South Carolina, Virginia, and Vermont. These laws allow a buyer to recover damages from a breeder who sells unhealthy animals. Usually, a breeder is considered to be an individual who sells more than nine animals a year. If your cat comes down with a contagious or life-threatening disease within the first 14 days in your home, the breeder will be responsible for paying any expenses you incur. Additionally, if the pet dies within this period, the breeder can be required to reimburse you for any vet bills and the original cost of the animal.

It is important to check that there is a clause relating to lemon laws in any contract you intend signing because often purchasers buy cats from breeders who live and operate in another state. Animal law professionals and cat registries are excellent resources for advice relating to such relevant clauses.

The Humane Society of the United States has created a database to allow pet owners to see if pet lemon laws have been proposed or are currently under consideration in their state.

cat's background, and shelter personnel are obliged to tell you what they know. They are usually very helpful in this regard because they want to place a cat in the best possible home. It's important to try to ascertain whether a fully grown cat who is up for adoption is comfortable around children and other pets. Often, if a cat lived with a single person, this would be the best possible situation for the cat a second time around.

Young adult and senior cats are always less likely to get adopted than a fluffy kitten. So, by making such a choice you are definitely giving an older cat a second chance. You will be paid back beyond your wildest dreams in love and wonderful companionship.

◄ Adult cats are less likely to be adopted than kittens, so you may want to consider opening your heart to an older feline companion.

Chapter 8

Bringing Your Cat Home

I am as vigilant as a cat to steal cream.

— William Shakespeare, *Henry IV*

Before bringing a new cat or kitten home, it's important to make your residence a safe and secure place. In fact, catproofing is a lot like childproofing. Cats are curious and tend to investigate both horizontally and vertically. So it's time to lock away harmful cleaning products and medicines—even pack away extra rolls of toilet paper—and put treasured possessions of outreach. Consider *everything* from the Persian rug to a priceless china ornament a potential cat toy.

The second step is shopping for all the items your new cat will need, from the carrier, to special feline furniture such as a cat bed and a kitty condo, to items such as collars and ID tags, to grooming equipment.

You'll also need a game plan for introducing your new cat to her new home and introducing the various members of the household to her. Introductions are critical; they must be done slowly and with care. *Patience* is the key word.

Catproofing Your Home

A cat's-eye view of your home will always focus on the humanly unattainable so it's a good idea to get down on the ground in every room and view it from this feline perspective. Things look very different from the ground up.

Bedrooms, Living Rooms, and Dens

It's probably a good idea to take pen and paper and make a list as you go through each room of your home. Think of it as a home inspection—which it is—checking everything

▶ Catproofing your home can be difficult because there is no telling what inappropriate items your new cat may find fascinating.

Smoke in the Carpet

Many breeders and adoption agencies will not allow their cats to go a home where there are smokers. Secondhand smoke is as dangerous to pets as it is to people. Apart from what hangs in the air, cats walk on carpeted areas, which are notorious for absorbing smoke. They then lick their feet, ingesting smoke-related toxins.

▲ Secure window screens are must-have items to prevent your kitty from getting out.

from broken screens to how many accessible power outlets you may have to block off. Make a note of loose-lying appliance cords. This may even be the time to purchase new items you have been delaying buying, such as a new rug to replace the one with a hole in it that a cat or kitten may pounce on and begin to chew because it's already unraveling.

Electrical Cords

Electrical cords are a top priority because chewing through wiring can give your cat painful burns on her tongue and mouth area. An electrical shock can lead to pulmonary edema, which is a buildup of fluid on the lungs. It can occur very quickly and can be fatal.

Block off plug sockets and buy special tubing to encase bundles of wires, especially those around computers and electronics. There are also special wire covers obtainable from both hardware stores and pet stores that are infused with citronella that acts as a deterrent for determined chewers.

Carpeting and Rugs

Many wall-to-wall carpets and the matting underneath them contain chemicals that can be toxic to pets (and people). Older carpeting may contain chemicals that are now banned from production, while newer ones may contain adhesives, stain protectors, mothproofing, and flame retardants known to cause nerve damage and respiratory illnesses.

This is a difficult issue to manage unless you are planning to recarpet, which will give you the opportunity to select coverings with a Green Label Plus certification from the Carpet and Rug Institute. This certifies that the listed floor

coverings are free of harmful toxins and chemicals, such as those made from natural fibers like wool, hemp, and corn husks.

Windows and Exterior Doors

Windows and exteriors doors can be dangerous places; you need to make sure they are safe and secure to prevent your cat from getting hurt or ending up on the wrong side.

Blind cords and curtain ties: The cords that operate blinds make great toys because they swing when batted by feline paws. It's important to secure them so that they don't dangle because if a cat gets tangled in one, she could choke. Be extra careful with decorative curtain ties, too.

Screens: All windows and doors with outside access should have screens as a safety measure. Make sure there are no holes in the screen material that a cat could work at with a paw to enlarge and eventually climb through. This needs to be checked regularly!

Exterior doors: It's a good idea to put a note on *both* sides of all exterior doors to remind family members to be watchful for the cat. Include a note on the door leading to the garage, too, because if the main garage door is left open, a cat could inadvertently get out. Keep a squirt bottle filled with water (at room temperature) on either side of any exterior door and squirt in the direction of the cat (not at the cat and definitely not in the face) if she appears to be coming too close. This is an excellent training method to prevent mishaps. Cans of compressed air work, too. Such tactics are considered remote training concepts. In other words, the cat won't blame you personally, just the can or the water—so you won't be creating any feline resentment toward you in the process.

Ornaments, Books, and Other Accessories

Ornaments, books, and household accessories should be packed away, at least temporarily. This will safeguard your possessions and simultaneously protect your new cat from a nasty accident. You can reintroduce some items as your cat settles in and you are better able to judge what presents a hazard and what doesn't.

Candles: Candles are a particular hazard. Never place them on a table with a tablecloth because a cat can jump at the cloth and pull it down, toppling the candles and

possibly starting a fire. If you enjoy the ambience of candles, consider purchasing flameless ones.

Other household accessories and books: Don't only look at low surfaces like coffee tables; items placed on high shelves may also be a feline target. Be wary of unstable bookshelves. Falling books can break feline bones. Cats can also nimbly climb up things that cannot hold a person's weight to gain access to a tiny window or a dangerous shelf. So be sure to restrict access.

Toy boxes: Children's toy boxes should have lids and be kept securely closed because curious felines have been known to chew on and swallow small game pieces or parts of toys. Never leave cat toys lying around unattended either, particularly those with strings attached to wands. If the toy box is large enough for kitty to become trapped inside, you may want to knock a few inconspicuous air holes in it—just in case.

Houseplants

Many common houseplants are toxic to both cats and dogs. These include asparagus ferns, calla lilies, dieffenbachia, cyclamen, tiger lilies, and poinsettias (a winter holiday favorite). See the sidebar "Safe Plants and Toxic Plants" to get an idea of what plants you should get rid of before you bring your new cat home and what not to introduce, as well as which plants are OK to have in your home permanently.

You will also have to be very careful about silk and plastic plants because they could cause a cat to choke if chewed.

To keep pets away from nontoxic plants, sprinkle pepper at the base, on the exposed soil. This will deter any further feline inquisitiveness. Cover the soil surface of potted plants with decorative stones to prevent them from being used as a feline toilet.

Bathrooms

It's essential to also lock away all cosmetics, shampoos, toiletries, and cleaning materials in

◄ If you like to burn candles or incense, keep them somewhere your cat cannot reach them.

Safe Plants and Toxic Plants

Many cat lovers are unaware that lots of very common and popular decorative houseplants are cat-safe for cats to nibble on. These include orchids, African violets, bamboo palms, and various ferns, along with lots of common garden flowers like zinnias and alyssum and herbs such as parsley, sage, thyme, and chickweed.

Nevertheless, there is also a long list of both indoor and garden plants that are *highly toxic* to pets. When you are catproofing your home, make a careful note of the following, which are listed as the ten most poisonous plants by the American Society for the Prevention of Cruelty to Animals (ASPCA)'s Poison Control Unit and be sure to remove them if they are within reach of your cat (both inside and outside).

Lilies

Cyclamen

Oleander

Lilies: All lilies are very popular indoor plants, especially around Easter time. As beautiful as they are, they are highly toxic to cats and can cause severe kidney damage.

Sago palm: These plants can potentially produce vomiting, diarrhea, depression, seizures, and liver failure. All parts of the plant are poisonous, but the seeds or "nuts" contain the largest amount of toxins.

Tulip/narcissus: The bulb portions of these plants contain toxins that can cause intense gastrointestinal irritation, drooling, loss of appetite, central nervous system depression, convulsions, and cardiac abnormalities.

Azalea and rhododendron: These plants contain substances known as grayanotoxins, which can produce vomiting, drooling, diarrhea, weakness, and central nervous system depression in animals. Severe azalea poisoning could ultimately lead to coma and death from collapse of the cardiovascular system.

Cyclamen: This plant contains cyclamine; the highest concentration of this toxic component is typically located in the tuber (root) portion of the plant. If consumed, it can produce significant gastrointestinal irritation, including intense vomiting. Fatalities have also been reported in some cases.

Marijuana: Ingesting this plant in any form can result in central nervous system depression, as well as vomiting, diarrhea, vocalization, drooling, increased heart rate, and even seizures or coma.

Oleander: All parts of the oleander plant are considered to be toxic because they contain cardiac glycosides that have the potential to cause serious effects, including gastrointestinal tract irritation, abnormal heart function, a significant drop in body temperature (hypothermia), and even death.

Castor bean: The poisonous component in this plant is ricin, a highly toxic protein that can produce severe abdominal pain, drooling, vomiting, diarrhea, excessive thirst, weakness, and loss of appetite. In severe cases, dehydration, muscle twitching, tremors, seizures, coma, and death can occur.

Kalanchoe: This plant can cause gastrointestinal irritation and also seriously affect cardiac rhythm and heart rate.

Yew: This plant contains taxine, which affects the central nervous system and causes trembling, lack of coordination, and breathing difficulties, as well as significant gastrointestinal irritation and cardiac failure, which can result in death.

The toxins in poisonous plants have varied effects on cats ranging from a skin rash to vomiting and diarrhea to serious convulsions, damage to the nervous system, kidney and liver failure, and death.

If your cat nibbles on the wrong thing, she is going to need urgent medical attention. Rush her to your veterinarian or nearest pet emergency room and take a sample of the plant with you. This will help the veterinarian with diagnosis and treatment.

Lists of both safe and toxic plants can be found on the ASPCA's website (aspca.org), the Cat Fanciers Association's website (cfainc.org), and CatChannel.com.

a cupboard with a childproof lock. If necessary, replace cakes of soap with liquid soap dispensers and replace open garbage bins with a peddle-type or swing lid so that a cat doesn't have access to the contents.

Toilets and toilet paper: Always ensure that all toilet seats are kept in a down position. Write notes to remind forgetful family members and friends. A kitten can drown in a toilet. Also, solid deodorizers placed inside a toilet bowl are toxic if licked. Make sure the toilet paper is rolled up; don't leave even the tiniest piece hanging because it could be construed by a cat as a toy and even eaten. Store extra rolls in a cupboard.

Showers: Always keep the doors to the shower cubicle closed because cats often enjoy the warmth after the shower has been used and may also lick the walls and floor. If you've just sprayed them with cleaning fluids, that's what they will be ingesting. If possible, it's a good idea to switch to using a nonchemical cleaner such as vinegar or pure lemon juice in case a door is inadvertently left ajar. There are also lots of other nonchemical cleaners to consider.

Dental floss: Be particularly careful about dental floss. Never leave it lying around, and wrap it securely in a tissue before placing it in a secure bin. If ingested, dental floss can be very dangerous because it can constrict a cat's intestines and result in a life-threatening emergency. Be sure everyone in the household is mindful of this.

Kitchens and Laundry Rooms

As with the bathroom, it's critical to lock away all the cleaning supplies and other chemicals in the kitchen and laundry room as well. Make sure garbage cans are inaccessible to felines here, too. Other safety measures to take concern food, appliances (hot stoves and open washing machines), and small spaces that can prove dangerous.

Food: Never leave food out on counters. This applies to food ready for preparation and ready to be served, as well as leftovers. Never leave food wrapped in plastic on counters to defrost. Certain seemingly harmless foodstuffs such as mushrooms and grapes and beverages like tea and coffee are

▲ Keep the toilet lid closed to prevent your cat from drinking the water or falling in.

toxic to cats. Some felines are also lactose intolerant, and milk can cause those kitties diarrhea. Specific foods that are dangerous to cats include:

- Store-bought baby foods because many formulas contain onions, which are toxic to cats
- Grapes, mushrooms, raisins, and chocolate
- Table scraps that include meat, fish, and chicken bones, which can cause a cat to choke
- Tea, coffee, and alcoholic beverages
- Human vitamin supplements in pill form
- Milk and dairy products because many cats are lactose intolerant
- Moldy and spoiled food that you intend to throw in the trash
- Raw eggs and chicken that may contain salmonella
- Raw fish—many cats are allergic to certain fishes
- Bread dough left on a counter to rise; if ingested, it can swell in the stomach and even rupture intestines

Stovetops and ranges: Cats should be discouraged from being on counters near the range. It's a good idea to use plate covers when the stovetop is not in use, just in case your cat hasn't gotten the message to stay away and decides to jump up to investigate the source of all those delicious cooking smells.

Shopping bags: Make sure shopping bags—no matter what materials they are constructed from—are not left lying around anywhere in the home. Cats can suffocate if they get caught up in a plastic bag. Even paper bags with rope-styled handles or "eco-friendly" bags can be dangerous if a cat tries to get inside and gets the handle caught around her neck.

Laundry equipment: In the laundry area, make it a rule to close both washing machine and clothes dryer doors immediately after removing items to ensure that a cat doesn't get inside by accident. Awful accidents involving cats trapped in laundry equipment have made headlines in the past. In addition, be extra careful when tossing out used fabric softener cloths from clothes dryers. They can be toxic if chewed.

Space around appliances: Block off any tiny spaces alongside major appliances such as the fridge, stove, washing machine, and dryer to prevent curious felines from exploring and possibly getting stuck.

Garages

This area should be off-limits to cats at all times unless the garage is used *only* as a storage area and the exterior door is *never* opened. Generally speaking, a garage can be a really dangerous zone. The garage door opening at odd times during the day may give a cat sleeping in there a fright and cause her to run out. In addition, cats like to sleep under cars and stand the chance of being run over. Furthermore, it's a no-go zone because such areas are often used to store products such as antifreeze, garden fertilizers, and woodworking adhesives. Such products are all highly toxic to cats. It's more difficult to lock all of these products away in a garage, so it's better to keep the cat out of the garage.

▼ If you can't keep kitty out of the laundry area entirely, always check that she isn't in the washer or dryer before you turn it on.

▲ Fireplaces and woodstoves must have proper screening to prevent your cat from getting burned—or just covered in ashes.

Safe Outdoor Enclosures

There's no question that cats live safer lives if they enjoy an indoor-only lifestyle. However, if you have space to build an outdoor enclosure for them to use with direct access from your home, it is guaranteed to be a popular attraction. These days, many cat doors can be programmed shut to keep such areas off-limits when necessary.

Having a cat is an excellent excuse to practice environmentally friendly gardening indoors as well as out by getting rid of all the toxic chemical fertilizers and sprays. If you have a feline-safe outdoor enclosure that contains plant material, be very wary of putting down poison pellets for caterpillars, slugs, and other leaf munching bugs because they often resemble treats and kibble. At the same time, remember that although coffee grinds may be eco-friendly, they are toxic to pets. (See "An Outdoor Enclosure and Nontoxic Gardening," page 212.)

Shopping for Your Cat

Like every member of the household, a new cat is going to need her own space in the home in the form of a comfy bed, kitty condo, or cat tree, as well as basic accessories. Shopping in advance and having everything in place will allow your new friend to settle down quickly into her new home. Here's a checklist of cat essentials:

Kitty Carrier

You're going to need a nice secure kitty carrier to bring the cat or kitten home. Because it's not an item that is going to be replaced regularly, choose the size carefully and ensure that it's large enough for a fully grown cat to stand up and turn around in. It must offer plenty of ventilation. If you plan to travel with your feline companion, ensure that the carrier meets the standard size requirements for airline travel so it can fit comfortably under your seat. Carriers with flaps that can be rolled down may help a cat who is nervous to feel more secure.

Line the carrier with a fleecy, washable mat or a towel. If you are getting the kitten from a breeder, it's a good idea to take (or mail) the mat or whatever liner you plan to use to the breeder in advance so that the kitten can become used to it beforehand and "endorse it" with familiar smells. This will help familiarize her when she gets to her new home.

Be sure that you immediately attach a luggage-type label to the carrier detailing your cat's name and your contact information, such as name, address, and a telephone number where you can *always* be reached.

When the carrier's not in use, make sure it's stored in an accessible place so that you can grab it quickly, especially in an emergency situation. This basic planning should be done in advance, too. Make sure that everyone in the household knows where it's kept. Whether you are purchasing a soft-sided carrier or a plastic one, keep it in a clear plastic bag. This way, it will remain dust free and will be usable at a moment's notice.

If you are planning to travel with your cat regularly, consider purchasing two carriers—one strictly for trips to the veterinarian. Your cat will learn to distinguish between dreaded trips to the vet's office and climbing into the carrier to go somewhere fun.

Collars and ID Tags

There's a myriad of designs and colors to choose from when it comes to collars and tags. Because kittens grow quite quickly, it's a good idea to purchase the next size up when you make your

Pet Theft

Pet theft is an increasing problem across the United States. Cats or dogs who are left outdoors are often taken and sold for medical experiments or other uses. If your pet is taken, it may be hard to discover what happened and who is responsible. If you are lucky enough to not only recover your pet but also identify the catnapper, that individual can be prosecuted for the crime. However, this is a very difficult crime to punish because individuals who steal pets are often successful at evading the law by using aliases and phony business names.

More commonly, owners lose pets not through theft but through a pet becoming lost. Although you may diligently search for your lost pet, you can lose your rights to get her back if someone else has found her and is taking care of her. In such instances, the owner cannot claim theft. Each state regulates this process differently. To protect your pet, always make sure she is secured properly. If your backyard is gated, make sure it is properly locked so that strangers do not have easy access. Additionally, if you cannot secure your cat outside, consider an indoors-only lifestyle to protect her from being stolen.

initial purchase. A soft fabric collar with a quick-release clasp is ideal. If you want to purchase something stylish in leather be sure it has a release clasp to ensure that your cat will be able to escape if she climbs somewhere and gets hooked. With a collar that fits correctly, you should be able to slip two fingers inside. Never make it too loose because the cat will figure out how to slip out of it—and of course make sure it's not too tight! Collars with an actual buckle—that is, with a hook that fits into a hole—are best. Often, when cats scratch the area around their necks, collars that don't close securely in this manner can come loose and fall off.

Have an identification tag made in the store when purchasing a collar and attach it immediately. It's a good idea to purchase a second ID tag as back up. Proper identification is a lost pet's ticket home, and in many states, it's becoming law to microchip pets before they leave a shelter. Nevertheless, it's still a good idea to add a tag to a collar and to ensure that the information is always kept up to date. A collar and ID tag is the first thing someone finding your cat will see and, outside a shelter or other place that can read microchips, that is all that the person will see. With a tag, your cat may be returned sooner.

Harnesses and Leashes

It's possible to train a cat to wear a harness and leash to go for walks. The sooner you start this training the better. Consider purchasing a soft puppy harness, which is more secure than the standard harness designed for cats. You may have to replace this item as your kitten grows. To be stylish, purchase accessories to match the collar. If the harness gets in the way of the collar, then be sure to purchase another ID tag to remain permanently affixed to the harness.

The best way to train your cat to walk on a leash is to start by leaving her harness and leash lying around the house; play with your cat or kitten in this vicinity. And be sure to give treats. Next, put the harness on your cat indoors and let her wear it around the house. Start with no more than five minutes and build up to thirty minutes or longer.

▶ You will need a carrier for your kitty for trips to the vet and in case of an emergency, such as a weather-related evacuation.

Next, attach the leash and walk her around indoors. Remember, during all this training, treats are your (and your cat's) best friend! Finally, you are ready for the great outdoors.

A six-foot (2 m) leash is a good starter length for initial outdoor excursions. Depending on how your cat reacts and how comfortable you feel outdoors with her, you can at a later stage consider a longer retractable-style leash. It's also a good idea to take a big towel with you for outdoor excursions in case you have to grab her quickly if a dog comes along. The towel will prevent you from being scratched.

Cat Beds

Chances are your cat will enjoy curling up and sleeping on the bed with you, or she may select a certain sofa or chair in the home as a preferred snooze zone. Nevertheless, most cats enjoy having their own beds, too.

Because cats like to sleep curled "in the round," select a round or oval-shaped bed. Small dogs beds work very well for felines so don't over look this department when shopping. If the bed doesn't come with a detachable cover, make sure the fabric is easy to keep clean. There are also plenty of plush beds that are fully machine-washable.

Food and Water Bowls

There is no shortage of stylish food and water bowls that will slot in beautifully with your home décor. Stainless steel, glass, or non-lead ceramic bowls are

▲ Cats can be trained to walk with a harness and leash, and these cats enjoy their outings.

hygienic because they are dishwasher safe and thus easy to keep clean. Avoid plastic, not only because it is more difficult to keep clean, but also because many cats are allergic to this material and break out in chin acne. When selecting food bowls, also remember that the flatter the bowl or plate, the better. Cats don't feel comfortable when their whiskers touch the side of a bowl. It's called *whisker stress*.

Many veterinarians consider raised food bowls a good idea because sitting upright is a far better position for good digestion. Similarly, consider a special tall glass pet flute as a water bowl. This looks similar to a glass vase with a wide bowl on a stand.

A lot of cats love to drink running water and will enjoy a drinking fountain. They run on very low-voltage electricity and will ensure that your pet has a constant supply of fresh water. There are different types to choose from: Some send the water cascading down, and others allow the water to bubble up. Always have at least two water sources in the home, even more if you have a multipet household.

Litter Boxes

Choose a litter tray with nice high sides, which will guard against the contents being flung out and

Leash Laws

Leash laws for cats are regulated by local city or country ordinances and do exist in states such as Georgia, North Dakota, and Texas. In essence, a leash law means that any cat found roaming free can be picked up and euthanized. Such laws are subject to ongoing controversy because opponents feel cats should be treated differently than dogs because they do not pose the same threats to property and human beings that dogs do. Such laws are also subject to constant change. Up-to-date information is available at www.municode.com.

scattered over a wide area. There are numerous shapes to consider, as well as a variety of automated boxes. The rule is one litter box per cat in the household even though each cat may not use one box exclusively.

A self-cleaning litter box is something you may want to consider at a later stage, once you have assessed your cat's personality. Many cats are scared by the noise the cleaning mechanism makes as a rake runs through the litter, pushing the solid waste into a receptacle on one end of the box, where it is covered up. The rake will comb through the litter until no more waste is encountered. The waste receptacle is disposed of every few weeks.

Another toileting system deemed suitable for cats looks like a square of lawn with a special drain system built-in underneath. They can be kitted out with either real or synthetic grass and can be kept inside or on a balcony.

Despite the many shapes and concepts for kitty toilets, behaviorists tend to favor large open boxes—the bigger the better, especially in multicat households, so that no cat ever feels trapped inside her box with no escape route.

Also, never place litter boxes side by side. Choose different locations in the household. In multicat

▲ A wide water bowl is the best choice for your kitty because cats don't like to have their whiskers touching the edges when they drink.

households, if cats are ambushing one another around the litter box, placing them next to one another is considered one giant litter box from a feline standpoint, and this could lead to one of the cats avoiding the boxes to go elsewhere for privacy.

Litter Type

If you are using a conventional litter box and you got your cat from a breeder, check with the breeder to find out what type of litter the kitten has been using and initially buy the same brand. You can always transition to something else later by adding the new preferred brand to the existing brand, gradually increasing the amount until you are switched over completely. A transition can take about a week to ten days.

The most widely used type of litter is a clay-based clumping formula. There is also a wide variety of long-lasting silica formulations, as well as a variety of eco-friendly litters made from wheat and coconut husks that can be safely flushed down a toilet.

Litter Box Accessories

A litter mat placed under the box will help contain litter and keep it from being tracked outside of the box. Litter box liners are designed for quick and easy removal of the entire contents of the box so it can be emptied and sanitized. Be sure to purchase thick plastic liners so that your cat doesn't claw through them. A litter scoop, of course, is essential. The latest litter scoops come on a telescope-style handle so that you don't have to bend to floor level. Add a brush and a pan to the shopping list to keep the area clean.

New litter box accessories are constantly making an appearance in the marketplace, such as handheld vacuums designed specifically for scattered litter pick-up and that also have a nozzle to remove cat hair from fabric surfaces. If necessary, there are certain nontoxic litter deodorizers that you can add directly to the litter to keep it odor-free.

Scratching Posts

Scratching is an instinctive feline trait. Cats scratch for various reasons: to sharpen their claws, to mark their territory, to reduce stress—and also as a form of exercise. They tend to scratch your favorite chair because they are attracted to it by *your* scent. Consequently, investing in a nice scratching post will preserve your furniture and give your cat an important enrichment tool.

Cats scratch both horizontally and vertically, and it's difficult to tell which they prefer. So, if your budget will allow, buy two different kinds of scratchers and you will soon learn your cat's preference. Those made from recycled cardboard are economical and eco-friendly. Sisal-covered posts are also popular with felines and very hard wearing. It's a good idea to avoid carpet-covered posts because some cats have difficulty differentiating between their scratching post and your expensive floor covering or priceless Oriental rug.

Where you position scratchers in the home is equally important because cats usually like to stretch and scratch after a nap. It's a good idea to place one near a cat bed or a favorite snooze zone. Over time, consider placing others around the house; it will be obvious which rooms of the home your cat spends more time in, such as the family living room. Once again, be sure to place a scratcher near a popular nap spot or next to a particular piece of furniture that your cat has been eyeing.

Introduce your cat to a new scratching post by scratching on the surface with your fingers. The cat will copy (cats are fast learners). A little catnip rubbed into the surface is another irresistible incentive. Keep in mind that you can never have too many scratching zones in the home. Consider taller scratching posts over shorter ones even if they are more expensive because they will allow your cat to get a really good stretch, too.

Kitty Condos and Cat Trees

Because cats enjoy spending time in elevated positions, a multistation kitty condo or a tall cat tree is a wonderful feline entertainment center. At the same time, such an item of feline furniture allows your cat the privacy of having her own space in the home. Look for a design that has a place where a cat can snooze or hide out, as well as an elevated observation platform. Such play stations often are accessorized with toys, such as dangling ropes, and may include a tall scratching post. If space is a

▼ Investing in a nice scratching post will preserve your furniture and give your cat an important enrichment tool.

An Outdoor Enclosure and Nontoxic Gardening

Most cats love the opportunity to sun themselves in a safe outdoor environment that offers them some plants to nibble on, a shady spot to snooze in, and even a tree to scratch on and climb. It's very easy to create an environmentally friendly organic area with some simple planning.

Before you even begin to think of an organic garden, it's important to find an ideal part of your outdoor area that can be safely enclosed for your cat to enjoy. Fencing is your first priority, and there are special cat-proof fences that can be erected over existing fences to prevent cats from escaping and coming into contact with predators or other dangers, such as traffic.

Consider turning an atrium or enclosed patio with planting areas into a cat-friendly outdoor area, too. If you are worried about birds flying in and falling prey to feline paws, roof the area with light netting or lattice work.

Preparing the Soil

Gardening organically instead of using chemicals is not only better for the environment, but it's also better for you, your family, and your pets. Proper soil preparation is key to successful organic gardening. (It can take up to three years for an area that has previously been treated with chemical fertilizers and pesticides to become all-natural again.) Your ultimate goal is a soil rich in organic nutrients that will produce lush plants.

Garden supply stores sell soil test kits if you want to check the exact acidity or alkalinity of your soil, so that you can improve or *amend* it for optimal plant growth. The best way to improve your soil is with organic compost. Organic compost can be bought from garden stores and nurseries, but its very easy to make your own simply by purchasing a compost maker and depositing in it all your natural household waste matter, such as lawn clippings, fallen leaves, vegetable peels, coffee grounds, and egg shells. As these items break down and decay, they become compost that will add nutrients and micronutrients to your soil, which, in turn, will product strong, healthy plants.

It's become very popular for the organically minded to invest in a worm farm. This is a special set of containers that become home to earthworms purchased specially to feed off your kitchen leftovers to produce compost, as well as turning their worm poo (called *castings*) into a rich fertilizer.

Bone meal is an excellent source of potassium and magnesium, but because it's an animal and fish by-product it is not acceptable to vegan gardeners. Compost is a vegan-friendly alternative. Chicken manure and bat guano are other sources of nitrogen and phosphorous. Bird guano is a mined product that will add nitrogen and phosphorous, depending on where it has been mined, and potassium sulfate is also a mined product that will add potassium and magnesium, depending on where it's been mined. Be sure to read the labels, and ask your local garden experts about plants that can add nutrients (such as nitrogen) to your soil, too.

Mapping It Out

What you plant is going to depend directly on the size of your area and the amount of sun or shade the spot receives. It's a good idea to draw a diagram and map out what you would like to include in your cat-friendly garden. Cats love a tree to scratch on and possibly even climb and watch the world go by. Depending on space, you may even want to secure a little cat lookout platform in a tree. (It's important to ensure that the branches do not reach a wall or other structure that the cat could access.) Or, consider building a wooden cat condo with hidey-holes for snoozing and attach weatherproof swing toys to it. Other great ideas for your cat-friendly outdoor space:

Calendula officinalis

- A feline "staircase" of shelves with planters on each step filled with catnip, cat grasses, and flowering edibles

- For the enclosed patio or paved atrium, a patch of grass grown in a framed box for easy maintenance

- An outdoor litter box—free standing or, if possible, dig a hole and recess it so that it's level with the ground but easy to take out for cleaning

Outdoor water sources, like bowls and flowing fountains are always a popular feline attraction. Water will attract birds and other small animals, however, so you may want to provide a separate catproof area for bird baths and feeders. Any outdoor water source provided must be cleaned out regularly to prevent algae build-up; use a solution of vinegar and baking soda instead of toxic cleaning agents.

Catnip

What to Plant

Cats love to nibble on plants and grasses in particular. There are lots of safe nontoxic herbs, flowers, shrubs, and trees to choose from. Always make sure that whatever you choose to plant will do well in your climate and with your soil conditions.

Herbs, Fruits, and Vegetables

- *Fruits:* melon, squash, strawberries

- *Herbs:* basil, cat grass, catmint, catnip, cilantro, dill, lavender, lemon balm, lemon verbena, thyme, and parsley

Lavender

- *Vegetables:* carrots, cucumber, lettuce, spinach, Swiss chard

Flowering Plants

- *Annuals: Alyssum, Aster, Calendula, Celosia, Iresine,* marigold (*Tagetes*), nasturtium (*Trapaeolum*), pansy (*Viola*), snapdragon (*Antirrhinum*), *Zinnia*

- *Ferns:* Boston fern (*Neprolepis exaltata*), button fern (*Pellea rotundifolia*), holly fern (*Cyrtomium falcatum*), mother fern (*Asplenium bulbiferum*)

- *Perennials:* aster cone flower (*Echium*), *Coreopsis*, gerbera daisy (*Gerbera*), coral bells (*Huechera*), polka dot plant (*Hypoestes*), African daisy (*Osteospermum*), bearded tongue (*Penstemon*), sage (*Salvia*), pincushion flower (*Scabiosa*)

Mock orange

- *Shade plants: Begonia,* cast iron plant (*Aspidistra elatior*), *Impatiens,* spider plant (*Chlorophytum*), wandering Jew (*Tradescantia zebrine*)

- *Tropical:* bamboo, banana (*Musa*), canna lily (*Canna*), ginger (*Zingiber officinale*), jungle geranium (*Ixora*)

Grasses and Ground Cover

- *Ground cover:* baby tears (*Soleirolia soleirolii*), ice plant (*Lampranthus*), Serbian bellflower (*Campanula*), spring cinquefoil (*Potentilla*), star jasmine (*Trachylospermum jasminoides*), wild strawberry (*Fragaria*)

Star jasmine

- *Lawn:* Bermuda (*Cynodon dactylon*), St. Augustine grass (*Stenotaphrum secundatum*), tall fescue (*Festuca arundinacea*)
- *Ornamental grasses:* blue fescue (*Festuca caesia*), Carex 'Frosty Curls', fountain grass (*Pennisetum*), sheep grass (*Festuca ovina*)

Shrubs

- Bush cherry (*Eugenia*), camellia (*Camellia japonica* and *Camellia sasanqua*), *Coleonema pulchellum*, glossy abelia (*Abelia grandiflora*), Japanese aralia (*Fatsia japonica*), 'Little John' dwarf bottlebrush (*Callistemon*), mirror shrub (*Coprosma*), mock orange (*Pittosporum tobira*), Natal plum (*Carissa macrocarpa*), roses (*Rosa*), star jasmine (*Tracylospermum jasminoides*)

Trees

- *Fruit trees:* orange and lemon trees are easy to control in size and shape and can be grown successfully in large containers; cats are not interested in eating these fruits. Put something moving and shiny in the branches of fruit trees to keep birds at bay.
- *Ornamentals:* crape myrtle (*Lagerstroemia indica*), pink melaleuca (*Melaleuca nesophila*), weeping bottlebrush (*Callistemon viminalis*), weeping fruitless mulberry (*Morus alba* 'Chaparral')
- *Palms:* bottle palm (*Beaucarnia recurvata*), kentia palm (*Howea forsteriana*), lady palm (*Raphis excelsa*), pygmy date palm (*Phoenix roebelinnii*), windmill palm (*Trachycarpus fortunei*)

How to Mulch and Fertilize

Adding mulch to your garden helps to prevent weeds, conserves moisture in the soil, and stabilizes soil temperatures. Organic mulch also helps to maintain the humus or organic content of the soil as it decomposes and keeps the top layer loose and airy. Layer mulch two to four inches deep over bare soil around your plants. You can use organic compost, grass clippings (which are high in nitrogen), bark or shredded wood chips, fallen leaves (but be sure to chop them small), pine needles, and even straw. Beware of cocoa mulch, which is a chocolate by-product and very toxic and possibly lethal to both cats and dogs.

Chemical fertilizers can also be toxic to cats, so choose safe organic alternatives instead. Organic fertilizers are, in fact, superior to chemicals because you are adding nutrients to the soil, rather than just giving plants a "quick fix."

Dealing with Pesky Pests

The toxic chemical pellets used as snail bait often resemble kibble and may be eaten by cats, and chemical pesticides sprayed onto leaves instantly make them toxic to pets who like to nibble on grass and greenery.

Organic pellets made from iron phosphate are a safe alternative to control slugs and snails. There are several organic pesticides on the market that are derived from spinosaid, a naturally occurring chemical produced by bacteria that kills insects. It's available in a liquid spray-on form. It takes care of worms, beetles, earwigs, sowbugs, and ants. Neem, derived from the Indian neem tree, is another natural insecticide that kills sucking insects like mealybugs, scale, and aphids. The efficacy of most organic pesticides is short, so you will have to reapply more often.

Grassy areas can also pick up fungus and other diseases and are home to insects pests and fleas. Use organic forms of lawn control that contain nematodes, a type of microscopic worm that feeds on bacteria, fungi, grubs, and the larvae of grubs and—most important for cat owners—fleas. Another good organic flea control product is diatomaceous earth, a chalky powder made up of the exoskeletons of diatoms, which are a form of algae; it is a powerful desiccant and will dry up and kill flea larvae on contact. Products that contain both diatomaceous earth and nematodes are available from online stores and specialized organic gardening stores.

Time to Enjoy

If you have space, be sure to include a bench, garden chair, or even a chaise longue so that you can enjoy some outside time with your felines too.

▲ If you have the space and the budget, your cat will surely love a kitty condo or cat tree.

concern, look for special designs that hook onto the back of a door or can be bolted to a wall.

Grooming Tools

If your kitten comes from a breeder, ask his or her advice on what grooming tools to buy in terms of your kitten's fur type. Here's a list to get you started, the basic at-home tools of the trade:

- A soft wire brush to remove tangles without irritating skin
- A comb with wide teeth for removing tangles, especially in longhaired cats
- A curry comb with long rubber teeth that removes loose hair and simultaneously massages the skin
- A de-shedding tool to remove thick undercoat as well as loose fur
- A grooming glove or mitt covered with a knobby rubber finish or a special hair-grabbing material
- A good pair of nail clippers, even if your cat has a scratching post
- Specially formulated feline grooming wipes

If you are unsure about how to clip your cat's nails, consider buying clippers that light up to show you where its safe to cut so that you don't cut into the quick and cause bleeding.

Remember that grooming is also a wonderful quality-time activity and plays an important socializing role in establishing a human–feline bond. Consequently, when shopping for grooming tools, look for those with ergonomically designed handles that you feel comfortable holding.

Toys

Every cat and kitten needs a well-stocked toy box, and there's no shortage of fabulous toys that cater specifically to feline needs, offering both mental and physical stimulation, as well as revving up their prey drive and honing their hunting skills. Remember that kittens teethe. So add to your shopping list special textured chew toys that can be placed in the freezer for an additional soothing effect. They are a good investment because they also promote healthy teeth and gums.

No cat can resist a wand with something feathery on the end. Small balls that roll and anything that crinkles will also be well received. Be sure to add a catnip-filled mouse to your shopping list, too.

Some young kittens appreciate sleeping with something warm and cuddly. A special slumber toy with a built-in heartbeat mechanism designed to sooth an anxious kitten who is spending her first nights away from her mother is worth considering. They are available in a variety of shapes and sizes. Alternatively, consider purchasing a soft floppy comfort toy and place a small alarm clock underneath it. The ticking effect is also soothing.

If you have young children in the household, ensure that your cat's toys have a different texture and feel to them than your children's favorite toys. In this way, a young child will be able to better understand which toys belongs to the cat and that *they* aren't allowed to touch and chew those toys.

Cats need toys that provide interaction, distraction, and comfort. You can buy basics in the beginning and add to the collection from time to time because cats, just like children, always enjoy something new.

Interactive toys are those, such as lasers and wand-type toys, that will involve you in the game. Distraction toys are those, such as food puzzle games, that keep the cat busy figuring out how to get to the goods and thus mentally stimulated. And comfort toys comprise anything soft and cuddly and preferably catnip-infused.

There is also a wonderful selection of battery-operated toys that can be pre-set to start up when your cat is home alone, such as a laser toy that can be pre-set for play and a little mouse going around and around on a track to provide both mental and physical stimulation.

Introducing Your New Cat

New surroundings can be daunting to a new cat or kitten. The best way to get her to settle in quickly is to initially place her in one room and let her familiarize herself within these confines first. Select a bright airy room that has little foot traffic.

Put the cat bed in a corner or on the side of the room away from drafty windows or doors, and position the food and water bowls close by. Be sure to place her litter tray at the opposite side of the room. Felines are fastidious about their toilet habits

▲ Different cats like different toys. Experiment with several types to see which your cat prefers.

and don't like food and water close to their toilet area. The best litter box location is one where the cat can see anyone approaching.

Most kittens have been trained by their mothers to use a litter box and will instinctively cover up their business with litter after they are done. However, in the beginning, it's a good idea to place your cat in the box at regular intervals, especially after meals. Natural instinct will kick in! Because cats are such clean animals, get into the habit of scooping the tray at least once a day. Otherwise, your cat may use a cleaner spot outside the box. If

▼ Kitty tunnels are another type of cat furniture your cat may enjoy.

this happens, you will only have yourself to blame! If you start out keeping a cat in one room, once you give her access to more space, you can slowly move the box until you are able to position it in its final location in the home.

Opinions vary as to how long a cat should initially be confined to a room. The time frame will have a lot to do with the makeup of your individual household in terms of children and other pets. If you live alone, a week may be fine. However, with young children and other pets around, you may want to extend the restriction to one room for as long as a month.

Initially, only one person should be in charge of all cat duties, from putting down food and water to scooping the litter box. Once the cat has been properly integrated into the household, however, these duties can be delegated. Even when a kitten is allowed free rein of the home, if you have to go out, it's a good idea to once again confine her to the initial room where she was housed on arrival. It's safer for the kitten, and you will have more peace of mind. In the beginning, you may want to consider doing this for a new adult cat, too.

Introducing the newcomers to all members of the household—human (adult and child), feline, canine, bird, rodent—takes time and patience. It's critical that you handle the introductions carefully, to ensure the best possibility for household harmony. No matter whom the cat is being introduced to, whether it's to family members or to other pets in the household, remember to reward positive behavior with treats—and that includes rewarding any human children!

Introductions to the Family

When it comes to introductions, take it slow and only allow one person at a time to come into the room to meet the newest member of the family. Naturally, children need to be accompanied by an adult, and the kid and feline house rules have to go into effect immediately. Save introductions to friends for a few weeks to ensure it's not all too overwhelming for the newcomer.

Hands-on attention is a very important part of socializing both a kitten and an older cat so that the

▲ Wands and other interactive toys are wonderful because they give you a way to play with your cat.

newcomer will settle down in her new environment and enjoy being with the family. In fact, the more handling a kitten receives during the early weeks of her life, the more sociable she will be as an adult.

It's during this time that a kitten is most open to exploring the unfamiliar, which consists of everything and everyone in its new world. So make sure the kitten has a good time in the company of different family members. By the same token, stroking and playing with an older cat will also help the newcomer to establish bonds and enjoy the companionship that everyone in the household has to offer.

Introductions to Other Family Felines

If you already have a cat, don't count on the fact that the newcomer and the established feline resident are of the same species to translate into instant friendship. How those first introductions go will have a lot to do with the personalities of the respective felines. If the incumbent cat is shy, she could even show signs of aggression because cats are naturally territorial, and a new cat could be viewed as an intruder. An incumbent cat is more likely to be tolerant of a kitten than of a fully grown cat, and female cats are known to be more aggressive than males. Ultimately, their individual personalities will rule. As far as members of the household are concerned, everyone needs to stay calm during these initial introductions. Cats are very intuitive and pick up on human emotions. Patience is key; go slowly.

Because the new cat will initially be confined to one room, you may find your incumbent cat coming to sniff at the door. In fact, introducing cats by smell is the best way to go. One way you can do this is with a pair of socks. Rub one sock with the smell of the newcomer and the other with the smell of your incumbent cat or cats. Then swop out the socks by placing the newcomer's sock in an area of the house where other animals are and vice versa. Do this daily for a couple of days.

When you ready for formal introductions, it's a good idea to place the newcomer in another room of the home and allow your incumbent cat or cats to go inside the room that the newcomer has just vacated and sniff around. Again, do this several times before taking it up a notch and allowing them to sniff each other.

If you have a baby gate, let them meet on either side of the gate. Alternatively, place the newcomer in a carrier so that she feels secure and allow your other cat(s) to sniff around.

It's important to gauge how you think it's proceeding before actually letting them meet up face to face, with no barrier between them. Plan the initial meet-up for when you have time, such as on a weekend or when you've scheduled a few days off from work.

Rubbing vanilla essence on both cats, on their shoulder blades and at the base of their tails where they will have difficulty licking at it, can be helpful with the initial meet-up because when they sniff each other, they will smell the same.

It's important that the first occasions spent together are positive experiences for both cats. Consider having the first "meet-and-greet sessions" be held over a tasty treat by putting them down next to each other with a separate bowl of tuna or kibble for each.

Expect some hissing and some deep-throated growling. It's a normal part of the "meet-and-greet" routine. Pet and play with both of them. However, if it turns physical, you may have to step in and separate

◄ Hands-on attention is a very important part of socializing a new feline companion so she will settle down in her new environment and enjoy being with the family.

them again. And, if the physical contact continues to get nasty every time you place them together, you may have to go back to square one, separate them for a week, and then start over.

Feline introductions can take a long time—even up to six months before they tolerate one another. With care and patience, they can go from toleration to friendship.

The bottom line is take charge. *Never* bring in a new cat and leave the cats to get on with it. This can be very stressful to all the cats involved, and sometimes the resulting animosity is permanent.

Introductions to the Family Dog

Once again, the sniffing game is a good place to start. Don't ever let your dog rush at your cat or kitten, even in play. After giving the animals time to get used to the smell of each other with the room-sniffing routine, move on to the next step: a face-to-face meeting, with precautions. For this meeting, keep the cat in a carrier and your dog on a leash. In this way, you can control your dog and can pull him away if necessary. Make sure you have treats handy and reward your dog, along with lots of "Good dog!" praises.

When you finally let your cat out of the carrier, continue to keep your dog on a leash so that you can separate them quickly if necessary. At all times, make sure that there is an easy escape route for the cat. It's a good idea to do initial introductions close to a cat condo so that the cat can easily get out of reach of the dog in a hurry. (It's a good idea to have a pet first-aid antiseptic spray on hand should they scratch or nip one another.)

Slowly allow them to spend more time together under strict supervision until you are sure that neither one is a threat to the other.

Introductions to Birds and Small Critters

It's important to bear in mind that cats are natural predators, and small critters such as hamsters, birds, and fish need to be kept out of harm's way at all times. Both bird cages and small animal cages should have a box inside them so that these pets can escape completely out of sight, too.

Be careful of your cat getting on top of the fish tank or reptile cage as well. The cat may knock over lights, filters, or heating elements, causing flood or fire. The cat could also go through the fish tank cover, which would not be good for the fish. If the tank is large enough, there might even be a chance your poor cat could drown.

Different animals can live harmoniously in a household. However, never leave a cat alone in a room with a small critter or a fish bowl. Natural instincts may just kick in when you are not there.

▼ With patience and careful management, your cat and your dog can be friendly toward—or at least tolerant of—each other.

▼ When introducing two cats to each other, intervene whenever hissing and spitting escalates to scratching and biting.

Chapter 9

Establishing a Health Care Regimen

Dr. Arnold Plotnick, DVM

The key to establishing a good health care regimen for your new kitten or adult cat is preventive care. The best way to achieve this is to find a good veterinarian and work closely with him or her to come up with a comprehensive preventative care program. Every cat is an individual, and your veterinarian can help you devise a program that is appropriate for your cat's particular needs. Immunization, for example, is a critical part of a preventive health care program for all cats. Cats who go outdoors, however, may require vaccinations that differ from those for cats who reside strictly indoors. As cats progress through the different stages of life, the diagnostic tests that are part of a comprehensive wellness program will differ accordingly. It is important that you choose a veterinarian with whom you feel comfortable, so that you can communicate your observations and concerns candidly and comfortably, enabling you to work together to maximize your cat's health and longevity.

Selecting A Veterinarian

Choosing a veterinarian is similar to selecting a family doctor or dentist. It is a very personal choice, and the same criteria apply. Many people choose a veterinarian based solely on proximity. However, there are many factors to consider when choosing a veterinarian, including the services offered, the cost, and the doctor's bedside manner. Personal referrals are an excellent way of finding a good veterinarian. Before simply consulting the Internet or

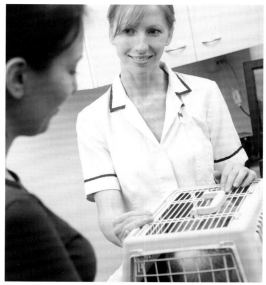

▶ Choose your veterinarian carefully. You need to be comfortable with the vet, his or her staff, and the office environment.

checking local Yellow Pages for the nearest clinic, ask your cat-owning friends, relatives, or neighbors for recommendations (make sure they are satisfied with the veterinarians they recommend). If you have a specific breed of cat, contact the local breed club for recommendations for veterinarians familiar with your breed; breed clubs can be a good all-around source of information. Cat owners may want to consider going to a feline-exclusive veterinary facility because the doctors there will be more familiar with feline disorders than those at a general veterinary practice.

Once you have the name of the recommended veterinarian or veterinary clinic/hospital, pay a visit to meet the veterinarian so you can discuss your cat and your expectations. Ask for a tour of the facilities. The clinic should meet your standards for cleanliness and organization, and the veterinarian should be someone who makes you feel comfortable and who is willing to answer all of your questions. The technicians, receptionists, and other staff should be friendly and professional. You may wish to visit several practices before making your final decision.

Pets don't always get sick between 9:00 a.m. and 5:00 p.m. If you find yourself in the unfortunate position of having to deal with a veterinary emergency, it's important to know where to go for help. Not all veterinary clinics offer twenty-four-hour or emergency care. If your veterinarian does not offer emergency services, ask him or her where to take your cat in the event of an emergency. Although veterinary clinics offer a name and phone number of a nearby emergency facility on their answering machine recording if you call after hours, you should be familiar with the location before any emergency arises. Don't squander precious time searching for the facility if your cat is in dire straits.

Immunization

Vaccines have been an integral part of preventive health care programs for several decades. In fact, no other medical development has been as successful as vaccination in controlling deadly diseases in companion animals. Vaccination is a medical procedure, and the decision to vaccinate is made

Vaccine-Induced Sarcomas

Certain types of vaccines contain a chemical substance called an *adjuvant*. Adjuvants cause a strong inflammatory response at the injection site, and this enhances the immune response to the vaccine. In rare instances, however, the exuberant inflammatory reaction can give rise to a cancerous skin tumor called a sarcoma. Other factors, such as genetic susceptibility, may also play a role in some cats. The incidence of vaccine-induced sarcomas is low—approximately 1 or 2 per 10,000 vaccines administered.

based on the risks and benefits for each individual cat. Although vaccination should not be considered a totally benign procedure (see Vaccine-Induced Sarcomas sidebar on this page), choosing not to vaccinate our pets is not an option. The threat of their contracting infectious, often fatal diseases is too great. The goal is to devise a reasonable strategy for vaccination that maximizes our ability to prevent infectious disease while minimizing the occurrence of adverse events associated with vaccination.

Core vs. Noncore Vaccines

Vaccinations can be divided into two broad categories: core vaccines—those recommended for *all* cats, and noncore vaccines—those that may or may not be necessary, depending on the individual cat's lifestyle and circumstances. Currently, vaccines against panleukopenia, herpesvirus, calicivirus, and rabies fall into the core vaccine category. The most commonly used vaccine against panleukopenia, herpesvirus, and calicivirus is a *multi*valent vaccine: it contains viral antigens for several diseases together in the same dose, and it is commonly abbreviated as the FVRCP vaccine. The rabies vaccine is usually a *mono*valent vaccine: it contains viral antigens for one virus, the rabies virus.

Vaccines against feline leukemia virus (FeLV), feline immunodeficiency virus (FIV), feline infectious peritonitis (FIP), ringworm (a skin fungus), *Chlamydophila* (a respiratory pathogen, formerly called *Chlamydia*), and *Bordetella* (another respiratory pathogen) are considered to be noncore. Some of the noncore vaccines have questionable efficacy and are not generally recommended.

Pediatric Vaccination Protocol

Kittens are the main target population for vaccination because they are more susceptible to infection than adult cats, and they tend to develop more severe disease than do adults. The currently recommended vaccination protocol is as follows:

- The kitten vaccination series should begin at six to eight weeks of age. Kittens should initially receive an FVRCP vaccine, with additional boosters given every three to four weeks until sixteen weeks of age. Kittens older than twelve weeks of age should receive an initial FVRCP vaccine, followed by an additional FVRCP booster three to four weeks later.
- Kittens should receive a rabies vaccine at twelve to sixteen weeks of age.
- The FeLV vaccine is a noncore vaccine in adult cats; however, all kittens should be vaccinated against FeLV because the lifestyles of kittens may change after adoption, potentially increasing their risk for FeLV exposure. A

▼The vaccination regimen for kittens normally starts when they are six to eight weeks old.

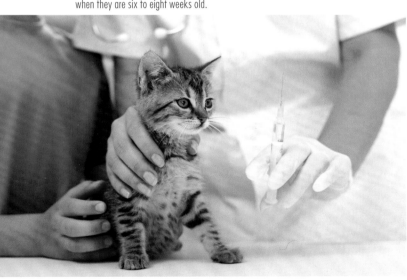

booster vaccine should be given one year later in cats who remain at risk for exposure to FeLV.

- One year after the last vaccination, an FVRCP vaccine and a rabies vaccine should again be administered.

Vaccines against infectious diseases have done much to reduce sickness and death in companion animals, and vaccination is the cornerstone of preventive veterinary medicine. As with any medical procedure or decision, the advantages must be balance against the risks, and you and your veterinarian should discuss all of the options available to determine the best vaccine protocol for your cat.

Adult Vaccination Protocol

Cats older than sixteen weeks of age who have never been vaccinated against panleukopenia, herpes virus, and calici virus should receive two doses of vaccine, three to four weeks apart. A single booster against panleukopenia , herpesvirus, and calicivirus is given one year later, and then every three years thereafter.

How often the rabies vaccine should be given depends on the vaccine. Some are labeled for annual revaccination. Others are to be given every three years. The FeLV vaccine is given annually in cats determined to have continued risk of exposure.

Healthy older cats, and those with chronic but stable conditions, should be vaccinated in the same fashion as if they were younger adults. Sick cats, however, whether kitten or adult, should not be vaccinated until they have recovered from their illness.

Health Care Issues for New Kittens

There are few things in life more endearing and enjoyable than a fuzzy new kitten. Caring for a kitten, however, is a great responsibility, a commitment that can last fifteen or even twenty years. To ensure that your kitten completes her kittenhood

Cat Years

Cats are considered to be adults at one year of age, the age when kittenhood officially ends. Although there is no consensus among veterinarians as to when middle age ends and "old age" begins, most veterinarians (and many pet food companies, if you go by how they label their "lifestage" cat foods) would say that adulthood/middle age lasts from the age of one to seven years, and that cats are "elderly," "geriatric," "senior," or "mature" from the age of seven onward. A recent classification by the Feline Advisory Bureau makes the distinction between "prime" cats, "mature" cats, "senior" cats, and "geriatric" cats. Exactly when a cat is considered to be senior or geriatric is not well-defined. Cats can be thought of as being "mature" from the ages of seven to ten years, "senior" from the ages of eleven to fourteen years, and "geriatric" at age fifteen and older.

Advances in veterinary medicine have allowed cats and dogs to live longer than ever before. Your average indoor well-cared-for housecat lives, on average, sixteen to seventeen years. Feral cats and cats who go outdoors live shorter lifespans.

The notion that dogs (and cats) age at a pace of seven years for every one actual year is a persistent myth. If you think about it, it is not uncommon for some cats to live to be eighteen or nineteen years old. If they aged seven years for every one year, then an eighteen-year-old cat would be equivalent to a 126-year-old person, which is clearly not very likely. The "seven-to-one" rule is just not true. Cats age faster when they're younger, but the aging process slows down as they get older.

The Feline Advisory Bureau divides a cat's life into six stages—kitten (zero to six months), junior (seven months to two years), prime (three to six years), mature (seven to ten years), senior (eleven to fourteen years), and geriatric (fifteen years and older). This chart shows a comparison of cat's age to human age.

CAT'S AGE	HUMAN'S AGE	CAT'S AGE	HUMAN'S AGE
0–1 month	0–1 year	11 years	60 years
2–3 months	2–4 years	12 years	64 years
4 months	6–8 years	13 years	68 years
6 months	10 years	14 years	72 years
7 months	12 years	15 years	76 years
12 months	15 years	16 years	80 years
18 months	21 years	17 years	84 years
2 years	24 years	18 years	88 years
3 years	28 years	19 years	92 years
4 years	32 years	20 years	96 years
5 years	36 years	21 years	100 years
6 years	40 years	22 years	104 years
7 years	44 years	23 years	108 years
8 years	48 years	24 years	112 years
9 years	52 years	25 years	116 years
10 years	56 years		

with flying colors, you need to consider several common health issues. Helping your kitten reach adulthood can pose a challenge, as bacterial, viral, fungal, and parasitic diseases lurk around every corner. Awareness of the symptoms of common kitten diseases, followed by prompt veterinary intervention, maximizes your kitten's ability to reach adulthood.

Upper Respiratory Infections

Upper respiratory infections (URIs) are very common in kittens and are usually caused by a virus—the herpes virus, the calici virus, or both. They often result in sneezing, discharge from the eyes and nose, drooling, congestion, fever, and poor appetite. The herpes virus (also called the rhinotracheitis virus) is the most common culprit and causes profuse sneezing and a watery or mucoid nasal discharge. Calici virus causes milder respiratory signs; however, it can cause ulcers in the mouth and on the tongue, resulting in drooling and difficulty eating. Conjunctivitis (informally known as pinkeye) in both eyes often accompanies these symptoms. Conjunctivitis can be viral, but it can also be caused by *Chlamydophila*, a common bacteria isolated from cats with viral URIs. Treatment of URIs requires supportive care with oral antibiotics, antiviral drugs, medicated eye ointments, and nutritional supplements such as the amino acid lysine. Fortunately, most kittens recover from respiratory infections.

External Parasites

Ear mites and fleas are both parasites that live on the skin surface. Ear mites mainly affect kittens, whereas fleas are equal opportunity tormenters, affecting kittens and cats alike.

Ear Mites

These tiny mites feed on debris in the ear canal. Symptoms include ear scratching, head shaking, and a dark brown, crusty ear discharge. Often, some trauma occurs around the ears and face because of the intense itching caused by the mites. Many veterinary and over-the-counter products

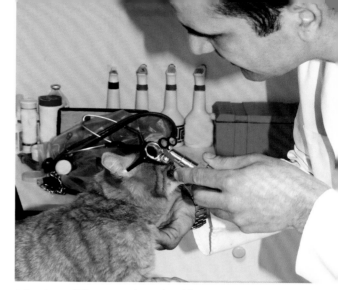

▶ Ear mites are fairly common in kittens, but adult cats are not immune. Your vet will definitely check your new feline for these pests.

require frequent application to the ears of an often-uncooperative kitten, making the process time-consuming and labor intensive. However, newer topical products that are put on the skin have made treatment of these pesky mites easier for cat owners.

Fleas

Fleas have always been a source of much misery for pet cats. They feed on blood and can cause life-threatening anemia in cats, especially kittens. At best, the fleas will make your kitten itchy and uncomfortable. At worst, they can transmit pathogens to your cat, such as tapeworms and *Bartonella*, and to humans as well. Oral and topical preparations, usually administered once a month, have revolutionized our ability to control fleas. Some of these products, however, carry age or weight restrictions and should be used cautiously with kittens, especially sick or debilitated ones.

▲ The cat flea will not only make your kitty itchy, it could transmit tapeworms to her.

Ringworm

Despite the name, ringworm is a fungus, not a worm. It can affect the skin and can spread to other cats and to people. Symptoms of ringworm include small patches of hair loss, scaling, redness, and crusting on the body. Ringworm commonly appears around the head—especially around the eyes, ears, nose, and lips. Treatment usually involves a combination of oral antifungal medication and a topical therapy, such as a shampoo, a dip, or an ointment.

Intestinal Parasites

A variety of intestinal parasites can affect cats and kittens, including coccidia, *Giardia*, and roundworms.

Coccidia

Coccidia are protozoal parasites that rarely appear in adult cats but commonly affect kittens, especially those obtained from unsanitary, multicat environments. Diarrhea flecked with bright red blood, in association with straining and increased frequency of defecation, is a classic sign of coccidiosis.

Giardia

Giardia is a protozoal parasite that occasionally affects kittens. It causes soft, light-colored, greasy stools. Severe infections can cause growth retardation because of malabsorption of nutrients.

Roundworms and Hookworms

Roundworms are the most common kitten parasite, with most kittens becoming infected through nursing. Most infections produce mild clinical symptoms, such as diarrhea and a "potbellied" appearance. Heavily infested pets may become quite ill.

Hookworms, common in puppies, rarely affect

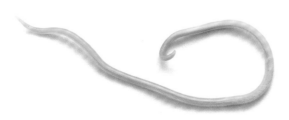

▲ Roundworms are the most common parasite veterinarians see in kittens.

kittens. Diagnosis of intestinal parasites is achieved by analysis of a fecal sample. Occasionally, kittens will vomit up a roundworm, allowing for a simple, on-the-spot diagnosis. There are many safe and effective dewormers that can treat intestinal parasites in kittens.

Viral Diseases

Kittens, with their poorly developed immune systems, are highly vulnerable to viral diseases.

Feline Leukemia Virus (FeLV)

FeLV is a serious viral infection of cats. The virus suppresses the immune system, leaving the kitten susceptible to a variety of infections and other disorders. The virus is transmitted through close contact, such as mutual grooming, sharing of food and water bowls and litter boxes, and from the mother to kittens in utero. Kittens are highly susceptible to the virus. No successful treatments for FeLV exist, and infected kittens often succumb quickly to the virus. All kittens should be tested for FeLV as early as possible, and vaccination against the disease is strongly recommended during kittenhood.

◄ Kittens are highly susceptible to the FeLV infection and should be vaccinated against this fatal virus.

Feline Infectious Peritonitis (FIP)

FIP is perhaps the most unforgiving and most misunderstood of the feline viral diseases. During their first few weeks of life, many kittens are exposed to a virus called the feline enteric corona virus, a relatively harmless virus that infects the intestinal tract and may cause mild self-limiting diarrhea or perhaps no symptoms at all. In some instances, however, the harmless intestinal corona virus mutates, gaining the ability to leave the intestinal tract and cause problems throughout the body. This more invasive strain of corona virus is now the deadly FIP virus.

FIP manifests in two forms: the "wet" form and the "dry" form. The wet form is characterized by fluid accumulation in body cavities, such as the abdomen or (less commonly) the chest. Fluid accumulating in the chest causes breathing difficulties. Fluid accumulating in the abdomen gives a pot-bellied appearance, similar to that seen in cats with intestinal worms. FIP in both forms also causes lethargy, poor appetite, weight loss, and a fever that does not resolve with antibiotics. The dry form normally takes more time to manifest than the wet.

No single blood test can definitively diagnose the disorder, making diagnosis difficult. Once diagnosed, no recourse exists for the patient; the disease is invariably fatal. A vaccine against FIP is available, but its efficacy is questionable, and it currently is not recommended by the American Association of Feline Practitioners.

Panleukopenia

Panleukopenia (sometimes referred to as feline distemper, although this is a misnomer) is another viral disease of cats. The panleukopenia virus attacks the intestinal cells and bone marrow, causing severe, often bloody diarrhea and a very low white blood cell count. Because cats need white blood cells to fight off infections, those affected with low white blood cell counts are at increased risk of contracting other infectious disorders. The virus spreads primarily through contact with contaminated feces from infected cats, although food bowls, litter boxes, and other contaminated surfaces may transmit the virus. Although infected kittens often succumb to the virus, some kittens survive with aggressive veterinary treatment. Fortunately, there is an effective vaccine against this virus.

Complementary Therapies/ Holistic Medicine

Alternative methods of treatment are not new. Acupuncture and traditional Chinese medicine go back more than 2,000 years. As modern Western medicine became the norm in the Western world at the end of the nineteenth century, veterinary practitioners discarded alternative therapies. Today, however, more and more people are seeking out alternative care for their pets (as well as for themselves) because they view these options as less dangerous and less invasive. Complementary and alternative veterinary medicine (CAVM) includes such modalities as aromatherapy, Bach flower remedy therapy, magnetic field therapy, acupuncture, chiropractic, physical therapy, massage therapy, homeopathy, nutraceuticals, and holistic medicine.

Although some veterinary practitioners are open to the idea of complementary modalities, many others are reluctant to utilize approaches that haven't been rigorously tested. Although numerous studies support the efficacy of acupuncture, chiropractic, and physical therapy for humans, studies in animals are still lacking. With other therapies, such as aromatherapy, even the efficacy with humans rests on anecdotal reports rather than studies proven by the scientific method. If you decide to use a veterinarian who embraces complementary and alternative therapy, make certain that he or she has the requisite skills and knowledge; for example, a veterinarian using acupuncture might be certified by the International Veterinary Acupuncture Society (IVAS), whereas one using chiropractic technique might be certified by the American Veterinary Chiropractic Association (AVCA).

Diagnostic Tests and Technology

Dramatic medical advances in the past few years have greatly increased the level of sophistication in veterinary medicine. Many of the same high-tech diagnostic tests and technologies that have been used to diagnose human problems, such as magnetic resonance imaging (MRI), are now available for our pets.

Diagnostic Tests

Veterinary science has entered an exciting time. New breakthroughs are allowing our pets to live longer and healthier lives. Unfortunately, the average pet owner is often unaware of all the specialties, diagnostic tests, and procedures available to their four-legged family member.

The following sections describe a list of veterinary tests that help veterinarians diagnose and treat illness and injury.

Cytology and Histopathology

Cytology is the microscopic evaluation of cells from the body. This test is commonly employed to evaluate skin masses and other tumors. A needle is inserted into the mass, and suction is applied to a syringe attached to the needle. A sample of the cells from the mass is aspirated into the hub of the needle. The material is then sprayed onto a microscope slide and stained. A cytologist evaluates the cells. The advantage of this test is

that anesthesia is rarely necessary to obtain the sample. The disadvantage is that, in some cases, the specimen obtained is inadequate to make a firm diagnosis. If that happens, a biopsy may be necessary to achieve a definite diagnosis.

Histopathology is the microscopic evaluation of a biopsy specimen by a trained pathologist. The advantage of histopathology is that it is much more likely to yield a definitive diagnosis. The disadvantage is that obtaining a biopsy specimen is more invasive and requires anesthesia and surgery.

Complete Blood Count

This test evaluates all of the important blood cells: the red blood cells (erythrocytes), white blood cells (leukocytes), and platelets (thrombocytes). The complete blood count gives information about whether a cat is anemic (too few red blood cells) and detects abnormalities in the white blood cell count— for example, to see if the white blood cell count is elevated, which is a common finding if there's an infection. An abnormally low platelet count can lead to blood clotting problems, and this would also be detected with a complete blood count. The complete blood count is often abbreviated CBC.

▼ If the need arises, talk to your vet in detail about the medical testing appropriate for your cat's specific health issue.

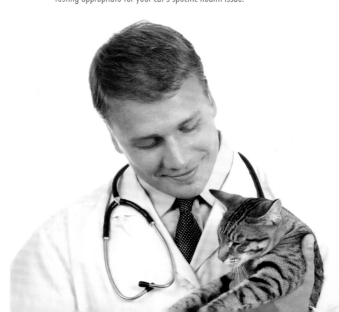

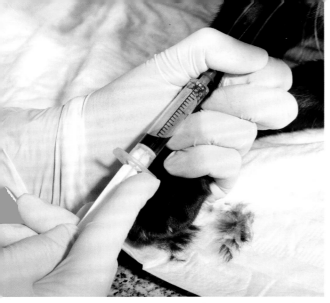

▲ A complete blood count and serum biochemistry panel can reveal a wealth of information about your kitty's health.

Serum Biochemistry Panel

This very important test evaluates between fifteen and twenty-five substances in the blood, giving important information about kidney function, liver function, blood sugar levels, blood lipids, electrolytes, and other substances.

Thyroid Evaluation

Hyperthyroidism is the most common glandular disorder of cats. This simple blood test is the most common method of achieving the diagnosis.

Urinalysis

Analysis of the urine is a very important test and yields key information regarding kidney function, as well as the presence of white blood cells (which may indicate a bladder or kidney infection), red blood cells (which could indicate infection, inflammation, or a blood clotting disorder), glucose (usually an indicator of diabetes), crystals (which could be a normal finding or could indicate the presence of bladder stones), and other significant substances.

Other Tests

A variety of other tests and diagnostic techniques are available to veterinarians to augment the process of obtaining a diagnosis. Blood tests are available that evaluate one particular organ in more detail. Examples of this are the bile acid test to evaluate liver function, the pancreatic lipase immunoreactivity (PLI) test to assess whether the pancreas is inflamed, and the low-dose dexamethasone suppression (LDDS) test to evaluate the function of the adrenal glands.

Serology involves assessing antibody or antigen levels in the bloodstream to see whether an infectious disease may be present. There are serologic tests for fungal diseases, such as blastomycosis and histoplasmosis, as well as for protozoal diseases like toxoplasmosis. The most common serologic tests performed on cats are for the viral diseases, such as FeLV and FIV.

Technology in Diagnostics

Veterinary medicine has gotten quite sophisticated, with veterinarians utilizing many of the same machines used in human hospitals. Some of these modalities (x-ray, ultrasound, endoscopy) may be found in a regular veterinary clinic, while others, such as computed tomography (CT) and magnetic resonance imagining (MRI), are typically limited to referral centers.

CT and MRI

Computed tomography (formerly known as a CAT scan) is a specialized type of x-ray. The cat, under anesthesia, is secured to a thin platform-type table and is slowly moved into the CT machine through a donut-shaped opening. The x-ray tube rotates around the patient while a computer collects the data. The collected images appear as a "slice" of the cat's body. Slices can be studied individually, or they can be placed together to create a three-dimensional image of the area being studied. This differs from MRI, which uses magnets and radio waves to create an image. No x-rays are used in MRI scans.

For MRI scans, the cat is secured to a table very similar to that used for CT scans. The cat is slid into a long cylinder, which is actually a very large magnet. Radio waves are sent through the cat's body, and hydrogen atoms in the cat's tissues emit a signal.

The signal is collected by an antenna and fed into a sophisticated computer, which produces the images. The images look similar to CT scans but provide higher detail in soft tissues. MRI scans are not very good with bony structures. CT scans, on the other hand, provide excellent detail of bony structures.

EKG

An electrocardiogram (EKG) is a measure of the electrical activity of the heart. The EKG is obtained by attaching small electrode clips to the cat's body and evaluating the waves either on a small monitor or by printing the EKG tracing onto paper. The EKG allows assessment of the heart rate—whether the heart is beating too fast or two slow—as well as the heart rhythm and whether it is normal or irregular. The EKG may also provide information about whether the chambers of the heart are normal-sized or whether they are enlarged. Performing an EKG is not painful, although cats

may be resent being restrained for the procedure. A continuous EKG tracing is usually performed when cats undergo dental and surgical procedures as part of the proper anesthetic protocol.

Endoscopy

Endoscopy is a procedure that allows your veterinarian to look inside your cat's body. This is done via the use of an endoscope, a long thin tube with a camera attached to one end. The endoscope is inserted into the region to be examined and an image is obtained for visual evaluation. The endoscope also has the capability to obtain biopsy specimens—small samples of the tissue being examined. This is an invaluable tool for achieving a diagnosis. Endoscopes vary in length depending on their purpose and can be rigid or flexible. Endoscopic procedures are named based on the body system being evaluated.

Arthroscopy: This is endoscopic evaluation of the

joints, for example, the elbow or knee joint. Minor surgical procedures (arthroscopic surgery) can be performed in this manner if warranted.

Bronchoscopy: This is endoscopic evaluation of the trachea (windpipe) and the lungs. In addition to obtaining biopsy specimens, a specially designed brush can be inserted into a channel in the endoscope and then brushed against the walls of the air passages to obtain samples for cytology.

Colonoscopy: This evaluation of the colon can be performed using either a flexible or rigid endoscope.

Cystoscopy: This is endoscopic evaluation of the bladder. The procedure is not commonly performed in veterinary medicine, although it is a useful tool for obtaining biopsy specimens of bladder tumors without doing surgery.

Rhinoscopy: This is endoscopic evaluation of the nasal passages. Tissue samples can be obtained for biopsy, and samples can be obtained for bacterial or fungal culture if an infectious disease is suspected.

Upper GI endoscopy: This refers to the endoscopic evaluation of the esophagus, stomach, and/or first part of the small intestine (the duodenum)—the gastrointestinal (GI) tract. Evaluation of the esophagus alone is called esophagoscopy. Gastroscopy is the endoscopic assessment of the stomach. The initial part of the small intestine is called the duodenum; duodenoscopy is the evaluation of this area using the endoscope. In addition to obtaining biopsy specimens, upper GI endoscopy is often performed to remove foreign bodies from the esophagus or stomach using special grasping forceps that can be inserted into a channel in the endoscope.

Radiographs

Radiographs (also known as x-rays) use an electromagnetic beam to produce images of internal organs and bones. As the x-ray beam is aimed at the body, different parts of the body allow some of the beam to pass through. Softer tissues, such as skin, fat, and muscle, allow most of the beam to pass through, resulting in a dark gray appearance on the x-ray film. Denser tissues, such as tumors or bones, allow less of the x-ray beam to pass through and appear white on the x-ray. If there is a break in a bone, the beam passes through the broken area and appears as a dark line in the white bone. Radiographs are an invaluable diagnostic tool that allows the veterinarian to peek inside the patient without doing surgery.

Ultrasound

Ultrasound differs from x-rays in that, rather than using an electromagnetic beam, ultrasound uses high-frequency sound waves to render images of internal structures. It is a very safe procedure. Ultrasound offers some advantages over x-rays. Ultrasound has better contrast resolution than x-rays and can differentiate between fluid-filled structures and solid structures. Ultrasound can confirm the origin of a tumor in the abdomen with more precision than an x-ray. The images seen with ultrasound are shown in real time, so that what

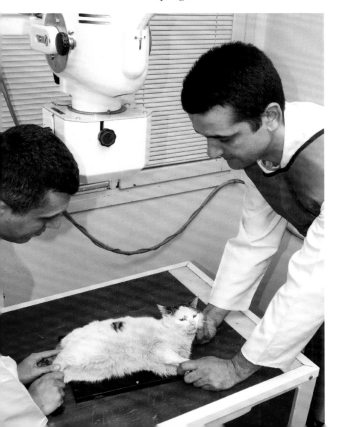

◄ Cat in the process of getting an x-ray or radiograph. This tool allows vets to peer inside your pet without surgery.

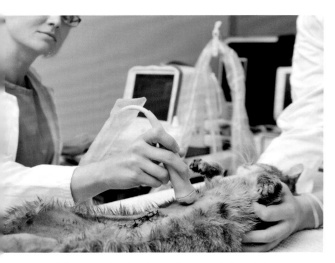

▲ An ultrasound provides images of organs and other soft tissues.

you see on the screen is what is actually happening inside the cat at the time of scanning. Ultrasound allows the assessment of the internal structure of the organs. For example, the heart valves can be seen opening and closing using ultrasound. Ultrasound has limitations, however. It is not useful for assessing the bony structures of the body. X-rays and ultrasound often complement each other, with each providing key diagnostic information.

Alternative Therapies for Pets

By Sandy Robins

With the growing trend for cat lovers to mimic popular human lifestyle trends for their pets' general health and well-being, there is a growing interest in alternative therapies—massage, acupuncture, and chiropractics—for pets. Today, there are courses and certifications in all these modalities for practitioners to legally work on animals.

Aromatherapy and Cats

Aromatherapy is a generic term that refers to the various uses of liquid plant materials known as essential oils for the purpose of affecting a person or animal's mood or health. An essential oil is liquid that comes from a single plant. These oils are extracted from flowers and other plant parts, including leaves, stems, roots, seeds, and bark. Apart from being mood enhancers, they have various medicinal and healing properties as well, and thus they promote general well-being. Aromatherapists believe that essential oils work in two ways. First, the fragrant aromas activate the limbic system and stimulate the emotional centers of the brain. Second, when applied to the skin, they are absorbed into the bloodstream, thereby allowing the body to register them and promote healing.

Flower essences are sometimes used in health-related products. For example, some anti-itch creams used to treat skin irritations contain chamomile oil, and some insect repellents use lavender oil as an ingredient. The most famous of all flower essences are those formulated by British physician Dr. Edward Bach in the 1930s. He created thirty-eight different essences, all of which are safe to use on a cat, including his famous Rescue Remedy calmative, which is now also specifically marketed for pets and readily available in stores and online.

Essential oils are very concentrated and hence extremely potent. In fact, undiluted essential oils are highly toxic to cats. Even one drop on your cat's paw can make her extremely ill and may even cause death. Felines lack the necessary enzymes in their liver to break down and excrete certain chemical compounds that exist naturally in essential oils. (Dogs and people are different.) Therefore, overdosing or overuse causes these compounds to accumulate in the body and can result in liver or kidney failure.

Symptoms of toxicity include vomiting, drooling, and uncoordinated movements. The toxic buildup is often slow and doesn't necessarily show up immediately. It could take weeks, months, or even years. Often,

◄ Aromatherapy is the use of essential oils derived from medicinal plants to affect the mood or health of the patient—human, feline, or other.

owners are unaware that their cat is suffering from any kind of poisoning until the vet does a general blood panel and the toxin shows up there.

Fortunately, you can buy ready-made dilutions of essential oils called *hydrosols*. These are water-based by-products that can be diluted even further for safe use. Before you proceed, consult a professional pet aromatherapist with regard to formulations for your cat and how to correctly administer them.

The Therapeutic Benefits for Cats

Apart from getting rid of parasites such as ticks and fleas, aromatherapy is used to treat mild skin inflammations, sore muscles, and stiff joints. It's also used to de-stress a variety of emotionally charged situations, such as traveling, moving, the introduction of a new pet or baby into a household, separation anxiety, and nervousness induced by thunder and lightning storms. While the hydrosols can be used individually, pet aromatherapists often blend several together.

A cat's nose is undoubtedly her most important organ. Cats have between 60 and 80 million

▼ Essential oils can be used to ward off fleas as well as to treat other problems, but they can also cause toxic reactions when used incorrectly.

olfactory cells, while humans have only between 5 and 20 million—which explains a feline's incredible sense of smell. Therefore, pet aromatherapists suggest that the best way to introduce your cat to a particular oil is to allow her to first sniff it while you watch for signs of acceptance. If the cat gets up and moves away, it's a clue not to proceed. If she shows interest by wanting to lick it or by rubbing against it, you can take this as a sign that the hydrosol in question will have a therapeutic effect and that your cat is giving you the green light to proceed. Never test a hydrosol by placing it on your cat's nose because this takes away her freedom of choice.

Difference Between Essential Oils and Flower Essences

Essential oils all have very potent individual fragrances. Flower essences (often known as flower remedies) are fragrance-free high-frequency electrical solutions distilled from fresh flower blossoms and contain the distinct vibrational energies of the plants from which they are derived. When properly applied, they help balance and strengthen the body's electrical system. In doing so, they remove any interference that can cause both physical and emotional discomfort. Thus, they work to alleviate both physical pain and discomfort and emotionally work to relieve stress.

Massage

For your stroking and petting movements to be officially considered a pet massage, the intent has to be to touch the animal for some beneficial effect. Pet massage therapists say that a cat has to give you permission to perform a therapeutic touching routine. If they're interested in pursuing the idea, they will automatically nuzzle up to you, lie down, or simply stay where they are, giving the go-ahead to continue. The most obvious rejection is to jump up and run off.

Massage improves blood circulation, increasing oxygenation and nutrition to the cells and tissues throughout the body. If your cat is on any medication, massage will help it work more efficiently and, at the same time, minimize side effects by removing the toxins and waste products from the system. Massage also reduces pain associated with illness or old age because endorphins, the body's natural pain relievers, are released into the system through massage. These natural mood enhancers allow your feline to feel better. In human terms, this translates into an upbeat mood. The gentle power of touch also releases lactic acid from sore muscles, decreasing swelling from inflammation. It definitely allows older cats suffering from arthritis and joint discomfort more flexibility of movement and could possibly help them negotiate stairs around the home well into their teens.

▲ When performed by a skilled practitioner, massage therapy can help a cat recover from injury or surgery.

Special infrared massage units made specifically for home use definitely help cats with poor circulation be able to move around better. This is also a useful tool for diabetic cats whose back legs are very weak as a result of their disease.

Although massage therapy is no substitute for veterinary care, more veterinarians are appreciating its benefits and seeing how it complements medical treatments. Thus, they are recommending massage therapy for cats who have undergone surgery or other trauma (including abuse) to help facilitate the healing process.

Shiatsu

Shiatsu is a Japanese form of massage therapy that's very similar to acupressure (see below). In fact, the word means, "finger pressure." The Shiatsu therapist usually applies pressure using his or her thumbs, although some may also use their fingers, palms, and even elbows to apply the required pressure to allow energy to flow freely. Often, some gentle massage is performed to the soft-tissue areas along the body's meridians—channels through which "*chi*" (life energy) travels—as well as some gentle stretching movements.

Thai Massage

This form of massage itself is not a therapy that applies to cats. However, many pet therapists do use traditional Thai herbal compresses in their massage routines. Heated herbal compresses are excellent for sore or pulled muscles and ligaments, back pain, arthritis, and even stress and anxiety disorders. Typical ingredients include cassumunar ginger, lemongrass, and kaffir lime leaves. Together, they are placed in a muslin cloth and then gently heated in a steamer or microwave. The compress is held in place for several minutes and is often used to end a pet massage therapy session.

Tellington Touch

This behavioral therapy was especially designed for pets by horsewoman Linda Tellington-Jones and first used on horses in the 1970s. The technique depends solely on the power of touch and doesn't involve any traditional massage movements or acupressure. The therapist uses circular finger and hand movements all over the cat's body to relax her and thus reduce stress and fears she may have. In cats, it's often recommended to treat extreme shyness, fear, and resistance to grooming, as well as to deal with excitability and nervous behavior. Although initially considered an animal therapy, these days, health care professionals use it on people to reduce stress and anxiety, particularly after an illness.

Reiki

The word *"reiki"* means "universal life energy," and this form of healing also originated in Japan. By placing his hands on strategic points of the body, the therapist acts as a conduit, channeling the healing energy from himself directly to his pet patient.

Acupuncture and Acupressure

These age-old healing techniques have their roots in both China and India. In the past decade, they have become increasingly popular for both people and their pets. They correct the imbalances of energy known as *qi* (pronounced *chee*) within the body and unblock obstructions in energy flow, thus allowing *qi* to flow freely again and the body to heal itself. Along with the free-flowing energy, endorphins are released into the system, which helps reduce sensitivity to pain and stress.

▼ Acupuncture is the use of needles to move healing energy in the body. It is used in cats to treat joint problems, muscular problems, asthma, and more.

Acupuncture

During treatment, a variety of small needles and sometimes a low-power laser are used to stimulate the acupuncture points on the body. Acupuncture is primarily used on pets to treat joint and muscular problems, but it is also said to aid pets being treated for cancer with chemotherapy. It's also an accepted form of treatment for respiratory problems such as chronic asthma, and it is used to stimulate the immune system to treat such diseases as FeLV and FIV. Only specially qualified veterinary acupuncturists or pet therapists who are also licensed veterinary technicians or who have some kind of medical background should perform this treatment. Ask for credentials before making an appointment.

Acupressure

Acupressure is best described as acupuncture without needles. It works on the same principle but, instead of needles or lasers, practitioners use finger pressure on specific points on the body. These pressure points are situated on channels or meridians along which the body's energy flows. Many pet therapists incorporate this modality into their general massage routine.

Animal Chiropractics

Veterinary chiropractic, also known as animal chiropractic, is an emerging subspecialization for doctors of veterinary medicine (DVMs) and doctors of chiropractic (DCs) to provide spinal manipulation, manual therapy, and other holistic and conservative techniques for animals. In concert with conventional veterinary care, the complementary use of veterinary chiropractic is primarily used for common neuromusculoskeletal conditions to enhance performance, function, and quality of life. Animal chiropractic techniques are more commonly used on dogs than on cats. Many veterinary practices have an association with an animal chiropractor; consult with your veterinarian to find out whether this form of additional treatment would be beneficial for your cat.

Chapter 10

Grooming Your Cat

I'm afraid I have to expel a rather ferocious
hairball. You're on your own, girl.

— Cheshire Cat in *Alice in Wonderland* by Lewis Carroll

Grooming is not just about making your cat the quintessential glamour puss; it's also a great way of spending quality time with your feline and strengthening the human–animal bond. And although it may be more efficient to groom on a flat surface, there is nothing wrong with grooming on your lap when you are both curled up together in front of the TV. So consider grooming to be something functional but also fun.

The term *human–animal bond* became the new buzz phrase at the birth of this millennium. In a 2008 study, neurology professor Adnan Qureshi and a team of researchers at the University of Minnesota's Zeenat Qureshi Stroke Research Center found that the relative risk of death from heart attack was 40 percent higher in people who had never owned a cat.

When presenting the findings, Qureshi said, "If we assume that cat ownership is directly responsible for the benefits, then the most logical explanation may be that cat ownership may relieve stress and anxiety and subsequently reduce the risk of cardiovascular diseases."

Animal behaviorists started to educate cat owners about the benefits of grooming, telling them it was a bone fide way of spending quality time with a feline, to mutual benefit. Cat grooming got a further

▶ Grooming is a great way to spend some quality time with your feline companion.

endorsement when educationists suggested that it was possible to make grooming a cat part of the owner's everyday lifestyle by multitasking. In other words, it's possible to brush and comb a cat while relaxing in front of the TV.

Thus, the grooming revolution has become part of every cat owner's lifestyle and is here to stay.

The History of Feline Grooming

Since ancient times when cats were first revered by the Egyptians, felines around the world have lived up to their sobriquet of "glamour puss." However, history shows that when courtesans started grooming dogs for kings and queens, especially during the seventeenth century, and when poodles graced the French court during the reign of King Louis XVI, cats weren't included in such beauty regimens.

They nevertheless still featured in artwork of the day and later in family photographs, sitting by their owners, looking picture perfect, no doubt relying on their universal reputation of being very efficient self-groomers.

The first mention of feline grooming techniques comes from Harrison Weir, who has been hailed as the father of the cat fancy. As noted in chapter 4, Weir was responsible for the first official cat show, held in London in July 1871 (see chapter 4, page 53). It's significant to remember that when cats were first entered in cat shows, more importance was given to their breed, colorings, and markings than to the actual condition of their fur. Then judges started remarking that this cat or that cat would have scored higher marks if her coat had been better cared for (better groomed). Even with the urging of the father of the cat fancy and the remarks by judges, it took time for the idea of grooming a cat for a show to catch on and for tools made specifically for feline grooming to become available to the general cat-owning public.

Early Grooming Advice

In his book, *Our Cats and All About Them*, Harrison Weir advised cat owners never to use a comb, especially on longhaired cats, for fear of breaking the hair and causing a rough and uneven coat. He wrote:

Should the hair become clotted, matted, or felted, as is sometimes the case, it ought to be moistened, either with oil or soft-soap, a little water being added, and when the application has well soaked in, it will be found comparatively easy to separate the tangle with the fingers by gently pulling out from the mass a few hairs at a time, after which wash thoroughly, and use a soft, long-haired brush; but this must be done with discretion, so as not to spoil the natural waviness of the hair, or to make it lie in breadths instead of the natural, easy, carelessly-parted flaky appearance, which shows the white or blue cat off to such advantage.

Weir made the point that cats dislike water and suggested:

If a cat is to be washed, treat it as kindly and gently as possible, speaking in a soothing tone, and in no way be hasty or sudden in your movements so as to raise distrust or fear. Let the water be warm but not hot, put

▼ Grooming was not part of the earliest cat shows, and the practice of grooming cats took some time to catch on.

▲ Your cat will spend a lot of time grooming herself, but there are still regular grooming chores you must perform.

the cat in slowly and when its feet rest on the bottom of the tub, you may commence the washing.

He recommended that his readers use a dog soap called Naldire Dog Soap and after the bath put the cat in a box filled with oat straw and place it near a fire to prevent her from catching a chill before she was properly dry.

Victorian cat expert Frances Simpson, whose 1903 book *The Book of the Cat* was the definitive cat bible of its day, also made the point that exhibitors needed to pay more attention to coat care.

In the dog, rabbit and pigeon fancy a great deal more attention is given to condition than among cat fanciers, who need waking up to the fact that nothing goes so far to propitiate a judge as superb show form and general good appearance.

Simpson suggested dampening a cat's coat with a solution of ammonia and water as an alternative to a bath. She also recommended that Pear's White Fuller's Earth be rubbed into the fur to remove grease and then brushed out using a soft brush. In another grooming tip, she told readers they could warm a large quantity of bran in the oven, then stand "puss in it and [rub] it over the fur for some minutes and then carefully [brush] it out."

Early Grooming Tools

Appalled by the conditions cats had to endure on the way to cat shows, Frances Simpson promoted the idea that owners should accompany their cats on the journey—as opposed to just boxing them up and shipping them to the event—because this would also present opportunities for extra grooming en route. "There is also the advantage," she explained, "that if you arm yourself with a brush and comb you are able to give some finishing touches to pussy's toilet previous to the judges' inspection and awards. Let me recommend a metal comb and a brush such as is used for Yorkshire terriers which has long penetrating bristles but is neither too hard nor too soft." We can assume that all cat grooming tool recommendations were for tools originally designed for other animals or humans because there seems to be no record of products actually being manufactured specially for cats.

Although cats were still being left largely to their own natural grooming efforts, professional dog groomers had been snipping and shaping and combing out for centuries. One swanky Dogs' Toilet Club in London, established in London around 1903, offered its canine customers egg yolk shampoos and other lavish services. The 1930s saw the advent of doggie barbershops, the forerunner of today's grooming salons. It is unclear whether they were patronized by dogs being groomed for the show ring or whether the upper classes brought their dogs here to be groomed simply to be clean and trendy. However, no consideration was given to felines at the time, and they were certainly not welcome in these canine establishments.

No Sharp Scissors!

Never tackle a seriously matted coat with a sharp pair of scissors because you could inadvertently cut into the skin, causing bleeding and possible infection. Mats and tangles must be attended to for the general health and well-being of your cat. So, if necessary, seek professional grooming help.

Grooming Your Cat

A Grooming Calendar

If you plan to groom your cat yourself, it's a good idea to design your own grooming calendar. Take a nice photograph of your cat and glue it onto a piece of cardboard. Next, make headings for daily, weekly, and monthly grooming routines and fill them in on the calender. It's a nice reference to ensure you don't forget to include such things as flea and tick treatments in your routine.

Here's a guideline:

Daily tasks

- Brushing for longhaired cats
- Check paw pads and eyes
- Check for strange lumps or redness anywhere on the feet, ears, and body

Weekly tasks

- General brushing for shorthaired breeds
- More intense work-over for longhaired cats
- Check ears and gums and eyes
- Wipe down for elderly cats
- Teeth cleaning (attempt to do as much as you can)

Monthly tasks

- Bath or full-body wipe down with wipes
- Nail trim and foot inspection
- General body check for lumps and bumps
- Flea and tick topical treatments (some last longer)
- Ears and mouth inspection, checking for any foul-smelling odors
- Inventory grooming products, checking for what needs replenishing

Around this same time, pet stores that primarily sold food and grain started to carry a few rudimentary grooming tools for dogs and animals such as horses—but no tools specifically for cats. The concept of brushing cats and clipping their nails at home on a regular basis—let alone the idea of having them professionally groomed—only began to gain ground when the role of the domestic cat changed during the second half of the twentieth century.

Grooming Revolution

Cats transitioned from essentially being housed in the backyard or barn and, to a large extent, allowed to roam free, to being brought indoors on cold nights and allowed to sleep in kitchens or laundry rooms (regarded as warmer rooms in the average house) to taking up primary or sole residence inside. This transition also brought about emotional changes and attitudes among cat owners and subsequently a change in feline status: the domestic cat came to be viewed as a companion animal, even a "fur kid." People now saw themselves as the protectors and caretakers of their cats, rather than simply the owners of good utilitarian mousers. And taking care of their cats meant not only feeding them but also grooming them. By the 1970s, people were able to pick up cat-specific brushes and combs in the local pet stores.

By the late 1990s, cat owners were also being offered various other grooming products and services that mimicked their own lifestyle needs and wants, from nail clippers to floral-scented shampoos and conditioners. And by the new millennium, the idea of sending the family feline to a pet spa for a nail trim and even a complete grooming makeover was no longer a gimmick but a recognized way in which to deal with grooming problems.

The feline grooming industry got a further boost when cat lovers were also faced with another reality check: statistics being released from various veterinary schools around the country were proving that it was much safer for domestic cats to enjoy an indoor lifestyle because they were thus protected from predators and parasites.

Cats living mostly outdoors shed seasonally twice a year. In contrast, cats subjected to controlled climatic conditions, such as air conditioning and heating, shed all year round. Furthermore, cats in the outdoors are able to take care of their nails by scratching on natural surfaces and climbing trees, and they keep their teeth clean by hunting and devouring prey such as mice and birds. Indoor felines commonly have longer, unmanageable nails that need regular attention. It also became evident that cats were developing serious dental issues.

Consequently, despite being universally recognized as efficient self-groomers, domestic felines now needed human help in dealing with common problems such as shedding and taking care of matted hair, as well as with nail and teeth care.

Furthermore, respected veterinary schools around the country started issuing reports that domestic pets were living much longer as the direct result of better nutrition in the form of specialized pet foods and also *better grooming*. Suddenly, for the first time, cat lovers were faced with having to care for geriatric felines and learning firsthand that elderly animals are often not able to care for themselves as conscientiously as when they were younger and more agile. Thus, cat lovers found themselves having to take care of an elderly cat's grooming needs on a full-time basis.

Consequently, in the past twenty years, many pet product manufacturers have been pandering to these specialized feline needs and, in so doing, the pet industry has grown to become a massive economic force, with an annual turnover that in 2013 was in excess of $55 billion. Today, there is a plethora of specialized grooming tools and toiletry items to aid a variety of health and beauty conditions, as well as ergonomically designed grooming aids to make regular grooming more pleasurable for both the pet parent and the cat.

A Grooming Routine

It's important to introduce a grooming routine as soon as a cat or a kitten comes into the household. In this way, she will quickly get used to the idea and not only tolerate the procedure but also learn to enjoy it. One of the additional benefits of such hands-on attention is that should the necessity arise to administer any oral or topical medications, it is much easier to treat a cat who is used to having her eyes, ears, and teeth cleaned.

It's a good idea to initially groom a cat in different locations in order to discover where the cat enjoys it most. Some cats like to be on the floor. Others will choose a particular level on a kitty condo. The couch or even on your lap may prove to be a preferred site. If you select a countertop, put down a towel to cover the slick surface to give the cat some grip and allow her to be more comfortable in such a location.

If you've acquired a cat or a kitten from a breeder, it's a good idea to ask him or her to suggest basic tools that are ideal for your specific breed. Another good place to learn hints and tips is at a cat show; the registry organizing a show often will hold special grooming workshops. Furthermore, exhibiters are always willing to offer grooming advice and recommend particular tools.

One of the best ways to learn about specific grooming tools is to page through mail-order catalogs or browse online; such venues usually have detailed descriptions of tools. Of course, you can shop remotely, too, but often it's a good idea for first-time cat owners to get the feel of the items in the store, especially as manufacturers place a lot of emphasis on ergonomic comfort to make grooming a pleasurable experience for the groomer, too.

◄ Start grooming your kitten when she is young, so she will quickly come to enjoy it as part of her routine.

Brushing

Before even picking up a brush, it's a good idea to stroke your cat all over. Why? First, this is calming. Second, because this is an excellent way of locating any matted fur that will require extra attention and need to be dealt with before the primary grooming. A dematter—a comb-shaped tool with elongated razor-like prongs that work their way through the mat, teasing it out in small parts—is the best grooming aid to deal with mats or any foreign matter that may be caught up in the fur, such as twigs or burrs. Alternatively, a medium- to fine-toothed comb will also do the job. Although where to begin brushing is not set in stone, cats love long brushing strokes beginning at the neck in a downward motion toward the tail. So this would be great way to start. Always brush in the direction of the fur. If you begin on the back, take the movement down the legs and the tail. Gently push the cat onto her side so that you can work the area of the chest and belly. Be extra gentle because this can be a sensitive area, especially on a female cat with slightly protruding nipples. It's a good idea to use a softer nylon brush or a curry brush to work between the ears and under the chin.

A bristle brush and a rubber curry brush and even mitts are basics for regular shorthaired cat grooming. For longhaired cats, double-sided wire and bristle brushes are useful, as are a small slicker brush and a wide-toothed comb to maintain tangle-free fur. All cats shed; it's nature's way of removing dead hair and replenishing new fur. Feral cats who live completely outdoors will adhere to nature's routine of shedding seasonally twice a year: in the spring to lose the thicker winter coat and in the fall to allow new fur to grow. However, domestic cats who are exposed to constant air conditioning and heating tend to shed continually and consequently need regular help through brushing. The amount they shed is also governed by the number of hours they are exposed to sunlight. This is known as the *photoperiod* and it triggers the natural shedding process. There are special deshedding tools on the market to help keep the situation under control; a deshedding tool is an essential item in every cat's owner's toolbox.

It's important to never allow the hair to get so matted that the cat's entire body has to be shaved. However, should this happen, its best to have the cat shaved by a professional groomer who will have

▼You may be amazed at how much hair comes off your cat during a grooming session.

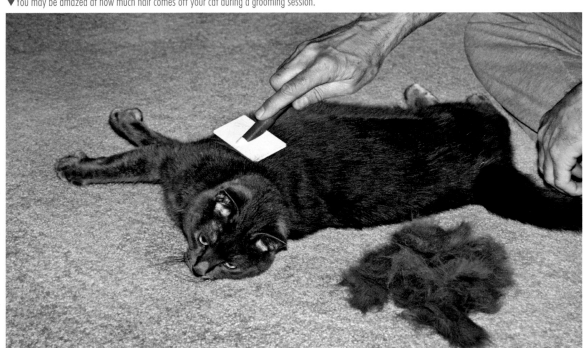

▲ Always comb and brush your cat in the same direction her fur goes.

been bathed before, introducing a regular a bathing ritual could be problematic. It's important to remember that pitiful meowing is a stress indicator. If your cat does this when you try to bathe her, consider less stressful alternatives that will do the job of keeping her clean.

If you are brushing regularly, most cats can be bathed every couple of months or alternatively wiped down with specially formulated wipes and waterless shampoo-styled mousses on a monthly basis. It's a matter of establishing a routine that works best for you and your cat. Where you live and how exposed your cat is to dust and grime will also dictate your schedule.

the right tools to do it efficiently, making the ordeal less stressful. Never clip out a mat of hair with pointed scissors because you could easily cut into the skin without realizing it and cause profuse bleeding. There are special bull-nosed scissors designed for general use on cats. They are particularly useful for trimming hair between the toes.

Keeping fur short is also an excellent option for elderly longhaired cats who are no longer adept at attending to their own grooming needs. It's also a "style" worth considering if you live in a very hot climate.

Brushing a cat on a regular basis means that you are removing all excess hair that would otherwise be ingested during a typical self-grooming routine; such hair can cause hairballs and constipation. It is dangerous for a cat to ingest too much hair because it can lead to internal blockages and can even be life-threatening.

Bathing

The general perception is that cats hate water and thus hate being bathed. However, show cats tolerate regular bathing without problems, which proves that if a cat is introduced to a bath from a young age, she will learn to tolerate the procedure and not be stressed out. However, if you have adopted an adult cat who hasn't

Toolbox Check List

Here's what your basic toolkit should look like, based on whether you have a shorthaired or longhaired feline. As with your own personal brushes and combs, it's a good idea to regularly wash and disinfect your cat's grooming tools. Keep them all together in a little plastic container.

Shorthaired: Your basic tool kit should include a nylon bristle brush to give the coat a smooth silky look, a rubber curry brush that looks like a comb with large rubber teeth that magnetically lifts fur and massages, and a flea comb. Also consider a fine short-toothed comb to gently remove matted hair and for removing hair from the slicker brush. Also include a deshedder.

Longhaired: A double-sided wire and bristle brush is useful for general grooming. Consider a slicker brush for removing tangles, dead hair, and debris. These brushes also help to distribute healthy coat oils all over the body. A wide-toothed comb helps long hair to remain mat- and tangle-free, and a deshedding comb will keep the undercoat thinned without cutting the hair. Again, a deshedder is a "must-have" item.

Grooming Your Cat

Bath Time Preparation

Cats can be bathed wherever it's most convenient for you—in the kitchen or bathroom sink, the tub, or the shower stall. Wherever you decide, place a rubber mat or a towel on the surface to provide traction for the cat and make bath time less of an ordeal.

Sometimes, cats object more to the sound of handheld shower sprays than to the actual feel of the water. If you find your cat protesting pitifully when you turn on a sprayer, instead of using the shower spray to wet the fur and to remove shampoo, use buckets of warm water with a sponge and a cup to wet the fur and rinse out the shampoo.

Be sure to get everything ready before you start bathing your cat. Have at least two towels in place. Special pet absorbent towels are excellent for removing excess water before using an ordinary towel. It's a good idea, especially in colder climates, to warm the towels in advance by placing them in the tumble dryer.

Start by washing from the neck down to the toes and tail. Massage cleansing products into the fur. Dab shampoo and conditioner onto a cotton ball and work gently around the eyes, nose, and ears, and under the chin. Some cats may prefer the use of a pet wipe on the facial area or even a face cloth with ordinary warm water. If you are using any kind of special skin treatment shampoo, it should be applied twice during a bath for it to effectively treat the condition. If possible, leave the second application on for five to fifteen minutes to allow the active ingredients to be properly absorbed.

Rinse the fur well to remove all traces of shampoo and conditioner; use an extra bucket of water if necessary. If you are showering the products off, allow the water to run over your cat for at least five minutes to enable the skin to be properly hydrated. It's very important to rinse well because any residue can cause skin irritation. The residue may also be ingested when the cat begins her own after-bath grooming process.

Never allow water to enter a cat's ears. Fold them over when rinsing. It's not a good idea to place cotton balls in the ears in case you forget to remove them!

Longhaired cats should be gently brushed or combed after a bath so that their fur doesn't mat during the drying process.

Waterless Products and Wipes

Waterless spray-on products are formulated for cats who won't tolerate water. They all contain a diluted form of shampoo that is effective enough to clean but not strong enough to leave any residue on the skin or hair. For a very dirty coat, first spray a fine mist of warm water or wet the coat with a sturdy damp paper towel. You can also use the absorbent, sponge-type towels found in the household cleaning section of the supermarket.

Spray the product directly onto your hands. Then use your fingers to apply it directly to your cat's body, starting at the neck and working down the body and legs. Next, rub the product in with a warm, wet, squeezed-out washcloth, working all the way down to the skin. Rinse the cloth often, and keep wiping until there is no more product left on the hair.

▼ Bathe your cat every couple months, depending on how often your cat is exposed to dust and dirt.

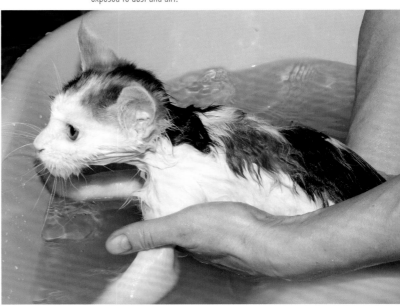

▲ Heating the towels you use to dry your kitty will help keep her from getting too cold after a bath.

Dry the coat with a paper towel, and brush or comb the coat immediately afterward.

To clean the facial area, dip a cotton swab or cotton ball into the product and apply it carefully to the areas around the nose, eyes, and mouth. Wipe it off with a tissue.

However, a better bet is a specially formulated wipe for cats. Never use wipes made for humans because they contain alcohol, which is extremely drying to feline skin and could cause skin irritations.

Wipes are also useful to remove dirty spots and very practical for grooming elderly felines who are no longer capable of grooming themselves properly. Look for products that clearly state they are "lick safe" and "nontoxic" and with a pH factor formulated for felines.

Shampoo and Conditioning Treatments

Shampoos for people are selected according to hair type (normal, oily, dry). Shampoos for felines are selected for skin type. A cat's skin can be affected by variety of things such as air conditioning and heating and various air pollutants; even air fresheners can result in a dry and itchy skin, further causing fur to become matted, static, or oily.

Moisturizers work to add moisture and rehydrate the skin and hair follicles. Conditioners are a combination of ingredients that coat the hair to make it shiny, glossy, and fluffy. They prevent static and stop fur from matting and tangling. Most products on the shelves for cats are a combination of both. Remember that the "hardness" or "softness" of water from the faucet will also affect the texture of a cat's hair.

It's worth investing in products that contain all-natural ingredients because many chemical ingredients in pet shampoo and conditioning products can cause skin allergies. Look for words such as *natural plant extracts* on the labels. Further look for labels that say the products are free of *parabens* (chemicals used as preservatives).

Here's a guide to finding the right products for various skin condition and what to look for on the product labels:

Dry, flaky skin: This requires both moisturizing and conditioning. Look for a shampoo containing

Dos and Don'ts of Grooming

With the recognition that a feline grooming routine is a *de rigueur* part of cat ownership comes a list of basic dos and don'ts to assist with the process. One of the most important don'ts is to not use products that are not specifically formulated and designed for felines. There are significant physiological differences between cats and other pets and cats and humans that make the use of non–feline-specific products detrimental to your cat's health.

For instance, feline fur has a different pH level to both human hair and dog hair. In addition, a cat's hair follicles have multiple hair shafts whereas human hair follicles have only one shaft. So, for example, a human shampoo on a cat produces different results and, in fact, will cause an oily buildup. Furthermore, humans have sweat glands all over the body whereas a cat only has sweat glands on her paw pads and the bridge of her nose. Cats have sebaceous glands all over the body whereas humans have sebaceous glands only in the facial region and the hair on their heads. All this points to the fact that human products are formulated for people, dog products for dogs, and specially formulated feline products are best for felines. There is no shortage of these products, so it's easier to buy the right grooming products in the first place.

Grooming Your Cat

protein and moisturizing ingredients such as aloe vera, borage oil, oatmeal, vitamin E, and vitamin B5 (panthenol) that will soften and soothe the skin as well as leave the coat shiny and glossy. You can use an all-in-one shampoo-conditioner.

Dry, itchy, or sore skin: This needs to be well moisturized and treated to heal skin irritations. If you reduce itching, it's possible to avoid secondary infections caused by scratching. Look for products that list ingredients such as coal tar and sulfur that have antibacterial and antiseptic properties. Plant extracts such as chamomile and comfrey also have excellent anti-inflammatory and soothing properties.

Greasy, flaky skin: This condition can be likened to sunburn in humans. Ingredients such as aloe vera and chamomile will help reduce oiliness and rejuvenate the skin. Other natural plant extracts such as ylang-ylang and lavender also control oiliness and have soothing properties. A greasy flaky skin could also be caused by a medical condition or by dietary issues, so be sure to check with your veterinarian.

Skin allergies: Allergies are best treated with a hypoallergenic shampoo. This means the product has no colorants or fragrance. Look for products that contain aloe vera, peppermint, and geranium,

▲ It's important to snip off only the clear part of the nail. Hitting the quick will cause pain and bleeding.

which have soothing properties. Be aware, however, that if skin allergies and redness persists they could be indicators of an internal problem that will also need veterinary attention.

Fleas and ticks: Shampoos provide some instant help but have no long-term benefits. Some insecticides can be toxic to cats and kittens and may even cause death. Current flea and tick treatments focus on the use topical products, some of which contain insect growth regulators (IGRs) that break the flea's life cycle. This approach has been deemed more effective than shampoos.

Nail Care

A cat's claws grow very fast. Consequently, nails should be trimmed monthly to prevent ingrown nails that can affect how your cat walks and also reduce damage from her scratching furniture around the home.

The best way to introduce nail trimming as part of the grooming routine is to gently massage your cat's in the normal course of a play session. In this way, she will get used to your pressing on her paw pads and splaying her toes and thus will be more tolerant when the nail clippers come out.

A quality pair of stainless steel "guillotine-styled" pet nail trimmers will do the job quickly and efficiently. Never use human nail cutters because they tend to split nails.

Watch the Bumps

Cats, just like dogs and even people, often develop lumps and bumps anywhere on their bodies. These are usually associated with age. Often they are benign, but it's important to check them out with your veterinarian. If you and the veterinarian deem it wisest to leave them alone, then make sure you identify them for the groomer with colored stickers. They should stay on long enough for the groomer to be able to identify the area. However, be careful if you put them on an area of the fur that the cat can reach and lick off and ingest! During your regular grooming sessions at home, avoid mishaps by simply putting your thumb on the lump or bump and carefully working around this tender spot.

As with any grooming routine, it's important to find a place where your cat will be the most comfortable. Some cats will simply lie on a couch or bed and let you trim. Others prefer to be sitting on your lap.

The easiest way to get the job done is to work with an assistant and use the "kitty burrito" method: wrap the cat up in a towel and only expose one foot at a time. Get your assistant to hold the cat facing you. Pick up a paw and press gently so that the nails are extended. The best way to decide where to cut is to look at the nail from the side to distinguish between the nail and the *quick*, the blood supply that is an opaque pink color at the base of the nail. (If you accidentally do cut into the quick, styptic powder will stop the bleeding. So will ordinary flour.)

Hold the clippers in a horizontal position and clip firmly. This will prevent the nail from splitting. Remember to include the dewclaw—the slightly thicker nail on the side of the front feet. On longhaired cats, it's a good idea to wet the fur to make it easier to see the dewclaw. Leaving this claw unattended will cause it to grow into the skin, which can be extremely painful and also cause an infection.

If you are unsure about the procedure, simply trim the very tips of the nails until you've built up more confidence. An ordinary nail file or a special pet nail file will help smooth any rough edges.

Whenever trimming the nails, look closely to ensure they are healthy and that nothing is caught between the toes, such as kitty litter. A cat nail fungus infection called *paronychia* can be a symptom of an internal medical condition that will require veterinary attention.

It's important to note that even trimming a cat's nails regularly will not necessarily stop her from attempting to scratch furniture. If she is scratching furniture, consider pasting specially designed claw covers over each nail to prevent damage. They are sold in kits with special adhesive and usually last up to six weeks. They are available at pet supermarkets and boutiques and are definitely a viable option to declawing.

Eye Care

Make wiping your cat's face with a warm damp cloth or a special nontoxic pet wipe a regular part of your grooming routine and simultaneously check that her eyes are clear and healthy. If she allows you to do so regularly, it will ensure that, should she ever need eye drops or ointments, she will be more tolerant of their application.

Once again, use this grooming time to take careful note of any changes in the eye color or the area surrounding the eye. Eyes should be clear, bright, and free of any discharge. Cats can lose their sight quickly for a number of medical reasons such as high blood pressure, hyperthyroidism, and diabetes. Sight deterioration can be rapid. A cat can also become blind from not being dewormed because the worms migrate around the body, including behind the eyes, which can destroy the optic nerves.

Although they are harmless, some cat owners consider tearstains unsightly. Tearstains are those brown streaks on the inside corners of the eyes running down the bridge of the nose. It is normal for the tear glands to produce secretions that lubricate the surface of the eye and drain down the tear ducts into the nose and throat. However, some liquid tends to accumulate on the skin of the eyelids. As it evaporates, the natural iron compound found in the tears mixes with oxygen in the air and causes a brown stain.

◀ Gently wipe the area around your kitty's eyes with a damp cloth as part of her normal grooming routine.

Paw Irritants

Salt and chemicals used to de-ice outdoor areas can cause skin irritations on a cat's paw pads. Most de-icing products are toxic to pets and could make your cat ill if ingested when she licks her paws; some products can be fatal if ingested. Be sure to wipe paws with a damp paper towel or soft cloth to remove residue *every time* a cat walks on such surfaces. For cats regularly exposed to such conditions, it's a good idea to rub a Shea butter paw balm into the paw pads. It offers protection to the paw pads against these harsh climatic conditions and is harmless if licked off.

Antifreeze is another product used regularly in parts of the country that are annually snowbound. It's important to be wary of any antifreeze that may have dripped on a driveway; cats are attracted to it because of its sweet smell and taste, but it's also highly toxic and can cause death.

It's a good idea to read the labels on the products you are using to clean hardwood floor and tiles as well. Look for pet-friendly nontoxic cleaning agents because cats walk on these areas daily and then lick their paws.

Tearstains are most noticeable on light-colored fur and more prevalent in certain breeds such as Persians because the shape and position of their eyes doesn't allow the tear ducts to drain effectively.

Numerous specially formulated products are designed to lighten these stains. Some are food or water additives; others are packaged as eye pads to be applied directly to the affected areas, and these can be used regularly as part of the grooming routine. It's always a good idea to consult a veterinarian if you are planning to treat tearstains on a permanent basis.

Ear Care

The inner surface of the ear should always be odor-free and feel slightly greasy to the touch. However, sometimes, the ears develop an excess of wax visible on the inside of the ear flap. This can be removed with special ear-wipes or with a cotton swab. *Never use* a swab to clean deep within the ear itself because you can damage the ear canal. It's important to note that ear mites are the most common cause of a gritty dark wax in a cat's ears. This needs veterinary treatment.

Dental Hygiene

A full-grown cat has thirty teeth. There are sixteen on the top and fourteen on the bottom. Kittens usually lose their baby teeth between the ages of two and four months and have all their permanent teeth by the time they are six months old.

Dental problems can plague felines from a very early age starting with a bacteria buildup on the teeth that causes plaque. As in humans, plaque irritates the gums and causes gingivitis, which in turn can cause periodontal disease when the bone around the teeth begins to deteriorate.

Even if you try to get your cat accustomed to allowing you to check her mouth from an early age, there's no question that it can be extremely difficult to efficiently clean a cat's teeth. Consequently, it's simply a matter of doing the best you can as opposed to doing nothing!

There are a plethora of dental products from brushes and pastes to finger gloves to dental gels and sprays all designed to control plaque. There are also tasteless additives for the water bowl.

Regular dental checkups at the veterinarian are important to your cat's overall good health because bacteria left untreated in the mouth will migrate internally, causing kidney and liver damage and other serious issues.

It's important to note that the "gentle dental" teeth-cleaning techniques done without anesthesia and often advertised in local newspapers have to be done by a licensed veterinarian or dental technician at a veterinary office. Beware of unscrupulous practitioners. Often, if the cat is nervous and squirms a lot, the overall treatment cannot be performed properly and is more or less useless. A veterinary technician can definitely do a better and more efficient job if the cat is sedated. Discuss the

▲ Including a massage as part of the regular grooming for an elderly cat can help to maintain flexibility and good blood circulation.

situation with your veterinarian first, especially if your feline is elderly.

Grooming an Older Cat

Because cats are living longer, often well into their teens and even into their twenties, stiffening joints make it difficult for them to efficiently groom themselves as they did when they were younger. You will notice it when your cat no longer grooms herself with that typical leg-in-the-air stance; suddenly, her fur appears a bit matted. When this happens, it's time to help her with her regular grooming by brushing her more regularly and wiping her down with pet wipes or a warm damp cloth.

Older cats also often have difficulty using a litter box and, as a result, fecal matter can get caught in the area around the anus, and clumping litter can become caught between the toes. This can be extremely uncomfortable when it hardens. A warm sponge or a pet wipe will usually take care of such issues. If you cat will allow you, dip her paw in warm water to loosen the trapped debris and then use a cotton ball or a paper towel to efficiently clean and dry between the toes.

It's a good idea to include a massage as part of the regular grooming of an elderly cat. Massage helps to maintain flexibility in the joins and ensure better blood flow to boost circulation. Pet massage therapists are becoming more popular, with pet massages being done at pet spas as well as at home. About twenty basic massage and touch techniques are used, including Swedish massage, shiatsu, Thai, reflexology, Reiki, and acupressure.

Although pet massage therapists draw from all these modalities, the most common techniques employed come from Swedish massage, which uses long and flowing strokes designed to increase circulation and blood flow and to limber up joints and relax tense muscles.

These are the five basic strokes:
- Effleurage: gliding strokes designed to warm up the muscles.
- Petrissage: gentle kneading and circular strokes.
- Friction: deep, circular rubbing.
- Tapotement: rhythmic tapping, administered in several ways—with the edge of the palm, the heel of the hand, with the fingers, or with short, rapid movements using the sides of the hand.
- Vibration movements: very fine, rapid shaking.

It is possible to gently massage your cat yourself practicing these stokes. Pet massage workshops and courses are available around the country to help you improve your technique.

For the ultimate comfort for senior pets, you may want to invest in a specially designed infrared

Pet Dental Month

February is officially Pet Dental month in the United States, when many veterinary offices offer a discount for what is called an ATP—assessment, treatment, and prevention checkup. This is a good time to get your cat in for a dental check, which is necessary and will include a state-of-the-art teeth cleaning done under anesthetic. Be aware, however, that in senior cats the veterinarian may suggest a blood panel to determine whether any internal problems exist that may make proceeding with the anesthesia unwise. It's important to discuss the process with your veterinarian. Cats suffering from medical conditions such as diabetes often are not good candidates for any kind of anesthesia.

Feline Grooming Aids

Here is a guide to feline grooming aids. Initially, when introducing your cat to a grooming routine, only brush all over with a soft nylon brush or a mitt. Once your cat is used to the idea, consider including other more specific routines to deal with the ears, eyes, teeth, and nails. Generally speaking, cats should be brushed at least once a week. Longhaired cats often require daily attention and a more intense session once a week.

Brush, pin: A brush with nylon bristles with round tips on the ends resembling sewing pins. Ideal for grooming longhaired cats.

Brush, slicker: This is an inexpensive wire brush designed to remove tangles, dead hair, and debris while distributing healthy coat oils. Dual-headed slicker brushes follow with the contour of the body and are more efficient.

Brush, wire and boar-bristle combination: The advantage of a combination wire and boar-bristle brush is that the wire section helps to separate the hair and the boar bristle works to distribute the natural oils through the hair and simultaneously stimulate the skin and boost circulation.

Brushes, nylon: Using a selection of brushes with nylon bristles gives the coat a smooth and silky look.

Calming cap: This special cap is designed to lessen a cat's anxiety during grooming by reducing its field visual of vision. It's available in two sizes for cats and kittens.

Chamois cloth, special: This is excellent for a rub down to bring a glossy sheen to shorthaired coats.

Comb, deshedding: A metal comb with alternating short and long tines that extract dead undercoat hairs.

Comb, flea: A metal comb with very closely spaced tines for extracting fleas and flea eggs. It can also be used for gently grooming facial areas and is excellent for removing hair from other grooming brushes.

Comb, rubber: A rubber comb with large teeth, also known as a curry brush, magnetically lifts loose fur and massages the skin.

Comb, short-toothed: A fine, short-toothed comb gently removes any matted hair from the fur. It can also be used to remove hair from the slicker brush.

Dematter: A comb-shaped tool with elongated, razorlike prongs that work their way through the mat, teasing it out in small parts at a time.

Deshedding tool: This "new age" grooming tool is designed for grooming efficacy; it is specifically designed to deal with feline shedding problems by doing the job of a brush and a comb simultaneously. Many have a special fur ejector button to make it easy to remove gathered hair from the gadget. There are several on the market, such as the FURminator and the ShedMonster.

Grooming wipes, hypoallergenic: Specially formulated for a feline skin, these grooming wipes are a quick coat-cleaning solution and also ideal for cleaning between the toes and attending to the tail area, especially on elderly kitties who have difficulty grooming these areas themselves. These all-natural cat wipes contain mild cleansers to deodorize and whisk away dirt, dander, and residual saliva on the fur.

Hair mitt: A hair-grabbing mitt has little rubber knobs on the underside or is manufactured from a special fabric that removes loose hair and also offers a nice massage at the same time.

Massage roller-brush: The rubber bristles on the roller are ergonomically designed to gently remove loose dead hair, dried dirt, and dander while providing a soothing body massage. Most models on the market have two speeds and a very silent motor that make this gadget very cat-friendly.

Nail clippers and nail files: There are a variety of nail clippers on the market. The guillotine style is best for cats. The latest hi-tech nail trimmers come with a built-in light so that it's easy to see where to cut. Some even have a light indicator that turns green when you are at the right place to clip. They are a worthwhile investment because a cat's nails can grow quickly, especially on the front paws, and most cats aren't very tolerant of this necessary procedure. There are also special battery-operated feline nail files that are designed to quickly and efficiently file down feline talons. However, if the noise spooks your cat, use an ordinary human nail file.

Oral hygiene rinse: This product is designed for cats who are notoriously uncooperative when it comes to brushing their teeth. An oral hygiene rinse sprayed into the cat's mouth will help to prevent plaque and tartar buildup and generally keep your feline's mouth in good condition.

Pet hairdryer: Human hairdryers are far too hot and will burn a cat's sensitive skin, even on the lowest heat setting. Consequently, specially designed pet dryers have heat settings tolerable to pet skin and hair and are relatively low-noise. They also clip on to a counter or have suction feet to allow you to use both hands for brushing and drying. Look for a model that offers the latest ionic technology that allows the negative ions in the air to break large water droplets on the hair into smaller drops. In turn, these smaller drops allow more water to be absorbed into the hair so it can dry more quickly and simultaneously retain moisture. The result is smoother and less static fur.

Scissors, blunt-tipped: This tool is useful for cutting into a knot of hair that won't separate using a comb or a brush. The scissors can also be used for trimming excess hair between the toes.

Styptic powder: This special antiseptic powder efficiently stops bleeding if you unintentionally cut into the nail quick.

A good kit to buy is the Scaredy Cut Silent Home Pet Grooming Kit. This innovative bright pink seven-piece kit includes six combs in various sizes that work in conjunction with a special pair of scissors. The combs snap in place under the scissor blades and trim fur safely and evenly. The combs are the very same combs used with standard electric grooming clippers and are designed to glide through hair. A pair of bull-nose scissors (as described above) can also be included in the kit on request.

▲ If you prefer taking your kitty to a groomer, one who specializes in cats is your best bet.

massager that has two heated massage heads—a large head for greater coverage and a small head for more concentrated areas. The heat and massage movement can be controlled separately. The unit is ideal for relieving stiffness and pain associated with arthritis, and it improves circulation and alleviates general stress.

Choosing a Professional Cat Groomer

For a cat, a pet spa or a grooming salon can be a noisy and very stressful environment. Therefore, it's important to do your homework to find out what exactly your cat is going to be exposed to in the grooming area, out of sight of the front desk.

It is important to be able to speak to the grooming professional personally. You need to make sure the groomer is someone who will listen to your requests, who will make recommendations that will improve the health and well-being of your pet, and, most importantly, will talk to and reassure your pet during the grooming process.

Don't be shy about asking to see the grooming area. Inquire about what services are included and what are considered extras. Ask about what type of products are used and inquire about dryers. If your cat is scared of handheld dryers, only consider a salon that uses cage dryers.

Avoid salons that require all pets to be checked in early in the morning and then left to wait their turn in the noisy holding area. Instead, seek out a salon that works by appointment only.

The best way to find a groomer who specializes in cats, or, if possible, a cats-only groomer, is to ask your veterinarian or inquire at your local pet boutique. Cat shows are another great source of local information. And, as with human stylists, personal recommendations are often the best.

During a typical professional grooming session, the groomer will trim your cat's nails and dewclaws, clean her ears with an antiseptic cleaner, and clean her teeth using a brush or a dental cleaning tip that fits over the groomer's finger. After these basics, the groomer will thoroughly brush the coat and remove any mats using a deshedding tool. A typical bath is from the neck down, and the face is usually wiped with a warm cloth or special pet wipe. Massage services are an extra. Some groomers are trained in basic massage techniques, while others work in conjunction with a pet massage therapist.

Cat-Friendly Mobile Groomers

If you are unable to take care of your cat's grooming needs and are not comfortable about sending her to a grooming salon, consider using a mobile grooming service that comes to your front door. Such a service may cost more, but the higher charge will be offset by the fact that you are saving gas and parking costs for two trips (there and back). The biggest saving is the fact that your cat will not be stressed out by the travel ordeal or the salon environment. Once again, look for a personal recommendation or ask for names at your veterinary office. Some services have a feline-only clientele.

Grooming Your Cat

Chapter 11

Feeding Your Cat

My cat's breath smells like cat food.

— Ralph from *The Simpsons*

In 2013, the pet food industry in the United States alone was estimated to be in excess of a $20 billion business. Nutrition is indeed one of the biggest sectors of the pet world, one that most closely mimics human lifestyle trends. If a trend exists for humans, such as foods with organic ingredients, wheat-free, and gluten-free, you can rest assured the same trends exist for pet foods, too. Organic pet foods now dominate more than 25 percent of the pet food market. And furthermore, pet food manufacturers are going to great lengths to source ingredients locally and proudly claim their foods are made in America.

History of Pet Food in America

The pet food business originated in Victorian England. Spratt's Patent Limited produced what is believed to be the first commercial dog food in 1860, a product originally intended for working and show dogs. The company opened an office in the United States in the early 1870s. In 1895, the company's catalog advertised a cat food called Patent Cat Food, an expensive food for the time at five cents a packet. By the 1930s, Spratt's was advertising several different dry cat foods, a feline version of their dog biscuits that had to be softened in milk.

▶ Before cat foods became available commercially, cats ate table scraps and whatever small animals they could catch.

According to Katherine Grier in her book *Pets in America* (2007), several US companies followed Spratt's into the pet food business in the early 1900s. Among them was the Walnut Food Company, which offered what could have been the first commercial wet cat food marketed in the United States; it was meant for show cats. Another pioneer of the early pet food industry was William Danforth, who, in 1902, started an animal feed company called the Robinson-Danforth Commission in St. Louis, Missouri. Although the original company name might not mean much to the average cat person, Robinson-Danforth evolved into the Nestlé Purina Petcare Company, one of the giants of the modern pet food industry. The Iams Company, established in 1946 by Paul Iams to make dog foods, also started small. Today it is part of the Procter and Gamble conglomerate.

Hill's Pet Nutrition, which today is a $2.2 billion global subsidiary of Colgate-Palmolive, started back in the 1940s, when a blind gentleman named Morris Frank met a veterinarian named Mark Morris at a luncheon and asked him to examine his guide dog, Buddy. Dr. Morris diagnosed that the dog was suffering from kidney failure and sent Frank home with a food he had developed called Raritan Ration B. This food, manufactured by a company that Dr. Morris was working with, namely the Hill Packing Company, later became known as Prescription Diet k/d Canine, and it became the forerunner of other prescription formulas manufactured to target specific medical ailments common to both cats and dogs. The company, which evolved into Hill's Pet Nutrition, is also known today for its Hill's Science Diet brand, which is now sold in more than ninety countries.

During the 1930s and 1940s, canned fish pet food products also began to emerge when commercial fishing companies saw this as a way of marketing fish parts that weren't considered edible for human consumption. Initially, these products were marketed for both dogs and cats.

All these new pet foods were considered supplemental to the table scraps being fed to pets— or, in the case of many cats, what they could catch for themselves.

Revolution in Nutrition

In the 1960s, the way Americans viewed their own diets and, in turn, the foods that they were feeding to their pets, began to change. American

◄ The first cat food sold commercially became available in 1895.

▲ Being carnivores, cats require a diet very high in protein. Some form of meat or fish should be the first ingredient in your feline's diet.

food writer and pioneer of the organic health food movement Adelle Davis spoke out passionately against processed foods and food additives and urged Americans to improve their diets. In doing so, she resurrected a phrase that had been used by nutritionist Victor Lindlahr in the 1920–1940s, telling Americans, as Lindlahr had, "you are what you eat."

Slowly, her words began to influence the pet food industry, too, and the focus began to shift from "just food" in a box or a can to highlighting better quality and nutritional content for this targeted market.

In the same decade, a French veterinarian named Jean Cathary, practicing in Aimargues, near Montpellier, saw a rising numbers of patients with skin and fur problems. Cathary recognized that these problems and other pet health conditions were the result of improper nutrition and decided to treat the cause of his patients' skin problems by developing his own pet food recipe. When he realized that his food was successfully curing his patients' skin problems, he decided to launch his product on the market under the name Royal Canin, another prominent industry name that is now owned by another pet food giant, Mars Incorporated.

Over the next few decades, all the major pet food companies worked to develop specific products within their brands with the goal of improving pet health. Feline nutrition also improved greatly with the advent of many smaller pet food companies that focused more intently on feline nutrition. There were also companies that introduced the first breed-specific diets, such one especially designed for Persians, with a specially shaped kibble that is easier for "flat-faced" cats to eat.

Even though pet nutrition was improving, by the 1990s, our cats were facing previously rare health issues, such as obesity and diabetes, which reflected the transformation of their domestic lifestyle from outdoor-indoor pets to indoor-only pets, leading safer yet also more sedentary lives.

The Next Level of Nutrition

By the start of this millennium, the American public was also battling a variety of health issues on a large scale, including obesity and illnesses such as type 2 diabetes. With the help of health gurus such as Dr. Mehmet Oz, who spoke out for a healthy lifestyle, once again Adelle Davis's message became a theme song for human diets.

By now, cats were no longer viewed as just household companions; they were being treated as fur kids in many American households, and a new trend emerged that focused on promoting a general regimen of good health and well-being for felines that mimicked the new lifestyle ideals that people wanted for themselves.

Cat owners were beginning to ask, "What's in the cat food?" The tainted pet food debacle that resulted in thousands of pet deaths and a massive food recall in 2007 really brought home the fact that owners who wanted to protect and promote the health of their cats had to be aware of exactly what they were feeding their pets.

Pet food manufactures, whose images had been badly damaged, rallied to help. They took on an educational role—teaching retailers more about the products they were selling and distributing a lot of nutritional education information to owners through their company websites.

In this, the second decade of the twenty-first century, education about feline nutrition is being taken to the next level, and the phrase "you are what you eat" is being dissected to explain dietary requirements and to educate cat owners about the benefits of certain ingredients.

Consequently, today's domestic cats are now given dietary considerations that take everything from their age, breed, present health, and general lifestyle requirements into account. The selection of different products on the food shelves of the average pet store is bigger than it has ever been. What's more, holistic pet food stores are popping up all over the country.

An even greater emphasis than ever before is placed on the benefits of organically grown, chemical-free ingredients. Adelle Davis would be very proud.

A Cat's Nutritional Needs

Cats are meat eaters (carnivores). That means they require two to three times the amount of protein that omnivores, such as humans, do. Consequently, they rely mainly on nutrients found in animals— high protein, moderate fat, and minimal carbohydrates—to meet their nutritional needs.

Protein

Proteins are the basic building blocks for cells, tissues, and organs. They can be either animal-based—such as chicken, lamb, turkey, fish, and eggs—or plant-based such as soy, vegetables, and cereals. In addition, cat food often contains by-products of animals or plants, the parts that people don't normally eat. The type of meat products that most closely resemble what a cat would catch for itself in the wild would be birds—such as chicken, turkey, and quail—and game animals—such as buffalo, ostrich, venison, and bison. In addition, animal-based proteins also contain complete amino acids, such as taurine, arginine, cysteine, and methionine. These are essential for cats whose bodies don't synthesize them in adequate amounts. In particular, taurine is essential to a cat's diet, and a deficiency is serious because it can cause blindness and fatal heart disease.

Because cats catch fish in the wild, too, fresh fish can be an excellent addition to their diet. Fish is high in iodine and beneficial omega-3 fatty acids that promote healthy skin and fur.

◀ Cats require an amino acid called taurine in their diet. Today's commercial cat foods contain the proper amount of this nutrient.

Fats

Fats are found in animal fat, fish oil, and vegetable oils. Luckily, felines don't suffer from cholesterol issues and in fact require quite high amounts of fats in their diet for energy, and proper brain and metabolism functionality, as well as to maintain healthy skin and fur. The fats they require are found in the form of unsaturated fatty acids such as omega-3 and omega-6. Grass-fed animals contain higher levels of omega-3 fatty acids, whereas cold-water fish such as wild salmon, sardines, mackerel, and trout contain good amounts of other essential unsaturated fatty acids known as docosahexaenoic acid (DHA) and eicosapentaenoic acid (EPA). Although carbohydrates also provide energy, cats use them less efficiently as an energy source. In fact, excessive carbohydrates can cause health issues in cats, such as bloating and obesity.

Fiber

Fiber is found in plant materials. There are two forms: soluble and insoluble. Soluble fiber, which partially dissolves in water, delays the time it takes for food to make its way through the intestine; insoluble fiber, which draws water into the colon, speeds up the time it takes to digest food in the intestinal tract and results in a softer stool. Examples of soluble fiber include oats and psyllium husks and vegetables such as Brussels sprouts and broccoli. Insoluble fiber is found in spinach, celery, pumpkins, zucchini, and carrots.

Generally, healthy cats don't need a lot of fiber in their diets. However, fiber is considered useful to treat constipation and diarrhea. Medical evidence shows that soluble fiber slows down glucose absorption and thus stabilizes blood glucose levels, making it a useful food ingredient for cats suffering from diabetes. (However, to control diabetes mellitus in cats, many veterinary nutritionists are now advocating a low-fiber, low-carbohydrate, high-protein diet.)

Vitamins and Minerals

Vitamins and minerals work in conjunction with one another to keep the body functioning, as in

Say "No!" to a Vegetarian Diet!

Cats are carnivores and require meat products in their diet. They can develop serious health problems on an all-vegetarian diet, even if it's supplemented with vitamins and minerals. Vegetarianism is one lifestyle that humans can't share with their cats—ever.

aiding digestion, ensuring muscle and bone growth and function, and maintaining healthy skin and fur. For good nutrition, cats also need vitamins, such as A, B, D, E, and K, as well as minerals, such as calcium and phosphorus.

Liver contains vitamins such as A and D that are essential to the feline diet. Vitamin B2, which is also known as riboflavin, is another essential found in organ meats, poultry, whole grains, and dairy products.

Essential minerals such as iron, potassium, and calcium are found in meat, including bones, as well as in vegetables and dairy products. Deficiencies can cause growth problems and weight loss, whereas an excess can result is serious medical issues such as high blood pressure, kidney disease, and urinary tract disease.

Commercially Manufactured Diets

Generally speaking, the majority of cat owners purchase commercially manufactured cat foods available in four main forms: dry, canned, semi-moist, and chunky with gravy. Although all of them may contain the same ingredients, they are processed in different ways. In general, cat food consists of water, proteins, fats, carbohydrates, vitamins, and minerals. How close your domestic cat's diet comes to that of its feral cousin's depends on what formula the cat food manufacturer uses.

Dry Foods

Dry food resembles tiny pellets in different shapes and sizes and is marketed in resealable bags. All dry pet foods are made in a machine called an extruder that combines a pressure cooker with a meat grinder. The contents are placed in the machine wet and are ground as they are pushed through the machine. The food is cooked with a steam process as it moves down the line. On exiting, the food is pushed between two plates that cut the food into different shapes and thicknesses. Different pressures inside and outside the machine causes the food to expand and puff up. Next, it is sprayed with tasty fat and flavoring to make it appealing to feline taste buds. Finally, it is dried and packaged. A similar process is used to make popular breakfast cereals for humans.

Canned Foods

A plethora of different canned cat foods on supermarket shelves offer a wide selection of food choices. They are all made in a similar process called *retorting*. First, red meat, chicken, or fish content is ground into small pieces. Then, water is added to form a mixture called a *slurry*. Next, the dry ingredients containing vitamins and minerals are added and blended into the mixture, which is then put into individual cans, sealed, and placed in a giant pressure cooker known as a *retort*. The retort cooks the ingredients for between 50 and 90 minutes at a temperature that will kill any bacteria. Balancing time and temperature to ensure that the food is safe to eat and that cats like the flavor makes the process complex. The cans are then cooled to room temperature and individually labeled.

Semi-Moist Foods

Semi-moist cat food has a soft chewy texture obtained from high levels of water. The process used is called *intermediate moisture technology*, which controls the water content by using ingredients that chemically bind with water. Additional preservatives make it possible to store on a shelf just like a canned food.

Cuts and Gravy

This type of food is made by first grinding all ingredients together into one smooth mixture. Wheat gluten is added to the mixture to thicken it until it becomes firm. The ingredients or mixture may be cooked at any time before it passes through

▼ Feeding cats and dogs specially prepared raw food diets is a growing trend, but it's also somewhat controversial.

The Raw Diet Controversy

In 2012, the American Veterinary Medication Association (AVMA) took a public stand on raw diets for both cats and dogs with the release of this statement:

Raw or Undercooked Animal-Source Protein in Cat and Dog Diets

The AVMA discourages the feeding to cats and dogs of any animal-source protein that has not first been subjected to a process to eliminate pathogens because of the risk of illness to cats and dogs as well as humans. Cooking or pasteurization through the application of heat until the protein reaches an internal temperature adequate to destroy pathogenic organisms has been the traditional method used to eliminate pathogens in animal-source protein, although the AVMA recognizes that newer technologies and other methods such as irradiation are constantly being developed and implemented.

Animal-source proteins of concern include beef, pork, poultry, fish, and other meat from domesticated or wild animals as well as milk* and eggs. Several studies reported in peer-reviewed scientific journals have demonstrated that raw or undercooked animal-source protein may be contaminated with a variety of pathogenic organisms, including *Salmonella spp*, *Campylobacter spp*, *Clostridium spp*, Escherichia coli, Listeria monocytogenes, and enterotoxigenic *Staphylococcus aureus*. Cats and dogs may develop foodborne illness after being fed animal-source protein contaminated with these organisms if adequate steps are not taken to eliminate pathogens; secondary transmission of these pathogens to humans (eg, pet owners) has also been reported.[1,4] Cats and dogs can develop subclinical infections with these organisms but still pose a risk to livestock, other nonhuman animals, and humans, especially children, older persons, and immunocompromised individuals.

To mitigate public health risks associated with feeding inadequately treated animal-source protein to cats and dogs, the AVMA recommends the following:

- Never feed inadequately treated animal-source protein to cats and dogs

- Restrict cats' and dogs' access to carrion and animal carcasses (eg, while hunting)

- Provide fresh, clean, nutritionally balanced and complete commercially prepared or home-cooked food to cats and dogs, and dispose of uneaten food at least daily

- Practice personal hygiene (eg, handwashing) before and after feeding cats and dogs, providing treats, cleaning pet dishes, and disposing of uneaten food

*The recommendation not to feed unpasteurized milk to animals does not preclude the feeding of unpasteurized same-species milk to unweaned juvenile animals.

The "Rawvolution" has always been a controversial in the pet world and no doubt will continue to be a topic for debate.

---

an extruder, where it is flattened into a sheet that is then diced into chunks, and gravy is added. It's usually sold in cans or pouches.

Alternative Diets

With the quest for optimum health for their cats, more cat owners are considering serving their pets alternative diets. Feline home-cooked meals are gaining in popularity. To prepare these meals, owners cook meat in a meat broth or fry it in olive oil and add carefully chosen vegetables (those on the safe list—see below). If you choose to go this route,

be aware that cooking destroys nutrients, which means you will have to add certain key ingredients or supplements.

Another alternative and much more controversial diet that some owners have tried offers completely raw foods. The reasoning behind this diet is that, in the wild, a cat eats a raw food diet and meets all her essential needs through it. When a cat catches a bird, a mouse, or even a fish, she consumes everything, often leaving not even a trace of the meal. The prey's internal organs provide essential proteins, fats, vitamins, and minerals. The

What's So Natural About That?

When it comes to pet foods, there are no official definitions for the terms *natural* and *organic*. Organic has to do with how a food source is grown and processed, usually without the addition of chemicals. *Organic foods* are grown with only animal or vegetable fertilizers such as manure, bone meal, and composted vegetation. The US Department of Agriculture (USDA) will only endorse products that meet these specifications.

Natural may mean that the product has no artificial flavors or colorants, and manufacturers may use the word to state that this is the case only if the ingredients of the product are in accordance with what is found or expected in nature.

Beware of labels that claim *100 percent All Natural*. According to the Pet Food Institute in Washington, most complete and balanced cat foods have vitamins and minerals in them, and those additives are usually artificial. The correct terminology would be *Natural with added Vitamins and Minerals*.

Words such *premium* or *ultra-premium* don't have any official weight; they are advertising terms used to suggest good quality. And there is no legal definition for the word *holistic*.

bones and even bird feathers are a source of fiber. However, a raw food diet presents a real danger of serious illness through contaminated meat, which is why the American Veterinary Medical Association (AVMA) took a stand against the raw food diet in 2012. The raw food diet is discussed here so that readers understand why some people advocate it and also why many authorities warn against it.

Home-Cooked Meals

Preparing homemade foods that are truly healthy and beneficial for your cat involves dedication in the kitchen. If this is the way you would like to go, it's important to discuss your cat's diet with your veterinarian and purchase a book dedicated to the subject of the feline diet that will offer all the necessary advice, along with some tasty recipes.

Healthy vegetables that can be a part of a cat's diet include carrots, pumpkin, sweet potatoes, zucchini, celery, parsnips, peas, and green beans. When cooking for cats, it's important to avoid the use of onions and other vegetables in the onion family, such as leeks and shallots, because they are known to cause Heinz body anemia, a condition in which the red blood cells are destroyed, resulting in anemia. Garlic should be avoided for the same reason. Common signs are weight loss, panting, lethargy, and general weakness. It should be further noted that red vegetables, such as tomatoes, eggplant, bell peppers, and red potatoes, cause digestive problems in cats.

Very often, cat lovers, while keen to ensure that their cat's diet promotes optimum health, do not have the time required to prepare homemade meals and rely on commercially prepared, ready-to-serve "homemade-style" foods. As with raw food diets, "homemade meals" are also are available in frozen form at specialist pet stores.

Raw Food Diet

BARF (biologically appropriate raw food) is the name given to a raw diet resembling what a cat would eat in the wild. An all-raw diet requires a lot of dedication on the part of the cat owner to ensure that the ingredients are fresh and not tainted by common bacteria such as *Salmonella* and *Escherichia coli* (*E. coli*) or parasites. Although such bacteria are not as harmful to cats as to humans, it's important to ensure raw cat food doesn't contaminate any foodstuffs intended for human consumption in the kitchen. These hazards also apply when thawing frozen meat because once meat reaches room temperature, it can activate parasites and microbes that, under certain temperature conditions, can multiply to levels that can lead to foodborne illnesses in humans.

It is possible to purchase commercial pre-mixed raw food that contains ground meat, organs, bones, and vegetables from specialist pet food stores. It's important to package it carefully and only use certain kitchen utensils to prepare it for serving to your cat.

▲ Read labels carefully to be sure you select a high-quality diet for your kitty.

Dehydrated cat food is a convenient way of storing and serving your pet raw, fresh food. It has a good shelf life and takes up very little room on the

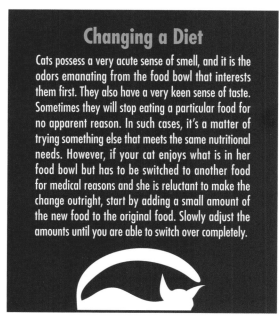

Changing a Diet

Cats possess a very acute sense of smell, and it is the odors emanating from the food bowl that interests them first. They also have a very keen sense of taste. Sometimes they will stop eating a particular food for no apparent reason. In such cases, it's a matter of trying something else that meets the same nutritional needs. However, if your cat enjoys what is in her food bowl but has to be switched to another food for medical reasons and she is reluctant to make the change outright, start by adding a small amount of the new food to the original food. Slowly adjust the amounts until you are able to switch over completely.

pantry shelf—a four-pound box can produce fifteen to seventeen pounds of fresh food.

Manufacturers of dehydrated cat food use human-grade organic ingredients such as eggs, potatoes, yams, organic flaxseed, zucchini, spinach, cranberries, and rosemary, along with free-range chicken. They add various vitamins and minerals that help maintain optimum feline health. Meal preparation involves rehydrating the food by adding warm water, and the process only takes a few minutes. Once prepared, uneaten food needs to be refrigerated and eaten within two days.

Pet Food Labels

Like human foods, pet foods are regulated under the Federal Food, Drug, and Cosmetic Act, and must be pure and wholesome and contain no harmful substances. They also must be truthfully labeled. Foods for human or pet consumption do not require Food and Drug Administration (FDA) approval before they are marketed, but they must be made with ingredients that are "generally recognized as safe" (GRAS) or ingredients that are approved food and color additives. If scientific data show that an ingredient or an additive presents a health risk to animals, the FDA's Center of Veterinary Medicine can prohibit or modify its use in pet food.

Pet food labeling regulations are mainly determined at the state level. Each state has a feed control official responsible for overseeing the marketing, including the labeling, of all animal feeds within that state. However, most states have adopted the regulations recommended by the Association of American Feed Control Officials (AAFCO). It is important to remember that not all pet foods are created equal. A manufacturer can claim that its food is formulated to meet the AAFCO nutrient profiles for a particular life stage. This details the content but doesn't indicate how digestible or nutritionally beneficial it may be for your cat.

Alternatively, the manufacturer can have the food undergo AAFCO feeding trials to establish nutritional adequacy, which ultimately shows that the content is nutritionally beneficial to your cat. Many manufacturers believe that feeding trials are the best way to document how a pet will perform when fed a specific food.

The AAFCO also issues specific rules regarding what can and cannot be placed on the labels of pet foods.

▲ Only feed a diet intended specifically for cats. Feeding your kitty a diet made for another species will not provide proper nutrition.

Standard Label Terms

Every label has to include the product name, net weight, statement of purpose or intent, ingredient list, guaranteed analysis, feeding directions, nutritional adequacy statement, and statement of responsibility.

Serving up Some Greens

Despite being carnivores, cats are very fond of nibbling on different grasses, and there is nothing wrong with placing some greens alongside their food bowl. Small containers of wheat grass are available in the produce section of supermarkets, and packets of grass seeds and sometimes little growing kits can be found at both pet and garden stores. These are cheap and very easy to grow. Cats don't eat greenery to induce vomiting, as many people believe. Often, the foliage is hard to digest, so they simply vomit to expel it from their stomachs.

Why do our little carnivores choose to munch on shoots of grass and other nonfleshy items? The truth is, we don't know. Researchers at the Veterinary Behavior Service at the University of California Davis School of Veterinary Medicine in Santa Cruz, California, however, are conducting the first-ever scientific study to find answers as to why grass and leaves, as well as certain barks, fruits, and vegetables appeal to feline taste buds. Anyone can take part in the study by completing the online survey found at this address: http://intercom.virginia.edu/SurveySuite/Surveys/PlantCat/index2.html.

The product name: The product name explains what kind of what food it is, highlighting the key ingredient, and the words used in the name must conform to AAFCO regulations. For example, a product cannot be named "chicken" unless it contains no less than 95 percent by weight of chicken, not including moisture content. If a product contains at least 25 percent but less than 95 percent chicken, then the product name may include chicken but must also have a descriptive term, such as chicken dinner or chicken entrée, in the name.

If a product contains two *key* ingredients, such as chicken and fish, then the product has to contain more of whichever one is named first, but together they must add up to 95 percent. Beware also that if the word *with* appears in the product name, for example, *Cat Formula with Chicken*, then the manufacturers are only required to include 3 percent of that named ingredient in the food.

The net weight: This has to state exactly what the food in the container weighs.

The statement of purpose or intent: Somewhere on the packaging it must state that the food is specifically for cats. This is to draw the consumer's attention to the fact that cats have specific nutritional needs; they must have certain things in their diet. In other words, you can't feed a cat dog food and vice versa.

Ingredients list: By law, pet food ingredients must be listed on the label in descending order by weight, and the protein should be top of the list. It's important to remember that the moisture content affects weight. So ingredients that are moisture-heavy, such as chicken or lamb, are listed higher on the ingredient list than the same ingredient when added in a dry form.

In addition, similar materials listed as separate ingredients may outweigh other ingredients that precede them on the list of ingredients. For example, chicken may be listed as the first ingredient, then wheat flour, ground wheat, and wheat middling. In this instance, although chicken may appear to be the predominant ingredient, when added together, all three wheat products may weigh more than the chicken.

Here's a quick guide to some of the most common ingredients:

- *Meat*: Cleaned flesh from chicken, lamb, turkey, cattle, and related animals that have been slaughtered specifically for animal feed purposes. However *flesh* means more than skin. It may include muscle (including the

diaphragm), fat, and nerves, blood vessels from the skin, the heart, esophagus, and the tongue.

- *Meat by-product*: Clean, non-flesh parts from the same animals mentioned above. This can include the blood, bone, brain, liver, lungs, liver, kidneys, and emptied stomach and intestines. There are no hooves, hair, horns, or teeth in meat by-products. Chicken by-products are feather free.
- *Beef tallow*: A fat made from beef.
- *Meal*: Finely ground tissue.
- *Bone meal*: Finely ground bone from slaughtered feed animals.
- *Fish meal*: Clean, ground whole fish or fish pieces. The fish may or may not still contain fish oil.
- *Ground corn*: Chopped or ground corn kernels.
- *Corn gluten meal*: A product that forms after corn syrup or starch is made.

Preservatives play a critical role in dry pet foods, acting as antioxidants to prevent the fat in foods from spoiling. Once a fat spoils, the food loses its nutritional value and can become unsafe to eat.

The preservatives used in cat food can be natural, such as vitamin E (tocopherol) or vitamin C (ascorbic acid). Artificial preservatives include butylated hydroxytoluene (BHT) and butylated hydroxyanisole (BHA); both are synthetic forms of vitamin E.

Because ingredient definitions and designations are standardized, it is difficult to determine the quality of ingredients. Ingredient quality can only be determined from laboratory analysis and animal feeding tests.

The guaranteed analysis: The analysis states the minimum or maximum amount of certain nutrients. The following four nutrients must be included on all pet food labels:

- Crude protein (percent minimum)
- Crude fiber (percent maximum)
- Crude fat (percent minimum)
- Moisture (percent maximum)

Pet Food Recall of 2007

On March 15, 2007, pet food manufacturer Menu Foods alerted the Food and Drug Administration to fourteen animal deaths in the United States—four cats and one dog reported by consumers and nine cats who died during routine taste trials conducted by the company. The animals were reported to have developed kidney failure after eating certain "cuts-and-gravy" style dog and cat food produced at Menu Foods' facilities in Emporia, Kansas, between December 3, 2006, and March 6, 2007.

In the following months, consumers and veterinarians reported cases of illnesses and deaths potentially associated with a wide variety of pet foods made by Menu Foods and other manufacturers.

On investigation, the FDA researchers found melamine and melamine-related compounds in samples of pet food. Melamine, an industrial chemical, and its related compounds have no approved use as an ingredient in animal or human food in the United States.

The FDA traced the melamine to products labeled as wheat gluten and rice protein concentrate imported from China and used as ingredients in pet foods. Cornell University scientists also found melamine in the urine and kidneys of deceased cats who were part of a taste-testing study conducted for Menu Foods.

The FDA's further testing showed that the vegetable protein products imported from China were mislabeled. American and Chinese authorities investigated the source of the contamination linked to the pet deaths, and Chinese authorities subsequently closed down two companies responsible for the contaminated products.

There were several other pet food recalls subsequent to this debacle that definitely changed the way American pet food manufacturers operate. Information about this recall, as well as ongoing research into pet foods can be found at www.FDA.gov.

This pet food recall made cat parents realize how important it is to read labels and learn about their cat's basic nutritional needs. These days, many pet food manufacturers have detailed information on their websites and have taken major steps in helping to educate pet food retailers about their respective products so that the sellers can, in turn, offer customers more informed choices.

▲ Whether you free-feed or give your cat a fixed feeding time will depend on your cat's eating habits and your preference.

For example, a food with a 25 percent minimum crude protein guarantee should contain at least 25 percent protein but could contain much more. The only way to determine the actual amount is by laboratory analysis.

Manufacturers may voluntarily include information about other nutrients, such as magnesium (percent maximum), taurine (percent minimum), ash (percent maximum), and linoleic acid (percent minimum), on cat food products.

The guaranteed analysis is an important tool when beginning to compare pet food formulas. However, it doesn't provide meaningful nutritional information. Using information on the energy content and nutrient density of a food is the only way to properly compare pet foods. This information is available from the manufacturer.

The feeding directions: Directions are important; they are a general guideline as to how the product should be fed to the cat. Due to the critical nutrient requirements for growth, kitten products should provide specific feeding rates related to age and weight. However, because these are only recommended feeding amounts, it's essential to get exact feeding instructions from your veterinarian.

The AAFCO Nutritional Adequacy Statement: This statement is required on all pet foods because it details for which specific lifestyle and age of cat the food is intended. Products may either be formulated, which means the product has been manufactured according to AAFCO nutritional guidelines, but not actually fed to cats or dogs prior to sale, or tested, which means that the product has been formulated, then fed to dogs or cats prior to sale to ensure it meets important criteria related to growth, maintenance, and/or reproduction.

Veterinary-exclusive products include statements such as "This product is intended for intermittent feeding only" and "Use only as directed by your veterinarian."

The statement of responsibility: This statement lists the name of the company responsible for making the product, as well as the address and, where possible, a toll-free phone number so that customers can quickly and easily obtain product information. In addition to stating that the product is guaranteed, the company should indicate what action would be taken to meet customer expectations, such as replacing the product or giving a money-back guarantee.

Making a Pet Food Complaint

Complaints about pet food must be made to your state's FDA Consumer Complaint Coordinators. A list of telephone numbers can be found on the FDA.gov website.

The following information must be provided:

- Exact name of the product and product description (as stated on the product label)
- Type of container (e.g., box, bag, can, pouch)
- If the product intended to be refrigerated, frozen, or stored at room temperature
- Lot number: This number is often hard to find and difficult to read. It is stamped onto the product packaging, typically includes a combination of letters and numbers, and is always in close proximity to the expiration date (if the product has an expiration date). The lot number is very important because it helps determine the manufacturing plant as well as the production date.

- Best-by or expiration date
- UPC code (also known as the bar code)
- Net weight
- Purchase date and exact location where purchased
- Results of any laboratory testing performed on the pet food product
- How was the food stored, prepared, and handled. Consumers often transfer dry pet food into other containers for easier handling. Hence, it's important to save the original packaging until the pet food has been consumed so that you can access needed information.

Description of the problem with the product such as:

- Foul odor, off color
- Swollen can or pouch, leaking container
- Foreign object found in the product; describe

If you think your pet has become sick or injured as a result of consuming a pet food product, also provide the following information about your pet:

- Species (cat)
- Age, weight, breed, pregnant, spayed/neutered
- Previous health status of pet
- Any preexisting conditions
- Do you give your pet any other foods, treats, dietary supplements or drugs?
- How much of the product does your pet normally consume?
- How much of the "suspect" product was consumed from the package?
- How much product remains?
- Clinical signs exhibited by your pet (examples: vomiting, diarrhea, lethargy)

- How soon after consuming the product did the clinical signs appear?
- Veterinarian's contact information, diagnosis, and medical records for your pet
- Results of any diagnostic laboratory testing performed on your pet
- How many pets consuming the product exhibited clinical symptoms?
- Are there any pets who consumed the product and are not affected?
- Does your pet spend time outdoors unsupervised?
- Why do you suspect the pet food caused the illness?

By-Products

By-products is a term that often gets a bad rap. It should be noted that not all by-products are inferior. According to the AAFCO official publication of 2008, the definition of a *by-product* is "secondary products produced in addition to the principle products." Thus, a by-product is something produced in the making of something else. For example, vitamin E is a by-product of soybeans. Vegetable oils, such as flaxseed oil, rice bran oil, and soy oil, are by-products extracted from the seeds produced for human consumption.

Often, which parts of a food animal that a cat owner may think inferior or unpalatable has more to do with that person's cultural background than with true inferiority. For instance, in many parts of Asia, chicken feet are part of a human's daily diet. It's also important to remember that, in the wild, cats don't differentiate between body parts. Often they will eat everything—including feathers!

Life-Stage, Breed-Specific, and Medical Diets

Cats have different nutritional needs during the different stages of their lives. A *life stage* refers to a particular developmental period, such as kittenhood, adulthood (which ranges up to seven human years), and the senior years (seven years and older).

It's important to note that the AAFCO has only established two nutrient profiles for cats to fit their life stages—growth/lactation and maintenance. A product intended for growing kittens or for pregnant or lactating females must meet the AAFCO's nutrient profile for growth and lactation. Products that meet the AAFCO's profile for maintenance are suitable for an adult, nonreproducing cat of normal activity level, but may not be adequate for an immature, reproducing, or hard-working animal. A product may claim that it is for "all life stages" if it is suitable for adult maintenance and also meets the more stringent nutritional needs for growth and reproduction. So, terms like "senior" or "formulated for large breed adults" mean that the food meets the requirements for adult maintenance—and nothing more.

However, in the past decade, pet food manufacturers trying to give pets the best possible well-being that can be obtained from diet have taken the initiative and branched out by introducing certain breed-specific cat foods and low-calorie lifestyle options designed for cats who have a more sedentary lifestyle.

A typical breed-specific food is one created for Persian cats. Studies have shown that the facial structure of a Persian makes it more difficult for this breed to pick up certain shaped dry foods. Special almond-shaped formulas are manufactured to deal with this

◄ Each cat in the house should have her own food bowl, although they will likely eat out of each other's bowls anyway.

problem. Furthermore, certain specialized diets for longhaired cats contain more fiber, which helps to minimize hairballs.

There are also special diets for cats with certain medical conditions like urinary tract disease, kidney disease, and allergies, as well as special weight-control formulas. These specialized formulas are only sold in veterinary offices, based on the premise that such a diet has to be supervised by a veterinarian. For example, a calorie-restricted formula will be boosted with additional vitamins that target the problem, such as L-carnitine, a nutrient that maintains muscle while the animal is losing fat.

Another new food trend has been the introduction of single-source protein foods. This can be a huge help to owners whose cats may be allergic to a particular protein ingredient because it allows them to completely eradicate the offending ingredient from the cat's diet without compromising its general nutrition. Popular single-source protein

Food Allergies

Symptoms of a food allergy include abdominal pain, bloating, vomiting, diarrhea, itchy skin, and swelling of the skin. Cats aren't born with a food allergy; it's something that develops and can occur in cats as young as five months old or even at an advanced age.

It's important to ascertain whether the cat has a food allergy or simply intolerance to a certain food, which means that she is unable to digest and process the food correctly. Take your cat to the veterinarian if she is showing any of these symptoms (see page 287 on allergies).

foods include those featuring duck, lamb, venison, and rabbit.

There is a misconception that corn is a major cause of allergies in cats and dogs. In fact, veterinarians say that is isn't a very common cause of allergies and is implicated in fewer allergy than common protein sources such as beef, dairy products, chicken, or soy.

▼Most veterinarians recommend feeding a cat kitten food until she is nine to twelve months old.

Nevertheless, this has brought about another trend in pet foods: namely, products that are advertised as grain-free and also often gluten-free.

Feeding Your Cat

A lot of cats are nibblers and, as such, like to visit their food bowls throughout the day and night. This free-feeding method is fine as long as you aren't topping up the bowl all the time and supplementing with human tidbits. If you prefer fixed feeding times, then it's suggested that you put out half the total amount in the morning and the balance at night. Many cat owners do a combined feeding schedule by putting out food in the morning and leaving down what is not initially eaten, then putting out the balance of the prescribed amount at night.

Cats can be notoriously fussy eaters, especially if adopted when they are already fully grown. Never leave food down for days and expect them to eat it. It will lose its nutritional value and possibly become unsafe, too. There is no shortage of choices on the product shelves. Try something else.

Cats also love to eat out of each other's bowls. And, in a multicat household, it can get complicated trying to ensure that each cat is getting the right amount of food, especially if the different felines are on different diets. If this is the case, then it's important to set up isolated, individual feeding places in an attempt to ensure that each cat eats mostly what has been allotted to her.

It's important to take veterinary advice about exactly how much food to give your cat each day. This amount can depend on, among other factors, the age of your cat, whether your cat is pregnant, the weight of your cat, and the amount of exercise your cat enjoys on a daily basis.

Feeding a Kitten

As with human babies, newborn kittens get all the nutritious food requirements they need from their mother's milk. They can be introduced to a prescribed kitten food when they are about four or five weeks old. Although they won't be weaned at this age, they can be fed up to six times a day until they are three months old. Between the ages of four

List of Foods to Avoid

Here is a list of foods published by the Humane Society of the United States that can be harmful and even toxic to cats:

- Alcoholic beverages
- Apple seeds
- Apricot pits
- Avocados
- Dough containing yeast
- Candy containing the sweetener xylitol
- Cherry pits
- Chocolate
- Coffee (grounds, beans, chocolate-covered espresso beans)
- Grapes
- Hops (used in home beer brewing)
- Macadamia nuts
- Moldy foods
- Mushrooms
- Mustard seeds
- Onions and onion powder
- Peach pits
- Potato leaves and stems (green parts)
- Raisins
- Rhubarb leaves
- Salt
- Tea (caffeine)
- Tomato leaves and stems (green parts)
- Walnuts

and six months, the meals can be reduced to four times a day and thereafter slowly reduced to three meals and finally to a twice-a-day feeding schedule.

Veterinarians recommend that kittens initially be fed a special formula designed to strengthen their immune systems and build healthy bones.

Currently, there is only one two-stage kitten feeding program on the market. The first formula is designed for young kittens between the ages of one and four months. It's a soft mousse texture designed to help them transition from milk to solid food. The dry food version is the tiniest of kibbles. Because the age range from four weeks to four months is a high growth period, the content of the products has a high percentage of energy from nutrients such as protein and fat. The second kitten formula is geared to kittens from four months to a year. The wet formula is a chunk and gravy style that has been specially textured for baby teeth and jaws, and the dry version a slightly larger kibble shape than that created for very young kittens. These formulas are geared toward building healthy muscle and bones.

These foods are believed to be revolutionary in the pet food industry because they are based on the latest research that outlines that cats have a preference for their food based on nutrient content rather than a taste preference. This preference is based on what is called the *macro nutrient profile* (MNP), which is described as the redistribution of energy provided by each macro nutrient in the diet—namely, proteins, fats, and carbohydrates—to support long-term palatability. The specific MNP of a cat varies according to the cat's age as well as its physiological condition.

The research behind these new kitten foods indicates that kittens can develop a texture preference, and, consequently, the type of food—wet versus dry—given to just-weaned kittens can initially influence the type of foods they will prefer to eat during their kittenhood and possibly throughout their adult life.

Many veterinarians suggest that kittens be introduced to a young adult food at around nine months so that they do not suddenly pick up weight because kitten formulas are intended for growth. Orphaned kittens or those who have had a poor start in life can be fed a supplement of bovine colostrum that can be bought in powdered form at pet supermarkets and mixed with bottled water.

Although all pet foods have feeding instructions on the packaging, it's important to check the

Food for Spayed/Neutered Cats

In late 2012, the first foods formulated specifically for spayed and neutered cats was launched onto regular pet food shelves nationwide by Royal Canin, also the first company to manufacture breed-specific formulas.

It's a well-known fact that the metabolism of cats who have been spayed or neutered can slow down by as much as 30 percent. In addition, these cats also experience a 20 percent increase in their appetites, which results in weight gain that can, in many cases, become clinically obesity. Although there are lots of low-calorie diets on the market, these formulas do not address the problem of increased appetite, which is the main reason for weight gain.

This new range of products has been special formulated by nutritional experts with a special blend of fibers to make cats feel full and thus consume less food. The kibbles are also specially shaped, with a larger surface area (the one for cats aged one to seven years resembles a tiny donut in shape) because this larger food surface has been known to make cats consume fewer pieces.

One product caters to spayed and neutered kittens from six to twelve months of age by promoting growth while maintaining weight control. The formulas for cats between the ages of one and seven years, and for cats aged seven to twelve years control appetite and promote vitality, helping felines in this age range maintain a healthy weight. The fourth formula is for spayed and neutered cats twelve years and older and contains ingredients for joint support and kidney health and, at the same time, is geared to weight maintenance.

Although the formulas target these specific groups with the correct amounts of antioxidants, reduced phosphorus levels, and increased amounts of omega-3 fatty acids for each age group, there will be no nutrition harm done in multicat households where cats of different life stages tend to eat out of each other's bowls.

correct amounts for your cat with your veterinarian and also inquire if and when the amounts should change. Keep a special measuring cup especially for meals. Color-code the cups for different cats in the household so as not to get confused. You can even make your own using the see-through plastic cups that hold ready-made gelatins or desserts in the supermarket. Cut them to hold the required amounts and label them accordingly.

It's a good idea to introduce a kitten to both wet and dry foods so that she will accept both formulas later on. Wet food is an excellent way of adding supplements or giving a cat prescribed medicine because it can be mixed into the food.

Feeding a Pregnant Cat

A pregnant cat will need at least 25 percent more than her usual food intake. She may require up to three times her normal amount of food while suckling her kittens. Special dietary consideration for pregnant and lactating cats should be discussed with a veterinarian.

Feeding an Obese Cat

Cats typically weigh between 5.5 and 16 pounds (2.5 to 7.3 kg). Some of the bigger breeds, such as Maine Coons, can weigh in at around 25 lbs (11.3 kg). However, obesity is becoming a huge issue among the feline population. As with humans, being overweight can lead to serious medical conditions such as diabetes and kidney disease, not to mention joint issues, which can hinder a cat's mobility and make it even more difficult for her to lose weight.

Cats don't lose weight easily so its better to control their feeding from the get-go to avoid having to deal with a weight loss issue later on. The best ways to do this is to be firm about the contents of the food bowl. Never feed human food and treats. Even specially formulated felines treats must be given sparingly. Treats should never make up more than 10 percent of your cat's daily diet. Always check the calorie content on the package.

A feline weight loss program must be properly supervised by a veterinarian to ensure the cat's

Turning Up Their Noses

Here is a question many cat owners ask: Why does my cat literally turn up her nose at food?

a. She is checking to see whether it's the same food she was served the night before.

b. She has a very keen sense of smell.

c. It's just a twitch and means nothing.

d. The food is going bad.

Answer:

b. Cats have between 60 and 80 million olfactory cells. Humans have only between 5 and 20 million. So felines definitely have a keener sense of smell. They also have a special scent organ called the *Jacobson's organ* located in the palate. It analyzes smells and, when it's working, cats often appear to be turning their noses up to food.

nutritional intake is *not compromised* in any way during the weight loss process. Although it requires a proper medical opinion to determine if a cat is underweight or overweight, it's possible to gauge appropriate weight with the following guidelines:

- In a healthy cat, the leg shape should be clearly defined from the side, and the chest area should dip to create a waist when viewed from above.
- In an underweight cat, the ribs and hips will protrude.
- Overweight cats are a distinct pear shape with a sagging tummy that makes their back legs look much shorter. The more pear-shaped, the more obese.

Providing Supplements and Vitamins

A cat fed a proper and balanced diet should not require any additional vitamin supplements in her daily diet. However, supplements can be beneficial for boosting the immune system in ill or elderly pets, in treating certain skin conditions, in pregnancy, and for improving joint flexibility and offering relief from arthritic discomfort. Always seek veterinary advice to ensure that you are giving the correct dietary supplements and the correct dosage. Such supplements come in both pill and capsule form. For cats who refused to take pills, they can be disguised in a soft "pill pocket" (a flavored dough-like cat treat), and the contents of a capsule can be sprinkled onto food.

A well-balanced multivitamin will contain the following ingredients:

- Calcium ascorbate
- Copper sulfate
- Dicalcium phosphate
- Dl alpha acetate
- Ferrous fumarate
- Gelatin
- Magnesium silicate
- Magnesium stearate
- Manganese sulfate
- Niacinamide
- Potassium chloride
- Potassium iodide
- Pyridoxine hydrochloride
- Riboflavin
- Safflower oil powder
- Thiamine mononitrate
- Vitamin B supplement
- Vitamin D3 supplement
- Zinc oxide

Nutraceuticals are dietary supplements made from a food or part of a food that provides both medical and health benefits, including the prevention and treatment of disease. Glucosamine and chondroitin tablets are classified as nutraceuticals. Studies have shown that glucosamine, a 2-amino derivative of glucose, and chondroitin, which is found in animal cartilage, have a therapeutic effect on joint and cartilage problems in cats. Another popular nutraceutical for cats is an omega-3 fatty acid supplement derived from fish oil.

The FDA does not regulate nutraceuticals. Consequently, although products may look the same, dosage and quality may differ. Read the labels carefully!

▼ Many cats enjoy drinking from the faucet. You can even buy a pet fountain, so your cat has access to running water all the time.

Providing Drinking Water

A regular supply for fresh drinking water is essential to every cat's diet, especially those who eat a dry formula. It's a good idea to have several water bowls around the house and refresh them regularly. Algae can develop in a water bowl, so be sure to wash bowls out properly on a weekly basis. It's a good idea to give cats who suffer from urinary tract infections or kidney disease distilled water in their water bowls to ensure they are drinking water in its purest form.

Pet drinking fountains offer cats a continuous supply of fresh flowing water and have the added benefit of filtering the water, too. They are a worthwhile investment, especially in a multicat household. However, even with one installed in a central location, it's a good idea to have additional bowls around the home.

Drinking fountains emulate the flowing water that cats enjoy in the wild, and there are many styles from which to choose. Some allow the water to "bubble up" into the bowls; others allow the water to flow downward. Although there is no scientific research to back this up,

many observers believe that cats with a drinking fountain tend to drink more water, which is good.

Many cats love to drink water out of glass receptacles—just ask any cat owner who has to share a glass of water on the night stand with a cat. Special tall glass drinking flutes on a stand are available from pet boutiques and online stores. You can find one by searching for the phrase "pet drinking flute."

Chapter 12

The Cat Body

By Arnold Plotnick, DVM

If you want a cat who will be as healthy as possible inside and out, from the first day you bring her home to last day of her long, happy life, then you need to learn all about every square inch of her body. It is not enough to just admire the long, flowing locks of a Persian's coat or the striking color of a Siamese's eyes. You need to understand what each part of the cat's body does to keep her safe and you need to know what can go wrong with each part. In this chapter, we begin by taking a look at the different parts of the fascinating feline body from the outside in.

Skin and Coat

The hair coat and skin make up the outer covering of the body. The coat is the first barrier to mechanical trauma. The thick coat and orientation of the hairs of some cats repel water, so that it doesn't reach the skin surface. Certain breeds, such as the Norwegian Forest cat, have coats that are very repellant to water. In fact, some show judges will let several drops of water fall onto the hair coat to see if the drops roll off without wetting the cat. The hair coat also is an effective barrier to visible light and ultraviolet light. (White cats and those with very light coats are at increased risk for some types of cancers that are known to be induced by frequent exposure to the sun.)

The skin is the largest and one of the most important organs of the body. It forms an essential barrier between the cat and her environment, protecting her from infections,

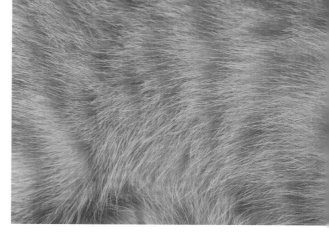

▶A cat's fur is her first barrier to injury, and it also protects her skin from ultraviolet light.

▲ Although they can't see in total darkness, cats require only one-sixth the amount of light to see as a human does.

parasites, and the elements. The skin consists of an outer layer (epidermis) and an inner layer (the dermis). The epidermis consists of tough cells containing a protective protein called *keratin*. As keratinized cells are shed from the skin surface, new ones are continuously formed. The dermis, located beneath the epidermis, contains blood vessels, nerves, connective tissue, hair follicles, and various glands. The skin also prevents dehydration and protects against infection by microorganisms and harmful chemicals. The skin is also where vitamin D is synthesized.

The coat and skin play a significant role in thermoregulation. The thick hair coat and subcutaneous fat cells protect the cat during cold weather. Blood vessels in the dermis also play a role in temperature regulation. Vasodilation (expansion of the blood vessels in the skin) allows for heat loss, whereas vasoconstriction (contraction of the blood vessels in the skin) prevents heat loss from the circulation. The skin also plays a sensory role through free nerve endings in the skin that recognize such sensations as heat, cold, pain, and itchiness. Specialized structures contained within the skin allow for recognition of pressure and touch.

The skin and coat are often a good reflection of the general state of a cat's health.

Ears and Eyes

The cat's ear is divided into three parts: the external (outer) ear, the middle ear, and the inner ear. The outer part of the ear—the part you can see when you glance at your cat—is called the *pinna*. The pinna acts like a funnel that catches sound vibrations and transmits them to the eardrum, via the ear canal. The eardrum separates the external ear from the middle ear. Vibrations from the eardrum are transmitted through small bones in the middle ear to the vestibular window. From the vestibular window, vibrations enter the inner ear, where the cochlea turns them into nerve impulses that travel to the brain via the auditory nerve. Within the inner ear, too, is the vestibular system, which is responsible for maintaining the sense of balance.

Cats can distinguish among sounds better than can dogs or humans. They can also hear sounds at a higher pitch (up to 65 kHz) than can humans.

The eye is made up of three layers. The outer layer is the fibrous layer, the middle layer is the vascular layer, the inner layer is the nervous layer. The outer fibrous layer consists of the sclera (the white of the eye) and the cornea (the clear part of the eye). The thick middle layer is called the uvea, and it is composed of the choroid (the blood-vessel containing layer behind the retina), the ciliary body (a structure that produces the fluid in the front chamber of the eye), and the iris (the colored part of the eye that surrounds the pupil). The muscles in the iris that surround the pupils are able to narrow the pupil into a vertical slit in bright light and open fully in dim light, allowing maximum illumination to enter the eye.

In humans as well as in animals, the role of the visual system is to collect light and focus it onto the retina, where specialized cells convert this light energy into nerve impulses. The amount of light that passes through the cornea is controlled by the pupil. Similar to the aperture of a camera, the pupil adjusts to different light levels by dilating to let in more light during dim conditions or by constricting to limit the amount of light in bright conditions.

The lens, located just behind the pupil, focuses the light coming through the pupil onto the retina. The retina at the back of the eye acts like the film in a camera. When light strikes the retina, light-sensitive photoreceptor cells (rods and cones) are stimulated, causing them to produce impulses that travel to the brain via the optic nerve. Rods are sensitive to dim light; cones are sensitive to bright light and colors.

As nocturnal creatures, cats are more sensitive to light than humans. Although they can't see in total darkness, cats require only one-sixth the amount of light as a human to see. Their pupils can dilate three times larger than a human's, and the feline cornea is bigger, allowing more light in. The feline retina also contains reflective cells that amplify the light coming into the eye. These reflective cells (the *tapetum*) are responsible for the glowing appearance of the eyes when light strikes them.

Eyesight in cats is geared to assist in hunting. Being predators, their eyes are placed on the front of the head. This results in a larger area of binocular vision, allowing for more accurate depth perception and coordination of body movements with visual events. Cats, however, cannot see detail very well.

Visual acuity is the ability to see the detail of an object separately and clearly. A person with 20/20 vision can discern the details of an image (such as letters on a chart) perfectly from 20 feet away. Applied to animals, dogs are said to have a visual acuity of 20/75. The average cat is believed to have a visual acuity between 20/100 and 20/200. Simply put, cats are nearsighted.

Cats can see color, but they do not have as many color-sensitive photoreceptors as humans do. Colors that would appear to be very rich to us are more pastel-like to the cat. Cats respond to the blue and yellow wavelengths best, having trouble with green and red. What appears to us as *red* is simply *dark* to cats. A fraction

◄ Cats start losing their baby teeth at about four months of age and have all their adult teeth by six months.

of the green spectrum in cats is indistinguishable from white. Cats would see a green, grassy lawn as a whitish lawn, and a green rosebush with red roses would appear as a whitish bush with dark flowers. Cats, however, are very good at distinguishing many different shades of gray.

Teeth

Kittens are born with no teeth. At one to two weeks of age, the deciduous teeth (baby teeth) erupt. At six weeks of age, all twenty-six baby teeth should be present. At four to five months of age, the baby teeth are shed, and the permanent teeth erupt. By six months of age, all thirty adult teeth will have erupted. The thirty teeth include twelve little incisors in front, four canine teeth (the two upper and two lower *fangs*), ten premolars, and four molars. The periodontium consists of the structures around the teeth, namely, the periodontal ligaments that attach the gums to the teeth, the alveolar bone (the "tooth socket"), and the gingiva (the gums).

The Declawing Debate

Perhaps no topic involving feline welfare is more controversial and ignites more passion than the topic of declawing. Declawing is the surgical removal of the cat's claws. In most cases, only the front feet are declawed. The surgery involves the amputation of the last digit of each toe with the cat under general anesthesia. There are several techniques for removal of the claws.

Traditionally, the individual claws are dissected out using a scalpel blade or similar instrument. In recent years, laser declaw surgery has become more readily available and may offer quicker recovery times and less discomfort. If declawing is to be performed, it is best done in kittenhood. Because of their small size, kittens bear less weight on their feet after the procedure and recover more quickly. Because the claws are a major method of defense, declawed cats should never be let outdoors.

▲ Nail caps.

There are several reasons why cat owners choose to have their cat declawed. They range from a desire to protect furniture and furnishings from destruction to preventing or reducing the chance of a cat's scratching children or others to protecting the health of household members who are immunocompromised.

Those who are against declawing believe that the surgery is unnecessary and that cats can be trained not to scratch the furniture or people and to use appropriate items like scratching posts instead. They argue that the procedure is painful and can lead to behavioral and health problems for the cat later on. Many people feel that the procedure is cruel and amounts to mutilation, and they point to the fact that many countries outlaw the procedure for this reason.

Yet even some who are against declawing in general might feel that declawing is acceptable as a last resort if it prevents a cat from being relinquished to a shelter. Destructive behavior is a common reason for pets to be relinquished to shelters.

There are alternatives to declawing. One is a surgical procedure wherein the tendon attached to each nail is severed, resulting in the inability of a cat or kitten to extend the nails. This is known as a *digital flexor tendonectomy*. However, because the nails are still present, cat owners opting for this alternative to declawing must trim their cat's nails regularly. If they don't, the nails can overgrow and penetrate the skin and pads of the feet, causing pain and infection.

Another alternative to declawing, one which might appeal more to those who are against any surgical procedures, is to apply soft plastic nail caps to the claws. These nail caps are available under the brand name Soft Paws. The nail caps are glued into place. Cat owners utilizing this product need to be aware that the nail caps have to be replaced periodically, usually once every four to six weeks. The application of Soft Paws is not painful and can usually be performed without sedation. (Exceptionally grumpy cats, however, may need a sedative or tranquilizer.)

Paws

A cat's front paws differ slightly from the back paws. Front paws normally have five toes; back paws normally have four toes. Some cats have a harmless genetic trait that causes them to have extra toes on the front feet, back feet, or both. This is called *polydactyly*.

Each feline toe has a pad and a claw associated with it. In the center of each paw is a large paw pad. Some cats have pink paw pads. Others have black paw pads. Some cats have both colors, sometimes within the same pad. The skin of the paw pads is thicker than the skin on the rest of the body, providing the toughness necessary for walking and jumping. Despite the added thickness, the skin on the paws is capable of sensing vibrations and temperature changes. Paw pads also contain sweat glands, making them the only places on a cat's body that sweats. Longhaired cats can have tufts of hair growing between the toes.

Cats' claws, like the claws and nails of all animals, are made of the protein keratin. Beneath the claw is a pink structure, the quick, which contains blood vessels, nerves, and cells that give rise to the keratin that makes the nail. Cats use their claws for climbing, for killing prey, and for defense.

Musculoskeletal System

Making up a large part of the cat's weight, the musculoskeletal system comprises all of the bones and muscles in the cat's body. The skeleton supports the body and provides the framework for the muscles. The bones have other functions as well, such as mineral storage and the formation of blood cells, which occurs in the marrow within the bones. Cats have approximately 230 bones in their body, approximately twenty-five more than humans have. Most of those extra bones are found in the tail.

The skeleton can be divided into two parts: the *axial skeleton*—the skull, spine, ribs, and sternum— and the *appendicular skeleton*, which comprises the front and hind legs. Although cats are very limber and coordinated, their bones are fairly fragile and orthopedic injuries such as broken bones are common.

Muscles can be divided into three basic types: skeletal, smooth, and cardiac. *Skeletal muscle* is responsible for voluntary movement such as running, jumping, and walking. *Smooth muscle* is found in internal organs such as the intestines and bladder and is involved in involuntary actions within the body. *Cardiac muscle*, found only in the heart, is a specialized type of muscle that is capable of contracting rhythmically and spontaneously.

▼The cat skeleton. Cats have approximately 230 bones.

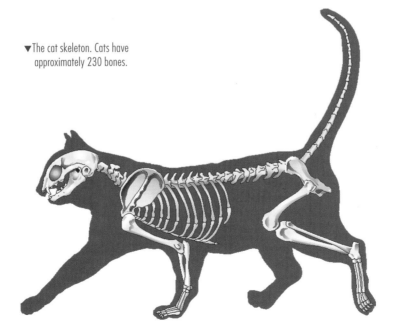

The Immune System: Ready for Battle

The immune system can be thought of as an "army" whose job is to defend the body against "invaders." These invaders come in the form of bacteria, viruses, parasites, toxins, and other foreign materials.

The immune system comprises various organs and cells located throughout the body. The main organs of the immune system are the lymph nodes. They are small structures located throughout the body in areas such as the neck, armpits, groin, chest, and abdominal cavity. As blood flows through the lymph nodes, *antigens* (proteins found on invading viruses, bacteria, and so on) are filtered and trapped by the lymph node. The nodes contain large numbers of *lymphocytes*, the white blood cells that are the key players in the immune response. Other organs involved in the immune response are the lungs, the liver, the intestine, the thymus, and the blood. The spleen is an important component of the immune system; it filters and traps antigens directly from the blood stream. The bone marrow is another major component of the immune system and is the site where most of the infection-fighting white blood cells are produced. A variety of white blood cells participate in the immune response. Some white cells attack and kill invading bacteria and viruses directly. Others produce antibodies (also called *immunoglobulins*), specialized proteins that play an important role in the immune response, especially against viruses.

The organs of the immune system connect and communicate with each other via the lymphatic system, a network of vessels that is very similar to the circulatory system. The cells of the immune system and the materials that they produce (antibodies, for example) circulate through the lymphatic system so that they can be deployed to those areas of the body that are most in need.

The immune system is programmed so that it recognizes *self* (the cat's own body) and *nonself* (bacteria, viruses, parasites, and so on). Occasionally, the immune system goes awry and directs itself against the body's own components, resulting in *immune-mediated* disorders. The cat is susceptible to a number of these disorders, such as pemphigus, lupus, and immune-mediated hemolytic anemia. Some viruses, such as the feline immunodeficiency virus (FIV), attack the immune system itself, leaving the cat susceptible to other infectious diseases. Cancer of the immune system can also develop in the form of a solid tumor (for example, as lymphoma of the lymph nodes) or as a circulating leukemia of the white blood cells.

Tendons are strong bands of connective tissue that attach the skeletal muscles to the bones. When a muscle contracts, it pulls on the tendons, which pull on the bones and result in movement. *Ligaments* are strong pieces of connective tissue that connect bones to other bones. Tendon and ligament injuries are not as common in cats as in dogs, but they do occur.

Cardiovascular System and Respiratory System

The cardiovascular system of the cat is similar to our own. A heart, consisting of four chambers—the left atrium, left ventricle, right atrium, and right ventricle—pumps the blood through arteries that carry blood away from the heart, through smaller vessels and capillaries where oxygen is exchanged, and then through veins that return the blood back to the heart. The heart rate in the cat can vary, but is generally between 160 and 240 beats per minute—much faster than the human heart. Heart disease can occur in any age cat. Fortunately, unlike in humans, diseases of the blood vessels that supply the heart itself, such as atherosclerosis, are very rare in cats.

The heart and the respiratory system are intimately connected (hence the familiar term *cardiopulmonary*, which refers to both the heart and the lungs). The heart pumps blood to every inch of the body. The lungs make sure that blood is properly oxygenated and remove carbon dioxide at the same time.

The respiratory system of the cat consists of the nasal cavity and mouth, the pharynx (back of the throat) and larynx (voice box or "Adam's apple"), the trachea, bronchi and lungs, the diaphragm, and the muscles of the chest. Cats, like humans, have two lungs. The lungs are divided into smaller sections, called lobes. Within the lobes, the large air passages (bronchi) divide into smaller branches called bronchioles. These split into progressively smaller tubes, in much the same way that a tree divides into smaller and smaller branches. At the end of the smallest bronchioles are the alveoli. It is here that gas exchange occurs; carbon dioxide is removed and oxygen is delivered. The respiratory system, working together with the tongue and mucous membranes of the mouth, serves another important function: heat regulation. This is important, because cats have a poorly developed mechanism for sweating.

The cat's upper respiratory system begins at the nostrils. Occupying the space from the nostrils to the back of the throat is the nasal passage. The nasal passage is divided into the right and left side by the septum, which runs down the middle and is composed partly of bone and partly of cartilage. The nose and mouth are responsible for taking air into the body. Fine hairs that line the nasal cavity and mucus produced by the cells in the nasal cavity help to filter debris from the air before it enters the body. The nasal cavity also warms and moistens the air. At the back of the nasal cavity is the olfactory region; as air passes over this region, the sense of smell is activated. Further along, beyond the end of the nasal cavity is the pharynx (the throat). The lower part of the pharynx that is part of the oral cavity is the oropharynx. The upper part of the pharynx that is part of the respiratory system is called the nasopharynx.

The nasopharynx connects the back of the nasal cavity to the larynx (voice box or "Adam's apple"). The larynx is composed of muscle and cartilage. The cartilages at the front of the larynx act as a valve or doorway to the trachea (windpipe), closing and covering it during swallowing so that food does not enter the trachea. When open, it allows air to pass from the nose to the trachea. The larynx also contains the vocal folds, which are necessary for vocalization, such as meowing or growling. Cats use their voices to communicate and have a vocabulary of several types of meows, such as the *demand* meow ("feed me," "I want to go outside"), the *pleading* meow, the *hunting* meow, the *trilling* meow that mother cats use with their kittens, and *caterwauling*—an aggressive call between two males.

▲ Cats are carnivores, so they need very little fiber in their diet.

Digestive System

Although we don't usually think of it this way, the gastrointestinal (GI) tract is basically a long hollow tube lined by different types of cells. Within the walls of this tube are a variety of glands, muscles, and nerves. These structures, as well as the diameter and shape of the tube, vary depending on which region of the GI tract one is observing. The gastrointestinal system is responsible for digesting food and absorbing nutrients. It is also responsible for collecting waste material and expelling it from the body.

The GI tract starts at the mouth, where food is taken in. As food is swallowed, it passes through the pharynx and enters the esophagus, which is located in the cat's neck and chest. The esophagus contains muscles that rhythmically propel food down its length toward the stomach. Food then enters the stomach. The stomach contains glands that produce enzymes and acids that help digest the food. The

▲The kittens in a single litter can have different fathers.

walls of the stomach also contain muscles that mix and grind the food. From here, the partly digested food moves into the longest part of the tube, the small intestine. It is in the small intestine that most of the absorption of nutrients occurs.

The first part of the small intestine is called the *duodenum*. Digestive enzymes from the pancreas and gall bladder enter the small intestine through ducts that lead into the duodenum. The next section of the small intestine is the *jejunum*. In this portion, food continues to be digested and nutrients are absorbed. The short, final section of the small intestine is the *ileum*. From here, digested food moves into the large intestine.

The large intestine participates in the last phase of digestion, absorbing water and electrolytes from the food. It also forms and stores feces, and it produces enzymes that further help break down difficult to digest material. The large intestine is composed of the *cecum, colon,* and *rectum*. The cecum is a small pouch located at the junction between the ileum and the large intestine. The colon consists of three sections. The first portion is the ascending colon. Beyond that is the transverse colon. The last portion is the descending colon. The descending colon leads into the rectum, which receives undigested food and expels it through the anus.

Urinary System

The feline urinary system consists of two kidneys, two ureters, the bladder, and the urethra. These organs work together to eliminate waste materials from the body. The urinary system also regulates the amount of water and the levels of electrolytes in the body. The kidneys filter toxins from the bloodstream. Urine that is produced in the kidneys flows through the ureters, which connect the kidney to the bladder. The bladder stores the urine until it is eliminated through the urethra, the tube that connects the bladder to the exterior, during urination. Typically, feline urine is yellow and clear and has a mild smell. It may be cloudy or bloody, however, if a urinary tract infection is present. Urine from tomcats (unneutered males) has a particularly strong odor.

Reproductive System

The major parts of the male reproductive system are the testes, the scrotum, and the penis. The testes are located in the scrotum. The testes (also called testicles) produce sperm. Sperm production is influenced by testosterone, a hormone produced by the testicles. Testosterone also influences some male behaviors, such as territorial aggression. Normally, there are two testes present, which an examiner should be able to feel in the scrotum of a kitten by six weeks of age. However, sometimes neither testicle, or only one testicle, can be seen or felt in the scrotum. This condition is called *cryptorchidism* (crypt = hidden; orchid = testicle). If neither testicle is present, it is called bilateral cryptorchidism. This is very rare. More common is unilateral cryptorchidism, when only one testicle is present. When removing the testes during neutering, it is imperative that the veterinarian locate and remove the retained testicle(s) or else the cat will develop (or continue to exhibit) behaviors such as mounting and/or spraying. The urine will also continue to retain its characteristic pungent tomcat odor. Retained testicles also have an increased probability of becoming cancerous.

Rough little spines called papillae protrude from the penis's surface in intact male cats. These rough projections are responsible for stimulating the female cat to ovulate during mating. Neutering the cat causes the spines to disappear.

The major organs of the female reproductive tract are the ovaries, the fallopian tubes, the uterus, the vagina, and the mammary glands. The mammary glands run in two rows along the outside of the abdomen, from the groin to the chest. Cats typically have four or five pairs of mammary glands, which store and secrete milk. The ovaries, fallopian tubes, and uterus are located inside the abdomen. The right and left ovaries are situated just behind the kidneys. Ovaries produce eggs, as well as important hormones (estrogen and progesterone). The ovaries are connected to the uterus by small ducts called fallopian tubes (also called oviducts). The uterus is shaped like the letter Y, with the arms of the Y representing each uterine horn. The uterine horns extend from each ovary. The uterus is the site where fertilized eggs develop into fetuses. The uterus houses the fetuses until they are ready to be delivered. The base or stem of the Y represents the body of the uterus.

The very tip at the base of the Y is the cervix. The cervix is a muscular tube that remains closed during pregnancy to prevent infection occurring in the uterus. During fertilization and birth, the cervix is relaxes and opens. The cervix separates the uterus from the vagina. The vagina provides a passage way from the outside of the body to the uterus. It also provides a protected passageway for the fetuses as they travel from the uterus to the outside during birth.

Chapter 13

External Conditions, Diseases, and Disorders

By Arnold Plotnick, DVM

T he previous chapter gave you an idea how the body of the domestic cat is put together, the external parts as well as the complex internal systems and how they function. In the remaining chapters of this section, we take a look at some of most common and most serious conditions, diseases, and disorders affecting the different parts and systems of the cat. In this chapter, we discuss external conditions, injuries, diseases, and disorders of the skin and coat, ears and eyes, teeth, and paws and nails.

Skin and Coat Injuries and Diseases

The skin of cats is thinner than that of dogs and thus more prone to injury. Careless or rough handling, such as using improper grooming equipment or cat fights, can easily damage the skin, resulting in lacerations and punctures, which in turn can lead to infections and abscesses. Parasites, bacteria, and allergies can also lead to skins diseases as well as hair loss.

Abscesses

Cat fights and their resultant injuries are a common reason for veterinary visits. Although cats living together indoors occasionally fight over territory or for owner attention, such scraps rarely lead to serious injury. Cats who encounter other cats outdoors, however, are more likely to fight, to fight more often, and to fight more seriously, usually over territory.

▶ Fights and overenthusiastic playing between cats are among the most common causes of injury to pet felines.

Causes and symptoms: Cats' teeth are sharp, and when they bite, they inflict puncture wounds. Cats have a tremendous amount of bacteria in their mouths, which are injected into the skin with a bite. Because puncture wounds in cats seal over quickly, this bacteria becomes trapped. The bone marrow sends out many white blood cells to help fight this infection. The white blood cells and bacteria accumulate to form a painful pocket of pus just beneath the skin. This collection of pus is an abscess. Abscesses are common in cats, owing to the tough, elastic nature of feline skin that so readily seals over contaminated puncture wounds and allows for pus to accumulate beneath it.

▲ Abscesses require veterinary care. This cat is having the abscess in her tail flushed and drained.

Trauma and infection are not the only concern regarding cat bite injuries. Cat bites have the potential to transmit several life-threatening infectious diseases to other cats, such as the feline leukemia virus (FeLV), the feline immunodeficiency virus (FIV), and rabies.

The majority of abscesses are seen in cats who go outdoors. Intact males are at higher risk than neutered males or females because they're more likely to roam and fight over territory. Typically, a cat who has been bitten appears fine after the encounter. Over the next two to four days, bacteria deposited in the wound begin to multiply, and as they do, the cat develops a fever, becomes lethargic, and often stops eating.

Diagnosis and treatment: Many cats are taken to the veterinarian at this stage, when the abscess appears as either a firm or soft painful swelling. In most cases, puncture wounds or small lacerations are present, and the area may feel warm. If not discovered in this early stage, the abscess will continue to swell, burrowing through tissues and accumulating more pus. The abscess may then burst through the overlying skin, releasing creamy yellow or brownish, foul-smelling pus. Overlying hair may become matted with dried discharge. Common locations for abscesses are the face and neck, tail, back, and legs, although any part of the body can

be bitten during a fight. If a bite wound occurs in a location that does not have much loose overlying skin (a leg, for example), the infection can dissect its way through the tissues, causing a diffuse swelling instead of a discrete collection of pus. This diffuse swelling is called *cellulitis*.

The earlier that treatment is instituted, the better the chances of the wound healing without complications. In most cases, the cat is anesthetized so that an incision can be made into the abscess. The wound is then flushed with an antibacterial solution to further remove pus and other debris. If the abscess is detected and addressed at an early stage, lancing and flushing (plus antibiotics) may be all that is required. If it's discovered at a later stage, when significant tissue damage has occurred beneath the skin, the veterinarian may need to debride the wound (that is, remove dead or compromised tissue). In some cases, the veterinarian may find it necessary to insert a drain (a piece of soft rubber tubing that exits the skin at the lowest point of the wound) to allow any future accumulation of fluid or pus to escape. After debriding, if the wound is large, sutures may be required to partially close it. Most wounds, however, are left open to drain and heal on their own. Very large skin defects may require some type of reconstructive skin surgery after the infection has resolved.

The prognosis for a properly treated abscess is excellent. However, cats who engage in frequent fights are at high risk for contracting serious illnesses such as FeLV and FIV. Cats who contract these viruses may then spread them to other cats in future encounters. Cats with FeLV or FIV also have weakened defenses against infection and may have difficulty defeating an infection if bitten by other cats. Outdoor cats should be regularly tested for these viruses. Cats who go outdoors should also be current on their vaccinations, especially rabies and FeLV, and perhaps FIV. The best prevention is to keep all cats indoors and prevent them from roaming and fighting. (See chapter 16, pages 360, for more information on FeLV and FIV.)

Cysts

A cyst is a hollow sac containing fluid or solid material. In cats, cysts appear as small bumps within the skin. They often feel like peas or marbles.

Causes and symptoms: One of the most common types of cyst that develop in cats is the *sebaceous cyst*, sometimes called an *epidermal inclusion cyst* or an *epidermoid cyst*. These cysts contain material secreted by the sebaceous glands. Sebaceous glands are located next to the hair follicles; they secrete sebum, an oily substance that protects and lubricates the skin. If a hair follicle becomes obstructed (blocked), sebum can accumulate abnormally and form a cyst.

Diagnosis and treatment: A diagnosis can be made by a technique called *fine-needle aspiration*. In this technique, the cyst is pierced with a needle, and the cyst material is aspirated into the hub of the needle and dispersed onto a microscope slide. Evaluation of the cystic material usually leads to proper diagnosis. In some instances, a skin biopsy may be necessary for definitive diagnosis. Sebaceous cysts are not painful (unless they become infected, which is uncommon) and are of no consequence. Treatment is rarely necessary. Other types of cysts that can be present in the skin include follicular cysts, dermoid cysts, and apocrine cysts.

The vast majority of cysts are benign and have no clinical significance. Occasionally, however, a cyst may grow to a size large enough to bother the cat. In these cases, the cyst should be removed. Likewise, if the cyst material is infected, the material may need to be drained or the cyst may need to be surgically removed. Cats who cannot undergo surgery (due to ill health or financial concerns) can have the cyst drained rather than removed. Be aware, however, that although draining will reduce the size of the cyst, doing so is a temporary measure because the cyst will refill with material over time.

Most cysts are discovered by the cat owner while petting the cat; sometimes the veterinarian finds them during a physical examination. If the veterinarian is unsure whether the skin lesion is a cyst, removal and biopsy may be recommended to make sure that it is not something dangerous, like cancer. If you find any kind of lump or bump on your cat, always bring it to the attention of your veterinarian.

Allergic Dermatitis

Skin allergies are a common finding in cats. When an allergic cat encounters an offending allergen, the immune system responds by sending inflammatory cells into the skin in an attempt to fend off the allergen. These inflammatory cells release substances that can cause the skin to become red, inflamed, and itchy. The most common types of allergic dermatitis in cats are food allergy, flea allergy, and atopy (allergy to inhaled substances). Clinical signs for each of these diseases often overlap, making diagnosis challenging.

Food Allergy

Allergy to food is a significant cause of itching and scratching in cats. Males and females are equally affected, and there is no particular age preference, although the majority of cats are young to middle-aged (two to six years old). A sudden change in diet is not necessary for food allergy to develop, and, in fact, most cases of food allergy develop after a cat has been fed the same food for a long time.

Causes and symptoms: The most common offending substance in the food tends to be a protein source such as beef, lamb, or seafood.

However, allergies can also develop to corn, soy, dairy components, and gluten. Food allergy can affect the gastrointestinal tract, causing vomiting and/or diarrhea, or it can affect the skin. In some cases, both systems are affected. When the skin is affected, the primary sign tends to be itching, which causes excessive licking, biting, scratching, and chewing at the skin. Hair loss is common because an itchy cat will pull out her hair. Ear infections are occasionally seen. Cats with food allergy also tend to show itching around the head and face. Itching tends to be year-round, not seasonal.

Diagnosis and treatment: Diagnosis of food allergy is made by conducting a food trial. This consists of feeding a food that contains a protein and carbohydrate source that the cat has never encountered before. Prescription pet food manufacturers offer diets that are designed for food-allergic cats, such as venison and green pea or duck and green pea. When undergoing a food trial, the cat can consume absolutely no other food items except the prescription diet and water or the results

will be inconclusive. The diet should be fed for at least twelve weeks before making a final assessment of the response. Once the signs resolve, feeding the cat her original diet and seeing the clinical signs return will be definitive proof of food allergy.

Your veterinarian may want to do some diagnostic tests to rule out other disorders that have similar clinical signs. These tests may include blood work, skin scrapings, fungal cultures, and a skin biopsy. Some veterinary laboratories offer a blood test for diagnosis of food allergy; most veterinary dermatologists, however, do not believe that these tests are accurate. Skin testing, which is accurate for diagnosing inhalant allergies in cats, is also ineffective for diagnosing food allergy. Conducting a hypoallergenic food trial is the only effective means of diagnosis. Once the diagnosis is made, treatment consists of avoiding the offending allergen and feeding only a hypoallergenic diet.

Occasionally, a cat will develop an allergy to the new food. In these cases, switching to a diet with a novel protein and carbohydrate source may

▼ Food allergies can be tricky to diagnose. Doing so involves feeding the cat proteins and carbohydrates she has never eaten before and checking her reaction.

▲ Most cases of food allergy develop after a cat has been fed the same food for a long time, not when the diet is changed.

again be necessary. Some prescription pet food manufacturers offer a "limited antigen" diet, which is a diet in which the protein has been hydrolyzed (broken down and digested) into fragments that are small enough to escape detection by the immune system, thus preventing them from triggering an allergic response. These hydrolyzed diets may be necessary in cases of recurrent food allergy.

Flea Allergy

Flea allergy dermatitis (FAD) is a very common skin disorder in cats.

Causes and symptoms: When fleas bite a cat, they inject saliva into the skin. Cats who are allergic to the flea saliva will become very itchy after being bitten and will scratch themselves repeatedly, damaging the skin and increasing the risk of acquiring a skin infection. Any area of the body can be affected, although the lower back and base of the tail are the most common spots. Cats with flea allergy may show *miliary dermatitis*—tiny little scabs throughout the hair coat. Hair

loss is common, resulting from excessive licking or pulling of the fur. As few as one or two flea bites can trigger the reaction. Unlike food allergy, FAD tends to be seasonal, being worse during the summer and early fall.

Diagnosis and treatment: FAD is diagnosed based on the clinical signs in conjunction with the discovery of fleas or flea dirt on the cat, and the ruling out of other skin disorders. This may require various tests, including blood work, skin scrapings, fungal cultures, and skin biopsy. Intradermal skin testing, in which a small amount of flea antigen is injected into the skin, is a more objective measure of the presence of FAD, but this test is rarely necessary. Treatment includes strict flea control using topical once-a-month flea control products that kill fleas before they bite. All cats in the household should be treated. Frequent vacuuming of carpets and upholstery is beneficial in removing flea eggs and larvae from the environment. In cases of severe infestation, treatment of the premises with flea sprays or bombs may be warranted. Antibiotics may be necessary if a secondary bacterial skin infection is present. Corticosteroids, antihistamines, and omega-3 fatty acids may be beneficial for controlling itchiness and inflammation.

Allergic Inhalant Dermatitis

Allergic inhalant dermatitis (atopy) is an allergy to airborne substances such as pollens or dust. It is a common cause of itching in cats. In most cases, the itching is seasonal; however, many cats with atopy can be itchy all year round if the allergen persists in the environment.

Causes and symptoms: Atopy is an inherited disease, passed on to the cat by one or both parents. Although it can strike cats at any age, most cats begin showing signs of atopy when young, usually by one year of age. Cats with atopy are itchy and may show red, inflamed skin due to constant scratching, particularly around the face, feet, and ears.

Diagnosis and treatment: Diagnosing atopy can be challenging. Clinical signs that are seasonal are suggestive of atopy. Intradermal skin testing, in which tiny amounts of allergenic substances are injected into the skin and the reaction recorded, is the chief way in which atopy is diagnosed. Blood tests designed to test whether a cat is allergic to plants native to a particular geographic region, as well as to common household dust and mites, are thought to be inaccurate and unreliable. Intradermal skin tests should be performed by an experienced veterinary dermatologist because the skin response to the injections can be subtle and more difficult to interpret in cats than in dogs.

To rule out other common causes of itching and hair loss in cats, your veterinarian may need to perform some tests, such as blood work, skin scrapings, fungal cultures, and skin biopsy. The ideal treatment for atopy is avoidance of the offending allergen, although this is rarely possible. Treatment may include antibiotics to treat secondary bacterial skin infection if present; corticosteroids, antihistamines, and omega-3 fatty acids to control

▲ Flea allergy dermatitis is very common in cats. The best way to prevent it is to keep your cat indoors and practice strict flea control.

itching; and soothing shampoos. Immunotherapy, in which the cat is given a series of allergy shots to modify the immune response to the offending allergens, is another possible therapy. The allergy shots are prepared by a veterinary dermatologist based on the results of the cat's individual intradermal skin test results.

Bacterial Skin Infection

The term *pyoderma* means bacterial infection of the skin. Bacterial infections of the skin are uncommon in cats.

Causes and symptoms: Signs of bacterial skin infection may include red, itchy skin, miliary dermatitis (tiny little scabs throughout the skin), small pimples, and oozing or draining sores. Skin-fold pyoderma occurs in folds of skin that are difficult for the cat to keep clean. Persian cats are especially prone to develop skin-fold pyoderma within the facial skin folds. This "dirty-face syndrome" commonly seen in young Persian and Himalayan cats is thought to be an inherited disorder and is usually accompanied by waxy ear infections.

Most cases of pyoderma in cats occur secondary to some other itchy skin problem. Flea allergy, for example, can cause itching, and the self-trauma that the cat causes when scratching can damage the skin, compromising the protective barrier function of the skin and allowing bacteria to colonize it. Cats who are immunosuppressed, such as those infected with FIV, are at increased risk for infections, including bacterial skin infections. The most common skin infections in cats are caused bacteria of the genus *Staphylococcus*.

Diagnosis and treatment: Diagnosis is usually made by visual inspection of the skin; however, culturing the skin, microscopic examination of the contents of a pustule, and skin biopsy are occasionally required to make a definitive diagnosis, especially if the infection recurs after treatment. Antibiotic therapy is the appropriate treatment for bacterial skin infections. Antibacterial shampoos may be beneficial in stubborn cases. Cats with red, inflamed skin lesions may require clipping of the hair around the affected area and cleaning with an antiseptic solution. The development, several years ago, of a long-lasting injectable antibiotic for the treatment of skin infections in dogs and cats has been a significant advance in pyoderma therapy. One injection lasts for fourteen days, alleviating the need to administer oral liquid or tablet antibiotics. This is a very welcome development for cat owners because cats can be challenging to medicate orally.

Ringworm

Ringworm is the most common infectious skin disease in cats. Despite the name, ringworm is not a worm; it is a skin fungus. *Microsporum canis* is the species of ringworm that most commonly affects cats. Ringworm is a zoonotic disease—meaning it can be transmitted to people.

Causes and symptoms: Cats become infected with ringworm when they're exposed to infective spores through contact with an infected animal, a contaminated object, or a contaminated environment. Spores are small and may also be carried on air currents and on dust particles. Once the spores reach the coat, if they survive the cat's natural defense mechanisms (for example, grooming and sunbathing), they adhere to and invade cells called *keratinocytes* on the hair shaft and skin (and occasionally, the nails) and they germinate, initiating the infection. Hair shafts become weak, brittle, and easily broken. Hair fragments and skin scales are shed into the environment, along with thousands of spores. Spores can remain in the environment for months or years, serving as a reservoir of infectious material for humans and other cats brought into the environment.

Many factors, including young age, concurrent disease, drugs that suppress the immune system, compromised immune status, poor nutrition, stress, and overcrowding will predispose cats to acquiring ringworm. Cats in animal shelters and catteries are much more likely to harbor ringworm than pet cats, and isolation of this fungus from even one cat or kitten in a cattery warrants treatment of the entire cattery.

▶ Feral kittens commonly have ringworm, something that anyone who works in shelters or does cat rescue should be aware of.

Cats of any age, sex, or breed are susceptible to infection. Kittens and geriatric cats, however, are more frequently affected, as are longhaired cats. Longhaired cats are believed to be more susceptible because the long hairs protect the spores from being removed by grooming. Long hair can get matted, and matted hairs are also more susceptible to ringworm infection. When cats groom themselves, they're engaging in an important activity that helps limit ringworm infection.

Kittens in general are the most susceptible population, with the head, face, ears, and forelimbs primarily involved. It is speculated that the face and ears are commonly affected spots in kittens because these areas, although groomed well by the mother, tend to be not very well groomed by kittens. Interestingly, lesions often appear in kittens at or around the time of weaning, which supports this hypothesis.

Concurrent disease can have an effect on the susceptibility to infection. For example, cats infected with FIV are three times more likely to acquire ringworm than are uninfected cats. Genetics may also play a role in a cat's susceptibility to ringworm. Studies have shown that chronic ringworm problems are most common in catteries in which members were genetically related, and breeders may be unintentionally selecting for susceptible cats when they breed for certain coat characteristics.

Grooming is one way that cats help to remove ringworm spores from their coat. Persians, Himalayans, and other longhaired cats tend to be less efficient groomers, making them more inclined to acquiring ringworm infection. Genetic influences, however, may play a role in these breeds as well.

The classic clinical appearance of ringworm includes one or more areas of patchy hair loss with mild or moderate crusting, but ringworm in cats can have a wide variety of presentations. Infected cats can present with any combination of the following:

- blackheads—ringworm infection occasionally causes blackheads on the chin in young cats
- crusting and scaling—ringworm lesions tend to be exfoliative. Usually, the scaling is mild, but in some cats it's quite severe.
- hair loss—ringworm causes hair loss; this may be subtle or dramatic, and may show a symmetrical pattern or be totally asymmetrical
- hyperpigmentation—ringworm infection can cause a darkening of the skin in some cats
- nail infection only—a few cats with ringworm develop crusty or greasy nail infections as their only clinical sign of ringworm.
- overgrooming—cats with hair loss from apparent overgrooming will sometimes be found to have ringworm infection.
- pruritus (itchiness)—in general, ringworm is not an especially itchy disease, although some cats have mild itchiness, while others are

▼ Himalayans and other longhaired cats tend to be less efficient groomers, making them more inclined to acquire ringworm infection.

▲ Shampoos containing a combination of miconazole and chlorhexidine are very effective against ringworm.

severely itchy and will scratch to the point of self-mutilation.

- redness—areas of hair loss are often reddened when they first develop.

Diagnosis and treatment: Diagnosis is made through fungal culture. Hairs from affected areas are plucked with a sterile hemostat and placed on a special fungal culture medium. If the ringworm fungus starts to grow on the culture medium in a few days, the diagnosis is confirmed. Shining a fluorescent light, called a Wood's lamp (named for its inventor, physician Robert W. Wood), on the hair coat may help better identify infected hairs, for better sampling for the fungal culture. Half of the strains of *Microsporum canis* will glow apple-green under the lamp.

Cats who test positive for ringworm need some kind of treatment. Treatment plans may vary somewhat for each cat, but all plans involve some combination of clipping the hair coat, topical therapy, systemic (oral) antifungal medication, and environmental decontamination. Environmental decontamination suggestions when treating ringworm include:

- Discard all blankets, brushes, cat rugs, collars, and fabric toys.
- Discard any cat objects that cannot be easily disinfected, repeatedly scrubbed, and/or frequently vacuumed.
- Purchase a new, inexpensive vacuum cleaner with hose attachments that can be thoroughly cleaned.
- Remove and clean all drapes and decorations. In multicat households, remove and clean all heating duct and vent plates, and install disposable house dust filters behind the duct plates before replacing them. This will keep spores out of the heating ducts.
- Put a fan in the window, if possible, so that it draws air out of the room to the outside.
- Vacuum all surfaces of the room.
- Dust all surfaces and ledges with a disposable electrostatic cloth (such as a Swiffer).
- Scrub all surfaces with a detergent that is safe to use around cats. Rinse all surfaces well. Apply a 1:10 dilution of bleach to all nonporous surfaces. Leaving the bleach solution on the surface for fifteen minutes is ideal.

- Using a portable dehumidifier is beneficial because humid environments allow spores to remain viable.

Step 1 of therapy involves clipping the hair coat. Clipping the coat removes infected hairs and minimizes continued shedding of hair fragments and spores. It also allows for more thorough penetration of topical antifungal shampoos. As a general rule, if a shorthaired cat has five or more discreet spots of ringworm, the entire coat should be clipped. If a shorthaired cat has fewer than five discreet spots, the hair around the individual spots can be clipped. If the cat is longhaired, the entire coat should be clipped regardless of how many discreet ringworm spots are visible on the coat. Once the coat is clipped, cats are ready to undergo topical therapy with a medicated shampoo. Topical therapy minimizes the spread of infective spores into the environment and helps remove infective crusts, scales, and spores from the coat. Without topical therapy, treatment will take longer and will be more costly.

There are many effective topical products. Shampoos containing a combination of miconazole and chlorhexidine are very effective against ringworm. Cats should be bathed twice weekly. For the shampoo to be effective, it is important that there be a contact time of ten minutes with the cat's fur.

The cornerstone of treatment for ringworm is systemic therapy with an oral medication. Drugs that have been shown to be effective include griseofulvin, itraconazole, ketoconazole, and terbinafine. Cats receiving treatment for ringworm usually show marked improvement in clinical signs within two to four weeks of therapy. Four weeks after beginning treatment, cats should be reexamined. A fungal culture should be performed at every recheck. Once a negative culture is obtained, weekly fungal cultures should be performed. Two consecutive negative fungal cultures indicate successful treatment.

Ringworm spores can persist in the environment for a long time, perhaps eighteen to twenty-four months. The spores are microscopic and can be spread easily by air currents and contaminated dust, and through heating ducts and vents. To minimize environmental contamination in households where only one single pet cat is infected, the cat or kitten should be kept in a small, easily cleaned room (such as a bathroom) that does not have carpeting. The cat should be quarantined in this room until it has received oral antifungal medication for two weeks, and a minimum of four medicated baths. At this point, the cat can be given greater access in the home, ideally in uncarpeted and easily cleaned rooms. Thorough and repeated vacuuming and wiping of surfaces on a daily basis should prevent the home from becoming contaminated. Cat beds and blankets should be washed daily in hot water and bleach. Bathrooms and smooth surfaces can be disinfected

◀ EGC can be triggered by an allergic response to mosquito bites, but most of the time, the underlying cause is never discovered.

with a bleach solution (1 part bleach, 9 parts water). Routine cleaning and disinfecting should continue until the cat is considered cured of ringworm. Indoor cats are unlikely to become reinfected once the ringworm is treated successfully.

Eosinophilic Granuloma Complex

The eosinophilic granuloma complex (EGC) is a collection of skin disorders that are often grouped together because they have the same basic underlying characteristic—infiltration of the skin by eosinophils. An eosinophil is a type of inflammatory blood cell that is commonly associated with allergic or parasitic diseases. There are three manifestations of the feline EGC: the indolent ulcer, the eosinophilic plaque, and the eosinophilic granuloma.

Causes and symptoms: The cause of EGC is not known; however, an underlying allergy such as flea allergy, atopy (allergy to inhaled environmental allergens), or food allergy has long been suspected. A genetic predisposition to EGC has also been postulated. In some cases, EGC are triggered by an allergic response to mosquito bites. Most of the time, the underlying allergen is never discovered. Any age cat may be affected, but EGC is most common in young to middle-aged cats. In some cats, more than one type of eosinophilic skin disease can occur at the same time.

The *indolent ulcer* (sometimes referred to as *rodent ulcer*) commonly appears as an eroded spot on the margin of an upper lip. Both lips can be affected, but in most cases, it is unilateral. The ulcers appear reddish brown and are well-demarcated and hairless. Sometimes they are painful and affect a cat's willingness to eat.

Eosinophilic plaques can appear anywhere on the skin, but they are most commonly found on the abdomen and the inside thighs. They may be singular, or there may be multiple lesions. They appear raised, red, moist, and well circumscribed.

▲ Keeping your cat indoors will reduce the chance she will ever become infested with lice or mites.

They are very itchy, and cats lick them constantly. Analysis of the blood often reveals an increased number of eosinophils in the bloodstream as well.

Eosinophilic granulomas (also called *linear granuloma* or *collagenolytic granuloma*) often occur down the back of the thigh, on the face, and in the mouth, especially on the tongue or the roof of the mouth. When they occur on the skin, they tend to be yellow or pinkish in color, raised, hairless, with a characteristic linear configuration. When they occur on the face or in the mouth, they tend to appear more nodular. One manifestation is to cause the lower lip to swell, giving the appearance of a "fat lip."

Diagnosis and treatment: Diagnosis of eosinophilic skin disorders is usually made based on their visual appearance. However, a biopsy is sometimes necessary to rule out disorders with similar appearances. The optimal treatment is avoidance of the offending allergen. Strict flea control is essential because flea allergy may be a potential trigger for EGC. A feeding trial with a hypoallergenic diet may be needed to identify

Tearing Their Fur Out

"I've been tearing my hair out over this!" Sound familiar? If you haven't said it yourself, you've certainly heard other people use the phrase when they are frustrated or anxious over a situation. Fortunately (in most cases anyway), they're not speaking literally, and no bald patches appear on their heads.

This is not the case with cats, however. Stressed or anxious cats often pull, chew, or excessively groom their fur. In fact, psychological disturbances are a very common cause of self-inflicted hair loss in cats. In many instances, the cause of a cat's stress is obvious: a move to a new apartment, a short stay at a boarding facility, a new pet or baby in the household, territorial competition in a multiple-cat household, to name a few examples. In some cases, the cause of the stress is not so obvious to us.

Grooming is a comfort behavior, often used by cats to relax themselves. Think about the last time your cat did something foolish or klutzy, like misjudge a leap or accidentally tumble off the sofa. We might chuckle, but the cat immediately grooms. Whether they feel embarrassment is debatable, but cat lovers recognize this reflexive grooming behavior in their cats whenever uncertainty arises. It shouldn't be surprising that, in the face of stress, they may turn to excessive grooming to dispel their anxiety.

Once parasites, allergies, and other medical problems have been ruled out, *psychogenic alopecia*—hair chewing and overgrooming due to psychological factors such as stress, fear, anxiety, or nervousness— must be considered. Psychogenic alopecia is a diagnosis of exclusion. Cats of Asian lineage (Siamese, Abyssinians, Burmese. and Himalayans) are apparently more susceptible to psychogenic alopecia, presumably because of their high-strung, nervous temperaments.

Ideally, the treatment of psychogenic alopecia would involve the elimination of the potential stressors in the cat's environment. Unfortunately, this is often impossible or impractical, and antianxiety or antidepressant medications are often warranted to control the problem.

---

an underlying food allergy. In most cases, the allergen cannot be identified, and administration of immunosuppressive drugs is necessary to control the clinical signs. These drugs can be given in pill form or as a long-acting injection. The prognosis varies, with young cats often having a better prognosis.

Hair Loss

The medical term for hair loss is *alopecia*. There are many possible reasons for hair loss in cats. Spontaneous hair loss (that is, the hair is falling out) can be the result of systemic diseases, especially glandular disorders. This is common in dogs, but uncommon in cats. Self-inflicted hair loss is the more common scenario in cats. Cats will lick, bite, or pull their hair out because the skin feels itchy or for a variety of psychological reasons. There are numerous causes for itchy skin, with parasitic infestations, fungal infections, and hypersensitivities/allergies being some of the more common reasons.

Parasitic Infestations

External parasites such as lice, mites, and fleas will always be a problem for companion animals. Few creatures living on earth today have had as much impact on world history as the common flea. From the black plague during the fourteenth century to the present day, fleas have been the cause of much grief. They make your cat itch, especially if she is allergic to flea bites, which is quite common. External parasites are a well-known cause of hair loss in cats.

Causes and symptoms: Pediculosis (lice infestation) has been reported to cause itching and hair loss in cats, although the condition is quite uncommon. Infestation with scabies mites is uncommon in cats, although it has been reported in cats with potentially immunosuppressive disorders, particularly FIV infection. Signs of scabies infestation varies widely, with some cats barely showing any itchiness and others showing intense skin discomfort and subsequent hair loss from overzealous grooming. Demodicosis (infestation with mites of the genus *Demodex*) can cause itching and hair loss, although it, too, is relatively uncommon in cats.

Flea infestation and flea allergy, however, are very common causes of hair loss in cats. Fleas deposit their saliva into a cat's skin before they draw their blood meal, and flea-allergic cats may show a severe reaction to the saliva, even from one flea bite. The itching can be intense, and cats may lick and chew excessively at their skin, especially around the base of their tail.

Diagnosis and treatment: Parasitic infestations are diagnosed by carefully inspecting the skin for parasites (such as fleas), as well as by performing skin scrapings and microscopic examination to look for mites. Flea problems should be suspected if fleas or flea dirt is noted during the exam. Even if fleas are absent, flea allergy can be issue. For cats who are allergic to flea bites, it only takes a single bite to produce an intense and sometimes prolonged reaction.

Flea infestation is easily remedied with once-a-month topical flea control products. These products can be obtained only through your veterinarian. (Do not purchase over-the-counter monthly flea control products from drug stores or pet stores. These often mimic the veterinary products in appearance, but

may contain insecticides that can cause serious harm to your cat.) Cats with severe inflammation and itching may experience some relief with a short course of oral corticosteroids and/or antihistamines.

Hypersensitivities/Allergies

Allergies are a common reason why cats overgroom and pull out their fur. Flea allergy, food allergy, and atopy (allergy to airborne substances) are the three common causes of allergy in cats.

Causes and symptoms: Adverse reactions to food may manifest themselves via the skin. Severe generalized itching; tiny little scabs and crusts throughout the hair coat (called *miliary dermatitis*); itching around the head, neck, ears, and face; and self-inflicted hair loss due to overgrooming may be seen. Food allergy may show up first in the skin as small red spots. These can turn into scabby or crusty sores that become infected as the cat rubs or scratches them.

Allergies to airborne substances, such as pollens or dust, can lead to itching and subsequent excessive grooming and hair loss. Itching that is seasonal is suggestive of atopy, although many cats with atopy can be itchy all year-round as well.

Diagnosis and treatment: Itching around the head and face is a common sign of food allergy in cats; however, there are many cats whose only sign

▼ Cat showing evidence of self-inflicted hair loss or overgrooming. A variety of physical and psychological problems can cause this behavior.

of food allergy is self-induced hair loss. Dietary elimination trials, in which the cat is fed a diet containing a protein source she hasn't encountered before (such as duck, rabbit, or venison) are necessary to obtain a definitive diagnosis. These trials require patience on the part of the cat owner, as it may take anywhere from three to twelve weeks before improvement is noted.

Making a diagnosis of atopy can be challenging. Blood tests can be performed to see if the cat is allergic to plants that are native to a particular geographic region, as well as to common household dusts and mites, although many dermatologists feel the blood tests to be unreliable. Intradermal skin testing, in which tiny amounts of allergenic substances are injected into the skin and the skin reaction noted, is a more meaningful diagnostic test. Dust mites and molds are the most common airborne allergens, with some cats having concurrent reactions to seasonal pollens. Intradermal skin tests should be performed by an experienced veterinary dermatologist.

Cats who are diagnosed with food allergy should continue to be fed their hypoallergenic diet.

Specific treatment of an airborne allergy is possible if the allergen(s) can be identified and avoided or removed from the environment. Often, this is not practical, especially in patients allergic to airborne pollens. *Hyposensitization*—serial injections of progressively larger amounts of the offending allergen—is probably the most appropriate long-term control method for cats with a prolonged allergy season. Other therapies that can be considered are antihistamines, omega-3 fatty acids, and corticosteroids. Although steroids have the potential to have side effects, the doses necessary to control allergic dermatitis are unlikely to cause problems, especially in cats, because cats are more resistant to the undesirable side effects of steroids than are dogs.

Fungal Infection

The fungal infection best known to cause hair loss in cats is ringworm.

Causes and symptoms: Ringworm, as noted earlier, is the most common infectious skin disease in cats, and it may cause hair loss. Any age, sex, or breed of cat may be affected, although young cats, older cats, and longhaired cats are more frequently affected. Although ringworm, in general, is not thought of as an especially itchy condition, this is very variable. It can cause a lot of itching in some cats, so one has to consider ringworm in the list of itch-inducing skin disorders in cats. The itching may occasionally result in self-induced hair loss.

Diagnosis and treatment: Ringworm is a *zoonotic* disease—it can be transmitted to humans. If your cat has a circular crusty skin rash, and you have a similar rash, you can be almost certain that ringworm is the culprit. A definitive diagnosis is achieved through fungal culture.

▶ Ear infections are more common in dogs than in cats.

Ringworm treatment options vary, depending on the situation (an individual cat vs. cattery or multiple-cat household, longhaired cats vs. shorthaired cats), but may involve some combination of clipping the coat, topical therapy (usually shampooing), oral medication, and environmental decontamination. Treatment is often successful if clients are diligent about following the prescribed protocols.

Ears and Hearing Injuries and Disorders

Although ear infections are not as common in cats as they are in dogs, they do occur. If untreated, some can lead to compromised hearing and deformity.

Otitis Externa

Otitis externa refers to any inflammatory disease of the external ear canal, although the term is mostly used to describe an outer ear infection. Most ear infections are due to bacteria.

Causes and symptoms: Most cases of ear infection occur secondary to some other disease state or because of some predisposing factor. Foreign bodies (such as plant material, dirt, sand), parasites (such as ear mites), trauma (excessive scratching by the cat), food allergy, ear canal tumors, atopy or some other kind of general skin disease, and excessive moisture in the ear are examples of possible causes of ear infections in cats. Once the skin inside the ear is compromised, bacteria and yeast that normally live in the ear can overgrow, causing an infection. The inside of the ear can become red, and a foul-smelling discharge can develop. Cats will often shake their heads, scratch at their ears, and react in pain when their ears are touched or rubbed. Severe, untreated infections can result in stenosis (a narrowing or closing) of the ear canal.

Diagnosis and treatment: A diagnosis is usually made on physical examination. Your veterinarian will look into the ear with a device called an otoscope to identify ear mites, the degree of debris buildup, foreign bodies, tumors or polyps, and whether the eardrum is intact. In some cats, this might require sedation. Examination of exudate

(a mixture of fluid, cells, and debris) from the ear under the microscope provides immediate diagnostic information and helps determine the types of microorganisms and parasites that might be present within the canal. A culture of the exudate from the canal allows identification of any bacteria that might be causing infection. Yeasts do not usually grow on culture; yeast is best identified on microscopic examination of the exudate. If a tumor is visible in the ear canal, a biopsy may be necessary to identify the type of tumor.

Successful treatment requires correcting any underlying factors; accurately identifying specific bacteria, yeast, parasites, or foreign bodies in the ears; thoroughly cleaning all of the debris, exudate, and wax from the ears; and administering the proper medications at home. Antibiotics are indicated when a bacterial infection is present. Antibiotics are given topically (instilled into the ear). In some cases, oral antibiotics are given in addition to the topical ones. Topical antifungal medication is given when fungal (yeast) infections are present. Insecticides are given (either in the ear or on the skin) if ear mites are identified.

Otitis Media and Otitis Interna

Otitis media refers to infection of the middle ear; otitis interna refers to infections of the inner ear.

Causes and symptoms: Otitis media occurs, in most cases, when an external ear infection breaks through the eardrum and enters the middle ear. Other possible causes include polyps, tumors, and the spread of an upper respiratory infection from the throat, up the eustachian tube, and into the middle ear. Middle ear infections can extend into the inner ear, where the vestibular system resides, causing problems with balance and coordination.

Signs of otitis media include shaking of the head and pawing at the ear, similar to that seen with otitis externa. Running through the middle ear is the facial nerve; when it is affected by otitis media, paralysis of the lip on the infected side occurs and a decreased or absent blink reflex of the eye on the affected side may be seen. If the inner ear becomes involved, cats may develop a head tilt and an uncoordinated gait, in which they lean, stumble, or fall when they walk.

Diagnosis and treatment: Diagnosis is made mainly by clinical signs. Head shaking, a head tilt, circling, rolling, stumbling, leaning to one side, involuntary beating of the eyes from side to side (this is called *nystagmus*), or signs of facial nerve abnormalities strongly suggests otitis media and/or otitis interna. Other signs may include pain when the head is touched or when the mouth is opened. Examination of the ear canal with an otoscope may reveal a ruptured or bulging eardrum. If the eardrum is bulging, a procedure called *myringotomy*, in which the eardrum is punctured with a needle, may be helpful for draining the fluid, obtaining samples for microscopic evaluation and culture, and flushing the middle ear. X-rays of the skull, taken with the cat under anesthesia, can reveal changes in the bony structures that house the ear. If they are

available, computed tomography (CT) or magnetic resonance imaging (MRI) scans provide additional useful diagnostic information.

Treatment involves administering antibiotics orally for four to six weeks. In recurrent or nonresponsive cases, surgery may be necessary.

Nasopharyngeal Polyps

Nasopharyngeal polyps are benign growths that can arise from several sites, including the nasopharynx (the back of the throat); the nose, where they occupy the nasal cavity; the middle ear, where they can break through the eardrum and enter the external ear canal; and the external ear canal itself, usually very close to the eardrum.

Causes and symptoms: The cause of the polyps is unknown. Nasopharyngeal polyps are most commonly seen in young cats, usually less than two years old. The clinical signs can vary depending on

▼ If your young cat has noisy breathing, chronic sneezing, and difficulty swallowing, she may have nasopharyngeal polyps and will need veterinary care.

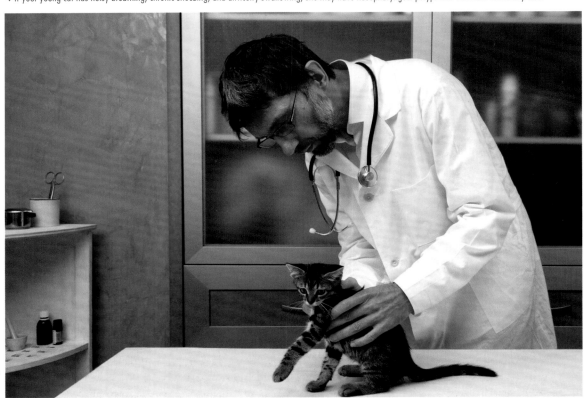

the location of the polyp. Cats with polyps in the nasal cavity often have loud, noisy breathing; heavy snoring; frequent sneezing; chronic nasal discharge; and occasional problems with swallowing. In the middle ear, they can affect balance and hearing. If she has a polyp in an ear canal, a cat may have discharge from the ear and an ear infection. A foul smell may be noted coming from the ear canal. A polyp in the ear may be misdiagnosed as a simple ear infection that does not respond to antibiotics.

Nasopharyngeal polyps should be suspected in any young cat with very noisy breathing, chronic sneezing, nasal discharge, and difficulty swallowing. Polyps that occur in the nasal cavity may cause a downward displacement of the soft palate, which may be visible when the oral cavity is examined.

Diagnosis and treatment: Polyps that occur in the external ear canal may be seen with an otoscope. X-rays of the skull often reveal the presence of a polyp. If available, CT and MRI images are superior imaging techniques for detecting polyps, especially if the middle ear is involved. If the mass is above the soft palate, rhinoscopy, in which a flexible tube with a camera on the end is inserted into the mouth and then flexed backward, may allow direct visualization of the polyp.

Treatment involves grasping the polyp with forceps at the base and applying gentle traction until the polyp is removed. Failure to remove all of it may result in regrowth. If a CT scan or an MRI shows a polyp in the bulla (the bony structure surrounding the middle ear), surgery should be performed to open the bulla and remove the polyp. This surgery is called a *bulla osteotomy.*

Aural Hematomas

An aural hematoma is a collection of blood that has accumulated between the inner and outer surfaces of the ear.

Causes and symptoms: Aural hematomas are believed to be caused by trauma, such as excessive shaking or scratching of the ear. Common reasons for excessive shaking and scratching are severe ear infection or ear mite infestation. Normally, the

▲ If left untreated, eye conditions can lead to visual impairment, so seek prompt veterinary care if your cat show signs of an eye infection.

inner surface of the pinna (the external, visible part of the ear) is firmly attached to the skin. After trauma, hemorrhage occurs and accumulates between the cartilage and the skin. The blood dissects the skin away from the cartilage, forming a hematoma or pocket of blood. The pinna appears swollen, bulging mainly inward, partly occluding the ear canal. If left untreated, the hematoma matures and contracts, causing the ear to become thickened and deformed—the so-called cauliflower ear.

Diagnosis and treatment: Diagnosis is made on physical examination, where a large, warm, fluid-filled swelling is noted on the ear. A concurrent ear infection may also be noted.

Aural hematomas are treated surgically. Any underlying problem, such as ear mite infestation or an ear infection, needs to be treated as well. Surgery will

▲Veterinarian examining a cat who may have conjunctivitis.

remove the hematoma, and it offers the best chance of retaining the natural appearance of the ear.

Eyes and Vision Injuries and Disorders

The eyes are important and delicate organs. A veterinarian should be consulted—ideally within twelve hours—when an eye problem is suspected. Signs of an eye problem include squinting, tearing, swelling or redness of the eyelid or eyeball, protrusion of one or both eyes, or discharge from one or both eyes. If left untreated, many eye conditions can lead to visual impairment or even blindness, thus any abnormality should be reported to a veterinarian. Some of the most common eye disorders in cats include cataracts, conjunctivitis, corneal ulcers, glaucoma, and uveitis (inflammation of the inner layer of the eye). The third eyelid (known as the *nictitating membrane* in medical jargon) is a membrane located in the inside corner of the eye. It produces a portion of the tear film, helps distribute this tear film over the surface of the cornea, and protects the cornea from damage. Elevation of the third eyelid on one side only is often a sign of local irritation or trauma to that eye.

General malaise from a variety of systemic illnesses can cause bilateral elevation of the third eyelid (often described by cat owners as a "film over the eyes"). Whenever this symptom appears, a thorough ocular and systemic examination is warranted.

Eyelid Problems

The eyelids of the cat, like those of humans and other animals, are designed to protect the eye. Although eyelid disorders are uncommon in cats, they do occur. Examples of eyelid disorders include blepharitis (inflammation of the eyelid) and eyelid agenesis (a birth defect in which the eyelids are missing).

Causes and symptoms: The most common eyelid defect in cats is entropion, a rolling inward of the edge of the eyelid, usually the lower lid. Entropion can affect one eye or both. Some cases are breed associated, especially in purebred cats with flat faces, such as Persians and Burmese. Entropion can also occur secondary to other conditions, such as spasm of the eyelid in cats with painful corneal ulcers, or as a result of chronic herpes virus infection. When the eyelid rolls inward, the hair on the eyelid rubs against the cornea, causing continual discomfort and irritation. Clinical signs include tearing, squinting, rubbing at the eyes, redness or swelling of the tissues surrounding the eyes, and wetness on the hairs adjacent to the eyelids.

Diagnosis and treatment: Entropion is diagnosed on physical examination. Surgery is required to roll the eyelid outward and correct the condition. This should be done by a veterinarian with experience in this technique.

Corneal Ulcers

Corneal ulceration is a painful and potentially vision-threatening condition that occurs when the corneal epithelium (the outermost layer of cells on the cornea) is damaged or lost.

Causes and symptoms: Superficial ulcers can occur as a result of trauma, such as from a fight with

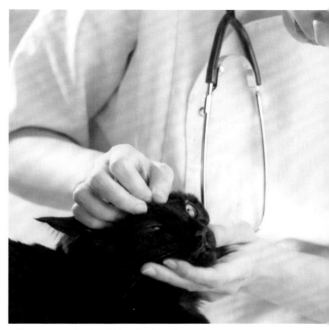

▲The treatment of conjunctivitis varies depending on the cause.

Administering Eye Medication

Therapy for most eye disorders entails administering drops or ointments. Drops are often easier to administer, although many drops require frequent administration. Ointments have the advantage of providing lubrication and allowing for increased contact time for the medication; they are especially useful given at bedtime. Application involves using the thumb or forefinger to gently roll the cat's lower eyelid downward. Ointment is then squeezed into the exposed space (called the *conjunctival sac*), and the eye is opened and closed by hand several times to evenly distribute the ointment over the eye. Approaching the eye from the outside corner can prevent the cat from seeing the tip of the tube, making administration a bit easier. Eye drops are instilled with the cat's nose tilted slightly upward. To prevent contamination, the tip of the dropper bottle or ointment tube should not be touched by fingers or any other surface; to prevent injury it should not come into direct contact with the eye.

another cat, or as a result of herpes virus infection. Other causes include abrasion from hairs on the eyelid (entropion—see above), foreign bodies, and chemicals. Although any cat can be affected, breeds with naturally bulging eyes (such as Persians) are at increased risk.

Regardless of the cause, ulcers must be treated promptly. The feline cornea is only 0.5 millimeters thick. Delaying therapy for corneal ulcers can result in perforation, leading to blindness. Signs that a cat might have a corneal ulcer include squinting, discharge from the eye, rubbing at the eye, excessive tear production, and inflammation of the soft tissues surrounding the eye.

Diagnosis and treatment: Diagnosis of a corneal ulcer is achieved through special staining techniques. A drop of a fluorescent dye is placed on the cornea. If the cornea is intact, the dye washes over the eye as a smooth film. If a scratch or abrasion is present on the cornea, the dye will adhere to the exposed tissue layer beneath the corneal epithelium, making the ulcerated area fluoresce bright green and allowing assessment of the size and depth of the ulcer.

Corneal ulcers are treated with antibiotic drops or ointment to prevent the cornea from becoming infected. Antiviral drops or ointment may be indicated if herpes virus infection is suspected. Atropine drops or ointment is administered to the eye to dilate the pupil and paralyze the ciliary muscle of the eye, preventing painful spasm. An Elizabethan collar may be necessary to prevent the cat from rubbing the eye and causing further damage. Deep corneal ulcers may require surgery to prevent potential rupture of the eye. A soft contact lens is sometimes warranted to protect the cornea from further damage. Oral antiviral medication, as well as the amino acid lysine, may be helpful in the treatment of ulcers caused by feline herpes virus. Most superficial, uncomplicated ulcers heal within seven days. Deep ulcers and nonhealing or progressive ulcers may require ongoing evaluation by a veterinary ophthalmologist.

Conjunctivitis

Disorders of the conjunctiva— the membrane that lines the lids and covers the eyeball—are some of the most common eye conditions affecting cats. Inflammation of this structure is called *conjunctivitis*.

Causes and symptoms: By far the most common cause of conjunctivitis in cats is a viral upper respiratory infection (mainly the herpes virus and the calici virus). Bacterial infections of the conjunctiva often develop secondarily in cats with viral conjunctivitis, as bacteria take advantage of the inflamed conjunctiva and colonize the eye. *Chlamydophila* (formerly *Chlamydia*) is a common cause of bacterial conjunctivitis in cats. Herpes conjunctivitis is usually bilateral, whereas *Chlamydophila* often begins in one eye and progresses to bilateral involvement in about a week. Kittens are particularly susceptible. Other reasons for conjunctivitis include any other cause of infection and inflammation of the eyelids and cornea, as the conjunctiva is so closely associated with these structures.

Signs of conjunctivitis include redness of the eye, excessive squinting or blinking, and discharge from the eye. If concurrent upper respiratory infection is present, sneezing, nasal congestion and discharge, fever, lethargy, and poor appetite may also be present.

Diagnosis and treatment: Diagnosis is based on physical examination findings of a red, inflamed conjunctiva. Treatment of conjunctivitis involves treating any underlying causes, if identified. Topical antibiotic and antiviral drops or ointments are the standard treatment. Oral medications may be recommended in severe cases. Lysine, an amino acid, may be beneficial in treating conjunctivitis due to the herpes virus.

▼Feral kitten with severe eye inflammation and secondary cataracts.

Glaucoma

Glaucoma is excessive pressure inside the eyeball. The normal pressure inside the eye is maintained through a delicate balance in the production and exit of aqueous humor, a watery fluid inside the eye.

Causes and symptoms: Glaucoma occurs if the normal outflow pathway of aqueous humor becomes obstructed. If the fluid cannot drain properly, the pressure in the eye increases, causing damage to the retina and optic nerve. This ultimately leads to vision loss.

▲ If your cat contracts an infectious eye condition, you may need to administer eye drops.

Primary glaucoma is a type of glaucoma that occurs spontaneously, for no apparent reason. In cats, this type is uncommon. The more common form is secondary glaucoma, in which the condition occurs secondarily to some other eye disorder, such as inflammation, displacement of the lens, trauma, or cancer.

Signs of glaucoma include an enlarged bulging eye, squinting, tearing, redness, a cloudy or "steamy" appearance to the cornea, and a dilated pupil. Most cases are unilateral (one eye affected).

Diagnosis and treatment: A diagnosis is made by measuring the pressure inside the eye with an instrument called a *tonometer*. Normal pressure within the eye is 15–25 mm Hg. Elevated pressure inside the eye (greater than 25 mm Hg) confirms the diagnosis. A thorough eye examination is necessary to determine if concurrent eye diseases are present because glaucoma can occur secondarily to other eye problems, and correcting the underlying problem may help control the glaucoma.

Treatment is either medical or surgical. Medical therapy consists of giving medication, both oral and topical, to decrease the production of fluid inside the eye and to reduce eye inflammation. If medical therapy isn't successful, surgery can be attempted. Surgery is aimed at destroying the structure in the eye that produces aqueous humor. This is achieved through cryosurgery (freezing) or laser surgery. In cases in which the glaucoma cannot be controlled, or those in which the glaucoma is caused by a tumor in the eye, enucleation (surgical removal of the eyeball) may be necessary.

The prognosis for glaucoma is guarded. Glaucoma is difficult to treat. Medications are necessary for the rest of the cat's life and must be given at the proper intervals.

Cataracts

A cataract is a cloudiness or opacity of the lens of the eye. The function of the lens is to focus light onto the retina in the back of the eye. To do this properly, the lens must be clear. A cataract within the lens may block the transmission of light onto the retina, affecting vision. Cataracts are much less common in cats than they are in dogs.

Causes and symptoms: Most cataracts develop secondary to some other eye problem, such as inflammation. Trauma is another cause of cataracts. Any penetrating injury to the eye has the potential to cause a cataract. Diabetes can result in cataracts in dogs, but not in cats. Inherited cataracts are rare in the cat.

As cats get older, the lens can become cloudy simply as a result of aging. This benign condition, called *nuclear sclerosis*, is often mistaken as cataracts. Unlike cataracts, however, it does not affect vision.

Signs of cataracts may include a white or gray color change within the eye, redness or inflammation of the eye, signs of pain or squinting, or signs of blindness (such as bumping into things, reluctance to jump on furniture, avoidance of the stairs).

Diagnosis and treatment: Diagnosis is usually made during a complete eye exam with your regular veterinarian; however, consultation with a veterinary ophthalmologist may be necessary. Surgery is the only option to restore vision. Whether a cat is a candidate for cataract surgery can be determined by a veterinary ophthalmologist. There is no medical treatment to reverse or shrink a cataract. Because most cataracts in cats are a result of some

Drooling

Cats show that they're happy in a variety of ways. They will purr, knead their paws, and sometimes offer up a couple of head butts. Occasionally, cats who are really on cloud nine will drool on their owners. If you are not doing something to make your cat super-happy, however, drooling is more likely to be a sign that something is amiss.

Saliva is continuously produced by the salivary glands. Excessive production and secretion of saliva is called *ptyalism*. Oral problems and nervous system disorders are common reasons for ptyalism and subsequent drooling. Ptyalism should not be confused with *pseudoptyalism*, in which a normal amount of saliva is being produced and overflows from the mouth due to anatomic abnormalities such as malocclusion (abnormal alignment of the teeth) or to an inability or reluctance to swallow because of pain associated with swallowing.

Disorders of the teeth and gums are the most common reason for drooling. Periodontal disease and the accompanying gingivitis, if severe, can lead to halitosis (bad breath), dysphagia (difficulty eating), and drooling.

The initial step in determining the cause of a cat's drooling is a thorough oral examination. This may require sedation, tranquilization, or even general anesthesia because cats with painful mouths are often head shy and won't allow a comprehensive exam. During the oral exam, your veterinarian will check to see if your cat can close her mouth properly. Some cats cannot, due to malocclusion. Although congenital and developmental disorders are common causes of malocclusion, oral tumors can cause misalignment of the teeth and/or jaw leading to improper closing of the mouth and subsequent drooling.

underlying systemic disease, cats with cataracts should be evaluated thoroughly by a veterinarian for concurrent illness.

Retinal Detachment

Retinal detachment occurs when the retina at the back of the eye peels away from the layer beneath it.

Causes and symptoms: The most common cause for this is high blood pressure. When cats have high blood pressure, fluid will leak out through blood vessels beneath the retina. This fluid accumulates beneath the retina, causing the retina to detach from the underlying layer. High blood pressure in cats is usually caused either by chronic kidney failure or by hyperthyroidism. Less commonly, retinal detachment can occur secondary to conditions that cause excessive viscosity or thickness of the blood. Excessive viscosity can occur in certain cancers, such as multiple myeloma or leukemia, or from excessive production of red blood cells (a condition called *polycythemia*). Retinal detachment may also occur if blood accumulates beneath the retina. This can happen if the cat has a blood clotting disorder, such as a low platelet count, or because of the ingestion of some types of rat poison. Trauma to the eye, with subretinal hemorrhage, can lead

to detachment. Any infection that causes retinal inflammation can lead to retinal detachment, for example, fungal infections such as histoplasmosis and cryptococcosis. Congenital retinal detachment (being born with detached retinas) is another possibility, but this is rare in cats.

Cats with retinal detachment will experience vision loss in the affected eye. The amount of vision loss depends on the severity of the detachment. If only one eye is affected, it may be difficult to tell if the cat is blind in that eye. If only a small section of the retina is detached (partial detachment), the cat often retains some degree of vision. Detachment secondary to high blood pressure is usually sudden in onset and affects both eyes.

Diagnosis and treatment: The most striking clinical sign of retinal detachment is widely dilated pupils that do not respond to a bright light. Evaluation of the retina using either an instrument called an ophthalmoscope or using a bright light and a special hand-held lens confirms the diagnosis. Some cases are difficult to diagnose, however, and may require special instrumentation and consultation with a veterinary ophthalmologist.

Once a diagnosis of retinal detachment is made, further tests may be necessary to determine an underlying cause. Since high blood pressure is the most common cause of retinal detachment, measurement of the blood pressure is of paramount importance. Other tests include a chemistry panel and urinalysis to determine if kidney failure is present and thyroid hormone measurement to check for hyperthyroidism. Blood clotting assessment, chest and abdominal x-rays, and other tests may be warranted.

Treatment involves addressing the underlying cause if possible. The detachment itself is difficult to treat. Detachments due to high blood pressure should be addressed immediately because a rapid normalization of the blood pressure may lead to partial reattachment and some restoration of lost vision. Depending on the cause of the detachment, other therapies may include antibiotics or antifungal drugs for bacterial and fungal infections, respectively. Chemotherapy may be warranted in some cases that are caused by cancer. Vitamin K therapy is the treatment for rat-poison induced hemorrhage. Hyperthyroidism is treated with oral medication, surgery, a prescription diet, or radioactive iodine.

Dental Problems

Dental problems are among the most common medical conditions seen in pet cats. They can lead to bad breath, swollen and bleeding gums, loose teeth, oral pain, and difficulty eating. Cats are secretive by nature, and sometimes it can be difficult to tell if a cat is experiencing oral discomfort. Occasionally, cats will reveal that their mouths are hurting by pawing at them, drooling, or deliberately turning their heads to one side as they eat to avoid chewing on the side of the mouth that's painful. Some cats will completely stop eating due to dental pain. Others may stop eating dry food and only eat wet food. Owners often mistakenly think their cats have become finicky about their food when in actuality the cats would prefer to eat the dry food but can't because it's become painful to crunch on kibble.

Periodontal Disease

Periodontal disease is an inflammation of the periodontium—the tissues surrounding the teeth.

Causes and symptoms: Periodontal disease is caused by plaque—the sticky bacteria-laden coating on the tooth surface—and the body's response to those bacteria and the toxins they release. As the immune system responds to the plaque, the gums become inflamed. This is the first phase of periodontal disease: gingivitis. As the inflammation progresses, the second phase of periodontal disease—periodontitis—occurs. Periodontitis is a condition in which both soft and bony tissues are affected, and cats may develop receding gums and experience bone loss. If not removed, plaque mineralizes into *tartar* (also called *calculus*) in a few days. Calculus requires mechanical removal by your veterinarian.

Periodontal disease is very common in cats. Untreated, it can lead to oral pain, abscess formation, osteomyelitis (bone infection), and tooth loss. Oral bacteria can enter the bloodstream through diseased oral tissues, affecting other organs as well, most notably the heart valves and kidneys.

◄ Dental problems are among the most common medical conditions seen in pet cats.

Diagnosis and treatment: Fortunately, the first stage (gingivitis) is reversible, so long as a professional cleaning is performed and a home care program is instituted. The early stages of periodontal disease are characterized by gingivitis and halitosis (bad breath). Up to 80 percent of cats three years of age and older suffer from gingivitis. The signs of gingivitis include red, swollen, or bleeding gums; bad breath; finicky eating habits; and reluctance to eat hard food. Veterinarians must look for these red flags of gingivitis and begin professional cleaning when warranted.

In cats, however, gingivitis can occur as young as 6 or 8 months, often associated with little or no calculus accumulation. We call this condition "juvenile-onset gingivitis." If left untreated, by 1 to 2 years of age, there may be irreversible periodontal disease. The exact cause of this condition is unknown, but genetics may play a role, since purebred cats, especially Siamese, Abyssinians, and Persians, are predisposed. Daily home care is essential in cats with this condition to avoid tooth loss.

If not addressed promptly, gingivitis develops into periodontitis and advanced periodontal disease. Treatment of periodontal disease requires professional cleaning. This is done under general anesthesia. Most cases of advanced periodontal disease can be prevented if detected early and treated appropriately.

By taking care of your cat's teeth, you're helping care for her overall health. Regular veterinary checkups and follow-up exams are necessary to maintain good dental health, especially if home dental care is not provided or tolerated by your cat.

Tooth Resorption

Tooth resorptions, formerly known as feline odontoclastic resorptive lesions (FORLs), are cavity-type erosions that develop in the teeth of some cats.

Causes and symptoms: FORLs are not caused by bacterial enzymes and decay and therefore are

▲ Regular veterinary checkups and follow-up exams are necessary to maintain good dental health.

technically not cavities. Rather, they are the result of the cat's own body resorbing the teeth. In fact, the veterinary dental community now prefers the term *tooth resorption* rather than FORLs. Conceptually, however, it is easiest for us to think of them as cavities. They occur typically at the gumline or just below it. Tooth resorption is often classified according to the severity, with stage 1 being the mildest and stage 5 being the most destructive. Although there are several theories as to why some cats develop tooth resorption, the exact cause remains unknown. In the early stages, most affected cats do not show any clinical signs. As the erosion progresses into the pulp cavity of the tooth, the tooth becomes sensitive to heat, cold, and touch and becomes very painful. Affected cats may salivate and experience difficulty eating. Some cats may switch from eating hard food to soft food due to pain experienced from crunching on the hard food. With the pulp cavity exposed, bacteria in the mouth may infect the pulp cavity and travel to the apex of the tooth root, causing a tooth-root abscess.

Diagnosis and treatment: A diagnosis of tooth resorption is usually made upon visual inspection of the mouth during a routine veterinary visit. Touching the tooth with a cotton-swab at the site of a resorptive lesion often causes pain, evidenced by jaw spasm. Often, the gums will overgrow and cover the erosion in the tooth, giving the appearance of a red spot on the tooth. Dental radiographs confirm the diagnosis. Because tooth resorption can be progressive and painful to the cat, extraction of affected teeth is the recommended treatment. To date, there is no known proven method to prevent tooth resorption.

Tooth Root Abscesses

A tooth root abscess is an infection involving the root(s) of a tooth.

Causes and symptoms: Oral bacteria may enter the central pulp cavity of diseased or broken teeth and migrate to the root of the tooth, where they can cause infection. A pocket of pus develops at the root of the tooth. The abscessed tooth root is painful and uncomfortable for the cat. A swelling may develop on the cat's face near the infected root.

Diagnosis and treatment: Treatment of these abscesses requires drainage of the accumulated pus, followed by antibiotic treatment. Antibiotic therapy alone is rarely effective for these abscesses because the infection is trapped inside the tooth root.

Drainage is best achieved through extraction of the affected tooth. Sometimes the abscess is so severe that the trapped bacteria tunnel a hole through the skin of the face to allow drainage. Once the tooth is removed, the gums will heal and the cat's mouth will no longer be painful.

Lymphocytic/Plasmacytic Gingivitis and Stomatitis

Lymphocytic/plasmacytic gingivitis and stomatitis (LPGS) is a painful inflammatory condition that causes a great deal of discomfort to many cats.

Causes and symptoms: Cats with LPGS exhibit chronic, severe inflammation and ulceration of the gums, back of the throat, and often other structures inside the mouth. The exact cause of LPGS is unknown, but it is most likely a combination of various factors. One theory is that some cats' gums are hypersensitive to bacterial plaque. Small amounts of plaque will cause the immune system to overreact and mount an exuberant inflammatory response, sending large numbers of inflammatory cells, mainly lymphocytes and plasma cells (hence the description "lymphocytic/plasmacytic"), into the gums and oral tissues. Suppression of the immune

▼ Veterinarian extracting a tooth from a cat.

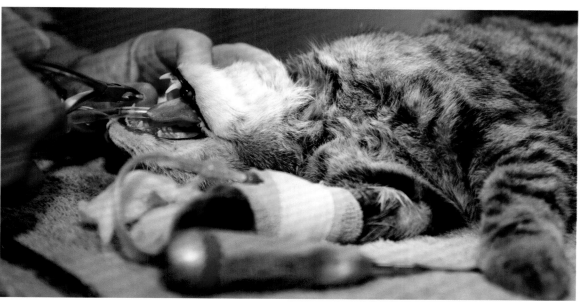

system has also been theorized as a cause or contributing factor in LPGS. Infection with FeLV and/or FIV is known to suppress the feline immune system and may play a role in some affected cats, although many other factors including stress and other environmental influences can weaken a cat's defenses and predispose her to illness. Other infectious causes have been implicated, including feline calicivirus. Some veterinarians feel that infection with the bacterial organism *Bartonella* may play a role in the disease, but this remains controversial. It has been suggested that a genetic predisposition is likely in some breeds.

▲ Normal, healthy cat's paw. Toepads on the same foot may be different colors.

Oral pain is probably the most common sign of LPGS. This can manifest in a variety of ways. Cats may have difficulty eating or may stop eating entirely. Some will drool excessively, with the drool being blood tinged on occasion. Some cats approach the food dish as if they're interested in food (which they usually are), but then run from the food dish because eating is painful. A few cats will paw at their mouths and may develop an aversion to having their faces touched. Some cats stop eating their dry food, which can be painful to chew, and will only eat canned food. (This is often misinterpreted as being "finicky.") Cats tend to be relatively secretive about their illnesses and may manifest their oral discomfort in more subtle behavioral ways, such as being reclusive, irritable, or aggressive. Grooming may become uncomfortable, and cats may develop an unkempt hair coat as a result. Often, cats with LPGS have halitosis (bad breath).

Diagnosis and treatment: A definitive diagnosis of LPGS is achieved by biopsy of the affected tissues, although a presumptive diagnosis is often made based on the results of a thorough oral examination. General findings include extremely red, proliferative (swollen and overgrown), and ulcerated oral tissue that bleeds easily when touched. The most frequently affected tissues are the gums, although other areas of the mouth are commonly affected, such as the roof of the mouth, the fauces (the lateral walls at the back of the throat that surround the tonsils), the tongue, and sometimes the lips. Various degrees of dental and periodontal disease may be present because this often contributes to the severity of LPGS. Oral x-rays may reveal the presence of retained tooth roots and resorptive lesions—painful tooth erosions similar to cavities. In most cases, the cat needs to be sedated for a proper, thorough oral examination to be performed; general anesthesia is usually required if dental radiographs are to be taken.

The goal of treatment is to decrease the inflammatory response. Control of plaque and tartar is the cornerstone of therapy, and therefore a thorough dental scaling and polishing should be performed. Ideally, cats' teeth should be brushed regularly after the dental scaling; however, cats with LPGS have mouths that may be too painful to tolerate brushing. Oral rinses or gels may be of benefit, but again, many cats find any manipulation of their mouths intolerable. Unfortunately, even with thorough dental scaling and subsequent home care, the condition often progresses. Antibiotics may help some cats during flare-ups of oral pain. Many cats need an occasional short course of anti-inflammatory drugs during flare-ups. Ideally, the anti-inflammatory medication is given at initially high doses to control the inflammation, and then the dosage is tapered to the lowest dose that keeps the condition under control. However, as stated earlier, most cats won't allow oral administration of medication. In these cases, an injection of a long-acting steroid is often the only alternative. The use of antibiotics and anti-inflammatory drugs, however, offers only a short-term "fix." Eventually, most cats become nonresponsive to medical treatment and will require extraction of all of the teeth except the canines (the "fangs"). In most cases, extraction alone successfully reduces the inflammation and allows the cat to eat and live normally. Cat owners often worry that their cat won't be able to eat after full-mouth extraction. Most cats, however, tolerate extractions very well and can eat moist food readily,

Polydactylism

Normally, a cat has eighteen digits. The front paw has five toes: four toes and one dewclaw (the small toe on the medial side of the foot that doesn't touch the ground). The normal rear paw has four toes. Polydactylism (from the Greek: *poly* = "many," *daktulos* = "fingers") is the anatomical abnormality of having more than the usual number of digits on the paws. It is a natural genetic variation that occurs in many animals (as well as in humans), and it is a common trait among cats.

Polydactyl cats are occasionally referred to as "mitten cats," "thumb cats," and "Hemingway cats," the latter name referring to the writer Ernest Hemingway. In the 1930s, Hemingway established a home on the small island of Key West, Florida, which he eventually shared with several cats, including a six-toed polydactyl named Snowball. Today, Hemingway's home has gone to the cats—some fifty of them—at least half of them polydactyls, all descendants of Snowball. Many other six-toed cats can be found elsewhere on the island as well.

Most polydactyl cats have one or two extra toes on each foot, with the extra toes appearing on the thumb side of the foot. Most cases of polydactylism affect the front feet only. The hind feet are less often affected. When they are, it is usually in addition to having polydactyl front feet. It is quite rare to find a cat with polydactyl rear paws and normal front paws. The gene for polydactylism can give rise to either extra toes or extra dewclaws. When polydactylism occurs on the hind paws it tends to cause extra toes rather than a dewclaw.

Genetically, polydactylism is a simple autosomal (not related to gender) dominant trait. Cats with extra toes have the dominant gene. A cat needs only one copy of this gene from either parent to have the trait. If one parent has it, 40–50 percent of the kittens will have it, too. Because many polydactyl cats carry the gene for normal toes, the trait is never "fixed." In other words, even breeding two polydactyls doesn't guarantee all the kittens will be polydactyl. There will always be a few normal-toed kittens in the litter because of the recessive gene.

Polydactylism doesn't affect cats adversely. It offers them no advantages, nor does it yield any disadvantages. It is an anomaly—a deviation from the norm—rather than a deformity, and most cat owners regard it as an enchanting quirk. The toenails associated with the extra toes tend to be normal nails, although occasionally, the extra toe is incompletely formed, and the nail bed is deformed, leading to claw problems like ingrown or overgrown claws. The extra nails of polydactyl cats, like all nails, require regular trimming.

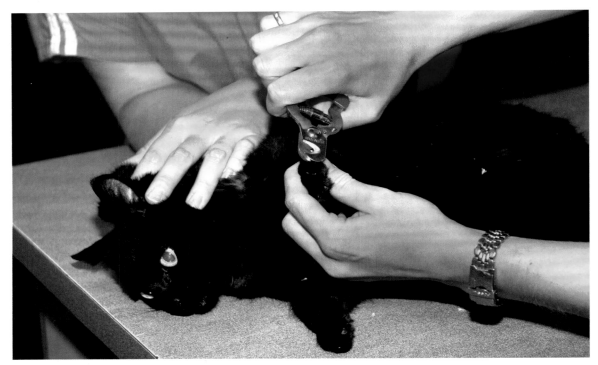

▲ Keeping your cat's claws trimmed will prevent her from getting them stuck in something and possibly pulling out the nail.

with many cats able to crunch on dry food after the extraction sites have fully healed.

Cats with LPGS are likely facing a lifetime of frequent veterinary visits and treatments. With vigilant monitoring and conscientious veterinary care, cats with LPGS can live comfortable happy lives.

Paw and Nail Injuries and Problems

Cats claws are made of the protein keratin. Beneath the claw is a pink structure, the quick, which contains blood vessels, nerves, and cells that give rise to the keratin that makes the nail. Cats use their claws for climbing, for defense, and for killing prey. Like any part of the body, the feet are susceptible to injuries and illnesses.

Paw Injuries and Diseases

Your cat's paws serve a greater purpose than just standing and walking. Cats use their paws for predation, for territorial marking (via secretions from glands located on the pads), and for regulating body temperature through sweating. Like any part of the body, paws are susceptible to injury and illnesses.

Eosinophilic Granuloma

Eosinophilic granulomas are inflammatory lesions that commonly affect feline skin, including the lips and occasionally inside the mouth. This condition can also present as ulcerative lesions around the edges of the foot pads, often on several feet. It tends to occur in young cats (most affected cats being less than one year of age.) In most cases, it does not affect the cat's ability to walk; however, because the feet come into contact with dirty surfaces like the floor and the litter box, the ulcerated areas are susceptible to infection. Treatment with antibiotics can control infection, but anti-inflammatory medications must also be given so that the lesions resolve.

Pemphigus

Pemphigus foliaceus (PF) is a skin disorder in which blisters and pustules develop on the skin, affecting primarily the face, feet, and ears. It is more common in middle-aged and older cats. PF is an autoimmune disorder, a disorder in which the cat's immune system attacks a specific component of its own body—in this case, the skin. This causes the outermost layer of the skin to separate from the layers below, forming blisters or pustules. Although the face and ears are initially affected, the feet usually become affected, including the footpads. Eventually, the entire body becomes involved. Biopsy of the affected skin is usually required to make a definitive diagnosis. Treatment with anti-inflammatory medications often brings the disorder under control; however, the drugs must be given for the remainder of the cat's life.

Plasma Cell Pododermatitis

Feline plasma cell pododermatitis is an uncommon disorder characterized by soft, usually painless swelling of several of the foot pads. In some cases, ulcers may develop on the swollen pads and may lead to secondary infection and pain. A tentative diagnosis is made on physical examination, due to the characteristic swollen, puffy appearance of the main weight-bearing pads (leading to the nickname "pillow paw" disease). Definitive diagnosis requires biopsy of an affected pad. The cause of the disorder is unknown, although the response to immunosuppressive medications suggests an autoimmune disorder (i.e., one in which the immune system inappropriately sends inflammatory cells into the pads).

Nail Injuries and Problems

Toenail injuries in cats are relatively common; however, they are usually of minor significance. The most commonly seen disorders of the nails in cats are broken nails and overgrown nails.

Broken Nails

Broken nails are a common problem in cats; if not removed promptly, they can result in pain and infection.

Causes and symptoms: Cats can get their claws stuck in a carpet or something similar, and when they pull their feet loose, they can tear a nail. Sometimes the tail is torn completely off. In most cases, the nail is partially torn and is dangling, causing pain every time the nail is moved. A partial or total avulsion of the nail will expose the underlying tissue, which is called the *quick*. The quick contains many nerve endings and is very sensitive. Cats may limp on the foot or refuse to bear any weight on it at all.

Diagnosis and treatment: Torn nails should be evaluated by a veterinarian. If the nail is partially torn, your veterinarian will remove the dangling nail. The exposed quick, besides being sensitive, is also at risk of becoming infected since cats scratch around in their litter boxes, which contain many bacteria. Your veterinarian will prescribe antibiotics and possibly pain medication. Switching to a new type of litter, such as shredded or pelleted newspaper, may help minimize the chance of infection. A new nail will regrow from the exposed quick over the course of a few weeks. Keeping the nails trimmed will prevent torn nails from occurring.

Overgrown Nails

If a cat's nails are not trimmed regularly, they can grow too long and inflict injuries.

Causes and symptoms: Normally, when cats groom their feet, they remove the outer nail sheath with their teeth. They also remove their outer nail sheaths when they use their scratching posts. If these sheaths don't get removed, they can grow too long, curling all the way around and piercing the pad of the affected toe.

Diagnosis and treatment: If the nail pierces the pad, your veterinarian will have to trim the nail and treat the wound that it created. If the wound is infected, antibiotics will be prescribed. In some cases, soaking the foot in an antiseptic solution may be beneficial. Overgrown nails can be prevented by keeping your cat's nails trimmed. If you cannot trim your cat's nails yourself, take your cat to your veterinarian or a groomer to have it done regularly, approximately every six to eight weeks.

Chapter 14

Musculoskeletal and Nervous System Injuries, Disorders, and Diseases

By Arnold Plotnick, DVM

Even though cats walk on all fours, compared to humans who walk upright, the feline skeleton and the human skeleton are fairly similar. Cats have more bones than humans (230 vs. 206), but that's primarily due to the tail bones. Feline muscles are strong and well-constructed, as you'd expect for such an agile hunter. The nervous system can be divided into two main portions: the central nervous system (CNS) and the peripheral nervous system (PNS). The CNS includes the brain and the spinal cord. The PNS is made up of all of the rest of the nerves that are found throughout the body. The nervous system and the musculoskeletal system work together like a well-oiled machine, allowing the cat to finely coordinate her activities, like running, jumping, and pouncing. Despite their exceptional athletic ability, cats do not always land on their feet; injuries and disorders of the musculoskeletal and nervous system do occur in cats, although less commonly than in their canine counterparts.

Musculoskeletal Injuries and Disorders

The skeleton can be divided into two parts: the *axial skeleton*—the skull, spine, ribs, and sternum—and the *appendicular skeleton*, which comprises the front and hind legs, as well as the hips and shoulder blades. Although cats are very limber and coordinated, their bones are fairly fragile, and orthopedic injuries such as broken bones are common. Ligaments are strong pieces

▶ Despite the adage, a cat does not always land on her feet, and a fall from a height can cause her injury.

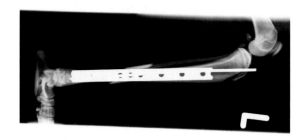

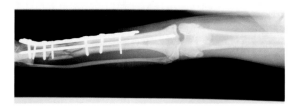

▲ Radiographs showing metal plates implanted to fix a cat's fractured leg.

of connective tissue that connect bones to other bones. Ligament injuries are not as common in cats as in dogs, but they do occur.

Luxating Patella

The patella is the kneecap. In order for the rear legs to flex and extend properly, the patella needs to glide within the natural groove that is present at the end of the femur (thigh bone). In some cats, the patella does not glide properly in the groove. It slips out of the groove, usually toward the inside (medial) part of the leg (as opposed to the outside or lateral part). Cats with this problem are said to have a medial patellar luxation (MPL). It is much more common in dogs, however, than in cats.

Causes and symptoms: The most common cause of MPL in cats is developmental; cats are born with a tendency to develop the problem, usually within the first year of life. Severe cases may lead to lameness problems early in the cat's life, but this is rare. Most cases show no symptoms at all. As the cat ages, mild cases of MPL may progress in severity, eventually leading to persistent lameness. Again, this is uncommon. Cats with this condition are rarely bothered by it. Trauma is the second most likely cause of MPL in cats, usually as a result of being hit by a car.

The main clinical sign of MPL is lameness. This can vary from a very mild limp to a complete lameness, with the cat's not being able to bear weight on the affected limb.

Diagnosis and treatment: Diagnosis is based mainly on physical exam findings. During an orthopedic examination, the veterinarian will manipulate the patella to see whether it is firmly in its groove or can easily be displaced. Both knees will be evaluated. In many cases, the luxation is bilateral, although there may be differing degrees of severity between knees. x-rays may be useful in confirming the diagnosis.

Treatment varies, depending on the severity of the MPL and the cat's clinical signs. Mild cases may not require treatment or may be managed with a short course of pain medication. More severe cases may require surgery. The most common surgery for MPL involves deepening the groove that the patella glides in, making the kneecap less likely to pop out of place. Most cats respond well to surgery and are walking normally several weeks later. However, arthritis is likely to develop in the joint later in life.

Ruptured Cruciate Ligament

The cruciate ligaments are two bands of fibrous tissue found in the knee joint, one running toward the front of the joint (the cranial cruciate ligament), the other situated toward the rear of the joint (the caudal cruciate ligament). The ligaments cross in center of the joint—hence the name *cruciate*, from the Latin, meaning "cross"—keeping the tibia (shin bone) and the femur (thigh bone) stable and properly aligned relative to each other. Although not a common occurrence in cats, a cruciate ligament (specifically, the cranial cruciate ligament) can suffer a tear or rupture, leading to lameness.

Causes and symptoms: By far the most common cause of a torn cruciate ligament is some type of trauma, such as landing improperly after a jump, falling from an elevated height, or being hit by a vehicle. The severity of the lameness depends on the type of injury. An acute, sudden tear can lead to lameness so severe that the cat cannot bear weight on the limb at all. Tears that occur as a result of a slow, progressive breakdown of the ligament usually cause milder clinical signs such as an intermittent limp.

Diagnosis and treatment: Diagnosis is made on physical examination. After observing your cat walk, your veterinarian will perform an orthopedic exam on the affected rear leg. While holding the tibia and the femur firmly, your veterinarian will see whether the tibia can be moved excessively in a forward motion compared with the femur. This excessive movement is called *cranial drawer* and indicates that the cranial cruciate ligament is torn. x-rays may be helpful in supporting the diagnosis.

Most cats require surgery to repair the ligament. Some cats may be able to recover from their lameness without surgery, but healing takes time, and the cat has to be restricted from exercising the affected leg. This may require confinement in a cage for several weeks. Cats who do not respond to conservative treatment (rest and anti-inflammatory medication) will need to have the ruptured ligament surgically repaired. Most cats do well after surgery, although the affected knee may become arthritic as the cat ages. Overweight cats do much better if they are put on a diet to lose weight.

Soft-Tissue Injuries

Although cats are very agile creatures, they occasionally suffer sprains and other soft-tissue injuries to the limbs and joints. In most cases, the tissue damaged is a ligament.

Causes and symptoms: The most common cause of these injuries is trauma—such as being hit by a car, falling from a window or other high area, or as a result of running or playing. Signs of a sprain include pain, swelling, and lameness in the affected limb. The signs can vary in severity, from a barely perceptible limp to a complete non-weight-bearing lameness.

Diagnosis and treatment: In most cases, the diagnosis can be based on the physical exam

▼Kitten with a broken leg. Falls are the most common cause of broken bones in cats.

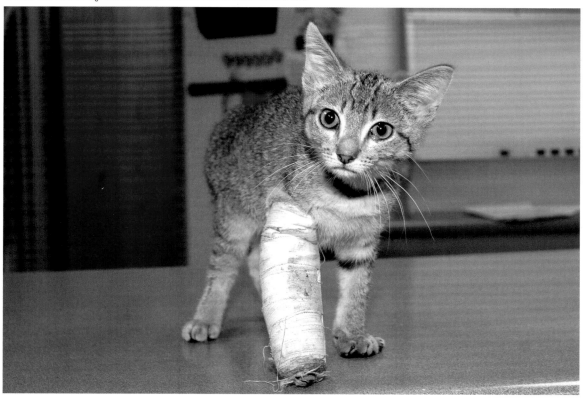

findings along with a history of trauma. x-rays may be necessary to rule out a fracture or dislocation, which can have similar clinical signs.

Mild sprains and soft tissue injuries heal on their own over the course of a few days. Anti-inflammatory medication may be warranted for cases in which there is obvious discomfort. More severe cases may require a splint to protect and support the affected joint, as well as strict confinement. The incidence of sprains (and more serious traumatic injuries) can be reduced by keeping cats indoors.

Nervous System Disorders, Diseases, and Injuries

As with the other body systems, the nervous system is susceptible to a variety of ailments. Diagnosing neurological disorders can be especially challenging because many of the clinical signs are subtle, intermittent, or subjective. Sophisticated equipment is often required to achieve a definitive diagnosis of some neurologic disorders, such as disc disease and brain or spinal tumors, and may warrant a visit to a referral center or veterinary university.

Brain Tumors

Brain tumors are uncommon in cats, but they do occur. Tumors can be *primary* (the tumor originated in the brain) or *secondary* (the initial tumor originated elsewhere in the body and has spread to the brain).

Causes and symptoms: The most common brain tumor in cats is a *meningioma*. This is a tumor that arises from the membranes that cover the brain. The next most common brain tumor is *lymphoma*. Clinical signs of a brain tumor depend on the size, location, and rate of growth of the tumor. Primary brain tumors tend to grow slowly, initially allowing the brain to adapt. During this time, there may only be vague, subtle behavioral changes. Clinical signs progress as the tumor continues to grow. Common signs include altered mental attitude, seizures, blindness, walking in circles, and compulsive pacing.

Diagnosis and treatment: Making the diagnosis can be challenging. Common tests, such as blood tests or x-rays, rarely allow for a diagnosis. Advanced imaging techniques, such as computed tomography (CT) or magnetic resonance imaging (MRI), are often necessary.

▼ Intervertebral disc disease is less common in cats than in dogs, but it can occur in cats of any breed.

Depending on their location, some meningiomas can be surgically removed. Cats typically show marked improvement within several days after surgery. Cats who had seizures before the surgery may continue to have seizures after the tumor is removed and will continue to require anticonvulsant medication. Brain surgery in cats requires special equipment that is often only available at universities and referral centers.

Although lymphoma is generally not treatable via surgery, it may respond to chemotherapy, radiation, or a combination. For tumors that are not amenable to surgery or that fail to respond to chemotherapy and/or radiation, palliative therapy with anti-inflammatory medications may lead to significant improvement in clinical signs. Unfortunately, this is usually short-lived. Unless the tumor can be removed completely, most cases of brain cancer have a guarded to poor prognosis.

Disc Disease

Between the individual bones of the spine (the vertebrae) are structures called *discs*. The discs have a hard outer surface and a soft inner core, similar to a jelly doughnut. The discs act as cushions between the vertebrae.

Causes and symptoms: Intervertebral disc disease (IVDD) is a condition that occurs when one or more discs get compressed between the vertebrae. This causes the "jelly" inside to leak out, or *herniate*, irritating or damaging the spinal cord just above it. Herniation of disc material can occur suddenly as a result of trauma, or it can happen gradually. IVDD is much more common in dogs than in cats.

The signs of IVDD can vary, from mild back pain to complete paralysis of the front and/or rear legs. In most cases of feline IVDD, the disc problem occurs in the mid to lower spine. If paralysis occurs, the front legs are often spared, with only the rear legs affected. Other possible signs of IVDD include reluctance to play, crying in pain when picked up or petted along the spine, reluctance to jump or climb stairs, and an uncoordinated gait.

Diagnosis and treatment: To diagnose IVDD, your veterinarian will perform a complete

Landing on Their Feet

Despite their flexible muscular bodies and excellent righting reflex, many cats have acquired severe injuries after falling only a short distance. Any windows that a cat has access to should have strong, intact screens, and rooftops and unscreened balconies should be off limits to your cat.

neurologic examination. Once a neurologic problem is confirmed, other diagnostic tests will likely be necessary. X-rays can sometimes help point to the suspected area of the spinal cord that is being compressed, but a definitive diagnosis often requires more advanced techniques such as a CT scan, an MRI, or a myelogram. A myelogram is a procedure in which a dye is injected into the spinal canal, allowing for better visualization of the spinal cord on X-rays. The exact location of the spinal cord compression can then be determined.

Treatment for IVDD depends on how severely the cat is affected. Mild signs of IVDD can often be treated with strict cage rest, anti-inflammatory medication, and muscle relaxants. More severe cases may require surgery to remove the extruded disc material and relieve the pressure on the spinal cord. The prognosis in mild cases is favorable. For cats who require surgery, the prognosis depends on how severely the spinal cord was damaged and whether the surgery to remove the extruded disc material was done in a timely fashion. It may take several weeks or months for a cat to recover from a spinal cord injury.

Feline Hyperesthesia Syndrome

Feline hyperesthesia syndrome (FHS) is an uncommon, mysterious condition that manifests as a variety of behavior changes, the most common being a heightened sensitivity to touch especially over the lower back and rump.

Causes and symptoms: Most affected cats will become fixated on their tails, swishing them back and forth, chasing them, frantically overgrooming them, or viciously attacking them. The skin along a cat's back may twitch or ripple, and a cat may show sudden bouts of bizarre hyperactive or aggressive behavior. Other signs that may accompany this condition are sudden mood swings, in which cats can go from extremely affectionate to aggressive, increased vocalization, and apparent hallucinations, manifested in behavior such a cat's appearing to follow the movement of something that isn't there or running away from some unseen adversary. Some people find this behavior amusing and will jokingly describe their cat as being "possessed." Abyssinians, Burmese, Himalayans, and Siamese are especially prone to the condition, although any breed may be affected.

The cause of FHS remains elusive. Some people think that it is some type of seizure activity. Others feel that it is a form of obsessive-compulsive behavior. The fact that Oriental breeds are somewhat predisposed to FHS suggests a possible inherited tendency. Stress is considered to be a factor in this disorder.

Diagnosis and treatment: There is no specific test for FHS. Diagnosis is based on the clinical signs and ruling out other medical disorders, such as hyperthyroidism or skin allergies.

Treatment involves reducing stress in the cat's environment. Some behaviorists recommend allowing the cat to "blow off steam" by encouraging predatory play activities using interactive toys such as feather toys on a string or a wand and laser toys. This helps reduce any bottled-up prey drive the cat may have. Actions that trigger the behavior, such as petting or scratching near the base of the tail or the rump should be avoided. In cases in which the symptoms occur spontaneously or where symptoms are severe, medical therapy may be warranted. Anti-obsessional drugs, such as fluoxetine (Prozac), have been shown to be effective. Anticonvulsant medication, such as phenobarbital, is also effective

▶ The Abyssinian is one of the breeds that is most susceptible to feline hyperesthesia syndrome.

for this condition. Severely affected cats can usually live a normal life if treated appropriately.

Idiopathic Vestibular Disease

The vestibular system in the cat comprises nerves and sensors that start in the brain and extend to the inner ear. It is responsible for a cat's balance and coordination. Occasionally, a disorder of the vestibular system arises, and cats become dizzy and lose their balance.

Causes and symptoms: This disease is typically manifested through a variety of clinical signs, such as tilting the head, walking in circles or as if drunk, stumbling, falling, incoordination, and nystagmus (a back and forth beating motion of the eyes). In severe cases, the cat may not be able to stand at all. Although vestibular disease can occur as a result of inner ear infections, thiamine deficiency, poisonings, and tumors or polyps in the middle ear, in most cases an underlying cause is never determined and the condition is referred to as *idiopathic* (meaning "no known cause").

Diagnosis and treatment: In dogs, idiopathic vestibular disease typically affects older animals. In

▲ If your cat has a seizure, take her for examination by a veterinarian as soon as possible after the seizure ends.

cats, however, the disorder can strike at any age. The sudden onset of signs can be drastic and frightening to owners and often causes them (and some veterinarians) to mistakenly diagnose cats as having suffered strokes. It is *not* a stroke, and euthanasia should *not* be considered. Idiopathic vestibular disease in cats usually shows rapid, dramatic improvement over twenty-four to seventy-two hours, and most cats are completely back to normal two weeks after the initial onset of clinical signs. Severely affected cats may need to be isolated to a small area so that they don't injure themselves by trying to go up or down stairs or jump on furniture. Obviously, they should be prevented from going outdoors until fully recovered. If confinement at home isn't possible, the cat can be admitted to the veterinary hospital and kept in a cage with blankets and protective soft bedding to prevent injury. Cats who developed a head tilt at the onset of clinical signs may continue to have one after recovery; the head tilt has no effect on the cat (other than giving him an unusual appearance).

Seizures/Epilepsy

Few things are more upsetting for a cat owner than witnessing his or her beloved companion in the throes of a seizure. Luckily for cat owners, feline seizure disorders are fairly uncommon. Whereas epilepsy affects up to 3 percent of the canine population, cats are much less susceptible.

Causes and symptoms: Seizures can vary in severity, from a mild episode of acting spacey to a severe episode in which a cat falls on her side, gnashes her teeth, salivates, paddles all four limbs, and loses bowel and bladder control.

The term *primary epilepsy* implies that the seizures are due to a primary brain disorder. Trying to prove that a cat has primary epilepsy can be difficult. Epileptics appear normal on physical examination and on neurological examination, and diagnostic tests, including advanced imaging tests like CT or MRI, show no abnormalities. This, in fact, is how the diagnosis of primary epilepsy is achieved: by exclusion of other causes of seizures.

Burmese Craniofacial Defect

Burmese breeders in North America bred their cats toward a different physical conformation than breeders in Europe and much of the rest of the world. While European breeders maintained the semi-foreign conformation and a wide range of colours (which preserved a wide gene pool), North American breeders selected for a cobbier Burmese with a more domed head and stuck to the four original colours. This meant a small number of stud cats, with the desired domed head shape, were much in demand, and their genes became widespread in the American Burmese gene pool. In later generations, when carriers were bred together, deformed kittens appeared. As a result of the craniofacial defect, British cat registries banned the use of imported American Burmese as outcrosses for the European Burmese.

Affected kittens have a normal lower jaw and tongue, but the upper jaw, the upper part of the muzzle, and the roof of mouth are duplicated. The area above the muzzle is incomplete; the ears and eyes are malformed and the skull doesn't close completely, leaving part of the brain covered with skin only. Affected kittens are usually stillborn or die soon after birth. Those that survive must be euthanized due to the devastating nature of this deformity.

Responsible breeders have identified and neutered carriers of the defect, and the deformity is encountered less often. It is not possible to completely eliminate recessive mutations without genetic screening. Some lines of American Shorthair are affected by a similar syndrome, also due to breeders wanting to create a more domed head shape.

Secondary epilepsy suggests that the seizures are associated with an underlying structural disorder, such as inflammatory disease, trauma, or cancer. This is seen more commonly in cats than in dogs. Metabolic diseases and toxicities can lead to seizures in cats. Infectious causes that should be considered in cats with seizure disorders include feline infectious peritonitis (FIP), feline leukemia virus (FeLV), feline immunodeficiency virus (FIV), *Cryptococcus* (a fungal infection), and rabies (extremely rare). Toxoplasmosis is an uncommon cause of seizures in cats. Up to 20 percent of cats presenting with acute onset of seizure activity may have *cerebral ischemic encephalopathy*, a condition in which the brain is damaged due to decreased blood flow to a part of the brain (similar to a stroke). In most cases of cerebral ischemic encephalopathy, the cause is never determined. Cancer is a possible cause of seizures in cats, with the most common brain tumor being a meningioma, a tumor arising from the membranes covering the brain. Another possible cause of acute seizure activity in cats is the larva of the parasite *Cuterebra* migrating through the brain.

Diagnosis and treatment: If your cat has a seizure, don't panic. Take note of the time the seizure begins. It may seem like forever but, in fact, most seizures last from thirty seconds to two minutes. Clear away any objects that the cat might hit during the seizure, such as furniture, and protect her from stairs or water. Do *not* attempt to hold the cat's mouth open or closed; airway obstruction by the tongue rarely occurs. Provide gentle restraint during the seizure by holding a light blanket or towel over the cat. Afterward, confine the cat and monitor breathing and pulse. Do not be alarmed if your cat vocalizes or stumbles after the seizure ends; this is common.

Cats who have experienced a single, short seizure should be evaluated by a veterinarian as soon as practical. If, however, the seizure lasts longer than three or four minutes, or if more than one seizure has occurred in a twenty-four-hour period, or if a new seizure begins before the cat has fully recovered from the first seizure, the cat should be taken to an emergency clinic for immediate evaluation. A thorough history and a comprehensive physical and neurologic exam, including an eye exam that evaluates the retinas, should be done in all cats with a history of seizures. A complete blood count, serum biochemistry panel, urinalysis, and evaluation of infectious disease status (FeLV, FIV, FIP, *Toxoplasma*, *Cryptococcus*) should be performed or considered. If neurologic abnormalities are detected on physical examination, further testing is advised. This may include doing a "spinal tap" and obtaining a sample of the cerebrospinal fluid (the fluid that bathes the brain and spinal cord), as well as advanced imaging tests such as a CT scan or MRI.

Cats with seizures may require anticonvulsant medication. Unfortunately, the number of drugs that have been developed or recommended for seizure control in cats is limited. Phenobarbital remains the first choice of anticonvulsants in cats. For cats who do not tolerate phenobarbital, diazepam (Valium) is usually the second choice of most veterinarians. Recently, the drug levetiracetam (Keppra) has shown promise in controlling seizures in cats who do not respond well to phenobarbital. Once cat starts taking anticonvulsant medication, it needs to be continued for the remainder of the cat's life.

Spinal Trauma

Trauma to the spinal cord is an uncommon occurrence in cats, but when it does happen, the effects can be devastating.

Causes and symptoms: The most common cause is vehicular trauma, although gunshots and falling from a height are other possibilities. Signs of spinal cord injury often reflect on the cat's ability to walk. Affected cats will show varying degrees of lameness, from a mild limp to incoordination to complete paralysis.

Diagnosis and treatment: Cats with suspected spinal injuries should be evaluated by a veterinarian immediately. To prevent further injury, immobilize the cat before transporting her. Lay her on a board and immobilize her with straps, cords, or tape, paying special attention to the head and neck. Alternatively, wrap the cat in a blanket or a coat to immobilize her. Gently lower the immobilized cat into a large box or secure container for transport to a veterinarian. Diagnosis is based on a history of recent injury, physical examination, and other diagnostic tests, such as x-rays, a CT scan, or an MRI.

Treatment depends on the type and severity of injury. Treatment can be medical, surgical, or both. Medical therapy involves giving anti-inflammatory drugs to prevent swelling and inflammation of the spinal cord. Surgery may be necessary in cases of fracture or dislocation or in cases in which the neurologic signs are getting worse despite medical therapy. Severe fractures or dislocations may not be treatable with surgery or medical therapy, and euthanasia should be considered in these cases.

Spinal Tumors

Tumors of the spinal cord are uncommon in cats. Of the tumors that do occur, the most common one affecting the feline spinal cord is lymphoma.

Causes and symptoms: Most affected cats are young (average age is twenty-four months), and most of these cats are concurrently infected with FeLV. In fact, the virus is believed to be the cause of the lymphoma.

Spinal lymphoma tends to grow slowly, progressing over several weeks or months. The clinical signs of spinal lymphoma vary depending on where in the spinal cord the tumor is located and how rapidly the tumor is growing. Tumors that involve the meninges (the membranes covering the spinal cord), the spinal nerves, or the nerve roots may cause varying degrees of pain, from mild discomfort to extreme sensitivity. Lameness, progressing to partial or total paralysis, is commonly seen.

Diagnosis and treatment: Diagnosis can be challenging and often requires advanced imaging techniques, such as a CT, an MRI, or a myelogram. As noted earlier, a myelogram is a procedure in which a dye is injected into the spinal canal to allow better visualization of the spinal cord. This procedure often reveals the location of the spinal tumor. Other tests, such as a complete blood count, a FeLV test, and a bone marrow analysis, may yield information supportive of the diagnosis.

Treatment depends on the location and severity of the tumor. Surgery may be warranted to relieve pressure on the spinal cord. Some tumors, such as a meningioma (a tumor arising from the membranes covering the spinal cord) may be treatable by surgical removal. However, the most common tumor—lymphoma—is usually not amenable to surgery. Currently, the recommended treatment for cats with spinal lymphoma is radiation and chemotherapy. Although cats may initially respond to treatment, the prognosis in general is poor, with most cats succumbing to their illness a few weeks or months after treatment.

Chapter 15

Cardiovascular and Respiratory Disorders and Diseases

By Arnold Plotnick, DVM

The cardiovascular system includes the heart and the blood vessels (arteries, veins, and capillaries). This system is responsible for pumping and delivering blood to the rest of the body. This system is of vital importance because the blood contains oxygen, nutrients, hormones, and antibodies, all of which are essential substances for survival. The respiratory system is usually divided into the upper respiratory system (nasal cavity and sinuses) and the lower respiratory system (bronchi and lungs). The respiratory system is closely affiliated with the cardiovascular system. The heart pumps blood to the lungs, and the lungs give off carbon dioxide and take up oxygen, which is then delivered to the rest of the body via the circulatory system. Respiratory illnesses in cats are very common, running the gamut from minor illnesses, such as viral respiratory infections, to potentially serious illnesses, such as asthma. Disorders of the heart are also surprisingly common and are a significant cause of mortality in cats.

Cardiovascular Disorders and Diseases

Heart disease is a common occurrence in cats and can occur at any age. Disorders of the heart valves occur, but are much less common in cats than they are in dogs. Disorders of the heart muscle itself, however, are very common and can have serious health consequences. Fortunately, the most common heart disorder in humans—atherosclerosis (build up of plaque in the blood vessels that supply the heart)—is almost never seen in cats.

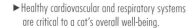
► Healthy cardiovascular and respiratory systems are critical to a cat's overall well-being.

Valve disorders

The heart has four valves. The mitral valve is on the left side of the heart, between the left atrium and left ventricle. The tricuspid valve is on the right side of the heart, between the right atrium and the right ventricle. The pulmonic valve mediates blood flow from the right ventricle to the lungs, and the aortic valve controls blood flow from the left ventricle, out through the aorta to the rest of the body. The job of these valves is to keep blood flowing in the proper direction. If the valves become defective and malfunction, the tight seal that the valve makes is compromised, and blood may escape around the valve.

Causes and symptoms: Valve disorders are often detected as heart murmurs during physical examinations. Valvular defects can lead to heart enlargement and eventual congestive heart failure (CHF). This can happen in younger animals as a result of a congenital malformation or in older animals as a natural result of aging. Valve disorders are much less common in cats than in dogs, however, and CHF secondary to valvular problems is rare.

Diagnosis and treatment: Definitive diagnosis of a valvular disorder is made via cardiac ultrasound. Medication may or may not be prescribed by your veterinarian, depending on whether there is concurrent heart disease present.

Hypertrophic Cardiomyopathy

Cardiovascular disease is the number one cause of death in people in the United States. Most cat owners probably don't realize that heart diseases are also quite common in cats. In fact, disorders of the *myocardium* (heart muscle) are the major cause of heart failure in cats. The most common feline cardiomyopathy (heart muscle disorder) is *hypertrophic cardiomyopathy* (HCM). This condition occurs when the heart muscle, especially that of the left ventricle, becomes excessively thickened.

The job of the left ventricle is to pump blood out through the aorta to the rest of the body. When the wall of the ventricle becomes thickened and stiff, the ventricle cannot hold as much blood, and less blood is sent to the body with every pump.

Heart Murmurs

A heart murmur is an abnormal sound that is caused by turbulent blood flow through the heart. Although the presence of a murmur is not necessarily something to be worried about, all murmurs should be investigated because they could be the first sign of serious heart disease. Cardiac problems that can cause a heart murmur include cardiomyopathies (diseases of the heart muscle), disorders of the heart valves, and congenital defects.

Murmurs are graded on a scale from 1 to 6, with 1 being barely audible and 6 being intense enough to cause vibrations that can be felt by touching the chest. The intensity of the murmur does not correlate with the severity of the condition, and not all murmurs are indicative of heart disease. Heart murmurs can be the result of other systemic diseases or conditions, for example, anemia or high blood pressure. In some cases, a murmur may be completely benign and not be associated with any illness at all. Murmurs are common in older cats. Some kittens are born with murmurs and then outgrow them. To investigate the cause of a murmur, diagnostic tests are necessary and may include blood tests, blood pressure measurement, chest X-rays, an EKG, and an echocardiogram (ultrasound examination of the heart).

Frequently, the septum (the wall that separates the right side of the heart from the left) becomes thickened, too. This makes it even more difficult for blood to flow out of the aorta and puts a big strain on the heart. The chamber above the left ventricle, called the left atrium, tries to pump blood into the thickened left ventricle, but it is not easy because the thickened ventricle is stiff and much less compliant. This causes increased pressure in the atrium, and the atrium gets larger and larger. The increased pressure in the atrium may be transmitted to the lungs, resulting in fluid retention in the lungs and eventual CHF.

Causes and symptoms: Although there are specific conditions that can cause the heart muscle to become thicker (such as hyperthyroidism and high blood pressure), HCM is considered to be a primary disease because in most cases an inciting cause cannot be found. In Maine Coons, however, a genetic predisposition for HCM has been discovered. Eventually, through selective breeding, the gene responsible for HCM in Maine Coons may be eliminated. If HCM is identified in any cat, it is advisable not to breed the affected cat and to carefully screen closely related family members. The majority of cases, however, are domestic shorthaired cats without any family history of disease.

Cats of either sex can be affected, although males are predisposed. Most cases occur in middle age, usually between the ages of four and eight, although the disease has been reported in cats as young as three months and as old as seventeen years.

Diagnosis and treatment: The clinical signs of HCM can vary greatly from cat to cat. Some cats present with nonspecific signs, such as lethargy, decreased appetite, weight loss, hiding, and reluctance to socialize with the owner and with other cats. Coughing, which is common in dogs with heart disease, is rare in affected cats. In a majority of cases (55 percent), cats have no clinical symptoms, and a diagnosis is pursued only after some abnormality—a heart murmur or an abnormal

rhythm—is detected during a routine physical exam when the veterinarian listens to the chest with the stethoscope. A lesser but substantial number of cats are discovered to have HCM when they present to the veterinarian already in CHF. An even more upsetting (and dire) scenario is the discovery that a cat has HCM when it presents as an emergency with sudden painful hind limb paralysis. This devastating complication of HCM occurs when a blood clot (also known as a thrombus) forms within the left atrium and a small piece of this clot (called an embolus) breaks off from the main clot and travels down the aorta, becoming lodged at the end of the aorta and rapidly cutting off the blood supply to the legs. This condition is known as arterial thromboembolism (ATE).

X-rays, electrocardiograms (EKG), and echocardiograms (cardiac ultrasound) are the common diagnostic tests performed on animals with suspected heart disorders. For cats with HCM, however, x-rays are of limited usefulness. X-rays tend to be normal in the early stages of the disease. As the disease progresses and the cat goes into heart failure, pulmonary edema (fluid in the lungs), and/or pleural effusion (fluid in the chest cavity) may be visible on the x-rays. Although most EKGs are normal in cats with HCM, an EKG can provide the veterinarian with useful information because disturbances in the electrical conduction system of the heart occur in about 30 percent of cats with HCM.

Ultimately, a definitive diagnosis of HCM is achieved by means of echocardiography (cardiac ultrasound). Ultrasound allows for evaluation of many parameters, including the size of the chambers, the thickness of the heart muscle, the function of the valves, how well the heart is contracting, how efficiently the blood is flowing through the heart, and whether there is a blood clot in the left atrium.

The goals of treating cats with HCM are to improve the ability of the ventricle to fill, prevent or delay the onset of CHF, and prevent such

◄ Although cats of either sex can contract HCM, it is more common in males.

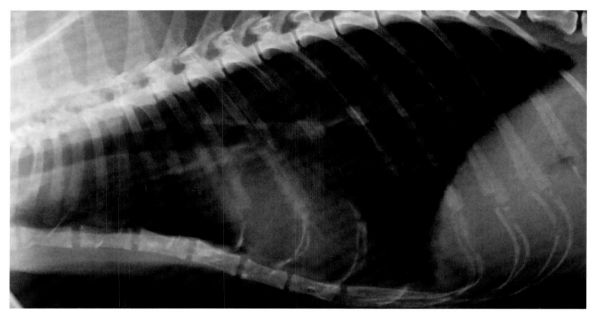

▲ Radiograph showing a cat's lungs.

complications as arterial thromboembolism. Medications may be prescribed to slow down the heart (beta blockers), so that there is adequate time for the stiff ventricles to fill, and to relax the heart muscle (calcium channel blockers), again to facilitate filling of the stiffened chambers. Cats who are in heart failure and have fluid accumulation in their lungs often benefit from having diuretics administered. Another category of drugs, called angiotensin converting enzyme (ACE) inhibitors, has been shown in some studies to be useful in managing HCM. Which drug or drugs are prescribed depends on the ultrasound findings, whether the cat has concurrent CHF, and the personal preference and experience of the veterinarian or veterinary cardiologist. To reduce the chance of a thrombus forming within the heart, veterinarians often give cats medications that reduce the blood's ability to clot, such as aspirin, heparin, or clopidogrel (Plavix).

The prognosis for HCM varies. Hypertrophic cardiomyopathy can progress rapidly in some cats, whereas in others the condition remains relatively static for years. Many cats will have slowly progressive disease that ultimately leads to CHF.

A significant number of cats with HCM will be fine for a while, only to develop sudden rear limb paralysis due to ATE. When the heart muscle becomes thickened, the coronary arteries have trouble supplying enough blood to the heart muscle. The areas of inadequate blood supply may serve as a site where abnormal rhythms are generated. These abnormal heart rhythms can lead to fainting, or in some instances, sudden death.

Cats who develop blood clots tend to do poorly. Those who survive their initial twenty-four hours have a median survival time of two to six months. Cats with CHF fare somewhat better, surviving for three to eighteen months. Those with no symptoms survive, on average, three to five years after the diagnosis.

Arterial Thromboembolism

A significant number of cats with HCM develop ATE. This is one of the most serious complications associated with HCM and is one of the most common causes of hind limb paralysis in the cat. Cats with HCM are at increased risk of developing a blood clot (also known as a *thrombus*) in the left atrium of the heart.

Causes and symptoms: Arterial thromboembolism occurs when a piece of this thrombus—the piece is called an *embolus*—breaks free from the main thrombus and enters the circulation. The embolus eventually becomes lodged in a vessel, cutting off the blood supply to that area. Smaller emboli may travel into small arteries and affect blood flow to a limb or to other sites such as the brain, lungs, or kidneys. The vast majority (more than 90 percent) of emboli become lodged at "the aortic trifurcation"—the area at the very end of the aorta where it branches off to supply the left and right rear legs and the tail. This area has also been called the "saddle" area, and a blood clot lodged in this area is sometimes termed a "saddle thrombus." Cats are literally normal one second and paralyzed in the next second.

Diagnosis and treatment: A diagnosis is usually made based on clinical signs at presentation. Most cats present with acute onset of lameness, partial paralysis, or complete paralysis of the affected limbs. The hind limbs are often cold, and the nail beds are cyanotic, that is, they have a bluish tinge due to lack of blood flow. No pulses can be felt in the rear legs. Many of the cats with ATE show signs of shock. Virtually all cats with ATE are in obvious and considerable pain, as evidenced by excitement, frenzy, vocalization, rolling, and panting.

Some cats diagnosed with ATE were diagnosed with HCM not long before. Others may have been diagnosed with HCM months or even years before, with no clinical signs until that day. Some cats with CHF that is well controlled may suddenly fall victim to ATE. The majority of cats with ATE, however, present without any evidence of preexisting heart disease. For these cats, diagnostic tests such as cardiac ultrasound invariably confirm that there is heart pathology and that a blood clot is present within the left atrium. Ultrasound machines are able to evaluate arterial blood flow. During the cardiac evaluation, the ultrasound probe can be placed on the inside of the thigh to evaluate arterial blood flow to the rear limbs. An inability to detect arterial blood flow supports the diagnosis of ATE.

The ultimate goal of managing the acute episode of ATE is to pull the cat through this initial critical phase. Controlling pain, improving cardiac blood flow, and treating CHF if present are the top priorities. Restoring blood flow to the rear limbs

▼Arterial thromboembolism is a serious complication of HCM and one of the most common causes of paralysis in cats.

is of secondary importance; making sure the cat survives takes center stage. Many cats do not survive the initial episode; they either die or are euthanized within the first 48 hours of the onset of paralysis.

Pain control is essential because these cats are in great discomfort. Improving circulation using intravenous fluids is of paramount importance. This can be a challenge, however, because fluid therapy must be administered cautiously in cats with heart disease.

Acepromazine, a sedative, has been used by some clinicians to decrease anxiety and improve blood flow to the affected areas by dilating the blood vessels. Anticoagulants are recommended during the acute crisis to prevent any new thrombi from forming in the heart and to prevent the embolus from growing in size and further reducing the blood flow to the affected region. Drugs are available that have the potential to dissolve a thrombus or embolus. They are expensive, however, and can have significant side effects. Whether these drugs offer any real benefit remains controversial. Without treatment, in the natural course of disease, blood flow will often resume to the affected area as the body eventually dissolves the clot on its own. Vessels in the tissues adjacent to the blocked vessel experience a gradual increase in blood flow as they learn to adapt to their injury.

Preventing ATE is a logical goal, but few studies on how to do so have been performed in veterinary medicine, and therapeutic recommendations are lacking. Platelets play a significant role in the development of ATE, and antiplatelet drugs such as aspirin are a logical choice for prevention of ATE. Aspirin treatment, however, has not been reported to result in dramatic reduction in the prevalence of ATE. Clopidogrel (Plavix), an antiplatelet drug commonly used in humans, has recently been shown to be safe and effective in helping reduce the incidence of ATE.

HCM is a frustrating disorder to treat, and it becomes even more frustrating when ATE complicates the picture. Although there is no predicting which cats with HCM will be stricken with ATE, continued research in the areas of prevention and treatment will allow for more successful management of this devastating disease in the future.

▼A cat who is breathing through her open mouth possibly has a respiratory illness.

Dilated Cardiomyopathy

Dilated cardiomyopathy (DCM) is a heart muscle disorder in which the walls of the right and left ventricles—the chambers that pump blood out of the heart—become thinner and thinner. As this happens, the contractions get weaker and weaker, and the heart is unable to pump blood with sufficient force, leading to heart failure.

Causes and symptoms: In 1987, researchers discovered that a deficiency in the amino acid taurine was a significant cause of DCM. Pet food manufacturers supplemented their diets with adequate amounts of taurine, and the incidence of DCM plunged. Now, very few cases can be attributed to taurine deficiency. Most cases diagnosed today are idiopathic; that is, they have no known cause.

The clinical signs of DCM may include poor appetite, lethargy, and inability to play or exercise. Cats in heart failure secondary to DCM may show labored breathing or a distended abdomen. Unfortunately, by the time DCM is diagnosed, nearly all cats are in CHF.

Diagnosis and treatment: A diagnosis of DCM is made after various tests are performed, such as chest x-rays, an EKG, and an echocardiogram. x-rays usually show an enlarged heart and may show patchy accumulations of fluid in the lungs (pulmonary edema) and enlarged veins around the heart. The EKG may be normal or may show an abnormal rhythm. The most informative test is the echocardiogram, which typically shows severe dilation of all chambers of the heart in combination with weak cardiac contractions. Blood levels of taurine should be evaluated in all cases of DCM.

Treatment may include drugs that help the heart contract more strongly, such as digitalis or pimobendan, as well other drugs to control CHF if present. Taurine supplementation is recommended for cats with low taurine levels. Periodic echocardiograms are necessary to monitor the course of the disease.

Cats with DCM secondary to taurine deficiency have an excellent prognosis if they receive taurine supplementation and their CHF is under control.

Change in Voice

Occasionally, cat owners will become aware of a change in their cat's voice. The most common cause is a viral upper respiratory infection. Most viral URIs result in runny eyes, snotty nose, and lots of sneezing. Occasionally, they result in laryngitis—a "sore throat"—and this can lead to hoarseness and a change in voice. Cats with oral tumors involving the throat or the vocal cords may experience a change or loss of voice. There is also a condition called laryngeal paralysis in which the cartilages and muscles that control the vocal folds in the throat become dysfunctional, causing the larynx to not open properly and leading to a change of voice. This is much more common in dogs than cats. Even though most cases are due to upper respiratory infections that are fairly benign, a change in voice should be evaluated by your veterinarian. He or she may want to sedate the cat and perform a thorough oral exam, looking at the back of the throat and even trying to pass an endotracheal tube down the trachea to see if there is a mass or other obstruction. X-rays may be necessary to look for masses that are in the trachea or in the neck.

Cats with idiopathic DCM and CHF have a guarded to poor prognosis. Medication helps stabilize the patient but doesn't alter the progression of the heart failure. Most cats survive only a few months after the diagnosis is made.

Respiratory System Disorders and Diseases

Disorders of the feline respiratory system can be generally divided into disorders of the upper respiratory system (the nasal cavity and sinuses) and the lower respiratory system (the airways and the lungs). Examples of disorders of the upper respiratory system include infections and nasopharyngeal polyps. Asthma is the most common lower respiratory disorder in cats. Infectious bronchitis is less common. Heartworm disease is frequently diagnosed in dogs but is still quite rare in cats.

Upper Respiratory Infections

Upper respiratory infections (URIs) are a common, contagious disease in cats.

Causes and symptoms: The most common cause of upper respiratory infections is viral, with the feline herpes virus (FHV) and the calicivirus (FCV) accounting for 80 percent of all feline URIs. Bacteria and fungi can also cause URIs in cats. Cats can acquire these infections through several means, including coming into contact with another cat who has a URI, contact with aerosolized virus particles when an infected cat sneezes, contact with items such as infected food or water bowls, or contact with human hands that have touched an ill cat. Young kittens are at greatest risk of infection. The most common way that kittens contract URIs is via nursing, around the time of weaning. Cats exposed to other sneezing and ill cats, such as in a shelter environment or a cattery, are also at increased risk, as are unvaccinated cats and cats with immunosuppressive disorders.

Once exposed to the virus, cats experience an incubation period lasting two to five days, after which signs of infection develop. These may include lethargy, decreased appetite, sneezing, conjunctivitis, watery discharge from the eyes and/ or nose, congestion, and fever. Corneal ulcers can develop, especially in cats infected with FHV. Ulcers in the mouth and on the tongue commonly develop in cats infected with FCV, and cats may drool as a result.

Diagnosis and treatment: Diagnosis of URI is based mainly on clinical signs. Determining specifically whether FHV, FCV, or both are responsible for the infection is rarely necessary because treatment is symptomatic regardless. Treatment is usually aimed at preventing a secondary bacterial infection from occurring by administering antibiotics. The amino acid lysine is thought to improve recovery from these infections and is often prescribed as well. Most cases resolve in five to fourteen days. In stubborn cases, antiviral drugs, such as famciclovir, can be administered. Cats with conjunctivitis or corneal ulcers may also require topical eye medications. Cats with severe nasal congestion may experience poor appetite because they cannot smell their food. These cats may need to be fed with a syringe or given appetite stimulants until the congestion resolves. Hospitalization is rarely necessary.

Once infected, cats become carriers of the virus and may periodically have bouts of URI during times of stress.

Vaccines against viral URIs are available. They can reduce the potential for infection in cats who have never been exposed to the virus. Most cats, however, are exposed to the virus during kittenhood and are carriers. Vaccination does not eliminate the carrier status of previously infected cats, and it does not prevent viral shedding. However, vaccinated cats experience milder symptoms when the virus reemerges from dormancy.

Using an Inhaler

Inhaled steroids are the most potent inhaled anti-inflammatory drugs available. Inhaled steroids like fluticasone (Flovent) are of a large molecular size and thus do not pass into the bloodstream when inhaled. As a result, they do not cause the unwanted side effects that pills or injections do. Many cat owners find that giving inhaled steroids is faster and seems to bother the cat less than trying to administer oral medication.

The inhaler for these drugs fits on one end of the chamber, and a specially designed facemask attaches onto the other end. Cat owners can be taught by their veterinarian to gently place the facemask over the cat's mouth and nose, and the cat is allowed to inhale and exhale the medication seven to ten times with the mask in place. The facemask needs to fit properly. Flat-faced cats (Persians, Himalayans) may have difficulty achieving a tight fit.

The Original Cat Fancy Cat Bible

▲ Unfortunately, asthma is a common illness of cats.

X-rays of the skull may be useful in making or confirming the diagnosis. Polyps that have invaded the ear are diagnosed by visualizing the polyp deep in the ear canal using an instrument called an otoscope. In some cats, sedation is required for a proper, thorough ear exam. If the polyp is located deep in the middle ear, a computed tomography (CT) scan or magnetic resonance imaging (MRI) can give additional information as to its full extent.

Polyps located above the soft palate that extend into the back of the throat are treated by grasping them with a hemostat at the base of the polyp and plucking them out. This usually causes instant improvement in breathing and a complete resolution of clinical signs. Polyps that extend into the middle ear require a more complex surgery. The prognosis for recovery is excellent, although if the polyp is not completely removed there is a possibility of recurrence.

Asthma

Asthma in humans is a lower airway disease that causes people to cough and wheeze and limits their ability to exercise. These clinical signs occur because the airways in asthmatic humans are hyperreactive and may undergo spontaneous constriction when exposed to certain stimuli. A remarkably similar condition exists in cats.

Causes and symptoms: Asthmatic cats experience recurrent bouts of coughing, wheezing, and labored breathing. The condition affects approximately 1 percent of the general cat population, and more than 5 percent of Siamese cats. Some cats have only a brief history of coughing episodes before presenting with acute, severe respiratory compromise, the so-called asthma attack. When not having episodes of coughing or wheezing, most cats behave completely normally.

Clinical signs of asthma in cats may be acute or chronic. In acute cases, there is a history of sudden onset of labored breathing. In most cases, however, asthmatic cats are presented to veterinarians with a complaint of chronic coughing.

Diagnosis and treatment: There are no simple laboratory tests that can diagnose feline asthma with 100 percent certainty. A diagnosis is usually made

Nasopharyngeal Polyps

Nasopharyngeal polyps are benign masses that may arise in a cat's nose, pharynx (back of the throat), or middle ear. Those arising in the middle ear may extend through the eardrum, into the external ear canal.

Causes and symptoms: Why nasopharyngeal polyps occur is unknown, but they're most commonly seen in young cats; the average age at the time of diagnosis is one and a half years. The clinical signs of a polyp vary, depending on the location. Polyps in the nasal cavity cause noisy breathing or snoring, nasal discharge, coughing, and sometimes trouble swallowing. Those that occur or extend into the ear canal may cause ear infection, ear discharge, and vestibular signs (loss of balance, tilted head).

Diagnosis and treatment: In many instances, a diagnosis can be achieved via oral examination with the cat under anesthesia or heavy sedation. The soft palate is pulled back with a surgical instrument, and if a polyp is present it is usually readily apparent.

based on the history, physical examination findings, and x-rays of the chest. Radiographs (x-rays) provide the most information for veterinarians presented with a coughing cat. Radiographs help eliminate other causes of coughing and wheezing, such as heart failure, pneumonia, lung cancer, and inhaled foreign bodies. Identification of thickened air passages (seen as "doughnuts" and "train tracks" on an X-ray) is the most important radiographic finding in a diagnosis of feline asthma. Other helpful tests include a complete blood count and a heartworm test. Occasionally, if clinical signs, x-rays, and blood tests are ambiguous, other tests such as bronchoscopy may be necessary. Bronchoscopy involves the use of an instrument with a tiny fiberoptic camera (the bronchoscope) to examine the inside of the lungs and collect specimens for cytology or biopsy.

The ideal treatment of asthma would be to limit the cat's exposure to the offending allergen. However, it is often impossible to definitively determine which allergen is triggering the bronchitis. People should not smoke or apply perfume around asthmatic cats, and dusty cat litters should be avoided.

Corticosteroids are the most effective long-term treatment of feline asthma. These drugs are anti-inflammatory, and they help in removing the inflammatory cells that surround the airways in affected cats. Humans who receive oral steroids often experience serious side effects that may preclude their routine use. Fortunately, cats are fairly resistant to the health-threatening side effects of corticosteroids. Prednisolone, initially given at high doses for two weeks and then slowly tapered down to every-other-day therapy, remains the most consistent, reliable, and effective treatment for asthma in cats.

Bronchodilators are drugs that reverse airway constriction, allowing the air passages to open. Bronchodilators may be used as adjunct therapy, but they shouldn't be used as sole treatment. Chronic inflammation is the root of the problem, and treatment of this inflammation using steroids is the cornerstone of therapy.

Some cat owners find it nearly impossible to orally medicate their cat. In this situation, an injectable long-acting steroid may be given. This is a less desirable approach to treatment, however, as these injections vary in how long they last (anywhere from three weeks to three months) and may be associated with side effects such as transient diabetes. When the effects of the injection wear off, the clinical signs usually return.

Administration of medication via inhaler is an alternative therapeutic option. Metered dose inhalers (MDIs) are commonly used in asthmatic humans. They allow high concentrations of drugs

▶ Using a dust-free litter, such as wood pellets, can help reduce the incidence of feline asthma attacks.

Steroids, such as prednisolone, are very effective treatment for feline asthma.

to be delivered directly to the lungs, avoiding or minimizing systemic side effects. Inhaled drugs relieve symptoms of asthma much faster than oral or injectable drugs. The inhalers are designed for people to coordinate the activation of the device during a slow, deep inhalation for optimal lung delivery. Obviously, this cannot be controlled in children or in animals. Addition of a spacer allows the MDI to be used in children and pets. The spacer is a plastic chamber about the size of an inner roll of toilet paper. (See Using an Inhaler.)

Feline asthma is not a curable disease. Recent advances in our understanding of the disorder, however, have allowed veterinarians to devise more effective treatment plans, and cats are breathing a little easier as a result.

Chronic Bronchitis

The bronchi are the tubes that transport air from the trachea (windpipe) to the lungs. Within the lungs, the bronchi divide into smaller branches called bronchioles. Inflammation of the bronchi and bronchioles is called *bronchitis*, and when the inflammation is persistent it is called *chronic bronchitis*. Although chronic bronchitis is more common in dogs than in cats, some cats do suffer from it.

Causes and symptoms: The cause of most cases of chronic bronchitis is not known; in some instances, the condition develops as a result of a longstanding infection. Chronic exposure to environmental irritants, such as cigarette smoke, has been suggested as another possible cause of chronic bronchitis in cats. Cats with chronic bronchitis may show clinical signs related to the respiratory system, including coughing, rapid and/or labored breathing, and wheezing, as well as general signs of illness such as poor appetite and lethargy. The respiratory compromise may affect the cat's ability to play or exert herself.

Diagnosis and treatment: Diagnosis is usually made through evaluation of chest x-rays. In some instances, more advanced diagnostic tests are required, the best one being bronchoscopy. For this test, the cat is anesthetized and a long thin snake-like tube with a fiberoptic camera on the end (the bronchoscope) is inserted into the trachea and then down farther into the bronchi. This allows visualization of the airways, where samples of material from the airways can be evaluated for cytology, biopsy, and culture.

Treatment of chronic bronchitis depends on the diagnostic findings. It an infectious agent is isolated from the culture specimen, treatment with antibiotics is warranted. Chronic bronchitis that is inflammatory in nature often requires anti-inflammatory medications such as corticosteroids. Bronchodilators (drugs that widen the air passages) and cough suppressants may be indicated, depending on the severity of the condition. Chronic bronchitis cannot be cured, but it is often controllable through the use of medication. Obesity worsens the condition; cats should be maintained

Cardiovascular and Respiratory Disorders and Diseases

at their ideal weight. Environmental irritants such as chemical fumes, dust from renovations, and cigarette smoke can further irritate the airways and should be minimized.

Heartworm Disease

The name *heartworm disease* is somewhat of a misnomer in cats; the heartworms primarily affect the lungs, not the heart. Heartworm disease is usually thought of as a dog disease. Feline heartworm disease (FHD), however, is more prevalent than once believed. It is now understood that whenever heartworm infection exists in the local canine population, it will also be found in the feline population. There are significant differences, though, between FHD and its canine counterpart.

Causes and symptoms: Cats acquire heartworm disease when a mosquito carrying heartworm larvae bites the cat. The larvae enter the skin through the bite wound and develop into juvenile worms. The immature worms enter a blood vessel and travel in the bloodstream. When they finally arrive at the lungs, they cause a dramatic inflammatory reaction. In many cases, the immune system of the cat reacts against the juvenile worms causing them to die, which results in an even more severe inflammatory response. In some cats, all of the juvenile worms die and the cat clears the infection. In other cats, a few juvenile worms escape destruction and develop into adult worms. Although most cats end up with only one or two adult worms in the pulmonary arteries of the lungs, even a small number of worms are potentially life-threatening.

The adult worms suppress the immune system, allowing them to live in the heart or lungs for months or even years, often causing no problems. When the adult worms die, however, a major, severe inflammatory reaction can occur. Pieces of dying heartworms can obstruct the pulmonary vessels, resulting in thromboembolism, which often leads to severe illness or fatal acute lung injury. The respiratory signs that develop when the juvenile worms arrive at the lungs and subsequently die are often misdiagnosed as asthma or bronchitis, when in fact it is part of a syndrome termed *heartworm-*

associated respiratory disease (HARD). Even if the cat clears the infection, the initial damage to the lungs can be significant. Cats who go outdoors and have increased contact with mosquitoes are at increased risk of infection, but that doesn't mean that indoor-only cats are safe from the disease. In one study, 28 percent of cats diagnosed with heartworms were indoor-only cats.

The signs of heartworm disease vary widely. Many cats show no clinical signs at all. Most cats have signs of respiratory disease such as coughing, wheezing, or rapid or labored breathing. Other possible clinical signs include intermittent vomiting (unrelated to eating), diarrhea, poor appetite, weight loss, seizures, and fainting. A heart murmur is sometimes heard on physical exam.

Diagnosis and treatment: Heartworm disease can be difficult to diagnose in cats. The most useful tests are heartworm serology, chest x-rays, and echocardiography. Serologic tests involve testing the blood for heartworm antibodies or heartworm antigens. A positive antibody test means that the

▼ In cats, heartworm actually affects the lungs more than the heart. Keeping your cat indoors lowers her risk of contracting heartworm.

▲ Heartworm is completely preventable using monthly oral or topical medications.

cat has been exposed to heartworms but doesn't necessarily mean that the cat is currently infected with heartworms. A positive antigen test indicates that the cat is currently infected with adult female worms. In most cases, both tests are run to provide as much information as possible. Chest x-rays may provide additional information but are rarely definitive in making the diagnosis. In cats who are infected with adult heartworms, an experienced ultrasonographer may detect the worms via ultrasound. Detection of worms in this way allows for a definitive diagnosis.

Treatment of FHD varies depending on the individual cat. If the cat shows no clinical signs despite being infected, the cat should be closely monitored. The anti-inflammatory drug prednisolone is often administered to these nonsymptomatic cats in tapering doses, as medical supportive therapy. Cats who become acutely ill from heartworm disease need more aggressive medical attention, which may include hospitalization, intravenous steroids and fluids, drugs to relax the airways, and supplemental

oxygen. The drugs that are used in dogs to kill off the adult worms are, unfortunately, not safe for use in cats. If adult worms have been identified via ultrasound, surgical removal of the worms by inserting a special catheter into right jugular vein and advancing it down toward the pulmonary vessels may be attempted in cats who are infected with several worms or in cats in critical condition from their illness. This procedure is very difficult and must be done by an experienced specialist at a referral center.

Heartworm disease is completely preventable. Monthly preventatives, either oral or topical, should be administered to cats at risk (that is, those in heartworm endemic areas). Both indoor and outdoor cats should be protected. Heartworm preventatives should be administered starting thirty days before the estimated onset of mosquito season and continued for thirty days after mosquito season has ended. In fact, the best option is to administer the monthly preventative every month, year-round. In endemic areas, prevention should begin in kittens starting at eight weeks of age.

Chapter 16

Digestive and Urinary Disorders and Diseases

By Arnold Plotnick, DVM

All cat owners know firsthand that cats pee and poop. Occasionally, they also puke and have the runs. Most cat owners try not to think about these ghastly things. However, when faced with a malodorous mound of diarrhea in the litter box, stepping into a pile of cat vomit upon coming home from work, or discovering that Tigger has urinated on your computer keyboard, thinking about such delightful topics becomes unavoidable. Read ahead, for a candid description of the disorders of these two prominent body systems: digestive and urinary.

Digestive System Disorders and Diseases

An occasional bout of digestive system disorders such as colitis, constipation, diarrhea, and vomiting may not be anything to worry about, but persistent occurrences can be symptoms of something serious, which is why it's important to understand both common and uncommon causes behind these problems. It can be even more crucial to recognize the symptoms of critical diseases ranging from inflammatory bowel diseases to gastrointestinal (GI) cancer.

Colitis

Colitis is defined as an inflammation of the colon. An occasional episode of colitis is not uncommon in cats; recurrent episodes, however, may signal a more serious problem and should be addressed by your veterinarian.

▶ All cats will experience an occasional digestive upset. Don't be overly concerned unless the episodes become frequent.

Causes and symptoms: There are several possible causes for colitis, including a sudden change in diet, eating something unusual, overeating, inflammatory bowel disease, food allergy, colon cancer, bacterial infection, parasites such as *Giardia*, and stress. Cats are very sensitive to changes in their environment and may experience a bout of colitis in response to a disruption in their routine (for example, relatives visiting for the holidays, a move to a new home, a drastic change to the owner's work schedule, a new cat in the household). Cats with colitis usually have diarrhea, often with blood or mucus in the feces. They may strain while defecating and may visit the litter box more frequently than normal. There may be vomiting, too, often at the same time the cat is straining to defecate or soon afterward. There is usually a sense of urgency associated with defecation, and some cats cannot make it to their litter box in time and will defecate on the floor.

Diagnosis and treatment: To diagnose the cause of colitis, your veterinarian may need to run several tests, including a complete blood count, chemistry panel, urinalysis, fecal examination, and fecal culture. x-rays or abdominal ultrasound may be warranted, and in some cases colonoscopy may be necessary to obtain a diagnosis. This requires general anesthesia.

Treatment of colitis depends on the cause. Treatment may include changing the diet to a high-fiber or hypoallergenic one or administering probiotics, dewormers, antibiotics, or anti-inflammatory drugs. In many cases, a cause cannot be identified and cats are treated symptomatically. Typically, this involves withholding food for twelve to twenty-four hours and then gradually introducing a bland, nonirritating diet followed by gradual reintroduction of the cat's normal diet. Sudden changes to the diet should be avoided, and stressful events (any abrupt change in environment) should be kept to a minimum to avoid recurrences.

▲ A cat with colitis may run to her box but not quite make it in time.

Constipation

Constipation is defined as infrequent or difficult defecation with passage of hard, dry feces. All cats experience a bout of two of constipation over their lifetimes. Recurrent constipation, however, is not normal, and you should consult your veterinarian about it.

Causes and symptoms: There are many causes of constipation, the most common being dietary. Diets low in fiber may predispose cats to constipation. Cats with limited access to water may develop very firm stool. Cats who swallow a lot of hair when grooming may also develop constipation. Cats may retain feces and become constipated if their litter box is dirty. Some drugs can cause constipation. Constipation can occur if the passage of feces is blocked, perhaps by a tumor or other stricture. Cats may avoid defecation and become constipated if defecation is painful, for example, if cats have an anal sac abscess or a pelvic fracture. Certain metabolic, endocrine, and neurologic disorders can also result in constipation.

Constipation should be suspected if very little or no feces are seen in the litter box, or if the cat is observed to be straining to defecate yet produces little or no feces. On occasion, a small amount of liquid feces will be produced after prolonged straining; this can be mistaken for diarrhea, when it is actually just some excess mucus produced by the irritated colon. Some constipated cats will show decreased appetite or occasional vomiting.

Diagnosis and treatment: A diagnosis of constipation is made based on a description of the cat's defecation behavior along with physical exam findings. On examination, most constipated cats have a large amount of feces that can be felt by the veterinarian. x-rays of the abdomen can confirm this and give information regarding the extent of the constipation. Blood, urine, and fecal tests may be warranted to provide further information as to the possible cause of the constipation.

If an underlying cause for the constipation can be identified, it should be corrected if possible. A change in diet may be advisable. Laxatives or stool softeners may be prescribed. Cats with significant impaction of feces may require brief hospitalization and one or more enemas.

Diarrhea

Like vomiting, an occasional bout of diarrhea in cats is not uncommon and is usually no cause for concern. Persistent diarrhea, however, is not a normal and requires veterinary attention. Left untreated, diarrhea can result in dehydration and electrolyte imbalances.

Causes and symptoms: There are many possible causes of diarrhea in cats. Some common causes include a sudden change in diet, eating inappropriate items, GI infections (bacterial, viral, protozoal), parasites, food allergy, pancreatitis, and inflammatory bowel disease. The presence of blood and/or mucus in the diarrhea indicates that the large intestine is involved and that the cat may have colitis. Depending on the cause, cats with diarrhea may have no other signs of illness other than loose stool, or they may be systemically ill and show signs such as fever, poor appetite, weight loss, and vomiting.

Diagnosis and treatment: Cats who are systemically ill should be checked by a veterinarian. Acute cases may respond to symptomatic therapy such as withholding food for twelve to twenty-four hours and then feeding a highly digestible prescription diet. Simple cases of intestinal parasites may only require routine deworming. Some cats cannot tolerate a particular brand of food or a particular form of the diet (dry vs. canned); in these cases, switching to a more appropriate diet resolves the problem. Cats with diarrhea for several days may require subcutaneous fluids and antidiarrheal medications. Over-the-counter antidiarrheal drugs intended for humans should not be given to cats with diarrhea because many of these medications contain substances that may be dangerous or toxic to your cat. Always consult your veterinarian.

Depending on the severity and duration of the diarrhea, your veterinarian may want to perform some tests such as a complete blood count, chemistry panel, urinalysis, fecal exam, fecal culture, abdominal x-rays, ultrasound, and perhaps

▼ Swallowing a lot of hair during grooming puts a cat at risk of hairballs and constipation.

endoscopy, colonoscopy, or exploratory abdominal surgery to obtain a diagnosis. Treatment of diarrhea will vary depending on the cause. Infectious causes may require antibiotics or other antimicrobial drugs. Food allergy often responds to a hypoallergenic diet. More serious conditions such as GI cancer may require surgery and/or chemotherapy. As with chronic vomiting, the prognosis for chronic diarrhea depends on the cause.

Vomiting

Every cat vomits occasionally. Most of the time, there is a harmless explanation for it, such as a sudden change in diet, eating too fast, or hairballs. In some instances, however, vomiting can be a serious sign of illness; consult with your veterinarian.

Causes and symptoms: Cats can vomit from a GI disorder such as food allergy or inflammatory bowel disease. They can also vomit from systemic disorders that have nothing to do with the GI system, such as kidney disease; if the kidneys can't remove toxins from the bloodstream, the toxins accumulate, leading to nausea and vomiting. Other potential causes of vomiting include intestinal parasites, diabetes, motion sickness, pancreatitis, heartworm disease, ingestion of foreign bodies, liver failure, and constipation.

An acute bout of vomiting in a cat who seems normal otherwise is seldom a cause for concern and can be treated symptomatically at home by withholding food for a few hours and then gradually reintroducing the diet. Cats who have vomited multiple times in one day or several days in a row may need to be examined by your veterinarian.

Diagnosis and treatment: Because vomiting has so many potential causes, diagnosing the reason for the vomiting can be challenging. Your veterinarian will likely want to run a number of tests, such as a complete blood count, chemistry panel, urinalysis, fecal exam, x-rays, and perhaps ultrasound or endoscopy. In some cases, abdominal surgery is necessary to make a definitive diagnosis.

Treatment of vomiting depends on the underlying cause. Some cases, such as food allergy, can be treated with a simple diet change. Mild cases may require subcutaneous (injected under the skin) fluids, antivomiting drugs, and a prescription diet designed for cats with GI problems. More severe cases, such as GI cancer, may require surgery and chemotherapy. The prognosis will vary depending on the cause.

Inflammatory Bowel Disease

Inflammatory bowel disease (IBD) is an uncontrolled or excessive inflammatory response resulting in the infiltration of inflammatory cells into various segments of the GI tract. Most affected cats tend to be middle-aged or older, although any age cat can be affected. Inflammatory bowel disease is often mistakenly called irritable bowel syndrome.

Causes and symptoms: The most common symptom of feline IBD is weight loss. This may be accompanied by a decreased appetite, vomiting, or diarrhea. In most cats, physical examination tends to be normal. Occasionally, thickened or fluid-filled intestines are evident when the abdomen is examined. Routine laboratory tests tend to be normal. Increased liver enzymes are occasionally reported in cases of feline IBD and may indicate that the cat has concurrent inflammation of the liver and bile ducts (cholangiohepatitis) and/or pancreatitis.

▼ Cats who eat strange or new foods often develop upset stomachs.

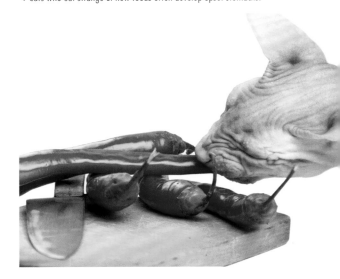

Ingested Foreign Bodies

A foreign body is a nonfood object that results in a GI problem when eaten. Dogs are much less discreet than cats about what they put in their mouths and will often be found to have ingested rubber balls, toys, clothing, corn cobs, coins, and so on. Cats tend to avoid solid objects. The majority of foreign bodies cats ingest are strings, ribbons, thread, and rubber bands. These are often referred to as "linear" foreign bodies. Gastrointestinal foreign bodies can become lodged in the GI tract and cause a life-threatening GI obstruction. Cats of any age are susceptible, but young cats (less than two years old) are particularly vulnerable. Although strings and ribbons can sometimes pass through the GI tract intact, in most cases they get lodged, resulting in serious digestive problems.

The reason why linear foreign bodies can cause so much damage is the manner in which they cause an intestinal obstruction. Usually, one end of the string becomes anchored, either by wrapping around the base of the tongue or by getting lodged in the pylorus (the part of the stomach that leads to the small intestine). The peristaltic waves generated by the intestines try to propel the free end of the string along the intestinal tract. Because the leading end of the string is lodged, it cannot be pulled along. What happens instead is that the intestines "climb" up the string, causing them to become pleated. Food cannot pass through the pleated intestines, resulting in an obstruction. Initially, the cat tries to eat, but vomits when the food encounters the obstruction. Eventually, the cat stops trying to eat. Cats may stop drinking as well. Most affected cats are extremely lethargic and may show signs of abdominal pain. The fluid loss from vomiting and not drinking can lead to severe dehydration.

A linear foreign body can sometimes be diagnosed during the physical exam because the string or thread may be visible lodged under the tongue. Abdominal x-rays may reveal a linear foreign body, although in many cases the foreign material is radiolucent and not visible on the x-ray. Pleating of the intestines is sometimes visible, suggesting the presence of a linear foreign body. A barium x-ray may be necessary to make the diagnosis. In this type of x-ray, the cat is given liquid barium, which appears bright white on the x-ray film. This type of x-ray will reveal if the intestines are pleated or bunched up and may reveal the foreign material itself.

Some foreign objects can be retrieved from the stomach using an endoscope. Grasping forceps can be inserted through the endoscope, and the foreign object can be grabbed. Linear foreign bodies, however, cannot be grabbed this way. They must be removed surgically. Most cats recover well after surgery. However, if the obstruction has been present for several days, the intestines can become inflamed, and toxins from the intestinal contents can seep through the intestinal wall, causing peritonitis. This is a serious complication that can lead to septic shock and death. Some cats who swallow thread will also swallow the sewing needle that is attached to it. If the needle perforates the intestine, this, too, can lead to peritonitis and septic shock.

Foreign body ingestion can be prevented by not allowing your cat access to objects that can be easily swallowed. If you suspect your cat has swallowed a string or other object, visit your veterinarian immediately. The sooner a diagnosis is made, the better the prognosis.

There are many disorders that can cause or mimic GI inflammation, including intestinal parasites, viral infections such as feline leukemia (FeLV) or feline immunodeficiency virus (FIV), food intolerance, food allergy, GI cancer, and metabolic disorders such as hyperthyroidism. These must be ruled out before a diagnosis of IBD can be considered.

Diagnosis and treatment: x-rays and ultrasound may be necessary to rule out a GI obstruction or an abdominal mass. x-rays alone, however, are ineffective for diagnosing IBD. Increased intestinal wall thickness and enlarged intestinal lymph nodes may be visible on ultrasound in suspected cases of IBD. These findings, however, are suggestive, not diagnostic, of IBD. Ultimately, a definitive diagnosis requires obtaining biopsy specimens from the GI tract.

Biopsies can be obtained either via endoscopy or exploratory surgery. Endoscopy is a procedure in which a long, flexible snakelike tube (the endoscope) enters the GI tract through the cat's mouth (upper

▲ Endoscopy or colonoscopy may be necessary for an accurate diagnosis of several digestive disorders.

GI endoscopy) or anus (lower GI endoscopy) to visualize the internal lining of the tract and obtain biopsy specimens. Endoscopy is less invasive than surgery and allows for direct examination of the mucosal surfaces (innermost lining) of the GI tract. The limitations of endoscopy are that the biopsy specimens obtained by this method consist only of the mucosal lining rather than a full-thickness biopsy of the intestinal tract, occasionally resulting in a misdiagnosis if the disease process primarily involves a deeper layer of the intestinal wall. Another potential disadvantage of endoscopy is that the endoscope can only reach the stomach and the duodenum (the first part of the small intestine). The jejunum (the next part) and the ileum (the final part) cannot be reached with an endoscope. In most cases of IBD, however, the GI tract is diffusely affected, and samples from the stomach and duodenum are sufficient to achieve a diagnosis.

Abdominal exploratory surgery may be more appropriate, however, if concurrent abnormalities are detected, such as increased liver enzymes, enlarged lymph nodes, or an abnormal liver or pancreas is seen on ultrasound, because biopsy specimens of these organs can be obtained at surgery. Both procedures—endoscopy and abdominal exploratory surgery—require general anesthesia.

The typical finding on biopsy specimens in cases of IBD is an increased number of inflammatory cells infiltrating the walls of the GI tract. Inflammatory cells may be detected in the stomach, the small intestine, or the colon. The degree of severity is often graded mild, moderate, or severe by the pathologist.

Treatment of feline IBD can be challenging. The goal of treatment is to identify and remove the cause of the inflammation and to suppress the immune response. This is usually accomplished through the use of immunosuppressive drugs and prescription diets. No single diet is suitable for all cats with IBD. For some cats, a highly digestible diet may be most beneficial. For others, a hypoallergenic diet may be the most effective. A hypoallergenic diet is a diet that contains a protein source to which the cat has not previously been exposed. Hypoallergenic diets alone, however, are usually inadequate at inducing long-lasting remission in cats with IBD, and immunosuppressive drugs are required.

Corticosteroids are the most commonly prescribed immunosuppressive drugs for the treatment of IBD. Typically, oral prednisolone is given for at least two to four weeks. If clinical signs resolve, the dosage of prednisolone is slowly tapered until the lowest effective dose is reached. In cases of severe inflammation in which a dietary change and prednisolone are ineffective, other immunosuppressive drugs can be added. Although IBD isn't curable, the prognosis is good for adequate control of the disease.

Megacolon

Megacolon is a condition involving extreme, irreversible dilation of the colon. The colon loses its ability to propel the feces, causing the feces to accumulate.

Causes and symptoms: Although chronic, recurrent bouts of constipation can eventually lead to megacolon, megacolon can also develop on its own, in cats with no history of previous constipation problems. In fact, this is the most common scenario.

Megacolon is seen most often in middle-aged cats; the average age is six years. It is more common in males. The clinical signs of megacolon are the same as those in cats with simple constipation: straining to defecate and passage of small amounts of hard, dry feces. As a result of a prolonged inability to defecate, cats may show systemic signs of illness such as poor appetite, lethargy, weight loss, abdominal discomfort, and vomiting.

Diagnosis and treatment: On physical examination, a very large colon full of hard feces is felt through the abdomen. x-rays of the abdomen can help determine the severity of the condition and whether there are predisposing factors such as a foreign body or a pelvic fracture.

Treatment for a cat with megacolon may initially require the administration of one or more enemas at the veterinary hospital. If enemas do not effectively remove the impacted feces, anesthesia and manual removal of feces will be necessary. Once the colon is emptied, long-term home management can be instituted. Motivated clients with cooperative cats may be taught to give their cat an enema at home, if warranted. Enemas available for over-the-counter purchase at human pharmacies should never be used on a cat at home. Instead, enemas designed specifically for companion animals should be obtained from your veterinarian. Your veterinarian or one of his veterinary technicians will demonstrate

Food Allergy

Although food allergy is not a very common problem in cats, it does occur. Most people assume that a sudden change in diet is necessary for a food allergy to develop, but, in fact, the opposite is true. In most cases, the allergy develops to ingredients that have been fed over a long period. The ingredients most commonly responsible for food allergies in cats are chicken, beef, and fish. Eggs and milk are also commonly implicated in food allergies in cats.

The cause of food allergy is genetic. It is an immunological condition that is passed on from one or both parents. Most cases of food allergy manifest themselves as skin problems—scaling, redness, scabs, ear infections, hair loss, and itching, especially around the head and face. Less commonly, food allergy results in GI signs, mainly vomiting and/or diarrhea.

Diagnosis of food allergy is achieved by performing what is called an "elimination food trial"; that is, feeding a hypoallergenic diet and seeing if the clinical signs resolve. A hypoallergenic diet is one that contains a protein source that the cat has never been exposed to, such as rabbit, venison, or duck. Absolutely no other food can be fed during this trial period or the results will be inconclusive. Gastrointestinal signs usually resolve in a few days. Dermatological signs may take several weeks (as long as eight to twelve weeks) before signs resolve. Once signs resolve, feeding the previous diet and seeing the clinical signs return is definitive proof of food allergy. Because there are so many other illnesses that can cause vomiting and/or diarrhea, your veterinarian may want to perform some diagnostic tests such as blood work and x-rays to rule out other reasons for vomiting and/or diarrhea.

Treatment of food allergy involves continued feeding of the hypoallergenic diet and avoiding foods containing the protein (or carbohydrate) source known to trigger the reaction. A recently developed diet that contains hydrolyzed protein may be more effective for cats prone to developing food allergy. Hydrolyzed protein is protein that has been converted into molecules small enough to evade detection by the immune system so that they cannot trigger an allergic reaction.

the proper technique for administering an enema in the home setting, if such treatment is necessary.

Long-term management of megacolon will likely involve a change in diet. Formerly, high-fiber diets were recommended; now, however, many veterinarians feel that a highly digestible diet may be equal or superior to high-fiber diets. Your veterinarian can make recommendations, and he or she will likely prescribe laxatives or stool softeners as well. Another treatment option is to give "prokinetic" drugs. These are drugs that help the colon to contract and propel the feces. Although most cases of megacolon respond to therapy initially, many cases become refractory to medical therapy. In these patients, surgical treatment in which most of the colon is removed may be the only remaining option. The prognosis for cats with megacolon is guarded.

Gastrointestinal Cancer

Gastrointestinal cancer can strike cats of any age, although it is mostly seen in older cats. Although the GI tract is susceptible to several types of cancer, lymphoma is the most common.

Causes and symptoms: Exactly why lymphoma develops in some cats is not clear, but viruses may play a role. The feline immunodeficiency virus is associated with an increased risk of lymphoma. Cats infected with FIV are 5.6 times more likely to develop lymphoma than are FIV-negative cats. Infection with FeLV dramatically increases the risk of developing lymphoma; FeLV-positive cats are 62 times more likely to develop lymphoma than their negative counterparts. Most cats who develop GI lymphoma, however, are negative for these two viruses.

Gastrointestinal lymphoma usually involves the small intestine. The stomach and colon are less likely to be affected. The average age of cats with GI lymphoma is nine to thirteen years. The most common clinical signs of GI lymphoma are decreased appetite and weight loss. Vomiting occurs in about 50 percent of cases and diarrhea in about 30 percent.

Diagnosis and treatment: To obtain a definitive diagnosis of GI lymphoma, biopsies must be performed. Biopsy specimens can be obtained to two ways. One is endoscopy, in which a long snakelike tube with a camera on the end is inserted into the cat's mouth and then advanced into the stomach and small intestine. Biopsies are then obtained using special forceps that are inserted

▼ Successful treatment of your cat's IBD requires that you identify and eliminate the ingredient in her diet causing the inflammation.

through the endoscope. The other way to obtain biopsy specimens is via abdominal surgery. Both procedures require general anesthesia.

Once a diagnosis is achieved, the lymphoma is categorized into one of two general types: low grade (also called *small cell* or *lymphocytic*) or high grade (also called *large cell* or *lymphoblastic*). The type of lymphoma is significant in terms of prognosis. Low-grade lymphoma has a significantly better prognosis than does high-grade lymphoma.

Chemotherapy is the treatment of choice because lymphoma is the considered the most chemotherapy-responsive cancer. Combination chemotherapy, in which several drugs are administered sequentially, is the primary method of treatment. In cases in which the lymphoma is causing a complete or partial intestinal obstruction or an intestinal perforation, immediate surgery may be necessary, followed by chemotherapy.

The prognosis for GI lymphoma varies, depending on type. The median survival time with chemotherapy for high-grade lymphoma is only 2.7 months. Cats with low-grade lymphoma fare much better. Median survival of 18–24 months has been reported, and it is not uncommon for cats to survive even longer.

Urinary System Disorders and Diseases

Disorders of the urinary system are common in cats. In fact, kidney failure is one of the most common disorders of geriatric cats. Cats who urinate in places other than their litter box should be evaluated for a medical problem before being accused of a behavioral problem because inflammatory and infectious disorders are a frequent cause of inappropriate urination.

Kidney Infection

A bacterial infection of the kidney is called *pyelonephritis*.

Causes and symptoms: Infection of the kidneys can occur if bacteria from a bladder infection travel up the ureters toward the kidneys. Disorders that suppress the immune system, such as FIV or diabetes, put cats at increased risk. Signs of

pyelonephritis may include increased frequency of urination, straining to urinate, and bloody urine. Cats with pyelonephritis are often systemically ill and may show fever, decreased appetite, lethargy,

Anal Gland Problems

Just inside the cat's anus are two small glands: the anal glands. These glands produce a foul-smelling secretion that is normally released in small amounts when the cat defecates. Occasionally, when cats get excited or frightened, they may express the contents of these glands, resulting in a very foul musky odor. Diseases of the anal glands include impaction, abscess formation, and tumors (common in dogs, uncommon in cats). Sometimes, the duct leading from the gland to the anus becomes clogged with dried secretions. The gland becomes distended, which causes discomfort to the cat. Cats may show signs of discomfort by "scooting" or dragging their anus on the floor or the carpet, or they may spend an inordinate amount of time licking or cleaning the anal area.

In cases like this, your veterinarian can express the anal glands manually, relieving the pressure within the gland. This is usually sufficient to solve the problem. Occasionally, the entrapped anal gland secretion will become infected and pus will begin to accumulate within the gland, forming an abscess. If the pus cannot exit the gland through the duct, it will burrow through the skin and eventually drain out. If it does not drain on its own, it may need to be lanced while the cat is sedated or under anesthesia. After lancing, oral antibiotics are prescribed. Warm compresses to the area are also beneficial after lancing. High-fiber diets have been recommended for cats with recurrent anal gland problems. The fiber causes a bulkier stool, which puts more pressure on the anal glands during defecation, allowing them to express more efficiently. Cats who suffer repeated impactions or abscesses may require surgical removal of the anal glands.

vomiting, excessive thirst and urination, and pain in the area of the kidneys.

Diagnosis and treatment: Diagnosis of pyelonephritis requires, at minimum, a urinalysis and urine culture and may require additional tests such as a complete blood count, serum chemistry panel, abdominal x-rays, or abdominal ultrasound. Unlike cats with simple urinary tract infections (UTIs), cats with kidney infections may require hospitalization, intravenous fluid therapy, and intravenous antibiotics for several days. Mild cases may be treated with antibiotics on an outpatient basis.

Chronic Kidney Disease

Chronic kidney disease (CKD)—the slow progressive loss of kidney function—is a common cause of illness in cats, especially in older cats. While the condition is often still referred to as chronic renal failure (CRF), the term is falling out of favor, and the condition is now more commonly referred to as chronic kidney disease (CKD).

Causes and symptoms: Although kidney infections, ingestion of toxins, and other diseases of the kidney can lead to a decline in kidney function, in most cases a cause is never identified. Signs of kidney disease include increased thirst, excessive urination, decreased appetite, weight loss, and vomiting.

Diagnosis and treatment: Diagnosis of CKD is usually made through blood and urine tests. The kidneys filter toxins out of the bloodstream and put them in the urine. When the kidneys fail, the toxin level rises, and the urine becomes dilute. Cats with CKD may also have elevated levels of phosphorus, have low levels of potassium, be anemic (have a low red blood cell count), and have high blood pressure.

For many cats, a diagnosis is made after the veterinarian runs routine blood and urine tests during a wellness exam. These cats do not require hospitalization and can be treated on an outpatient basis. Cats who are acutely ill with CKD require

▲ Kidney disease is one of the most common disorders of senior cats.

hospitalization, intravenous fluids, and other supportive measures. Unless the underlying cause of the initial renal injury can be discovered and treated, CKD invariably progresses. With the exception of a kidney transplant, it is difficult or impossible to improve kidney function in cats with CKD.

It is possible, however, to delay the progression of renal failure, improve the cat's quality of life, and extend a cat's survival time through a variety of diet and drug interventions. If a cat is not acutely ill or her condition improves and she is sent home, she should be fed a prescription diet designed for cats with CKD. It has been proved that cats with CKD who eat these diets do better and live longer. Nausea is a common occurrence in cats with CKD, contributing to the poor appetite and vomiting. Antacids such as famotidine (found in the brand name Pepcid) have proven beneficial in some cats with CKD.

Some cats with CKD will develop low levels of potassium in their blood. This can accelerate the progression of the CKD. Potassium supplements can correct this problem. Twenty percent of cats with CKD have high blood pressure. This, too, can accelerate the CKD as well as damage the eyes, heart, and nervous system. Cats with CKD and high blood pressure should be given medication to control the latter. Some cats with CKD are found to have excessive levels of protein in their urine. These cats tend to have shorter survival times. Fortunately, this can also be corrected with proper medication.

Cats with CKD tend to develop anemia over time. Severe anemia can be treated with injections of a hormone that causes the bone marrow to release more red blood cells.

As the kidneys continue to fail, the blood phosphorus level may begin to rise. Elevated phosphorus levels can be detrimental to the kidneys. For cats with high phosphorus levels, a phosphate binder can be mixed into the food. These supplements bind the phosphorus in the food so that it is not absorbed by the cat.

Cats with CKD should be encouraged to drink as much water as possible. This can be done by feeding canned food, adding water or broth to the food, and using fountain-type water bowls. Cats with an inadequate water intake can be given fluids subcutaneously (under the skin) at home. Although this sounds daunting, cat owners can quickly master this skill, once shown the proper technique.

Many advances have been achieved regarding the treatment of CKD. Although CKD is not curable, cats can live for many years after diagnosis if treated appropriately.

Acute Renal Failure

As mentioned in the previous section, the kidneys filter toxins from the bloodstream and put them in the urine. The kidneys also regulate the amount and composition of the fluid in the bloodstream. Acute renal failure (ARF) is a sudden decrease in kidney function. This is a serious condition that, if not recognized and addressed quickly, can lead to rapid decline and possible death.

Causes and symptoms: Cats with ARF are usually very sick. Loss of appetite, vomiting, extreme lethargy, weakness, and decreased urine production are common signs of ARF. Unfortunately, most of the signs of ARF are nonspecific and may result in delayed recognition that the cat is ill.

The most common causes of ARF in pet cats are ingestion of ethylene glycol (antifreeze) and ingestion of lilies. Other possible causes include

▼ Excessive thirst is one sign of kidney disease, but that symptom also has other, less severe causes.

kidney infection, misguided administration of toxic drugs (for example, ibuprofen), and any situation that results in decreased blood flow to the kidneys (for example, anesthesia).

Diagnosis and treatment: Diagnosis is based on results of various tests, which may include a complete blood count, chemistry panel, urinalysis, x-rays, ultrasound, ethylene glycol test, and perhaps a kidney biopsy. A thorough medical history is very important as well. For example, cats who reside totally indoors are unlikely to encounter antifreeze. The presence of a lily plant in the house raises the possibility of lily toxicity.

Aggressive treatment is the key to survival for cats with ARF. Cats must be hospitalized and given intravenous fluids as well as drugs that increase the blood flow to the kidneys and promote urine production. Electrolyte abnormalities are common and must be monitored and corrected. The most problematic electrolyte disturbance is an elevated blood potassium level. Potassium, if not excreted in the urine, accumulates in the bloodstream and can lead to serious heart disturbances if not corrected promptly. Induction of vomiting may be beneficial if recent toxin ingestion is suspected as a cause of the ARF. Treatment is more likely to be successful if the underlying cause of the ARF can be identified and corrected.

If affected cats do not begin to produce urine despite medical treatment, dialysis may be the only remaining option to save the cat's life. There are two types of dialysis— peritoneal dialysis and hemodialysis. These are advanced procedures that can only be performed at specialty practices and are very costly.

The prognosis for cats with ARF is guarded and is dependent on the cause of the damage, the severity of the damage, and the response to therapy.

▶ If your cat stops using her litter pan, a urinary tract infection may be the cause.

Urinary Tract Infections

Bacterial UTIs are less common in cats than they are in dogs. This is because feline urine is typically very concentrated and is an unfriendly environment for bacteria to grow in.

Causes and symptoms: It is easier for bacteria to live in dilute urine. Disorders that cause dilute urine, such as kidney failure, increase the risk of UTIs. Diabetes is a risk factor because the urine is dilute, and the sugar in the urine is a nutrient source for the bacteria. Grooming problems can also cause UTIs. Longhaired cats may not groom their anal area very effectively, which may result in feces stuck to the fur being pressed up against the opening of the urinary tract when the cat sits, increasing the risk of fecal bacteria migrating into the urinary tract. This is especially true for female cats because females have a shorter urethra, and their urinary tract is located closer to the anus than that of males. Older cats may have trouble grooming their anal/genital area because arthritis has reduced their flexibility to groom. Overweight cats are less efficient at grooming their anal/genital area, putting them at risk for UTIs.

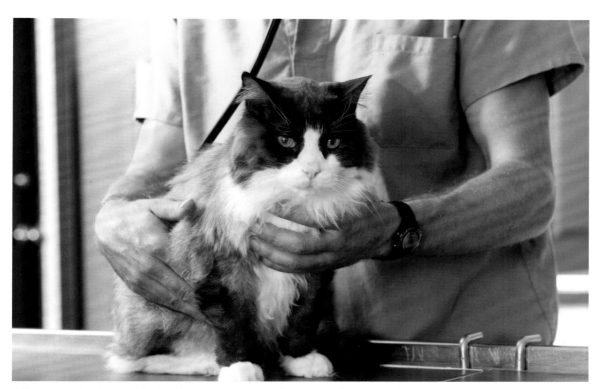

▲The symptoms of a urinary tract infection and urinary stones are very similar; see your vet for an accurate diagnosis.

Diagnosis and treatment: Cats with UTIs often show signs such as frequent trips to the litter box, straining to urinate, urinating in inappropriate places, and possibly having blood in the urine. To diagnose a UTI, a urine sample needs to be analyzed and cultured. Typically, there will be an increased number of white blood cells in the urine, and the culture will grow the specific organism(s) responsible for the infection. Diagnostic laboratories test a variety of antibiotics against the organism they isolate to see which antibiotics are most effective. While waiting for culture results, your veterinarian will likely place your cat on a broad-spectrum antibiotic. If the culture results show that the organism is sensitive to the chosen antibiotic, that therapy is continued, usually for fourteen to twenty-one days. If the organism is revealed to be resistant to the chosen antibiotic, your veterinarian will switch your cat to an antibiotic that has been shown to be effective.

Urinary tract infections are not only uncomfortable for your cat but also can worsen if left untreated. Bacteria can migrate from the bladder to the kidneys, leading to a kidney infection. This is a more serious condition. Cats with untreated UTIs may develop inappropriate urinary elimination behavior. The incidence of UTIs can be reduced if the predisposing factors can be controlled. Overweight cats should be put on a diet. Longhaired cats who cannot keep their anal area properly cleaned should have the hair in that area trimmed or shaved. Arthritic cats who cannot groom properly may require arthritis medication.

Most cats with UTIs respond rapidly to antibiotic therapy, although recurrences are possible if underlying conditions, such as renal failure or diabetes is present.

Urinary Stones

Calculi (stones) can be found anywhere in the urinary tract. When found in the kidneys, they are called *renal calculi*. When found in the bladder, they are called *cystic calculi*. The bladder is the most common place in the urinary tract for calculi to form. The more familiar term is *bladder stones*.

Causes and symptoms: Why stones occur in some cats and not in others is something of a mystery. Genetic and dietary factors are suspected of playing a role, as are other potential factors, such as metabolic disorders, congenital problems, and bacterial infections of the urinary tract. In most cases, a cause is never identified.

Cats with bladder stones may have signs similar to those seen in cats with UTIs: straining to urinate, urinating in inappropriate places, frequent trips to the litter box, and sometimes having blood in the urine.

Diagnosis and treatment: Diagnosis of bladder stones is usually made by taking x-rays. The two most common types of stones—struvite stones and calcium oxalate stones—are usually visible on x-rays. Other types of stones, such as cystine and silica, are quite rare. In some cases, stones may not be dense enough to be seen on an x-ray but may show up on an abdominal ultrasound.

There are two possible treatments for bladder stones: surgical removal or dietary intervention. Of the two most common types of stones found in cats, one type—struvite stones—may be treated by feeding the cat a special diet designed to dissolve the stone. Calcium oxalate stones cannot be dissolved using diets. Your veterinarian cannot tell which type of stone is in your cat's bladder based on x-rays or ultrasound. If a urine specimen from the cat contains crystals, it is reasonable to assume that the type of crystal seen in the urine is a reflection of the type of stone in the bladder. If no crystals are seen, your veterinarian can make a guess based on the pH of the urine (calcium oxalate tends to form in acid urine; struvite tends to form in alkaline urine), although urine pH measurements aren't very precise and there is a lot of overlap.

If the stone is presumed to be struvite but is actually calcium oxalate, it will not dissolve on the diet and the cat's clinical signs will remain. Surgery is a faster and more effective way to remove the stones; of course, it is also more invasive. Once the stones are removed, they can be analyzed to determine their mineral composition. Cats with

▲ Urinary illnesses can be life-threatening; take your cat to the vet if you suspect she has one.

bladder stones should be fed a prescription diet designed to prevent their recurrence. Several companies manufacture these diets, and most veterinary offices sell them. Cats at risk for developing bladder stones should be encouraged to drink more water.

Feline Lower Urinary Tract Disease

As mentioned in the previous sections, it is fairly common for cat owners to observe their cat showing a number of clinical signs associated with a urinary tract problem. The combination of some or all of these clinical signs is a condition or syndrome that has been given several names over the years. The term *feline urologic syndrome* (FUS) was coined in 1970 to describe cats with these types of symptoms; however, the term currently favored in veterinary medicine is *feline lower urinary tract disease* (FLUTD).

Causes and symptoms: Symptoms include straining to urinate, urinating more frequently, urinating very small amounts, and doing it in inappropriate places, that is, places other than the litter box. Occasionally, blood may be seen in the urine. Although there are many possible causes of FLUTD, most cases of FLUTD occur for no known reason. These cases are termed *idiopathic*, a technical way of saying that we don't really know why it happens.

Diagnosis and treatment: Before a cat can be said to have idiopathic disease, recognized causes of urinary tract disease must be eliminated, such as UTIs, bladder stones, anatomical defects involving the bladder or urethra, and neoplasia (cancer).

Blood work is usually normal in cats with signs of FLUTD. Urinalysis results, however, can be variable. Sometimes, crystals are present in the urine. Crystals can irritate the bladder lining, causing capillaries (tiny blood vessels) in the bladder wall to bleed. Occasionally, bacteria are present, indicating that a UTI is the cause of FLUTD.

Blood is a common finding, either grossly (the urine appears pink or red) or microscopically (red blood cells detected only when the urine is viewed under the microscope). x-rays are usually normal, although special studies in which a dye is injected into the bladder may reveal a thickened, irregular bladder wall. This occurs as a result of chronic irritation. Occasionally, a bladder stone or an anatomic defect is identified on x-rays.

Treatment of FLUTD can be very frustrating for the veterinarian and the owner. If the urinalysis reveals the presence of bacteria, the urine should be cultured and antibiotics should be prescribed (see the section on UTIs). If crystals are present, an appropriate diet should be prescribed. Struvite crystals (the most common type) form in alkaline urine, so in these cases a diet that acidifies the urine should be prescribed. Calcium oxalate crystals form in acid urine; in these cases, an alkalinizing diet should be prescribed. Several companies make prescription diets designed to alter the pH of the urine, so that new crystals do not form. More

◄ Feline urethral obstruction is seen almost exclusively in male cats.

Encouraging Your Cat to Drink More

Cats with kidney disease, constipation problems, and urinary issues should be encouraged to drink more water because this has been shown to have therapeutic benefit. There are several ways to accomplish this. Feeding canned food instead of dry food is an important first step. Adding a few spoonfuls of water to the food creates a broth that cats will often consume with the food. Cats are often attracted to water in a novel location. It is not unusual to find a cat drinking from a glass of water left unguarded on a coffee table. This interest can be exploited by placing additional water bowls in atypical areas, such as the corner of a bedroom or an office. Many cats are attracted to flowing water and will often drink from a leaking kitchen or bathroom tap. Fountain-type water bowls are ideal for cats fascinated with running water. Like humans, cats prefer their water fresh and cool. Rather than adding more water to a bowl that is half empty, discard the entire contents of the water bowl and replaced it with cool, fresh water.

recently, prescription food manufacturers have marketed new diets that prevent formation of both types of crystals. These diets work by making the urine very dilute and preventing crystals from forming. For finicky cats who won't eat these prescription diets, it is possible to obtain urinary acidifiers or alkalinizers from your veterinarian and mix them into the cat's regular diet. If x-rays reveal a bladder stone, surgery and medical dissolution are the current treatment options (see Urinary Stones, page 350).

The most difficult cases are those in which there is no obvious cause for the urinary tract disease. In these cases, urinalysis typically reveals adequately concentrated urine. Blood is often the only abnormality detected in the urine. x-rays are normal—no bladder stones or anatomical defects are visible. Ultrasound reveals no tumors. Urinalysis reveals no crystals. Urine culture reveals no infection. A variety of terms have been used to describe this condition, including idiopathic FLUTD, idiopathic cystitis, and feline interstitial cystitis (FIC).

Currently, there is still no universally accepted treatment for the idiopathic form of FLUTD. In most cases, the condition resolves on its own after a few days, regardless of the treatment prescribed. Feeding a diet designed to prevent crystal formation may be helpful, even if crystals do not seem to be the cause of the problem. Although clinical proof is lacking, anecdotally, supplements containing glucosamine and chondroitin sulfate, which are

typically given to cats with arthritis or other joint problems, may help decrease the frequency and severity of recurrences in some cats.

Recent studies suggest that stress may play a role in the development of idiopathic FLUTD. Single cats who live indoors may experience stress in the form of boredom or monotony. Cats in multiple-cat homes may suffer from the stress of constantly engaging in territorial battles or of being the most subordinate cat on the totem pole. Treatment of idiopathic FLUTD and prevention of future episodes should include actively making the indoor environment more stimulating for cats. Cats enjoy surveying their environment from high places, so providing them with cat trees or a wall-mounted shelf is helpful. Appropriate scratching surfaces (both horizontal and vertical) should be provided, so cats can stretch their muscles and engage in natural scratching behavior. Owners should engage in interactive play with their cats at least twice daily. Toys on a wand or "fishing pole" are especially appealing. When cats are home alone, toys that encourage solo play should always be available. Toys should be rotated often, so that cats don't get bored. Toys that mimic prey and allow cats to engage their natural hunting instincts, such as stalking, pouncing and capturing, are ideal. Videos designed for cats, featuring bugs, birds, small mammals, fish, and natural sounds, are available commercially and are mesmerizing to many cats. By incorporating some of these suggestions and reducing environmental stress, you can actively minimize the risk of future bouts of idiopathic FLUTD.

Urethral Obstruction

Feline urethral obstruction (UO) is a life-threatening urinary disorder seen almost exclusively in male cats. Obstruction occurs when crystals in the urine come together and form sand; the sand combines with mucus and other inflammatory debris to form a plug in the urethra that obstructs the flow of urine. Less commonly, the flow of urine may be obstructed by a tiny bladder stone that gets lodged in the urethra during urination.

Causes and symptoms: Exactly why some cats develop UO while others do not has not been determined, although genetic and dietary factors are suspected. Indoor, overweight cats with a sedentary lifestyle are at increased risk of developing UO.

Cats with UO may go in and out of the litter box, repeatedly squatting and straining to produce urine. The amount of urine passed may be small (just a few drops), or there may be no urine produced at all. Some cats cry or yowl during these attempts. Cats may groom their genital area excessively. Some cats will urinate in inappropriate locations. Clearly, these cats are uncomfortable. Cat owners sometimes mistakenly interpret the unsuccessful attempts to urinate as a sign of constipation rather than a urinary obstruction. As time goes on, if the obstruction is not relieved, cats will become lethargic, will stop eating, and may begin to vomit. Some cats resent being picked up because their bladder is distended and tender, and they will cry when lifted.

Diagnosis and treatment: UO is a serious veterinary emergency. Male cats with these clinical signs need to be evaluated by a veterinarian immediately. If your regular veterinary hospital is closed, the cat should be taken to a twenty-four-hour veterinary emergency center. Diagnosis is usually made on physical examination; most cats with UO have a large, rock-hard distended bladder that can be readily felt in the abdomen. In overweight cats, an abdominal x-ray or ultrasound may be necessary for the diagnosis.

Treatment consists of sedating the cat and relieving the obstruction by placing a urinary catheter into the urethra and flushing the bladder with sterile fluid. Once the obstruction is relieved, a sample of the urine can be analyzed to obtain more information as to the possible cause of the obstruction. Blood can be collected while the cat is sedated to evaluate kidney function and electrolyte levels. An intravenous catheter is also necessary to correct the serious electrolyte and acid–base derangements that may occur during UO. Pain medication may be prescribed to help with urinary discomfort. Cats with long-standing obstructions (greater than forty-eight hours) may develop cardiac problems due to elevated levels of potassium in the bloodstream. An electrocardiogram (EKG) may be necessary to monitor the cat's heart rate and rhythm. Cats with very high potassium levels may need to be given medications immediately to help quickly lower the potassium level and prevent adverse effects on the heart.

After a day or two, the urinary catheter can be removed. The cat will remain in the hospital and be monitored very closely to ensure that he is able to urinate normally. Re-obstruction is a common occurrence during the first twenty-four to forty-eight hours after the urinary catheter is removed, so this close monitoring is necessary. Once the cat is urinating normally, he can be sent home.

Cats who have experienced a urethral obstruction should be encouraged to drink water. Obesity should be corrected or prevented. Prescription diets designed to prevent formation of urinary crystals must be fed to minimize future incidents of UO. Ideally, only the canned version of these diets should be fed due to their higher water content. Although most cats never experience a second episode once preventive measures are taken, a few cats will suffer a recurrence. In these cats, a surgical procedure called a perineal urethrostomy (often referred to as a "PU") may be recommended to prevent future episodes. This surgery results in a shortening and widening of the male cat's urethra. This may increase the incidence of future UTIs, but it greatly reduces the chances of another life-threatening UO.

Chapter 17

Infectious Diseases and Parasites

By Arnold Plotnick, DVM

L ike most mammals, cats are susceptible to problems caused by a variety of creatures and critters—specifically, bacteria, viruses, fungi, protozoa, fleas, ticks, mites, and worms. Some of these organisms are relatively harmless, while others can have serious health implications. Advances in veterinary diagnostics and therapeutics have made detection and treatment of these malignant microbes and pesky parasites much easier. A few, however, remain a challenge for cat owners and veterinarians.

Infectious Diseases

Of all the infectious agents that affect cats, viruses remain one of the most common and the most frustrating. I've included *Chlamydophila* in this section on viruses because, although it is a bacterium, it often teams up with the respiratory viruses to compound the grief they cause to our kitties.

Herpesvirus

Feline herpes virus (FHV) is a major cause of upper respiratory disease in cats. FHV is very contagious between cats. Most cats become exposed to FHV at some time in their lives, and the majority of exposed cats become infected.

  Causes and symptoms: Cats typically develop a mild upper respiratory infection—sneezing, conjunctivitis ("pink eye"), runny eyes, nasal discharge—which often resolves on its own. In

▶ Respiratory infections pass easily between cats.

▲Vaccination against FPV is routine, and the vaccine provides cats with excellent protection from the disease.

some cats, the virus induces severe upper respiratory disease, and a few of these cats may develop persistent upper respiratory symptoms for years. The herpesvirus can also cause a variety of eye disorders and may cause skin disease as well. Although cats of all ages are susceptible, kittens appear to be affected more severely than adults.

Diagnosis and treatment: A presumptive diagnosis is made based on evaluation of the cat's history and clinical signs. After a cat recovers from the initial infection, the virus remains in the body as a latent infection. The dormant virus can be reactivated during times of stress, crowding, and concurrent illness, resulting in a recurrence of clinical signs. During these recurrences, infected cats shed the virus profusely in their ocular, nasal, and oral secretions, increasing the risk of infecting other cats. Although there are antiviral drugs that can be administered to cats showing symptoms of herpesvirus, there are currently no drugs that eliminate FHV from the body. A vaccine is available, and it is considered to be a core vaccine— all cats should be immunized against this virus.

Calicivirus

The feline calicivirus (FCV) is an important cause of upper respiratory and oral disease in cats.

Causes and symptoms: Respiratory signs caused by calicivirus (sneezing, ocular discharge, nasal discharge) tend to be milder than those caused by the herpesvirus; however, calicivirus may cause ulcers on the tongue of cats and kittens. The virus is mainly transmitted by direct cat-to-cat contact, but indirect transmission via contamination of the environment or through contaminated objects is also possible. Acutely infected cats will shed the virus in oral, ocular, and nasal secretions for two or three weeks, although some cats become chronic carriers and will shed the virus persistently for months or even years. Cats of any age are susceptible, although kittens are most susceptible. Cats housed in groups, such as in boarding catteries, shelters, and breeding colonies, are at increased risk for contracting FCV.

A more serious form of calicivirus infection, caused by virulent systemic calicivirus (VS-FCV), has been reported in recent years. Disease caused by VS-FCV tends to be more severe and may be fatal.

Diagnosis and treatment: A presumptive diagnosis is made based on evaluation of the cat's history and clinical signs. Vaccines against FCV are available. The vaccine is commonly combined with the vaccines for the herpesvirus and the panleukopenia virus (the FVRCP vaccine). A vaccine against VS-FCV, the more virulent strain of calicivirus, was introduced to the market in 2007. All cats should be immunized against the common calicivirus. Whether a cat needs to be inoculated against VS-FCV or not is a matter to discuss with your veterinarian.

Chlamydophila

Chlamydophila (formerly called *Chlamydia*) is a common cause of conjunctivitis (pink eye) in cats. Cats often acquire the infection through close contact with other infected cats. Although the majority of upper respiratory tract infections (URIs) are caused by the herpesvirus and calicivirus, approximately 10–30 percent of cats with URIs are also infected with *Chlamydophila*. Kittens between the age of two and eleven months are most likely to be infected.

Causes and symptoms: *Chlamydophila* is primarily an eye pathogen, causing redness, swelling, and discharge. It usually occurs in only one eye; occasionally it spreads to the other eye after a day or two. Sometimes nasal discharge and sneezing accompany it.

Diagnosis and treatment: A definitive diagnosis of *Chlamydophila* can be made by scraping or swabbing the conjunctiva of the affected eye(s) and sending the material to a laboratory, where the organism can be identified. Most veterinarians, however, make a presumptive diagnosis based on the clinical signs. The drug of choice for treatment is tetracycline, in the form of an eye ointment. *Chlamydophila* infections can be stubborn, and it may take several weeks before clinical signs completely resolve. A vaccine is available. Although the vaccine is considered to be a noncore (that is, not required for every cat) vaccine, it may be beneficial in shelters, catteries, and other multicat environments where disease caused by *Chlamydophila* has been confirmed.

Panleukopenia

Panleukopenia is a highly contagious viral disease caused by the feline panleukopenia virus (FPV).

Symptoms: Cats infected with the virus often show signs of lethargy, poor appetite, fever, vomiting, and severe diarrhea. The word *panleukopenia* means "a decrease in white blood cells," and that is what is seen on the blood work of affected cats. In young cats, the disease is often fatal. Queens, if infected during pregnancy, may give birth to kittens with a condition called *cerebellar hypoplasia*, a neurologic disorder that causes severe incoordination. The virus is spread mainly through contact with feces; however, it is very stable in the environment and can also be spread via contaminated food bowls, water bowls, litter boxes, and health care workers.

Diagnosis and treatment: Diagnosis is made based on clinical signs (mainly fever, vomiting, and profuse diarrhea), a low white blood cell count, and detection of the panleukopenia virus in the feces.

▼ Although FIV and FeLV are serious diseases, cats infected with the virus can live long, happy lives.

Because the virus is of a type called a *parvovirus*, the rapid in-house test that is used to detect parvovirus in dogs can be used to diagnose the virus in cats. Treatment consists mainly of supportive care—hospitalization, fluid therapy, antibiotics, and nutritional support. With aggressive care, some cats survive the infection; most young kittens, however, succumb to the virus. Vaccination against FPV is a routine part of feline health care, and the immunity conferred by this core vaccine is considered to be excellent.

FeLV and FIV

The feline leukemia virus (FeLV) and the feline immunodeficiency virus (FIV) are among the most common—and most serious—infectious diseases of cats. Fortunately, the prevalence of both viruses in the cat population is low (approximately 2.3 percent for FeLV and 2.5 percent for FIV). The prevalence of FeLV infection has decreased over the past twenty years, due to testing programs, vaccination, and general awareness of prevention methods. The prevalence of FIV infection, in contrast, has not changed significantly since the virus was discovered in 1986. Cats who have outdoor access and exposure to other cats are at increased risk for infection. Male cats, particularly those that who not been neutered, are especially at risk.

Causes and symptoms: Both viruses can cause a variety of clinical signs in infected cats. FeLV and FIV suppress the immune system, making cats more susceptible to secondary infections. Cats infected with FeLV (and to a lesser extent, FIV) are at increased risk of developing lymphoma, a cancer of the lymphatic tissues. FeLV, as its name suggests, may cause cats to develop outright leukemia (cancer of the blood). FIV often causes or contributes to oral problems in cats. All cats who are sick, regardless of age and despite any previously negative test results, should be tested for the retroviruses. Previously tested cats may have become infected since the cat's initial testing. Don't wait

for illness to have your cat tested, however. Because of the serious health consequences of infection, all cats should be tested for both viruses at some point. This includes all cats about to be adopted or brought into a new household and adult cats and kittens of any age.

Diagnosis and treatment: Because the prevalence of both viruses is low in the feline population, a negative test result is likely to be truly negative. Because of the significant implications of a positive test, cats who test positive for either virus should have the test repeated a few days later using a fresh blood sample to confirm the results. As noted earlier, kittens may be tested for FeLV and FIV at any age. A positive FeLV test strongly suggests that the kitten is infected with the FeLV virus; this should be confirmed by retesting a few days later. A positive FIV test in a kitten, however, should be interpreted carefully. The FIV test detects antibodies against the virus. The test can detect antibodies passed to the kitten from the mother. This can be mistaken for infection in the kitten. Kittens who test positive for FIV antibodies should be retested every sixty days up to six months of age. By six months of age, any antibodies that came from the mother are gone. If, after six months of age,

▼ If your cat has been diagnosed with FeLV and/or FIV, keep her indoors so she won't infect other cats.

▲ Outdoor cats who fight with other cats are at high risk for infection with FIV and should be vaccinated.

the results are still positive, the kitten should be considered infected with FIV.

To date, no treatment has been shown to reverse a FeLV or FIV infection in cats. Although reports on the use of various drugs and supplements appear occasionally in the veterinary literature, large controlled studies are lacking regarding antiviral drugs or alternative therapies for FeLV or FIV. However, no cat should be euthanized based solely on the presence of a FeLV or FIV infection. Cats can live for many years after infection. Recent studies report the median survival of cats diagnosed with FeLV to be 2.4 years; for FIV-infected cats, 4.9 years. Every cat is an individual, however, and some cats can survive much longer, especially those with FIV. Cats diagnosed with FeLV and/or FIV should be confined indoors, both so that they do not infect other cats and to decrease their exposure to infectious agents in the environment. Because FeLV may be transmitted through mutual grooming,

sharing of food bowls, water bowls, and litter boxes, cats with FeLV should be isolated and prevented from interacting with other housemates. In general, FIV transmission is low in households with stable social structures where housemates do not fight. No new cats should be introduced into the household, to reduce the risk of changing the social structure and inciting territorial aggression.

Vigilant veterinary care is required in cats who test positive for either virus. Raw foods should be avoided because of the risk of parasitic infections or exposure to food-borne bacteria. Infected cats should be examined at least twice yearly and at the first signs of illness. Internal and external parasite control is imperative. Infected queens should not be bred, and cats should be spayed or neutered if their condition is stable enough to permit surgery.

Vaccines are available for both retroviruses. Both are considered noncore; that is, they are optional, based on the risk assessment of the individual cat.

Infectious Diseases and Parasites

361

Cats living in a FeLV-negative, FIV-negative, indoor environment are at minimal risk.

FeLV vaccination: Because kittens are so susceptible to FeLV, it is currently recommended that all kittens be vaccinated for FeLV. Furthermore, the lifestyles of kittens often change after adoption, increasing their risk for FeLV exposure. Cats who go outdoors, cats who come into direct contact with other cats of unknown status (such as those going to foster homes or other group housing situations), and those living with FeLV-positive cats should also be vaccinated. Cats should be tested and confirmed negative prior to FeLV vaccination. Administering FeLV vaccines to cats already infected with the virus confers no benefit.

FIV vaccination: Outdoor cats who fight with other cats are at high risk for infection and may be candidates for vaccination. Because FIV is spread mainly through biting, cats living in households with an FIV-positive cat may be at lower risk for FIV infection if a stable social structure exists and fighting does not occur. In this situation, whether or not to vaccinate should be discussed with your veterinarian. If the decision falls in favor of vaccination, cats should test negative immediately prior to vaccination because vaccination of cats who are already infected, while not harmful, confers no benefit. Cats who are vaccinated against FIV will subsequently test positive for FIV antibodies. Fortunately, a test has been developed that can distinguish whether FIV antibodies are the result of infection or vaccination.

Feline Infectious Peritonitis (FIP)

Of all of the infectious diseases that cats can acquire, feline infectious peritonitis (FIP) is perhaps the most devastating. FIP is a viral disease caused by a type of virus called a coronavirus.

Causes and symptoms: Most cats are exposed to, and become infected with, the coronavirus as kittens. At worst, kittens may get mild diarrhea. Many show no clinical signs at all. The immune system makes antibodies against the virus but does not eliminate it, and the virus continues to reside in the intestinal tract, usually causing no further problems for the cat.

Occasionally, however, for reasons not fully understood, the harmless intestinal coronavirus mutates, gaining the ability to leave the intestinal tract and cause problems. The immune system tries to defeat the virus, but the virus manages to evade it. This mutated intestinal coronavirus is now the evil FIP-inducing coronavirus.

The FIP virus causes damage to blood vessels, allowing fluid to leak through the vessel walls. Effusions (collections of fluid) can develop in the abdominal cavity, chest cavity, and pericardium (the sac around the heart), resulting in what is referred to as the "wet" form of FIP. Some cats develop nodular accumulations of inflammatory cells called granulomas throughout many of the body's organs. This form of the disease is known as the "dry" form of FIP.

Diagnosis and treatment: Diagnosis of the disease is difficult because clinical signs are vague. Most affected cats are young (usually less than one year) and show lethargy, weight loss, poor appetite, and a fever that doesn't respond to antibiotics. A serum chemistry panel often only shows elevated protein (mainly in the form of increased globulins)

▼ Fleas are the most common—and one of the most irritating—external parasites seen in cats.

biopsy of the affected organs or tissues remains the only way to definitively diagnose FIP.

FIP is progressive and fatal. Cats with FIP tend to succumb to the disease rather quickly, in a few days or weeks. The "wet" form of FIP tends to progress faster than the "dry" FIP. Treatment is generally symptomatic and supportive. Nutritional support, antibiotics, and corticosteroids may produce a temporary alleviation of clinical signs, but the disease invariably progresses. Ultimately, nearly all cats diagnosed with FIP are euthanized to alleviate suffering. Studies of investigational drugs have shown potential in the treatment of some cases of FIP. Polyprenyl immunostimulant (PPI), for example, has shown promise in the treatment of the dry form of FIP; controlled studies, however, are pending.

Although a commercial FIP vaccine is available, the efficacy of the vaccine remains questionable. The American Association of Feline Practitioners and the Academy of Feline Medicine, in their regularly published guidelines for feline vaccination, currently do not recommend the FIP vaccine.

Parasites

Like all household pets, cats have their share of parasites, both external and internal. Some are clearly visible with the naked eye. Others require a microscope for definitive identification. Although some of these parasites are mostly a nuisance, some can cause significant illness in cats. Fortunately, recent breakthroughs in parasite control have made treatment a much simpler and effective endeavor.

External Parasites

External parasites include fleas, ear mites, ticks, and a variety of other less common critters that can affect the skin, such as *Cheyletiella*, *Demodex*, and scabies.

Fleas

Few creatures living on earth today have had as much impact on world history as the common

unless the virus has begun to affect the kidneys or liver, in which case the liver and kidney parameters may be abnormal. The wet form is easier to diagnose because the presence of fluid in the abdomen or chest is relatively easy to detect, and fluid analysis can give additional information supporting the diagnosis. The dry form remains challenging to diagnose.

There is no simple blood test for FIP. Many laboratories offer veterinarians an "FIP test," but these tests tend to only measure antibodies to coronaviruses in general. The tests cannot tell whether the antibodies are there due to the cat's being infected with the harmless intestinal version of the coronavirus or the deadly FIP version of the coronavirus. A positive test does not mean that the cat has FIP. Until a rapid reliable test is developed that allows veterinarians to make a diagnosis,

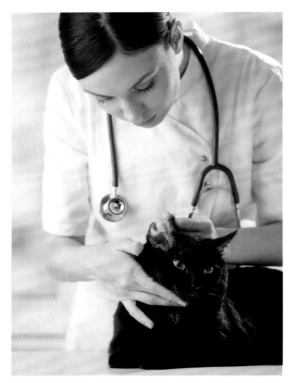

▲ Cats commonly contract ear mites, but fortunately these pests are not difficult to eliminate.

flea. From the black plague during the fourteenth century to the present, fleas have been the cause of much grief. They make your cat itch, especially if the cat is allergic to flea bites, which is quite common. In fact, flea allergy dermatitis is the most prevalent small-animal skin disease.

It is important for cat owners to understand the life cycle of the flea. Once a flea jumps on a cat, it stays for its entire life. Fleas do not jump from one cat to another. Although the flea spends its entire life *on* the cat, the majority of the flea's life cycle is completed while *off* the cat. When a female flea jumps onto a cat, it begins feeding on blood within minutes. Ingestion of blood is required for the flea to reproduce. By twenty-four hours, the flea starts to lay eggs, about forty to fifty per day. The cat then moves around the house, acting like a living salt-shaker, as flea eggs fall off and accumulate in the areas where the cat sleeps or rests. Within a week, larvae hatch

from flea eggs. The larvae try to avoid light and burrow into carpets, cracks in hardwood floors, and other humid areas such as concrete floors in damp basements. Five to twelve days after that, larvae spin a cocoon in which they develop into pupae. Fleas emerge from pupae within one to three weeks. These newly hatched fleas wait for the cat to pass by, and then they hop onto the cat and the life cycle starts all over again.

The entire flea life cycle takes three to six weeks. When all of the life stages of the flea are looked at as a population, adult fleas compose only about 5 percent. Eggs make up 50 percent of the population, with larvae at 35 percent and pupae at 10 percent. If you're seeing adult fleas on your cat, you can be sure that there is a veritable flea factory nearby.

Even if a cat spends her entire life indoors, she can still get fleas. Fleas are hitchhikers—they jump onto our clothing, and we bring them back home, where they hop onto our cats.

Causes and symptoms: The most common sign that a cat has fleas is scratching. Cats who are allergic to fleas will often experience additional signs such as hair loss, redness, and miliary dermatitis—small scabs throughout the hair coat.

Diagnosis and treatment: Diagnosing fleas is easy if fleas are seen crawling through the hair coat. Sometimes, fleas may not be seen, but "flea dirt" (flea feces) is present. Flea dirt has the appearance of pepper shaken onto your cat. Combing this dark material out of the hair coat on to a moistened paper towel will resuspend the digested blood in the feces, leaving a red stain. This is a simple test and confirms the diagnosis.

Fleas can cause health problems in cats in addition to severe skin irritation and flea allergic dermatitis. Fleas are also responsible for transmitting tapeworms to cats. Heavily parasitized cats, especially kittens, can develop anemia due to blood loss from flea bites. Fleas pass *Bartonella*, the organism responsible for cat-scratch disease, from one cat to another. Most cats infected with *Bartonella* are clinically normal; however, infection in cats can sometimes lead to uveitis (an inflammatory condition of the eye).

Traditionally, the most effective approach to flea control has been the three-step method: treatment of the yard, the home, and the cat. Excellent compounds are available that can be applied directly to the soil in moist, shady areas around the house where immature fleas are most likely to live. These compounds are reasonably priced, long-lasting, and environmentally friendly. As for the home environment, there are safe and effective compounds that can be applied to carpets and upholstered furniture in cases where the flea problem is especially severe, although in most instances, simply vacuuming and thoroughly washing your cat's bedding may be sufficient. Repeated vacuuming of carpets, furniture, and floors mechanically removes flea eggs and larvae from the environment. Steam cleaning reduces flea larvae in carpets.

In recent years, many new flea control products have been marketed that are truly among the most effective and important formulations in the war against fleas. In fact, these products are so effective that, in most cases, the cat alone needs to be treated; treatment of the yard and the house is often no longer necessary. Many of these products are applied to the cat's fur once a month. Some are given orally.

Talk to your veterinarian about which product is right for you and your cat because different products have different benefits. Some of these products not only kill fleas but also prevent ticks from attaching and may treat intestinal parasites and other parasites such as ear mites.

Ear Mites

Ear mites are pesky little bugs that live in the ear canal of cats. They feed on skin debris, blood, and tissue fluids.

Causes and symptoms: The mites irritate the ceruminous (wax-producing) glands of the ear, causing the ear canal to fill with wax, blood, and mite feces. This material has a characteristic reddish brown appearance, resembling coffee grounds. Ear mites cause itching and discomfort. Ear mite infection is a very common disorder. Kittens often acquire the infection from their mother or from contact with another infected kitten. Affected cats often shake their heads and may scratch their ears so vigorously that bleeding results.

Diagnosis and treatment: Diagnosis is made by examining some of the crusty ear material under the microscope. The mites, which are fairly large, will be readily apparent. Treatment typically involves applying medication directly into the ears for several days. A relatively new topical product containing 0.01 percent ivermectin can be applied directly into the ear; only one dose is required. There are topical products, however, such as selamectin, that can be applied to the skin. The selamectin is absorbed into the skin and gets distributed throughout the body, including inside the ears, where it kills ear mites. Topical treatment is preferred because cats do not like (and will often fight) having medication introduced into their ears and because some mites can colonize the skin around the ear and neck. Medication instilled into the ear might not kill

Ticks

Ticks are less of a nuisance in cats than in dogs. Researchers speculate that the meticulous grooming habits of cats allow them to remove most ticks before they attach. Cats are also fortunate in that they are much less susceptible to, and thus rarely fall victim to, dangerous tick-borne diseases such as Lyme disease, ehrlichiosis, and Rocky Mountain spotted fever than dogs. Although most once-a-month flea products do not claim to be effective against ticks, some newer products are effective against both fleas and ticks.

mites that have strayed out of the ear into the surrounding skin. Topical selamectin kills those stray mites. Removing as much debris and mites as possible before treatment is beneficial and makes treatment more successful, especially if medication is to be instilled into the ear.

Cheyletiella

Cheyletiella are mites that can affect dogs, cats, rabbits, and people. They live on the surface of the skin, completing their entire life cycle on the host animal.

Causes and symptoms: The most common sign of *Cheyletiella* mange is itching and dandruff, although the itching is not as intense as that caused by other mites such as Demodex or Notoedres. The itching is mainly on the back, but it can also be anywhere on the trunk. Dry white scales are often present down the back. When a cat infested with *Cheyletiella* is examined closely, the dandruff can be seen to be moving, which explains the name "walking dandruff" that is often used to describe *Cheyletiella*. The movement is actually caused by the mites moving around beneath the dandruff flakes.

▼This poor cat is possibly suffering from a scabies infestation.

Cats can develop small scabs all over their body, and symmetrical hair loss can be seen along the sides of the body where the cat might be overgrooming from the itchiness.

Diagnosis and treatment: Diagnosis is made by examining skin scrapings under the microscope; however, because the mites live on the surface of the skin, they may be detected using the "Scotch tape" technique, in which a piece of clear tape is applied to the scaly part of the skin and is then stained and adhered to a slide for microscopic evaluation. Treatment involves weekly use of a medicated dip for six to eight weeks. Other treatment options include medicated sprays, oral ivermectin, or topical selamectin. The house needs to be treated with sprays in a manner similar to that done for fleas. All cats in the household should be treated.

Demodex

Demodicosis (also called *demodectic mange*) is a skin disorder that affects both cats and dogs. In cats, demodectic mange is caused by mange mites of the species *Demodex cati*, or *Demodex gatoi*. Demodectic mange is much more common in dogs than in cats. Although all ages and breeds of cats are susceptible, Burmese and Siamese cats are at increased risk.

Causes and symptoms: Two forms of the disease are possible: the localized form and the generalized form. The localized form is more common, with symptoms (hair loss, scaly skin, itching) usually limited to the eyelids, head, neck, and ears. The generalized form looks similar, but involves the body and legs as well. Cats with generalized demodicosis usually have some sort of underlying immunosuppressive disease, such as FeLV infection, FIV infection, or diabetes. In some cases, demodicosis develops after a cat has been on immunosuppressive drugs, such as corticosteroids.

Diagnosis and treatment: A diagnosis is achieved upon microscopic detection of *Demodex* in skin scrapings. Treatment requires medicated baths or dips using lime sulfur. The drug ivermectin, given orally, has been used successfully as well. All cats in the household should be treated because the mite is contagious between cats. Antibiotics are occasionally necessary if a secondary bacterial skin infection is present.

Notoedres

The *Notoedres cati* mite causes feline scabies (also known as *notoedric mange*), an uncommon, contagious skin disease of cats and kittens. This mite can also infest other animals, including humans. Although scabies is much more common in dogs than cat, a different species of mite is responsible for canine scabies.

Symptoms: Scabies is an extremely itchy disease, affecting mainly the face, ears, and neck. If not addressed promptly, the skin lesions spread to cover the entire body. The affected skin takes on a thick, crusty, scabby appearance. Cats will scratch the affected areas until they become red, raw, and inflamed.

Diagnosis and treatment: Diagnosis is achieved by doing skin scrapings of the crusty areas and observing live mites and eggs under the microscope. Scabies is commonly treated with a drug called ivermectin or selamectin. If a secondary bacterial skin infection has developed, antibiotics may be warranted.

Internal Parasites

The internal parasites of most concern in cats are those that affect the gastrointestinal tract. These include *Coccidia, Giardia,* hookworms, roundworms, tapeworms, and *Tritrichomonas.*

Coccidia

Coccidia are parasitic protozoans (one-celled organisms) that mainly affect the small intestine.

▲ Outdoor kittens typically have worms. If you adopt a feral kitten, ask your veterinarian to screen her for worms.

Cats acquire coccidial infections mainly by ingestion of soil contaminated with infected cat feces. Ingestion of infected rodents is another way of acquiring a coccidial infection, but this is less common. Most kittens acquire the infection from the feces of their infected mothers.

Causes and symptoms: Affected cats often show minimal clinical signs, although diarrhea, bloody or mucoid stools, and dehydration are sometimes seen. Kittens are more severely affected than adult cats. Cats kept in crowded or unsanitary conditions are at increased risk of becoming infected. Cats who are immunosuppressed are also at increased risk. The organism is very contagious from one kitten to another. Coccidian parasites of cats and dogs do not infect humans.

Diagnosis and treatment: Diagnosis is made upon identifying coccidial oocysts in a fecal sample. Treatment requires administration of anticoccidial

Infectious Diseases and Parasites

▲ Cats get *Giardia* infestations from drinking contaminated water.

medications. Most infected cats respond well to treatment; however, debilitated kittens may die from overwhelming infections.

Giardia

Giardia is a protozoan parasite that affects mainly the small intestine, although it can occasionally affect the large intestine. *Giardia* lives as two different forms: a cyst form and a live trophozoite form. The cyst form is shed in the feces and infects other animals. *Giardia* is acquired by ingestion of contaminated feces or contaminated food or water. Once a cat eats a *Giardia* cyst, the cyst makes its way to the small intestine, where it opens up and releases a trophozoite, the active swimming form of the organism. The trophozoites attach to the inner surface of the intestine and reproduce by dividing in two. After this brief reproductive period, the trophozoite forms a wall around itself and becomes a cyst, which is passed in the feces. The cysts can survive for several months in the environment. The trophozoites damage the intestinal wall and are responsible for the resultant clinical signs.

Symptoms: *Giardia* mainly causes diarrhea, although occasionally it can cause vomiting,

borborygmus (loud stomach growling noises), and weight loss. The diarrhea may be acute (sudden onset), intermittent, or chronic (persistent). Diarrhea caused by *Giardia* is often very watery and foul smelling and may contain blood and/or mucus. Many cats show no clinical signs at all. *Giardia* is seen more commonly in cats living in crowded or unsanitary conditions and in cats whose immune system is suppressed. People can contract *Giardia* infections, although whether the cat is a source of infection for people is a topic of debate. Until we know for certain, it is best to consider giardiasis to be a potentially zoonotic disease—one that can be transmitted to people. Immunocompromised people should avoid handling cats who have been diagnosed with *Giardia*.

Diagnosis and treatment: Diagnosis is made by detecting *Giardia* cysts on analysis of a fecal sample. However, diagnosis can be challenging because not every stool sample from an infected cat will have detectable cysts. Testing a fecal sample daily for three consecutive days increases the accuracy of diagnosis. Occasionally, cysts and/or live trophozoites are seen on direct microscopic examination of fecal sample. Another method of diagnosis involves testing for *Giardia* antigens in the feces using an in-house test that is similar to the type of test used to diagnose FeLV and FIV. This test is more accurate than microscopic fecal analysis.

Either metronidazole or fenbendazole has traditionally been used to treat *Giardia*. A recent study, however, showed that giving both drugs in combination is the most effective method of treatment. Most cats respond very well, and their diarrhea resolves after treatment. Because cysts may persist in the environment, the potential for reinfection exists, especially in cats who go outdoors. Because *Giardia* infection is often seen in cats with compromised immune systems, all cats with *Giardia* should be tested for FeLV and FIV. Cats infected with either of these viruses may have a more difficult time eliminating the organism.

Hookworms

Hookworms are nematode parasites that, like roundworms, live in the small intestine. There are three main species of hookworm in cats: *Ancylostoma tubaeforme* (most common), *Ancylostoma braziliense*, and *Uncinaria stenocephala*. Cats acquire hookworms by either ingesting an infected host (rats, for example) or more commonly via ingestion of contaminated feces. Hookworms are not transmitted via nursing. Hookworm infection is not as common as roundworm infection.

Causes and symptoms: Hookworms attach to the wall of the small intestine and suck blood. Clinical signs are more severe in kittens than in adults and may include vomiting, diarrhea, and weight loss or failure to gain weight. Because they are bloodsucking parasites, hookworms can cause severe anemia, especially in kittens. Hookworms are zoonotic—that is, they can infect people. Human infection occurs when the skin comes into contact with soil or sand containing hookworm larvae. The larvae penetrate the skin and cause cutaneous larval migrans or "creeping eruption." The lesions appear as red lines under the skin and cause severe itching.

Diagnosis and treatment: Diagnosis of feline hookworm infection is made by seeing hookworm eggs upon microscopic examination of a fecal sample. There are many oral and topical dewormers available for treatment, most of which treat roundworms as well as hookworms. Dewormers from a pet store or from the pet section of a supermarket are not recommended because the main ingredient in some over-the-counter dewormers is piperazine, which is effective against roundworms but not hookworms.

Roundworms

Roundworms are nematode parasites that live in the small intestine. There are two main species of roundworm in cats: *Toxocara cati* (most common) and *Toxocara leonina*. Cats acquire roundworms by either ingesting infected hosts (mice, birds, insects) or more commonly by coming into contact with contaminated feces. Kittens may also acquire roundworms from ingestion of milk from an infected mother while nursing.

Causes and symptoms: Kittens are more commonly affected, and they show more severe signs than do adult cats. This includes vomiting, a

▼ Cats who lose weight but have a normal appetite may have some type of digestive parasite.

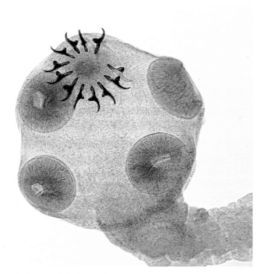
▲ Magnified image of the head of a tapeworm.

Roundworms are zoonotic—that is, they are a human health hazard. Their larvae may cause a condition in people called visceral larval migrans, whereby roundworm larvae migrate throughout the body. The condition occurs most often in young children who play in soil infested with roundworm eggs. Most cases are caused by the canine roundworm, although *Toxocara cati* has been implicated in some cases.

Tapeworms

Tapeworms are long, flat worms that live in the small intestine, absorbing nutrients through their skin. Adult worms can grow up to 20 inches (51 cm) in length. The worms consist of a head and neck followed by many segments. New segments are formed and added to the neck region of the worm, while segments at the tail end of the tapeworm break off as they mature. These segments contain tapeworm eggs.

Causes and symptoms: Tapeworms rarely cause any clinical signs in the cat. Very heavy infestations may cause deprivation of nutrients, causing the cat to lose weight, although this is uncommon. Cats acquire tapeworms from ingesting an infected flea.

Diagnosis and treatment: A diagnosis of tapeworm infection is usually made by finding individual segments on the rear end of the cat, in the cat's feces, or in areas where the cat rests or sleeps. The worm segments are small and white, resembling a grain of rice. The worm segments may dry out when exposed to the air for a while, taking on the appearance of a sesame seed. Occasionally (and shockingly, for most cat owners), a live segment can be observed wriggling directly out of the cat's anus or on the nearby fur. When the segments crawl out of the anus, they may cause itching, and the cat may scoot its rear end on the floor or carpet. A diagnosis of tapeworms in the cat is proof that the cat has had contact with fleas. It is very uncommon for the feline tapeworm to infect people; however, there are rare reports of tapeworm infections in children.

Treatment of tapeworms in cats is achieved using a dewormer prescribed by your veterinarian.

distended abdomen, weight loss or failure to gain weight, and diarrhea. Because the life cycle of *Toxocara* cati involves migration of worms through the lungs, coughing may also be a clinical sign of infection in kittens. Occasionally, live worms will be seen in the vomit and/or the diarrhea. Adult worms live in the small intestine and get their nourishment by absorbing nutrients from the cat's intestinal juices. Mature roundworms produce eggs that pass out into the cat's feces.

Diagnosis and treatment: Diagnosis is made by seeing roundworm eggs upon microscopic examination of a fecal sample or by seeing a live roundworm in the vomit or feces. Roundworms are long and thin and look like a strand of spaghetti. There are many oral dewormers available for treatment, as well as topical products that are applied to skin. Kittens should be routinely dewormed for roundworms even if fecal examination is negative because eggs may escape detection on a fecal analysis. A second treatment two to three weeks following the initial deworming is necessary to make certain that all worms were killed. Although treatment is usually successful, roundworm eggs may persist in the environment for years and can lead to reinfection, especially in outdoor cats.

▲ If your cat has an intestinal parasite, your veterinarian likely will prescribe an oral deworming medication.

Over-the-counter dewormers from pet stores or supermarkets are not recommended because they most likely do not contain the proper medication required to treat tapeworms.

Tritrichomonas

Tritrichomonas (try-trick-a-*moan*-us) is a protozoan that mainly affects the large intestine of cats. Cats become infected via ingestion of contaminated feces.

Causes and symptoms: *Tritrichomonas* causes intractable, foul-smelling, watery diarrhea, often with blood or mucus. Excessive gas, increased frequency of defecation, and straining to defecate is common. Cats of any age can be affected, although infection is most common in kittens and young cats. Cats kept in crowded or unsanitary conditions, such as shelters and breeding catteries, are also at increased risk. *Tritrichomonas* is not believed to be zoonotic, so it cannot be transmitted to people. However, people coming in contact with infected cats should practice basic hygiene, such as washing with soap and water after handling the feces or litter box of infected cats. *Tritrichomonas*

is often confused with *Giardia* because they cause similar clinical signs.

Diagnosis and treatment: Microscopic examination of a fecal specimen is unlikely to lead to diagnosis. Instead, a diagnosis is made via culture of the stool or by a test called polymerase chain reaction (PCR). The PCR test is the most accurate, although the test is not widely available. Treatment can be frustrating. If untreated, the diarrhea often spontaneously resolves; however, that can take as long as two years. The drug ronidazole has been shown to be effective, but the drug is not approved for use in cats, so any use of the drug would be considered "off-label" usage requiring written consent from the cat owner. Although most cats tolerate the drug, some have developed neurological signs, such as twitching and seizures. These signs usually resolve when the drug is discontinued. Ronidazole can cause severe birth defects and should never be given to pregnant cats. A highly digestible diet or a diet high in fiber may cause partial resolution of the diarrhea caused by *Tritrichomonas*.

Chapter 18

Life Cycle Needs

By Arnold Plotnick, DVM

Maintaining the health and well-being of a cat through all the stages of life is a great responsibility. To be able to accomplish this, owners must know and understand each stage of a cat's life, how needs change from one stage to another, and what kind of daily and veterinary care is required as a cat progresses from kitten to adult to senior. First, we look at reproduction. Even though the majority of cat owners today will adopt their cats from shelters, already spayed or neutered, it's important to understand the unique reproductive life of cats, how that affects their health, and how it has led to the urgent need for programs to spay and neuter. If, for some reason, you do end up with a pregnant cat under your care, this section also lays out basic health care needs of the mother and her newborn kittens. Knowing how to care for an orphaned kitten can also be important. Finally, cats are living longer than ever before. It is no longer a rarity to see cats reach the age of twenty. We conclude this chapter by addressing the special issues and needs of the elderly cat.

Reproductive Care

Cats have long been recognized for their fertility. Bastet, the Egyptian goddess of fertility, is depicted as a cat in artwork, and the ancient Egyptians worshipped cats as a symbol of fertility. When it comes to making babies, cats are one of the most prolific of domestic pets. Like rabbits, they are capable of multiple pregnancies within a single reproductive season.

▶ It is your responsibility to care for your feline through all the stages of her life.

Some aspects of the cats' reproductive capabilities are truly remarkable. A female cat in estrus or "heat" may allow several males to mate with her, and it is possible for kittens in a litter to have different fathers. (The technical term for this is *superfecundity*.) Lactation (production of milk) does not suppress the heat cycle, and cats who are actively nursing kittens can come into heat as soon as two weeks after giving birth. Even being pregnant doesn't necessarily suppress the heat cycle. In fact, 10 percent of female cats come into heat between the third and sixth week of pregnancy. Although these cycles are rarely fertile, it is theoretically possible for a cat to be carrying fetuses of different ages, resulting from separate matings in different heat cycles! (The scientific term for this is *superfetation*.)

The unique reproductive features of the cat—polyestrous (multiple heat cycles during the reproductive season), early onset of puberty, extreme fertility, heat cycles not suppressed by lactation, and short gestation period (sixty-five to sixty-seven days, on average)—all contribute to the sad fact that there are many more cats than there are homes for them. In the United States, an estimated 3 to 4 million cats are euthanized every year.

Puberty

Although the average age at which queens reach puberty and have their first heat cycle is between five and nine months, some cats experience puberty as early as three and a half months and at a body size as small as 4½ pounds (2 kg). Male cats become sexually mature approximately one to two months later than females do.

There are many factors that affect the onset of puberty. General health, physical condition, nutritional status, social environment, time of year, and breed can all influence puberty. In general, domestic shorthaired cats come into heat at an earlier age than do domestic longhaired cats, and mixed breeds come into puberty earlier than do purebreds. Persian cats are especially late in reaching puberty, often not experiencing their first heat until twelve months of age. Females are at their most fertile between the ages of one and a half

▲ On average, female cats can first get pregnant at the age of five to nine months.

and eight, although they can reproduce up to about fourteen years of age. Males can reproduce several years longer.

If allowed to mate naturally, a typical queen having two or three litters a year, with three or four kittens per litter, can have anywhere from 50 to 150 kittens in her lifetime.

Mating

Estrus is the period in which the female will allow males to mate with her. This period varies in length between five days to three weeks. If the female does not mate with a male during the heat cycle, she will experience repeated cycles every twelve to twenty-two days. In the Northern Hemisphere, as the days get longer in late January and early February, queens begin to cycle, coming into heat approximately every two weeks. This usually continues until late September. In October, November, and December, cats tend to stop cycling until the new

Spaying and Neutering

Cat overpopulation is a very serious problem. A major part of the responsibility of cat ownership is guaranteeing that your cat doesn't reproduce. Neutering and spaying are two of the most commonly performed elective surgical procedures. Not only do they help curtail cat overpopulation, they also bring many health and behavior benefits to both you and your cat.

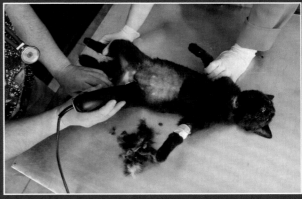

▲ Cat being shaved just prior to her spay surgery.

Spaying is the surgical procedure performed on female cats. The medical term for this surgery is *ovariohysterectomy*—removal of the ovaries and uterus. The advantages of spaying are no more heat cycles; no more crying, yowling, or trying to escape outside; no more unwelcome visits by unneutered male cats in the neighborhood; no uterine infections; and a greatly reduced incidence of mammary tumors if the cat is spayed before experiencing her first heat.

Neutering or castration is the procedure used for males; the actual medical term for the procedure is *orchiectomy*. In this procedure, the testicles are removed. The advantages of neutering are a reduced urge to roam, stopping the mating drive, stopping or preventing urine spraying, and less territorial aggression (which reduces the risk of cat-fight abscesses or acquiring FeLV or FIV from another cat through fighting).

Many cat owners are concerned that spaying or neutering their cats will result in undesirable behavioral changes. One concern is that the cat will become fat and lazy. Although the metabolism does slow down a bit after spaying and neutering, most cats gain weight because they are fed too much and they don't get enough exercise—not because of the operation. After spaying or neutering, monitor your cat's appetite and activity patterns and adjust the diet accordingly.

Some people feel that neutering a male cat will result in him feeling like less of a male. These concerns are unwarranted. Cats don't have any concept of sexual identity or ego and don't suffer any kind of emotional reaction or identity crisis when neutered.

A popular misconception is that it is better for a female cat to have one litter before spaying. Medical evidence, however, shows the opposite to be true. Dogs who are spayed before their first heat rarely, if ever, develop mammary tumors. The same holds true for cats. This is important because feline mammary tumors are much more malignant than those seen in dogs and they carry a worse prognosis.

Cats are not being deprived of parenthood by being spayed. Unlike people, cats do not experience a sense of emotional fulfillment by giving birth or by the mothering process.

Some people want to breed their cat because they are hoping that the kittens will be exactly like the mother or father in appearance and/or temperament. This is a misconception. Breeding two purebred animals rarely results in offspring who are exactly like one of the parents, and with mixed breeds it is virtually impossible to have offspring who are exactly like one of the parents.

The idea that a cat should have a litter so that children can witness the miracle of birth is disconcerting. There are countless books and videos available to teach children about birth in a responsible manner. Letting a cat produce offspring that the family has no intention of keeping is teaching children irresponsibility. Millions of dogs and cats are euthanized in shelters each year. Approximately 75 percent of all cats entering shelters are euthanized. While you may be able to find homes for all of the kittens in your cat's litter, each home you find means one less home available for cats at shelters and humane organizations who truly need them. Having your cat neutered or spayed is the ultimate sign of responsible pet ownership.

▲ An average cat pregnancy is sixty-five to sixty-seven days, but an individual cat may give birth a few days early or a few days late. Be prepared.

season resumes in late January. For housecats, the actual parameters of the reproductive season can vary due to the effects of artificial lighting on the reproductive cycle, although most housecats stop coming into heat during the winter months. Siamese cats are less affected by photoperiod than other breeds and often cycle year round.

The signs that a cat is in heat include excessive vocalization, becoming very affectionate, rubbing her head and neck against people and objects (more than she usually does), rolling and squirming, assuming the mating posture (the rump in the air, tail deflected to the side, and back arched downward), and making "treading" movements with her back legs.

When a female goes into heat, the smell she gives off and the vocalizations she produces alert the tomcats in the neighborhood. If several tomcats are nearby, they may gather around the female, engaging in fights with rivals. The victorious male will then pursue the female, who appears to play "hard to get." Premature attempts to mate by the male often elicit a very aggressive rebuff by the female. After a while, however, the female becomes ready to mate and will

assume the mating posture described above. The male will grasp the female by the skin over the nape of her neck and begin copulation. When the male ejaculates, the female produces a loud shriek, hisses aggressively, and violently swats the male away. The female's reaction is believed to be due to pain upon withdrawal by the male, caused by the barbs on the penis. After mating, the female rolls around on the ground while the male retires a discrete distance away. This mating process is often repeated several times, and females may mate with more than one male during their heat cycle. The males depart after the heat cycle and do not participate in the care of their kittens.

Pregnancy

As the winter turns to spring and the weather begins to get warm, the longer periods of daylight stimulate the reproductive hormones in the cat. The pituitary gland in the brain releases follicle stimulating hormone (FSH), which causes the ovaries to produce eggs. The act of mating causes the pituitary gland to release another hormone called luteinizing hormone (LH). This hormone stimulates the release of eggs (ovulation) from the ovary. Once released, the eggs travel down the fallopian tubes, where they encounter sperm from the male and become fertilized. The fertilized eggs implant themselves onto the wall of the uterus. The ovaries then secrete progesterone, the primary hormone responsible for maintaining pregnancy.

About thirty days into the pregnancy, fetuses can be felt through the abdominal wall by a veterinarian. (Cat owners should not attempt this, to avoid potential damage to the fetuses.) Fetuses can be detected even earlier than this (about fifteen days in) by ultrasound.

Pregnant cats should be kept indoors. The nutrition requirements of the pregnant cat will increase, and she may eat twice as much as before. A high-protein, high-energy diet should be fed during this time and during nursing.

About ten days before the kittens are born, the progesterone levels begin to drop and the estrogen levels start to rise. These hormonal changes give rise to behaviors that indicate labor and delivery are approaching. Cats may seclude themselves and exhibit nesting behavior as they search for the most suitable place to give birth. Provide your cat with a nesting box—a comfortable box or bed for her to have her kittens. The box should contain towels or easily shredded material, such as paper.

The birthing procedure is a natural process for cats and usually proceeds without any problems. If possible, the owner should stay by the cat's side to monitor delivery. The birth process proceeds in stages. Initially, the cervix relaxes and the uterus begins to contract. The contractions become stronger and more frequent, propelling the first fetus toward the pelvis. When the fetal head fully enters the pelvis, its pressure causes the cat to voluntarily contract her abdominal muscles. This deliberate push helps propel the fetus through the pelvis. Once the head emerges from the vulva, one or two more pushes from the female should result in delivery. Each kitten is covered with fetal membranes. As each kitten is born, the queen will tear open the membranes and clear the kitten's mouth and nose. She will also bite off the umbilical cord and eat the placenta that emerges after the kitten has been born. The interval between kittens is variable. On average, it takes approximately an hour between kittens; however, in some cases kittens can be born as quickly as ten minutes apart. Although the average litter size is four, it can range from one to twelve.

Problems during the birthing process are rare. If problems do develop, however, veterinary attention should be sought immediately.

Orphaned Kitten Care

Most people will never have to take care of an orphaned kitten, but if circumstances bring a neonate into your life, it is critical that you understand the proper care.

A kitten who does not have a mother to look after it during the first few weeks of life is said to be orphaned. If an orphaned kitten is to survive, it requires proper nutrition, hygiene, and medical and emotional support.

◄ A queen may have between one and twelve kittens in a litter, but the average litter size is four.

Nutritional support is of utmost importance. Orphaned kittens should be fed kitten milk replacer. This can be purchased at pet stores and is composed of water, proteins, fats, carbohydrates, vitamins, and minerals in proportions similar to feline milk.

Cow's milk it not an appropriate substitute and should not be used. Kitten milk replacer should be warmed to 100°F (38°C) before feeding. How much to feed will depend on the weight of the kitten and the schedule of the caretaker. The label on the kitten milk replacer will give detailed instructions.

The best method of feeding orphaned kittens is by nursing bottle, provided that an appropriately sized bottle and nipple are used. A nipple that is too small can be swallowed. A nipple that is too big can prevent proper nursing. The opening in the nipple must also be appropriate size. A hole too small will restrict the flow of milk. A hole too large can lead to an excessive amount of milk exiting the nursing bottle, which may result in aspiration of the milk into the lungs. Kittens under ten days of age may need to be fed via feeding tube since kittens this young have an absent or poorly developed swallowing reflex. Your veterinarian can provide you with the proper sized tube (typically a 5 French tube for kittens weighing less than 300 grams and an 8 French tube for kittens weighing over 300 grams) and can demonstrate the proper procedure. After each feeding, kittens should be burped to remove any swallowed air from the stomach. For the first three weeks of life, kittens will need to be stimulated to urinate and defecate after every feeding. This is accomplished by wiping a warm moist cotton ball on the genital and anal area.

Newborn orphan kittens should be fed 6 to 8 times a day. As the kitten approaches two to three weeks of age, the frequency of feedings can be reduced to three to four times per day. Newborn kittens typically weigh around 100 grams and are expected to gain about 10 grams per day. At 6 weeks of age, kittens should weigh around 500 grams. Caretakers of orphaned kittens should obtain a scale so they can monitor the kittens' weight gain.

▲ Newborn orphaned kittens should be fed six to eight times a day.

A log should be maintained for each kitten. The log should note the weight, amount that the kitten ate, urination and defecation, deworming history, and vaccination history.

By three weeks of age, solid food can be offered to the kitten. Initially, a thin gruel of canned kitten food mixed with kitten milk replacer is fed. Bottle feedings should be continued during this time. Over a two-week period, the gruel should be gradually made thicker. By 6 to 8 weeks of age, the food should be nearly solid in consistency. Fresh water should always be available during this time.

Orphaned kittens need a well-regulated environment. Kittens should be kept in a box or container that is warm and free of drafts. A heat lamp, light bulb, or heating pad covered with towels should be used to provide heat. The temperature in the box should be 85 to 90°F (29.5 to 32°C) during the kittens' first week of life, and then 80 degrees (26.5°C) for the next four weeks. A thermometer should be kept nearby to accurately measure the temperature. Once they reach 6 weeks of age, a room temperature of 70°F (21°C) is acceptable. To reduce the risk of infection, exposure to other animals or multiple people should be avoided. Wash your hands before and after each handling, and clean all equipment after use. The nesting box should be kept clean using towels or newspapers that can be easily changed when soiled. Kittens should be handled only when being fed to avoid interrupting their sleep pattern.

At two weeks of age, kittens should be dewormed. This should be repeated two weeks later. Orphaned kittens should receive their initial vaccinations at approximately 4 to 6 weeks of age.

Geriatric Care

Pets today are living longer and better-quality lives than ever before, thanks to improved nutrition, better veterinary care, and educated owners. This increased longevity means that more cats are reaching an older age, and cat owners will be faced with the special demands and problems that become apparent with age. Understanding the aging process and the most common problems that face the elderly cat is the first step in providing the best possible care for your geriatric cat.

It is important to realize that aging itself is not a disease; it is simply a stage of life. Increasing age causes a gradual decline in the body's ability to repair itself, maintain normal body functions, and adapt to the stresses and changes in the environment. Many changes occur in cats as they age. Metabolism changes, for example, so less food is required. Housecats in general have a more sedentary lifestyle, and older cats specifically are usually less active, so weight gain and obesity are common problems. The lack of exercise contributes to reduced muscle tone and strength, further adding to the potential for obesity.

With time, cats begin to have a gradual decline in their sense of hearing, smell, vision, and taste. Decreased taste sensation can contribute to anorexia, especially if the cat becomes ill. It is not uncommon for older cats to spend more time sleeping and have more difficulty being roused. Metabolic and endocrine problems, organ dysfunction, and cancer are all seen with increased frequency in the geriatric feline population. Cancer is generally a disease of older animals, so it should come as no surprise that the prevalence of cancer in cats is increasing. This is the fateful price cats must pay for their increasing longevity.

Exactly when a cat is considered to be senior or geriatric is not well defined. Most veterinarians would classify cats as being *mature* at ages seven to ten, *senior* at ages eleven to fourteen, and *geriatric* at ages fifteen and older. In the following sections, the terms *senior*, *elderly*, and *geriatric* are used synonymously.

Wellness Program

Most veterinary hospitals have designed a wellness program specific for geriatric cats. These programs consist of a thorough physical examination and a variety of diagnostic tests designed to ensure that the early stages of disease are identified and appropriate preventive measures and treatment plans are instituted. The most effective way of maintaining excellent health in a geriatric cat is to participate in your veterinarian's geriatric wellness program. Practicing prevention is always better than treating a disease already present. In the long run, preventive medicine improves quality of life and is more cost effective than waiting for problems to appear.

The most common diagnostic tests performed as part of a complete geriatric work-up include the following.

Complete medical history: It is very important to obtain a thorough geriatric health history. Some veterinarians have specific geriatric health history

▼A cat is considered a senior when she is eleven years old.

questionnaires that can be filled out by the owner. In addition, any problems or concerns that owners have about their cat should be discussed; some problems that an owner may simply attribute to "old age" are very often signs of underlying diseases that may be treatable.

Thorough physical examination: This should be performed to attempt to uncover specific problems. The eyes are examined, and a retinal exam may be performed if there is some question as to whether your cat may be experiencing some loss of vision. The ears are examined for signs of infection, parasitism, or allergies. The mouth, gums, and teeth are evaluated, with dental disease and gingivitis being common findings. Lymph nodes and the thyroid gland are evaluated for enlargement. The skin and quality of the hair coat are observed. Skin tumors or swellings are noted. A poor hair coat or a lack of grooming may be signs of allergies, parasites, infections, or systemic illness. The heart and lungs are evaluated with the stethoscope, and any abnormalities or murmurs are noted. The abdomen is palpated for any masses or organ enlargements. Finally, the general body condition is scored, and the weight is recorded.

Complete blood count: This test evaluates the circulating blood cells—the red cells, white cells, and platelets. Abnormalities in the complete blood count are common in elderly cats. Anemia can be seen as a result of kidney failure or inflammatory or cancerous conditions. Changes in the white cell count may indicate inflammatory or infectious conditions.

Biochemical profile: This profile is a very valuable test in the geriatric animal. Information about the liver, kidneys, blood sugar, and electrolytes is obtained through this important test.

Thyroid testing: Hyperthyroidism is the most common glandular disorder in elderly cats. Untreated, it can lead to serious health consequences. Thyroid testing enables veterinarians to diagnose this very treatable disorder.

Urinalysis: Analysis of the urine can help detect underlying urinary tract infection, kidney problems, and diabetes. If the urinalysis suggests the presence of an infection, a urine culture may be recommended.

Fecal examination: Since gastrointestinal parasites may be more debilitating in geriatric animals, a yearly fecal exam is recommended.

Feline immunodeficiency virus (FIV) and feline leukemia virus (FeLV) testing: Both of these viral diseases may cause suppression of the immune system and can contribute to many other systemic illnesses. In cats who are at risk of exposure to these viral diseases (i.e., outdoor cats or cats who have contact with other cats), routine blood testing is recommended. If the viral status of a cat is unknown, testing is also advised. Cats who have previously tested negative and have had no possible exposure to other cats may not need this test.

These tests represent the most routine diagnostic tests that are recommended for senior cats. Based on the history, physical examination findings, and initial test results, common additional testing might include:

Blood pressure measurement: Hypertension (high blood pressure) is often identified in the geriatric cat. Hypertension is usually associated with other disease conditions such as kidney disease and hyperthyroidism.

▼The most effective way of maintaining excellent health in a senior or geriatric cat is to participate in your veterinarian's geriatric wellness program.

▲ Cats often become less active once they enter their senior years.

Aspiration of skin masses: A common finding on the physical examination of older cats is small masses on or in the skin. Many times, these are benign tumors or cysts that grow slowly and rarely cause problems. However, cats do have a higher incidence of malignant skin tumors than do dogs. Because of this, it is usually recommended that skin tumors on cats be aspirated (a needle is inserted into the mass) and the recovered cells evaluated microscopically for evidence of malignancy. The size and location of all masses should be recorded in the medical record so that changes in previous masses or the development new masses can be noted.

Radiographs: Radiographs (x-rays) may be advised based on the initial tests or physical exam findings. Chest radiographs are part of a cardiac investigation if a heart murmur is discovered, as well as a screening test for cancer. Abdominal radiographs might be needed if organ dysfunction is suspected or organ enlargement or masses are detected during the physical examination.

Cardiac (heart) evaluation: If there are signs of potential heart disease, such as a newly discovered heart murmur or labored breathing, a more complete cardiac evaluation is indicated. Chest radiographs, an electrocardiogram (EKG), and an echocardiogram will help better define the extent and cause of potential cardiac disease and whether treatment is necessary.

Abdominal ultrasound: Abdominal ultrasound offers a noninvasive method of visualizing masses and organs within the abdomen. Generally, more detail can be obtained with an ultrasound than with radiographs.

Endoscopy: Evaluating the stomach and intestines through the use of endoscopy is a valuable diagnostic tool. Inflammatory bowel disease (IBD) and gastrointestinal lymphoma are common gastrointestinal disorders seen in senior cats. Endoscopy offers a relatively noninvasive method of obtaining gastrointestinal biopsies for establishing a diagnosis.

By participating in and following a geriatric health plan, disorders can be detected early enough so that prompt medical or surgical intervention can be provided, allowing for significant improvements in the quality of a cat's life.

Conditions Associated with Aging

Although most cats age very gracefully, many suffer from some of the same conditions and diseases that aging humans do, including arthritis, hearing and vision loss, and cognitive dysfunction. As with people, for instance, arthritis can be present in cats of all ages, but it is more common in older cats. A study of cats of all ages showed that 22–33 percent of cats have x-ray evidence of arthritis and that the incidence increases with age. Furthermore, 90 percent of cats over the age of twelve have radiographic signs of arthritis. The elbows and hips are the most commonly affected joints. Many cats have multiple affected joints.

Arthritis

Arthritis is a well-recognized problem in dogs but is often overlooked or unrecognized in cats. This lack of awareness is due to several factors. Cats with arthritis are less likely than dogs to show true lameness because cats are adept at redistributing weight bearing to unaffected limbs. The feline lifestyle is also a factor. When an arthritic dog can no longer jump into the back of the van or has to stop and rest during long walks, the owner immediately recognizes that there's a problem. When a cat can no longer jump onto the windowsill or bed, she merely chooses a new favorite place to sleep or meditate, and the owner simply thinks the cat has discovered a novel location for her lounging. Many cat owners don't consider that their cats might be suffering from arthritis. As we've noted before, cats are very good at hiding their signs of illness or pain.

Arthritis can be categorized as either primary or secondary. In primary arthritis, there is no clear underlying cause of the arthritis. With secondary arthritis, an underlying cause is identified or suspected, such as hip dysplasia or previous joint trauma. Most cases of arthritis in cats are primary.

Symptoms: Unlike dogs, lameness is not a typical clinical sign in cats. Cats with arthritis will often show signs such as inappropriate elimination (urinating and/or defecating outside the litter box) because their normally very flexible spine

▲ An arthritic cat may spend more time on the floor because it is too difficult for her to jump up to her favorite resting spots.

become stiffer and less compliant as they develop spinal arthritis, making it difficult to squat in the litter box. Often, the cat will urinate or defecate immediately outside the box instead. Decreased grooming, matting of hair, or an unkempt coat may be seen because stiffness of the spine can make it difficult to twist the torso properly to groom the rear parts of the body. You may also see reluctance to jump up or down, inability to jump as high as before, sitting down and standing up more slowly than in the past, hiding, becoming annoyed about being combed or groomed, and sleeping more. These signs are often incorrectly attributed to simple aging, leading cat owners to delay or avoid seeking veterinary advice.

Diagnosis and treatment: The diagnosis of arthritis is usually based on a history of behavioral changes associated with arthritis and physical examination findings. Radiographs confirm the diagnosis, but the clinical signs of arthritis do not always correlate well with the radiographs. In other words, a cat with mild x-ray changes may experience significant discomfort, whereas a cat with severe radiographic changes may feel OK. Joint fluid analysis may help to support or confirm the diagnosis, but this is rarely necessary.

Treatment may involve lifestyle changes as well as pharmacological and nonpharmacological therapies. Food bowls should be placed in areas that do not require jumping for access, and litter boxes with high sides may need to be replaced with a low-sided box for easier access. Steps or ramps can be constructed to allow cats to have continued access to their favorite spots. As in dogs, obesity is suspected to contribute to the development and clinical signs of arthritis. Overweight cats should be placed on a diet with close veterinary monitoring. Exercise using toys (a laser pointer and other interactive toys) can encourage weight loss and keep joints limber.

The cornerstone of pharmacological management of arthritis is the use of nonsteroidal anti-inflammatory drugs (NSAIDs). Cats, however, often have trouble metabolizing drugs of this type, and some of these drugs can be toxic if given to cats. Meloxicam, an NSAID, has been reported to be effective in treating or controlling arthritis pain, but its use in cats is controversial, and it should only be considered as a last resort, in cases of crippling arthritis.

Nonpharmacological management may include administering nutraceuticals such as glucosamine and chondroitin sulfate. These compounds are believed to slow the progression of cartilage degradation and promote cartilage health by providing the necessary ingredients to repair and maintain cartilage. Several formulations for use in cats are available. Polysulfated glycosaminoglycans (under the brand name Adequan) have also been shown to be helpful in treating arthritis. This nutraceutical is approved for use in dogs and horses, but has been used in cats by many veterinarians (myself included), with dramatic results in some cases. Acupuncture has also been used to treat arthritis in cats with varying success.

Arthritis is an irreversible, progressive disease that cannot be cured by medical treatment. Although arthritis may not be as well documented in cats as in other species, it is essential that cat owners recognize the clinical signs associated with arthritis, especially now that cats are enjoying longer lifespans.

Cognitive Dysfunction

As cats get older, they sometimes experience a decline in mental ability or *cognitive function*. Changes in memory, learning, perception, and awareness are well documented in aging people, and similar changes have been described in aging pets.

Symptoms: In cats, this decline may reveal itself in several ways. Some cats may forget previously learned behaviors, such as housetraining. Sometimes a cat will acquire new fears and anxieties. Other signs may include failure to recognize people, places, and other pets; altered sleep–wake cycles (such as sleeping more overall, but less at night); aimless activity, such as wandering or pacing; and acting generally "disoriented." Sometimes, when cats become geriatric, they may begin vocalizing excessively; cognitive dysfunction (CD) needs to be considered as the possible cause of this vocalization.

▼ Senior cats with cognitive dysfunction may cry excessively for no discernible reason.

In lay terms, CD would be equivalent to senility or senile dementia in humans. Some cats as they age become mentally feeble, and this may express itself as increased, seemingly pointless vocalization.

Diagnosis and treatment: Cognitive dysfunction syndrome (CDS) is a clinical syndrome defined as the development of one or more geriatric-onset behavior problems that cannot be attributed to an unrelated medical condition such as cancer, infection, or organ failure. Studies have shown that about 55 percent of cats aged eleven through fifteen years develop at least one geriatric-onset behavior problem and that the percentage increases to 80 percent for cats aged sixteen through twenty. Although cats show similar types of geriatric behavior problems as dogs, the percentage of cats who are affected with CDS is much lower. As we noted before, cats age very gracefully.

Treatment options for cats with cognitive dysfunction syndrome are limited. The drug L-deprenyl (Anipril) is approved for use in CDS in the United States but only for dogs. Although there are no published studies on the use of L-deprenyl in cats, anecdotal reports of cats being given the drug off-label suggest that some cats might benefit from this drug. Cat owners should be aware that administration of medication for CDS is not approved for cats. A nutritional supplement containing s-adenosyl-methionine (SAMe) has been marketed under the brand name Novifit and is designed to help support cognitive function in aging cats and dogs.

Hearing Loss

Cats have an amazing sense of hearing, being able to hear high frequencies that humans cannot. They can locate the source of a sound with pinpoint accuracy and can hear sounds at much greater distances than can humans. Unfortunately, hearing is another of the senses that diminish as cats age. Deafness that occurs in one ear only usually goes unnoticed by most cat owners because cats compensate very well.

Symptoms: Cats who are deaf in both ears may show signs of hearing loss such as responding only when they can see you, sleeping more than normal, turning their heads in the wrong direction when called, not responding to noises that formerly elicited a response (such as the opening of a can of cat food or the shaking a packet of cat treats), and not waking up unless physically touched.

Diagnosis and treatment: Specialized tests are available at referral centers to definitively prove a cat's deafness, but these are expensive and are rarely necessary. A simple test is to make a loud noise while the cat is asleep and see if the cat awakens. The item that makes the noise should not cause vibrations (such as a door slamming) because as this can confuse the assessment. Cats suspected of being deaf should be evaluated by a veterinarian to be certain that the deafness isn't due to a treatable condition. Sensorineural deafness, the kind that occurs as a natural part of the aging process, cannot be treated. (The use of hearing aids has been attempted in dogs and cats, but the majority of animals do not tolerate the presence of the hearing aid in the ear canal.) A deaf cat may no longer come when you call her, so consider attaching a bell to your deaf cat's collar so that you can more easily locate her. Deaf cats should never be allowed outdoors because they cannot hear dangers, such as cars.

▼ If your cat has become blind, don't move the furniture, litter pan, or food and water bowls from their familiar places.

Vision Loss

Many cat owners notice that their elderly cat's eyes have a cloudy appearance. This is often mistaken for cataracts. In fact, this condition is called lenticular sclerosis and is a benign clouding of the lens that occurs naturally as cats age. It does not cause significant vision impairment.

When elderly cats do go blind, it can occur gradually as the visual system gradually degenerates with age, or it can be sudden, as is seen in cases of acute retinal detachment. Retinal detachment can occur as a result of high blood pressure. The most common cause for high blood pressure is chronic kidney disease, a very common disease of geriatric cats. Many owners don't notice that their cat is blind right away because the senses of hearing and smell can often compensate for the loss of vision. When vision loss is gradual, cats memorize their surroundings and owners may notice that their cat is blind only when the cat's surroundings are altered.

Symptoms: Signs of blindness include bumping into objects, acting easily startled or fearful, an inability to locate their food and water dishes, excessive sleeping, and decreased interest in toys, especially those that incorporate motion, like a laser pointer.

Diagnosis and treatment: Acute vision loss should be evaluated by a veterinarian promptly so that a cause can be determined. Cats with vision loss that occurs secondary to retinal detachment from high blood pressure may have some of their vision restored if the blood pressure is quickly brought to normal. Vision loss that occurs due to age-related degeneration, however, cannot be restored.

Cats adjust to their blindness just like humans do, relying on their other senses, especially smell and hearing, which are very well developed in the cat. It may take time, however, for a blind cat to adjust to her vision loss, especially if the blindness occurred acutely. The most important thing is to keep the environment as consistent as possible. Furniture should not be rearranged. Clothing, toys, or other items should not be discarded on the floor. A consistent area for eating, sleeping, and

▲ Blind or deaf cats should not be let outside, but they can still enjoy a screened-in porch.

eliminating is essential. Do not move the cat bed, litter box, or food and water bowls. Try to feed your cat around the same time every day to establish a routine. Remove or cover any sharp objects or edges, especially those at the cat's eye level. Keep the toilet lid closed. Cats navigate their way using their other senses as well as their memory. Do not carry the cat from one area to the other because this can be confusing to her. Blind cats do better if they walk from area to area. A familiar voice encouraging your cat to come toward you can help a cat who seems lost or disoriented. Taking your cat to the same familiar spot, such as the feeding area, is a good way to reorient her. Block your cat's access to stairways, balconies, and terraces.

When she is sleeping, use your voice or some other kind of noise, rather than touch, to wake her up. Some blind animals may become startled when touched and may scratch or bite. Once awakened by a noise or your voice, you can gently touch her. Blind cats still enjoy playing with toys, but they should be toys that stimulate the other senses. If your cat responds to catnip, a catnip-scented toy can be a treat. Toys that make sounds can provide stimulation.

Obviously, blind cats should never be allowed to go outdoors unattended. In the unlikely event that your cat escapes or finds her way outdoors, she is

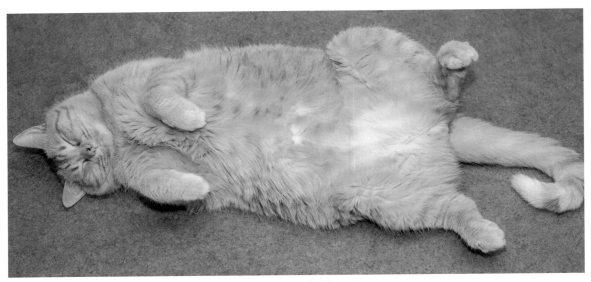

▲ Obesity may contribute to diabetes in cats, so do your best to keep your kitty at a healthy weight.

unlikely to find her way back home. Make sure she always has some identification on her, either a collar (with a medical alert tag that says that she is blind), a microchip, or both. If you do let your cat outside, a harness or leash should be used. A screened porch is a safe way for your blind cat to enjoy the outdoors.

Metabolic and Cancerous Conditions Seen in Aging Cats

Geriatric cats also have problems with periodontal disease (see chapter 13, page 305) and kidney disease (see chapter 15, page 346). They are also more likely than young cats to succumb to diseases such as diabetes, hyperthyroidism, and cancer.

Diabetes occurs when the pancreas fails to produce adequate amounts of insulin, a hormone necessary for controlling blood glucose (sugar) levels. Most cats diagnosed with diabetes are over seven years of age. Males are almost twice as likely to become diabetic as females. Overweight cats are more likely to be afflicted with diabetes.

Hyperthyroidism is a common cause of weight loss in senior cats. A variety of other clinical signs can accompany the weight loss, most notably a dramatic increase in appetite. It occurs when the thyroid gland produces excessive amounts of thyroxine, the major thyroid hormone.

Hyperthyroidism is a disorder of elderly cats. The vast majority of hyperthyroid cats are over twelve years of age.

Cancer is unrestrained cell growth and replication. Normally, cell replication is tightly regulated. Occasionally, a single cell may experience one or more genetic mutations and cancer may arise. Control of cellular replication becomes unregulated, resulting in a tumor. Exactly what causes a cell to mutate into a cancerous cell remains unknown, although some environmental agents have been shown to be able to induce cancerous changes in cells, such as viruses, chemicals, radiation, and some hormones. The effects of these agents can accumulate over time, explaining why, although it does occur in younger animals, cancer more commonly affects older ones. Another word for cancer is *neoplasia* (new growth), and tumors are sometimes referred to as *neoplasms*. Tumors are classified as benign or malignant. Benign tumors remain at their original site of occurrence. Malignant tumors can invade surrounding tissues and gain access to the bloodstream or lymphatic vessels and then be transported to nearby lymph nodes or other parts of the body. This process is called *metastasis* and is commonly how cancer spreads. Cats are susceptible to a variety of cancers. Among the most common are mammary (breast) cancer, lymphosarcoma, and squamous cell carcinoma.

Diabetes Mellitus

Diabetes is one of the most common endocrine (glandular) disorders in cats, affecting about 1 in 400 cats in the United States. Although the exact cause of diabetes in not known, obesity, genetic predisposition, pancreatic disease, hormonal imbalances, and certain medications have all been incriminated.

Symptoms: Most cats are presented to the veterinarian with the classic signs of diabetes: excessive urination, excessive thirst, very good appetite, and weight loss. In a small number of diabetic cats, the nerves supplying the hind legs may be affected, resulting in an abnormal gait.

Diagnosis and treatment: Diabetes is usually easy to diagnose. High levels of sugar in the blood and the presence of sugar in the urine allow for a straightforward diagnosis. Occasionally, the clinical signs can be misleading and the blood and urine tests can be equivocal, making the diagnosis somewhat tricky. In these instances, some additional tests may be necessary before a definitive diagnosis can be reached.

Caring for a diabetic cat takes a strong commitment from both the cat owner and the veterinarian. You must be able and willing to provide a high level of care on a daily basis. Although a few cats will experience remission of their diabetes if their blood sugar is aggressively controlled with insulin and diet, most cats require lifelong insulin therapy. Every day, you will have to give your cat insulin injections, watch her diet, and monitor her behavior.

The initial cost of treating a diabetic cat can be significant. In some cats, the diabetes can be brought under control fairly quickly, with only a few visits to the veterinarian and a minimal number of adjustments to get the insulin dosage right. Other cats require more frequent initial visits and more dosage adjustments. The initial attempts to regulate the diabetes involve simple blood or urine tests and outpatient visits. As you and your veterinarian get

closer to discovering the exact amount of insulin required to control the disease, your cat may need to be hospitalized for ten to twelve hours so that a "glucose curve" can be performed. This involves taking a tiny sample of blood every one to two hours and determining the blood sugar level. The glucose curve allows the creation of a blood glucose profile in the form of a graph, giving information about your cat's unique pattern of response to its insulin. In most cases, a glucose curve is not necessary, and progress can be monitored by measuring a cat's fructosamine levels. The fructosamine level is a reflection of the cat's average blood sugar level over the previous two weeks.

Advances in home monitoring systems are leading some veterinarians to recommend that blood glucose curves be obtained in the home setting. Blood glucose concentrations are measured at home by collecting blood from the ear of the cat using a lancing device.

▼ Diabetic cats require daily insulin injections and a special diet—and a loving and committed pet parent.

This can be demonstrated in the office for the client. Collection of blood from the ear does not appear to be painful to the cat, and the puncture sites are barely visible, even after multiple collections.

Once the initial testing is accomplished and the insulin requirements are determined, subsequent costs (insulin, syringes, prescription diets, progress examinations) decrease dramatically and are quite manageable.

Treatment of diabetes involves medication and special diets. Although some diabetic cats may respond to treatment using oral glucose-lowering drugs, these drugs work poorly and have fallen out of favor. The majority of cats will require twice-daily insulin injections.Many studies have also shown that a high-protein, low-carbohydrate food is the ideal diet for diabetic cats. These diets are available as prescription diets and can be purchased at nearly all veterinary offices.

Many cat owners cringe at the idea of injecting their cats. However, owners soon learn that most cats find injections far less stressful than pilling and get the technique down fairly quickly. Your veterinarian and his or her technicians will teach you the technique.

Insulin must be given at the same time(s) every day. The majority of cats receive insulin twice daily. Choose the time frame that works best for you. If you're most likely to be home at 6 a.m. and 6 p.m., give the injections at these times. If 9:00 a.m. and 9:00 p.m. works better for you, this is fine too. As long as you're consistent, there should be few problems.

Reusing needles is not recommended. After one use, needles are no longer sterile and bacteria from the cat's skin can contaminate the entire bottle of insulin when a used needle is stuck back into the vial. Needles also become dull very quickly, and dull needles are more likely to sting a little when they're inserted into the skin.

Although most diabetics remain reasonably healthy before they present to the veterinarian, some cats can develop a condition called *ketoacidosis*, in which the cat may become extremely lethargic with signs such as vomiting, diarrhea, loss of appetite,

Signs of Hypoglycemia

These signs include weakness, lack of coordination, acting spacey or confused, and occasionally coma. Dogs often experience seizures when they become hypoglycemic. Cats may have seizures, but this is less common. Instead, cats seem to act "drunk" and confused. If a diabetic cat experiences an episode of hypoglycemia, contact a veterinarian immediately. While waiting for veterinary assistance, give your cat corn syrup or honey slowly, using a syringe to squirt it into her mouth. If she is able to eat, offer her normal food. If your cat is having seizures or is semi-comatose, rub a tablespoon of corn syrup or honey onto her gums. A noticeable effect should be seen within five minutes of administering the syrup. Overdoses can happen if an incorrect insulin dose is being measured on the syringe. A more common scenario that leads to overdosing is that one family member has given insulin to the cat not realizing that another family member already gave it. If more than one person is handling the medication of a diabetic cat, good communication between family members is essential to avoid this situation.

dehydration, and coma. Ketoacidosis is considered a potentially life-threatening emergency, and any diabetic cat with these clinical signs should be evaluated by a veterinarian immediately. Diabetics are also more prone to infections, with oral and urinary tract infections being most common.

Without insulin, your cat cannot survive. Too much insulin, however, is just as bad as too little. A potentially dangerous condition called *hypoglycemia* (low blood sugar) can result from an overdose of insulin. This is sometimes referred to as "insulin shock." Any cat undergoing treatment for diabetes must be watched carefully for signs of hypoglycemia. (See Signs of Hypoglycemia on this page.)

Although the concern that a cat owner feels when told that his or her cat has diabetes can be overwhelming, it should be kept in mind that the prognosis for diabetic cats is good; diabetic cats do not go blind from cataracts like diabetic dogs do, and they do not suffer circulatory problems or other problems that human diabetics experience. Diabetes is a treatable condition, and cats can live normal, happy, healthy lives for many years after the diagnosis.

Hyperthyroidism

Hyperthyroidism is a glandular disorder of geriatric cats. It occurs as a result of the thyroid gland (located in the neck) producing excessive amounts of thyroid hormone.

Symptoms: Cats with hyperthyroidism can have any of a number of clinical signs, the most common being weight loss despite an excellent appetite. Other possible signs include excessive thirst and urination, vomiting, diarrhea, panting, restlessness, excessive shedding, and increased vocalization.

Diagnosis and treatment: Fortunately, hyperthyroidism is easily diagnosed by a simple blood test, and the disorder is very treatable. In fact, it is curable. The ideal treatment is the administration of radioactive iodine. A dose of radioactive iodine is given subcutaneously (under the skin). The iodine travels to the thyroid gland (because the thyroid is where all of the body's iodine is stored), allowing for the radiation to

treat the condition. A single dose of radioactive iodine is effective in approximately 95 percent of cases. The main advantage of radioactive iodine therapy is that it is curative, safe, and noninvasive; anesthesia and surgery are not required. The main disadvantages are the cost (at the time of this writing, the typical cost for this procedure is $1,500 to $2,000) and the requirement that the cat stay at the treatment facility for seven to ten days. Treated cats cannot be released to their owners until the level of radioactivity in the urine and feces decreases to an acceptable amount. Because this treatment requires the use of radioactive materials, it must be performed at a referral center.

Thyroidectomy (surgical removal of the thyroid) is another curative procedure. However, the risks of anesthesia, the invasiveness of the procedure, and the fact that the cost is the same (or more) than radioactive iodine therapy have made surgical treatment nearly obsolete.

The most common treatment is administration of medication that suppresses the release of thyroid hormone from the thyroid gland. The drug, methimazole, must be administered twice daily, doses approximately twelve hours apart. Although

▼ Hyperthyroidism can cause cats to become thin and shed excessively.

the medication is usually in tablet form, it can be compounded into a liquid form for cats who resist being pilled. For cats who resist any form of oral medication, the methimazole can be prepared (by a compounding pharmacy) into a gel that is applied to the inside, hairless portion of the ear. The methimazole is absorbed through the skin into the bloodstream.

Recently, a diet has been marketed that, if fed consistently, controls hyperthyroidism in cats. The diet is severely iodine restricted and works by depriving the cat of the iodine necessary to synthesize thyroid hormone. The diet must be the only food that the cat consumes. Absolutely no other food, including treats, can be given. The diet is available in both canned and dry formulations, and most cats find the diet palatable. If a cat who initially finds the diet palatable develops an aversion to the diet (as cats are known to do), an alternative treatment will be necessary to control the condition.

Left untreated, hyperthyroidism can have serious health consequences. Cats can develop heart failure and may also develop hypertension (high blood pressure), which can affect other body systems, namely the nervous system, the eyes, and the kidneys. To not treat is not an option. With appropriate treatment, the prognosis for cats with hyperthyroidism is excellent.

Lymphoma

Lymphoma (also called *lymphosarcoma*; the terms are often used interchangeably) is a cancer arising from lymphoid tissues. It is the most common cancer in the cat, accounting for one-third of all feline cancers. Affected cats range in age, on average, from two to six years although any age cat is susceptible. Infection with FeLV increases the risk of developing lymphosarcoma. This is especially true of younger cats. Older cats who develop lymphoma are less likely to be concurrently infected with FeLV. Cats infected with FIV are also more likely to develop lymphoma later in life. Exposure to second-hand cigarette smoke has also been shown to increase the relative risk of developing lymphoma.

▲With proper treatment, cats with hyperthyroidism have an excellent prognosis.

Lymphoma is often categorized by anatomic location. The five common types are mediastinal (involving structures inside the chest), alimentary (digestive system), multicentric (the lymph nodes), leukemic (the bloodstream), and extranodal (other organs, such as the kidneys, eyes, nervous system, nasal cavity, and skin). In cats, the most common sites are the gastrointestinal tract, the mediastinum (structures in the chest such as the thymus and associated lymph nodes), the liver, spleen, and kidneys.

Treatment: Once a diagnosis of lymphoma is made, there are three options: no treatment, euthanasia, or treatment. Some cat owners choose not to treat because of the financial, emotional, and time commitment involved. Lymphoma is one of the most treatable cancers in the cat, however, and for those who choose to treat a variety of options exist. Lymphoma is fairly responsive to chemotherapy, and your veterinarian can devise a protocol suitable for your cat's particular type of lymphoma. If more advanced therapies are appropriate, such as radiation or the use of investigational drugs, referral to a veterinary oncologist may be warranted. Lymphoma is controllable, but it is not considered curable by any currently available treatment. (For more information about gastrointestinal lymphoma, see the section on Gastrointestinal Cancer, chapter 16,

Mammary Cancer

Studies estimate that 1 out of 4,000 cats develop breast cancer. Although this may seem like a small incidence, breast cancer is in fact the third most common tumor in cats, accounting for 10–12 percent of all diagnosed feline tumors.

The average age at onset is ten to twelve years. Siamese females are at twice the risk of developing this type of cancer compared with other cat breeds. Siamese also tend to develop these tumors at a younger age. Males of any breed rarely develop breast cancer.

Unspayed cats are at an increased risk of breast cancer. Spaying a cat, especially before her first heat, greatly reduces this risk. Spaying a cat prior to six months of age leads to a 91 percent reduction in the risk of mammary cancer development. In other words, a cat spayed prior to her first heat (around six months of age) has only 9 percent of the risk of mammary tumor development that an unspayed cat does. If a cat is spayed after six months, but before one year, the risk is 14 percent compared with an unspayed cat. After a year (or two heat cycles), spaying offers no reduction in the risk of future tumor development.

Symptoms: Cats have four pairs of mammary glands: the four on the left side form the left chain, and the four on the right comprise the right chain. The glands are numbered one to four, with gland 1 being closest to the head and gland 4 being closest to the tail. Most cats with mammary tumors are brought to the veterinarian after the owner notices a lump associated with the mammary gland(s). Sometimes, however, the lump is detected by the veterinarian during a routine physical examination. Cats may have a tumor involving a single gland or multiple glands.

Diagnosis and treatment: Diagnosis is made by discovering the presence of a mammary mass on physical examination. Mammary tumors should be removed surgically. There is no way to determine whether a mammary tumor is benign or malignant solely from the visual appearance of the tumor. In dogs, 50 percent of these tumors are benign. Of the 50 percent that are malignant, half of them can be removed completely, resulting in a cure. The other half will either recur or metastasize (spread to other parts of the body) following surgery. In cats, the picture is grimmer: approximately 86 percent of tumors are malignant.

Because most affected cats are elderly, a full presurgical evaluation of the patient is important. A complete blood count, serum biochemistry panel, thyroid evaluation, and urinalysis should be performed. Radiographs should be taken as well, to determine if the cancer has already spread to the lungs at the time of surgery. If the cancer has spread, surgery won't be curative and it may be best to cancel the surgery and instead focus all efforts on supportive care to keep the cat comfortable. If the tumor is ulcerated and bleeding or infected, it may be necessary to proceed with surgery even if the tumor has already spread to the lungs or elsewhere.

The goal of surgery is to remove the entire tumor by the simplest procedure possible. Single tumors may be removed by a *mammectomy*—removal of the entire mammary gland. If tumors are present in multiple glands, they may be removed individually, or via a *chain mastectomy* in which the entire chain of mammary glands is removed via one long incision. Again, the choice of procedure depends on ease of removal of all affected tissue. Because each gland within a mammary chain is connected to each other by lymphatic vessels, some surgeons feel that a

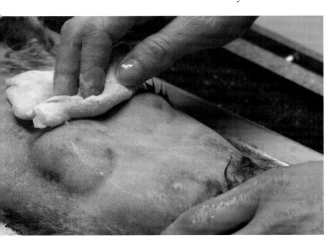

◄ Cat with mammary cancer being prepared for surgery.

Three Treatment Options for Cancer

Once cancer is diagnosed, there are three common treatment options: surgery, chemotherapy, or radiation.

Surgery: Surgery affords the best chance a cure by removing the affected tissue. Surgery is curative only if the cancer hasn't already spread and if the affected area can be removed completely. For cancers such as leukemia, which involves the bloodstream, surgery is obviously not an option.

Radiation: Radiation is an option for localized tumors that cannot be treated surgically or were treated surgically but all of cancerous tissue could not be removed. Radiation works by aiming a penetrating beam of high-energy gamma rays or streams of radioactive particles at the tumor. When irradiated, the DNA of the cancer cells is fatally damaged; cancer cells can no longer divide and spread, so they die. Some cancers are very susceptible to radiation treatment whereas others are resistant. Anesthesia is necessary, so that the cat is completely immobile and the radiation or particle beam can be precisely focused onto the tumor. The equipment necessary for radiation treatment is expensive and highly specialized and is only available at universities or referral centers. Side effects of radiation are usually temporary and can vary depending on the area of the body being irradiated. Redness and irritation at the site of radiation are the most common. Hair loss at the site of irradiation is often seen.

Although the lost hair usually grows back, the hair color may change. If radiation is administered to areas in or near the mouth, the oral tissues may become inflamed or irritated, and the cat may become reluctant to eat and/or drink. These cats may need to be handfed or have a feeding tube inserted. Radiation administered to areas near the eye may result in the vision being affected, or the cat may experience a reduction in tear production. There is always some risk associated with the anesthesia necessary for radiation treatment; however, the duration of anesthesia is usually short and cats are monitored closely throughout the procedure. Radiation therapy can be exceedingly expensive, and many cat owners find this option to be cost prohibitive.

Chemotherapy: Chemotherapy is another common option, especially for cancers involving several body sites or at sites that aren't amenable to surgery or radiation. Although many veterinary chemotherapy drugs are the same as those used for humans, they're not given with the same expectations. Chemotherapy for animals is not intended to be curative. The goal is to reduce the number of cancer cells and slow the progression of disease for as long as possible while maintaining good quality of life. Therefore the drugs are typically not used in the high concentration in cats than they are in people, which means that most cats tolerate chemotherapy very well. Chemo drugs are still potent, however, and cats must be monitored for side effects such as vomiting, diarrhea, and poor appetite. Generalized hair loss is uncommon, but shaved hair (shaved for intravenous catheter placement or surgery) is slower to grow back, and cats may lose their whiskers.

radical chain mastectomy is the procedure of choice, even if only one tumor is detected, since mammary tumors initially spread via the lymphatic vessels.

There are differing opinions regarding the efficacy of chemotherapy for feline mammary gland tumors. Some veterinary oncologists recommend chemotherapy as adjunct therapy in cats whose tumors show evidence of invasion into the blood vessels or lymphatic vessels. Others recommend chemotherapy in all cases, given the high metastatic potential of feline mammary tumors. A consultation with a veterinary oncologist would be prudent to assess whether a particular cat is an appropriate candidate for postsurgical chemotherapy.

Prognosis depends on several factors, the most important being the size of the tumor at the time of diagnosis. If the tumor is less than 2 centimeters in diameter, the prognosis is better; cats often survive more than three years. Tumors larger than 3 centimeters are associated with a survival time of only four to six months. These statistics clearly illustrate what has essentially become common knowledge regarding cancer in people and animals: early detection is of paramount importance.

Squamous Cell Carcinoma

Squamous cell carcinoma (SCC) accounts for 15 percent of all feline skin tumors. These tumors usually involve light or unpigmented skin. Sun exposure increases the risk of developing SCC. The most common locations are the hairless area of the nose, the eyelids, and ears. Older cats are at higher risk; the mean age for affected cats is twelve years. Siamese cats, with their pigmented skin, are less likely to develop SCC than other breeds. A more common—and more devastating—scenario is when SCC affects a cat's mouth. Oral SCC is the most common oral malignancy in cats. Its occurrence is often disastrous, as oral SCC is much worse than the skin form. The oral tissues that are commonly involved include the tonsils, the tongue, the gums, and the mandible (lower jaw bone).

Symptoms: The most common symptoms of oral SCC in cats are difficulty or inability to eat and/or groom. Cats may drool if the tumor prevents proper closure of the mouth. The saliva may be tinged with blood if the tumor becomes ulcerated. A foul odor from the mouth may be present if the tumor becomes infected. If the upper or lower jaw is the primary site of the tumor, a swelling on the face may be noted before clinical signs develop.

The primary symptom of the cutaneous (skin) form of SCC is the presence of a mass on the skin, mainly on the face or ears. In many cases, the mass will ulcerate and appear as a sore that fails to heal.

Diagnosis and treatment: Squamous cell carcinomas are diagnosed by biopsy of the affected tissues. This requires anesthesia. SCC of the skin is often amenable to treatment. Surgery, radiation therapy, and intralesional chemotherapy (in which the drug is injected directly into the tumor) have all been shown effective in treating this cancer.

Unfortunately, most cases (95 percent) of oral SCC are diagnosed only after the cat is showing overt clinical signs. Treatment of oral SCC is often unrewarding. Thus far, surgery has offered the best chance for survival but most of the time the disease has progressed too far for surgery to be of any benefit. Chemotherapy, like other treatment, has mostly been ineffective. However, Palladia, a new FDA-approved drug for treatment of some canine cancers has shown some promise in slowing the growth of oral SCC in cats.

▼ Cats with pale fur and skin are at an increased risk for squamous cell carcinoma.

Chapter 19

Activities with Your Cat

When I play with my cat, who knows whether she is not amusing herself with me more than I with her.

— Montaigne

There is no question that cats who have an exclusively indoor lifestyle are much safer than those exposed to predators, diseases, and other dangerous situations outside the home. As a result, they live longer, healthier lives (as statistics show). Those of us who bring our cats indoors, however, must remember that cats are predatory creatures and that part of their normal exercise routine is based on physical activities driven by their inherent prey drive. If we simply domesticate our felines without providing them with indoor alternatives, then we are all too likely to turn them into couch potatoes, a state that leads to obesity and the medical complications associated with it. A lack of daily activities also leads to behavioral issues associated with boredom and an unstimulated lifestyle, such as scratching furniture and chewing and even chasing their own tails and pulling out their fur.

Consequently, it's critical that an indoor cat's life be enriched with activities, toys, and lots of feline interaction with people and, possibly, other pets (see chapter 8, "Introducing Your New Cat") to ensure that she is getting plenty of physical and mental stimulation. (A good reason for adopting two cats from the same

▶ It's important to enrich the life of your indoor cat with activities, toys, and plenty of interaction.

litter is that they most likely will play with and entertain each other.) Fortunately, the pet industry at large is cognizant of the need for toys and quite happy to fill it. There's a plethora of wonderfully innovative products to pique feline curiosity and take care of various emotional, instinctual, and physical needs. Then there's the fabulous selection of creative cat condos and furniture designed to enhance the indoor feline lifestyle.

You don't stop at activities at home; there's plenty to share with your favorite feline outside the walls of your house. Properly equipped, you can take your cat for a stroll or a walk about the neighborhood, to visit friends (who don't have their own pets), or even to a special event. If you are feeling particularly adventurous, and your cat seems a candidate for it, think about entering her in agility competitions. Or, if your cat meets the qualifications, and you and she have the wherewithal for it, you might consider another type of competition—a cat show.

Whatever toys you get, whatever activities you take part in, don't forget it's really important to spend quality time with your cat every day. Try to spend forty minutes a day interacting with your feline, whether it is grooming or petting her or simply playing games or relaxing together on the couch. Remember, you can multitask: watch TV while you scratch her behind the ears. Consider breaking up the time you spend together into short sessions spread throughout the day. Such interludes should never be considered "a task" but a wonderful way of interacting with your pet, building her social confidence, and, most importantly, strengthening your human–feline bond.

Activities and Entertainment at Home

It's important to introduce toys and games from kittenhood. Always be in control and never encourage rough games that allow a kitten (or a fully grown cat) to bite, claw, and draw blood. If a cat is prone to such behavior, learn to time your play sessions accordingly and end the game just before the claws come out.

It's important to remember that, apart from the physical exercise fun and games provide, they also give your cat much-needed mental stimulation and help hone her inherent instincts to hunt and pounce.

Cat Toys and Games

Cats can be very inventive and turn just about anything from a crumpled piece of paper to a shopping bag into a plaything, and toy

▼Toys are fun, but they are no substitute to spending quality time with your feline companion.

▲ Most cats cannot resist laser pointers.

manufacturers have used this inventiveness to design some fabulous gadgets. Cat toys can be divided into three main categories.

Interactive toys are playthings that involve human and feline interaction. Distraction toys and games (often also referred to as enrichment toys) are designed to distract and keep a cat busy when she's on her own. This category is especially important if cats are home alone for lengthy periods. (It's a good idea to place toys in a cat tree or condo because cats love to play with things in their own private space, too.) And last, there are comfort toys—some cats, just like some dogs, love to carry around small plush toys in their mouths, wrestle with them, and then curl up to sleep with them.

Interactive Toys and Games

Interactive toys and games can be a lot of fun for both you and your cat. They fall into the following categories:

Wands and fishing rods: Wands can sport a variety of furry materials, feathers and bells, and stretch fabrics that will "jump" when pounced on and fly off in another direction. There are even bugs on wires that "fly" and fish on the end of realistic-looking rods that can be reeled in. Some wands also

have a battery-operated toy on the end that makes a realistic buzzing or fluttering noise to really pique a cat's prey drive and makes the games even more fun. Make sure you move the wand across and away from yourself to prevent your cat accidentally clawing you. Train your cat that such games take place in an open space to ensure that valuable ornaments and electronic equipment don't bear the brunt of such feline fun.

Laser toys: Lasers also rev up a cat's prey drive as they chase after the little red dot that seems to slip just out of reach with every paw pounce. Lasers come with different heads that change the shape of the beam. Such toys are great to keep handy when you are doing chores around the house because you can pick the laser toy up at intervals and introduce a couple of rounds of chase and catch. Be sure to let the beam rest in a spot long enough for your cat to pounce and try to capture her prey. Never shine a laser beam directly at her face and eyes. It's important to remember that laser games are not really fair play because the feline participant never gets the opportunity to catch and enjoy her prize. So give her a treat at the end of the game and be sure that the next toy you bring out is one that she can actually capture and kick around with her paws.

Ball games: Cats can be quite inventive when it comes to ball games because just about anything from the silver paper used to wrap chocolate to a scrunched piece of writing paper is considered a *ball* in feline terms. There's even a line of feline stationery items made from catnip-infused paper that can be scrunched up into paper balls that will really put the capital "P" in "play." There's also an enormous variety of commercial balls to add to the toy box, from high-velocity bouncing rubber ones to woolen ones with feathers. Many are made from nontoxic and eco-friendly materials. Some have bells inside; others chirp and make interesting noises that notch up the fun level. Be sure to include a variety of balls with soft materials that a cat can actually hold with her paws and toss about on her own. Although many people might not believe it, it's easy to engage a cat in ball games of fetch. Often, they initiate such play themselves by retrieving the ball and, like a dog, bringing it to you to throw over and over again. Some may even drag a wand with a furry creature on the end over to you and drop it at your feet to initiate play.

Cat-and-mouse games: No cat can resist little furry mice, especially when they are stuffed with catnip and make realistic squeaky noises. Other mice have bells and rattles, too. Most cats bite these toys to pieces to "attack" the noise, so be sure to remove the remnants to keep your cat from accidentally swallowing anything. Soft fabric mice usually contain a pouch that you can fill with catnip and constantly refresh to keep games stimulating and amusing. Some of them even have little wheels to help them scurry across the floor. And there are remote-control mice to rev up the fun, too!

Bubbles of fun: Because both cats and kids love bubbles, this is an ideal activity for them to engage in together. Although ordinary bubble soap purchased from a toy store or supermarket can be fun, a special catnip-infused bubble solution, available from most pet stores, will maintain feline interest for even longer periods.

Battery-operated toys: These days, the variety almost equals the selection for children—from battery-operated mice that scamper on all surfaces, to a Barbie-styled room of furniture with plastic mice on a special track that scurry around "the room" to pique feline curiosity. There are also laser units that can be pre-set to flash different light patterns around a room. Some of these items are so sophisticated they can be programed to switch on and off at regular intervals to initiate play when cats are home alone; these toys are definitely worth the investment. There are huge mental and physical stimulation benefits for a cat engaging with such toys when home alone, and, fortunately, the selection available grows bigger by the day.

Distraction or Enrichment Toys and Games

There are lots of innovative distraction toys on the market. They fall into the following categories:

Kitty gyms and activity centers: This selection of easy-to-assemble toys offers cats a variety of on-tap entertainment items that spin, dangle, whirl, and twirl. Some have tassels with bells and balls too.

◄ Cats love bubbles, and pet stores even carry catnip-infused bubble solutions.

▲ Puzzle games are great at keeping kitty occupied. This ball dispenses a treat when the cat hits it just right.

Certain designs are combined with a scratching pad or include birds on spring devices that move at the touch of a swatting paw. Be sure to remove and replace any parts that look worn and torn so your cat doesn't accidentally swallow something.

Scratching posts: Because cats scratch instinctively, a well-designed scratching post can also be considered an activity center. Some of the newest designs are made out of corrugated recycled cardboard, with ramps and hidey-holes that will provide endless hours of fun and games and, at the same time, take care of an instinctive feline need. Cats usually like to stretch and scratch, so place scratchers strategically near a popular snooze zone. The more scratchers around the home, the less likely it is that your cat will attempt to shred furniture and drapes.

Kitty condos and cat trees: Cats instinctively enjoy elevated positions. So, whether you have one or more cats, a multistationed cat tree is essential feline entertainment. Not only will it keep your cat out of mischief (such as going on a hunt and attacking various items in the house), but it will also provide endless hours of amusement. Space permitting in your home, look for a design that offers places to snooze, hide, and scratch, as well as some built-in activities, such as a toy on a spring or something that dangles and twirls. If space is really an issue, there are wonderful condos that can be attached to a wall or can even attach to the back of a door. Special floor-to-ceiling designs are specially made to fit into a small corner and can be made to look like a decorating feature. Cat trees made from real bark (some even have branches of silk leaves) and sisal are very decorative and will look fabulous in any stylish interior, as well as offering excellent feline enjoyment. Where possible, try and position the condo close to a window so that your cat can enjoy a view of the garden or street.

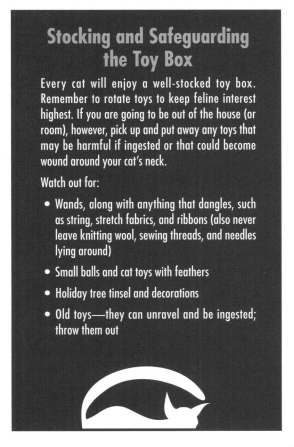

Stocking and Safeguarding the Toy Box

Every cat will enjoy a well-stocked toy box. Remember to rotate toys to keep feline interest highest. If you are going to be out of the house (or room), however, pick up and put away any toys that may be harmful if ingested or that could become wound around your cat's neck.

Watch out for:

- Wands, along with anything that dangles, such as string, stretch fabrics, and ribbons (also never leave knitting wool, sewing threads, and needles lying around)
- Small balls and cat toys with feathers
- Holiday tree tinsel and decorations
- Old toys—they can unravel and be ingested; throw them out

Puzzle games: Apart from providing endless hours of fun, puzzle games intellectually challenge your cat while allowing her to hunt and generally entertain herself. Some of the most stimulating games include large square boxes with balls or toys trapped within the framework but able to move around, or a wheel-shaped tunnel with a fast-moving ball that spins when batted.

Feline board games are the latest version of puzzle toys that allow treats or small toys to be hidden under plastic covers that adept paw manipulation can remove to retrieve the rewards. Another version of a feline board game consists of a selection of tubes of different heights slotted into a tray. Cats are very adept at removing treats with their paws and will spend hours working it out! This can also be a great way of feeding them part of their normal food allowance because it means they really have to work for it!

Hide-and-seek games: Cats love tunnels and bags that they can climb into to play games of hide-and-seek with themselves or other felines in the family. Some toys resembling brown paper bags make a crinkly noise when moved. Others even have toys

inside that move around to keep your cat intrigued. You can hide treats and other toys in there, too.

For a more elaborate game, set up a feline treasure hunt around your home using your cat's favorite toys and treats. This is a great way to keep cats occupied when they are home alone. Place the toys and treats in different hiding places around your home and leave her to seek them out and have some fun—and some munchies! Include special treat balls that dispense treats as they roll around, and even hide treats in accessible places near cat scratchers and on different levels on the kitty condo. It's a good idea to vary the locations and the toys to always keep things fresh.

Comfort Toys

Interestingly, despite the fact that many cats love soft cuddly toys, there are very few plush toys made specifically for cats, other than soft life-size mice. If you can't find a plush cat toy, shop at a toyshop or in the dog section at a pet store. Be wary of anything with glass or plastic eyes that could be pulled off and swallowed. Dog toys that have no stuffing

▼If you want to take your cat on outings, start training her on a harness and leash at an early age.

usually turn out to be kitty favorites. (Even though dog toys may have squeakers in them, because cats usually carry them around or toss them, they usually don't activate the squeakers.) My preference is for soft baby toys for your favorite feline because they are usually designed to high safety standards.

Feline Amusement Park

You can create your own feline amusement park by taking certain items you have around the home and linking them together. For example, try placing a cat tunnel next to the circular hidey-hole on the ground level of a kitty condo. On the other end, position an ordinary cardboard box with holes cut in it. To make the box attractive, paint it with nontoxic paint or cover it with carpet tiles or fabric. Put your imagination to work. Your cat will appreciate your efforts. There is also a system of corrugated boxes called Catty Stacks that can be combined in a variety of different ways to provide endless hours of fun. You can add other cat accessories to these structures, such as a sleeping mat or an attached wand toy for additional play. When it comes to feline amusement, it's all about variety.

Videos and TV Entertainment

Studies have shown that some cats do watch videos and television. Consequently, there is an enormous selection of cat videos to capture feline attention with flying objects and the noises of other animals and birds. Some cats also love to watch sports such as tennis and horseracing—TV channels such as Animal Planet and certain sports channels are an excellent source of feline entertainment. So, when you're planning to be out for a lengthy period of time, let modern technology baby-sit your feline by leaving the TV on a good cat-watching channel or inserting a special cat Blu-ray disc set on replay.

Outdoor Adventures with Your Cat

Ready to venture outside with your cat? Barring restrictions at a certain destination, you can take a cat just about anywhere with you as long as you have the right equipment and/or mode of transportation. If you want to take your cat for outings, begin

▲ A leash-trained cat can safely enjoy tree climbing as long as you are securely holding the leash.

training her to walk wearing a harness and leash at an early age. First, leave the harness lying around the house on its own and let her interact with it by placing a treat or two close to it. Then do the same with the leash. You can also play with it to pique kitty interest. Next, let her wear just the harness around the house on several occasions. After she's comfortable and totally ignores it, attach the leash and let her drag it around after her. Once she's comfortable with this scenario, you will be ready to take her for short walks outside. Always choose routes that are not known to be heavily populated by dogs or people so that she doesn't get spooked.

Alternatively, teach your cat to sit in a specially designed pet stroller. There are many designs to choose from. Those that have a carrier that clips onto a fold-up base are probably the safest for cats because it's not necessary to transplant them from a standard carrier into the stroller at your destination or reverse the procedure for the journey home.

Start by leaving the stroller inside your home in an open position so that she can jump in and out. Chances are, when you are least expecting it, you will probably find your cat curled up asleep inside it. Then start by taking her for short jaunts about the neighborhood. Gradually increase the distance of your outings. Your cat will grow to consider such outings normal events and enjoy the mental and physical stimulation of being out and about.

Taking your cat places also means that she has the opportunity to serve as an ambassador for all felines. Often, people who claim that they do not like cats have never met one. Because most cats are usually closeted in our homes, such people never get the opportunity to get up close and personal with a feline to learn to appreciate them. So taking your cat out and about is a great public relations opportunity to promote felines and possibly convert some self-proclaimed dislikers of cats into cat people. There was a certain famous Scottish Fold that did so while traveling the world (see the next chapter for his story).

Very sociable cats and those who are comfortable on a leash or don't mind traveling in a car often enjoy the stimulation of going shopping at a pet supermarket. If your cat is leash-trained and unnerved by the hustle and bustle of a store, she may be quite happy to sit in the shopping cart and enjoy the indoor part of the outing from there.

The alternative for such outings is, of course, a pet stroller. Many outdoor malls have a pet-friendly policy, allowing your cat to enjoy window-shopping with you. A cat in a stroller will be welcome at any outdoor eating area, giving you the opportunity to meet a friend for lunch or a quick coffee.

Catcentric websites and local newspapers are a good place to starting looking for pet-friendly events in your area. Furthermore, hotel groups that put out the welcome mat for pets, such as Kimpton Hotels, regularly hold pet-related events that a well-socialized cat may enjoy attending. A typical outing is a Christmas event to come and meet Santa Paws and have a photograph taken.

Don't forget visits to friends who love cats and don't have a pet; they are sure to make your feline happy with lots of attention. In particular, visit the elderly people you know, especially those who live alone and are likely to cherish time spent playing with a cat.

Cat Agility Competitions

If your cat seems to need more rigorous outlets than playing with toys at home and going on walking and stroller outings, consider getting her involved in cat agility, a recognized feline sporting activity. In cat agility tournaments, which are organized by International Cat Agility Tournaments (ICAT) and held around the country, cats compete

Cat Strollers

Apart from shopping trips and visits to friends, taking your cat for walks around the neighborhood is another good reason to invest in a cat stroller. Cats, because they are curious by nature, are fascinated by their surroundings. Cats who are allowed outdoors usually sit under a bush and watch their surroundings, and they can do the exact same thing from the safe confines of a stroller. And you will get much-needed fresh air and exercise, too.

Elderly cats in particular enjoy having "wheels" and will benefit from the mental stimulation gained from going for a ride. Pushing a stroller is a great form of daily exercise and comes with the built-in opportunity of spending quality time with your cat.

If you live in a neighborhood that also has wildlife such as coyotes, bobcats, mountain lions, and even large birds of prey, it is really not safe to let your cat outside unattended. Instead, let her enjoy the great outdoors from the safe confines of a stroller. It will also give you peace of mind as far as her safety is concerned. For multicat households, there are very large strollers (designed especially for 150-pound dogs) that will comfortably accommodate two and possibly three cats.

▲ If your cat is a glamorpuss, she may be the perfect candidate for a cat show.

against the clock for the fastest time on a course similar to that popularized in dog agility. Felines, especially the very athletic breeds, such as Bengals and Abyssinians, really enjoy the challenge. Professionally organized events are open to all cats, pedigreed and mix-breed.

To determine whether this is something your cat will enjoy, set up an agility course in your living room. An agility course usually comprises a number of stations, with bars to jump over, hoops to leap through, and tunnels to navigate. Check out professional agility kits for pets online to get an idea of the type of equipment needed and then improvise with items in your home. Turn chairs upside down and place a broom across them for a bar. Set out your cat tunnel, and, if you still have a hula-hoop in the garage, include it in the course. Alternatively, use items from a standard dog agility kit. Use a wand with a feather on the end to lure your cat from

station to station. Cats quickly get the hang of this and will pick up speed and have fun.

If your cat enjoys this type of fun at home, then it's a good sign that she may be willing to turn professional. Watch the notice board in your local pet store or supermarket because agility events are often held at such venues.

The Cat Show World

Even if you don't have a pedigreed feline with a family tree charted with champions, there is a place for your cat in the show world, and being involved in the cat fancy can be a fun and rewarding activity for both of you. The two main cat registries that rule the feline show world in the United States are the Cat Fanciers Association (CFA) and the International Cat Association (TICA). Both organizations include a section for household cats in their regular cat shows.

Activities with Your Cat

Cat shows take place practically every weekend in some part of the country, varying in size and importance on the feline show calendar. From both the spectator and participant viewpoints, they can be likened to mini-fairs. The show rings and judging form only one aspect of the day's proceedings; the variety of other activities range from informative workshops, adoption booths, and feline agility courses to numerous booths selling a cornucopia of cat-related wares.

Becoming involved in the cat fancy can be a time-consuming pastime. A lot of cats love the hoopla and attention and enjoy the mental and physical challenges of this pastime. But first, the best way to find out whether *you* would enjoy being involved in the cat fancy is to go to a few different shows as a spectator. As far as your cat is concerned, you will have to judge whether she would enjoy taking part in such events by how much she enjoys going out and about with you to the pet store or how she reacts around people in general. If she seems reluctant, remember the saying "When in doubt, don't!"

From the spectators' viewpoint, CFA- and TICA-organized events are set up along similar lines. Rows of cages (the benching area) house the feline participants waiting to be judged in a number of show rings, with each ring presided over by a judge

Shopping, Shopping, Shopping

The shopping area at a typical cat show is a great place to stock up on a variety of merchandise for yourself and your feline. Booths sell everything from cat-themed people apparel to the latest cat toys, carriers, and grooming products. You will find novelty cat items, some that are sold in pet stores, but several unique to the shows, such as a cat exercise wheel resembling a mini-Ferris wheel that offers a great workout to any cat curious enough to try it out.

and a clerk to keep a record of the proceedings. The judging in the various rings goes on concurrently.

Cat shows are often two-day events. Learning the ropes at a cat show can be confusing because the CFA and TICA each has its own set of competitive categories, methods of scoring, and awards system. Both organizations have very comprehensive information about the way they conduct competition on their websites: www.CFA.org and www.TICA.org.

CFA Cat Shows

The judging rings at a CFA show are classified either as *all-breed shows*, where all cats, regardless of coat length or type, compete for various awards, or *specialty shows*, where only cats of similar coat length or type are allowed to compete against one another. Males and females are initially judged separately within their breed's color classes. All the cats or kittens then compete for best and second best of breed.

Understanding CFA Categories

Both all breed and specialty shows are held for the following categories of cats. Cats who have been declawed are not permitted to compete in *any* of these categories.

Kittens: Kittens are classified according to their age. They have to be not younger than four months and not older than eight months. All kittens are judged collectively, irrespective of whether they have been spayed or neutered. Kittens can only win ribbons, not titles.

Championship Class: The Championship Class category is for unaltered (not spayed or neutered) pedigreed cats over the age of eight months. Premiership is the equivalent for all altered (spayed and neutered) pedigreed cats over the age of eight months.

Household Pets: The Household Pets Division is for nonpedigreed cats and pedigreed cats with a disqualifying trait that would disallow them from being shown in the regular classes. Nonpedigreed kittens between four and eight months can also compete with adults in the Household Pet category. However, if the cats are older than eight months, they have to be spayed or neutered.

▲The CFA has division for household pets so that even nonpedigreed cats can compete in the show.

Veteran: The Veteran Class is for both male and female, altered (spayed or neutered) or unaltered (not spayed or neutered) pedigreed cats who are more than seven years of age on the opening day of the show.

Provisional and Miscellaneous: Provisional and Miscellaneous categories are for breeds that have not as yet achieved championship status as recognized by the CFA.

Decoding CFA Show Categories and Color Ribbons

Every CFA-registered cat over the age of eight months starts its show career in what is known as the Open Class category. In this introductory level of competition, first place wins a blue ribbon, second place is red, third place is yellow (for both male and females). The overall winner's ribbon is red, white, and blue and is awarded to the best male and best female open in each color class.

A cat has to collect six winners' ribbons in this category to move up to become a *champion* or a *premier*.

In the champion or premier level of competition, when cats in the same color group are judged, they receive blue, red, and yellow ribbons.

The next level of competition is the Grand Champion class. Here, cats also compete for blue, red, and yellow ribbons within the color classes for males and females. The black ribbon denotes Best of Color Class and a white ribbon denotes second place.

Once a judge has evaluated all the cats in every color class within a breed (or color division within a breed), the brown Best of Breed ribbon is awarded. Second place receives orange. The Best Champion of Breed is awarded a purple ribbon and receives points for the number of other champions defeated. To achieve the Grand Champion title requires 200 points plus awards in judges' finals.

The very top of the awards pyramid is the final in each category, and the ultimate prize is a rosette along with points toward Grand Champion, Regional, or National wins. Rosettes can be any color.

Household Pets are judged in one group without regard to sex, age, coat length, or color, and they are judged simply for their unique appearance in addition to good condition and pleasing personality. In this category, cats can win red and white merit award ribbons.

If you are keen to learn the intricacies of the judging procedure, the CFA website (www.CFA.org) is a great place to start. They also hand out informational brochures at cat shows to help newcomers navigate the system.

Tracking Cat Shows

Both the CFA and TICA also post events on their respective websites. Their calendars detail shows planned for the next couple of years. Local newspapers are also an excellent source of information about cat shows. *Cat Fancy* magazine also lists the major shows around the country during a calendar year. Don't overlook notice boards in coffee shops, supermarkets, and the veterinarian's office.

▲ A show cat needs to become accustomed to being handled by many different people.

TICA Cat Shows

TICA also has two kinds of rings: all-breed and specialty. However, its title award system is based on a combination of points earned within color classes and divisions, along with the finals points. Kittens are also classified by age (four to eight months) and can't win titles.

Cats eligible for titles must make a given amount of points and reach the finals for each of the awarded titles. The points are tallied to ultimately award titles. To earn the Supreme Grand Champion, a cat must have earned a Best Cat after it's earned four Best Champion awards (Quadruple Grand Champion). Every TICA judge presides over his or her own awards for the top ten cats in each group in his or her ring. Because there are more judging rings at a TICA show than at a CFA show, there are more opportunities for awards.

Understanding TICA Groups

The main TICA groups are longhaired kittens, shorthaired kittens, unaltered (not spayed or neutered) adult longhaired, unaltered (not spayed or neutered) adult shorthaired, altered (spayed or neutered) adult longhaired, altered (spayed or neutered) adult shorthaired, altered (spayed or neutered) longhaired household pets, altered (spayed or neutered) shorthaired household pet, longhaired household pet kittens, and shorthaired household pet kittens, as well as a group known as "new breeds and new traits" accepted by TICA and endorsing the fact that the cat fancy continues to evolve.

In all of the adult groups, fully grown cats can compete for titles that range from Champion for unaltered pedigreed cats, Champion Alter for altered pedigreed cats, and Master for Household Pets. Other titles include, Grand Champion; Double, Triple, and Quadruple Grand Champion; and, finally, Supreme Grand Champion. Titles are not available for new breeds and new traits.

Decoding TICA Award Colors

The Best of Color award for each cat of a particular color is blue. The runner-up gets red. Third place is yellow, fourth place is green, and fifth is white. The judges then select the top three in each of eight divisions within four categories (Traditional Colors, Sepia, Mink, and Pointed), making a total of thirty-two divisions. The Divisions in each category are Solid, Tortie, Tabby, Silver/Smoke, Solid and White, Tortie and White/Tabby and White, and Silver/Smoke and White.

The Best of Division receives a black ribbon. Second is purple, and third is orange. Next, the judge selects the top three in the breed. The Best of Breed is gold. Silver ranks second, and bronze rates third. Judges are only required to name the breed placement. Most of the time, there isn't a ribbon for the breed. Breed placements don't actually earn any points.

In the final round in each category, rosettes are also given to the top ten cats. Like CFA, rosettes can be any color depending on the time of year or the theme of the event. For example, at Christmas time, they are usually red and white.

In the TICA title computation, the finals also count in points toward Regional and International wins.

TICA's awards systems can be complicated, to say the least. So, understandably, the best way to learn the different systems is to go to and keep going to cat shows of all kinds.

Other Cat Show Need-to-Know Facts

Just like the CFA, TICA also has ambassadors/ guides at their events wearing buttons who say things like "Ask Me," so information is readily available. Often the exhibitors, if they are not busy with their cats, are also happy to chat. You will learn a great deal from those chats, so don't be shy.

If you are interested in the show world but feel your present cat would not be a happy participant, this is an excellent place to meet breeders and even purchase a kitten with the potential to compete. If a kitten has show cat parents, which those offered by show breeders do, that kitten is likely to have the right temperament to enjoy participating in the show world, too.

Other facts you need to know about the cat show world:

- If you have purchased a pedigreed cat or kitten, it's a good idea to ask the breeder to be your mentor.
- You will have to register your feline with the organization of your choice. Both the CFA and TICA have basic guidelines, including information for household cats, posted on their websites.
- Not every cat has the temperament for the show ring. Preparation begins at home by getting your feline accustomed to being handled by different people.

- Showing your cat is a commitment in both time and money. Apart from the traveling, there's a lot of grooming involved at home and at a show. Exactly how much varies according to the chosen breed.
- To ensure your cat's comfort in a show environment, it's a good idea to bring her favorite blanket and toys.
- Your will also need cage curtains to cover the top, back, and sides of the cage to seclude your cat and keep her calm. You can begin your show career using sheets and towels and progress to fancy curtains that complement the color of your cat.
- Most cat shows provide litter, but each cat owner is responsible for the litter box and the provision of food and water during the event.
- Entry forms and payment can often be done online. Always ensure that you allow plenty of time to register and check in on the day of the event.
- If you are a newcomer, often the organizers will place you between experienced show-goers so that you can learn the drill from them.
- Many cat shows offer seminars and workshops to acquaint first-timers with grooming techniques, scoring arrangements, and general information about what the judges are looking for within particular breeds.
- Ensure everything you bring to the show is well marked with your name and details—and this includes your cat, in the form of a microchip implanted for identification. (Although this is not a show requirement in the United States, as it is in Europe, it is still a wise precaution.)
- A cat should always be transported in a well-ventilated and sturdy carrier with proper locking devices.

The Cat Library

The Cat Library in Glendale, California is the only known collection of its kind in the world. It is housed in the main Glendale City Library and only open to the public by appointment. Among its thousands of books are the works of Harrison Weir, the organizer of the first cat show in Britain, and Frances Simpson, who was probably the most renowned feline authority and author of her day. If you love cats, the library is definitely worth a visit to appreciate these valuable volumes and enjoy reading the English writing style of the Victorian era. The library is located at 222 E. Harvard St. Glendale, CA 91205. The direct telephone number for an appointment is 818-548-2037.

Chapter 20

Traveling with Your Cat

Every adventure requires a first step.
Trite, but true, even here.

— Cheshire Cat in *Alice in Wonderland*

Recent changes in the travel and leisure industry in both America and Europe have seen doors opening and the welcome mat being put out for pets. And this travel invitation is definitely being extended to cats too.

Consequently, it's easier than ever before to travel with a cat. Currently, the American travel industry does not monitor information about peripatetic felines. However, according to the 2013–2014 American Pet Products Association (APPA) National Pet Owners Survey, the number of felines who travel annually with their owners has doubled from 3 percent to 6 percent since 2012. In numbers, that's approximately 5.7 million felines. Only 1 percent of feline travelers go on plane trips. According to the survey, of those felines who travel with their pet parents, an average of six trips are taken by the family cat via other means of transport in a twelve-month period. Furthermore, people with two or more cats are more likely to travel with their felines than if they have only one cat. Both airline and hotel staff around the country concur that the number of furry feline travelers is definitely on the increase.

Ensuring Pet Identification

Yes, I have said this before, but it bears repeating, especially when you are about to take your cat away from home. Making sure that your cat can be identified if you are separated is critical. Apart from having

►Some cats really enjoy traveling and will be ready to go at any time.

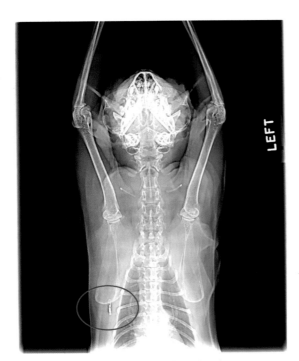

▲ Radiograph showing an identifying microchip implanted near the shoulder.

a microchip implanted, a cat leaving its home environment should be wearing a collar with a tag or disc engraved with current contact information, including you name and your telephone number. Some tags allow you to add your city and state, too. If you travel often, it's a good idea to also enroll your pet in a pet recovery program and ensure that the animal has that relevant disc on her collar, too. Should your pet go missing, these services offer twenty-four-hour help by notifying shelters in the area the cat was last seen to aid with a faster recovery. This can be useful if something occurs during a road trip. If you are planning to make lots of stopovers during a journey, it's an excellent idea to add to the collar a small lightweight paper tag purchased at a stationery store that carries the address and local-contact phone number for each destination/stop on your itinerary. Yes, paper tags can be scratched off the collar, but it's worth trying to keep them intact.

As a side note, although there are GPS systems that will help you track your cat efficiently to where she is in real time, currently, the units that fit onto a cat collar are bulky and, because they get warm, could be uncomfortable if worn permanently. I am sure that as the technology improves, these issues will be addressed, so it's worth monitoring what becomes available.

Buying Travel Gear

Now, on to what you need to outfit yourself and your cat for the trip. As part of this new cat-friendly travel policy, the pet industry continues to focus on designing and manufacturing a fabulous array of pet travel accessories that make it more comfortable for cats to be away from home. On the following pages, you will find a summary of some of the main items you'll need for both plane travel and road trips.

Carriers

Most cats associate carriers with trips to the vet. Therefore, it's an excellent idea to purchase a special carrier for vacationing, so that it can be associated with good times and fun stuff. The selection of carriers on the market is large, so choices need to be governed first by whether you are planning to travel by airline or by car. Next, you will also want to add certain items such as a soft pad and your cat's favorite blanket or toy. Make sure, no matter how you're traveling, that the carrier is properly labeled with your home address as well as information about your intended destination. If you are staying at different places en route, update information as you go using paper tags for labels.

The Airways or the Highway

Currently, most of the major airline carriers in the United States allow cats to travel in-cabin in a well-ventilated soft-sided carrier that will fit comfortably under the seat. The airline industry is trying to standardize carrier specifications to ensure that a carrier can be used on a variety of airlines. However, size specifications still differ from airline to airline so it's best to check before booking a flight. Fortunately, all the major carriers have extensive pet information listed on their websites.

The GOB Program

In the past, travelers with cats have been turned away by airlines because their pet's carrier hasn't met airline safety requirements. In an effort to standardize pet travel bags, the Sherpa Pet Group, the originator of the pet in-cabin carrier bag, has teamed up with major American air lines to introduce the Guaranteed on Board (GOB) Program. This is a free insurance plan that guarantees cats traveling in-cabin will never be refused to fly because the carrier doesn't meet standard airline regulations.

Travelers need to check the carrier requirements for their airline before purchasing a bag and subsequently register the bag at www.FlyGOB.com. Members are issued with documentation to show airport officials that will guarantee them on board. However, should a situation arise that prevents them boarding a particular flight because airline officials question the carrier for some reason, travelers are guaranteed full reimbursement of the cost their air ticket and their pet's travel expenses, too. An up-to-date list of participating airlines can be found at www.FlyGOB.com.

Veterinarians agree that cats are less stressed when they travel in-cabin with their family. However, for international air travel, aviation regulations insist that they travel in a specially ventilated cargo hold situated under the front section of the plane. The carrier requirements for this form of travel insist on a hard-cased carrier made from a sturdy plastic or wood frame with plenty of ventilation. The animal must be able to stand up and turn around inside. Once again, up-to-date information can be found on individual airline websites. It's very important to ensure that the crate locks securely, too.

For road trips, both the rectangular soft-sided and hard-cased options for air travel can be used. Basically, it comes down to what you consider most comfortable for your cat during a long car ride. However, because cats usually enjoy napping curled up in a round sleeping position, the latest circular-shaped carriers, such as the Sleepypod, are the most conducive shape to meet this feline need. The added advantage is that the top section of the carrier unzips and can be completely removed, converting it into a comfy bed for use at your destination. Furthermore, the designs have additional optional straps that allow them to be secured with a vehicle's seatbelts for added safety.

As with children, it's important that carriers be placed in the backseat area of a vehicle. If the carrier is not restrained with seatbelts, it should be placed on the floor section of the rear passenger section where it has the least chance of being thrown around should the driver suddenly apply the brakes.

▶ Choose the type of carrier that is suited to how you want to travel.

Cat Beds and Pee Pads

Whether you are traveling by air or land, if you don't have a carrier that converts into a bed, consider taking along a soft throw, a pet sleeping bag that resembles a rolled-up mattress, or purchase a simple cat cocoon that will be easy to pack. Don't forget to leave it lying around the house well before the road trip to give your cat the opportunity to discover it and become familiar with it.

Most carriers come with a nice soft cushion. If not, be sure to purchase one. In addition, it's an excellent idea to cover the cushion with a puppy pee pad to absorb any accidents that may occur en route. These pads, like diapers, are designed to absorb the liquid and leave the top layer dry for the pet's comfort. Always make sure you travel with a stock to replace used ones.

Harness and Leash

If you plan to travel regularly with your cat, you will need a harness and leash for her. As discussed in the previous chapter, it's a good idea to get her used to wearing them from kittenhood or at least

as far enough ahead of time as you can. This will make it much easier to make travel stops to give your pet some exercise and possibly a potty break. These days, many airports around the country have specially allocated pet potty areas; cats are welcome if they don't mind sharing with dogs.

Numerous harnesses are made specifically for cats. Be sure to choose a design that fastens on the back. Cats don't like to be strapped in with closures that fasten at their tummy area, unless it closes with strong Velcro, which is easier to work than buckles and straps. Soft padded or mesh harnesses that fit across the shoulders are the most comfortable for feline wearers, and you stand less chance of a cat being able to wiggle out of them. As explained in the previous chapter, to get your cat used to wearing a harness, put it on for short periods around the house. Then add the leash. It takes time for a cat to get used to the idea of actually walking with you in this manner, so it's important to start such training well in advance of any travel plans. During a road trip, it's a good idea to leave the harness on so that you only have to clip on the leash when necessary.

▼ Be sure to bring a portable kitty bed, so your feline will have a nice spot to sleep in your hotel room.

Bear in mind that even when your cat is wearing a harness, she should be wearing her collar, with all its necessary identification.

Disposable Litter Boxes

There is an excellent selection of disposable litter boxes that fold shut when not in use. Be sure to purchase one for a road trip and additional ones should you be staying at a hotel that doesn't supply them. Remember to call ahead to check with the hotel about what it does and doesn't supply. If your cat is fussy about the type of litter she uses, add some of her favorite brand. If necessary, give her a disposable box at home to try out ahead of time so she will be familiar with it before the journey.

Food and Water

It's never a good idea to feed a pet before a flight or a road trip. However, it's essential to take along her favorite food.

Food and water: Wet food options come in small packages and cans that are good for travel. Be sure to place dry food in tightly sealed plastic containers. Many airtight containers have screw-on tops that convert into food bowls, and these are ideal for travel.

Whether you're travelling by plane or car, it's a good idea to freeze water in a small plastic container so that your pet can lick it en route. Be sure to pack the lid to prevent it spilling when the ice melts. Of course, if you're traveling by plane with your cat in the cabin, you can take a collapsible bowl and ask the airline staff for ice during the journey.

Bowls: A selection of special travel bowls with disposable plastic liners are available that make

▲ It's essential you bring your kitty's leash and harness so she can get out and enjoy the sights with you.

an excellent option for cats, particularly if you are serving wet food. They are hygienic and there's no additional washing up required. Alternatively, you can use disposable food storage containers that you find in any grocery store. There's also a wonderful selection of collapsible travel bowls made from a variety of materials such as silicone and waterproof nylon, as well as water systems that have lids that, once removed, convert into drinking bowls.

Medication

If your cat is taking prescription medications, place each item separately in a plastic bag and keep them all in a small waterproof bag cooled with ice packs. Don't forget to pack pill pockets and syringes for liquid medications.

As with your own medicines, it's important that you travel with copies of any prescriptions for your cat. Some airlines and hotels require a vaccination certificate for local travel. Check directly with the airline or hotel because this information often is not on websites. However, you will definitely need such documentation for international travel, along with a passport for your pet.

Toys for the Outing

Cats are homebodies by nature so taking along some favorite toys will help your cat settle into a strange environment. Something with catnip will no doubt be popular. Lasers will kick-start games in a new environment. If you are traveling by car, it's also a good idea to put an older cat scratcher in the trunk, which you can toss if necessary before heading home again.

Traveling with Your Cat

413

Getting Ready to Fly

Your cat's carrier is going to be her home away from home during a vacation (this is also true for a road trip). So it's a good idea to purchase a carrier well in advance and leave it lying around your house for feline inspection. Some cats will happily climb inside and go to sleep.

Because felines are such intuitive creatures, they can sense when an excursion is about to happen. Prior to your actual departure, be sure to lock your cat up in a room that you can easily retrieve her from, such as a bathroom. Avoid bedrooms because cats are notorious for hiding under the bed just out of reach.

At an airport security checkpoint, carriers have to go through electronic screening. *Never* take your cat out of her carrier while in line; if you do so, you will have to carry her through the X-ray detection machine and this may spook her. By law, you may request a private screening in an enclosed room, which will ensure your cat's safety at all times. This is the time to be assertive, and don't let any official tell you otherwise!

Here are other steps to take ahead of time for safe air travel, including international travel.

An Airline Reservation

It's important to check that your airline does fly pets. For both local and international travel, it's imperative to make a reservation as much ahead of time as possible because airlines can restrict the number of pets per flight. When flying with a cat, book the most direct route. If you are changing planes and possibly flying another airline, you must check that the other airline is pet-friendly, too.

Many airlines have temperature restrictions, especially if the cat is flying in the hold. If it is above 85 degrees (29.5°C), airlines have the right to refuse to board a pet. If it's less than 45 degrees, the airline will request a letter of acclimation from a veterinarian stating that the pet can withstand the colder temperatures. It's also essential that you and your pet are booked on the same flight so you can personally monitor the situation. After all, weather changes daily. Temperature restrictions are particularly important for traveling with short-nosed (brachycephalic) breeds such as Persians.

A Passport for Your Cat

Undoubtedly, the most famous international feline traveler was a curmudgeonly Scottish Fold named Norton who, together with his owner author Peter Gethers, traveled the world and caused hilarious chaos wherever he went. (See the sidebar titled "A Most Well-Traveled Feline.")

Planning an international trip with pets is like planning to travel with small children—details, details, details! Although the quarantine laws between the United States, Britain, and Europe have been removed, there's still a lot of paperwork to be done before your pet can fly. Quarantine laws still apply in many countries around the world, such as Australia. The website http://www.dogfriendly.com has excellent up-to-date information relating to travel requirements for both dogs and cats.

The British Pet Travel Schemes (PETS) allows pets to travel freely from the United States (including Hawaii) to England and European Union countries. There's a standard procedure to follow to apply for a passport for a furry traveler. In Europe, pets are issued a document that resembles a person's passport, including a photograph inside. In the United States, by contrast, a pet receives a paper certificate; but let's hope that American pets will also be able to acquire authentic-looking documentation in the not-too-distant future. The PETS scheme is currently still operational, but it regularly comes up for review. So, for an up-to-date status check when you are planning to travel, check their website at http://www.defra.gov.uk.

Pet Passport Documentation Checklist

Health certificates have to be dated no more than ten days prior to your date of departure to ensure that your cat is free of parasites and generally healthy to travel. Many countries have a specific form they require to be filled in. You will need to check with the consulate in question. If not, you can use the International Health Certificate USDA-APHIS 7001 form available from your veterinarian.

Your pet has to be microchipped with an International Standards Organization (ISO)-readable chip since tattoos and other forms of identification such as standard ID tags are no longer accepted as official identification.

Cats also have to be vaccinated against rabies. Even if you have vaccinated your pet in the past twelve months, it will have to be done again. Your veterinarian will need to provide documentation showing the vaccination worked, so there is a twenty-one-day delay from the date of the shot. It's a good idea to vaccinate at the same time as you get the microchip implanted, and make sure your veterinarian includes all the following information on the paperwork:

- Your pet's date of birth and age written out in full
- The microchip number, date of insertion, and location of the microchip on the animal
- The date of rabies vaccination
- The vaccine product name and the batch number
- The date booster vaccinations are due (this is calculated by reference to the vaccine manufacturer's data sheet)

If you are traveling to Britain, your cat is required

▲ It's wise—and likely required—to have your cat get a health check and new vaccinations before she travels internationally.

to be treated against ticks and tapeworm between twenty-four and forty-eight hours before departing.

This preparation can only be done by a veterinarian accredited by the US Department of Agriculture—most veterinarians are accredited, but be sure to check. The documentation then has to be sent to your state veterinarian for final approval. The fee is nominal and varies from state to state. Furthermore, some countries require all the information to be translated into the official language of the country you're visiting, so, once again, be sure to check with the relevant consulate office.

To Tranquilize or Not to Tranquilize

The most common tranquilizer used for airline travel is acepromazine (Atravet, PromAce). Others, including diazepam (Valium), are often used. Significant tranquilization usually lasts about two to three hours, and then a gradual recovery occurs over the next two to three hours.

The problem is that flights from the United States to Europe can be ten hours long, and across the country five hours or more. This means that medication can wear off in the air and leave the pet very confused. And that's without taking delays into consideration. In many cases, the pet's general state of health and age also must be taken into account, so it's very important to have a discussion with your veterinarian on this subject.

It is a very controversial topic. Consequently, many veterinarians are suggesting spraying the carrier before take-off with stress-reducing spray such as Feliway and adding a few drops of a holistic remedy called Rescue Remedy to the water bowl before freezing it. In this way, the pet can lick the ice as it melts and stay calm throughout the journey. This advice also applies to road travel. There are also special collars infused with natural calming ingredients, such as chamomile, which will help relieve travel anxiety. The efficacy of such a collar lasts a month, and it should be worn in conjunction with a regular collar that carriers your cat's ID tags.

▲Tranquilizing a cat for travel is a controversial topic. Discuss the pros and cons with your veterinarian.

A Most Well-Traveled Feline

The adventures of the Scottish Fold Norton and his human, Peter Gethers, are told in three best-selling books by Gethers: *The Cat Who Went to Paris, A Cat Abroad,* and *The Cat Who'll Live Forever.* This well-traveled cat flew back and forth across the Atlantic, from New York to Paris, on the now defunct Concorde and visited many other places in Europe, too. He drank milk at a café on the streets of Paris and charmed the hotel staff at the ritzy Tremoille Hotel. He nearly caused a riot in Italy over his penchant for sardines and, while traveling in the States, grabbed paparazzi attention away from Sir Anthony Hopkins, outshining him at a movie premiere in the Hamptons. He was also regularly fêted in Beverly Hills with a special pizza at Spago made by celebrity owner-chef Wolfgang Puck. He even made canine friends at the dog run in New York's Washington Square Park, proving himself a true ambassador for felines everywhere. Through it all, Norton's and Gethers' unique relationship came to define the ultimate human—feline bond.

An antistress garment called a ThunderShirt is now also available for cats. It works on the same idea as swaddling a baby: it wraps around the cat's body and makes her feel more secure and less anxious in unfamiliar surroundings and circumstances.

Frequent Flyer Programs for Pets

Many pet-friendly airlines are now offering frequent flyer programs as an incentive to encourage pet travel. Some programs allow pets to redeem miles toward a free trip for themselves; others allow those points to accrue to the cat owner's frequent flyer account. Other airlines hand out gifts such as grooming certificates and designer bowls when pets reach a certain milestone. These travel programs keep changing, so it's a good idea to ask your airline of choice whether they have such a scheme, and, if so, to take advantage of it.

Relocating with Your Pet

Relocating, whether it's to another state or another country, takes a lot of careful planning. And paperwork! If you are unsure about the travel arrangements for your cat, it's a good idea to call in a pet-relocation specialist, who, for a nominal fee, will be able to organize everything on your behalf. They are experts in this field and will have answers to all your questions. From personal experience, it's definitely worth working with a pet-relocation specialist because you can rest assured that they will cover all bases.

If you are relocating to Europe and would prefer not to fly your cat in the cargo hold of an airline, there is a viable, albeit expensive alternative: although cruise ships in general don't allow pets on board, Cunard's flagship, the *Queen Mary 2*, does. This ship crosses the Atlantic between New York and Southampton, England. It has a state-of-the-art pet boarding facility on board with round-the-clock attention. Passengers aren't allowed to take cats to their cabins, but they can visit their pets in their quarters on the pet deck instead.

Checking into a Hotel or Staying Elsewhere

There is no shortage of pet-friendly accommodations to suit every pocket. There are motel and hotels chains, inns and resorts, as well as the homes of family and friends along the way. The AAA brings out an annual directory of pet-friendly accommodation in the United States, and the current publication lists more than 14,000 properties.

It's important to inform a hotel, inn, or resort in advance that you are traveling with your cat because some establishments reserve special rooms for guests with pets. Many hotels employ a pet concierge who will offer your cat a welcome pack on arrival that contains toys and treats. Others even have litter boxes and scratchers on request and will present a special door tag to alert hotel staff that a cat is in residence. It's quite common for hotels to offer special pet menus, too, with a selection of chicken and salmon dishes.

It's feline etiquette to keep your cat in her carrier and to be present when the room is being serviced. Many hotel chains don't limit the number of cats in your room but may request a cleaning deposit. It's important to ask about the facility's pet policy in advance of your arrival.

As for family and friends, it's also a wise—and polite—idea to call ahead to make sure that an

The Cypress Inn

The Cypress Inn in the quaint Californian beach town of Carmel is believed to have been one of the first pet-friendly hotels in America. Co-owned by legendary singer, actor, and animal advocate Doris Day, the hotel has invited both dogs and cats to stay since it first opened its doors more than twenty-eight years ago and thus many believe pioneered the current pet-friendly hospitality trends. Cats can catch the morning sun's rays in the hotel's courtyard and join their owners for a pre-dinner sherry around the roaring fire in the lounge.

overnight (or several nights') visit from you and your cat is convenient at the particular time you're planning on visiting.

Major US Hotel Chain Pet Policies

Here are the pet policies for some of the major hotel chains in the United States, current as of this writing. Be aware that pet policies within hotel groups can vary, especially if it's a franchised property where owners are allowed to determine their own requirements. For that reason, as well as to double-check for policy changes and to get specific fee information, it's a good idea to call ahead.

Four Seasons Hotels: Cats in public areas must in a carrier and cannot be left unattended. However, there are no pet charges or deposits required and no limit to the number of pets per room.

Hilton Hotels: The Hilton's pets-welcome policy allows one cat in specially designated pet-friendly rooms. There are no additional charges or fees required. The pet amenities provided include a bed made from special Crypton "mess-resistant" fabric, but no doubt kitty would prefer her own as these are geared more toward dogs. The company also owns, manages, or franchises Conrad Hotels and Resorts, Doubletree, Embassy Suites Hotels, Hampton Inn, Hampton Inn and Suites, Hilton Garden Inn, Hilton Grand Vacations, Homewood Suites by Hilton, and the Waldorf Astoria Collection. Policies can vary in franchised establishments, so be sure to call in advance.

▲ Check ahead with your hotel to make sure cats are allowed and what their pet policies are.

Hyatt Hotels: This group adopted a pet-friendly policy in 2012. Their Pampered Paws Program invites both cats (and dogs under 50 pounds) to stay for a nominal daily fee of about thirty dollars. Your feline will be given VIP treatment, which includes a food bowl, treats, toys, and a cat litter scooper; the hotels are BYODB (bring your own disposable [litter] box).

Intercontinental Hotels Group: This is the umbrella name for well-known chains such as Hotel Indigo, Crowne Plaza, Holiday Inn, Holiday Inn Express, Candlewood Suites, and Staybridge Suites. All Hotel Indigo properties accept pets. However, rules regarding deposits vary by property; guests should call ahead or check the website. Pet policies vary by location at both the InterContinental Hotels and Crowne Plaza Hotels, too. About 50 percent of the country's 900 Holiday Inns are pet friendly. Cats are welcome at about 1,800 Holiday Inn Express hotels countrywide. This chain also doesn't have a standard policy, so it's important to check in advance with your hotel.

Kimpton Hotels: Cats get VIP treatment at this chain of trendy boutique hotels. There is no pet deposit required, no additional room fees, and no limit to the number of pets checking in. Pet guests are greeted by name, and the hotels will even put a fish bowl holding a guppy in the room to keep your cat company. (They do, however, frown upon fishing.) The concierge desk offers excellent cat-related information about amenities in the vicinity of the hotel, such as pet stores and veterinary assistance.

La Quinta Inns: This chain of more than 700 properties doesn't charge pet-related fees or deposits. There is no limit to the number of pets either.

Loews Hotels: This chain charges per day fee for pets in the room. Two pets are allowed per room. The special pet room service menu varies at each hotel but features dishes such as roasted salmon and roasted chicken for finicky felines. On check-in, guests can request the "Kitty Pager" service, which equips pet-owners with a pager or cell phone to allow hotel staff to contact them immediately if there is a pet-related emergency.

Motel 6: Reputed to be the first pet-friendly chain in the United States; without a doubt, Motel 6 establishments have been welcoming furry friends since the 1960s. Today, the chain has about 900 properties. There are no additional fees or deposits required, and there is no limit on the number of pets.

Quality Inn: This chain allows three pets per room. Pets may not be left alone in the room unless crated or secured in a carrier. Some establishments may require a refundable deposit. This hotel chain is part of the Choice Hotels group that generally has a pet-friendly policy. Most properties within the group have designated rooms for people traveling with pets.

Staybridge Suites and Candlewood Suites: All the Staybridge Suites hotels and all the Candlewood Suites hotels throughout the country are pet friendly. These brands offer apartment-style accommodations with kitchens and are a good choice for extended stays. Pet policies vary, and you may have to show proof of up-to-date vaccinations.

W Hotels: Cats are very welcome at this trendy hotel chain. Guests traveling with pets will be required to sign a waiver at check-in, agreeing to uphold the guidelines of the hotel's pet policy, which requests that pets be leashed or in a carrier while in public areas and that the Welcome Desk be notified if pets are to be left unattended in the guest room. Basic amenities, such as a bed and a bowl, are provided, and the chain has an excellent selection of pet accessories at their Whatever/Whenever stores.

Westin Hotels: Cats get the "people welcome" here, too. There are no additional charges or deposits required, and there are no restrictions on the number of cats per room. Furthermore, furry guests get to sleep on a Heavenly Bed, a unique pet bed with Westin's signature white-on-white striped fabric, offering the same level of comfort as their people beds do.

Family and Friends

Many family members or close friends will welcome your cat as a visitor for an overnight visit or even a lengthy stay. Still, it's never a wise idea to presume that now is a good time to visit or that it's all right to include your cat. You may not realize that some people you know are allergic to cats or might

▲ Even at a pet-friendly hotel, there will be areas that are off-limits to your cat, such as the swimming pool.

expecting other visitors who are. Then there are others (hard to believe) who find a cat in your home fine but not in theirs. Don't take it personally, but do make sure of your welcome before dropping by.

Assuming you and your cat are welcome, be sure to provide all the cat basics, such as litter box, scratcher, food bowls, and a bed. If you visit a particular house often enough, your cat will come to regard it as a safe home away from home and settle in quickly on future visits. Nevertheless, if you're staying for more than one night, it's a good idea to ask the homeowners if you can put a note on all exterior-opening doors to gently remind everyone that there is a cat in residence. Again, if you visit frequently, ask if you can leave all your basic cat accessories there; have a box you can pack them up in so you can tuck it all into an out-the-way closet. Your cat will appreciate the familiarity.

Chapter 21

Pet Care Partners

*There are two means of refuge from the
miseries of life: music and cats.*

— Albert Schweitzer

There will be times when you will be away from home, and it's important to have a plan in place that will give you peace of mind knowing that your pet is being taken good care of during your absence. Cats are homebodies and consequently are much happier and less stressed if they can remain in their home environment, with its familiar sights, sounds, and smells. Despite the fact that they are self-sufficient creatures, it's never a good idea to leave them home unattended, even for a couple of days. Accidents happen around the home. Your cat can be left without sustenance, too, if the water bowl gets tipped over and ants invade the food bowl.

Long weekends and the holiday season are busy times, so it's important to make arrangements well in advance, especially if you are looking for a reservation at a cat-hotel or require the services of a professional pet sitter.

Kitty Day Care

It's an established fact that animals left home alone for long periods suffer from intense boredom. They may even begin to suffer from medical conditions such as separation anxiety and issues such as excessive licking and hair pulling. These concerns can develop into severe behavioral problems and cause destruction around the home.

▶ In general, cats are happiest if they can be left
at home while their owners are away, rather
than being boarded at a kennel.

Dog owners address such problems by employing a dog walker if they are not able to walk their pets themselves several times during the day. Some even send their pets to doggy day care and special dog camps so that their pets are kept both mentally and physically stimulated.

Believe it or not, there are now establishments that offer kitty day care, too, so that your cat doesn't have to spend endless hours home alone and bored. One such place is Pet Camp's Cat Safari in San Francisco, a specially landscaped greenhouse that offers felines the unique opportunity to enjoy the feel of the great outdoors within this safe enclosure. Surrounded by trees and plants, there are glass towers full of tropical fish and aviaries of twittering birds so that felines can look but not munch. Felines are allowed to play here on their own so there are no catfights. Pet Camp is a well-known pet care facility and boarding establishment with a special cattery for sleepovers at their main location. However, your cat doesn't have to board to be able to play at Cat Safari. Local cat owners as well as tourists visiting San Francisco are encouraged to bring their cats for a day's outing, for some mental and physical stimulation. Unfortunately, such fabulous facilities are not yet available everywhere throughout the United States. Let's hope this unique idea will become more popular in time.

It's very important to entertain cats in their home environment by ensuring they have plenty of safe toys to play with and a kitty condo to explore.

If you are worried about your cat spending long hours home alone, consider getting a cat-sitter to come in during the day. There are lots of elderly and retired people who, for various reasons, are unable to keep a cat of their own and would be only too happy to come and enjoy the company of a feline friend. Consider posting a notice in your veterinarian's office, local pet store, and even at local retirement and assisted living establishments. You may have a relative who would enjoy some feline company for a nominal fee—or for free!

▼There are now establishments that offer kitty day care so that your cat doesn't have to spend hours alone and bored.

Pet Sitter for Your Cat

It's a good idea to consider setting up a reciprocal plan with a pet-owning neighbor to keep an eye on each other's pets; attend to basic food, water, and litter box needs; and spend a bit of time playing with the animals, too. However, it has to be someone who understands cats and will be careful about opening doors so that your cat doesn't escape. Never ask a child be a sitter; taking care of a pet is a huge responsibility.

If you're planning to travel during a busy time of year, such as the holiday season, and you are unable to take your cat with you, it's probably a better idea to call upon the services of a professional sitter. A neighbor may be overwhelmed with other things to attend to during holiday time. Pet sitters do much more than simply provide food and water and scoop the litter box. They will spend quality time playing with your cat so that, although you will be missed, your pet won't feel abandoned.

Finding the correct pet sitter is just like finding a competent person to take care of your child. It's important to remember that just because someone calls himself or herself a pet sitter doesn't mean he or she is qualified for the job. Popular sitters are often booked well in advance. So make sure you never leave something this important for the last minute.

Where to Find a Sitter

Ask other friends with cats for recommendations. Or ask your veterinarian or the staff at a local pet store. Often, members of their staff are licensed and bonded pet sitters, too. Or just look at their boards; vet offices and pets stores frequently display the business cards of pet sitting businesses. Alternatively, check out advertisements in local community newspapers. There are also nationwide professional organizations—such as Pet Sitters International, Fetch! Pet Care, and the National Association of Professional Pet Sitters—that are geared to finding someone best suited to meet your needs.

Working with a professional organization ensures that their recommended sitters are licensed, have completed pet care study courses, and are competent to take care of the pets in their charge. (There are also independent licensed professionals.)

A Digital Cat Sitter

Consider leaving the TV on during the day to keep your cat company. There are also excellent cat-sitting videos that show cats at play, along with a variety of different small animal and insect videos to peek feline interest. Alternatively, a radio left on a talk radio station will offer some vocal companionship.

Nevertheless, whether you are working independently or through a professional organization, the onus is on you to check out your potential sitter's credentials. Before reaching any arrangement, invite the prospective sitter over so you can conduct an interview face to face and introduce him or her to your cat.

What to Ask

Here is a useful checklist of points to cover at this initial meeting:

- Ask to see written proof that the pet sitter has commercial liability insurance to cover accidents and negligence and is bonded to protect against theft (by the pet sitter).

▶ It's best to have the sitter over to meet your cat and for you to meet the sitter before you go away.

▲ Even with a good sitter, your kitty will be anxious for you to come home.

- Ask for phone numbers of other clients who have agreed to serve as references and subsequently follow-up by making a few phone calls.
- Inquire into what kind of training the pet sitter has received.
- Ask for a written contract that spells out the services the pet sitter agrees to perform relating to your cat, as well as other services, such as bringing in the mail and putting out the garbage, and be clear about the fees involved.
- If it's a live-in arrangement, specify the times you definitely want the sitter to be home with your pet.
- If it's not a live-in arrangement, make sure the pet sitter knows where to switch on and off the lights when checking in on your pet in the evenings. Arrange in advance if you want a specific light left on at all times.
- Be sure to stipulate how much time the sitter needs to spend with your cat on a daily basis.

- Inquire whether the person or organization has backup coverage in case of illness.
- Find out if the pet sitter is willing to take your pet to your veterinarian and, if not, what particular veterinary office he or she will take your cat to if the need arises. Make sure the sitter know where the nearest emergency animal hospital is located. It's a good idea to leave MapQuest-styled directions on the refrigerator—just in case.

It's also important that the pet sitter understands your cat's temperament. Not all cats are outgoing and friendly toward strangers, and your pal may be a bit reticent at first. Spell everything out, going over how your cat may react at first and what the sitter should do.

Don't forget to point out the salient features of your home, such as an alarm system and where you keep the remote control for the garage door. If you have one of those televisions that requires more than one remote to use it, take pity on the sitter and write out instructions, especially if you want that person to leave the TV on for the cat when she or he isn't there.

Tasks Before You Leave

Make sure you've written out all instructional information regarding your pet's food, medication, and general routine. Remember to pin your contact information up in a prominent place so you can be reached at any time, and give the pet sitter at least one neighbor's name and phone number. It's also good idea to leave an additional key with someone trustworthy in case your pet sitter gets locked out. (It happens, especially if you have a self-locking front door.) And don't forget to stock up with all you cat's needs, such as food, litter, and medications, before you go.

Cat Hotels and Boarding Facilities

The alternative to an at-home arrangement is boarding your cat. Many veterinary offices will look after your cat. This can be an advantage if your cat is on specialized medication and requires constant medical attention, such as the daily administration of insulin shots for diabetes or fluids to control kidney-related issues. Boarding your cat at the vet means that she's probably going to be caged for most of the time. Be sure to ask whether the cats are taken out at all and exercised in a secure place. It wasn't that long ago that boarding facilities for pets resembled stark, cold animal shelters offering caged areas with concrete floors and little else. Pet owners were required to bring with them all their pets would need.

Although it's still a good idea to take along your cat's favorite blanket and toys for comfort and security, these days, many pet care establishments have earned the right to call themselves pet resorts and hotels. Your cat can expect five-star treatment in establishments that offer a home-away-from-home ambience. Some pet hotels have installed webcams so that you can keep a close watch on your pet via computer and smartphone while you travel. Many places offer "in-house" entertainment, such as Animal Planet 24/7 or fish tanks for nonstop

amusement. Furthermore, there are resorts that specialize in cats only. Such a resort has obvious advantages, the main one being that your cat will not be stressed out listening to barking dogs.

How to Find a Hotel or Other Facility

It's important to research a facility in advance. Find out whether the accommodation is a multitiered

Stats on Traveling Cats

According to the 2013–2014 National Pet Owners Survey, published by the American Pet Products Association (APPA), seven out of ten cat owners make arrangements for their cat's care when they are away from home for at least two nights.

Here are the detailed statistics from the survey:

- When cat owners are away from home for at least two nights, six out of ten will have family/friends/neighbors come to their homes to feed and care for their cats.

- Only 5 percent or fewer will board their cats,

- 9 percent leave their cats with friends or family

- 6 percent of cat owners hire a professional pet sitter.

- Cat owners who travel in the car with their cat usually have only one child in the household.

- More cats who travel in the car live in the northeastern region of the United States than in other regions

- Cats traveling in the car also have owners with higher incomes who own their homes and travel; these cats more frequently have female owners as opposed to male pet parents.

- Only 1 percent travel by plane. Although there are no official statistics, pet friendly airlines say that a number of feline passengers travel on a regular basis for leisure and not just for cat shows

▲ Boarding at the vets is a good option, especially if your cat is on meds or has special needs.

"condo" so that your cat in fact has a sleeping area separated from the food and litter tray. Some places also have designated play areas with tall cat trees and tunnels, and each cat is given daily time to play in a secure environment under strict supervision. All-feline resorts usually offer cat owners the option of boarding multiple cats together as well.

What to Ask

If you are considering a cat hotel-styled facility, here are some important questions to ask before you book:

- Is somebody on the premises 24/7? If not, you may want to consider another facility. Although you may not be home every hour of the day, when you're boarding your cat in an unfamiliar environment, you want to know there is someone there watching out for her.
- Is the area climate controlled so that your cat remains in a constant-temperature environment similar to what she has at home? For example, make sure her designated condo isn't in full sun for some part of the day, which would make it very hot. (Establishments should know better, but it's your responsibility to check.)
- Will the staff adhere to the feeding schedule that your cat is used to at home? If not and your cat is on a special regimen, you definitely need to look elsewhere.
- How often is the litter box cleaned? Boxes should be scooped daily, preferably twice daily—morning and night. After all, you are paying for special service for your cat.
- Is there a veterinarian on call to come to the establishment if there is a medical emergency? If not, ask the staff what arrangement they have for a medical emergency. If the answer is not "rush the cat to the veterinarian or emergency

animal hospital, which is just down the road," look for another boarding facility.

- What type of food does the facility serve? If you're worried your cat won't eat whatever it is, try feeding her some ahead of time. Or ask if you can bring your cat's own food. Many establishments will allow you to do so.
- Will the staff meet the special needs of your cats, such as administering medications and daily supplements and even hand out treats at a certain time each day? If not, once again, you obviously need to find a place that will.
- What vaccinations must your cat have before boarding? Not only is this essential information for having your cat ready in time for boarding (vaccinations must occur at two weeks before boarding), but also if the answer is "none," you may want to consider boarding at another place. A recognized establishment will insist that your cat has all the standard cat vaccinations

Installing a Pet Video Monitor

In late 2013, Motorola, well-known manufacturer of baby monitors, introduced the first WiFi pet video monitor that allows pet parents to view their pets at home from their smartphone, tablet, or computer. The Scout 1 Pet Video Monitor video camera allows pet owners to view, listen, and speak to their pets when away from home. Apart from communicating with your pets, the camera also allows pet parents to play music to their pets. The sophisticated camera can pan and tilt to get the best views of a room and also has excellent night vision.

(see chapter 9, pages 222-223), as well as a rabies vaccine. Although there is a trend not to vaccinate indoor cats, you will have to toe the line if your cat is going to be boarded. When asked for proof of vaccinations, always submit copies of the vaccinations, never the originals.

◄ Your cat's vaccinations must be up to date before boarding her at a clinic or pet hotel.

Chapter 22

Emergency Situations

Be Prepared—the meaning of the motto is that a scout must prepare himself by previous thinking out and practicing how to act on any accident or emergency so that he is never taken by surprise

— Sir Robert Baden-Powell

Thanks to technology, meteorologists are able to predict when weather-related disasters are going to happen, giving people in harm's way an opportunity to get ready for the pending situation and, if necessary, evacuate. Nevertheless, accidents, especially those that happen within the home, can occur suddenly and without any prior warning. That's why it's so necessary to observe the Boy Scout motto and "Be prepared!"

Be Prepared at Home and Away

Even with the most meticulous pet-proofing precautions in place, accidents can happen. In addition, there's little you can do to prevent sudden illness. This is why it is so important, as we discussed in chapter 9, to find a veterinarian and veterinary practice in your area and establish your cat or kitten there right away. (See chapter 9, Establishing a Health Care Regimen, for further discussion on finding a veterinarian.)

It's also important to know their office hours and whether the office is open on weekends. Even a

▶ It's important to know your vet's emergency hours and emergency policies before you need them.

veterinary practice with weekend hours, though, is unlikely to be open 24/7. However, most veterinary practices have an affiliation with a twenty-four-hour emergency pet hospital. Ask whether this is the case and get contact information.

As a matter of routine preparedness, contact the emergency pet hospital to ensure it also has all of your pet's information on file. Be polite but insistent if the staff is not keen to take on potential patients. Even in an emergency, the pet hospital won't treat your pet before all the laborious paperwork is in place. If necessary, prepare an information sheet and ask the staff to have it on file to save time, should an emergency arise.

Make sure you have all the contact information for your veterinarian and the emergency pet hospital (along with the hours that your vet clinic is open) prominently displayed in your home. Because most kitchens are the nerve center of the household, use the inside of a kitchen cupboard door to tape up all the information and include directions and even a map. That way, should you not be home when an emergency occurs, someone else can easily step in and take charge.

Find out if there is an emergency pet ambulance service in your area and keep that information prominently displayed as well. It's also a good idea to have the number of a local taxi service that will allow pets to ride in their vehicles as another emergency measure. To be really prepared, program relevant veterinary numbers into your home phone and all family cell phones, and program the address of the veterinarian's

clinic and the pet emergency hospital into your car's GPS system.

While you are putting all this emergency paperwork in place, be sure to put decals on the exterior of your home alerting neighbors and emergency service first responders to the fact that there are pets inside and detail exactly how many and what species. These decals can be purchased from online stores and many pet boutiques. Animal welfare organizations often give them away from free so check websites such as ASPCA.org. Good locations include the front door, the back door, and the garage door.

The Feline First-Aid Kit

It's essential to also have a basic feline first-aid kit handy. (Take it with you when you're traveling.) You can buy specially prepared, cat-specific first-aid kits from various online stores, but it's very easy to assemble one yourself.

Start off with a shoebox-size plastic container that seals tightly and label it accordingly. Keep it in a bathroom cupboard or where you keep other pet supplies and be sure that everyone in the household knows how to access it in a hurry.

A well-equipped first-aid kit should include the following items:

- Antiseptic ointment or solution
- Small bottle of table salt (a teaspoon of salt added to a large glass of warm water will make a saline solution for cleaning minor cuts and scrapes)
- Bottle of hydrogen peroxide (as an alternative to a salt solution)
- Small stainless steel or plastic bowls for solutions to bathe wounds
- Cotton balls, cotton swabs, and a roll of cotton padding
- Sterile dressing pads
- Liquid bandage for pets (available from veterinary offices and online pet pharmaceutical supply websites)
- Small flashlight and fresh batteries to look inside a mouth (check regularly to maintain working condition

Safer Indoors

Keeping a cat indoors on a permanent basis definitely reduces the number of dangers and emergency situations that she would otherwise be exposed to.

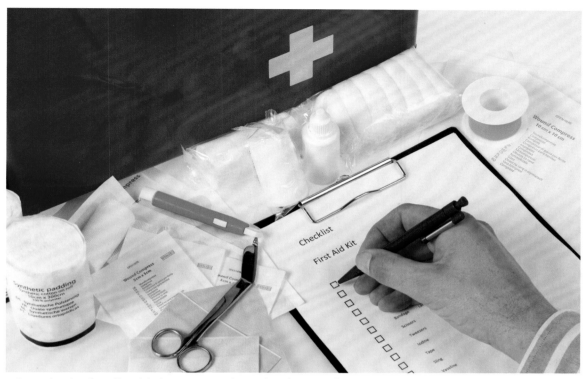

▲ Put together a kitty first-aid kit and check its contents every few months, replacing items that are expired or used up.

- Tick Key, a gadget to safely remove ticks without leaving any poisonous discharge behind (can be found at www.tickkey.com)
- Self-adhesive bandage (you can purchase special pet bandages)
- Roll of narrow adhesive tape
- Latex gloves
- Sharp tweezers
- Small blunt scissors
- Pet digital rectal thermometer
- Tube or jar of lubricant jelly to lubricate the thermometer before insertion
- Sterile eye wash solution (the human kind is suitable)
- Eyedropper
- Syringe to administer liquid medicine
- Hydrocortisone ointment or antihistamine spray for insect stings
- Glucose powder to make a rehydrating fluid; use one tablespoon of glucose and add a teaspoon of salt to a liter of water (1¼ pints)
- Corn syrup to revive a cat in a diabetic coma; simply rub a little on the gums
- Ice pack in the fridge marked accordingly for a pet emergency; keep a small towel in your kit to wrap it in for use
- Small blanket or large towel (place alongside your first-aid box if it won't fit inside) to wrap the cat "burrito-style" while administering medication or attending to a wound
- Elizabethan collar to prevent the cat from interfering with a dressing or bandage; you can purchase soft collars from online stores and boutiques that do the same job but are far more comfortable than the hard plastic type
- Small mirror (to be used in front of a cat's nose to determine if she's breathing)

A variety of pet-specific first-aid products are on the market. They are worth researching and including in your kit. Put all bottles in plastic bags in case they leak, and be sure to replenish what you use and to periodically check the date stamps on ointments and liquids. Always bear in mind that a first-aid kit is there for *first* aid. It should never be a substitute for a visit to the veterinarian.

The ABCs of First-Aid Basics

It's essential to know the best way of handling a variety of emergency circumstances that can occur at home so that you can give your cat the best chance of surviving what could potentially be a life-threatening injury. This begins with the first-aid ABCs: airway, breathing, and circulation.

Airway: Your first priority is to ensure that nothing is blocking the airway. If there is, gently remove it. You may have to wrap your cat in a towel so that she doesn't interfere with your efforts. Cats often instinctively bite when scared or stressed, so be careful.

Breathing: Next check that your cat is breathing. If you are not sure, place a mirror in front of her nose and see if it fogs up slightly. If your cat has very shallow breathing, her tongue is a blue-black color, and you've established that there is nothing blocking the throat, gently lift her chin to extend her neck, open the airway, and slowly begin administering artificial respiration:

1. Hold the cat's mouth closed and cover her entire nose with your mouth.
2. Gently breathe up the cat's nose—count out 30 breathes per minute. Take your mouth away from her nose in-between breaths so that she has the chance to exhale.
3. Keep this routine up until she begins to breathe or professional help arrives.

Circulation: Finally, check that her heart is beating. The best way to check for a pulse is to place two fingers on the inside of the cat's thigh in the groin area (you would do this behind an ear on a person). If the heartbeat is slow (or appears to be nonexistent), begin cardiopulmonary resuscitation (CPR), which is an emergency technique to help a person's or an animal's heart start functioning normally again. To do this, begin chest compressions as follows:

1. Place one hand on either side of the cat's chest, just behind her elbows.
2. Squeeze the chest by using a flat hand to compress. Do not use too much force or you could crack ribs.

CPR works together with the artificial respiration technique described earlier. Give two breaths to every four hand compressions and keep it up until the heart begins to beat or professional help arrives.

It is always best to work on a hard surface and most effective if the cat is lying on her side.

Many groups and organization offer basic pet first-aid classes. If such a class is available in your area, it's certainly worth taking.

Bleeding Wounds

If you can tell it's nothing serious, clean the cut and bandage it using items from your first-aid kit.

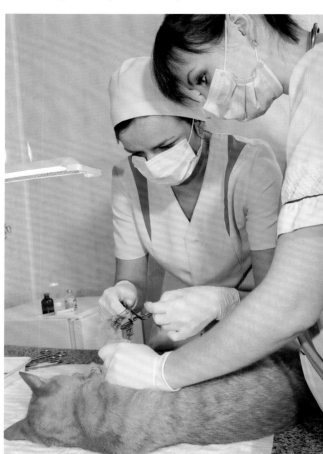

▶This cat is being treated for a paw injury.

However, if you suspect a gunshot wound or can see something impaled in the cat (yes, this can happen with outdoor cats), don't attempt to remove anything because it could make the bleeding worse. Don't apply a tourniquet unless you are trained in first-aid procedures and know what you are doing because you could, in fact, make the situation worse by cutting off the blood supply. Take your cat immediately to the veterinarian or emergency pet hospital. Even what you may consider to be a minor cut may need stitches. Let the veterinarian be the judge.

Bite Wounds

Cats who have access to the outdoors can get bitten by a number of animals. It's often difficult to determine what has caused the bite: it could be another cat invading your cat's territory, a rodent (which could be dangerous because rodents carry so many diseases), or a snake. If you are not sure, try to keep her as still as possible because, if it is a snakebite, you need to prevent the venom from spreading quickly through her body. Wrap her in the towel from your first-aid kit to immobilize her and take her immediately to the veterinarian office or emergency pet hospital.

It's much easier to assess a bite wound if your cat has an indoor lifestyle. If it's not the result of an altercation with another pet in the household, then perhaps she's caught herself on something sharp and the wound simply looks like a bite. Cut away the fur as best you can and clean the wound using swabs and antiseptic solutions from your first-aid kit. If it's a puncture wound, take your cat to the veterinarian right away to have it checked out.

Choking Cat

It's very important to establish that the cat is actually choking and not just gagging. A choking cat will paw at her face, cough, and appear distracted and frantic. If you cannot see anything—and it's very difficult to peer into a cat's mouth when time is of the essence—try lifting her up and holding her with her head pointing toward to the ground, then giver her a sharp knock on the

shoulder blades. This can be sufficient to dislodge something that has been swallowed and gotten stuck.

If you are still concerned, try the Heimlich maneuver as follows. But be careful; it requires force, and you don't want to break bones.

- Stand behind the cat.
- Make a fist with one hand; place your other hand over it and position both hands just below the rib cage.
- Compress the abdomen several times with quick pushes.

If this doesn't work, seek emergency attention immediately. Even if you have been successful, it's a good idea to follow-up with a veterinary visit.

Drowning Cat

Most cats can swim, but they may have difficulty extricating themselves from a swimming pool or river. Get the cat out the water and immediately try to drain as much water as possible from the lungs by her tilting her sideways until she is upside down. Two pairs of hands may be better than one if she is resisting. Then lay her on her side and rub her body vigorously to help expel more water. If she's not breathing, immediately begin artificial respiration or CPR.

Once again, seek veterinary help right away.

Electrocution

Never touch a cat who has been electrocuted. First, switch off the main power source. Then use a wooden object, such as a broom, to move her away from the wiring. Wrap her in a blanket and, if she is not breathing, begin mouth-to-mouth resuscitation. If there isn't an immediate response—or even if there is—seek emergency veterinary help.

Emergency Situations

433

Insect Stings

Cats are naturally drawn to things that flutter and fly around. It's always a good idea to get rid of any bees and wasps that fly into your home before your cat attempts to "help."

A cat who gets stung will immediately try to paw the area. Unlike wasps, bees leave a stinger behind. If you can locate it in thick fur, you may be able to pull it out with tweezers. Cats often chomp on a bee and get stung in the mouth. This could be dangerous because bee venom can cause swelling of the mouth and throat that could inhibit breathing. Treat the situation as an emergency because your cat will need an antihistamine injection to counteract swelling. Take her to the veterinarian or emergency pet hospital.

▲ Because cats like to chase small flying things, they can easily be stung by wasps, hornets, and other insects.

Ticks

Ticks pose a huge problem to both pets and people because they carry numerous nasty diseases, such as Lyme disease, and can cause tick bite fever. Covering ticks with petroleum jelly doesn't kill them, and using tweezers may only remove half the tick.

A handy gadget called a Tick Key removes these deadly parasites quickly and effectively without squashing them and leaving behind the blood or saliva that could cause infections and diseases harmful to both animals and humans.

It works by placing the specially shaped key over the tick and pulling in an upward motion away from the skin. It's an excellent investment for all pets and people in the home. Make sure there's one in your first-aid box. Another new product is Tick-SR. It works by dissolving the "glue" that creates a bond between the tick and the cat. At the same time, it impedes the blood flow to the affected area and thus the tick's ability to feed. With the glue and food supply disrupted, the tick can be more easily removed and then destroyed.

Poison

A variety of household cleaning products and plants are toxic to pets. Cats allowed outside can also eat rat poison or fertilizer and are also exposed to someone's putting out poisoned meat to lure them to their death. Feline bodies are not equipped to deal with any kind of toxins, and the first signs of a problem are usually extreme lethargy and profuse salivating. Keeping the ASPCA poison hotline number accessible at all times is a good idea, especially if you are unable to get immediate veterinary attention. The poison hotline does charge for calls, but it's worth it because they can give you step-by-step instructions on how to force your cat to vomit. However, even if you do manage to induce

If You Are in an Accident...

If you are in an accident that requires hospitalization, it's important that those taking care of you know that you have pets alone at home. Keep a card with this information in your wallet. It's even a good idea to engrave a dog tag and clip it onto your keys or even wear it as a piece of jewelry.

vomiting, your cat is still going to need urgent veterinary attention.

Cats often go into a state of shock immediately after a traumatic ordeal. Typical signs are very pale lips and gums, skin that's cold to the touch, and a blank stare in the eyes.

Keep her calm and quiet, and wrap her in a blanket to keep her warm. To promote blood circulation, gently massage her body or legs. If she won't let you touch these areas, try her paws.

Sunburned or Scalded

A cat lying in the hot sun can suffer from sunburn. If her paws are burned, try standing the cat in ice water to reduce the pain. Cats with pink noses and paw pads can easily suffer from sunburn on these areas. (A sunscreen with a minimum of 15 SPF is an excellent preventative measure. There are special pet sunscreen products on the market, but you can use a human product, too.)

Scalds from hot water can be initially treated the same way. Then wrap the cat firmly in a towel and seek veterinary attention.

Trapped in a Burning Building

If you and your cat are in a burning building and you don't have a carrier handy to put her in, grab a pillowcase, place her inside, and keep it tightly shut until you are out of harm's way. Any burns are going to need professional help from first responders. Wrap your cat in a blanket to prevent her going into shock and to keep her from licking herself because her fur will be covered in poisonous smoke. Try to keep her somewhere quiet until help arrives. Fortunately, most emergency fire services around the country have special pet oxygen masks and will be able to administer oxygen if required. As soon as possible, seek emergency veterinary help.

Moving an Injured Cat

If the accident occurred outside the home, check the locale carefully to ensure that you are not in danger, too. If the cat is in the road, get someone to stand in the road to alert motorists while you get a flat board. You can use anything from a plank, a flattened but firm cardboard box, a kitchen tray, or even a skateboard if necessary. Slowly place the

▼ Cats can be poisoned by eating mice or rats that have ingested rat poison.

▲ Having an evacuation plan worked out in advance of an emergency increases the likelihood both you and your cat will be okay.

cat on this makeshift stretcher by sliding both your hands under the body and, maintaining a horizontal position, slowly move her out of harm's way. Try to involve as few jerky movements as possible in case there are internal injuries that you can't see.

In the case of road accidents (or a cat being run over in a driveway), be aware that, even if injured, cats can jump up and run off. Don't chase. But lure her slowly to you and seek immediate veterinary help. Internal bleeding can be life-threatening.

Be Prepared When Disaster Strikes

Earthquakes, hurricanes, tornados, floods, wildfires, and even toxic spills can happen anywhere, often with little warning. If you have to evacuate with your pets, the most important thing is to have a safe place to go to or, if necessary, to leave your pets where they will be properly cared

for until the situation improves. A safe place could be a friend's house, a pet resort, an animal shelter, or even a pet-friendly hotel. Fortunately, more and more hotels are accepting pets these days, and such establishments usually come forward in an hour of need by offering evacuees really cheap rates.

It's important to have a list of possible places to go in all directions within a 50-mile radius. That's because you never know what area will be affected and how far from your home you will have to travel and in what direction. A list compiled in advance, in different directions, at different distances, with full addresses of prospective safe places along with telephone numbers, will save time in a true emergency.

Although with floods and fires there are usually official warnings from city personnel and possibly the opportunity to evacuate before it becomes mandatory, never leave anything until the last minute when animals are involved. Disaster may come sooner than predicted or may be worse than predicted or may be unpredicted. At the first sign of trouble, take out your pet carriers and keep them inside the house and ready to go.

It's a good idea to attach a few blank paper tags to each carrier so that you can write any last-minute information on them, such as your name and telephone numbers and the place where *you* will be staying if it's different from the animal shelter that will be temporarily housing your pet. Having several tags handy gives you the opportunity to update if necessary. These tags can be attached to your pet's carrier as well to her collar.

Proper identification is also your pet's ticket to being reunited with you should something happen to separate you. Make sure that your cat is wearing a collar with her name and your address and telephone number on it. It's important for your pet to have a microchip implanted, too, because collars can come off. As discussed in other chapters, there are lots of different services that you can subscribe to that will help you trace a lost pet. If you belong to such a service, be sure that your pet is wearing that tag, too. Simply put, your pet can never have too much identification.

It's always a good idea if someone you know and trust who lives near you has keys to your home should you be away at the time of a mandatory evacuation.

Evacuation Checklist for Your Cat

You are also going to need to have a kit ready to take care of your cat's needs. Here are the basic items I recommend including in your evacuation kit:

- Medicine bag: Place all medications in a cool bag well in advance and keep the whole bag in your refrigerator. Even if you have to work out of the bag for a couple of days, it's worth being prepared so that, when the time comes, you can just grab and go. If you give your pet fluids under the skin, place a couple of bags in a larger cooler bag and put it next to the medicine bag, along with the necessary needles and tubes needed for the procedure.
- Medical records: Be sure to take copies of all medical records, especially if your pet is allergic to certain medications. Be sure to include copies of all vaccination certificates.
- Carrier: Make sure it has ID tags and is lined with a puppy pee pad in case your pet has to be confined for a long time.
- Bowls for food and water
- Litter box and litter to last at least a week (you can purchase throwaway kits)
- Disposal bags for used kitty litter (a roll of dog poop bags is a good idea)
- Food: Cans and pouches are easy to pack; dry food must be packed into an airtight container. Make sure you have enough food for seven days.
- Bottled water: Allow enough water for seven days for each pet you are evacuating.
- Take a favorite toy and a favorite blanket.
- Pet first-aid kit
- Photographs of pets: Be sure you have current photographs of your pets should you become separated.
- Pet information sheet: An information sheet that details your veterinarian, medical conditions, and any behavioral issues.
- Portable radio: So you can keep abreast of the situation wherever you are.
- Flashlight

◄ If you and your cat are separated during an evacuation, proper identification is your ticket to a happy reunion.

Emergency Situations

Evacuation Without Your Cat

In an emergency situation, if you have no alternative but to leave your cat inside your home, you must do the best you can to protect her until emergency responders are able to come. Contain her in a safe room with plenty of food and water. If possible, make it a bedroom that has access to a bathroom, too, so that you can fill the sink with additional water. If you have a dog, do the same in another room to control the food and water situation.

Place notices prominently outside your front and back doors advising what pets are inside and explain where they are located. Provide a phone number where you can be reached, as well as the name and number of your vet. Remember, such actions are a last resort.

PETS Evacuation Act

The PETS Act (Pets Evacuation and Transportation Standards Act) was signed by President George W. Bush and made a federal law in October 2006 after thousands of pets perished when Hurricane Katrina devastated the shores of the Gulf Coast in August 2005. People fleeing the rising flood waters were not allowed to take their pets with them, and a small child crying for his dog, Snowball, became the impetus for this law when the story hit the headlines, drawing attention to the large numbers of pets who were left behind.

Many people refused to leave their homes because they didn't want to abandon their beloved companions. According to reports, as many as 50,000 companion animals died during this national disaster, and hundreds of thousands more were never reunited with their families.

The PETS Act requires that local and state emergency management plans include preparation for evacuating family pets and service animals along with their owners. It also allows the Federal Emergency Management Agency (FEMA) to provide funding to create pet-friendly shelters and assist with the development of localized emergency management plans. The PETS Act is one of the positive changes that came out of the Katrina disaster.

The impact and value of this legislation was apparent during the evacuations prompted by Hurricane Gustav in August 2008. Citizens who didn't have independent transportation were able to bring their pets to staging areas for evacuation. Cats, dogs, rabbits, and other small pets were issued bar-coded bands that matched those provided to their owners. The animals were then loaded into pet carriers and transported in air-conditioned tractor-trailers to predesignated shelters. The PETS Act continues to help to save pet lives every year during hurricane season.

This legislation is not limited to evacuations due to hurricanes; the PETS Act applies to all disasters, including floods, fires, earthquakes, tornadoes, and

◄ Make sure both your cat and her carrier have identification on them, including your contact information.

▲ After the ordeal of an evacuation, your cat may be skittish, hide a lot, or exhibit other nervous behavior.

other declared states of emergency. The law's intent is to not only protect pets and service animals but their owners as well.

The PETS Act, which is fact is an expansion of the 1988 Stafford Act, stipulates that in order for a community or state to be eligible to receive federal emergency funding, a detailed plan outlining emergency transportation and shelter plans for household pets and services animals must be submitted to FEMA. Although this legislation has been in place for almost seven years, sixteen states, including Katrina-affected Mississippi, have not submitted plans that are compliant with the PETS Act. An up-to-date map of the states that have plans in place and a list of resources can be found on the American Veterinary Medical Association's website (www.AVMA.org). FEMA has also produced a DVD called *Animals in Emergencies: What Planners Need to Know*. More information

about this presentation and how to receive a copy is available by contacting FEMA at www.fema.gov. Another excellent website that details disaster preparedness laws, as well as other pet laws, is the Animal Law and Historical Center website (http://www.animallaw.info) run by the Michigan State University College of Law.

After a Disaster

After a disaster, it's really important to check your home from the standpoint of your cat's safety to ensure that there is no access to the outside. If necessary, confine your cat to one safe room until all damage has been repaired. If this is not possible, make arrangements to board her as close to home as possible until you know your home is once again secure. It's also necessary to watch your cat's behavior for signs of stress, which can happen after a major catastrophe.

Chapter 23

Lost Cats

Read the directions and directly you will be
directed in the right direction

— Doorknob in *Alice in Wonderland*
By Lewis Carroll

Sadly, thousands of pets go missing around the country every day. For cat owners (as for other pet owners), there's nothing worse than that hollow feeling in the stomach when the realization hits home that their companions are nowhere to be found. To distraught owners, it often seems as if their cats have vanished without a trace, and panic starts to take over. When this happens, owners stop thinking clearly and miss taking the steps most likely to help them find their cats.

The best way to keep panic at bay is to know what those steps are in advance. The steps discussed in this chapter are ones that searchers have found most effective over the years. Pet detectives—professional animal finders—have devised some methods and refined others to help find lost cats as quickly as possible.

Not panicking doesn't mean you shouldn't take immediate action. If your pet fails to appear at mealtime, *don't* simply assume she will turn up. The sooner you begin searching, the better. And don't give up too soon. Cats can hide for weeks before coming out to be found.

▶ If your cat is lost, the most important things are to not panic and to search for her methodically.

Searching for a Lost Cat

Cats love to climb into things and go to sleep. So it's important to first check around your home looking in the most likely (and unlikely) places, such the mattress lining under the bed—some cats like to pull the lining of the mattress down and create a "hammock" to snooze in. Check laundry baskets, shelves, cupboards, and even between clothing items, such as stacks of sweaters. Cats can be inventive, and it's important to know their secret places so you can check there first before taking your search outside.

Indoor cats who only rarely venture beyond the front door (and then in carriers) are automatically out of their comfort zone when they accidently find themselves outside. Consequently, they tend to hide and go silent. Under such circumstances, it's important to remember that even the friendliest cat won't necessarily come when you call.

In fact, the temperament of your cat is one of the biggest influences regarding how your pet gets lost and what distance she's likely to travel. That temperament will affect how your cat will react and how her instinctive reactions may change when she goes into typical feline survival mode.

Other influential factors include the weather (such as thunderstorms or snowstorms), the population density of the area, and the terrain.

Understanding Lost Cat Behavior

Pet detectives who earn their living recovering lost and stolen pets stress that it's important never to assume that when a cat is lost she will exhibit the same behavior patterns that she displays in the comfort of her own home. Out of familiar territory, cats go into survival mode, avoiding contact with people, hiding during the day, and moving around looking for food at night, using the cover of darkness as a security blanket.

That said, however, pet detectives stress that missing cats do display four basic behavior patterns, based on their personality type: *curious*, *careless*, *cautious*, and *xenophobic*. It's important to recognize which category your cat fits into and paste this vital information up inside a kitchen cupboard. If she goes missing, you need to remain calm and think clearly, and this will help.

The Curious Cat

Gregarious cats who are outgoing and friendly get into trouble easily because they will run up to anyone and aren't afraid of anything. When displaced, they may hide initially but are most likely to travel.

Strategy for recovery: Place fluorescent posters within at least a five-block radius. Interview neighbors in a door-to-door search, thoroughly searching possible hiding places in yards of houses and other areas within a close proximity to the escape point. Never assume that your cat will come when you call her. Don't overlook crawl spaces under buildings, including sheds and other small structures.

The Careless Cat

Aloof cats who appear a bit detached and distant don't seem to care much about people. When a stranger comes in, they stand back and watch.

Strategy for recovery: When displaced, initially, they are more likely to hide than travel, then

Wrong Side of the Door

Make sure your cat doesn't get out when people come in, people who may not close doors. Whenever you have workers in your home, it's a good idea to secure your cat before their arrival and put a warning note on the door to the room in which she has been secured. Be sure to place food, water, and a litter box in the room, too.

This routine is also a good idea whenever you've having a party or even casual company over. Cats are curious; they will often inspect a door left slightly ajar and suddenly find themselves on the wrong side of it.

▲ Lost cats usually stay within five blocks of home, so concentrate your search there.

eventually they break cover and come back to the door and meow. Of course, there is the possibly that the cat could travel. The strategy should be to search hiding places nearby and closely search neighboring yards. If these efforts do not produce results, consider setting a baited humane trap.

The Cautious Cat

Cautious cats are friendly but shy. When a stranger comes to the door, they dart and hide, although they eventually come out to investigate. If lost, they will most likely immediately hide in fear.

Strategy for recovery: If not scared out of their hiding place, they will typically return to the point where they escaped, or they will meow when their owner comes to look for them. Typically, this behavior is observed within the first two days (after the cat has built up confidence). Sometimes, however, it takes seven to ten days, when their hunger or thirst has reached a critical point, for

them to respond. Do a very detailed search of neighbors' yards and set baited humane traps.

The Xenophobic Cat

Xenophobic cats are afraid of everything new or unfamiliar. They will hide when a stranger comes into the home and are easily disturbed by any change in the environment.

Strategy for recovery: When displaced, these cats bolt and hide in silence. They tend to remain

Check Every Hidey-Hole

Cats who are out of their comfort zone and possibly injured, will hide. Their survival instincts kick in, and they go silent so as not to alert a predator of their location. So don't assume your kitty is out of hearing range when you call for her; check every hidey-hole you see.

▲ Lost cat signs should be large, brightly colored, and placed in high-traffic areas.

in the same hiding place, immobilized with fear. If someone other than their owners finds them, they are typically mistaken as untamed or "feral." The primary strategy to recover these cats is to set baited humane traps. Xenophobic cats who become "lost" are routinely absorbed into the feral cat population.

Searching Beyond the Home

It's important to start your search in earnest the moment you are aware that your cat is not tucked away safely inside your home. If possible, try to ascertain the escape route: Is there an open window, was the front door inadvertently left open?

Because it's an established fact that your cat may not immediately come to you, it's important to go outside and establish your own scent trail around your house or apartment building so that if your cat is hiding close by, it will help alert her olfactory senses that you are in the neighborhood. This doesn't mean, however, that she will immediately run to you.

If you do spot her, do not rush up to her because this may cause her to bolt and run. Remember, displaced cats do not behave as they would within the confines of their home environment. Patience is key to success.

It's very important to take a flashlight with you, even in the daylight hours, and search every corner under your house. You should search around your neighbors' homes as well. Even if you're not on particularly good terms with some of them (it happens), this is a time when you have to put your personal feelings aside, knock on doors, and ask permission to search around their homes.

Pet detectives say that cats are more than likely to remain within a five-block radius than to run miles. Often they are much closer to home than you think. As with a search for a missing person, work in a tight grid—the more searchers, the better—and literally leave no stone unturned.

Pet detectives who search for lost pets on a daily basis say that they often find that pets run to the right-hand side of their home. Although there is no scientific data to back up this claim, it's certainly worth considering in your search strategy. I have been in a situation where one of my cats got out and hid. Luckily, she did cautiously appear after we had set up a scent trail around the property. And yes, she came from the right-hand side.

If you are lucky enough to spot your cat, putting down food may lure her to you. However, you may have to resort to using a humane trap to finally get her safely back where she belongs. You can get one from your local animal shelter or veterinarian. A shelter or rescue organization won't charge you but would appreciate a donation. Often, volunteers will offer assistance with the trapping process.

Kat Albrecht, a former police detective and K9 trainer, is one of the United States' foremost pet detectives. She is the author of *The Lost Pet Chronicles* and *Dog Detectives: Train Your Dog to Find Lost Pets* and founder of the website Missing Pet Partnership (www.missingpetpartnership.org). The Missing Pet Partnership website offers lots of excellent advice for locating a lost animal, such as how to go about recruiting volunteers to help with your search.

For designing effective posters, Albrecht has develop a method she calls her "Five + Five + Fifty-Five Rule," based on the premise that, at any typical intersection, motorists only have five seconds to read five words. So it's imperative to get your message over in five words.

Albrecht offers these helpful design tips:

- Make your posters giant sized so people driving by cannot miss them.
- Make them fluorescent so the color attracts the attention of everyone.
- Put them at major intersections near where you lost your pet (and in areas of sightings).
- Keep them brief and to the point.
- Let them convey a visual image of what you have lost.

Here are some other helpful hints for searching:

- Make sure you always have current color photographs of your pet that shows any special markings.
- Apart from putting up posters, when you've searched the neighborhood, search again!
- Make flyers. Talk to as many people as possible and hand them your flyers instead of just slipping them under the gate. Yes, this includes ringing the doorbell of neighbors you would rather avoid! Time to bury the hatchet.
- Contact all shelters and animal organizations in your area, as well as your veterinarian's office.
- Change the message on your answering machine and direct calls to a cell phone that will be answered immediately.
- Be proactive. Notify everyone around you as quickly as possible. Don't listen to those who tell you that "the cat will eventually come back."
- Seek professional help sooner rather than later.
- Be aware of your cat's daily habits. When does your cat eat? When does she sleep? Where is she likely to hide in your home?
- Explore every possible direction your cat could have gone after escaping. Think like a scared cat, not like a person.
- Cats have a keen sense of smell, which may also work to your advantage. For example, if your cat likes to sleep on clean laundry because she likes the scent of the fabric softener sheets, put towels in your humane trap that have the scent of your fabric softener sheets; the familiar scent may encourage her to get into the trap.
- Put a litter tray outside to lure her, too. If you have no other pets at home to worry about, leave it near an open window or sliding door.
- Keep traps propped open with food available. Dry food stays fresher and is more appetizing for a longer period of time. Other animals, including your cat may come to rely on the traps as a feeding station, which increases your potential for catching her.

◀ Keep a fresh bowl of your kitty's favorite food on your porch to lure her back home. Even better: put the food in a humane trap.

Employing a Pet Detective

Fortunately, there is a wide network of qualified pet detectives around the country and there are websites such as www.lostapet.org that will link pet owners to the nearest detective in their area. Most pet detectives work with search dogs who are trained to find cats. As with a search for a lost person, they will often let the dog smell the cat's bedding or litter box to help establish a scent trail. I personally know of many success stories in which pet detectives with a cat-sniffing canine have found lost pets. Consider it money well spent.

Ensuring Proper Identification

Proper identification is a lost pet's ticket home—even if it takes years. And yes, such miracles do happen and often make widely read headlines. Furthermore, there's no such thing as your pet having too much identifying information—on or even in them. All pets, even if they enjoy an indoor-only lifestyle, must wear a collar with up-to date information in case they escape or inadvertently find themselves outside of their home environments. Unusual situations can leave them on the wrong side of the door, from fear or curiosity. In a home invasion, for instance, burglars won't considerately close doors and windows to keep your cat in as they make off with your goods. In disaster situations (as occurred in 2005 with Hurricane Katrina and in 2012 with Hurricane Sandy), many pets are never reunited with their owners because the pets have no form of identification or lose it in the chaos of a natural disaster.

Because it's important for cats to wear breakaway collars in case they get caught on something, to truly ensure that they can be identified, you should have a microchip ID implanted as well. A microchip is the size of a grain of rice and is injected under the skin in the area of the shoulder blades. Each chip has a unique identification number that shows up when scanned, linking your cat to a database that has all your information on hand.

Although different companies marketing microchips for pets have different scanners to read them, more and more shelters are now routinely scanning pets as they come in and are also keeping universal scanners that can read all microchips, thus improving the chances of a lost pet being reunited with her owner.

A plethora of pet recovery systems on the market offer different means of recovery. Some work strictly with information in a database correlating with the ID number on a microchip. Other tracking systems have a twenty-four-hour hotline in place that will send out alerts to shelters within a fifty-mile radius of where your pet was last seen.

Global positioning systems (GPS) offer another way of tracking your pet. There are even phone applications to help you track her. Most have been designed for dogs, but manufacturers are now looking to make units to affix to a collar that are light enough for a cat to wear permanently, too. If you are unsure of which system to use, ask your veterinarian which is most prevalent in the area in which you live. Always remember that if you move, you need to update your current information on the database that you subscribe to as well. The more identification your cat has, the more peace of mind you will have.

When a cat goes missing, the biggest problem is that people give up the search far too quickly. A cat can hide for weeks in the neighborhood. Just keep looking.

Bring in the packing paraphernalia a good few weeks beforehand. Most cats love boxes, so let curiosity rule and allow your cat some fun. It will help put a more positive spin on the experience of transitioning to a new environment. It's also a good idea to have the carrier accessible so that your cat sees it around. Worst-case scenario, she'll think you have a trip to the veterinarian planned!

The moment the packing begins in earnest, make a point of confining your cat to another room. Cats have been known to jump into a box and snuggle down amid the contents, out of sight. Next thing you know, you can't find her because she's packaged to go!

Preventing Loss During a Move

Because cats are territorial creatures, moving to a new home can be a very traumatic event, and cats sometimes literally get lost in the transition. Consequently, it's important to think outside the moving boxes to make the transition both as stress free and as safe as possible.

Proper identification, as always, is critical. In line with the importance of proper identification, have a new tag made in advance of the move, with your new telephone and address details on it so you can add it to your cat's collar on moving day. It's a good idea to let your cat wear two tags for at least the first two weeks after your move. (Some cats will try to return to their old homes, but if you keep her well secured in your new home, she won't have an opportunity to try to return to your previous address. This is just a precaution.)

If your cat is usually allowed outside, stop letting her out at least two weeks before moving day. This will prevent her from possibly disappearing beforehand in an attempt to escape the upheaval of last-minute packing. During times when there's heavy foot traffic coming and going through the front door in preparation for the move, confine her to one room.

Executing Your Modus Operandi

You should have your modus operandi for moving day set ahead of time. Here is the one I have found to be most effective.

Before the movers arrive, confine your cat to a room that's not going to have any

◄ Inquisitive cats have been known to get into moving boxes. Keep track of kitty as you pack.

removal activity, such as a bathroom. Put her litter box, favorite blanket, and food and water tray down and add a note on the outside of the door instructing everyone to keep this cat zone secured. Place the carrier in there, too, so it isn't mistakenly loaded onto the moving van.

A move usually means all hands on deck, but if there is a responsible older child in the household or a friend you can call on, ask him or her to stay with the cat, who will appreciate the company. Felines can sense abnormal activity in the household and become agitated. Warn the sitter to be extra careful when opening the door; an upset cat is even more likely to take flight.

Wait until the movers have delivered everything and left the premises before transferring your cat to your new address. Choose a room and make it her temporary home for at least a week, putting everything in place before her arrival. In this way, when your cat steps out of her carrier, she will immediately begin to feel comfortable in her surroundings.

It's also a good idea to plug a synthetic feline pheromone diffuser into a floor-level electrical socket to help reduce her stress levels. Adding some Rescue Remedy to her water bowl will help keep her calm, too. Another option is a pheromone collar worn in conjunction with her standard collar for a couple of weeks. If you decide to try a collar, put it on your cat two weeks before the move and leave it on for two weeks after. The collar remains effective for a month.

Adjusting in the New Environment

Take time from your unpacking to give your cat lots of extra attention. You will be able to gauge how she's settling in and when she's ready to explore other rooms. Before she begins her walkabout, spray feline pheromones at strategic points throughout the home. This will encourage her to make her

▲ If possible, transfer your cat to your new home after your belongings are in place and the movers have left.

▲ Kitty will be happy to help you unpack!

own scent markings—all part of the settling down process. Cats are much safer if they enjoy an indoors-only lifestyle, and I strongly recommend going this way. You'll substantially lower her chances of injury from other animals, insects, and people if you do. However, if you are planning to give her access to outside, put on a harness and leash to introduce her to the new outdoor areas. By using a lightweight retractable leash, you will be able to slowly extend her boundaries.

Even if your cat enjoys an indoor lifestyle permanently, it may be a good idea to take her outside on a leash from time to time so that she can sniff the environment and be slightly familiar with her immediate outside surroundings. In this way, the environment immediately outside your front door is not quite so alien, which means your cat is less likely to panic and run away if she gets out because she will recognize the area.

Make sure she's wearing her new identification tag (and the old one in the initial period after the move, especially if you've moved a short distance). Be sure also to inform any lost-pet protection services to which you subscribe, the microchip database company, and your veterinarian of your change of address. It is a good idea to inform your neighbors at the old address of your move in case your cat tries to return to her old home and someone finds her in the vicinity and asks where she belongs.

Chapter 24

The End of Life

When you are sorrowful look again in your heart, and you shall see that in truth you are weeping for that which has been your delight.

— Kahlil Gibran

Research done over the past decade by Professor Bonnie Beaver of the College of Veterinary Medicine and Biomedical Sciences at Texas A&M University in College Station has shown that cats are definitely living longer and healthier lives. In 1975, the average age for a cat was between three and fours years. Today, thanks to excellent nutrition, general care, and state-of-the-art veterinary medicine, cats are living well into their teens and some even into their twenties.

As discussed in chapter 17, this extension of life has brought with it physical problems that were rarely seen a couple of decades ago. Owners need to be aware of what problems can occur and be ready to accommodate their homes to their cats' new physical limitations. Those with elderly cats must pay even closer attention to their health, including taking them to the veterinarian for general wellness checkups more often. It's a recognized fact that cats don't visit the veterinarian often enough. One of the reasons is that they are very good at masking their symptoms, leaving owners unaware of issues. As a concerned pet parent, it's our job to keep an eye on things by making sure our cats get a regular general wellness checkup.

▶ More cats are now living into their late teens and twenties.

All of us who love and cherish our cats also need to prepare ourselves, as our cats age, for that final good-bye.

The Senior Years

Elderly cats, just like humans, slow down in activity and suffer from age-related sight loss and deafness, as well as from many other diseases associated with advanced years. However because, unlike humans, cats never go completely gray or show other cosmetic signs of aging, their owners have to watch closely for typical signs of old age. Aging also means more regular checkups with the veterinarian to determine what is going on with your feline. There are serious diseases experienced by elderly cats, such as cancer, diabetes, and kidney disease, and equally challenging albeit less dire ones, such as arthritis. In this section, we talk about some of the less serious problems, as well as what alterations you can make at home to accommodate your cat's physical changes. By making those accommodations, you can help your older cat enjoy her golden years.

Regular Senior Checkups

Cats are considered to be seniors from the age of seven years onward. While it's wise to have annual checkups throughout your cat's life, as already mentioned, it's a good idea to have an older cat checked out more frequently as she ages. Cats are very stoic about pain and very good at masking signs of distress and serious illnesses. It's not necessary to be an alarmist, but any noticeable changes in behavior or everyday lifestyle patterns are often a sign of something amiss.

This is also the time to discuss with your veterinarian age-related diets. A simple dietary change, such as adding a little warm water to dry kibble to soften it a bit, can help an older cat eat more comfortably, especially if she has lost teeth. Because wet food has higher water content, your veterinarian may suggest offering an elderly cat both wet and dry foods. Remember to inquire about dietary supplements such as glucosamine and chondroitin that can aid joint mobility, and ask

▶ It's a good idea to take senior cats to the veterinarian for checkups more frequently than younger cats.

whether it is appropriate to continue giving her regular vaccinations. Some veterinarians consider it unnecessary to continue annual vaccinations, especially if the cat enjoys an exclusively indoor lifestyle.

Many veterinarians have a high regard for various complementary modalities such as acupuncture and massage to offer physical comfort to an elderly pet, and it's worth discussing such options with regard to your cat, too. It may not be necessary to take your cat for weekly massage therapy treatments because simply working your hands in fluid movements over her body and limbs can help improve her circulation; you can do this when you stroke her. The pet industry also is very cognizant of the aging pet population and consequently is manufacturing accessories to support an aging lifestyle, such as special hand-held massagers and therapeutic memory foam beds.

Common Problems and Accommodations

Here is a brief look at some of the common problems senior cats deal with and some of the accommodations you can make in your home to compensate for them. For a lengthy discussion about senior (or geriatric) medical problems, how to recognize them, and what treatments are available, see chapter 17, "Life Cycle Needs," in the section titled "Geriatric Care" (page 379).

Problem: Being Less Active

Just like their human counterparts, elderly felines tend to run about less and sleep more. This is a primary reason why older cats suffer from obesity and the various diseases associated with it, such as kidney disease and heart problems. Physical health is important for their overall well-being, and they need to be encouraged to get up and frolic (or just move about more).

Accommodations: One idea to help initiate exercise is to pick up your geriatric cat and take her to the place in the home that is farthest from her food bowl. She will definitely gravitate toward it on her own. Two trips a day will increase her mobility. Encourage her to climb pet steps inside the home too (see below). You can also encourage her to play more

▲ If your senior cat has become inactive, try carrying her far away from her food bowl twice a day.

games by playing with her more frequently rather leaving her to her own devices.

Problem: Not Drinking Enough Water

Senior cats often drink less than younger cats.

Accommodations: Encourage greater water intake by placing more water bowls around the home for easier access. Often, installing a pet fountain (if you don't already have one) will be an incentive to more water drinking because many cats are drawn to running water.

Problem: Stiffness and Lack of Mobility

Geriatric felines can suffer from stiff joints and may suddenly have difficulty (1) getting in and out of a litter box, (2) lowering their heads or crouching down to eat food and drink water, and (3) grooming.

Accommodations:

1. Increase the amount of litter used in the box, raising the level on the inside, and consider adding a ramp for easier accessibility. Alternatively, place a puppy pee pad alongside

the litter box for a pet to use who really has difficulty negotiating climbing in and out of a box at any height. These accessories are available from all pet and online stores.

2. Raised food and water bowls are an excellent option for elderly cats because they don't have to bend down to access food. There is an excellent selection available in various heights. The correct height is determined by your cat's sitting position. Look for bowls that are raised between three and a half and eight inches (9 and 20 cm) off the ground. This way, she is sitting to eat and not crouching.

3. When a cat suddenly stops grooming herself because she lacks the mobility to reach various parts of her body, it's time for you to take charge. Give your cat a daily brushing and other general grooming. Specially formulated pet wipes are an excellent way of keeping dust and dirt off fur. Consider grooming sessions as a wonderful way of spending quality time together.

You can also use grooming sessions as an all-over inspection of her body, looking for any changes such as the development of growths, swollen paws (which could be a circulation issue), or a sign of some other medical situation. Check her mouth too; swollen or inflamed gums are common in elderly cats and require veterinary attention.

Problem: Not Able to Jump Anymore

One of the biggest physical changes in senior cats is the loss of the ability to jump up on to counters and favorite napping places. This may also be caused by stiff joints or weak back legs as a result of diabetes.

Accommodations: Invest in pet steps. There are many designs on the market. If you have a cat who has several sleeping places, such as the bed and a favorite chair in the living room, steps made from high-density foam are lightweight and easy to carry around the house and set up in different places. Or invest in more than one set. This simple accessory will improve your cat's quality of life and give her the independence to still enjoy her favorite places.

Initially, an elderly cat may need some

encouragement to use the stairs. Treats placed on the steps offer a positive incentive. Once you have successfully trained her to ascend, repeat the process in the other direction to teach her how to descend. Having steps also means your cat will also get some exercise using them.

Problem: Feeling Cold

Elderly cats often feel the cold (just as elderly people do) more than their frisky young counterparts do.

Accommodations: You will probably see an increase in the number of sunny resting places your cat seeks out. Increase her comfort by adding a pet bed or a blanket in at least a couple of her favorite sunny locations. (Do the same if she enjoys napping outside on a sunny, secure balcony.) Wonderful orthopedic memory-foam beds are perfect for making elderly

▼ A heated cat bed is just the thing for an older cat who has become sensitive to the cold.

▲ Making difficult decisions for your cat is part of the responsibility of having a pet.

joints more comfortable. Consider purchasing a heated pet bed for your senior cat as well; many different kinds are available.

Problem: Loss of Hearing

Elderly cats often lose their hearing.

Accommodations: Little changes in routine will help a deaf cat greatly, such as always approaching her from the front and never from behind and giving her a fright. Cats all rely on vibrations to sense anyone approaching, so stepping firmly as you approach will alert her that someone is coming. This tactic will work for cats who suffer from impaired sight, too.

Problem: Loss of Sight

Elderly cats often lose their eyesight.

Accommodations: It's important not to move furniture or leave large objects lying around so that an elderly kitty with minimum or no eyesight can continue to negotiate her surroundings as before. Remember to engage a sight-impaired cat in games with toys that make a noise.

If you previously allowed your cat access outside, sight and hearing disabilities mean that you need to restrict that access now and make your cat an indoors-only cat. She will no longer be able to protect herself outside, so even if she objects, to keep her safe, keep her inside.

When It's Time to Say Good-Bye

We are lucky today; we have more years with our cats than ever before. Yet no matter how much time we have to enjoy their company, it's never enough. There will come a day when you suddenly recognize that your ailing elderly cat is struggling more and more with all of her activities, from getting up from her bed in the morning to eating her food to using her litter box to simply walking a few steps. She may even refuse to take medications and supplements. This may be her way of letting you know that she is struggling and possibly suffering in silence. That is the day you will need to ask yourself the toughest question any cat lover must ask: What is the quality of my cat's life? Answering that question can be difficult because it demands that you not only be totally honest but also be completely selfless. You need to set aside your grief at the thought of losing your precious companion and think only of her pain and suffering. Ask yourself, how bad is it for my cat? Has it gotten so bad that she can no longer function unaided and without pain, even in the smallest thing that she does? If the answer is "yes," then it is probably time to ease her way to a better place, where she will no longer feel pain, where she will be at peace. As difficult as this decision is, no responsible pet parent wants to let a beloved pet suffer.

You may want to consult your veterinarian before

making your final decision. An end-of-life decision is one of the reasons it's so important to establish an excellent rapport with your veterinarian because a veterinarian who has overseen your cat's health and well-being over the years will be able to offer you an honest, well-informed medical opinion on your pet's condition and aid you in evaluating whether it is indeed time to say good-bye. The final decision is still yours, but having your veterinarian's opinion can help.

Euthanasia

Euthanasia is a peaceful and humane way to end your cat's suffering. If you decide it is time to let your cat go, discuss your options on where the procedure will take place and other details about it with your veterinarian. The staff of a veterinary clinic will always offer you and your pet the respect you both deserve in that final hour. The alternative is to ask your veterinarian it if can be done at home.

Euthanasia involves administering an overdose of a strong anesthetic, which immediately stops the cat's heart and lungs from functioning. It is quick and painless and likened to going into a deep sleep. Effectively, it puts your cat to sleep. It's important to mention that when this happens, all the internal organs also relax and thus the period immediately afterward can be messy as bodily fluids are released. This is not something many loving and grieving pet owners are prepared for. So the facts should be discussed with your veterinarian if you want to be present throughout.

Most veterinarians usually administer a strong sedative first and allow you to sit with your cat while it takes effect and then suggest that a veterinary technician takes your place for the final injection. Remember the effect of the sedative will

▲ The other pets in your house will also grieve, so give them extra attention.

make your cat unaware of her surroundings and you. She will already be at peace, and you will hold a perfect picture in your memory.

The Final Arrangements

Consideration also has to be given beforehand regarding your wishes for burial or cremation. This is something that the veterinary office can arrange on your behalf. Private cremations cost more, but you will get a certificate from the pet mortuary ensuring that the ashes presented to you afterward are those of your pet alone. Most veterinary offices can offer you a choice of a box or an urn for the ashes. If you want something special, however, there are many online pet stores that offer an excellent selection of commemorative urns and boxes with compartments in which you can place a collar, a favorite toy, and even a fur keepsake. This is something you should purchase in advance. The advantage of cremation is that no matter where you may move in the world, you can take your pet's ashes with you.

Alternatively, there are many pet cemeteries and crematoriums around the country that will help you plan a service for your cat. These sensitive professionals can take care of the casket or urn, the service, and even a floral tribute. The International Association of Pet Cemeteries and Crematories, a nonprofit organization, can help you find a reputable place in your area (visit www.iaopc.com).

When selecting a cemetery, be sure to pick a place that you can visit regularly. A good pet cemetery will keep your pet's gravesite well maintained, which helps to make each visit a positive experience.

Depending on where you live, some city municipalities allow pets to be buried on private property. Once again, you need to research this possibility in advance. Many pet stores and online stores sell either ready-made or customized memorial stones or plaques to mark the private burial site. Even if you choose burial in a pet cemetery or cremation, you can consider having a plaque made to place in your garden.

Memorializing Your Cat

A wonderful way to remember a special feline friend is to offer a memorial scholarship to a veterinary school. If your pet died of a particular disease or illness, think about creating a fund in her name so that you can be actively involved in raising money to aid future medical research. Even giving the medications she no longer needs to a welfare group is a way of memorializing her and helping others in her name. Consider donating a nice kitty condo to a shelter or even making a monetary donation in your cat's name. It doesn't have to be a huge amount; it's the thought that counts.

Coping with Grief

Losing a cat who has been both a best friend and a beloved family member leaves a huge void in the household. The empty bed or favorite snooze spot, her food and water bowl, and even special toys are a poignant reminder of the unconditional love you've lost and the huge empty space that remains.

It's all right to grieve. A constant lump in the throat and uncontrollable tears are all normal signs of grief. It's also important to grieve so that you can come to terms with your loss and begin to heal. Don't be shy; let your family members, friends, and even coworkers know what you are going through. Other pet lovers will empathize and can be a wonderful source of support. You might even consider joining a pet-loss support group. Your veterinarian or local animal shelter can help you locate one.

Helping Your Other Pets Grieve

It's important to remember that other pets in the household, both cats and dogs, will be feeling the loss, too. It's not unusual for surviving pets to search the house looking for their missing friend. Some even stop eating, become listless and lethargic, and show other unusual behaviors. Comfort grieving pets by spending extra quality time with them. If you are thinking of introducing another pet to the household immediately, don't. Your other pets need time to adjust, too. Eventually, they will settle and stop searching.

It's a cliché, but time does help you heal and put things in perspective. You will instinctively know when the time is right to consider adopting another cat and giving it a loving home. If incumbent cats in the household are seniors, they may bond better with an adult cat than with a curious and energetic kitten. And, because kittens usually find homes more quickly than older cats, your decision to adopt an older cat will be a good deed and could truly be life-saving.

However, when the time comes, you will need to discuss your decision with a veterinarian who knows your other cats' health records and temperaments. Often a young kitten brought into a senior household will give older cats a new lease on life. I speak from experience!

◀ There are many pet cemeteries that will help you plan a service for your cat.

Chapter 25

Feline Communication

It is a very inconvenient habit of kittens that whatever you say to them, they always purr. If they would only purr for "yes" and mew for "no," or any rule of that sort, so that one could keep up a conversation! But how can one deal with a person if they always say the same thing?

— Lewis Carroll, *Through The Looking Glass*

ats have their own ways of communicating with other cats, with different household pets, and with people, a communication style that goes beyond vocal cues to include their amazing olfactory and aural senses and their own unique body language.

What makes the domestic cat so endlessly fascinating is what eminent British zoologist Desmond Morris describes as the cat's double life: the ability to switch from a tame and cute household pet to a wild animal in hunt mode, and then back again to that content creature manicuring its toes, all within seconds.

It's probably because of this aptitude that they have a reputation for being such independent creatures. And although they can be self-sufficient and can look after themselves if forced to do so, it's important to remember that originally cats chose to become domesticated

▶ Every pet parent wants to know what his or her cat is thinking.

▲ Only cats who feel very secure will share a food bowl.

by seeking out human company. Consequently, in a modern domestic setting, they thrive on love and companionship and that's why learning to communicate with them is vital.

A true understanding of all forms of feline communication means that you can enhance your relationship with your cat and you can even take it to the next level by training her—yes, cats can be trained—to come when called, sit on command, and even run to greet you at the front door.

As with human relationships, a human–feline bond flourishes not only on understanding but also on acceptance of their typical feline ways. And, in the same way that the human relationships often breakdown with "irreconcilable differences" being cited as the reason, many cats find themselves in shelters or simply abandoned because of human error in failing to accept them for the species that they are by learning to understand and interpret their body language and their postures.

This Is My Territory

All cats, whether they live outdoors or enjoy an indoor lifestyle, are territorial. They have what's called a *home range* and a *territory*. The home range is the area that the cat lives in, and the territory is the area that the cat defends. The territory is smaller than the home range and is described more precisely as the area that represents a safe environment and a plentiful food supply.

Although domestic cats don't have to hunt—because they have a regular supply of food in the warmth of the family kitchen—they have not lost the desire to stake their claim to an area and be protective of a territory, particularly what is known as the inner core of that territory, which, in a home environment, would be around the food bowl.

This is particularly important to remember in a multicat household because cats are not only solitary hunters but also solitary eaters. That's why it's important that each cat has a designated food bowl. And it's a good idea to put the bowls in different places. Admittedly, cats will often eat out of one another's bowls, but only very secure cats will share a food bowl simultaneously. They may often appear "territorial" by "fluffing up" or even hissing over the use of a cat door or even a door or entrance to another part of the home.

Studies have shown that domesticated male and female cats who are allowed outdoors stake their claim to different sized areas. Normally, a female will consider her home range to be the immediate area (garden) of her home and that of the adjoining properties. A male cat's range can be equated to twenty city blocks.

I've Scent You a Message

Cats establish their home ranges by scent marking them. In a typical urban neighborhood, cats have learned to tolerate the presence of other cats more than they would in the wild. Males will physically defend their ranges from other males, but females usually share or overlap their home range with other females.

Cats have scent glands all over their bodies, particularly on their flanks, their faces, and their paw pads. Consequently, they keep a regular check on their ranges by patrolling the areas they have laid claim to by rubbing up against poles, fences, trees, and anything else that they can brush against or scratch and deposit their scent. They also like to climb up on

Hands Off!

Never force a cat to sit on your lap. When they've had enough, it's time to go. They will return when they choose to do so and simply jump back up, settle down, and pretend they never left.

objects—walls, trees, and so on—and look down to see what's going on in their designated zones. In an indoor setting, they do exactly the same thing, rubbing up against furniture, walls, potted plants, and even the people who they love—not to mention scratching on their owner's favorite chair, which is an indirect way of laying claim to their people.

Cats also do what's called chinning, when they rub with the side of their mouth against objects or people. Rubbing and chinning is more than simply

▼ Cats have scent glands on their faces and rub them up against things—including people and other pets—to mark them as their own.

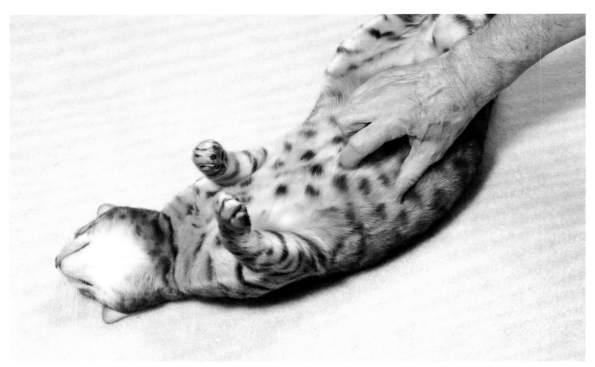

▲ A cat lying on her back with her belly exposed feels very happy and is seeking attention.

"being cute"; once again, they are sending scent messages that say "this is mine" or, in the case of a person, "you're mine too—I love you." In a multicat household, other cats check out these different scent messages. This is, in fact, a very satisfactory form of communication because it informs one cat that another has just been there and to stay away, thus avoiding possible conflict over any territorial rights.

Cats also use urine to mark their territory and communicate with other felines. When male cats spray, they lift their tails and quiver them while paddling backward with their back feet. In doing so, a cat is leaving a scent message at the height of other cats' noses, which makes for easy reading.

Cats also use feces to demarcate. This practice is called *middening*. The feces are intentionally left uncovered to ensure that other cats don't trespass. Middening is also a way of boosting the cat's own feelings of safety and security in the cat's designated zone.

Cats can be aggressive when defending territories and fearful when threatened. Very insecure and timid cats often spray and defecate indoors to make themselves feel more at home. People who don't understand this will often punish a cat for dirtying the house. This can set up a negative chain reaction and escalate the unwanted behavior because it causes the cat to feel even more insecure.

That's why it's important for the people around cats to understand that they are not being difficult or temperamental; they are simply doing what comes naturally to them.

Watch My Moves

Cats have very distinct body language using their tails, ears, eyes, whiskers, and body posture to communicate with each other and with people to divulge what they may be thinking or feeling. It's its very important to learn to read all these physical signs.

Common Postures; Simple Phrases

Here are some of the most common feline postures and what they mean.

Hello—I'm Friendly

When a cat puts a tail up and curls the end into a question mark, this is a friendly greeting. Very often, this posture is accompanied by a raised front paw, which means the cat is poised to come forward for a more personal greeting, such as being rubbed and tickled on the ear. The cat will reciprocate by rubbing up against your legs.

Attention, Please!

When a cat stands tall, with ears and tail up, it means she's being extra friendly and, in fact, is seeking your attention. Often entwining herself around your legs follows this pose and possibly even some vocal meows to indicate "pet me" or "feed me."

Hello! *More* Attention Please!

A totally relaxed cat seeking attention and lying on her back exposing her tummy, with her legs stretched out in different direction and her head facing upward, is having "an attack of cute." The message is "I am irresistible, come on, tickle or play with me. *NOW.*" A belly-up posture is an extremely vulnerable position for a cat to lie in, so a cat in this posture is very happy and content.

Something's Out There

When a cat sinks her body close to the ground, pulls her ears back, drops her tail, and slinks off, or, alternatively, crouches close to the ground holding this posture, it means that she's wary, tense, and watchful. You can feel her intense gaze. This means the cat is feeling unsure about something, sensing a potential threat. The cat is trying to make herself as small as possible so that she isn't noticed by whatever is making her feel that way.

I'm Seriously Worried Here

A worried cat will tuck her tail under her haunches and squat, putting most of her weight on her hind

You Lookin' at Me, Witch?

When territorial issues are at stake, the claws may come out and a real physical fight ensue, hence the slang terminology of a *catfight* referring to two women physically setting upon one another. Such physical feline combat is usually accompanied by vocal interaction such as hissing, growing, and yowling. The fight can sound deadly serious and just plain awful.

A cat who arches her back—with the hairs along the spine spiked up and the tail hairs bristled, making her appear twice her size—is ready to attack. This stance is often nicknamed the *witch's cat posture.* Usually, when she's all fluffed out like this, she will also stand sideways to the threat in an attempt to appear even larger and more threatening.

Sometimes, cats in a household will suddenly spat in this manner for no apparent reason. In fact, a typical scenario is when two cats are curled into one another grooming each other and dozing and, all of a sudden, one will jump the other and a quarrel will ensue. In this kind of surprise attack, the defending cat will roll over onto her back with her paws in the air, ready to kick out at the attacker. This upside down position is a defense posture, and the cat is getting ready for her next move. Then the games begin: the aggressor will circle around the defendant in the witch's cat posture. Sometimes, they will continue to spar like this. Other times, they will chase one another, flying around the room and tumbling about.

Then, as quickly as the fight heated up, it cools down and all goes quiet. The former combatants may even go back to grooming one another, leaving you wondering what *that* was all about.

Another typical feline scenario is when a cat is sitting quietly and another feline family member just walks past, prompting the first cat to raise a paw and hiss. This often happens at feeding time when the food bowls are being put out. It's a gentle feline warning to a housemate to eat out of her own bowl—no sharing!

▲To cats, a stare is a threatening gesture, so if your kitty is staring at something she is getting ready to pounce.

paws. This means that she is getting ready to strike out with her front paws if necessary. The ears are wide and slightly back, and the whiskers also point backward. A cat who feels threatened by another animal in the household and thus is getting ready to take off often adopts this poise. Frequently, cats will meow loudly to draw your attention to the fact that they would like your help to sort things out.

Ah, This Is the Life

When a cat stretches out with her back legs out to the side and her front paws curled inward and sometimes under, she's totally relaxed in her environment. If her ears are pricked, it means she's aware of what is going on around her but is perfectly content.

Now This Is Fun!

When a cat lies on her side with her back paws brought forward to meet with her front paws, she's usually in play mode and having lots of fun with a particular toy or an object she's made into a toy.

Shhh—I'm on the Hunt

When a cat sinks low to the ground, her tail out behind her, her ears forward and eyes wide, and she holds this position completely motionless, she's in stalk motion, gleaning as much information about her prey as possible before she pounces. When the tail starts swinging from side to side, the moment of execution is imminent. In this mode, she will probably ignore you in an attempt to concentrate on the pending attack.

Are You Going to Attack Me?

A cat who crouches with her head drawn back and her ears flattened is in a submissive pose and

Rare Catfights

Real catfights are rare; when they do occur, they are usually over quickly. During a fight, the defensive cat will roll over onto her back so that she can use all four feet—claws and all—as weapons.

is probably getting ready to be pounced upon by another cat. Sometimes, this position is adopted when a playful scrap is about to ensue. Other times, the situation can be seriously aggressive, especially if it involves feline territory. A sign that your cat feels really threatened is when the hairs along her back spike up.

Blinks and Stares

Every blink of the eye or stony stare also has a special meaning. A blink is a very reassuring signal and is used between cats to communicate with each other and with people. Slowly blinking at your cat is often called giving your cat blink kisses, and they usually respond back the same way. And, if they add a yawn, that's the ultimate compliment that they are enjoying your companionship.

In contrast, a stare is threatening. Cats in a conflict situation will often try to outstare each other. When a cat realizes she's being stared it, she will stop what she's doing to assess the situation and

A Yawning Hello

After a long snooze, a cat will wake up and give a big yawn. This is a sign of reassurance that all is well and also is a greeting—it's a casual "hello." Often, they will simply turn around, reposition, and go back to sleep.

However, if the food bowl is "calling," the cat will most likely get up and stand tall, giving a good stretch by arching her back and then proceed to stretching out front and back legs. Behaviorist Roger Tabor calls this routine "feline isometric wake-up-warm-up exercises."

will only resume when she knows that there's no real threat. Often, after such a staring match, cats go into grooming mode.

Generally speaking, cats have excellent peripheral vision. Consequently, they tend never to stare directly at something unless they are setting their sights on it and getting ready to pounce.

Looking at your cat's pupils is another way of reading the message she's sending. As well as dilating or contracting according to the amount of light around, a cat's pupils also contract or dilate to indicate mood. Dilated pupils accompany fear, aggressive excitement, and mild excitement, such as that experienced upon seeing a favorite person, a feline friend, or even dinner! The more fearful a cat is, the wider the pupils expand.

Tail Signals

A cat's tail can tell you a lot about what she's thinking, feeling, and planning to do next. It's important to understand the following tail language:

- An upright tail that quivers gently is a sign of happiness and excitement.

◀ Siamese are among the more vocal breeds.

- A slightly raised tail with a gentle curve means that something has piqued the cat's interest in a nonthreatening way.
- A gentle downward curve with the tip curled upward is a sign of contentment.
- A tail that is still except for the very tip, which twitches continuously, is an indicator that something is annoying or irritating the cat.
- A tail that swishes from side to side in a fast motion denotes a very angry feline.
- A sleeping cat who's curled up in a ball with her tail following the curve of her body is very relaxed and contented and is using her tail as a wrap for warmth.

Listen Closely

Feline behaviorists say that there are at least nineteen different types of *meow* that differ in pitch, rhythm, volume, tone, pronunciation, and the situations in which they are used.

Cats also make a variety of other different sounds such as growling, hissing and chirping, chattering their teeth, and yowling and screaming.

The number of sounds a cat makes depends on its breed because some cats, such as the Siamese, are

▲ Kittens begin to purr when they are only a few days old. This signals to mom that all is well.

considered far more vocal than others. It also has a lot to do with how they interact with other cats in the household or who they may come into contact with and the type of human–feline bond they experience with the people in their lives.

There is no question that if you talk to your cat, she will talk back and soon learn the sounds that elicit a response. A cat who is the only feline in the household is often more vocal with people than are cats who share a home with other felines. People also sometimes reinforce their cat's vocalizing by answering back and by interacting with the cat by petting her or picking up a toy with the intention of initiating play.

The Purr

There is nothing that quite sums up a feeling of pure contentment than a purring cat. A queen purrs when she's giving birth and guides her newborns through the vibrations of her purr to her nipples. (Predators are attracted to little cries and meows, but not so much to the purr vibrations, and since kittens are very vulnerable, the purr helps keep them safe.)

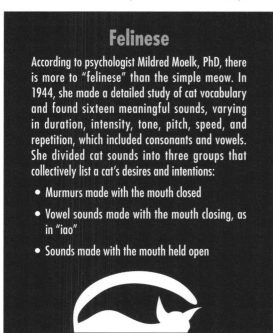

Felinese

According to psychologist Mildred Moelk, PhD, there is more to "felinese" than the simple meow. In 1944, she made a detailed study of cat vocabulary and found sixteen meaningful sounds, varying in duration, intensity, tone, pitch, speed, and repetition, which included consonants and vowels. She divided cat sounds into three groups that collectively list a cat's desires and intentions:

- Murmurs made with the mouth closed
- Vowel sounds made with the mouth closing, as in "iao"
- Sounds made with the mouth held open

Kittens begin to purr when they are days old and are suckling their mother while gently kneading her tummy with their tiny paws. It's a signal to the mother cat that all is well with her babies. Adult cats often continue to knead your lap and purr throughout their lives. Some cats purr so loudly it sounds like a low-grade rumble; others purr silently—you can hardly hear them, but if you put your fingers under their chins you will feel a rhythmic vibration.

However, cats don't only purr out of contentment. It can also be a sign that the cat is stressed, sick, or injured and in pain. The reason is that cats find the sound of their own purr very soothing, and it helps them to heal. In fact, studies indicate that endorphins, nature's pain relievers, are released when cats purr. Dying cats have also been known to purr.

The Meow

There's no question that if you live with a cat long enough, a very definite form of communication will be established between the two of you. Nicholas Dodman, director of Animal Behavior Clinic at the Tufts Cummings School of Veterinary Medicine in Grafton, Massachusetts, says cats communicate partly by instinct but also by learning how humans react to certain sounds. Dodman says that cats remember what sounds achieved the desired effect, and they also watch and copy what other cats do. He also believes that cats recognize a particular human's voice. Other behaviorists believe that cats can in fact even recognize specific words.

Author and naturalist Jean Craighead George, who writes about the language of cats in her award-winning book *The Cats of Roxville Station* and has studied cats in nature, endorses this idea that the different ways in which a cat meows have special idiosyncratic meanings. She has categorized some feline vocalizations as follows. They are written phonetically to emphasize the different sound and tones.

Kittens:
- Mew (high pitched and thin)—a polite plea for help
- MEW! (loud and frantic)—an urgent plea for help

▼ When meeting a cat, it helps to get down on her level.

Sometimes Cats Just Can't Get Along!

Cat lovers bringing new cats into the household often are unaware of the social issues that can occur. They feel sorry for a kitten they've found and introduce the newcomer to the family simply by leaving her to fend for herself without properly preparing the household to accept a change brought about by another cat. The premise is for the cats to "work it out" or "determine who is boss."

Bad idea! If cats don't accept cats outside of their social circle in the wild, there is no guarantee that they will accept and like one another in a domestic situation. Consequently, if there is conflict, it *never* goes away. And, in fact, you are trapping them in a toxic environment for the rest of their lives!

According to Margaret M. Duxbury, DVM, DACVB, of the University of Minnesota Veterinary Behavior Service at the College of Veterinary Medicine, studies have shown that unmanaged cats in a natural outdoor environment may regularly explore from as little as one acre to more than 400 acres. Such cats are highly social within their own groups, but tend not to interact amicably with cats they do not know.

Feline social groups typically consist of related individuals (females and their offspring) and are resistant to new members. In a restricted household environment where there is little room to roam and where they do not even have the benefits of predatory stimulation and exercise, the problem of dealing with newcomers is exacerbated.

"Limited physical space exacerbates conflict between unbonded household cats that might choose to avoid each other in more open and complex environments, but who are forced to cope with close proximity encounters with a cat perceived as an intruder," explains Duxbury. "Consequently, household cats, and especially those that are brought together as adults, may not form affiliative relationships despite years of living together."

Fortunately, in a domestic situation, you can take steps to create a state of nonconfrontational co-habitation.

First, every time you bring a new pet into a household, it's important to do proper introductions (see Chapter 26, page 481). (This applies to dogs too.) When introducing a new cat to an incumbent cat, confine the newcomer to one room with food, water, and a litter box for a week, possibly longer. (It can take as long as a month.) Introduce her to the incumbent cat first by smell. To do this, take a pair of socks, rub one on her and one on your incumbent feline and exchange the socks with the cats. After they are used to the smell of each other in this way, bring them face-to-face for supervised visits until you are comfortable leaving them alone.

The two cats may turn out to love each other, or they may be indifferent to each other but get along. In these instances, the initial hissing and growling will subside.

But then there is the situation in which they can't stand each other, and the problem is permanent, characterized by ongoing overt aggression with open-mouthed, sustained vocalizations and physical altercations.

According to Duxbury, cat owners also often miss signs of covert or passive aggression, such as staring and blocking physical space like the exit from the litter box. Such overt and passive conflict can be diminished, possibly removed, depending on the spatial arrangements in the household.

Cats have a harder time avoiding each other in homes with narrow hallways, lots of corners, and small rooms. So, consider dividing up your home by placing litter boxes, food, and water in different areas of the house so that every cat in the household can get what she needs without encountering a feline bully.

"This is especially important in order to promote successful litter box use by all cats in a household," says Duxbury. "In homes with inter-cat conflict, cats are often reluctant to use litter boxes that are covered, in enclosed cubbies, or accessible only after passing through a narrow hall or doorway." So make sure you have large open pans and place them so that the user can see who is approaching from all sides.

Another way to avoid conflict is to increase the space in the home by "going vertical" and adding perches and runways at ceiling height. You can add more options, such as lofty hidey-holes, and create new exits and entrances through walls at this elevated level so that cats can come and go without feeling trapped.

Behaviorists also suggest putting a bell on the collar of the most assertive feline in the household to give warning to other felines that she's approaching.

Also consider creating a safe zone by kitting out one room of your home with a computerized cat door that only cats wearing the proper microchip on their collar can access.

Such changes can go a long way toward decreasing social pressure and improving quality of life for all the felines in the household. And, in so doing, it's much less stressful for the humans who live there, too!

Adult cats:

- Mew—plea for attention
- Mew (soundless)—a very polite plea for attention (Craighead George believes this is what author Paul Gallico termed the "silent Miaow," which is probably a sound pitched too high for human ears)
- Meow—emphatic plea for attention
- MEOW!—a command
- Mee-o-ow (with falling cadence)—protest or whine
- MEE-o-ow (shrill whine)—stronger protest
- MYUP! (short, sharp, single note)—righteous indignation
- MEOW! Meow! (repeated)—panicky call for help
- Mier-r-r-ow (chirrup with lilting cadence)— friendly greeting

Tomcats:

- RR-YOWWW-EEOW-RR-YOW-OR— caterwaul
- Merrow—challenge to another male
- Meriow—courting call to female

Mother cats:

- MEE-OW—come and get it!
- MeOW—follow me!
- ME R-R-R-ROW—take cover!
- Mer ROW!—No! or Stop It!
- Mreeeep (burbled)—hello greeting to kittens and disarming greeting to adult cats (also used between adult cats and humans)

If you take the time to observe your cat, you'll find it's easy to understand what is being said. That's what communicating with your feline is all about.

What You Are Saying to Your Cat

A new study by Japanese researchers at the University of Tokyo, published in 2013 in *Animal Cognition* magazine, has revealed that cats can really understand their owner's voices and, in fact, do pay attention when they are spoken to.

Behaviorists say that *how* words are spoken is really important because cats are very sensitive and can feel safe or threatened by the tone of voice and its volume. Cats are more apt to respond and

Smokey the Cat with the World's Loudest Purr

On May 5, 2011, a twelve-year-old British Shorthair living in England named Smokey was officially listed in the Guinness Book of World Records as the cat with the world's loudest purr. Her winning purr measured 67.7 decibels. Pet parent Ruth Adams, of Northampton, says that Smokey has even been known to purr as loudly as 90 decibels. Most cats purr at around 25 decibels.

socialize with their people when spoken to in a soft and calm voice. And they can certainly learn to understand their names and come when called. However, if you have to use a strong tone of voice to indicate displeasure, never use their name and the word "no" in the same sentence because cats find this very confusing.

Communicating with your cat isn't only about words; it's also about human actions and the way in which cats interpret them and thus understand what we are trying to say or do.

Here are some human–feline communication tips.

How Do You Do? How To Introduce Yourself to a Cat

A handshake is the universal sign to a friendly introduction between people, and a closed fist is a sign of threatening aggression. If you are introducing yourself to a cat, the very opposite applies. Cats consider an open hand as a possible aggressive sign that you are going to pounce and attack them. A closed fist—with your forefinger slightly extended—is a sign that a cat will understand as you trying to be friendly, introduce yourself, and say hello.

It's important to remember that cats have very different personalities, ranging from shy and timid to outgoing and friendly. The best way to make a formal feline introduction is to start by getting down to their level, whether this means kneeling on the floor or lowering yourself into their line of vision if the cat happens to be snoozing on the back of the couch. Slowly extend your cupped hand with an

▲ In general, cats don't enjoy "drive-by" petting. If you're going to pet your cat, stay and hang out with her for a few minutes.

extended finger and allow the cat to make the next move by coming closer to sniff your finger. After the initial "sniff test," the cat may then rub her neck along your finger indicating that it's okay to scratch gently behind the ear or on the shoulders. Then you can notch it up a level by talking softly so that the cat can relate to the tone of your voice. Cats are, in fact, no different than people; you only have one opportunity to make a good first impression!

Kiss Kiss

Its become very popular (especially in Hollywood) to "air kiss" people by leaning past their cheek and kissing fresh air. The feline equivalent is matching your cat's direct gaze and slowly opening and closing your eyes in long blinking movements. Cats understand this to mean love and affection and will return the kisses by blinking back at you. And, very often, when they are "kissing" you back, their faces are relaxed, causing their ears to swivel slightly outward to form a "smile." Cats understand real kisses from their favorite people, too, and often will respond by licking you on the face or hand.

Hey! Don't Bother Me I'm ...

You know what it's like when you are working at the computer and stop to think things through in your head. To an onlooker, it appears that you are doing nothing but staring into space, which makes people think its okay to interrupt. By the same token, cats find "drive-by" petting very irritating. If you happen to walk by while they are grooming or sleeping, and you suddenly give them a quick pet and carry on with what you were doing, you are in fact disturbing them. From the feline perspective, this action is annoying. After all, you interrupted while they were busy sleeping, grooming, or doing an intense manicure on the left hind foot. They have no real way of telling you its annoying other than to ignore you and go back to sleeping, eating, or switching over and manicuring the right hind foot. It all boils down to mutual respect. Don't yank them away from their projects when, in fact, you are not planning to hang about and spend quality time with them but are simply passing by!

How Does One Gauge Feline Intelligence?

According to Dr. Nicholas Dodman, head of the Small Animal Behavior Clinic at the Cummings School of Veterinary Medicine at Tufts University in Grafton, Massachusetts, feline cognitive skills can be gauged in terms of their behaviors.

"Cats are smart and are especially good in their own biological niche. They excel in vision and image permanence testing because that's what a cat does when it comes to hunting for food in their natural habitat. Anyone who has watched a cat chase a mouse into a hole will know what I mean. They know it's in there and have the cognitive capacity to hold that thought. Thus they will sit patiently, sometimes for hours, knowing that it will reappear.

The consequences of a behavior predict if a behavior will be repeated. In other words, your cat has learned that when he does a specific behavior, such as bringing you his cat toy, and you respond by playing with him, his intelligence shows that he is able to repeat this behavior when he wants to play with you."

American psychologist Edward Lee "Ted" Thorndike (1874–1949) is believed to have pioneered the field of animal behaviorism as a means of gauging intelligence. His doctoral dissertation, *Animal Intelligence: An Experimental Study of the Associative Processes in Animals*, was the first in psychology in which the subjects were nonhumans.

His goal was to discover whether animals could learn tasks through imitation or observation. Although he worked with different species, cats were his most popular test subjects. He created special puzzle boxes approximately 20 inches long, 15 inches wide, and 12 inches tall. Each box had a door that was pulled open by a weighted string on a pulley system.

The cat inside the box had to learn by trial and error how to maneuver the string and open the box to exit and was subsequently rewarded with a treat.

By observing and recording the cats' escapes and escape times, Thorndike was able to draw a feline learning curve. It showed that the cats had difficulty escaping at first, but eventually "caught on" and escaped faster and faster with each successive puzzle box trial.

He reasoned that if the animals were showing insight, then their time to escape would suddenly drop to a negligible period. He found that cats "got it" and that they consistently showed learning abilities.

Fast forward to the twenty-first century. Swedish pet toy designer Nina Ottosson is known for her extensive range of dog and cat puzzles toys that offer different levels of difficulty for pets to test their abilities. All the puzzles offer rewards in the form of treats or food. Ottosson says that her inspiration comes from the way animals in the wild hunt for their food, relying their amazing olfactory senses or their exceptional vision skills.

As a result of Ottosson and other innovators like her, there is a plethora of games and activities that offer cats both mental and physical stimulation, from puzzle toys to "board" games such as a battery-operated mouse on a track that works to hone their hunting and pouncing techniques and keep them mentally engaged.

And there is no question that today's generation of kittens is very adept at playing with such toys and enjoying the challenges they offer.

When it comes to children, parents commonly remark that each generation seems to be born smarter. So, with all the buzz about pets toys and games that promote both feline mental and physical well-being, is the current generation of kittens smarter and more savvy than littermates born 10 or 20 years ago?

Dodman says "no." He points out that evolution is a long and slow process and that, in his opinion, feline levels of intelligence haven't changed in the last 100 years.

Chapter 26

Socialization and Training

Ignorant people think it's the noise which fighting cats make that is so aggravating, but it ain't so; it's the sickening grammar they use.

— Mark Twain

Cats are great mothers. If they are given the opportunity to rear their kittens—in other words, if the kittens aren't taken away from the mother too young (which happens for various reasons)—the mothers will teach their offspring many of the feline life skills they will need throughout their lives. Among those skills is socialization.

Although certain cat breeds are known to be characteristically friendly around people, there's no question that both kittens and older cats will definitely be more companionable if encouraged to socialize in a household. Therefore, it's up to the people they share a home with to ensure that they are social and well-adjusted in a domestic setting. Cats who have been handled by people since kittenhood and grow up in a friendly household are definitely less timid and generally more comfortable around people.

Social Stages of Kittenhood and First Teachers

All kittens are born with their eyes shut. They have an inherent sense of smell and touch and thus are instinctively able to find their mothers and suckle. (In fact, a mother cat

▶ Kittens get their first lessons in socialization from their mother.

guides her newborns to her nipples through the vibrations of her purrs.) In the first few days, they are very weak and can't move around, relying on their mother to pick them up by the scruff of the neck and place them where she wants them. When they are about seven days old, their eyes begin to open slightly. By the time they are two weeks old, their eyes are fully open, their fur has fluffed out, and they no longer look like little rats but the epitome of very cute kittens. At three weeks old, they are strong enough to begin walking about and continue to grow quickly. By the time they are a month old, their ears are upright and they can stand properly with their little tails in the air.

At about the age of four to five weeks is the time that veterinarians suggest supplementing their all-mother's milk diet with kitten food so that the mother cat can slowly begin to wean her offspring off her teats and give herself a break from all the rambunctious clowning around that goes with raising a litter.

At six weeks old, kittens are very alert, their inherent curiosity becomes apparent, and they begin to take an interest in small toys and everything

▲ Cats learn from their siblings how to play without using their claws.

around them, climbing on everything they can—and falling off. The great feline exploration has begun!

Behaviorists say that the initial two to seven weeks of a kitten's life is a critical socialization and training period.

Feline Teachers

In these early weeks of life, kittens get their first lessons in socialization from their mother. The mother cat will teach her kittens manners, how to interact with one another, and even to hone instinctive skills such as pouncing and hunting. Kittens also learn from their littermates. They start playing with each other from the time they are about three weeks old, and then get into full swing at about ten weeks old, chasing, stalking, and pouncing on each other and really enjoying objects of play, getting more rambunctious by the day.

Such play is important because it helps kittens not only to develop their motor skills but also to learn to set boundaries with one another. If a kitten gets hurt while rolling around, for instance, she will instinctively back off. She and her littermates learn about bite inhibition and how to "pull their claws" during play, so it doesn't become something serious.

Human Teachers

At about six weeks of age, kittens will start displaying friendly behavior toward humans in

The Crucial Feline Family

A very important reason to wait until kittens are twelve weeks old before separating them from their siblings and mom is because they learn extremely important socialization skills from their interactions and play with both their littermates and their mother. Social play not only develops body muscle and tone but also helps to develop motor skills and set boundaries during play. It's common to find cats with biting behaviors that are a result of being separated too early from their mothers and littermates.

the household by purring, making noises that phonetically sound like "mhrrrn," and rubbing and rolling around and playing with lightweight toys that are easy for little paws to bat about.

Even before six weeks, kittens are impressionable around people. As noted above, the first two to seven weeks of life are a critical socialization and training period. That's why many breeders like their kittens to be "underfoot," which means they live in a designated area in the home as opposed to a more sterile cattery environment. This allows them to have a lot of interaction with people in the household and learn to trust them.

Foster and Adoptive Teachers

Ideally, kittens should be around twelve weeks old when they leave their mother. By this age, they have been toilet trained and learned certain typical hunting and socialization skills through play and interactions with both their mother and their littermates. Unfortunately, cats with kittens are often abandoned and, as a result, the kittens find themselves separated from their mother from a much younger age. Often, shelters and rescue groups strive to put very young kittens into a foster home situation with experienced caretakers so kittens can get an opportunity to learn basic social skills, including being comfortable around people. Without the opportunity to learn these skills with a patient foster parent, many more young kittens would be returned to the shelter or rescue organization by an adoptive family that just couldn't cope with the extra socializing.

Whether you are adopting a kitten or an adult cat, it's important to make your new feline feel at home by exposing her to positive experiences in the company of different family members and friends, as well as other cat-friendly pets in the household.

Basic Training and House Rules

Turns out that when animal communicator Dr. Doolittle—celebrated in book, film, and song—chatted away with Jip the dog and Gub-Gub the pig, he was not as outside the norm as we thought—at least when compared with most cat owners. In

---

How Cats Greet Each Other

By Marilyn Krieger,
Certified Cat Behavior Consultant

Cats have evolved an elegant and formal protocol for greeting each other. When you're meeting a feline for the first time, play copycat and follow the same protocols; this allows the cat to find out something about you, and it will build trust between the two of you.

Do not try to pick up a cat you don't know (and *never* chase one). Instead, extend your finger toward the cat at about nose level. Make sure there is some distance between the two of you so she doesn't perceive the gesture as a threat.

The next move is up to the cat. When she's ready to say "hello," she will walk up to your extended finger and touch it with her nose. Next, she will move her head so that your finger is on her mouth, then she moves her head so that your finger is on her cheek. If she wants to continue with the meeting, she will rub your finger and your hand with her cheek, marking you. Cats have scent glands on their cheeks that produce "friendly pheromones." This is similar to humans shaking hands. After she marks you, you can now gently pet her under her chin, on the side of her head, then on top of her head.

You are furriends!

---

their 1986 study "Social Behavior of Domestic Cats," behavior consultant Peter Borchelt, PhD, and Victoria Voith, DVM, PhD (Department of Clinical Studies School of Veterinary Medicine at the University of Pennsylvania) found that in 96 percent of the households surveyed owners spoke to their cats at least once a day. In 65 percent of them, owners addressed their cats as they would another adult or a child.

Although you and your cat are not going to reach the word-for-word level of understanding that Doolittle and his pack did, you can teach your cat to understand quite a bit of "human" language. Cats can learn some words. Even more than words, however, cats learn to understand your meaning by your tone of voice and body language (see chapter 25). As you socialize with your cat and your cat learns to understand your language, you are also training your cat to respond to your voice. Consequently, training and socialization go hand in hand, and the tone of your voice can be a very strong training tool to use to teach your cat around the home.

The moment a young kitten or an adult cat comes into your home and has settled in, it's important to allow her to learn her way around the house while you slowly introduce her to your house rules so that good behavior patterns—like not clawing furniture—are established right away. When teaching basic house rules, it is important to use the right tone of voice, which should be firm but gentle and encouraging.

Being consistent is also crucial. Tell other family members the basic house rules for your cat, including which are the *no kitty zones*, so that everyone is on the same page. You should also give them a lesson in how to teach your new feline what is acceptable and what isn't, so your cat will learn fast and not be confused. Be aware that cats, even adult ones, like children, will test the boundaries for acceptable behavior and often push you to the limits. A firm tone and consistency will eventually get the job done.

What will *not* work—at all—is physical punishment. Physical punishment not only will fail to correct unwanted behavior but also is very likely to escalate that behavior and cause other undesirable behaviors to develop. That is because two of the main effects of such punishment are that you will damage or even break the bond you are trying to establish with your cat and that you will make the cat feel very insecure and unsafe. Your cat needs to have a strong rapport with you and needs to feel safe at all times. She cannot function and blossom if she does not.

According to behavior scientist Karen Pryor, cats, when threatened or hurt, instinctually go right into fight-or-flight mode. They don't move out of your way as cattle do or apologize and pee on the floor as puppies do. If you shout angrily at your cat or hit her to reprimand her, you become something she must defend herself against or seek cover from. Neither is a role you want; if you take one on in a thoughtless moment, you may never be able to shed it, and your cat may never recover from it.

Behaviorist Pam Johnson-Bennett, who has authored several popular behavior-training guides (including *Think Like A Cat: How to Raise a Well-Adjusted Cat—Not a Sour Puss, Cat vs. Cat*, and *Starting from Scratch*) believes in a threefold training technique to teach good manners. The technique consists of remote control training, redirection, and positive reinforcement. Other behaviorists and trainers endorse these three training concepts and recommend various ways to implement them, too.

Remote Control Training

Remote control training, Johnson-Bennett explains, means that you, the owner, aren't directly associated with the training so that it doesn't interfere with the bond you're trying to establish. For example, if you spray a cat with water to stop her doing something, she must blame the water and not you! It's also an ongoing method

◄ For ideal socialization, kittens should start interacting with people by the age of six weeks.

Nature or Nurture or Both?

"Nature or nurture" is the handy catch phrase people use when they are asking the question about whether a person or an animal is born with a certain trait (nature/genetics) or raised to have that trait (nurture/taught). In cats, that speculation extends to the trait of friendliness. Prospective cat owners would like to know ahead of time that the cat or kitten they choose will be friendly. That's harder to tell in a kitten who still has a lot of growing up to do. Since there's no specific test to see whether a kitten will grow up to be a friendly cat, prospective owners are left to ponder the nature/nurture factors.

On the nurture side, there is no doubt that growing up in a friendly environment imprints on a kitten's social behavior. If the mother cat seems sociable and the kitten has been interacting with humans from the start, the kitten will probably be sociable and friendly.

The nature side is more difficult to ponder. Exactly what role and how large a one nature (genes) plays in determining sociability and friendliness is not so clear cut. There has, however, been a study that has made a connection between the disposition of father cats and their offspring. In *The Domestic Cat: The Biology of Its Behaviour* (Cambridge University Press, 2nd ed., 2002), edited by D. C. Turner and P. Bateson, researchers, in a series of controlled tests, found that a "bold" father cat was likely to produce bold kittens. Because the father had no interactions with his offspring, researchers could conclude that the trait was a genetic one. How does boldness translate to friendliness? *Boldness* here refers to how readily a cat or a kitten will approach something new, be it person or object. A kitten who is more likely to come up to you is more likely to be friendly.

Some people have taken the results of this study to mean that the mother's genes play a less significant role in determining friendliness. That's not the case, however, because the study was never set up to test the maternal genetic contribution to boldness/friendliness. That's because it's easier exclude the father from the family circle than the mother when raising kittens! An additional genetic factor that's been considered is based on breed because certain breeds have a reputation of being exceptionally people-friendly. This, too, can be difficult to prove with certainty. All that said, given a father who's bold/friendly, a mother who is sociable/friendly, and people who have been interacting with the kitten from day one, the odds are in your favor that your kitten will be friendly, too.

Bear in mind, though, that every kitten is an individual and even kittens born in the same litter and nurtured by the same mother can be quite different. Some kittens, for instance, just don't like to be held much, a trait they are evidently born with and keep. That doesn't mean, however, that they aren't social. Although they don't like being held, they may enjoy hanging out with their people and even cuddling next to them on a couch or a bed. Whether you are bringing a kitten or an adult cat into your home, the best thing you can do is let your new feline's personality unfold on its own.

of training that you don't have to be present to apply, a way to teach, or continue to teach, your cat the correct behavior when away from home or out of the room. A typical example of this type of training is "booby-trapping" an area where you don't want your cat to access. This allows the cat to decide for herself that the area is not a fun place to be. Taping down bubble wrap securely on the kitchen counter or on a piece of furniture that you don't want the cat to sit on—or to scratch—is an example of remote control training. A few leaps onto popping bubbles and slick plastic surface and your cat will soon learn that it's unpleasant to sit or stand on the counter or chair and she will avoid it.

Behaviorists all offer their own ideas about useful remote anti-cat devices, such as squirt water bottles (never aim it at the face), a compressed air canister that will emit a loud hissing noise, and cans filled with coins. Bitter Apple is a nondamaging spray that can be used on drapes or other fabrics, for instance, to indicate that they are out of bounds; sheets of special sticky plastic are perfect for placing on fine furniture to deter scratching.

Cats are clever, and it will only take a few visits to a sticky counter or a tacky sofa for your cat to lose interest and seek out feline-friendly alternatives. When that happens, remove the booby traps and return the house to normal.

▲ If your kitchen counters are off-limits to kitty, enforce that rule consistently and make sure everyone in the house does, too.

Redirection

Redirection means turning the cat's attention away from the negative behavior and refocusing it on an acceptable alternative. An important aspect in being able to do this successfully is understanding the feline thinking or instinct that underlies the problem behavior. For example, your counter-loving cat is instinctively seeking a high place as a refuge from earthbound predators and a good platform from which to survey her territory and search for potential prey. With that in mind, before you set up your bubble wrap booby trap on the kitchen counter, make sure to provide your cat with another elevated surface—such as a cat tree or a cat-designated snoozing chair—nearby. *Redirection* means giving the cat an alternative option, one that is acceptable to both of you.

When training a cat or kitten, it's important to remember that scratching in an innate behavior. The simplest way to redirect scratching to a permissible location is to invest in good scratching posts. (Yes, plural!) Some cats like to scratch horizontally and prefer scratching pads. Make sure all posts and pads are easily accessible, a good distance from your favorite leather couch, and near a place where your cat likes to sleep because felines inherently love to scratch and stretch after a good snooze.

Positive Reinforcement

Finally, positive reinforcement is key to a cat's successfully learning a behavior or house rule. This entails giving out a tasty treat when your cat does something you want her to do. For it to be successful, you must give the treat as close as possible in time to when your cat performed the desired behavior. You also must give out the treat consistently until your cat definitely understands what she is doing to earn the treat. With positive reinforcement, you can teach your cat good house manners, such as sitting on command before being fed and not rushing to an open door.

In addition to good manners, you can use positive reinforcement to teach a cat basic commands—ones usually considered canine not feline—such as *come* and *sit* (as just described) and even to play fetch. Teaching such commands and even fun tricks such as giving a high-five paw to hand or playing *Three Blind Mice* (at least the first two bars) on the piano can all be done with patience and a positive reinforcement technique such as clicker training.

Clicker training is a method in which the trainer uses a handheld clicker to "click" and tell the cat that she's done the right thing and instantly offer a reward. The "click" identifies the behavior you plan to pay for with a treat the instant it happens.

When training, it is common to used a target or pointer such as a stick or a pencil to "identify" the behavior you are teaching. For example, if you are teaching a cat to shake your hand, you would start by getting the cat to touch a pencil with her paw and the moment she does so, click and treat. Eventually you would replace the pencil with your hand, and click and treat.

One important note: never add the cat's name when saying and teaching what "No" means. The cat's name should only be used to enforce positive behaviors.

Clicker Training: What You Need

Here are the simple tools you will need to embark on clicker training sessions:

- *A clicker*: This is available from online stores, pet supermarkets, and specialist pet boutiques. For a deaf cat, use a flashlight. You can even train deaf and blind cats by using an object that vibrates.
- *Treats*: Choose something your cat considers a real treat so she is motivated. Make it tiny so you don't fill her up (see below).
- *A target*: This can be any sticklike object, such as a pencil, a chopstick, or a wooden spoon. Later, you can substitute a favorite toy, such as a feathered object on a stick.

Clicker Training: Getting Started

The behavior terms used in clicker training are *shaping* and *capturing*. Start by teaching your cat to touch the target (stick) with her nose. Do so by presenting the target to the cat, that is, by putting one end of it near her face while holding the other. It's inevitable that she will touch it when she sniffs it. Click just as the cat touches the target—do not click prematurely, when her nose is close to the target but hasn't touched it yet. The click must happen the instant the action that you are reinforcing occurs. Now give your cat a treat. It's important to remember that every time you click, you *must* treat.

Target. Touch. Click. Treat.
Target. Touch. Click. Treat.

What you are doing is pairing the sound (click) with something positive (the treat). Initially, your cat will not understand that these tasty tidbits are not random events but that you are in fact shaping a behavior. And in shaping it, you are capturing it.

Initially, a total of five clicks and treats are considered enough of a training session for a cat who is new to the idea. So keep training sessions

▼ If kitty is not allowed on counters or bookcases, give her a cat tree so she'll have an elevated perch of her own.

▲ Keep training treats very small, so they don't overly interrupt training time.

short and always quit while she's still interested. Be sure to hide your target when it's not in use.

There are specific books on clicker training cats such as *Naughty No More* (i5 Press, 2010) by certified behaviorist Marilyn Krieger, which is worth getting if you want to seriously train your cat to do certain behaviors and tricks.

If you are worried about weight gain from the training-session treats, put aside 10 to 20 percent of her regular food intake and use that during training.

Social Behavior in Feral Colonies

Despite the fact that they are territorial, cats who live in urban feral colonies or in the wild still socially interact with each other. In fact, other queens (female adult cats) will act as midwives to a mother birthing kittens, helping to chew off umbilical cords and clean the newborn bundles of fur. Sometimes they will even babysit the kittens or bring the new mother food.

It's also a good idea to schedule training sessions before meal times.

Learning Through Play

As already mentioned, kittens learn a lot from their mothers and each other through play. As part of your socialization and training time, take it to the next level by playing with your cat and initiating fun and games. Just like clicker training, playtime can be used as a significant behavior modification tool, one that allows you to raise a confident cat who enjoys interacting on a social level.

A fair amount of a cat's play techniques are based on its natural hunting and predatory behavior, and thus many cat toys on the market are designed to hone a cat's natural instincts.

No matter what toy you are using to engage in interactive play, whether it's a teaser/wand-type toy or something else, it's important to gauge when she's getting overstimulated and stop the game before it gets out of hand. In feline terms, that means stopping before your cat gets rough and you end up getting scratched.

Never encourage any rough games that allow your cat to bite or claw and possibly draw blood. Similarly, never encourage her to pounce on your feet. If she is starting to display such behavior, stop the game or immediately redirect these play behaviors by

Why Cats Scratch

Cats need to scratch for a variety of reasons. When cats scratch, they are communicating their presence to the world and are marking territory. Cats mark through the visual evidence they leave as well and from scent/pheromones deposited from the scent glands located on the bottom of their paws. They scratch to enjoy a good stretch; they scratch when playing and to disperse energy and stress. Additionally, they scratch when they feel conflicted. Cats also need to scratch for nail maintenance.

introducing appropriate toys, such as a catnip mouse that she can play with and toss about on her own and that will distract her from the foot-biting game.

Alternatively, walk away. That is the feline equivalent of giving her a time-out. By doing this, you are modifying her behaviors and teaching her what is acceptable and what is not.

Every interaction is, in fact, a social interaction with your cat. Preparing the food bowls and placing them down for a meal, brushing and grooming your cat, or simply relaxing with her and petting her are social interactions that go toward strengthening the feline–human bond.

Whether you are around or not, in a multicat household where the felines know that there is enough food and shelter to go around, and thus that there is no need for them to be territorial about these issues, they will display social behaviors toward each other such as sleeping together, grooming each other, rubbing against each other, greeting each

other, playing together, and swatting each other as part of their every day feline social habits. These interactions will continue to teach your new cat about socializing, lessons begun with her mother and littermates, and what is and isn't acceptable in her new home.

Introductions to Other Cats and Household Pets

Introducing a new cat to an incumbent feline requires patience and time (see chapter 8, page 217-219, for more discussion on this subject, and Chapter 25, which explains why some cats may never get along). There's no way of anticipating how long it will take for them to accept one another and hopefully become friends. A lot has to do with the age and sex of the new arrival and, needless to say, with the personalities of the cats in question.

As previously mentioned, it's often a good idea to initially keep the new arrival separate from your other cat as part of adjusting to a new home. Sometimes, you may have to keep them separated for a month. It's all going to depend on how accommodating your incumbent feline is going to be. And remember, even when you are well past the introduction stage, it's not a good idea to leave the newcomer alone and unsupervised with other animals in a household. Place them in different parts of the house for the duration of your absence. Make this a household rule, and make sure all family members remember.

◀ Never encourage play that involves scratching or biting—you are asking for trouble!

Chapter 27

Problem Behaviors

*We can't solve problems by using the same kind
of thinking we used when we created them.*

~Albert Einstein

It's a sad reality that a behavioral issue is the number one reason cited for why cats lose their homes and end up in shelters. Sometimes what we humans consider to be bad behavior is normal behavior for cats, behavior that can simply be redirected so it doesn't cause a conflict between human and feline residents. Sometimes undesirable behavior is a sign of emotional or physical distress in a cat; once the underlying cause is understood and addressed, the behavior usually disappears. That's why it is so important to understand how cats think, how they react, and what kinds of behavior problems may arise and why. There is a reason for everything a cat does. For example, teething kittens will chew for relief; giving them proper chew toys will solve the problem. In an adult cat, however, chewing could be a sign of boredom, stress anxiety, or even of a serious medical condition. If it's the first two, it's possible to redirect such behavior with toys and games to restore harmony to the home; if it's the last one, you'll need to visit the veterinarian immediately.

Other situations that commonly cause behavioral problems with cats include your going away on vacation, moving to a new residence, or introducing a new baby or another pet into your home. With a better

▶ Teething kittens need to chew, so give
yours something appropriate to chew on.

understanding of what causes behavioral problems in cats, owners can work to resolve the issues, rather than simply giving up on their cats. Such problems are no reason for a cat to lose her home.

Litter Box Woes

Litter box avoidance is undoubtedly the most common feline behavioral problem that can cause a cat to lose her home. Fortunately, feline behaviorists and behavioral clinics, such the Animal Behavior Clinic at the Tufts Cummings School of Veterinary Medicine (Grafton, Massachusetts), are putting the word out that this is not an insurmountable problem. Experts have identified several possible causes for this behavioral problem and ways to deal with them. So, once the reason for such behavior has been identified, an owner can easily put into effect a plan to fix the behavior and the cat can sleep securely in her own home.

Medical Causes

If your cat is displaying this behavioral problem, begin to address it with a trip to the veterinarian, who will examine her to make sure you aren't dealing with a medical issue such as a bladder infection or bladder stones. (Signs of a medical problem include straining or crying out while urinating, passing small amounts of urine, or blood in urine.) If your cat does show signs of illness, the veterinarian can start treatment right away. If she does not, don't think of it as a wasted trip. You had to begin by eliminating the most serious possibility from your list of likely causes.

Other Causes

Once you eliminate medical causes, consider a few other possibilities. Here are the most common and ways the handle them:

Litter box placement: Bad (from a cat's view) placement of the litter box can be a cause. Cats like privacy for their litter box duties and are often spooked if the box is put in a high-traffic

▶ If your cat stops using her litter box, the issue is likely to be medical, not behavioral.

area in the house. The box needs to be in an area where cats won't feel they can be ambushed or cornered by another cat; they need to be able to see the whole room and possibly even through a doorway. The worst places for a litter box include under a staircase, in semi-enclosed cupboards, and in small restrooms.

Cleanliness of box: Cats are very clean animals and expect to find their litter box the same way. Thus, a dirty box may be a cause for them to look elsewhere in the home to do their business. Boxes must be scooped at least once a day, possibly more times in a day if multiple cats tend to gravitate to a particular box. How often you change the litter depends on the type you use. Crystals will last longer than newspaper pellets.

Number and type of boxes: Ideally, in multiple-cat households, there should be a litter box for each cat even if the cats don't use one box exclusively. Some behaviorists actually say you should have an additional box to the number of cats. For example, two cats, three boxes and so on. The type of litter box may also play a role. If its sides are too high, an

Barring Access to Plants

As previously discussed in chapter 11 (Feeding Your Cat), some cats love to nibble on houseplants. This can be a problem for two reasons: First and most important, many plants are toxic to cats; find out what plants are on the toxic list and remove them before you even bring your cat home. Second, not all plants look good with nibble marks on them; if you wish to keep up the decorative appearance of plants, sprinkle pepper on the soil and the leaves. After a few sneezes. the cat will get the message. Alternatively, you can put decorative pebbles on the surface of the soil to make it more difficult for the cat to get to certain plants. This will is also prevent your cat from using your bigger potted plants as additional toilets.

elderly cat may have trouble entering and exiting. There are litter box ramps and numerous litter box styles that would solve this problem. Make sure that the box is not too small. Enclosed boxes offer a smaller space than they appear to.

Type of litter: Some cats even object to the type of litter in the box. When switching to a different kind, do it gradually, changing the ratio of old litter to new over a period of a couple of weeks.

Paw issues: Sometimes cats who have been declawed develop litter box issues. Declawing is amputative surgery, and often cats find it painful to scratch in the litter box, especially immediately after the procedure, because the litter hurts their paws. You may have to use puppy pee pads to line the box until the cat has healed. (Cats need their claws and this surgery should never be an option.)

Spraying and Urine Marking

Cat spray, which is a mixture of urine and glandular secretions, is a foul-smelling clear or slightly white liquid. Spraying, or urine marking, is usually done on vertical objects by male cats and should not to be confused with litter box avoidance. Male cats primarily do it to mark out their territories, warning other males away and letting females know whose territory it is. Spraying is most prevalent among unneutered males and can be common in multicat households, where a cat can feel an urgent need to establish boundaries. Some females will also spray, particularly nonspayed females in heat, who use urine marking as a way of attracting a mate. Females also spray as a way of marking territory. Spraying can also be caused by anxiety and stress, which can be triggered by a number of factors.

If you have a cat who is spraying, the first step in trying to eliminate such behavior is to have that cat neutered/spayed. In the majority of cases, neutering/spaying will solve the problem. If the spraying problem persists or your cat has already been spayed or neutered, the problem could be caused by anxiety, stress, or a similar factor.

For example, the cause could be an invasion of your cat's personal territory by a neighborhood cat. That invasion could be anything from your cat's spying a strange cat walking across your lawn through a window to that strange cat actually entering your home through a cat flap and walking right into your cat's space. In the first example, the solution is simple: pull down the shade or close the blinds. In the second, go more electronic and buy a special cat flaps that can be programmed to only allow incumbent cats in the household to use them. They are activated by a little device on the cat's collar. Such a cat flap could solve a trespassing problem.

Of course, you may not be able to figure out what triggered the spraying so quickly. Discuss the problem with a veterinarian or a behaviorist and find out what can be done. Depending on the reason for the spraying, your veterinarian may prescribe antianxiety medication for your cat. In addition or alternatively, the veterinarian or behaviorist may recommend an over-the-counter pheromone spray. These pheromone sprays mimic the natural comforting facial pheromone secreted by cats. When cats sense the facial pheromone in areas around their home, they are less likely to urine mark or scratch those areas. These sprays, along with the implementation of certain behavior modification techniques can eradicate spraying issues. (*Note*: pheromone sprays can also be used for litter box issues.)

Whatever approach you take to dealing with spraying, you must be certain to do a thorough cleanup of any area that has been hit by your territorial tomcat (or female enticer). Use a product with an effective enzyme cleaner that will remove all traces of the odor and will prevent cats from returning to the same spot.

Scratching Here, There, and Everywhere

It's important to remember that scratching is a very normal activity. Cats have scent glands on the underside of their front paws. So, as they scratch, they are in fact marking a particular item in your home with their own scent. They usually choose your favorite chair because they are attracted by your scent. Furthermore, the physical act of scratching helps to strip off old claw sheaths, sharpen the new ones, and stretch the muscles and tendons in their legs. Cats also scratch to release energy, when they are conflicted, when they are playing, and when they are stretching.

It is very easy to redirect scratching to acceptable scratching zones such as a scratching post. Because some cats scratch horizontally and others vertically, be sure to provide both kinds of scratchers and place them in different rooms around the home. Look for tall posts so that your cat can get a good

▲ Provide your cat with acceptable items to scratch, so she won't be forced to choose her own.

stretch. Both sisal and recycled cardboard are excellent scratching materials. The latest designs even include real tree branches. Try to avoid carpeting because some cats have trouble differentiating between the carpet surface on a post and your priceless Oriental rug. Because cats usually awake from a catnap and stretch, it's a good idea to have a post or scratch pad close to their favorite snoozing places.

A spray water bottle or a can of compressed air are also excellent remote training devices to keep cats away from areas where they are not permitted to scratch. Eventually, a cat will react simply on sight of the bottle or can and learn that the area is out of bounds. Special sticky sheets are another useful household item to redirect scratching elsewhere. Keeping nails regularly trimmed will also help. Another option is to apply special nail caps called Soft Paws. They are designed to prevent cats from damaging things by scratching and are a safe alternative to declawing.

Cats also scratch out of boredom. Be sure your cat has plenty of toys. Such feline enrichment, as

ThunderShirt for Cats

One way to lessen separation anxiety or stress is to put your cat in a ThunderShirt. This garment is based on the swaddling effect that mother's use to wrap small babies and is known to relieve anxiety and stress. Such a garment is particularly useful to de-stress trips to the vet's office. I have used it successfully with Ziggy, who now sings fewer "arias" in the car when we are traveling.

well as clicker training to teach your cats tricks, as described in the previous chapter, are excellent ways of giving your cat both the mental and physical stimulation she needs.

Play and Prey Aggression

We've all heard the expression "as playful as a kitten." Kittens love to pounce and chase one another in what behaviorists describe as attack-and-retreat behavior. They will jump on each other and wrestle around, clutching each other. When they get older, they continue to play in this mode and sometimes even hiss and growl. Although it may sound serious, they are still in play mode.

Cats also indulge in predatory play. They will lie in wait, hiding, crouching, getting ready to spring out and pounce as they would if they were hunting in the wild.

Pica: That's Not on the Menu!

When kittens who have been prematurely taken from their mothers suck on fabrics as substitute form of nursing, the behavior is sometimes labeled *pica*. According to Arnold Plotnick, DVM, however, this is not true pica behavior. In his 2006 article "Pica—Why Cats Eat Weird Things," he explains that pica "is the voluntary ingestion of non-edible materials. . . . The etiology of true pica is not known, although mineral deficiencies or psychological disturbances are often blamed." By contrast, "[w]ool-sucking is a commonly described abnormal ingestive behavior in cats . . . a compulsive, misdirected form of nursing behavior [that] should be distinguished from true cases of pica." Cats with true pica have been found eating clay litter and even licking silverware. True pica is a problem that definitely needs professional attention. Oriental breeds, such as Siamese, are more prone to pica issues than other breeds.

Very often cats transfer these play and prey tactics to the humans in the household, lying in wait and jumping out to attack legs and feet. Sometimes a calm and peaceful petting session suddenly turns aggressive when your cat gets overstimulated and bites down on a finger and brings both her front and back legs together to hold your arm in a vicelike grip.

When it comes to a petting or a play session, you need know to when to stop the game, which is *before* your cat becomes overstimulated and goes into attack mode. Learn to read the signs, such as a twitching tail or flashing eyes and flattening ears, that will herald a bite and stop petting or playing with the cat. Initially, keep a squirt bottle handy and squirt her paws, never her face, with your "free" hand. An alternative is redirecting the cat's attention elsewhere by throwing a toy. You can also walk away and call it a timeout.

◀ If your cat becomes overexcited during play, divert her attention from you to a wand toy.

Once again, remember *never* to resort to physical punishment because cats don't learn from it and it only introduces a new set of behavioral problems.

It's also an excellent idea to divert a cat's play and prey drive by engaging her in interactive games with toys such as wands with fluttery furry or buglike objects, such as Neko Flies, on the end. There are also wonderful battery-operated toys that cats love to chase around and attack that keep your hands and feet out of the equation. Always remember to pack them away when the games are over to prevent accidents such as cats choking themselves by ingesting things or wrapping the strings around their necks.

Cat-on-Cat Aggression

Changes in a household, such as the arrival of another pet, can upset social tranquility and result in feline feuds. That's why it's so important to take your time when introducing cats to a new feline member of the household. Often, territorial boundaries are the underlying cause of the dispute.

When this happens, separate the feuding felines and slowly reintroduce them to one another using the same tactics as when they were introduced in the first place.

If these spats continue, the problem needs to be discussed with a veterinarian, who may consider the use of antianxiety medication for the aggressor. Alternatively, discuss the problem with a cat behaviorist who is qualified to handle aggression issues. Many behaviorists not only consult in person but also by phone, which may be more convenient if they don't have an office in your area.

There are a number of reasons why cats suddenly attack one another. For example, a cat who has been to the veterinarian to be spayed or neutered may be hissed at on returning home because she or he smells differently. Even a routine checkup at the vet's office can trigger such a response. Once the strange smells wear off, things go back to normal.

One of the advantages for cats who have an indoor-only lifestyle or are only allowed out into a secured garden area is that they cannot hop the wall and pick a fight with a neighbor's cat, which will, of course, induce a new set of problems for the household, especially if they injure one another and you end up with the vet bills!

Separation Anxiety

Cats who develop really close bonds with their owners become distressed when left alone for long periods and can develop an obsessive-compulsive behavior such as *overgrooming*, licking or grooming a particular area until all the fur has been pulled out and the skin is red and raw, behavior known as *psychogenic alopecia*. This same problem can occur as a result of boredom.

Try alleviating your cat's distress by giving her things to do while you are out; for instance, leave toys out so she can spend her time playing and hide treats around the house so she can occupy her time on a tasty treasure hunt. A treat ball allows you to record a message so that she can hear your voice as she rolls the ball around to trigger the message and a treat. Another way to lessen separation anxiety and help your cat while away the hours is to provide her with visual entertainment. This can be in the form of a secure (in other words, has a sturdy lid and can't be toppled) fish tank or special cat videos played on the TV.

To comfort your cat in your absence, place some clothing you've worn or slept in around the house. She can breathe your scent for reassurance and when you come home, you may find her snuggled down for a nap in your sweatshirt.

If you think getting a second cat for company may be the answer to separation anxiety, consider all the possible ramifications before acting on the idea. Discuss it with your veterinarian or a behaviorist first. Sometimes this is not the answer and only causes more problems in the household, especially if your first cat becomes possessive and territorial about you and your home or is made to feel more anxious and insecure.

▲ Some cats become bored and lonely when left alone all day and start to suffer from separation anxiety.

Eating or Sucking Materials

Cats who love to chew on a blanket or a piece of cloth may be likened to young children who walk around sucking on pacifiers or hugging security blankets. This behavior often occurs in kittens who have been removed from their mothers too young and have not had the opportunity to nurse until their mothers properly weaned them. Soft cuddly fabrics become a substitute for mama cat.

The sucking itself is not a problem, but if the sucking turns into chewing and swallowing the fabric, then that can lead to problems such as gastrointestinal obstructions. Thus, it's important to redirect your cat to playing with proper feline chew toys that won't present the same problem (always get rid of a chew toy that has started to fall apart). There are several cat chew toys on the market. They are usually labeled for teething kittens, but adult cats can enjoy them, too.

Often the urge to suck on fabrics subsides as a kitten becomes an adult, although many cats will continue to knead your lap the way they knead their mother's tummy when drinking from her (as discussed in the previous chapter) if given the chance. However, the problem chewing can reoccur in adulthood as a defense mechanism for dealing with a stressful situation such as household tensions between cats or separation anxiety.

If it persists in older cats, the problem needs to be addressed by a veterinarian who may prescribe an antianxiety medication along with some behavior modification and lifestyle enrichment.

Chapter 28

Cats at Work

*As anyone who has ever been around a cat
for any length of time well knows, cats have
enormous patience with the limitations of the
humankind.*

~Cleveland Amory

The title of the chapter may cause some head scratching. If most of us were asked to name animals that work, the cat would not top our lists (nor appear on them at all). The dog, of course, would be right up there with the horse. From the time they were first domesticated, dogs have been bred and trained to perform a variety of functions, such as hunting and herding, for our benefit. Today, dogs are also trained in search-and-rescue work, as companions for the sight- and hearing-impaired, to sniff out drugs, and to detect materials and conditions from bombs to cancer. In fact, there are even dogs trained to sniff out cash and thus are helping to prevent tax evaders from getting on a plane and leaving a particular country!

By contrast, cats really domesticated themselves, their usefulness to humankind being the mutually beneficial act of rounding up rodents (see chapter 1). For this, cats required no training and operated pretty much on their own schedule. As domestic

▶ A cat can play a useful role in a therapy, day-care, library, or senior-center setting.

felines won their places in the homes and hearts of their owners (and mice became less of an issue in urban households), they settled down to cushy, nonworking lives. And it turns out that it is by being their laid-back feline selves in our environs every day that cats provide their greatest service to us. Studies have shown that people who are around cats suffer less stress and anxiety, conditions that could lead to fatal heart attacks.

The most important research highlighting how simply being around cats is "great medicine" was conducted by Dr. Adnan Qureshi, executive director of the Zeenat Qureshi Stroke Research Center at the University of Minnesota, in Minneapolis, who, in 2008, released the findings of his ten-year study. Qureshi and colleagues based their work on a previous National Health and Nutrition Examination Study that was conducted in the United States from 1976 to 1980. From this National Health and Nutrition Examination study, they extracted data on 4,435 Americans aged thirty to seventy-five. Of their sample, 2,435 of the participants were current or former cat owners, whereas the remaining 2,000 had never lived with a cat. These researchers highlighted causes of death in their sample, including stroke and other heart events, and found that over a ten-year follow-up period, cat owners showed a 40 percent lower risk of death from heart attacks compared with those who did not own cats.

Consequently, if one had to give the average cat who dispenses love and affection on a daily basis a job title, it would undoubtedly be Public Relations Officer Promoting Human Health and Well-Being. This is probably too much of a mouthful for most of us, which is why we simply refer to them as "therapy cats," whether they are "working" in their own homes or outside of it by visiting people of all ages and in all walks of life and giving them a dose of special feline "medicine."

Therapy Cats: The Power of the Purr

The health work of felines has had far-reaching effects, bringing about enormous benefits, especially for the elderly and the infirm. For example, as an acknowledgment of the health benefits of having a cat, many landlords around the country have relaxed and changed their "no pets allowed" policies for tenants. Many assisted-living centers and old age homes now "employ" a resident cat as a companion to the residents. Best of all, hospitals have started opening their doors to specially certified therapy cats, allowing them to visit patients on a regular basis and dispense their special brand of feline love and affection.

Although a therapy cat requires no special training, candidates for this type of work must have certain qualifications or characteristics. The therapy cat must be a lap cat, with a placid yet affectionate disposition, one who is comfortable meeting and interacting with new people and accepting of sights and sounds not usual in her home environment. A therapy cat also needs to be tolerant of petting that can be a bit rough at times, as well as of being poked and pulled a bit. It's not that the people a therapy

◄ A therapy cat can bring joy to those with mental and physical challenges.

Assisted Animal Therapy Organizations

Pet Partners (formerly the Delta Society), based in Bellevue, Washington, is a world leader in the field of human–pet relationship research. In 1990, the group launched its Pet Partners Program training volunteers and their animals to visit people in a variety of situations, from hospitals and hospices and assisted-living facilities to classrooms and children's homes. They currently have about 10,000 teams of people and pet therapists, and 200 of the teams include felines.

To be certified by the organization, all volunteers have to register for Pet Partner's one-day workshop, which provides information on how to identify stress in animals and how to work within different population groups. Volunteers can be as young as ten years of age but must have parental permission. The workshops are held around the country but can also be taken online through the organization's website.

Part of the certification process also includes an evaluation of both the volunteer and his or her cat to ensure that both have the right temperament for this time of work. For the cat owner, it can sometimes be very emotional work.

Pet Partners operates in all fifty states. Its network links volunteers with facilities in their own communities that request pet visitors and also helps pet partners contact new locations to visit. Volunteers working under the organization's umbrella are covered by the society's liability insurance. The society accepts individual volunteers, as well as families. Cat therapy work is a wonderful way of sharing your cat's love; the benefits derived by the recipients of this feline affection are instantaneous.

cat meet are trying to treat her roughly, but some are children who have to be instructed on touching a cat properly and others are too infirm or disabled to give the cat a gentle caress. Finally, she must enjoy traveling by car and possibly walking on a leash.

As the owner of a therapy cat, try to ascertain whether your feline has a preference for being around children or older people. If you are not sure how your cat will react to going to visit strangers, start with visits to family and friends and gauge her reaction to being in a different environment. See whether she interacts better with children or older people. Some cats are fine with both groups; if this is case, decide whether *you* have a preference for visiting hospitals and hospices as opposed to children's centers and schools.

Be sure to take treats along. Cats are quick learners, and your cat will soon associate a trip in the car with being placed next to someone who will pet her and give her a treat.

It's important to ensure your cat's vaccinations are always up to date and that she is in good health so that she doesn't endanger anyone you may visit who has an impaired immune system. Take your therapy cat for veterinary checkups every six months.

It's always a good idea to own two cat carriers; one that's strictly associated with trips to the vet and the other one for social outings such as therapy visits.

Grief Therapy

Grief therapy is a special type of counseling given to console people who have suffered severe trauma resulting from death and destruction that they have witnessed. Typical natural disaster scenarios are fires, floods, and earthquakes that have caused massive destruction and loss of life. Grief therapy is also used to console students whose school campuses have become battlegrounds involving shooting incidents, such as the Columbine High School massacre in Colorado in 1999, when two senior students went on a rampage, killing twelve students and a teacher and injuring many more. A similar incident took place on the campus of Virginia Tech in Blacksburg, Virginia, in 2007, when a lone gunman killed thirty-two students. And, again in 2012, when a gunman opened fire at a cinema in Aurora, Colorado. Feline therapy also played a huge role with the families who lost loved ones in the Sandy Hook Elementary School shootings in Connecticut. The Red Cross and other relief organizations also used grief therapy to console the families and friends of those killed in the terrorist attacks on September 11, 2001.

Initially, this type of therapy work was limited to volunteers with dogs. This has begun to change, however, as there is no question that the power of the purr can do wonders to help heal in such situations, too.

Literacy Therapy

Another type of therapy had its origins not long ago in the schoolroom. As teachers know too well, students with reading disabilities face two opponents when they try to improve their reading skills—their own disabilities and the taunting of their peers. In 1999, Intermountain Therapy Animals, a Salt Lake City organization, started the Reading Education Assistance Dogs (READ) program aimed at helping these students. Dogs were introduced into classrooms and libraries to serve as nonjudgmental and comforting listeners to children reading aloud, which helped them not only to improve their reading skills but also to gain self-confidence. As the concept of literacy therapy was taken up by other organizations, including Pet Partners, forward-thinking educators realized that cats, too, would make great reading buddies (naturally). Feline literacy therapists are happy to curl up in a lap and "listen" to the stories being read. This reading buddy system works and is encouraged in the home environment, too.

Other Forms of Therapy

The fact that cats have such a wonderful therapeutic effect on humans has prompted medical researchers to look at other areas where the power of the purr can be beneficial to humankind in general. Currently, cat therapy research is being conducted in several fields, including the ones below.

Cancer: Research done at the University of California-San Francisco has shown that owning pets helps to strengthen a person's immune systems as a result of their exposure to allergens in the household relating to pet hair. And as a result, cat (and dog) owners have a 30 percent less likely chance of developing non-Hodgkin's lymphoma (NHL).

Broken bones: Experts from the Fauna Communications Research Institute in North

▲ Having a therapy cat on hand can help distract a cancer patient from the effects of chemotherapy.

Carolina are speculating that cats' vibrational frequencies when purring at their dominant frequency range of 25–50 Hertz may also help heal and grow denser human bones.

Love hormones: According to New York psychologist and psychoanalyst Joel Gavriele-Gold, PhD, there's a great deal to be said for nonverbal contact and the simple companionship cats offer. Gavriele-Gold says that, in today's frenetic world, people often have trouble staying in touch with their emotions; interacting with cats offers a way for people to reconnect with their feelings and themselves. "Petting a cat or simply watching your pet curled up asleep somehow brings us closer to nature and a sense of oneness with the world."

Gavriele-Gold says that, for many people, the fear of reaching out and touching someone is based on the anticipation of rejection and criticism. Pets are a primary source of touching and being touched. People who are not ready for a deep human relationship seem to find more comfort in animals than in people, and, in these instances, it can be very comforting being around a feline. Researchers exploring the human–animal bond have discovered that the "love hormone," *oxytocin*, released by the body during childbirth and sex, comes into play when humans and animals bond, too. This is the subject of a book titled *Made for Each Other: The Biology of the Human–Animal Bond* by Meg Daley Olmert.

Public Cats: The Power of Personality

Cats have not limited themselves to the therapy field when it comes to the work world. Just as the power of the feline purr has offered many people great comfort, the power of the feline personality has given many people great delight. Cats have put their winning personalities to good use in libraries, hotels, retail businesses, show rings, and various entertainment fields.

Libraries

It was Reggie, the cat-in-residence at the Bryant Public Library in Sauk, Minnesota, who inspired librarian Phyllis Lahti to found the Library Cat Society in 1987. Since then, dozens of member libraries from around the world continue to exchange information on their cats whose job description includes attracting people to libraries, especially children and the elderly who possibly live alone and aren't able to keep a pet of their own.

Historically, there have been cats in libraries for decades. In the past, they were mostly feral and earned their keep doing rodent patrol. Modern-day

▼The Library Cat Society was founded in 1987, and there are dozens of member libraries across the globe.

▲ It's become common for used bookstores to have a resident feline.

library cats are more involved in "communications and public relations" with the library-visiting public, and many have been named after authors such as Brontë and Emily Dickinson or have appropriately "bookish" names like Page and Libris.

Undoubtedly, the most famous library cat was Dewey ReadMore Books, a ginger tabby who was found by Vicki Myron, director of the library in Spencer, Iowa, as a tiny bedraggled kitten in the library's book drop chute in 1988. Shortly after the kitten's rescue, city officials approved the library's cat-in-residence and a photo of the city's "new employee" sitting on the card catalog appeared in *The Daily Reporter* in Spencer. Residents were invited to help name the kitty, and 394 cast ballots.

It is unclear how Dewey catapulted to fame from greeting visitors to the library to appearing as Mr. January in a national cat calendar. Next came his role in the documentary *Puss in Books: Adventures of the Library Cat*, made by filmmaker Gary Roma. Finally, Myron wrote the cat's amazing life story,

titled *Dewey: The Small-Town Library Cat Who Touched the World*, which became an international bestseller. Dewey lived until he was 19 years old, and when he passed away in 2006, more than 200 newspapers across America ran his obituary.

Like Dewey, most current library cats were abandoned and rescued by caring library staff members. It's a great "job" for a cat, with excellent benefits in the form of love and care. Dewey certainly helped to popularize the current trend of library felines. In 1999, the Ocean Shores Library in Ocean Shores, Washington, created a special library cat position on its staff roster after a survey revealed that 98 percent of the patrons favored a furry staff member. A cat named Trixie was appointed and was even given her own checkbook to pay for food and veterinary bills.

Leisure and Retail

These days, many pet-friendly businesses are employing an official greeter, or "director of pet relations" as the pet involved is often called. Many small business owners who have placid cats have found that taking their felines to work draws people to the store.

Cats "work" well in bookstores, gift stores, and even in office situations. More recently, even corporate America has been opening doors to part-time feline employees by allowing staff members to bring their pets to work. If your cat has the temperament and your work place is a safe and secure environment, there's no reason why your cat can't get a job dispensing feline love and affection in the workplace.

In the case of the hotel and leisure industry, a feline greeter gives guests a "fur fix" when they are traveling and have had to leave their own cats at home. Undoubtedly, the world's most famous feline employed in the leisure industry is a Rag Doll named Matilda III who lives at the Algonquin Hotel in midtown Manhattan, where she's been in residence since 2010 greeting guests at this stylish boutique hotel off Times Square. Matilda, who began life as an abandoned kitty, receives e-mails from around the world on a daily basis, gifts on her birthday, and cards at Christmas. Some guests even write to tell her when they plan to visit again and ask if she would please pass on the information to the reservation desk.

As the Algonquin's Directfurr of Pet Relations, her perks include scrumptious meals from the hotel's kitchen, her own chaise longue in the hotel lobby, a private closet for her litter box and food, and a place to escape when guests get too noisy at her self-appointed nap times.

The hotel management believes that having Matilda on hand to greet everyone in the lobby instantly makes travelers, especially if they are on business, feel more at home. She befriends everyone and guests often write to her when they get home as if they're corresponding with a friend.

Advertising and Entertainment

The fact that cats and dogs (and other domestic animals) have come to be considered full-fledged members of the family has had a direct impact not only on pet products, but also on advertising and show business. In recent decades, cats and dogs have been playing more prominent roles in TV sitcoms and all forms of media advertising, and even more starring roles in Hollywood movies. Of course, some older films featured animals (see chapter 3, Movies), but undoubtedly feline and canine actors have been appearing more and more as the decades have passed. They don't necessarily have to play in a starring role; sometimes it's just a fleeting appearance as a member of a household. But this scenario in itself is cropping up more and more.

There are roles for both superbly coifed show cats—such as Mr. Bigglesworth, the svelte Sphynx cat who starred alongside Mike Myers as Dr. Evil in the Bond spoof *Austin Powers* (1997)—as well as typical cat-next-door types. In fact, cats with unusual markings don't often get roles because their markings may appear strange from certain camera angles, and it's more difficult to find a feline "body doubles" when filming a full-length feature. It's not unusual for several cats to play one role in the film.

Every day, pet talent agencies around the country are inundated by doting and starry-eyed pet parents

Products Tester

In recent years, the pet products industry has exploded and, according to the American Pet Products Association (APPA), in 2013 earned more than $55 billion. When it comes to cats, the focus has been on foods, home accessories from litter boxes to beds, and dinnerware and toys for feline enrichment. Although companies usually have their own feline testers, they are often looking for opinions from the public feline sector. If you are keen to get involved, the best way is to contact the companies concerned and make your cat available to be a tester. There is no pay, but you will get to keep the products that are the focus of the research.

▲ Some bed-and-breakfasts have an affectionate feline on the premises to prevent customers from going through cat withdrawal.

who are determined to carve out a lucrative career for their felines, hoping that, if not a starring role in a movie, then possibly a spokescat deal like the one Morris the Cat has for 9Lives pet food. (See chapter 1, The World's First Spokescat.)

Before you let your feline give up her day job as the competent inventor of 101 different snooze positions on the family couch, you should realize that feline stardom can be very hard to achieve. Cats need special training to be in front of the camera—and some very lucky breaks. Most of the cats who *do* have careers in the advertising and show business worlds are owned by professional trainers and are capable of reacting to both voice commands and hand directives.

If you still want find out something about these worlds, pet talent agencies offer training classes based on positive reinforcement techniques such as clicker training, and training never goes to waste. Bear in mind, though, that these types of classes can be more expensive than other training classes. So weigh the pros and cons before you take the next step. As with their human counterparts, cats, even the most gorgeous and talented, can have a hard time breaking into the entertainment business (and they don't make good waiters in restaurants!).

If you've decided to pursue a career for your cat, one way to get started, in addition to the training lessons, is to seek out local photographers in your area and ask them whether they need a cat or cats for a project. You may even consider having a set of professional photographs taken for future use.

Check out local film schools and make them aware of your feline's aspirations. Because all film school students need to make a film to graduate, this could be a way of getting your feline into the business.

A perfect example of this is Seattle-based filmmaker Will Braden, the creator of the famous Henri Le Chat Noir videos that have become a YouTube sensation. As a student at the Seattle Film Institute, he had to do a project for his class. The students had been watching black-and-white avant-garde French movies from the 1950s and '60s, and Braden decided to do a parody. He asked family members if he could use their cat, a black-and-white Tuxedo named Henry, for the film and he renamed him Henri for his cinematic debut.

The videos have a French soundtrack with English subtitles and won Braden a Lifetime Achievement Award at The Friskies Awards in 2012, honoring the best cat videos on the Internet. At the time this book went to print, Henri had more than 154,000 Facebook fans. The website sells a variety of merchandise in Henri's likeness, and there's a book in the works, too. Henri is famous around the world and has become a financial success for Braden, too.

Show World

Being a professional show cat can indeed be a full-time job because there are cat shows held on local, regional, and national levels every weekend of the year!

The show ring isn't the exclusive domain of pedigreed felines either, because most shows include a household section that is open to mixed breeds. House cats are judged collectively without regard to their sex, age, color, or coat length. Instead of being judged to a specific breed standard, the competitors are judged for their uniqueness, pleasing appearance, unusual marking, and sweet natures. However, they may not be declawed, and, if they are more than eight months old, they must have been spayed or neutered.

Every cat entered receives a red and white merit award as a testament to her good health and vitality. Getting your cat involved in the show world is a great way to connect with other cat people.

▲ If you are lucky, teaching your cat some tricks could lead her into a career in film or on stage.

However, it takes both time and dedication to learn how to groom your cat for the show ring. This is particularly important if you have a pedigreed feline and are taking the competition seriously. Furthermore, it's important to ascertain whether this time-consuming lifestyle will fit into your daily schedule and not be a drain on your finances.

Most importantly, you need to determine whether the show ring is right for your cat. Factors to consider include whether your cat has the temperament to be handled by strangers and whether she is spooked by crowds and loud noises. Does she have any objection to traveling and spending long hours in a show hall? Many people who show professionally say that their cats thrive on the attention, both in the show ring and from spectators and that it's an enjoyable "work experience" for all concerned.

Cat Blogger

Social media—specifically blogs and websites—are making different job opportunities available to cats and their owners. There are numerous cat blogs and websites "run" by cats. So if you have an excellent knowledge about felines at large, or your cat is adept at charity work and can raise money for animal shelters, then you and your cat may have a career as a cat blogger or website personality. There are many blogs and websites that are sponsored. You may not become rich, but you could develop it into a big enough business to earn a living.

Chapter 29

Careers with Cats

Saving one cat won't change the world but it will change the world for that cat.

~Author Unknown

Most cat owners have at one time or another declared that they would love nothing more than to stay home all day and be with their cats. The next best thing is a career that allows you to work with felines.

In recent years, the number of new career opportunities has mushroomed beyond expectations thanks to the phenomenal growth in the pet industry, which has been fueled by the "humanization" of our pets and the desire to give our cats a lifestyle that mimics our own (see The Humanization of Our Pets, page 502). Consequently, cat-related career and job opportunities are many and varied. Some require study; others are born out of ingenuity and necessity as the result of being around felines and understanding their wants and needs, and these have spawned many cottage industries.

It is interesting to note many careers, commercial enterprises, and industries linked to pets have proven to be more "recession-proof" than other spheres of the economic sector. Pet industry insiders like Bob Vetere, who heads the American Pet Products Association (APPA), believe this is because, in times of hardship, many people turn to their pets for stress relief, love,

▶ Many cat owners dream of a having a career involving felines.

Humanization of Our Pets

Not that long ago, a spa day for your cat that included a moisturizing bath, massage, and peticure or perhaps a dinner of New Zealand canned venison served to your favorite feline in a stylish raised bowl were simply considered gimmicks. Now, this imagery is simply a reflection of family life in many cat homes across America.

The keyword is *family*. According to various pet-related surveys recently commissioned and published by such diverse sources as business strategists and pet-manufacturing companies such as Hartz Mountain Corporation and Del Monte Foods, the majority of pet owners in this country now call themselves "pet parents." Consequently, many cats (and dogs) have lifestyles that mirror their pet parents' own health and well-being ideals. Thus, the "gimmicks" have morphed into a full-fledged trend aptly labeled *pet humanization*.

According to Michael Schaeffer, author of the book *One Nation Under Dog*, a well-researched look at our love affair with our pets, pet humanization is an almost inevitable reaction to our times. "A century ago, domestic cats and dogs were kept for economic reasons as guard dogs or rat catchers. Now, most people keep pets for love. So we apply the same instincts to caring and nurturing them as we do for our kids. And, since the way we nurture kids has changed a bit—we go for more natural food and less punishing education, we work longer hours and thus rely more on daycare—so has the way we nurture our pets."

In a 2011 study published by the Hartz Mountain Corporation of Secaucus, New Jersey, a company with an eighty-five-year-old history in the pet industry, 65 percent of the respondents felt that their pet's personality was far more important that its physical appearance or pedigree.

Nutrition and health care are two categories in the pet world that have possibly experienced the biggest impact from pet humanization. With nutrition being so important to people, a strong upward trend has emerged in the demand for premium, natural, and organic foods and treats for cats, too. And when it comes to general cat care, people are seeking out luxury and pampering for their cats just as they are in their own personal health care treatments. Other areas strongly reflecting pet humanization include vitamins and supplements, especially those targeting our aging pets.

Business strategist Mike Dillon, who also publishes annual surveys monitoring the pet industry, believes that, in fact, we are past talking about *humanization* because pets are already ubiquitous in American culture and business. He believes we are already on the next phase, which is *integration*, and that this phase will mature over the next three years (2013–2015). In this next stage, Dillon predicts that more industries not traditionally associated with pets will begin appealing to pet owners, extending popular brands and products into the pet segment. Traditional category boundaries will blur as integration spurs products that cross segment definitions. And there will also be more cultural and legal changes to reflect the status of pets.

And, on the subject of the way pet companionship affects human health, Dillon says that the integration of pets into health and wellness programs has already begun. Pet therapy is widely recognized across America, and studies like the one that claims cat owners are 40 percent less likely to suffer a heart attack are being taken seriously (see chapter 28, page 492).

His forecast is already finding roots in reality with the formation of the Human Animal Bond Research Initiative (HABRI), designed to form a central database for all research relating to the human–animal bond. The organization was officially launched at the Global Pet Expo in Orlando, Florida, in March 2011. Its founding sponsors are the American Pet Products Association, Pfizer Animal Health, and PETCO. The central database, known as HABRI Central, is with Purdue University in West Lafayette, Indiana.

The goal of HABRI is to be an umbrella organization that will support multidisciplinary research on the human–animal bond by providing scientific evidence for informed decisions in human health and pet ownership. Currently, there is a lot of anecdotal information than needs to be scientifically explored. The organization's work will focus on communicating with and educating Congress about the importance of providing $30 million to create a Human Animal Bond Research Center at the National Institute of Health and to continue to inform and educate the general public on the health benefits of pet ownership.

The ultimate goal of HABRI, of course, is to promote pet ownership by pet lovers, expanding pet families and introducing the idea of having fur kids to people who may never have considered bringing a pet into their lives before and affection and so will cut back on their own necessities to purchase items and health care to ensure that their pets' well-being isn't compromised. Too often, though, despite their best efforts, people simply can't afford to care for their pets. As a result, the numbers of pets being turned into shelters rises, which in turn opens new doors to those who want to dedicate their time to helping pets in need.

Because of all the new doors being opened up in the industry, it's becoming easier for people to direct their wide and varied educational skills into newfound pet-related careers, whether they are looking for full- or part-time employment, want to work in an office or workplace environment, or simply want to work from home with their own cats to "help" with everyday tasks.

Veterinary Care

From veterinarian to veterinary technician, technologist, and assistant, to animal chiropractor, there are many career options to consider in the field of veterinary medicine.

Veterinarian

Veterinary medicine is an obvious choice for a dedicated cat person. There are twenty-eight veterinary schools in the United States; each one has an excellent reputation both within this country and around the world.

To earn the letters DVM (doctor of veterinary medicine) or VMD (veterinary medical doctor, the degree granted by the University of Pennsylvania) behind your name takes eight years of college study but requires a lifetime of continued learning.

Modern Veterinary Practice

Veterinary medicine has benefited in so many ways from the state-of-the-art techniques and drugs developed for humans that veterinarians today have an enormous range of tools to give cats the best possible treatment to promote their health and general care. Veterinarians have fabulous opportunities to study further and qualify in specialized fields such as veterinary dentistry, orthopedics, dermatology, cardiology, and ophthalmology.

US Veterinary Medical Schools and Colleges

Auburn University

Colorado State University

Cornell University

Iowa State University

Kansas State University

Louisiana State University

Michigan State University

Mississippi State University

North Carolina State University

Ohio State University

Oklahoma State University

Oregon State University

Purdue University

Texas A&M University

Tufts University

Tuskegee University

University of California, Davis

University of Florida

University of Georgia

University of Illinois at Urbana-Champaign

University of Minnesota

University of Missouri

University of Pennsylvania

University of Tennessee

University of Wisconsin—Madison

Virginia-Maryland Regional College of Veterinary Medicine

Washington State University

Western University of Health Sciences

The majority of veterinarians work in private practice, whether it's a small facility or a full-scale veterinary hospital that offers everything from

▲Veterinary medicine is an obvious choice for a dedicated cat person, although the educational requirements are rigorous.

X-rays and surgical procedures to a variety of postoperative care and therapies. Although about 75 percent of all veterinarians work in private practices, the rest work in a variety of other venues. Many work for drug manufacturers or large pet food companies and play a major roll in the development of life-saving drugs and feline nutritional ideas that ensure future generations of cats are fed the best diet possible. Others have found themselves starring in animal-related shows on TV or even consulting behind the scenes and being on standby on a movie set. Some veterinarians have successfully turned entrepreneur, using their veterinary knowledge and expertise to invent gadgets that enhance the practice of veterinary medicine, as well as useful cat-related tools for the home.

Although most of the animals seen in private veterinarian practice are dogs and cats, most veterinarians must also be capable of treating a variety of small critters, including birds and reptiles. There are, however, veterinarians who specialize within species, too; for example, veterinarians can opt to work exclusively with farm animals while others opt to work exclusively with cats. In recent years, the number of feline-only practices has grown considerably around the world. There is even an association looking after the interests of such specialists, the American Association of Feline Practitioners.

Is Being a Vet Right for You?

Apart from knowing that it's going to take nearly a decade to qualify, potential veterinary students have to have the right personality for the job. Veterinary practice can involve long hours, the making of life-and-death decisions, and the emotional realization that no matter how qualified and skilled you are, there are times when it's not possible to save an animal that's sick or has been severely injured. There are also times when it's necessary to euthanize an animal. Most veterinarians say that is the most difficult part of the job.

Further, apart from a deep caring and love of animals, a veterinarian needs to have excellent people skills, including a good "bedside manner" and the ability to be a good listener, to instill confidence and trust in those who are entrusting him or her with the care of their beloved pets. Above all, a great veterinarian needs to be very sensitive to a pet owner's grief.

The Long Road to a DVM

For a young person interested in a career in veterinary medicine, it's a good idea to start preparing while still in high school because the college classes that veterinary students need to pass are very science- and math-focused. Therefore, high school students who take chemistry, biology, physics, and calculus, as well as other science and math courses, will have an easier time in college. By taking these classes, they are also more likely to be accepted into the college of their choice.

After graduating from high school, the next step is to embark on a four-year undergraduate degree. Although most students who are admitted to veterinary school have earned a bachelor's degree, this is not always a requirement. However, these schools require all students to complete a number of specialized college classes.

Core subjects required vary from school to school but generally include zoology (the study of animals), biology (the study of life and living organisms), inorganic chemistry (the study of the synthesis and behavior of inorganic and organometallic compounds), physics (the study of matter and energy and their interactions), organic chemistry (the study of substances produced by living organisms), biochemistry (the chemistry of living things), genetics (the study of hereditary), microbiology (the study of living organisms that can be seen only under a microscope), and English. Increasingly, courses in general business management and career development have become a standard part of the curriculum to teach new graduates how to effectively run a practice.

The Association of American Veterinary Medical Colleges, based in Washington, DC, lists all the accredited colleges in this country and in Canada, as well as in other parts of the world. It also has the enrollment forms for these colleges on its website and thus is an excellent resource for background information and the requirements needed to enter this profession.

Admission is tough, and although schools may that state their GPA requirement is between 2.5 to 3.2, students with a 3.0 or higher are usually the ones accepted. You also stand a better chance if you are a resident of a state that has a public state-funded veterinary college because the admission policies at these schools favor state residents.

In addition to satisfying pre-veterinary course requirements, applicants must submit test scores from the Graduate Record Examination (GRE), the Veterinary College Admission Test (VCAT), or the Medical College Admission Test (MCAT), depending on the preference of the college to which they are applying.

The four years spent at a veterinary school are divided into two phases. The first phase is academic and involves two years of intense science-related study. Students take classes in anatomy, physiology, pathology, pharmacology, and microbiology. Much of the time is spent in classrooms and in college laboratories. In addition, there's a lot of research to be

◀ Veterinary students attend school for four years in addition to their undergraduate program.

done, assignments to be written, and study work for exams. Because of the heavy workload, it is common for veterinary students to work and study at all hours of the day and night, including weekends.

The second half of veterinary school is the clinical phase. Students continue attending classes to learn about animal diseases, surgery, and other scientific and medical subjects. They also begin to apply what they have learned by working in an animal hospital or clinic. Most veterinary schools have teaching hospitals right on their campuses. These are actual clinics where people can take their pets for treatment. Under the supervision of instructors (who are licensed veterinarians), students gain hands-on experience. They learn how to give examinations, diagnose and treat diseases and injuries, and perform surgery.

During the fourth and final year, students do clinical rotations, which allow them to work with many different types of veterinarians. They may observe and assist veterinary surgeons,

dermatologists, oncologists, and ophthalmologists, as well as other specialists. Students also experience veterinary specialties such as aquatic medicine, exotic-animal medicine, and zoo-animal medicine. In most cases, veterinary students are not required to complete an internship during their college training. However, many choose to do so to gain valuable work experience. Students who want to specialize in a particular type of animal or area of medicine must usually complete a one-year internship after veterinary school.

Before graduates can practice veterinary medicine, they must be licensed with the state in which they plan to work. This certifies them as a DVM or VMD. Then they may set up their own practice or join a practice with other veterinarians. Yet, even though they have finished school, their education does not end there. To keep up with the latest knowledge and technology, veterinarians must read scientific journals and participate in professional seminars and workshops. Many states also require veterinarians to take educational courses to keep their licenses current. There are also lots of annual veterinary conferences held around the country that keep those in the profession up to date on the latest state-of-the-art gadgets and surgical techniques.

Veterinary Technician/Technologist

Many observers liken some of the work that veterinary technicians and technologists do for a veterinarian in a clinic, including routine laboratory and clinical procedures, to that done by nurses for a physician in a human medical practice or hospital. However, they also point out that the technicians and technologists do more in a clinic than a nurse would in an office, including assisting in dentistry, radiology, and surgery.

Although they perform the same tasks, veterinary technicians and veterinary technologists have different levels of education. Veterinary technicians are required to study for a two-year associate degree from an American Veterinary Medical Association (AVMA)–accredited community college with a program in veterinary technology. Veterinary technologists sign on for a four-year

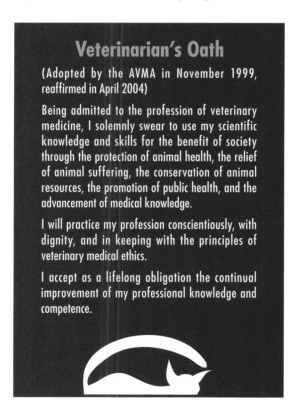

Veterinarian's Oath

(Adopted by the AVMA in November 1999, reaffirmed in April 2004)

Being admitted to the profession of veterinary medicine, I solemnly swear to use my scientific knowledge and skills for the benefit of society through the protection of animal health, the relief of animal suffering, the conservation of animal resources, the promotion of public health, and the advancement of medical knowledge.

I will practice my profession conscientiously, with dignity, and in keeping with the principles of veterinary medical ethics.

I accept as a lifelong obligation the continual improvement of my professional knowledge and competence.

▲ Being a veterinary technician is quite rewarding, and the requirements are not as daunting as those for becoming a veterinarian.

research facilities, where they administer medications orally or topically, prepare samples for laboratory examinations, and record information on an animal's genealogy, diet, weight, medications, food intake, and clinical signs of pain and distress. Other duties can include sterilizing laboratory equipment and providing postoperative care.

Because veterinarian technicians work alongside veterinarians, their work can also be physically demanding if they have to help restrain animals and emotionally stressful because they work directly with sick, injured, and abused animals, especially if the practice they work in has a care relationship with animals shelters and rescue organizations. In some animal hospitals, research facilities, and animal shelters, a veterinary technician is on duty twenty-four hours a day, which means that some may work night shifts.

According to the 2012–13 Occupational Outlook Handbook published by the US Bureau of Labor Statistics, the employment of veterinary technologists and technicians is expected to grow much faster than the average of all occupations through the year 2018. One of the reasons cited to spur this employment growth is that pet owners are becoming more affluent (because they are not spending money on human children) and, because of the humanization of pets, they are more willing to pay for advanced care. Furthermore, the rapidly growing number of cats as companion pets is expected to boost the demand for feline medicine and services. However, records continue to show

AVMA-accredited program. There are 131 AVMA-accredited veterinary technology programs in forty-four states. Students graduating from these programs can take their final credential exam, known as the Veterinary Technician National Examination, in any state in the country.

However, once they are working in their chosen field, they are both usually referred to as veterinary technicians.

Once qualified, their work can be in a private practice, animal hospital, or a research laboratory. Technologists and technicians usually begin work as trainees in routine positions under the direct supervision of a licensed veterinarian. In a private practice, as they gain more experience, they will perform various medical tests, such as urinalysis and blood counts, prepare tissue samples, and take blood samples, as well as assist veterinarians in a variety of tests and analyses involving the use of medical and diagnostic equipment. They will also assist with routine dental prophylaxis done on cats. Other duties can include taking and developing X-rays and providing specialized nursing care. They will also be allowed to obtain and record patients' case histories and discuss a pet's condition with its owners.

In addition to working in private practices and animal hospitals, veterinary technicians can work in

Pre-Studies for Vet Tech

Anyone interested in pursuing the vet tech career path is advised to take as many high school science, biology, and math courses as possible. Science courses taken beyond high school, in an associate's or bachelor's degree program, should emphasize practical skills in a clinical or laboratory setting.

Careers with Cats

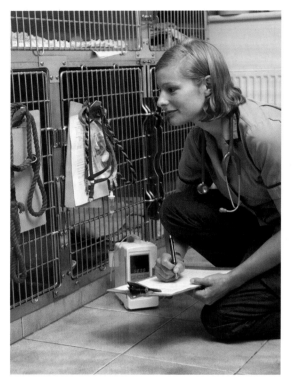

▲ A veterinary assistant may not do a lot of glamorous work, but they are essential to the smooth operation of a vet practice.

that dogs visit the veterinarian's office more often than cats do.

Veterinary Assistant

A veterinary assistant is someone who works in a veterinary office doing a variety of nonmedical tasks that are essential to the everyday working and functioning of a private practice or animal hospital. The position has neither educational requirements nor any national or state licensing procedures; the veterinary assistant learns the ropes through on-the-job training.

Typical duties include feeding, watering, monitoring, and exercising animals; cleaning and disinfecting work and cage areas; and sterilizing all surgical and laboratory equipment. For long-time employees, tasks can be extended to include limited postoperative care, the administration of medication both orally or topically, and the preparation of laboratory samples for examination under the supervision of either a veterinary technician or a veterinarian.

Animal Chiropractor

Chiropractic has always been an integral part of holistic health care for both people and their pets but was often considered an alternative approach at best, only to be undertaken if mainstream treatments failed. In the past decade, however, veterinarians have come to regard it as more mainstream, recommending such treatments for their patients and referring them to qualified animal chiropractors. Many veterinarians have even gone on to study this modality themselves.

The practice of chiropractic focuses on the relationship between structure (primarily the spine) and function (as coordinated by the nervous system) and how that relationship affects the preservation and restoration of health. It emphasizes the inherent recuperative power of the body to heal itself without the use of drugs or surgery.

The American Veterinary Chiropractic Association (AVCA) requires anyone wanting to study animal chiropractics to already be a qualified doctor of chiropractic and/or a doctor of veterinary medicine. Students of these professions currently enrolled in their last semester/trimester of study are allowed to enroll and learn this modality concurrently with their other studies.

Courses are offered by the Options for Animals College of Animal Chiropractic, a private postsecondary educational institution based in Wellsville, Kansas, and accredited by the Kansas Board of Regents and the US Department of Education.

The course consists of classroom and home study. Classroom study consists of a minimum of 210 hours of lecture and laboratory sessions. Classroom instruction is offered in a modular format; there are five modules, each module running for about four and a half days. Students average eight to ten hours of home study with each modular. All class and home study progress is monitored by written and practical examinations. The five modules must be completed within a two-year period; some students

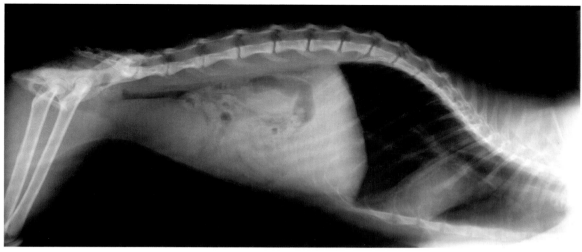
▲ Animal chiropractors learn to interpret radiographs and use them to decide on appropriate treatment.

go straight through, however, and complete the modules within five weeks.

The practice of animal chiropractic includes taking a thorough case history consisting of subjective information from the owner and information determined from examinations and X-rays, as well as previous diagnoses and therapies. The animal chiropractor will do a hands-on examination of the patient prior to any spinal, extremity, or cranial adjustments. Animal chiropractors usually work with horses, dogs, and cats. This type of treatment has been found to benefit animals that have sustained an injury or suffer from arthritis.

Animal chiropractors usually go to their patients' homes or, if they work with a veterinarian, will make special arrangements to treat your cat at the veterinarian's office.

Feline Well-Being

Apart from of the trend toward pet humanization, there is a genuine interest in trying to understand our feline friends and learn more about why they do what they do in our homes. Consequently, feline behaviorists have an important role to play in everyday cat care, as do groomers and animal massage therapists, who can help improve a cat's general health and well-being through the services and treatments they have to offer.

Animal Behaviorist

The work of an animal behaviorist with regard to domestic cats involves observing and treating feline behavior problems that exist in the home environment. Typical problems include intercat aggression, destructive scratching, and inappropriate urination. Cats who display such behavioral issues are often relinquished to shelters and, sadly, if it happens to be a kill shelter, they are euthanized. The work of an animal behaviorist is to resolve these issues and help the cat remain in her home.

The Animal Behavior Society (ABS) was the first organization in the United States to offer a certification program for applied animal behaviorists giving the applicants the right to call themselves Certified Applied Animal Behaviorists. There are now two other ways to get certified.

The International Association of Animal Behavior Consultants (IAABC) is an international organization headquartered in Pennsylvania that represents the professional interests of behavior consultants throughout the world. Certified members qualify in one or more species-specific divisions, including dogs, cats, horses, and parrots. All IAABC-certified members are required to procure a minimum of thirty continuing education units (CEUs) every two years, beginning with the year of certification, to ensure that they remain up to date in their education. At the time of this

▲ While some groomers work exclusively with cats, most also groom dogs.

writing, there are only fifty-two AABC-certified applied animal behaviorists in the United States.

The third option is to study to be a veterinary behaviorist and be certified through the American College of Veterinary Behaviorists. A veterinary behaviorist is a veterinarian with a special interest in animal behavior. Veterinary behaviorists have either completed residency programs after graduating from veterinary school or have done additional training and passed exams set by the American College of Veterinary Behaviorists. These veterinary behaviorists are known as board-certified diplomates of the American College of Veterinary Behaviorists.

A veterinary behaviorist is licensed to diagnose and treat problems in animals, whether they are medical or behavioral, and consequently can prescribe drugs and psychotropic medications (tranquilizers and antidepressants).

Animal behaviorists work by visiting the home and working with both the cat and the owner. Alternatively, they can dispense advice telephonically for a fee and follow up with subsequent phone calls. Some veterinary schools also run behavior clinics.

Each of the three organizations listed operate comprehensive websites detailing educational information and links to their member directories. These are the Animal Behavior Society (www.animalbehaviorsociety.org), the International Association of Animal Behavior Consultants (www.iaabc.org), and the American College of Veterinary Behaviorists (www.dacvb.org).

Groomer

Not only are professional groomers responsible for maintaining a pet's overall appearance from head to tail, but by the very nature of the profession, they also have the best opportunity to evaluate a pet's skin and coat, ears, dental hygiene, and nails and must be able to recognize any possible medical issues and convey this information to the client, suggesting that they seek veterinary attention. Therefore, individuals entering this profession should have a good working knowledge of the health and anatomy of the animals they plan to groom. Groomers should also have great people skills because it's important to establish a good relationship with a pet's owner.

Initially, groomers only specialized in dogs, but,

over the years, many have started to take on feline clients, too. However, because the number of cats that visit groomers are still a minority, plus the fact that owners of show cats usually prefer to do their own grooming, it may be difficult to make a living exclusively as a cat groomer. A lot will depend on your location; that is, whether you live in a community that will want such grooming services. There are some feline-only grooming salons and mobile feline grooming services located around the country; do a search online to get an idea of the places where they are doing business. As more people become aware that such services exist, there is definitely room for growth in this industry.

The first cat grooming standards specified within the grooming industry were set by the National Cat Grooming Institute of America (NCGIA) in 2007 to meet the needs of already certified dog groomers wishing to practice safer and better quality cat grooming, as well as for people wishing to specialize in feline-only grooming services. The NCGIA offers hands-on instruction as well as video, lecture, and written materials. Certification is earned upon completion of the hands-on classes and the exams that have been created to meet those standards. The course material covers a wide range of subjects including feline temperaments, coat types, colors, and patterns. The grooming elements include how to perform breed-specific face trims, the best order in which to apply a grooming routine, knowledge of grooming tools and equipment, and advice on operating a feline-only grooming service.

The grooming school run by the NCGIA is situated in Greenville, South Carolina. The school is fully equipped with state-of-the-art grooming equipment necessary to groom cats effectively. The best way to train is to attend a two-week course offered at the school. However, students can also

get their certification by attending workshops combined with a home study program.

Both written and practical exams can be taken at the end of the course or at any of the two three-day workshops held by the organization throughout the year. Written exams can also be taken at any trade show at which the NCGIA is in attendance. Some trade shows also allow for practical exams to be administered as well.

Certification with the accreditation of certified master cat groomer is also available through the Professional Cat Groomers Association of America (PCGAA). To obtain this title, you have to take ten courses and pass ten exams, with a passing grade of 85 percent or higher. The course can be studied at home, and examinations are conducted at the PCGAA Headquarters in Fairview Park, Ohio, at private grooming salons, and at other locations, and they are held throughout the year.

Because no governmental authority requires a groomer to have a license to practice, another way to learn the art of grooming is to get hands-on training in a salon as an assistant. This informal apprenticeship can last on average from a month

▶ Groomers often work in conjunction with pet boutiques and superstores, animal clinics, and pet hotels.

to three months. Trainees start with simple duties, such as bathing and drying, and graduate to learning how to use scissors, combs, razors, and nail clippers.

Once you have received adequate training, you can go to work for a feline-only salon, go to work for a general pet salon and become its feline grooming specialist, or, if you have the means, open up your own feline grooming salon.

Groomers often work in conjunction with pet boutiques and superstores, animal clinics, and pet hotels. Consequently, they are often required to be a jack of all trades, answering phones, selling products, and, most importantly, dealing with the people on the other end of the leash or, in the case of most feline clients, those toting the carrier.

However, a groomer who would like to specialize in cats would be well advised to consider operating a mobile grooming salon because many cat owners prefer that the groomer come to them rather than have their cats sit in a cage in a grooming salon. It's important to weigh up the costs of running such a van versus the costs of renting and maintaining premises. State-of-the-art mobile grooming vans are expensive to purchase. The success of any grooming business will depend on the location of the premises or, in the case of the mobile groomer, what competition exists from a standard grooming store. Mobile groomers can potentially do well in small towns, where there is not much competition and where neighbors with pets may get together and book the groomer to come to their street on a certain day.

Whatever avenue you pursue for your business, make sure that you have liability insurance. One of the advantages of membership in a professional organization is that it offers advice about insurance plans. (The National Dog Groomers Association of America has a special Professional Liability plan that insures its members against claims resulting from the performance of a member's professional services.)

Another advantage is that you have direct access to current information in the profession, which includes active message boards to share ideas and learn from others.

Massage Therapist

As with groomers, cat massage therapists have seen a rise in opportunities thanks to the growth in the pet care industry and the humanization of our pets. Cat massage therapists often combine several therapies in their treatments. All these therapies can be learned through study classes at pet massage schools and workshops held around the country. Many pet massage therapists work in conjunction with groomers or simply attend to their own clients' needs. Some work from home and others make house calls. In addition to general coat care, many groomers offer their clients massage as well as other services, such as reiki and Tellington touch therapy.

The International Association of Animal Massage and Bodywork was founded as a forum for animal massage and bodywork professionals to

▼ Professional pet sitting is one of the fastest-growing home-based businesses in the world.

▲ Most pet spas cater to dogs, but there are certainly opportunities for cat-focused spas in some communities.

network and support each other. The organization covers complementary and alternative veterinary medicine practices (such as acupressure, reiki, polarity, sound/music, healing touch, flower essence, aromatherapy, color and light therapies, and animal communication) and provides its members with information relating to the legal requirements to practice in all fifty states. It also lists training facilities around the country.

Caretakers and Hotel Owners and Staff

Small and large businesses have arisen to meet the needs of cat owners who must travel and leave their cats behind or simply want to know someone is watching out for their felines during the day while the owners are at work. There are lots of opportunities.

Cat Sitter

More and more cat lovers who are not keen to take their cats out of their home environment look to employ the services of a professional cat sitter to take care of their pets' needs on a daily basis. From a pet owner's standpoint, working with a professional gives peace of mind, knowing that such a caretaker will treat the job seriously and not absentmindedly leave doors open (as perhaps a friend or relative might) and allow their feline charge to escape.

In-home pet care provides a proven opportunity for entrepreneurs who love working with and caring for companion animals. Consequently, professional pet sitting is one of the fastest-growing home-based businesses in the world.

Pet Sitters International (PSI) is the world's largest educational association for professional pet sitters; it represents more than 8,000 independent professional pet-sitting businesses in the United States, Canada, and abroad. The association helps bring success to its members by giving them access to affordable bonding and liability insurance and to educational resources through the organization's accreditation program. Another organization that offers training help and advice about this profession is the National Association of Professional Pet Sitters (NAPPS), a national nonprofit US trade association for individuals with pet-sitting businesses. Its members are both full- and part-time pet sitters. Members are listed in the NAPPS referral network, which can be accessed by pet owners online or via phone. Listing in the referral network is a complimentary benefit. Associates can also purchase bonding, liability, and health insurance at discounted rates.

Some cat owners require you to simply check in on their pets daily, attend to their food and litter box requirements, and spend some quality time with

Pet Relocation Specialist

A pet-relocation specialist is first and foremost a very experienced travel agent registered with the various travel associations. He or she specializes in the relocation of pets around the country and around the world. These specialists handle the documentation and shipping processes from start to finish. They ship pets traveling on their own, as well as plan for passengers and pets relocating together. The job involves lots of paperwork and needs an in-depth knowledge of national and international laws relating to domestic pets, not to mention airline travel policies and medical records required.

A pet relocation specialist needs to be an accredited member of the International Airlines Travel Agent Network, an industry association responsible for the standard international codes for airlines, airports, hotels, cities, and car rental firms; a member of the Airlines Reporting Corporation, an airline-owned company serving the travel industry with financial services, data products and services, and ticket distribution; and also a member of the International Pet Animal Transportation Association, Inc. Pet-relocation specialists also require a handling license from the US Department of Agriculture. The training is on the job and involves building up excellent contacts within the industry. Pet-relocation specialists must have lots of patience and great people skills to handle overanxious cat lovers, especially when it comes to travel delays and unforeseen problems.

the pets. Other owners prefer a pet sitter who is prepared to move in and take on the responsibility of the entire household, including the pet's needs.

Some cat sitters also perform services such as visiting elderly pet owners on a daily basis to help with cat care. Cat-sitting is the type of profession that can be sculpted to suit your needs and the needs of your clients. Being an independent contractor allows you to work at your own pace and be selective about the jobs you are prepared to undertake.

If you want to go in a different direction, rather than being a sole operator you could run a cat-sitting service and employ people to work for you. Some existing pet-sitting businesses offer franchise opportunities that allow you to establish such a service in your neighborhood. The advantage of this is that the parent company helps organize the necessary insurance and licenses that you may need to operate and is on hand to offer business advice and allow you to benefit from the company's expertise. However, running a franchise operation does mean an ongoing financial link to the franchisor. Read the fine print.

Cat Hotel/Day Care Proprietors and Staff

One of the positive effects of United States' becoming such a pet-friendly nation has been the introduction of fabulous cat hotels and day care facilities around the country. The days of sterile boarding places are definitely over. Running a cat hotel can be fun for a cat lover, and, depending where you operate, you may have celebrity cats like Jay Leno's fur kid checking in when their famous owners have to travel and are unable to take their pets with them.

Running a cat hotel can also be financially rewarding. However, the success of such an operation will depend on the proprietor's business background and experience, possibly within the leisure industry. A cat hotel can operate in either a commercial or suburban setting depending on the local laws appertaining to running businesses in an urban area. It is also important to have a relationship with a veterinarian close by who will be on call 24/7 should an emergency situation arise.

Cat "suites" consist of individual enclosed areas and must be big enough to house a sleeping zone, food and water, and, of course, a litter box. Many of the upmarket facilities offer kitty condos consisting of two or three levels inside the cage whereby the cat's litter box is completely separated from its food station and bed. Some cat hotels provide TV sets playing cat-sitting videos and even have sealed aquariums so that feline guests can enjoy the entertainment value without eating the "talent."

Many such establishments are now installing video cams so that pet parents can check in on their felines for themselves from wherever they may be.

There must also be an enclosed area with kitty condos and toys where cats can be taken out to stretch and play under strict supervision. Some establishments offer quite elaborate play areas with bird aviaries, large aquariums, and tall trees, where feline guests are offered both mental and physical stimulation.

Although most cat hotels take guests for overnight stays, many will offer day care facilities to watch your cat. Any cat hotel advertising such a service will definitely attract business. Cat owners who are moving often need to put their cat in a secure room during the process, and this is definitely an option.

Most cat hotels ask their owners to provide their own food. So, you will need a well-organized kitchen facility to store and serve the food and enough refrigeration space to store any medications that guests may be required to take during their stay.

There is no limit to the ideas that you can add to your services to make cat owners feel comfortable about having their cat in your care, such as taking photographs and putting them up on your website and even writing a blog about the feline guests. The sky is the limit.

No matter how big or small the establishment, you will need to employ caretakers who love cats to help with daily tasks such as feeding and litter box duty, as well as with daily brushing, during which time they are able to interact with the cats so that they are not isolated from human companionship during their stay. If you are not in a position to set yourself up in a business, you can still work in one. In addition to caretakers to assist with daily tasks, a hotel will need to have someone sleeping on the premises at night, too. Working for such an establishment would probably be at the going hourly pay rate. However, if you enjoy working with animals and people, working in such an establishment is worthwhile considering as a second job.

Petrepreneurs in Commerce

One of the fastest growing segments in the pet industry relates to cats. Toys and gadgets for feline enrichment and wonderful housewares such as

▲ Gift stores that sell cat-themed merchandise as well as cat accessories have grown in popularity all over the country.

therapeutic pet beds and drinking fountains are popular items, along with pet-centric clothing and accessories for humans. Commercial ventures that cater to this market include traditional pet boutiques, general gift stores that may range from a cart in a mall to a fully fledged storefront, and, of course, Internet-based enterprises.

Pet Boutique/Store Owners and Staff

For anyone with a flair for retail and a love of cats, running a pet boutique or a store specializing in feline products and feline-themed merchandise means being surrounded by people besotted with cats all day long.

These days, pet retail stores serve the dual function of selling cat-related merchandise and educating the cat-loving public about the products they sell. Thus, entrepreneurs entering this field must have an in-depth knowledge about everything on their shelves. That's especially true when it comes to cat care products such as waterless shampoos and hairball remedies and foods. Ever since the pet food recall of 2007, cat owners are looking for more information about the foods they are serving their pets, which means the retailer needs to know a lot about the ingredients and manufacturing process and the different types of diets available.

Fortunately, most cat product and food manufacturers understand this thirst for knowledge and are providing a good deal of educational materials for storeowners to further educate their staff and, ultimately, cat owners.

Many pet-store owners work in conjunction with rescue and welfare organizations and host adoption days. Consequently, they also play an important role in helping pets find forever homes. Innovative entrepreneurs can hold contests, fashion shows, and special customer days to raise money for their favorite causes and thus assist those working in cat rescue and welfare.

Gift stores that sell cat-themed merchandise as well as cat accessories and basics have grown in popularity all over the country. Such business enterprises usually do very well when situated in an area with a lot of foot traffic or tourists.

Numerous pet-specific and gift trade shows are held around the country at regular intervals throughout the year, which makes it easy for a retailer to keep up with the latest trends and ideas and to stock the best selection of merchandise available.

If you are not in a position to own a store, there are certainly jobs for staff. Like the owners, staff members will need to be knowledgeable about the merchandise to meet the needs of the cat-loving public. A dedicated shop owner will go out of his or her way to ensure that those employed are properly trained and knowledgeable and thus an asset to the business and the pet community at large.

Manufacturer of Cat Products

The expression "necessity is the mother of invention" certain applies to the pet industry because many cat lovers have invented some fabulous toys and accessories by simply studying their own felines' wants and needs. Many a cottage industry has grown into a major manufacturing concern. Larger conglomerates have been known to then step in and buy up such companies. There is nothing to stop you starting small but thinking big!

Whether you are manufacturing toys, farming kitty grass, or designing unusually shaped scratchers or kitty condos, this is a wonderful opportunity to be working for the benefit of cats in general. Such businesses also usually have a few feline "staff members," too, whose sole job it is to test these products and snooze.

With the Internet, small start-up operations these days have the advantage of running their own stores online before venturing to sell their ideas to brick-and-mortar stores via distributors. The many cat shows held around the country on a weekly basis usually have a kitty mall and give start-up vendors the opportunity to take a booth. Craft fares, swap meets, and local pet expos are other places where it's possible to launch new products and ideas.

Millions of Cats

According to the American Pet Products Association's 2013–2014 National Pet Owners Survey, the number of home owners in America who have a pet continues to grow and currently stands at 82.9 million households. And, of that number, 45.3 million households have cats. Because there are on average 2.11 cats per household, this translates into 95.6 million cats with loving owners in the United States. This number of course excludes the feral cat colonies that are cared for by caring cat lovers and the numbers of cats in shelters looking to be adopted into loving homes. The same survey also highlights that pet owners have higher household annual incomes, compared to non-pet owning households and that the number of cat owners who buy gifts for their cats is also increasing, with $23 per gift being the average amount spent.

Animal Protection and Advocacy

Being involved with animal welfare and advocacy work can be a very rewarding way to make the world a better place for cats and all animals in general. Humane societies, city animal control units and shelters, as well as privately run animal welfare and nonprofit organizations offer a variety of career opportunities. Some careers can be very hands-on. Other jobs, such as a spokesperson, educator, or even professional fundraiser, collectively play an important role in the world of animal welfare.

Animal Control Officer

Cities across the United States, both big and small, have an animal control unit or at least one animal control officer who functions under the city's police or health department.

Gone is the stereotype of the animal control officer as a cruel inhumane "animal catcher" whose job it was to rid the streets of loose animals wandering about. Today, the role of the control officer is varied and includes reuniting lost pets with their owners and mediating neighborhood disputes relating to dogs and cats. Animal control officers investigate (dog) bite cases, cases of cruelty and neglect, and pick up dead or injured animals as well as strays.

Unfortunately, many city animal shelters or pounds still euthanize unwanted pets and thus there is still a certain stigma attached to the job. However, dedicated animal control officers are working within the system to stop the general euthanization of unclaimed pets and trying to change city ordinances that make it complicated for ordinary citizens to care for feral cat colonies in a quest to make the United States a no-kill country.

In their duties as investigators working to protect the health and safety of both people and animals, animal control officers need to be well versed in their city's local laws and ordinances, which they have the power to enforce. They can also make arrests.

Although many cities still offer their animal control officers on-the-job training, the National Animal Control Association (NACA) conducts three levels of training workshops, giving candidates certification as an animal control officer. This certification is now widely recognized across the country. The NACA's mission is "preserving the human/animal bond by insisting on responsible animal ownership." Many states are now insisting that their officers have this accreditation.

According to the NACA, animal control officers have much more contact with the public than other law enforcement officers. Therefore, officers must have great people skills for their day-to-day dealings with the public and be able to present a good image for the job that they do.

Animal Shelter Manager

An animal shelter manager wears many hats. This person is responsible for the day-to- day running of the shelter, supervising the work of shelter assistants and volunteers, and coordinating the treatment

◄ The duties of an animal control officer include reuniting owners with lost pets and investigating cases of animal cruelty.

provided by outside veterinarians and veterinary assistants who come to the shelter to perform procedures. Overseeing the training of shelter staff and volunteers is often part of the job as well. The job description also includes organizing adoption days and general fund-raising events. General office management experience is a definite advantage for this type of job.

The job also entails a lot of paperwork. This includes documenting the number of animals being brought to the shelter and adopted from it, all spay and neuter procedures and other medical care, and the number of animals being euthanized. Animal shelter managers also provide paperwork concerning animal abuse and neglect to local government agencies and prepare evidence for court cases.

The manager has many interactions with the general public and numerous ones with the city's animal control officers, other city and government agencies, and nonprofit animal organizations. This means that he or she needs to have good people skills. A shelter manager also needs to have a good public persona because he or she may be called upon to deal directly with the media.

City Shelter Attendant

The work of a shelter attendant or caretaker in a city-run animal shelter can be varied, with specific duties determined by how big the shelter is and how many people it employs. Generally, the duties

entail keeping the animals fed and groomed and their holding areas spotlessly clean. Attendants may also perform basic office tasks, such as answering the phones and handling the paperwork filed by potential adoptees. In addition to attending to the basic needs of the animals, caretakers at shelters keep records of the animals, including information about any tests or treatments performed on them.

City-run shelters have a working relationship with a veterinarian clinic to spay and neuter cats. Because most shelters do not have a full-time veterinary staff, shelter attendants may be required to take care of animals before and after surgery, checking on them and seeing that they are comfortable. As they gain more experience, they may be

▼ If you have a flair for training your cat to do tricks, you might consider becoming a professional trainer.

▲ A worker at an animal shelter normally will feed the animals, give them medication, clean cages, and help socialize them.

required to help with postoperative care, as well as the care of injured animals that enter the shelter. Experienced caretakers may vaccinate newly admitted animals under the direction of a veterinarian or veterinary technician and euthanize seriously ill, severely injured, or unwanted animals.

Shelter attendants have direct contact with the public both in the front office, dealing with members of the public dropping off unwanted animals or strays they have found, and behind the scenes where the animals are housed, accompanying people looking for their lost pets or looking for a pet to adopt. An attendant also may act as a co-coordinator overseeing volunteers working in the shelter. Many shelter attendants start out as volunteers and learn the workings of an animal shelter through on-the-job training. Many of the courses offered by the National Animal Control Association also stand potential shelter attendants in good stead in learning how to deal with the public and how to handle animal abuse situations.

Spokesperson, Educator, PR Officer

Many animal organizations such as the American Society for the Prevention of Cruelty to Animals (ASPCA), major adoption groups such as the North Shore Animal League America, and sanctuaries such as Best Friends Animal Sanctuary offer a variety of jobs such as public relations officer, spokespersons (although this often calls for a celebrity or someone with a recognizable face associated with cats), and educators.

Educators are often former teachers who have had classroom experience and can hold workshops and tour schools talking to children of all ages. The public relations field typically attracts people with a degree in communications. However, any experience of working with animals or any animal-related qualifications, such a veterinary technician or animal control officer, are taken into consideration. These organizations usually have a job section on their websites that details the type of work offered and the type of educational background and work experience they require.

Entertainment and the Media

These days, it's difficult to miss cats on TV, in print advertisements, and in the movies. They are everywhere! As they have moved up the ladder from being a mere household pet to being a beloved family member, they are being included in the entertainment and advertising world to show off

▲ Opportunities to work at wild cat sanctuaries exist, but they are rare and usually require specialized training.

their new position in pop culture. If you have aspirations to be part of the entertainment or advertising world and you love cats, here are some career options to consider.

Cat Trainer

Cat training in the entertainment field has come a long way since the 1980s, when famed Hollywood animal trainer Ray Berwick outlined a simple clicker training method for teaching show tricks to cats. Other well-known cat trainers include Karen Payne, owner and trainer of Princess Kitty ("The Smartest Cat in the World"), who could do more than 100 tricks on command and had a successful stage and TV career. Although there are numerous training academies and courses to teach trainers of dogs and exotic animals, there's still no generally recognized professional certification for cat trainers.

The Animal Behavior Institute offers an online program that includes specialized coursework in cat training and behavioral management. The more viable options available to cat owners nationwide, however, are still the self-help books and DVDs that promote positive-enforcement and clicker-training methods as training tools.

You will need to gain a good deal of experience and be out there training for a while before considering a career in cat training in the entertainment field. Novice trainers can earn excellent experience volunteering at cat adoption agencies and shelters using their techniques to help make cats more adoptable. Another avenue to put your cat training talents to work would be to start your own business and make house calls to train cat lovers how to work with their cats.

As you are mastering your cat trick training skills (and earning the money to finance your dreams), you will need to gain contacts in the industry. This is by no means easy. Often, animal trainers give demonstrations at cat shows and pet expos, so this would be a starting point in your networking. Among those contacts should be someone who can refer you to an agent; you will need an agent to approach studios on your behalf. And you will need to make a reel—film proof of your work—for the agent to submit to possible employers, which means finding a good videographer.

Many pet talent agencies offer training classes, and it is a good idea to approach such agencies and see if they are hiring. Breaking into the advertising world and film industry as a cat trainer is extremely difficult, but sometimes opportunities open up. Although film studios have their own trainers on contract, they do have a call for freelance cat trainers on set from time to time. Watch the job section on Craigslist. Studios and TV networks often put out a call on this platform, and all you have to do is respond. You just never know!

If you prefer to make your own opportunities and have the financing, consider a different approach. With the increase in the number of cats appearing in TV commercials, movies, and print advertisements, you could open your own cat talent agency, like Hollywood Paws in Los Angeles, and hire behaviorists on staff to offer in-house feline training.

Cat Photographer

We've all loved and admired those cute "chocolate box" photographs of cats and kittens. There's no question that being a successful cat photographer takes a true love of cats, an understanding of the feline mind, and lots of patience!

Clearly, if you don't already have it, you need to gain an in-depth knowledge of photography, especially as it's done in all of its wondrous forms today. There are numerous colleges that specialize in photography classes and teach students all aspects of the profession (including how to set up and manage a successful studio), as well as colleges with fine arts degree programs. Pet photographers usually start out taking photographs of their own pets to build a portfolio to show to others.

Before running off to enroll in a course, however, you need to determine whether you have the makings of a cat photographer. It takes a certain kind of person to work with animals, especially cats. You will need to build a rapport with cat parents and their doting fur kids. Cat parents with stars in their eyes behave just like parents trying to push their children to stardom. Cats, unless specially trained, will not do much on command. You will need to know the best ways to get certain shots and keep going until you get them. That means you have to have infinite patience! A cat photographer is often required to go to the client's home because pets, particularly cats, are much more relaxed in their own surroundings. The types of assignments are varied from private portrait sessions, magazine and advertising shoots, and pet catalogs to events such as cat shows. Most photographers are self-employed.

The spinoff, if you are successful, is that you can start producing your own pet calendars and stationery items. Then there are gift books, which are always perennial sellers. Make sure you get cat owners to sign releases so that you can use their pets' photographs.

▶ Being a successful cat photographer takes a true love of cats, an understanding of the feline mind, and lots of patience!

Chapter 1

"How Humans Created Cats," Rebecca J. Rosen. *Scientific American.* Dec. 2013. www.theatlantic.com/technology/ archive/2013/12/how-humans-created-cats/282391/

International Society for Endangered Cats www.wildcatconservation.org/

National Geographic Big Cats Initiative animals.nationalgeographic.com/animals/ big-cats-initiative/

Chapter 2

Alley Cat Allies
7920 Norfolk Ave. #600
Bethesda, MD 20814
Phone: 240-482-1980
www.alleycat.org

Animal Rescue League Boston
1 Appleton Street
Boston, MA 02116
Phone: 617-426-9170
E-mail: info@arlboston.org
www.arlboston.org

ASPCA
424 E. 92nd St
New York, NY 10128-6804
Phone: 888-666-2279
www.aspca.org/

Best Friends Animal Society
5001 Angel Canyon Rd.
Kanab, UT 84741
Phone: 435- 644-2001
www.bestfriends.org

Bideawee
410 East 38th Street
New York, NY 10016
Phone: 866-262-8133
www.bideawee.org/

The Blue Bell Foundation for Cats
20982 Laguna Canyon Road
Laguna Beach, CA 92651
Phone: 949-494-1586
www.bluebellcats.org/

Celia Hammond Animal Trust
High Street
Wadhurst
East Sussex
TN5 6AG
United Kingdom
Phone: 01892 783367
E-mail: headoffice@celiahammond.org
www.celiahammond.org/

Feral Cat Coalition
9528 Miramar Road
PMB 160
San Diego, California 92126
www.feralcat.com/

Hoarding of Animals Research Consortium
vet.tufts.edu/hoarding/index.html

Homeless Cat Network
P.O. Box 6
San Carlos, CA 94070-0006
Phone: 650-286-9013
E-mail: info@homelesscatnetwork.com
www.homelesscatnetwork.com/

North Shore Animal League
25 Davis Ave
Port Washington, NY 11050
Phone: 516-883-7575
www.AnimalLeague.com

Project Bay Cat
Email: ProjectBayCat@yahoo.com
www.facebook.com/ProjectBayCat

Chapter 3

Catster
www.catster.com

"Feline Folktails – Cats in Folklore and Superstition," Sarah Hartwell. 2010. messybeast.com/folktails.htm

Grumpy Cat
www.grumpycats.com/

"The Role of Cats in Myth and Religion," Sarah Hartwell. 2011. messybeast.com/feline-deity.htm

Romeo the Cat
www.romeothecat.com/

Simon's Cat
www.simonscat.com/

Sockington
www.sockington.org/

Chapter 4

American Cat Fanciers Association (ACFA, United States)
P.O. Box 1949
Nixa, MO 65714-1949
Phone: 417-725-1530
Email: acfa@aol.com
www.acfacat.com/

Cat Fanciers' Association (CFA, United States, Europe, Asia),
260 East Main Street
Alliance, OH 44601
Phone: 330-680-4070
www.cfainc.org/

The Feline Genome Project
www.vetmed.ucdavis.edu/Catgenetics/ Feline%20Genome%20Project/Feline_ Genome_Project.html

Governing Council of the Cat Fancy (GCCF,United Kingdom)
5 King's Castle Business Park
The Drove
Bridgwater
Somerset
TA6 4AG
United Kingdom
Tel: +44 (0)1278 427575
 www.gccfcats.org/

The International Cat Association (TICA, International)
PO Box 2684
Harlingen, TX 78551
Phone: 956-428-8046
E-mail: inquiries@tica.org
www.tica.org/

Sveriges Kattklubbars Riksförbund (SVERAK, Sweden)
The National Cat Association of Sweden
www.sverak.se/

Chapter 5

Fanciers Breeders Referral List
www.breedlist.com/index.html

Specialty Purebred Cat Rescue
www.purebredcatrescue.org/

National Abyssinian Cat Rescue
www.abyssinian-rescue.com/

Abyssinian Cat Association
www.theabycat.com/

American Bobtail Breeders' Club
www.americanbobtailbreeders.com/

Australian Mist Breed Council
www.australianmist.info/

The International Bengal Cat Society
www.bengalcat.com/

National Alliance of Burmese Breeders
www.burmesecat.org/

Burmilla Cat Club
www.burmilla.co.uk/

Planet Devon (Devon Rex information site)
planetdevon.com/

Korat World
www.koratworld.com/

LaPerm Cat Club of Great Britain
www.laperm.co.uk/

Maine Coon Adoptions
mainecoonadoptions.com/index.shtml

Norwegian Forest Cat Fanciers' Association
www.forestcats.net/

Ocicat Info
www.ocicatinfo.com/

Persian Cats
www.persian-cats.com/

Persian and Himalayan Cat Rescue
persiancats.org/

Official Pixiebob Website
www.pixie-bob.org/

RagaMuffin Associated Group
www.ragamuffingroup.com/

Savannahcat.com
www.savannahcat.com/public/index.php

Scottish Fold Rescue, Inc.
scottishfoldrescue.homestead.com/

Siamese Cat Rescue Center
va.siameserescue.org/

Siberian Cat Rescue Group
siberiancatrescue.com/

Snowshoe Cat Club
www.snowshoecatclub.com/

Sokokecat.org
www.sokokecat.org/

Sphynx Cat Dot Com
www.sphynxcats.com/

Tonkinese Breed Association
www.tonkinesebreedassociation.org/

…about Toygers
www.toygers.org/about.html

Turkish Van Cat Club
www.turkishvancatclub.co.uk/index.html

Chapter 6

"Tips for the First 30 Days of Cat Adoption"
www.petfinder.com/cats/bringing-a-cat-home/tips-for-first-30-days-cat/

"Top Ten Things to Do Before You Bring Your New Cat Home"
www.aspca.org/adopt/adoption-tips/top-10-things-do-you-bring-your-new-cat-home

Chapter 7

"Choosing the Right Cat for You"
http://www.humanesociety.org/animals/cats/tips/choosing_cat.html

Hybrid Law
www.hybridlaw.com/

Petfinder
www.petfinder.com

Chapter 8

Animal Poison Control
Emergency Phone Number: 888-426-4435
www.aspca.org/pet-care/animal-poison-control

"Cat-Proof Your Home in 12 Easy Steps"
www.humanesociety.org/animals/cats/tips/cat_proofing_your_house.html

"Catproof Your Yard"
www.instructables.com/id/Catproof-Your-Yard/

"Common Plant Questions and Answers"
www.catchannel.com/care/safety/article_6027.aspx

"How to Make Cat Toys"
www.wikihow.com/Make-Cat-Toys

"Pet Theft"
www.paws.org/pet-theft.html

"Plants and Your Cat"
www.cfainc.org/catcare/householdhazards/toxicplants.aspx

"Smoking and Your Cat"
www.catdoctor.com/dr.-mcfarland-s-information-center/smoking-and-your-cat.html

"Toxic and Non-Toxic Plants"
www.aspca.org/pet-care/animal-poison-control/toxic-and-non-toxic-plants

"What to Do if Your Pet Is Poisoned"
www.aspca.org/pet-care/animal-poison-control/what-do-if-your-pet-poisoned

Chapter 9

"Acupuncture for Cats," Diana Waldhuber
www.petmd.com/cat/wellness/evr_ct_acunpuncture_for_cats

American Veterinary Chiropractor Association
www.animalchiropractic.org/

Association of Feline Practitioners Veterinarian Finder
www.catvets.com/cat-owners/find-vets-and-practices

"Benefits of Cat Massage"
www.petfinder.com/cats/cat-care/cat-massage/

International Veterinary Acupuncture Society
www.ivas.org/

Small Animal Massage
www.smallanimalmassage.com/index.asp

Ten Best Pet Insurance list at Consumeradvocate.org
www.consumersadvocate.org/pet-insurance/best-pet-insurance.html?matchtype=e&keyword=pet%20insurance&adpos=1t2&subid=google&gclid=CPiE0f6qx70CFZJj7Aod-0EAtQ

Chapter 10

Ear Care
www.aspca.org/pet-care/cat-care/ear-care

Find a Groomer
www.findagroomer.com/

"How to Find a Good Groomer"
www.petfinder.com/dogs/dog-grooming/
how-to-find-a-good-groomer/

"How to Trim Your Cat's Nails"
www.wikihow.com/Trim-Your-Cat%27s-Nails

Chapter 11

Cat Nutrition
www.catnutrition.org/

FDA Consumer Complaint Coordinators
www.fda.gov/Safety/ReportaProblem/
ConsumerComplaintCoordinators/

"Feeding Your Cat"
www.vet.cornell.edu/FHC/health_
resources/FeedYourCat.cfm

"Feeding Your Cat: Know the Basics of
Feline Nutrition," Leslie A. Pierson, DVM,
Feb. 2013
www.catinfo.org/

Feline Nutrition Education Society
feline-nutrition.org/

"Making Cat Food," Leslie A. Pierson,
DVM
www.catinfo.org/?link=makingcatfood

Chapter 12

Declawing.com
www.declawing.com/

"Feline Vision: How Cats See the World,"
Tina Ghose, Oct. 2012
www.livescience.com/40459-what-do-cats-
see.html

"A Rational Look at Declawing"
www.bornfreeusa.org/facts.
php?more=1&p=357

Chapters 13 to 18

"Abscesses in Cats"
www.petmd.com/cat/conditions/skin/c_ct_
abscessation

"Allergic Dermatitis in Cats"
www.pethealthnetwork.com/cat-health/
allergic-dermatitis-cats

American Heartworm Society
www.heartwormsociety.org/

American Veterinary Medicine Association
1931 North Meacham Road, Suite 100
Schaumburg, IL 60173-4360
Phone: 800-248-2862
www.avma.org/Pages/home.aspx

"Asthma"
www.aspca.org/pet-care/cat-care/asthma

"Cancer in Cats: Types, Symptoms,
Prevention, and Treatment," Sandy Eckstein
pets.webmd.com/cats/guide/cancer-in-cats-
types-symptoms-prevention-and-treatment

Cathealth.com
www.cathealth.com/

Catwellness News
www.catwellness.org/

"Conjunctivitis in Cats"
www.vcahospitals.com/main/pet-health-
information/article/animal-health/
conjunctivitis-in-cats/75

Cornell Feline Health Center
www.vet.cornell.edu/fhc/

"Feline Asthma: a Risky Business for Many
Cats," Tom Ewing
www.vet.cornell.edu/FHC/health_
resources/Asthma.cfm

FelineDiabetes.com
www.felinediabetes.com/

"Feline Immunodeficiency Virus"
www.vet.cornell.edu/FHC/health_resources/
brochure_fiv.cfm

"Feline Obesity: An Epidemic of Fat Cats,"
Lisa A. Pierson, DVM, Feb. 2013
www.catinfo.org/?link=felineobesity

"Feline Vaccines: Benefits and Risks"
www.avma.org/About/AlliedOrganizations/
Pages/rbbroch.aspx

"Find a Low-Cost Spay/Neuter Program"
www.humanesociety.org/issues/pet_
overpopulation/tips/afford_spay_neuter.html

Healthy Cats
//pets.webmd.com/cats/

"Home Care for Cats" (from the American
Veterinary Dental College)
www.avdc.org/careforcats.html

Pet MD
www.petmd.com/

"Raising Orphaned Kittens"
www.feralcat.com/raising.html

"Ringworm in Cats"
www.cat-world.com.au/ringworm-in-cats

"The Special Needs Of Older Cats: Caring
For Your Elderly Feline," Ron Hines, DVM,
PhD, 2014
www.2ndchance.info/oldcat.htm

"The Special Needs of Senior Cats"
www.vet.cornell.edu/FHC/health_
resources/SeniorCats.cfm

"Ten Steps to Dental Health"
www.aspca.org/pet-care/cat-care/ten-steps-
dental-health

Winn Feline Foundation
www.winnfelinehealth.org/

Chapter 19

The Cat Library
222 E. Harvard St.
Glendale, CA 91205.
Phone: 818-548-2037

Games for Cats
www.ipadgameforcats.com/

International Cat Agility Tournaments
(ICAT)
catagility.com/index.html

"Seven Apps for Playful Cats"
www.techhive.com/article/2039061/seven-
apps-for-playful-cats.html

"Ten Easy Games You Can Play With Your
Cat," Susan Ng, Nov. 2009
susan-ng.hubpages.com/hub/
easygamesforcats

Chapter 20

British Pet Travel Schemes
www.defra.gov.uk.

"Cat Travel Tips," Helen Fazio
www.catster.com/cat-travel/

DogFriendly.com Pet Travel Guide
www.dogfriendly.com/

Guaranteed on Board
www.flygob.com/

"Traveling With Cats," Sandra Ballentine,
Karen Kaplan, and Jason Sweitzer
behavior.vetmed.ucdavis.edu/local-assets/
pdfs/Traveling_with_Cats.pdf

Trips With Pets
www.tripswithpets.com/

Chapter 21

National Association of Professional Pet Sitters
15000 Commerce Parkway, Suite C
Mt. Laurel, New Jersey 08054
Phone: 856-439-0324
E-mail: napps@petsitters.org
www.petsitters.org/

Pet Sitters International
201 E King Street
King, NC 27021.
Phone: 336-983-9222
www.petsit.com/

Chapter 22

Animal Law and Historical Center
www.animallaw.info

"Cat CPR – Step By Step Guide"
www.cat-world.com.au/cardiopulmonary-resuscitation-cpr-in-cats

"Disaster Preparedness"
www.aspca.org/pet-care/disaster-preparedness

"First Aid and Emergency Care, " Roger W. Gfeller, DVM, DipACVECC, Michael W. Thomas, DVM, and Isaac Mayo, Apr. 2014

www.veterinarypartner.com/Content.plx?P=SRC&S=1&SourceID=20

"First Aid Tips for Pet Owners"
www.avma.org/public/EmergencyCare/Pages/First-Aid-Tips-for-Pet-Owners.aspx

Chapter 23

Missing Pet Network
www.missingpet.net/
Missing Pet Partnership
P.O. Box 3085
Federal Way, WA 98063
Phone: 253-529-3999
E-mail: questions@pethunters.com
http://www.missingpetpartnership.org/contact.php

Chapter 24

ASPCA Pet Loss Hotline and Resources
Phone: 877-GRIEF-10 (877-474-3310)
www.aspca.org/pet-care/pet-loss

International Association of Pet Cemeteries and Crematories
4991 Peachtree Road
Atlanta, GA 30341
Phone: 800-952-5541
http://www.iaopc.com/

Petloss.com
www.petloss.com/

Rainbow Bridge
rainbowsbridge.com/hello.htm

Tufts University Pet Loss Support Hotline and Resources for Grieving
Phone: 508-839-7966
vet.tufts.edu/petloss/resources.html

Virtual Pet Cemetery
www.virtualpetcemetery.org/pet/index.html

Chapter 25

"Cat Communication – Body Language," Sarah Hartwell, 2009
messybeast.com/cat_talk2.htm

"How to Talk to Your Cat"
www.catster.com/cat-behavior/how-to-talk-to-your-cat

Chapter 23

"Clicker Training for Cats: The Basics"
www.catster.com/cat-behavior/clicker-training-for-cats

Karen Pryor Clicker Training
www.clickertraining.com/cat-training

"Socializing Shy Cats"
www.tenthlifecats.org/all-about-cats/cat-behavior/shy-cat-socialization

"Training Your Cat"
www.aspca.org/pet-care/virtual-pet-behaviorist/cat-behavior/training-your-cat

"Training Your Cat With Positive Reinforcement"
www.humanesociety.org/animals/cats/tips/training_your_cat_positive_reinforcement.html

Chapter 27

"Behavior Problems in Older Cats"
www.aspca.org/pet-care/virtual-pet-behaviorist/cat-behavior/behavior-problems-older-cats

"Cat Behavior"
www.aspca.org/pet-care/virtual-pet-behaviorist/cat-behavior

"Cat Behavior Issues"
drsophiayin.com/resources/cat_behavior

"Feline Behavior Problems: Aggression"
www.vet.cornell.edu/FHC/health_resources/brochure_aggression.cfm

"Feline Behavior Problems: House Soiling"
www.vet.cornell.edu/FHC/health_resources/brochure_housesoiling.cfm

"Preventing Feline Behavior Problems"
vet.tufts.edu/behavior/feline.shtml

Chapter 28

The Algonquin Cat
www.algonquinhotel.com/algonquin-cat

"ASPCA Animal Assisted Therapy Programs"
www.aspca.org/nyc/aspca-animal-assisted-therapy-programs

"How to Get Your Cat Certified as a Therapy Cat," Caroline Golon, Feb. 2013
www.catster.com/lifestyle/how-to-certified-therapy-cat

Library Cats Map
www.ironfrog.com/catsmap.html

Chapter 29

Animal Behavior Society
animalbehaviorsociety.org/

"How to Become a Veterinarian," Dawn Rosenberg McKay
careerplanning.about.com/od/veterinarian/tp/how-to-become-a-veterinarian.htm

International Association of Animal Behavior Consultants
565 Callery Road
Cranberry Township, PA 16066
iaabc.org/

National Animal Control Association
101 N. Church St.
Olathe, KS, 66061
Phone: 913-768-1319
E-mail: naca@nacanet.org
www.nacanet.org/

National Cat Groomers Institute of America
701 Pendleton St
Greenville, SC 29601
Phone: 864-787-6889
nationalcatgroomers.com/

Professional Cat Groomers Association of America
E-mail: procatgroomers@aol.com
www.professionalcatgroomers.com/

"Veterinarian Technician: Career Information," Dawn Rosenberg McKay
http://careerplanning.about.com/od/occupations/p/vet_tech.htm

Index

Photo Credits

Shutterstock: 41; Erik Lam/Shutterstock: 79, 89, 142 (top), 146, 427; Henrik Larsson/Shutterstock: 365; Alain Lauga/Shutterstock: 42; Lauraslens/Shutterstock: 56; Susan Legget/Shutterstock: 483; Gary Paul Lewis/Shutterstock: 196; Andy Lidstone/Shutterstock: 46 (top); Lindasj22/Shutterstock: 147 (top); Polina Lobanova/Shutterstock: 244; Lubava/Shutterstock: 473; Krissi Lundgren/Shutterstock: 71 (bottom), 103 (bottom), 159, 160; Leslie Lyons: 14; Tatiana Makotra/Shutterstock: 143 (left); Cosmin Manci/Shutterstock: 225 (bottom); Steve Mann/Shutterstock: 344; Dmitry Maslove/Shutterstock: 43; Mauro Matacchione/Shutterstock: 252; Efthyia Mavri/Shutterstock: 282, 439; Maximult/Shutterstock: 300; McCarthy's PhotoWorks/Shutterstock: 434; Mdmmikle/Shutterstock: 97, 150 (bottom); Medeia/Shutterstock: 132 (right); Ksenia Mernkova/Shutterstock: 339; Tomas Mikolanda/Shutterstock: 291; milias 1987/Shutterstock: 521; Modd/Shutterstock: 366; Monkey Business Images/Shutterstock: 221, 387, 508; Anna Morgan/Shutterstock: 399; Cimeron Morrissey: 30; Konrad Mostert/Shutterstock: 416; Catherine Murray/Shutterstock: 297; MW47/Shutterstock: 449; Nadinelle/Shutterstock: 201; Neftali/Shutterstock: 49 (center); Nelik/Shutterstock: back cover, 8, 69; Jeng Niamwhan/Shutterstock: 284; Nikolasfoto/Shutterstock: 401; Andreas Nilsson/Shutterstock: 362; Noko3/Shutterstock: 359; Tyler Olson/Shutterstock: 351; Sari ONeal/Shutterstock: 315; Martina Osmy/Shutterstock: 460, 518; Nataliya Ostapenko/Shutterstock: 382; Otsphoto/Shutterstock: 126 (top), 407; Alena Ozerova/Shutterstock: 278; Padmayogini/Shutterstock: 45; jakkrit panalee/Shutterstock: 330; panda3800/Shutterstock: 197; Parris Blue Productions/Shutterstock: 320; Bruno Passigatti/Shutterstock: 144 (bottom); patrimonio designs ltd/Shutterstock: 36; Ksinia Pelevina/Shutterstock: 294, 458; Mark William Penny/Shutterstock: 335; Pet Profiles/Lara Stern: 122 (bottom); Michael Pettigrew/Shutterstock: 499; Phant/Shutterstock: 272; Photomak/Shutterstock: 423, 447; Photopixel/Shutterstock: 205; La India Piaroa/Shutterstock: 321; Pichit/Shutterstock: 275; Tom Pingel/Shutterstock: 219 (right); Julia Pivovarova/Shutterstock: 199; Arnold Plotnick, MS, DVM, ACVIM: 328; Alin Popescu/Shutterstock: 215; Stuart G. Porter/Shutterstock: 145 (bottom); Praisaeng/Shutterstock: 235; Prateepp/Shutterstock: 255; project1 photography/Shutterstock: 39; Pshenina_m/Shutterstock: 71 (top); Pugovica88/Shutterstock: 470; Purple Queue/Shutterstock: 474; Dave Pusey/Shutterstock: 12; Jason Putsche: 29; Quintanilla/Shutterstock: 17; Walter Quirtmair/Shutterstock: 189; Daniel Rajszczak/Shutterstock: 186; Valentina Razumova/Shutterstock: 228; REDSTARSTUDIO/Shutterstock: front cover (bottom); Trevor Reeves/Shutterstock: 509; Julia Remezova/Shutterstock: 130 (right), 137 (top), 174 (top); Renkabora/Shutterstock: 496; Reystleen/Shutterstock: 443; Rigorosus/Shutterstock: 305; Sandy Robins: 50, 51; Alan Robinson: 86, 91; Robynrg/Shutterstock: 121, 125 (top); Christope Rolland/Shutterstock: 38; Roylee photosunday/Shutterstock: 369; S_E/Shutterstock: 438; S1001/Shutterstock: 204 (center); Saiko3p/Shutterstock: 1 (center); Silke Sandberg: 105 (right); R. Gino Santa Maria/Shutterstock: 114 (right); Jenifer Santee: 193; Satapat/Shutterstock: 393; Maria Sbtova/Shutterstock: 472; Susan Schmitz/Shutterstock: 130 (left); Nailia Schwarz/Shutterstock: 143 (right), 144 (top); Jean Schweitzer/Shutterstock: 338; Zina Seletskaya/Shutterstock: 111 (bottom); Sensay/Shutterstock: 18; Servantes/Shutterstock: 34; Alexey Shinkevich/Shutterstock: 424; Natalia Shmeliova/Shutterstock: 64; Shutterschock/Shutterstock: 204 (bottom); Sinelyov/Shutterstock: 341; Sippakorn/Shutterstock: 115; Skdiz/Shutterstock: 16; SMA Studio/Shutterstock: 337; Dwight Smith/Shutterstock: 410, 450, 517; Martin Smith/Shutterstock: 239; Vladyslav Starozhylov/Shutterstock: 74 (right); Viliers Steyn/Shutterstock: 13; Alexey Stiop/Shutterstock: 436; stock_shot/Shutterstock: 213 (center); stockphoto mania/Shutterstock: 295; Stokkete/Shutterstock: 500; Barcelona Studio/Shutterstock: 420; Stukkey/Shutterstock: 453; Mila Supinskaya/Shutterstock: 519; SvetoGraf/Shutterstock: 150 (top); Pavel Szabo/Shutterstock: 158; Magalena Szachowska/Shutterstock: 71 (center); tab62/Shutterstock: 179; Taiftin/Shutterstock: 166 (top); Tairen/Shutterstock: 274; Diana Talium/Shutterstock: 448, 481; TalyaPhoto/Shutterstock: 480; tankist276/Shutterstock: 149 (bottom); Andrzej Taranwczyk/Shutterstock: 53; Verkhovynets Taras/Shutterstock: 213 (bottom); Irene Teesalu/Shutterstock: 390; Serdar Tibet/Shutterstock: 429; Patrizia Tilly/Shutterstock: 498; Anatoly Timofeev/Shutterstock: 396; Timolina/Shutterstock: 200; toanne14/Shutterstock: 182; Trevor Allen Weddings/Shutterstock: 349; Sorapop Udomsri/Shutterstock: 455; v777999/Shutterstock: 261; Arno van Dulmen/Shutterstock: 66; Joost Van Uffelen/Shutterstock: 372; A. Vasilyev/Shutterstock: 163; Veera/Shutterstock: 98 (left), 479; Claudia Veja/Shutterstock: 180; Birute Vijeikiene/Shutterstock: 61, 68, 96 (top); Vikacita/Shutterstock: 90 (top); Christian Vinces/Shutterstock: 357; Illya Vinogradov/Shutterstock: 234; Vnlit/Shutterstock: 268, 281, 352; Kirill Vorobyev/Shutterstock: 81; VP Photo Studio/Shutterstock: 227, 327, 358; Henk Vrieselaar/Shutterstock: 391; Vvvita/Shutterstock: 31, 194, 461; Vydrin/Shutterstock: 246; Piotr Wawrzyniuk/Shutterstock: 419; Lawrence Wee/Shutterstock: 376; Ivonne Wierink/Shutterstock: 107, 108, 155 (top), 156 (bottom), 219 (left), 301; John Wollwerth/Shutterstock: 111 (top); Worldswildlifewonders/Shutterstock: 13 (top); Wrangler/Shutterstock: 467; Monika Wroblewska-Plocka/Shutterstock: 80, 456; Xseon/Shutterstock: 216 (top), 395; YangChao/Shutterstock: 49 (left); Yellowj/Shutterstock: 293, 371; Alaettin Yildirim/Shutterstock: 225 (top), 231; Elena Yutilova/Shutterstock: 258; Yykkaa/Shutterstock: 273, 346; Jakub Zak/Shutterstock: 236, 405; Faiz Zaki/Shutterstock: 452; Dora Zett/Shutterstock: 216 (bottom); Zigzag Mountain Art/Shutterstock: 213 (top center); Bildagentur Zoonar GmbH/Shutterstock: 52, 71 (top)

Special thanks to Helmi Fisk, Marianne Gerver, Pat Killmaier, Cimeron Morrisey at Project Bay Cat, Dr. Arnold Plotnick, Elizabeth Putsche and Jason Putsche at Alley Cat Allies, Sandy Robins, Silke Sandberg, and Jenifer Santee for their help locating photos.

Sandy Robins

Sandy Robins is an awarding-winning multi-media pet lifestyle expert, author, TV and radio personality and pet industry spokesperson. She is the 2013 recipient of the Excellence in Journalism and Outstanding Contributions to the Pet Industry Award presented by the American Pet Products Association to individuals in the media who have used their influence to positively promote the joys and benefits of pet ownership.

Her two cat books, *Fabulous Felines: Health and Beauty Secrets for the Pampered Cat and For the Love of Cats* have both won awards from the Cat Writers Association of America, of which she is a longtime member. She is also a member of the Dog Writers Association of America and has received more than 40 awards of excellence from both these organizations for her contributions to the pet world.

Her work focuses on lifestyle trends that improve our pets' general health and well-being, and ultimately enhance the human- animal bond—from state-of-the-art surgical procedures to the latest pet travel ideas, haute couture designs, and new home decor trends.

She is a regular contributor to popular sites, such as Today.com and AOL's PawNation, and to mainstream national publications such as *Consumers Digest* and pet centric magazines such as *Cat Fancy, Cats USA* annuals, various dog titles, such as *Dog Fancy, Modern Dog*, and *Fido Friendly*, and industry leaders such as *Pet Age Magazine*.

She works as a pet lifestyle spokesperson for Petco and appears monthly on their featured segment called *Pet Patrol* on the Weather Channel. She has worked with corporations such as Toyota to promote their "pet safety in vehicles" campaign. As spokesperson for Motorola, she helped launch the first pet video monitor. Prestigious pet food companies Sandy has been associated with include Merrick PetCare, Friskies, Temptation Treats, and Pedigree dog food. She worked with American Airlines to launch their pet carrier and to promote safe pet travel.

As a pet lifestyle consultant, she is often quoted in such prestigious publications as *Martha Stewart Living, The Wall Street Journal* and online on sites such as Oprah.com Foxnews.com and Kiplingers.com, and is also a popular TV and radio guest.

For the past four years, Sandy's blog *Bark.Sniff.Play* has appeared in *Modern Dog* magazine and she also blogs for Sergeants PetCare's popular blog called *Pet Health Central* focusing on feline issues. In 2014 she introduced her new bi-petual blog called *Reigning Cats and Dogs*.

You can connect with her at: www.SandyRobinsOnLine.com and www.ReigningCatsandDogsblog.com
Twitter: Twitter.com/PetSandy
Facebook: Facebook.com/SandyRobinsPetLifestyleExpert

Arnold Plotnick MS, DVM, ACVIM

Arnold Plotnick MS, DVM, ACVIM, has spent his career taking care of felines. He is a graduate of the University of Florida College of Veterinary Medicine. He achieved board certification in small animal internal medicine in 1997 and became board certified in feline medicine in 1999. He is the founder of Manhattan Cat Specialists, a feline-exclusive veterinary facility on Manhattan's upper west side. In addition to looking after his feline patients, Dr. Plotnick spends much of his time writing. He is the "Ask the Veterinarian" columnist for *Cat Fancy* magazine, a feline advice expert on CatChannel.com, and a regular contributor to *Catnip* newsletter. Dr. Plotnick enjoys traveling the world whenever possible, documenting his encounters with any street cats that cross his path in his blog, Cat Man Do. He lives in New York City with his two cats, Crispy and Mittens.

Lorraine M. Shelton

Lorraine M. Shelton is a research scientist, an author, a cat show judge for The International Cat Association (TICA), and a lecturer in the fields of avian and feline genetics. For two decades, her Featherland Cattery has specialized in rare-colored Persians, Turkish Angoras, Selkirk Rex, and Norwegian Forest Cats. She is the co-author of *Robinson's Genetics for Cat Breeders & Veterinarians*. She is a regular contributor to *Cat Fancy*, catchannel.com, and fanciers.com. She lives in Corona, California.

Sarah Hartwell

Sarah Hartwell, the originator of the messybeast.com website, is a writer on various feline-related topics, including breed history, behavior, rescue, senior cats, and care. Her articles have appeared in *Cat Fancy, Cat World, The Cat, FAB,* and other magazines and newsletters around the world. Sarah lives in Essex, England.

Praise for *The Original Cat Fancy Cat Bible*

"*The Original Cat Fancy Cat Bible* re-writes the 'Old Testament' history of cats in terms of the latest genetic research and highlights ways to enhance the human-feline bond, the newest trends in grooming and shedding solutions, and the latest information on feline nutrition and preventive care. It also introduces cat lovers to the Mew Testament—the current trends in feline enrichment, exercise, solving behavioral issues, and the role cats play in social media. This is the essential feline reference that cat lovers have always wanted."

—Dr. Marty Becker, "America's Veterinarian"

"Cats are such divine creatures and the information in *The Original Cat Fancy Cat Bible* will give all who own this book a rich resource for 'need-to-know' facts, figures and fun! With the information inside and a lifelong relationship with your veterinarian, you and your cat will share an enriched, healthy, and happy life!"

—Jane Brunt, DVM, founder "CHAT"-Cat Hospital At Towson;
Executive Director CATalyst Council

"What a terrific book. It has everything a cat lover could want. Superbly illustrated and packed with great information. Two paws up from this pundit. Meeeow."

—Professor Nicholas Dodman, BVMS, DVA, DACVA, DACVB
Dept of Clinical Sciences Cummings School of
Veterinary Medicineat Tufts University